To BP

$e^{\pi i} + 1 = 0$

Inside Microsoft® SQL Server™ 2005:

T-SQL Querying

Itzik Ben-Gan (Solid Quality Learning),
Lubor Kollar, Dejan Sarka

PUBLISHED BY
Microsoft Press
A Division of Microsoft Corporation
One Microsoft Way
Redmond, Washington 98052-6399

Library of Congress Control Number 2006921724

Printed and bound in the United States of America.

2 3 4 5 6 7 8 9   QWT   1 0 9 8 7 6

Distributed in Canada by H.B. Fenn and Company Ltd.

A CIP catalogue record for this book is available from the British Library.

Microsoft Press books are available through booksellers and distributors worldwide. For further information about international editions, contact your local Microsoft Corporation office or contact Microsoft Press International directly at fax (425) 936-7329. Visit our Web site at www.microsoft.com/mspress. Send comments to mspinput@microsoft.com.

Acquisitions Editor: Ben Ryan
Project Editor: Kristine Haugseth
Technical Editor: Steve Kass
Copy Editor: Roger LeBlanc
Indexers: Tony Ross and Lee Ross

Body Part No. X12-21118

Table of Contents

Foreword

As I thought about writing the foreword for this volume, the word "master" came to mind before ever opening the draft. As a transitive verb, "to master" means to gain thorough knowledge of something or to become skilled in its use. As a noun, "master" is a rich word with many subtle interpretations. In the context of this book, two interpretations come to mind: a master as someone who possesses consummate skill in some endeavor and a master as someone qualified to teach apprentices. I was amazed upon opening an early draft to find, as if by some synchronicity, the first chapter opening with a discussion of "mastering" the fundamentals of SQL programming.

SQL, the language, has that amazing property in that it is eminently approachable. You can walk people through the basics in a matter of minutes and quickly get them to the point of exploring a database. SQL is easily learned but not easily mastered. Mastery of the riches of SQL takes time but the rewards are plenty. There are many ways to do the same thing in the SQL language. When they first start to learn SQL, many people craft solutions to their queries in painful, contorted, and inefficient ways. Masters of SQL, on the other hand, often create simple, elegant solutions that are a joy to look at and learn from. This book is full of examples of these simple and elegant solutions that will help you master SQL.

In life, we encounter two classes of masters, those who share their mastery solely through their work and those who take on apprentices to further their craft–to pass it on and share it with others. Readers of this book have the opportunity to become apprentices of SQL from masters of the language and of the language's particular implementation in Microsoft SQL Server. Itzik Ben-Gan, this book's principal author, is a master of the SQL language. A recognized expert, Itzik is one of those people who redefine the medium. Often, when looking at a solution that Itzik has crafted, I am struck with that "I didn't realize you could do *that!*" feeling. Lubor Kollar, a program manager on the Microsoft SQL Server product development team, is a master at solving customers' problems. Sometimes I am the customer. Many times I have walked into Lubor's office asking about a particular way to solve some problem in SQL and, within minutes, Lubor will send me an e-mail message with a solution that ultimately finds its way into my notebook for future reference. Dejan Sarka, a well-known SQL Server MVP, is extremely knowledgeable in the pure relational realm but is also an expert in SQL Server 2005 BI, XML, and CLR integration. Dejan's principal contribution to this volume is to guide readers in determining when it is appropriate to employ XML or CLR integration in their solutions.

Inside Microsoft SQL Server 2005: T-SQL Querying starts where it should, separating the logical constructs of the SQL language from their physical implementation in Microsoft SQL Server. Like mathematics, a fundamental understanding of the logical constructs on which SQL is formed is required to build a firm foundation for further exploration. Chapters 2 and 3 go into the physical query processing aspects of how Microsoft SQL Server, the product, turns a logical query into an executable query plan that returns the results of the query efficiently. One would like to hold these logical and physical concepts completely separate. However, there are multiple ways to describe a query logically, and some of these are more easily translated than others by the SQL Server query optimizer into efficient plans. Chapters 4 through 8 form the basis for mastering SQL queries. In these chapters, you will learn to do things in several lines of SQL query text that many people who use, but have not yet mastered, the SQL language labor to do with cursors, temporary tables, or worse yet, imperative program logic. This is where you learn to ask the question as a SQL query and have SQL Server provide the answer, rather than coding the answer up yourself. You will find these chapters rich with many real-world examples with several alternative implementations and explanations of when to choose one over the other. Finally, Chapter 9 is truly the realm of masters. Many people who are not well versed in SQL or the relational model believe that graph structures cannot be represented in the relational world. Although this is patently untrue, there are few comprehensive treatments of this topic in existing SQL texts. This final chapter describes how to model graphs and trees through their essence—relationships. It presents a common data model to represent graph-like structures and then describes a number of techniques, including the use of new features in SQL Server 2005, to navigate these structures.

Inside Microsoft SQL Server 2005: T-SQL Querying, is not strictly a recipe book. It is not the place to look to cut and paste 20 lines of T-SQL code into your program. Although it contains explicit recipes and examples, *Inside Microsoft SQL Server 2005: T-SQL Querying* is a book about learning the craft of SQL. In reading it, you will learn to do things you didn't think were possible with the SQL language. When you encounter SQL challenges in the future that require techniques presented in this book, you will find yourself reaching for it on your shelf. Whether you are new to the SQL language and Microsoft SQL Server, have reached a plateau in your understanding, or are well on your way to becoming a master of SQL, I am convinced this book will help you further your craft.

Microsoft SQL Server is a tool or a platform. Everyone on the product development team takes great pride in delivering a great tool. In the end though, SQL Server's true value is only realized when placed in the hands of someone who creates something with it, just as a woodworker uses a tool in making a piece of fine furniture. Being a master woodworker requires knowledge of the fundamentals of the medium and techniques for working with it, a keen sense of design, and an intimate knowledge of the tools at hand. Craftsmen know their tools—how and when to use them as well as how to maintain them. *Inside Microsoft SQL Server 2005: T-SQL Querying* will show you the fundamentals of the SQL language. By reading it, you will get a keen sense of how to design elegant SQL solutions from masters of the craft and an appreciation for the unique aspects of Microsoft SQL Server as a tool for your use in mastering SQL to craft solutions by simple and elegant means.

David Campbell

General Manager, Microsoft SQL Server: Strategy, Infrastructure, and Architecture

Preface

This book and its sequel—*Inside Microsoft SQL Server 2005: T-SQL Programming*—cover advanced T-SQL querying, query tuning, and programming in SQL Server 2005. They are designed for programmers and DBAs who need to write and optimize code in both SQL Server 2000 and 2005. For brevity, I'll refer to the books as *Inside T-SQL Querying* and *Inside T-SQL Programming*.

The books focus on practical common problems, discussing several approaches to tackle each one. You will be introduced to many polished techniques that will enhance your toolbox and coding vocabulary, allowing you to provide efficient solutions in a natural manner.

The books unveil the power of set-based querying, and explain why it's usually superior to procedural programming with cursors and the like. At the same time, the books teach you how to identify the few scenarios where cursor-based solutions are superior to set-based ones.

The books also cover other much debated constructs—such as temporary tables, dynamic execution, XML and .NET integration—which hold great power, but at the same time great risk. These constructs require programmatic maturity. These books will teach you how to use them wisely, in efficient and safe ways where they are relevant.

The first book—*Inside T-SQL Querying*—focuses on set-based querying, and I recommend that you read it first. The second book—*Inside T-SQL Programming*—focuses on procedural programming and assumes you read the first book or have sufficient querying background.

Inside T-SQL Querying starts with three chapters that lay the foundation of logical and physical query processing required to gain the most from the rest of the chapters.

The first chapter covers logical query processing. It describes in detail the logical phases involved in processing queries, the unique aspects of SQL querying, and the special mindset you need in order to program in a relational, set-oriented environment.

The second chapter covers physical query processing. It describes in detail the way the SQL Server engine processes queries, and compares and contrasts physical query processing with logical query processing. This chapter was written by Lubor Kollar. Lubor was a group program manager during the SQL Server 2005 development, and his team was responsible for the "bottom" part of the Relational Engine—from query compilation and optimization to query execution, transactional consistency, backup/restore, and high availability. Table and Index Partitioning, Database Mirroring, Database Snapshot, Snapshot Isolation, Recursive Queries and other T-SQL query improvements, Database Tuning Advisor, and Online Index creation and maintenance were the major SQL Server 2005 features his team was working on. Few people in the world probably know the subject of query optimization as well as Lubor does. I find it a privilege to have one of the designers of the optimizer explain it in his own words.

The third chapter covers a query tuning methodology we developed in our company (Solid Quality Learning) and have been applying in production systems. The chapter also covers working with indexes and analyzing execution plans. This chapter provides the important background knowledge required for the chapters that follow, which discuss working with indexes and analyzing execution plans. These are important aspects of querying and query tuning.

The chapters that follow delve into advanced querying and query tuning, where both logical and physical aspects of your code are intertwined. These chapters are: "Subqueries, Table Expressions, and Ranking Functions"; "Joins and Set Operations"; "Aggregating and Pivoting Data" (including a section written by Dejan Sarka about CLR user-defined aggregates); "TOP and APPLY"; "Data Modification"; and "Graphs, Trees, Hierarchies, and Recursive Queries."

Appendix A covers pure logic puzzles. Here you have a chance to practice puzzles to improve your logic skills. SQL querying essentially deals with logic. I find it important to practice pure logic to improve my query problem-solving capabilities. I also find these puzzles fun and challenging. You can practice them with the entire family. These puzzles are a compilation of the logic puzzles that I covered in my T-SQL column in *SQL Server Magazine*. I'd like to thank *SQL Server Magazine* for allowing me to share these puzzles with the book's readers.

The second book—*Inside T-SQL Programming*—focuses on programmatic T-SQL constructs and expands its coverage to treatment of XML and .NET integration. The topics it covers include datatype-related problems, including XML and CLR user-defined types (UDT); temporary tables; cursors; dynamic execution; views; user-defined functions, including CLR UDFs; stored procedures, including CLR procedures; triggers, including DDL and CLR triggers; transactions, including coverage of the new snapshot-based isolation levels; exception handling; and service broker.

The material that covers XML and .NET integration (found in these chapters: 1, 6, 7, 8) were written by Dejan Sarka. Dejan is a SQL Server expert, and he is extremely knowledgeable about the relational model. He has fascinating views about the way these new constructs can fit with the relational model when used sensibly. I found it important to have someone with a strong grasp of the relational model cover these much debated areas of the product. All CLR code samples are provided in both C# and Visual Basic .NET.

The last chapter, covering Service Broker, was written by Roger Wolter. Roger is the program manager with the SQL Server development team in charge of Service Broker. Again, nothing like having the designer of a component explain it in his own words.

Last but not least, Steve Kass was the technical editor of the books. Steve is an extremely sharp guy. He is a SQL Server MVP, and he teaches mathematics at Drew University. He has extensive knowledge of SQL Server and logic, and his contribution to the books was invaluable.

And to you, the reader of these books, I'd like to say that for me SQL is science, logic, and art. I've been cooking up books such as these for a long time, and I've poured into these two books all my passion and many years of experience. I hope that you will find the books useful and interesting, and that you will find SQL a source of inspiration like I do. If you have any comments or corrections that you'd like to share, I'd love to hear them. You can contact me at *http://www.insidetsql.com*.

Sincerely, Itzik

Acknowledgments

Most readers usually skip the acknowledgments section, and many authors usually make this section very short. I really don't want to judge anyone; I can only guess that authors think it might look kitschy if they exposed their emotions, or that doing so is awkward. Well, many people contributed their heart and soul to these books, and I don't care how this section might seem. I'd like them to be recognized for their contributions!

My deepest gratitude goes to all those who contributed in any way to the books. Some spent countless hours directly involved in the project, and some of them had an impact on me and my work that implicitly affected the books.

To the guest authors Lubor Kollar, Dejan Sarka, and Roger Wolter: thanks for taking part in this project and adding your invaluable insight. It's been an honor and a pleasure to work with you. Lubor, your depth of knowledge and passion are a source of inspiration. Dejan, my good friend, I'm constantly learning new things from you. I find your views of the database world simply fascinating. Roger, I greatly appreciate the fact that you agreed to contribute to the books. Service Broker—your baby—brings an important dimension to Microsoft SQL Server that was never there before. I'm sure that companies will find it extremely valuable, and I'm eager to see how the queuing technology will be implemented—it has such great potential.

To Steve Kass, the technical editor of the books: Steve, I have no words to describe how much I value your contribution. You're simply brilliant and amazing, and one can only hope to have half the wit and logic that you were blessed with. Remind me never to end up in a battle of wits with you. You've spent so much time on the project and provided so many insightful suggestions that I feel that you've practically helped author the books. I hope that in future editions you will take an official authoring role.

To David Campbell and Lubor Kollar who wrote the forewords: your work and achievements are a guiding light to many of us. SQL Server has grown up to be a mature and fascinating product—one well worth dedicating our professional careers to and focusing our passions on. Thank you both for agreeing to write the forewords. This is truly an honor! To all contributors, I'm looking forward to doing many future projects together. I, for one, have already started cooking up ideas for future editions of the books.

Many thanks to the team at Microsoft Press: Ben Ryan, Kristine Haugseth, Roger LeBlanc, and probably numerous others who took part in the making of the books. Ben, I'm sorry to have been such a pain, and for wanting to be involved in every small detail that I could. Perfection and candor are my two guidelines, though one can only strive to achieve the former. I believe that by following this path, the end result can only improve, and regardless, I believe that there's no other path. Thanks for being so attentive. Kristine, you are simply great! Devoted, professional, caring, and steering the project so elegantly. On a more personal level, I feel that I've earned a new friend. Roger, I don't envy you for the countless hours you had to spend editing the books. Thanks for helping to improve their quality. And I'm sure there were many others at Microsoft Press who worked long hours behind the scenes to allow the books to see the light of day.

I'd like to thank Kalen Delaney. Kalen's previous *Inside Microsoft SQL Server* books were a bible to me with regard to SQL Server internals, and I'm eager to read her new coverage of SQL Server 2005's internals in her new volumes. Kalen was also the one who initially asked me to write the T-SQL volumes now that the product has grown so large.

Many people provided extremely valuable feedback by unofficially reviewing the books. Among them are members of the SQL Server development team, mentors from Solid Quality Learning, and MVPs. You didn't have to do this, so my gratitude goes to you from the bottom of my heart.

To the team at *SQL Server Magazine*: you're family to me. We've been working together for years and have grown and evolved together. I'm sure that I'm not the only one who believes that *SQL Server Magazine* is the world's best magazine for SQL Server professionals. These books are in great part due to what I absorbed and learned while working with you.

To my friends, partners, and colleagues at Solid Quality Learning: this company is by far the best thing that happened to me in my professional career, and in many ways in my personal life. It's simply a dream come true. With regard to the books, many of you contributed much to them through your reviews and through the work we've done together, which is naturally reflected in the books. But far beyond that, you're family, friends, and more than anyone could wish for. I still need to pinch myself to make sure this is reality and not a dream. And to Fernando: all of us share the opinion that you're the reason Solid Quality Learning came to life, and without you, it would not be. Your vision, patience, attentiveness, passion, and heart are an inspiration to us all. No words that I say or write can express the gratitude I have in my heart for you and how much I value your friendship.

I find that there are three key elements shaping a person's knowledge and ability: teachers, students, and passion. Passion is the seed that must come from within oneself, and I have great passion for SQL. I've been blessed with great teachers–Lubor Kollar and Sensei Leon Pantanowitz (Yehuda). Lubor, your passion and deep knowledge of SQL and its optimization, your seeking of new knowledge, your humility, the spark in your eyes, and your fondness for logic are all a source of inspiration to me. I'm so grateful that we came to know each other, and I cherish our friendship. Sensei Yehuda, though your world may seem to you to have nothing to do with SQL, to me, it has everything to do with it. Your advice, teaching, guidance, and friendship helped me in the SQL world in more ways than you will know. You and Sensei Higaonna are sources of great inspiration to me; you're living proof that nothing is impossible– that if we work diligently and constantly strive for perfection, we can improve and achieve great things in life. The focus on small details, never giving up, controlling excitement by thinking that "it's just another day in the office," honesty, dealing with the ugly parts of life... these are just a few examples of advice that has helped me in many ways. Writing for endless hours was extremely hard, but I attribute the fact that I managed to do it largely to you. I always thought of the experience as a long GoJu training.

To my students: I learned and continue to learn much through teaching. In fact, teaching is my true passion, and you are the main reason that I wrote these books. In the last few years, I've been traveling around the globe teaching. I spent very little time at home, sacrificing a lot to pursue my passion. My true hope is that after reading these books, we will end up meeting in class—my favorite dojo for learning and practicing SQL.

To my parents: my only regret in doing so much traveling is that it came at the expense of spending time with you. I remember a surrealistic moment where you sat in a session I delivered about partitioned tables and indexes in SQL Server 2005 to see me after we hadn't seen each other for three months. I apologize and hope you understand that I need to pursue my passion to be fulfilled. Pa, thanks for all the help in mathematics and logic. Ma, stop yelling at father when he gives me a new puzzle over the phone in cross-Atlantic calls; he can't help it, and I can't either.

Lilach, my love and my anchor: the only thing that keeps me sane while I'm away from home is the fact that you're with me. I think that the rest I will tell you in person; we don't want to embarrass ourselves in front of the readers. ;-)

Introduction

This book is targeted at experienced T-SQL programmers and database professionals who need to write or review T-SQL queries. The book covers advanced T-SQL querying, assuming that you already have a good grasp of the basic and intermediate levels of the subject matter and are ready to proceed to the next level.

Organization of This Book

This book is the first of two volumes. It covers advanced T-SQL querying. The second volume—*Inside Microsoft SQL Server 2005: T-SQL Programming*—covers advanced T-SQL programming. The second volume assumes that you read the first or have equivalent background. For more details about the organization of the two volumes, please see this book's Preface.

System Requirements

You'll need the following hardware and software to build and run the code samples for this book:

- Microsoft Windows XP with Service Pack 2, Microsoft Windows Server 2003 with Service Pack 1, or Microsoft Windows 2000 with Service Pack 4
- Microsoft SQL Server 2005 Standard, Developer, or Enterprise Edition
- Microsoft Visual Studio 2005 Standard Edition or Microsoft Visual Studio 2005 Professional Edition
- 600-MHz Pentium or compatible processor (1-GHz Pentium recommended)
- 512 MB RAM (1 GB or more recommended)
- Video (800 by 600 or higher resolution) monitor with at least 256 colors (1024 by 768 High Color 16-bit recommended)
- CD-ROM or DVD-ROM drive
- Microsoft mouse or compatible pointing device

For more details about the system requirements and about installing SQL Server 2005, please visit the section "Preparing to Install SQL Server 2005" in SQL Server 2005 Books Online.

Installing Sample Databases

This book requires that you create and use the Northwind and pubs sample databases. The Northwind and pubs sample databases are not installed by default in SQL Server 2005. These databases can be downloaded from the Microsoft Download Center at the following address:

http://go.microsoft.com/fwlink/?LinkId=30196

Alternatively, you can download the scripts that create the Northwind and pubs databases as part of the code samples for the book. Instructions for downloading the code samples for the book will be provided shortly.

Updates

You can find the latest updates related to SQL Server at the following address:

http://www.microsoft.com/sql/

You can find resources related to the book at the following address:

http://www.insidetsql.com/

Code Samples

All the code samples discussed in this book can be downloaded from the book's companion content page at the following address:

http://www.microsoft.com/mspress/companion/0-7356-2313-9/

Or alternatively, they can be downloaded at the following address:

http://www.insidetsql.com/

Support for This Book

Every effort has been made to ensure the accuracy of this book and the companion content.

Microsoft Learning provides support for books and companion content through the Web at the following address:

http://www.microsoft.com/learning/support/books/

To search for book and CD corrections, go to:

http://www.microsoft.com/learning/support/search.asp

If you have comments, questions, or ideas regarding the book or the companion content, or if you have questions that are not answered by querying the Knowledge Base, please send them to Microsoft Press using either of the following methods:

E-mail:

mspinput@microsoft.com

Postal mail:

Microsoft Press

Attn: *Inside Microsoft SQL Server 2005: T-SQL Querying* Editor

One Microsoft Way

Redmond, WA 98052-6399

Please note that Microsoft software product support is not offered through these addresses. For support information, please visit the Microsoft Product Support Web site at:

http://support.microsoft.com

You can also contact me through the Web site I created for the book at the following address:

http://www.insidetsql.com/

Chapter 1

Logical Query Processing

Observing true experts in different fields, you will find a common practice that they all share—mastering the basics. One way or another, all professions deal with problem solving. All solutions to problems, complex as they may be, involve applying a mix of key techniques. If you want to master a profession, you need to build your knowledge upon strong foundations. Put a lot of effort in perfecting your techniques; master the basics, and you will be able to solve any problem.

This book is about Transact-SQL (T-SQL) querying—learning key techniques and applying them to solve problems. I can't think of a better way to start the book than with a chapter on fundamentals of logical query processing. I find this chapter the most important in the book—not just because it covers the essentials of query processing, but also because SQL programming is conceptually very different than any other sort of programming.

The Microsoft SQL Server dialect of SQL—Transact-SQL—follows the ANSI standard. Microsoft SQL Server 2000 conforms to the ANSI SQL:1992 standard at the Entry SQL level, and Microsoft SQL Server 2005 implements some important ANSI SQL:1999 and ANSI SQL:2003 features.

Throughout the book, I will interchangeably use the terms *SQL* and *T-SQL*. When discussing aspects of the language that originated from ANSI SQL and are relevant to most dialects, I will typically use the term *SQL*. When discussing aspects of the language with the implementation of SQL Server in mind, I'll typically use the term *T-SQL*. Note that the formal language name is *Transact-SQL*, although it is commonly called *T-SQL*. Most programmers, including myself, feel more comfortable calling it T-SQL, so I made a conscious choice of using the term *T-SQL* throughout the book.

Origin of SQL Pronunciation

Many English-speaking database professionals pronounce *SQL* as *sequel*, although the correct pronunciation of the language is *S-Q-L* ("ess kyoo ell"). One can make educated guesses about the reasoning behind the incorrect pronunciation. My guess is that there are both historical reasons and linguistic ones.

As for historical reasons, in the 1970s IBM developed a language called SEQUEL, which was an acronym for Structured English QUEry Language. The language was designed to manipulate data stored in a database system called System R, which was based on Dr. Edgar F. Codd's model for Relational Database Management Systems (RDBMS). Later on, the acronym SEQUEL was shortened to SQL because of a trademark dispute. ANSI adopted SQL as a standard in 1986, and ISO did so in 1987. ANSI declared that the official pronunciation of the language is "ess kyoo ell," but it seems that this fact is not common knowledge.

As for linguistic reasons, the sequel pronunciation is simply more fluent, mainly for English speakers. I have to say that I often use it myself for this reason.

You can sometimes guess which pronunciation people use by inspecting their writings. Someone writing "an SQL Server" probably uses the correct pronunciation, while someone writing "a SQL Server" probably uses the incorrect one.

More Info   I urge you to read about the history of SQL and its pronunciation, which I find fascinating, at *http://www.wikimirror.com/SQL*. The coverage of SQL history on the Wikimirror site and in this chapter is based on an article from Wikipedia, the free encyclopedia.

There are many unique aspects of SQL programming, such as thinking in sets, the logical processing order of query elements, and three-valued logic. Trying to program in SQL without this knowledge is a straight path to lengthy, poor-performing code that is hard to maintain. This chapter's purpose is to help you understand SQL the way its designers envisioned it. You need to create strong roots upon which all the rest will be built. Where relevant, I'll explicitly indicate elements that are T-SQL specific.

Throughout the book, I will cover complex problems and advanced techniques. But in this chapter, as mentioned, I will deal only with the fundamentals of querying. Throughout the book, I also will put a lot of focus on performance. But in this chapter, I will deal only with the logical aspects of query processing. I ask you to make an effort while reading this chapter to not think about performance at all. There will be plenty of performance coverage later in the book. Some of the logical query processing phases that I'll describe in this chapter might seem very inefficient. But keep in mind that in practice, the actual physical processing of a query might be very different than the logical one.

The component in SQL Server in charge of generating the actual work plan (execution plan) for a query is the query optimizer. The optimizer determines in which order to access the tables, which access methods and indexes to use, which join algorithms to apply, and so on. The optimizer generates multiple valid execution plans and chooses the one with the lowest cost. The phases in the logical processing of a query have a very specific order. On the other hand, the optimizer can often make shortcuts in the physical execution plan that it generates. Of course, it will make shortcuts only if the result set is guaranteed to be the correct one—in other words, the same result set you would get by following the logical processing phases. For example, to use an index, the optimizer can decide to apply a filter much sooner than dictated by logical processing.

For the aforementioned reasons, it's important to make a clear distinction between logical and physical processing of a query.

Without further ado, let's delve into logical query processing phases.

Logical Query Processing Phases

This section introduces the phases involved in the logical processing of a query. I will first briefly describe each step. Then, in the following sections, I'll describe the steps in much more detail and apply them to a sample query. You can use this section as a quick reference whenever you need to recall the order and general meaning of the different phases.

Listing 1-1 contains a general form of a query, along with step numbers assigned according to the order in which the different clauses are logically processed.

Listing 1-1   Logical query processing step numbers

```
(8)  SELECT (9) DISTINCT (11) <TOP_specification> <select_list>
(1)  FROM <left_table>
(3)    <join_type> JOIN <right_table>
(2)      ON <join_condition>
(4)  WHERE <where_condition>
(5)  GROUP BY <group_by_list>
(6)  WITH {CUBE | ROLLUP}
(7)  HAVING <having_condition>
(10) ORDER BY <order_by_list>
```

The first noticeable aspect of SQL that is different than other programming languages is the order in which the code is processed. In most programming languages, the code is processed in the order in which it is written. In SQL, the first clause that is processed is the FROM clause, while the SELECT clause, which appears first, is processed almost last.

Each step generates a virtual table that is used as the input to the following step. These virtual tables are not available to the caller (client application or outer query). Only the table generated by the final step is returned to the caller. If a certain clause is not specified in a query, the corresponding step is simply skipped. Following is a brief description of the different logical steps applied in both SQL Server 2000 and SQL Server 2005. Later in the chapter, I will discuss separately the steps that were added in SQL Server 2005.

Brief Description of Logical Query Processing Phases

Don't worry too much if the description of the steps doesn't seem to make much sense for now. These are provided as a reference. Sections that come after the scenario example will cover the steps in much more detail.

1. **FROM:** A Cartesian product (cross join) is performed between the first two tables in the FROM clause, and as a result, virtual table VT1 is generated.

2. **ON:** The ON filter is applied to VT1. Only rows for which the *<join_condition>* is TRUE are inserted to VT2.

3. **OUTER (join):** If an OUTER JOIN is specified (as opposed to a CROSS JOIN or an INNER JOIN), rows from the preserved table or tables for which a match was not found are added to the rows from VT2 as outer rows, generating VT3. If more than two tables appear in the FROM clause, steps 1 through 3 are applied repeatedly between the result of the last join and the next table in the FROM clause until all tables are processed.

4. **WHERE:** The WHERE filter is applied to VT3. Only rows for which the *<where_condition>* is TRUE are inserted to VT4.

5. **GROUP BY:** The rows from VT4 are arranged in groups based on the column list specified in the GROUP BY clause. VT5 is generated.

6. **CUBE | ROLLUP:** Supergroups (groups of groups) are added to the rows from VT5, generating VT6.

7. **HAVING:** The HAVING filter is applied to VT6. Only groups for which the *<having_condition>* is TRUE are inserted to VT7.

8. **SELECT:** The SELECT list is processed, generating VT8.

9. **DISTINCT:** Duplicate rows are removed from VT8. VT9 is generated.

10. **ORDER BY:** The rows from VT9 are sorted according to the column list specified in the ORDER BY clause. A cursor is generated (VC10).

11. **TOP:** The specified number or percentage of rows is selected from the beginning of VC10. Table VT11 is generated and returned to the caller.

Sample Query Based on Customers/Orders Scenario

To describe the logical processing phases in detail, I'll walk you through a sample query. First run the code in Listing 1-2 to create the Customers and Orders tables and populate them with sample data. Tables 1-1 and 1-2 show the contents of Customers and Orders.

Listing 1-2   Data definition language (DDL) and sample data for Customers and Orders

```
SET NOCOUNT ON;
USE tempdb;
GO
IF OBJECT_ID('dbo.Orders') IS NOT NULL
  DROP TABLE dbo.Orders;
GO
IF OBJECT_ID('dbo.Customers') IS NOT NULL
  DROP TABLE dbo.Customers;
GO
CREATE TABLE dbo.Customers
(
  customerid  CHAR(5)     NOT NULL PRIMARY KEY,
  city        VARCHAR(10) NOT NULL
);

INSERT INTO dbo.Customers(customerid, city) VALUES('FISSA', 'Madrid');
INSERT INTO dbo.Customers(customerid, city) VALUES('FRNDO', 'Madrid');
INSERT INTO dbo.Customers(customerid, city) VALUES('KRLOS', 'Madrid');
INSERT INTO dbo.Customers(customerid, city) VALUES('MRPHS', 'Zion');

CREATE TABLE dbo.Orders
(
  orderid    INT       NOT NULL PRIMARY KEY,
  customerid CHAR(5)   NULL     REFERENCES Customers(customerid)
);

INSERT INTO dbo.Orders(orderid, customerid) VALUES(1, 'FRNDO');
INSERT INTO dbo.Orders(orderid, customerid) VALUES(2, 'FRNDO');
INSERT INTO dbo.Orders(orderid, customerid) VALUES(3, 'KRLOS');
INSERT INTO dbo.Orders(orderid, customerid) VALUES(4, 'KRLOS');
INSERT INTO dbo.Orders(orderid, customerid) VALUES(5, 'KRLOS');
INSERT INTO dbo.Orders(orderid, customerid) VALUES(6, 'MRPHS');
INSERT INTO dbo.Orders(orderid, customerid) VALUES(7, NULL);
```

Table 1-1   Contents of Customers Table

customerid	city
FISSA	Madrid
FRNDO	Madrid
KRLOS	Madrid
MRPHS	Zion

Table 1-2   Contents of Orders Table

orderid	customerid
1	FRNDO
2	FRNDO
3	KRLOS

Table 1-2   Contents of Orders Table

orderid	customerid
4	KRLOS
5	KRLOS
6	MRPHS
7	NULL

I will use the query shown in Listing 1-3 as my example. The query returns customers from Madrid that made fewer than three orders (including zero orders), along with their order counts. The result is sorted by order count, from smallest to largest. The output of this query is shown in Table 1-3.

Listing 1-3   Query: Madrid customers with fewer than three orders

```
SELECT C.customerid, COUNT(O.orderid) AS numorders
FROM dbo.Customers AS C
  LEFT OUTER JOIN dbo.Orders AS O
    ON C.customerid = O.customerid
WHERE C.city = 'Madrid'
GROUP BY C.customerid
HAVING COUNT(O.orderid) < 3
ORDER BY numorders;
```

Table 1-3   Output: Madrid Customers with Fewer than Three Orders

customerid	numorders
FISSA	0
FRNDO	2

Both FISSA and FRNDO are customers from Madrid who made fewer than three orders. Examine the query, and try to read it while following the steps and phases described in Listing 1-1 and the section "Brief Description of Logical Query Processing Phases." If this is the first time you're thinking of a query in such terms, it's probably confusing for you. The following section should help you understand the nitty-gritty details.

Logical Query Processing Phase Details

This section describes the logical query processing phases in detail by applying them to the given sample query.

Step 1: Performing a Cartesian Product (Cross Join)

A Cartesian product (a cross join, or an unrestricted join) is performed between the first two tables that appear in the FROM clause, and as a result, virtual table VT1 is generated. VT1 contains one row for every possible combination of a row from the left table and a row from the right table. If the left table contains *n* rows and the right table contains *m* rows, VT1 will contain *n* × *m* rows. The columns in VT1 are qualified (prefixed) with their source table names (or table aliases, if you specified ones in the query). In the subsequent steps (step 2 and on), a reference to a column name that is ambiguous (appears in more than one input table) must be table-qualified (for example, *C.customerid*). Specifying the table qualifier for column names that appear in only one of the inputs is optional (for example, *O.orderid* or just *orderid*).

Apply step 1 to the sample query (shown in Listing 1-3):

```
FROM Customers AS C ... JOIN Orders AS O
```

As a result, you get the virtual table VT1 shown in Table 1-4 with 28 rows (4×7).

Table 1-4   Virtual Table VT1 Returned from Step 1

C.customerid	C.city	O.orderid	O.customerid
FISSA	Madrid	1	FRNDO
FISSA	Madrid	2	FRNDO
FISSA	Madrid	3	KRLOS
FISSA	Madrid	4	KRLOS
FISSA	Madrid	5	KRLOS
FISSA	Madrid	6	MRPHS
FISSA	Madrid	7	NULL
FRNDO	Madrid	1	FRNDO
FRNDO	Madrid	2	FRNDO
FRNDO	Madrid	3	KRLOS
FRNDO	Madrid	4	KRLOS
FRNDO	Madrid	5	KRLOS
FRNDO	Madrid	6	MRPHS
FRNDO	Madrid	7	NULL
KRLOS	Madrid	1	FRNDO
KRLOS	Madrid	2	FRNDO
KRLOS	Madrid	3	KRLOS
KRLOS	Madrid	4	KRLOS
KRLOS	Madrid	5	KRLOS
KRLOS	Madrid	6	MRPHS
KRLOS	Madrid	7	NULL
MRPHS	Zion	1	FRNDO
MRPHS	Zion	2	FRNDO
MRPHS	Zion	3	KRLOS
MRPHS	Zion	4	KRLOS
MRPHS	Zion	5	KRLOS
MRPHS	Zion	6	MRPHS
MRPHS	Zion	7	NULL

Step 2: Applying the ON Filter (Join Condition)

The ON filter is the first of three possible filters (ON, WHERE, and HAVING) that can be specified in a query. The logical expression in the ON filter is applied to all rows in the virtual table returned by the previous step (VT1). Only rows for which the <join_condition> is TRUE become part of the virtual table returned by this step (VT2).

Three-Valued Logic

Allow me to digress a bit to cover important aspects of SQL related to this step. The possible values of a logical expression in SQL are TRUE, FALSE, and UNKNOWN. This is referred to as three-valued logic. Three-valued logic is unique to SQL. Logical expressions in most programming languages can be only TRUE or FALSE. The UNKNOWN logical value in SQL typically occurs in a logical expression that involves a NULL (for example, the logical value of each of these three expressions is UNKNOWN: $NULL > 42$; $NULL = NULL$; $X + NULL > Y$). The special value NULL typically represents a missing or irrelevant value. When comparing a missing value to another value (even another NULL), the logical result is always UNKNOWN.

Dealing with UNKNOWN logical results and NULLs can be very confusing. While NOT TRUE is FALSE, and NOT FALSE is TRUE, the opposite of UNKNOWN (NOT UNKNOWN) is still UNKNOWN.

UNKNOWN logical results and NULLs are treated inconsistently in different elements of the language. For example, all query filters (ON, WHERE, and HAVING) treat UNKNOWN in the same way as FALSE. A row for which a filter is UNKNOWN is eliminated from the result set. On the other hand, an UNKNOWN value in a CHECK constraint is actually treated like TRUE. Suppose you have a CHECK constraint in a table to require that the salary column be greater than zero. A row entered into the table with a NULL salary is accepted, because ($NULL > 0$) is UNKNOWN and treated like TRUE in the CHECK constraint.

A comparison between two NULLs in filters yields an UNKNOWN, which as I mentioned earlier, is treated like FALSE—as if one NULL is different than another.

On the other hand, PRIMARY KEY constraints, sorting, and grouping treat NULLs as equal:

- You cannot insert into a table two rows with a NULL in a column that has a UNIQUE constraint defined on it.
- A GROUP BY clause groups all NULLs into one group.
- An ORDER BY clause sorts all NULLs together.

In short, it's a good idea to be aware of the way UNKNOWN logical results and NULLs are treated in the different elements of the language to spare you grief.

Apply step 2 to the sample query:

```
ON C.customerid = O.customerid
```

Table 1-5 shows the value of the logical expression in the ON filter for the rows from VT1.

Table 1-5   Logical Results of ON Filter Applied to Rows from VT1

Match?	C.customerid	C.city	O.orderid	O.customerid
FALSE	FISSA	Madrid	1	FRNDO
FALSE	FISSA	Madrid	2	FRNDO
FALSE	FISSA	Madrid	3	KRLOS
FALSE	FISSA	Madrid	4	KRLOS
FALSE	FISSA	Madrid	5	KRLOS
FALSE	FISSA	Madrid	6	MRPHS
UNKNOWN	FISSA	Madrid	7	NULL
TRUE	FRNDO	Madrid	1	FRNDO
TRUE	FRNDO	Madrid	2	FRNDO
FALSE	FRNDO	Madrid	3	KRLOS
FALSE	FRNDO	Madrid	4	KRLOS
FALSE	FRNDO	Madrid	5	KRLOS
FALSE	FRNDO	Madrid	6	MRPHS
UNKNOWN	FRNDO	Madrid	7	NULL
FALSE	KRLOS	Madrid	1	FRNDO
FALSE	KRLOS	Madrid	2	FRNDO
TRUE	KRLOS	Madrid	3	KRLOS
TRUE	KRLOS	Madrid	4	KRLOS
TRUE	KRLOS	Madrid	5	KRLOS
FALSE	KRLOS	Madrid	6	MRPHS
UNKNOWN	KRLOS	Madrid	7	NULL
FALSE	MRPHS	Zion	1	FRNDO
FALSE	MRPHS	Zion	2	FRNDO
FALSE	MRPHS	Zion	3	KRLOS
FALSE	MRPHS	Zion	4	KRLOS
FALSE	MRPHS	Zion	5	KRLOS
TRUE	MRPHS	Zion	6	MRPHS
UNKNOWN	MRPHS	Zion	7	NULL

Only rows for which the <join_condition> is TRUE are inserted to VT2—the input virtual table of the next step, shown in Table 1-6.

Table 1-6   Virtual Table VT2 Returned from Step 2

Match?	C.customerid	C.city	O.orderid	O.customerid
TRUE	FRNDO	Madrid	1	FRNDO
TRUE	FRNDO	Madrid	2	FRNDO
TRUE	KRLOS	Madrid	3	KRLOS
TRUE	KRLOS	Madrid	4	KRLOS
TRUE	KRLOS	Madrid	5	KRLOS
TRUE	MRPHS	Zion	6	MRPHS

Step 3: Adding Outer Rows

This step is relevant only for an outer join. For an outer join, you mark one or both input tables as *preserved* by specifying the type of outer join (LEFT, RIGHT, or FULL). Marking a table as preserved means that you want all of its rows returned, even when filtered out by the <join_condition>. A left outer join marks the left table as preserved, a right outer join marks the right, and a full outer join marks both. Step 3 returns the rows from VT2, plus rows from the preserved table for which a match was not found in step 2. These added rows are referred to as *outer rows*. NULLs are assigned to the attributes (column values) of the nonpreserved table in the outer rows. As a result, virtual table VT3 is generated.

In our example, the preserved table is Customers:

```
Customers AS C LEFT OUTER JOIN Orders AS O
```

Only customer FISSA did not find any matching orders (wasn't part of VT2). Therefore, FISSA is added to the rows from the previous step with NULLs for the Orders attributes, and as a result, virtual table VT3 (shown in Table 1-7) is generated.

Table 1-7   Virtual Table VT3 Returned from Step 3

C.customerid	C.city	O.orderid	O.customerid
FRNDO	Madrid	1	FRNDO
FRNDO	Madrid	2	FRNDO
KRLOS	Madrid	3	KRLOS
KRLOS	Madrid	4	KRLOS
KRLOS	Madrid	5	KRLOS
MRPHS	Zion	6	MRPHS
FISSA	Madrid	NULL	NULL

Note   If more than two tables are joined, steps 1 through 3 will be applied between VT3 and the third table in the FROM clause. This process will continue repeatedly if more tables appear in the FROM clause, and the final virtual table will be used as the input for the next step.

Step 4: Applying the WHERE Filter

The WHERE filter is applied to all rows in the virtual table returned by the previous step. Only rows for which <where_condition> is TRUE become part of the virtual table returned by this step (VT4).

> **Caution**   Because the data is not grouped yet, you cannot use aggregate filters here—for example, you cannot write WHERF orderdate - MAX(orderdate). Also, you cannot refer to column aliases created by the SELECT list because the SELECT list was not processed yet—for example, you cannot write SFI FCT YEAR(orderdate) AS orderyear ... WHERE orderyear > 2000.

A confusing aspect of queries containing an OUTER JOIN clause is whether to specify a logical expression in the ON filter or in the WHERE filter. The main difference between the two is that ON is applied before adding outer rows (step 3), while WHERE is applied after step 3. An elimination of a row from the preserved table by the ON filter is not final because step 3 will add it back; while an elimination of a row by the WHERE filter is final. Bearing this in mind should help you make the right choice.

For example, suppose you want to return certain customers and their orders from the Customers and Orders tables. The customers you want to return are only Madrid customers, both those that made orders and those that did not. An outer join is designed exactly for such a request. You perform a left outer join between Customers and Orders, marking the Customers table as the preserved table. To be able to return customers that made no orders, you must specify the correlation between customers and orders in the ON clause (ON C.customerid = O.customerid). Customers with no orders are eliminated in step 2 but added back in step 3 as outer rows. However, because you want to keep only rows for Madrid customers, regardless of whether they made orders, you must specify the city filter in the WHERE clause (WHERE C.city = 'Madrid'). Specifying the city filter in the ON clause would cause non-Madrid customers to be added back to the result set by step 3.

> **Tip**   There's a logical difference between the ON and WHERE clauses only when using an outer join. When using an inner join, it doesn't matter where you specify your logical expressions because step 3 is skipped. The filters are applied one after the other with no intermediate step between them.
>
> There's one exception that is relevant only when using the GROUP BY ALL option. I will discuss this option shortly in the next section, which covers the GROUP BY phase.

Apply the filter in the sample query:

```
WHERE C.city = 'Madrid'
```

The row for customer MRPHS from VT3 is removed because the city is not Madrid, and virtual table VT4, which is shown in Table 1-8, is generated.

Table 1-8   Virtual Table VT4 Returned from Step 4

C.customerid	C.city	O.orderid	O.customerid
FRNDO	Madrid	1	FRNDO
FRNDO	Madrid	2	FRNDO
KRLOS	Madrid	3	KRLOS
KRLOS	Madrid	4	KRLOS
KRLOS	Madrid	5	KRLOS
FISSA	Madrid	NULL	NULL

Step 5: Grouping

The rows from the table returned by the previous step are arranged in groups. Each unique combination of values in the column list that appears in the GROUP BY clause makes a group. Each base row from the previous step is attached to one and only one group. Virtual table VT5 is generated. VT5 consists of two sections: the *groups* section that is made of the actual groups, and the *raw* section that is made of the attached base rows from the previous step.

Apply step 5 to the sample query:

```
GROUP BY C.customerid
```

You get the virtual table VT5 shown in Table 1-9.

Table 1-9   Virtual Table VT5 Returned from Step 5

Groups	Raw			
C.customerid	C.customerid	C.city	O.orderid	O.customerid
FRNDO	FRNDO	Madrid	1	FRNDO
	FRNDO	Madrid	2	FRNDO
KRLOS	KRLOS	Madrid	3	KRLOS
	KRLOS	Madrid	4	KRLOS
	KRLOS	Madrid	5	KRLOS
FISSA	FISSA	Madrid	NULL	NULL

If a GROUP BY clause is specified in a query, all following steps (HAVING, SELECT, and so on) can specify only expressions that result in a scalar (singular) value for a group. In other words, the results can be either a column/expression that participates in the GROUP BY list—for example, *C.customerid*—or an aggregate function, such as *COUNT(O.orderid)*. The reasoning behind this limitation is that a single row in the final result set will eventually be generated for each group (unless filtered out). Examine VT5 in Table 1-9, and think what the query should return for customer FRNDO if the SELECT list you specified had been *SELECT C.customerid, O.orderid*. There are two different *orderid* values in the group; therefore, the answer is nondeterministic. SQL doesn't allow such a request. On the other hand, if you specify: *SELECT C.customerid, COUNT(O.orderid) AS numorders*, the answer for FRNDO is deterministic: it's 2.

> **Note**   You're also allowed to group by the result of an expression—for instance, *GROUP BY YEAR(orderdate)*. If you do, when working in SQL Server 2000, all following steps cannot perform any further manipulation to the GROUP BY expression, unless it's a base column. For example, the following is not allowed in SQL Server 2000: *SELECT YEAR(orderdate) + 1 AS nextyear ... GROUP BY YEAR(orderdate)*. In SQL Server 2005, this limitation has been removed.

This phase considers NULLs as equal. That is, all NULLs are grouped into one group just like a known value.

As I mentioned earlier, the input to the GROUP BY phase is the virtual table returned by the previous step (VT4). If you specify GROUP BY ALL, groups that were removed by the fourth phase (WHERE filter) are added to this step's result virtual table (VT5) with an empty set in the raw section. This is the only case where there is a difference between specifying a logical expression in the ON clause and in the WHERE clause when using an inner join. If you revise our example to use the *GROUP BY ALL C.customerid* instead of *GROUP BY C.customerid*, you'll find that customer *MRPHS*, which was removed by the WHERE filter, will be added to VT5's groups section, along with an empty set in the raw section. The COUNT aggregate function in one of the following steps would be zero for such a group, while all other aggregate functions (SUM, AVG, MIN, MAX) would be NULL.

> **Note**   The GROUP BY ALL option is a nonstandard legacy feature. It introduces many semantic issues when Microsoft adds new T-SQL features. Even though this feature is fully supported in SQL Server 2005, you might want to refrain from using it because it might eventually be deprecated.

Step 6: Applying the CUBE or ROLLUP Option

If CUBE or ROLLUP is specified, supergroups are created and added to the groups in the virtual table returned by the previous step. Virtual table VT6 is generated.

Step 6 is skipped in our example because CUBE and ROLLUP are not specified in the sample query. CUBE and ROLLUP will be covered in Chapter 6.

Step 7: Applying the HAVING Filter

The HAVING filter is applied to the groups in the table returned by the previous step. Only groups for which the *<having_condition>* is TRUE become part of the virtual table returned by this step (VT7). The HAVING filter is the first and only filter that applies to the grouped data.

Apply this step to the sample query:

```
HAVING COUNT(O.orderid) < 3
```

The group for KRLOS is removed because it contains three orders. Virtual table VT7, which is shown in Table 1-10, is generated.

Table 1-10   Virtual Table VT7 Returned from Step 7

C.customerid	C.customerid	C.city	O.orderid	O.customerid
FRNDO	FRNDO	Madrid	1	FRNDO
	FRNDO	Madrid	2	FRNDO
FISSA	FISSA	Madrid	NULL	NULL

> **Note**   It is important to specify *COUNT(O.orderid)* here and not *COUNT(*)*. Because the join is an outer one, outer rows were added for customers with no orders. *COUNT(*)* would have added outer rows to the count, undesirably producing a count of one order for FISSA. *COUNT(O.orderid)* correctly counts the number of orders for each customer, producing the desired value 0 for FISSA. Remember that *COUNT(<expression>)* ignores NULLs just like any other aggregate function.

An aggregate function does not accept a subquery as an input—for example, *HAVING SUM((SELECT …)) > 10*.

Step 8: Processing the SELECT List

Though specified first in the query, the SELECT list is processed only at the eighth step. The SELECT phase constructs the table that will eventually be returned to the caller. The expressions in the SELECT list can return base columns and manipulations of base columns from the virtual table returned by the previous step. Remember that if the query is an aggregate query, after step 5 you can refer to base columns from the previous step only if they are part of the groups section (GROUP BY list). If you refer to columns from the raw section, these must be aggregated. Base columns selected from the previous step maintain their column names unless you alias them (for example, *col1 AS c1*). Expressions that are not base columns should be aliased to have a column name in the result table—for example, *YEAR(orderdate) AS orderyear*.

> **Important**   Aliases created by the SELECT list cannot be used by earlier steps. In fact, expression aliases cannot even be used by other expressions within the same SELECT list. The reasoning behind this limitation is another unique aspect of SQL, being an all-at-once operation. For example, in the following SELECT list, the logical order in which the expressions are evaluated should not matter and is not guaranteed: *SELECT c1 + 1 AS e1, c2 + 1 AS e2*. Therefore, the following SELECT list is not supported: *SELECT c1 + 1 AS e1, e1 + 1 AS e2*. You're allowed to reuse column aliases only in steps following the SELECT list, such as the ORDER BY step—for example, *SELECT YEAR(orderdate) AS orderyear … ORDER BY orderyear*.

Apply this step to the sample query:

```
SELECT C.customerid, COUNT(O.orderid) AS numorders
```

You get the virtual table VT8, which is shown in Table 1-11.

Table 1-11   Virtual Table VT8 Returned from Step 8

C.customerid	numorders
FRNDO	2
FISSA	0

The concept of an all-at-once operation can be hard to grasp. For example, in most programming environments, to swap values between variables you use a temporary variable. However, to swap table column values in SQL, you can use:

```
UPDATE dbo.T1 SET c1 = c2, c2 = c1;
```

Logically, you should assume that the whole operation takes place at once. It is as if the table is not modified until the whole operation finishes and then the result replaces the source. For similar reasons, this UPDATE

```
UPDATE dbo.T1 SET c1 = c1 + (SELECT MAX(c1) FROM dbo.T1);
```

would update all of T1's rows, adding to c1 the maximum c1 value from T1 when the update started. You shouldn't be concerned that the maximum c1 value would keep changing as the operation proceeds because the operation occurs all at once.

Step 9: Applying the DISTINCT Clause

If a DISTINCT clause is specified in the query, duplicate rows are removed from the virtual table returned by the previous step, and virtual table V19 is generated.

Step 9 is skipped in our example because DISTINCT is not specified in the sample query. In fact, DISTINCT is redundant when GROUP BY is used, and it would remove no rows.

Step 10: Applying the ORDER BY Clause

The rows from the previous step are sorted according to the column list specified in the ORDER BY clause returning the cursor VC10. This step is the first and only step where column aliases created in the SELECT list can be reused.

According to both ANSI SQL:1992 and ANSI SQL:1999, if DISTINCT is specified, the expressions in the ORDER BY clause have access only to the virtual table returned by the previous step (VT9). That is, you can sort by only what you select. ANSI SQL:1992 has the same limitation even when DISTINCT is not specified. However, ANSI SQL:1999 enhances the ORDER BY support by allowing access to both the input and output virtual tables of the SELECT phase. That is, if DISTINCT is not specified, in the ORDER BY clause you can specify any expression that would have been allowed in the SELECT clause. Namely, you can sort by expressions that you don't end up returning in the final result set.

There is a reason for not allowing access to expressions you're not returning if DISTINCT is specified. When adding expressions to the SELECT list, DISTINCT can potentially change the number of rows returned. Without DISTINCT, of course, changes in the SELECT list don't affect the number of rows returned. T-SQL always implemented the ANSI SQL:1999 approach.

In our example, because DISTINCT is not specified, the ORDER BY clause has access to both VT7, shown in Table 1-10, and VT8, shown in Table 1-11.

In the ORDER BY clause, you can also specify ordinal positions of result columns from the SELECT list. For example, the following query sorts the orders first by customerid, and then by *orderid*:

```
SELECT orderid, customerid FROM dbo.Orders ORDER BY 2, 1;
```

However, this practice is not recommended because you might make changes to the SELECT list and forget to revise the ORDER BY list accordingly. Also, when the query strings are long, it's hard to figure out which item in the ORDER BY list corresponds to which item in the SELECT list.

Important   This step is different than all other steps in the sense that it doesn't return a valid table; instead, it returns a cursor. Remember that SQL is based on set theory. A set doesn't have a predetermined order to its rows; it's a logical collection of members, and the order of the members shouldn't matter. A query that applies sorting to the rows of a table returns an object with rows organized in a particular physical order. ANSI calls such an object a *cursor*. Understanding this step is one of the most fundamental things in correctly under- standing SQL.

Usually when describing the contents of a table, most people (including me) routinely depict the rows in a certain order. For example, I provided Tables 1-1 and 1-2 to describe the con- tents of the Customers and Orders tables. In depicting the rows one after the other, uninten- tionally I help cause some confusion by implying a certain order. A more correct way to depict the content of the Customers and Orders tables would be the one shown in Figure 1-1.

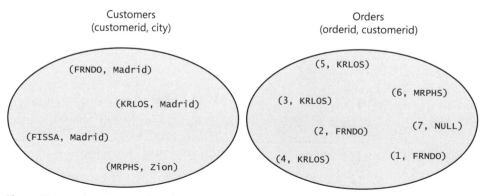

Figure 1-1   Customers and Orders sets

> **Note**   Although SQL doesn't assume any given order to a table's *rows*, it does maintain
> ordinal positions for *columns* based on creation order. Specifying *SELECT* * (although a bad
> practice for several reasons that I'll describe later in the book) guarantees the columns would
> be returned in creation order.

Because this step doesn't return a table (it returns a cursor), a query with an ORDER BY
clause cannot be used as a table expression—that is, a view, inline table-valued function, subquery, derived table, or common table expression (CTE). Rather, the result must be returned
to the client application that expects a physical record set back. For example, the following
derived table query is invalid and produces an error:

```
SELECT *
FROM (SELECT orderid, customerid
      FROM dbo.Orders
      ORDER BY orderid) AS D;
```

Similarly, the following view is invalid:

```
CREATE VIEW dbo.VSortedOrders
AS

SELECT orderid, customerid
FROM dbo.Orders
ORDER BY orderid
GO
```

In SQL, no query with an ORDER BY clause is allowed in a table expression. In T-SQL, there
is an exception to this rule that is described in the following step, applying the TOP option.

So remember, don't assume any particular order for a table's rows. Conversely, don't specify
an ORDER BY clause unless you really need the rows sorted. Sorting has a cost—SQL Server
needs to perform an ordered index scan or apply a sort operator.

The ORDER BY step considers NULLs as equal. That is, NULLs are sorted together. ANSI
leaves the question of whether NULLs are sorted lower or higher than known values up to
implementations, which must be consistent. T-SQL sorts NULLs as lower than known values
(first).

Apply this step to the sample query:

```
ORDER BY numorders
```

You get the cursor VC10 shown in Table 1-12.

Table 1-12   Cursor VC10 Returned from Step 10

C.customerid	numorders
FISSA	0
FRNDO	2

Step 11: Applying the TOP Option

The TOP option allows you to specify a number or percentage of rows (rounded up) to return. In SQL Server 2000, the input to TOP must be a constant, while in SQL Server 2005, the input can be any self-contained expression. The specified number of rows is selected from the beginning of the cursor returned by the previous step. Table VT11 is generated and returned to the caller.

> **Note**   The TOP option is T-SQL specific and is not relational.

This step relies on the physical order of the rows to determine which rows are considered the "first" requested number of rows. If an ORDER BY clause with a unique ORDER BY list is specified in a query, the result is deterministic. That is, there's only one possible correct result, containing the first requested number of rows based on the specified sort. Similarly, when an ORDER BY clause is specified with a non-unique ORDER BY list but the TOP option is specified WITH TIES, the result is also deterministic. SQL Server inspects the last row that was returned physically and returns all other rows from the table that have the same sort values as the last row.

However, when a non-unique ORDER BY list is specified without the WITH TIES option, or ORDER BY is not specified at all, a TOP query is nondeterministic. That is, the rows returned are the ones that SQL Server happened to physically access first, and there might be different results that are considered correct. If you want to guarantee determinism, a TOP query must have either a unique ORDER BY list or the WITH TIES option.

As you can surmise, TOP queries are most commonly used with an ORDER BY clause that determines which rows to return. SQL Server allows you to specify TOP queries in table expressions. It wouldn't make much sense to allow TOP queries in table expressions without allowing you to also specify an ORDER BY clause. (See the limitation in step 10.) Thus, queries with an ORDER BY clause are in fact allowed in table expressions only if TOP is also specified. In other words, a query with both a TOP clause and an ORDER BY clause returns a relational result. The ironic thing is that by using the nonstandard, nonrelational TOP option, a query that would otherwise return a cursor returns a relational result. Support for nonstandard, nonrelational features (as practical as they might be) allows programmers to exploit them in some absurd ways that would not have been supported otherwise. Here's an example:

```
SELECT *
FROM (SELECT TOP 100 PERCENT orderid, customerid
      FROM dbo.Orders
      ORDER BY orderid) AS D;
```

Or:

```
CREATE VIEW dbo.VSortedOrders
AS

SELECT TOP 100 PERCENT orderid, customerid
FROM dbo.Orders
ORDER BY orderid
GO
```

Step 11 is skipped in our example because TOP is not specified.

New Logical Processing Phases in SQL Server 2005

This section covers the logical processing phases involved with the new T-SQL query elements in SQL Server 2005. These include new table operators (APPLY, PIVOT, and UNPIVOT), the new OVER clause, and new set operations (EXCEPT and INTERSECT).

> **Note**   APPLY, PIVOT, and UNPIVOT are not ANSI operators; rather, they are T-SQL specific extensions.

I find it a bit problematic to cover the logical processing phases involved with the new product version in detail in the first chapter. These elements are completely new, and there's so much to say about each. Instead, I will provide a brief overview of each element here and conduct much more detailed discussions later in the book in focused chapters.

As I mentioned earlier, my goal for this chapter is to give you a reference that you can return to later when in doubt regarding the logical aspects of query elements and the way they interact with each other. Bearing this in mind, the full meaning of the logical phases of query processing that handle the new elements might not be completely clear to you right now. Don't let that worry you. After reading the focused chapters discussing each element in detail, you will probably find the reference I provide in this chapter useful. Rest assured that everything will make more sense then.

Table Operators

SQL Server 2005 supports four types of table operators in the FROM clause of a query: JOIN, APPLY, PIVOT, and UNPIVOT.

I covered the logical processing phases involved with joins earlier and will also discuss joins in more details in Chapter 5. Here I will briefly describe the three new operators and how they interact with each other.

Table operators get one or two tables as inputs. Call them *left input* and *right input* based on their position in respect to the table operator keyword (JOIN, APPLY, PIVOT, UNPIVOT). Just like joins, all table operators get a virtual table as their left input. The first table operator that appears in the FROM clause gets a table expression as the left input and returns a virtual table as a result. A table expression can stand for many things: a real table, temporary table, table variable, derived table, CTE, view, or table-valued function.

> **More Info**   For details on table expressions, please refer to Chapter 4.

The second table operator that appears in the FROM clause gets the virtual table returned from the previous table operation as its left input.

Each table operator involves a different set of steps. For convenience and clarity, I'll prefix the step numbers with the initial of the table operator (J for JOIN, A for APPLY, P for PIVOT, and U for UNPIVOT).

Following are the four table operators along with their elements:

```
(J) <left_table_expression>
       <join_type> JOIN <right_table_expression>
       ON <join_condition>

(A) <left_table_expression>
       {CROSS | OUTER} APPLY <table_expression>

(P) <left_table_expression>
       PIVOT (<aggregate_func(<expression>)> FOR
         <source_col> IN(<target_col_list>))
         AS <result_table_alias>

(U) <left_table_expression>
       UNPIVOT (<target_values_col> FOR
         <target_names_col> IN(<source_col_list>))
         AS <result_table_alias>
```

As a reminder, a join involves a subset (depending on the join type) of the following steps:

1. J1: Cross Left and Right Inputs
2. J2: Apply ON Clause
3. J3: Add Outer Rows

APPLY

The APPLY operator involves a subset (depending on the apply type) of the following two steps:

1. A1: Apply Right Table Expression to Left Table Input's Rows
2. A2: Add Outer Rows

The APPLY operator basically applies the right table expression to every row from the left input. You can think of it as being similar to a join, with one important difference—the right table expression can refer to the left input's columns as correlations. It's as though in a join there's no precedence between the two inputs when evaluating them. With APPLY, it's as though the left input is evaluated first, and then the right input is evaluated once for each row from the left.

Step A1 is always applied in both CROSS APPLY and OUTER APPLY. Step A2 is applied only for OUTER APPLY. CROSS APPLY doesn't return an outer (left) row if the inner (right) table expression returns an empty set for it. OUTER APPLY will return such a row, with NULLs in the inner table expression's attributes.

For example, the following query returns the two most recent orders (assuming for the sake of this example that *orderid* represents chronological order) for each customer, generating the output shown in Table 1-13:

```
SELECT C.customerid, city, orderid
FROM dbo.Customers AS C
  CROSS APPLY
    (SELECT TOP(2) orderid, customerid
     FROM dbo.Orders AS O
     WHERE O.customerid = C.customerid
     ORDER BY orderid DESC) AS CA;
```

Table 1-13   Two Most Recent Orders for Each Customer

customerid	city	orderid
FRNDO	Madrid	2
FRNDO	Madrid	1
KRLOS	Madrid	5
KRLOS	Madrid	4
MRPHS	Zion	6

Notice that FISSA is missing from the output because the table expression CA returned an empty set for it. If you also want to return customers that made no orders, use OUTER APPLY as follows, generating the output shown in Table 1-14:

```
SELECT C.customerid, city, orderid
FROM dbo.Customers AS C
  OUTER APPLY
    (SELECT TOP(2) orderid, customerid
     FROM dbo.Orders AS O
     WHERE O.customerid = C.customerid
     ORDER BY orderid DESC) AS OA;
```

Table 1-14   Two Most Recent Orders for Each Customer, Including Customers that Made No Orders

customerid	city	orderid
FISSA	Madrid	NULL
FRNDO	Madrid	2
FRNDO	Madrid	1

Table 1-14 Two Most Recent Orders for Each Customer, Including Customers that Made No Orders

customerid	city	orderid
KRLOS	Madrid	5
KRLOS	Madrid	4
MRPHS	Zion	6

> **More Info**   For more details on the APPLY operator, please refer to Chapter 7.

PIVOT

The PIVOT operator essentially allows you to rotate, or pivot, data from a state of groups of multiple rows to a state of multiple columns in a single row per group, performing aggregations along the way.

Before I explain and demonstrate the logical steps involved with using the PIVOT operator, examine the following query, which I will later use as the left input to the PIVOT operator:

```
SELECT C.customerid, city,
  CASE
    WHEN COUNT(orderid)  = 0 THEN 'no_orders'
    WHEN COUNT(orderid) <= 2 THEN 'upto_two_orders'
    WHEN COUNT(orderid)  > 2 THEN 'more_than_two_orders'
  END AS category
FROM dbo.Customers AS C
  LEFT OUTER JOIN dbo.Orders AS O
    ON C.customerid = O.customerid
GROUP BY C.customerid, city;
```

This query returns customer categories based on count of orders (no orders, up to two orders, more than two orders), yielding the result set shown in Table 1-15.

Table 1-15 Customer Categories Based on Count of Orders

customerid	city	category
FISSA	Madrid	no_orders
FRNDO	Madrid	upto_two_orders
KRLOS	Madrid	more_than_two_orders
MRPHS	Zion	upto_two_orders

Suppose you wanted to know the number of customers that fall into each category per city. The following PIVOT query allows you to achieve this, generating the output shown in Table 1-16:

```
SELECT city, no_orders, upto_two_orders, more_than_two_orders
FROM (SELECT C.customerid, city,
        CASE
          WHEN COUNT(orderid)  = 0 THEN 'no_orders'
```

```
       WHEN COUNT(orderid) <= 2 THEN 'upto_two_orders'
       WHEN COUNT(orderid)  > 2 THEN 'more_than_two_orders'
     END AS category
    FROM dbo.Customers AS C
      LEFT OUTER JOIN dbo.Orders AS O
        ON C.customerid = O.customerid
    GROUP BY C.customerid, city) AS D
  PIVOT(COUNT(customerid) FOR
    category IN([no_orders],
                [upto_two_orders],
                [more than_two_orders])) AS P;
```

Table 1-16   Number of Customers that Fall into Each Category per City

city	no_orders	upto_two_orders	more_than_two_orders
Madrid	1	1	1
Zion	0	1	0

Don't get distracted by the query that generates the derived table D. As far as you're concerned, the PIVOT operator gets a table expression called D, containing the customer categories as its left input.

The PIVOT operator involves the following three logical phases:

1. P1: Implicit Grouping

2. P2: Isolating Values

3. P3: Applying the Aggregate Function

The first phase (P1) is very tricky to grasp. You can see in the query that the PIVOT operator refers to two of the columns from D as input arguments (*customerid* and *category*). The first phase implicitly groups the rows from D based on all columns that weren't mentioned in PIVOT's inputs, as though there were a hidden GROUP BY there. In our case, only the city column wasn't mentioned anywhere in PIVOT's input arguments. So you get a group for each city (Madrid and Zion, in our case).

> **Note**   PIVOT's implicit grouping phase doesn't substitute an explicit GROUP BY clause, should one appear in a query. PIVOT will eventually yield a result virtual table, which in turn will be input to the next logical phase, be it another table operation or the WHERE phase. And as I described earlier in the chapter, following the WHERE phase, there might be a GROUP BY phase. So when both PIVOT and GROUP BY appear in a query, you get two separate grouping phases—one as the first phase of PIVOT (P1), and a later one as the query's GROUP BY phase.

PIVOT's second phase (P2) isolates values corresponding to target columns. Logically, it uses the following CASE expression for each target column specified in the IN clause:

```
CASE WHEN <source_col> = <target_col_element> THEN <expression> END
```

In this situation, the following three expressions are logically applied:

```
CASE WHEN category = 'no_orders'          THEN customerid END,
CASE WHEN category = 'upto_two_orders'    THEN customerid END,
CASE WHEN category = 'more_than_two_orders' THEN customerid END
```

> **Note** A CASE expression with no ELSE clause has an implicit ELSE NULL.

For each target column, the CASE expression will return the customer ID only if the source row had the corresponding category; otherwise, CASE will return a NULL.

PIVOT's third phase (P3) applies the specified aggregate function on top of each CASE expression, generating the result columns. In our case, the expressions logically become the following:

```
COUNT(CASE WHEN category = 'no_orders'
            THEN customerid END) AS [no_orders],
COUNT(CASE WHEN category = 'upto_two_orders'
            THEN customerid END) AS [upto_two_orders],
COUNT(CASE WHEN category = 'more_than_two_orders'
            THEN customerid END) AS [more_than_two_orders]
```

In summary, the previous PIVOT query is logically equivalent to the following query:

```
SELECT city,
  COUNT(CASE WHEN category = 'no_orders'
              THEN customerid END) AS [no_orders],
  COUNT(CASE WHEN category = 'upto_two_orders'
              THEN customerid END) AS [upto_two_orders],
  COUNT(CASE WHEN category = 'more_than_two_orders'
              THEN customerid END) AS [more_than_two_orders]
FROM (SELECT C.customerid, city,
        CASE
          WHEN COUNT(orderid)  = 0 THEN 'no_orders'
          WHEN COUNT(orderid) <= 2 THEN 'upto_two_orders'
          WHEN COUNT(orderid)  > 2 THEN 'more_than_two_orders'
        END AS category
      FROM dbo.Customers AS C
       LEFT OUTER JOIN dbo.Orders AS O
        ON C.customerid = O.customerid
      GROUP BY C.customerid, city) AS D
GROUP BY city;
```

> **More Info** For more details on the PIVOT operator, please refer to Chapter 6.

UNPIVOT

UNPIVOT is the inverse of PIVOT, rotating data from a state of multiple column values from the same row to multiple rows, each with a different source column value.

Before I demonstrate UNPIVOT's logical phases, first run the code in Listing 1-4, which creates and populates the PivotedCategories table.

Listing 1-4   Creating and populating the PivotedCategories table

```
SELECT city, no_orders, upto_two_orders, more_than_two_orders
INTO dbo.PivotedCategories
FROM (SELECT C.customerid, city,
        CASE
          WHEN COUNT(orderid)  = 0 THEN 'no_orders'
          WHEN COUNT(orderid) <= 2 THEN 'upto_two_orders'
          WHEN COUNT(orderid)  > 2 THEN 'more_than_two_orders'
        END AS category
      FROM dbo.Customers AS C
        LEFT OUTER JOIN dbo.Orders AS O
          ON C.customerid = O.customerid
      GROUP BY C.customerid, city) AS D
  PIVOT(COUNT(customerid) FOR
    category IN([no_orders],
               [upto_two_orders],
               [more_than_two_orders])) AS P;


UPDATE dbo.PivotedCategories
  SET no_orders = NULL, upto_two_orders = 3
WHERE city = 'Madrid';
```

After you run the code in Listing 1-4, the PivotedCategories table will contain the data shown in Table 1-17.

Table 1-17   Contents of PivotedCategories Table

city	no_orders	upto_two_orders	more_than_two_orders
Madrid	NULL	3	1
Zion	0	1	0

I will use the following query as an example to describe the logical processing phases involved with the UNPIVOT operator:

```
SELECT city, category, num_custs
FROM dbo.PivotedCategories
  UNPIVOT(num_custs FOR
    category IN([no_orders],
               [upto_two_orders],
               [more_than_two_orders])) AS U
```

This query unpivots (or splits) the customer categories from each source row to a separate row per category, generating the output shown in Table 1-18.

Table 1-18   Unpivoted Customer Categories

city	category	num_custs
Madrid	upto_two_orders	3
Madrid	more_than_two_orders	1
Zion	no_orders	0

Table 1-18   Unpivoted Customer Categories

city	category	num_custs
Zion	upto_two_orders	1
Zion	more_than_two_orders	0

The following three logical processing phases are involved in an UNPIVOT operation:

1. U1: Generating Duplicates
2. U2: Isolating Target Column Values
3. U3: Filtering Out Rows with NULLs

The first step (U1) duplicates rows from the left table expression provided to UNPIVOT as an input (PivotedCategories, in our case). Each row is duplicated once for each source column that appears in the IN clause. Because there are three column names in the IN clause, each source row will be duplicated three times. The result virtual table will contain a new column holding the source column names as character strings. The name of this column will be the one specified right before the IN clause (category, in our case). The virtual table returned from the first step in our example is shown in Table 1-19.

Table 1-19   Virtual Table Returned from UNPIVOT's First Step

city	no_orders	upto_two_orders	more_than_two_orders	category
Madrid	NULL	3	1	no_orders
Madrid	NULL	3	1	upto_two_orders
Madrid	NULL	3	1	more_than_two_orders
Zion	0	1	0	no_orders
Zion	0	1	0	upto_two_orders
Zion	0	1	0	more_than_two_orders

The second step (U2) isolates the target column values. The name of the target column that will hold the values is specified right before the FOR clause (num_custs, in our case). The target column name will contain the value from the column corresponding to the current row's category from the virtual table. The virtual table returned from this step in our example is shown in Table 1-20.

Table 1-20   Virtual Table Returned from UNPIVOT's Second Step

city	category	num_custs
Madrid	no_orders	NULL
Madrid	upto_two_orders	3
Madrid	more_than_two_orders	1
Zion	no_orders	0
Zion	upto_two_orders	1
Zion	more_than_two_orders	0

UNPIVOT's third and final step (U3) is to filter out rows with NULLs in the result value column (*num_custs*, in our case). The virtual table returned from this step in our example is shown in Table 1-21.

Table 1-21   Virtual Table Returned from UNPIVOT's Third Step

city	category	num_custs
Madrid	*upto_two_orders*	3
Madrid	*more_than_two_orders*	1
Zion	*no_orders*	0
Zion	*upto_two_orders*	1
Zion	*more_than_two_orders*	0

When you're done experimenting with the UNPIVOT operator, drop the PivotedCategories table:

```
DROP TABLE dbo.PivotedCategories;
```

> **More Info**   For more details on the UNPIVOT operator, please refer to Chapter 6.

OVER Clause

The OVER clause allows you to request window-based calculations. In SQL Server 2005, this clause is a new option for aggregate functions (both built-in and custom Common Language Runtime [CLR]-based aggregates) and it is a required element for the four new analytical ranking functions (ROW_NUMBER, RANK, DENSE_RANK, and NTILE). When an OVER clause is specified, its input, instead of the query's GROUP BY list, specifies the window of rows over which the aggregate or ranking function is calculated.

I won't discuss applications of windows-based calculations here, nor will I go into detail about exactly how these functions work; I'll only explain the phases in which the OVER clause is applicable. I'll cover the OVER clause in more detail in Chapters 4 and 6.

The OVER clause is applicable only in one of two phases: the SELECT phase (8) and the ORDER BY phase (10). This clause has access to whichever virtual table is provided to that phase as input. Listing 1-5 highlights the logical processing phases in which the OVER clause is applicable.

Listing 1-5   OVER clause in logical query processing

```
(8)  SELECT (9) DISTINCT (11) TOP <select_list>
(1)  FROM <left_table>
(3)    <join_type> JOIN <right_table>
(2)      ON <join_condition>
(4)  WHERE <where_condition>
```

```
(5)  GROUP BY <group_by_list>
(6)  WITH {CUBE | ROLLUP}
(7)  HAVING <having_condition>
(10) ORDER BY <order_by_list>
```

You specify the OVER clause following the function to which it applies in either the *select_list* or the *order_by_list*.

Even though I didn't really explain in detail how the OVER clause works, I'd like to demonstrate its use in both phases where it's applicable. In the following example, an OVER clause is used with the COUNT aggregate function in the SELECT list; the output of this query is shown in Table 1-22:

```
SELECT orderid, customerid,
  COUNT(*) OVER(PARTITION BY customerid) AS num_orders
FROM dbo.Orders
WHERE customerid IS NOT NULL
  AND orderid % 2 = 1;
```

Table 1-22   OVER Clause Applied in SELECT Phase

orderid	customerid	num_orders
1	FRNDO	1
3	KRLOS	2
5	KRLOS	2

The PARTITION BY clause defines the window for the calculation. The *COUNT(*)* function counts the number of rows in the virtual table provided to the SELECT phase as input, where the *customerid* is equal to the one in the current row. Remember that the virtual table provided to the SELECT phase as input has already undergone WHERE filtering—that is, NULL customer IDs and even order IDs have been eliminated.

You can also use the OVER clause in the ORDER BY list. For example, the following query sorts the rows according to the total number of output rows for the customer (in descending order), and generates the output shown in Table 1-23:

```
SELECT orderid, customerid
FROM dbo.Orders
WHERE customerid IS NOT NULL
  AND orderid % 2 = 1
ORDER BY COUNT(*) OVER(PARTITION BY customerid) DESC;
```

Table 1-23   OVER Clause Applied in ORDER BY Phase

orderid	customerid
3	KRLOS
5	KRLOS
1	FRNDO

> **More Info**   For details on using the OVER clause with aggregate functions, please refer to Chapter 6. For details on using the OVER clause with analytical ranking functions, please refer to Chapter 4

Set Operations

SQL Server 2005 supports three set operations: UNION, EXCEPT, and INTERSECT. Only UNION is available in SQL Server 2000. These SQL operators correspond to operators defined in mathematical set theory. This is the syntax for a query applying a set operation:

```
[(]left_query[)] {UNION [ALL] | EXCEPT | INTERSECT} [(]right_query[)]
[ORDER BY <order_by_list>]
```

Set operations compare complete rows between the two inputs. UNION returns one result set with the rows from both inputs. If the ALL option is not specified, UNION removes duplicate rows from the result set. EXCEPT returns distinct rows that appear in the left input but not in the right. INTERSECT returns the distinct rows that appear in both inputs. There's much more to say about these set operations, but here I'd just like to focus on the logical processing steps involved in a set operation.

An ORDER BY clause is not allowed in the individual queries. You are allowed to specify an ORDER BY clause at the end of the query, but it will apply to the result of the set operation.

In terms of logical processing, each input query is first processed separately with all its relevant phases. The set operation is then applied, and if an ORDER BY clause is specified, it is applied to the result set.

Take the following query, which generates the output shown in Table 1-24, as an example:

```
SELECT 'O' AS letter, customerid, orderid FROM dbo.Orders
WHERE customerid LIKE '%O%'

UNION ALL

SELECT 'S' AS letter, customerid, orderid FROM dbo.Orders
WHERE customerid LIKE '%S%'

ORDER BY letter, customerid, orderid;
```

Table 1-24   Result of a UNION ALL Set Operation

letter	customerid	orderid
O	FRNDO	1
O	FRNDO	2
O	KRLOS	3
O	KRLOS	4

Table 1-24   Result of a UNION ALL Set Operation

letter	customerid	orderid
O	KRLOS	5
S	KRLOS	3
S	KRLOS	4
S	KRLOS	5
S	MRPHS	6

First, each input query is processed separately following all the relevant logical processing phases. The first query returns a table with orders placed by customers containing the letter O. The second query returns a table with orders placed by customers containing the letter S. The set operation UNION ALL combines the two sets into one. Finally, the ORDER BY clause sorts the rows by *letter*, *customerid*, and *orderid*.

As another example for logical processing phases of a set operation, the following query returns customers that have made no orders:

```
SELECT customerid FROM dbo.Customers
EXCEPT
SELECT customerid FROM dbo.Orders;
```

The first query returns the set of customer IDs from Customers ({FISSA, FRNDO, KRLOS, MRPHS}), and the second query returns the set of customer IDs from Orders ({FRNDO, FRNDO, KRLOS, KRLOS, KRLOS, MRPHS, NULL}). The set operation returns ({FISSA}), the set of rows from the first set that do not appear in the second set. Finally, the set operation removes duplicates from the result set. In this case, there are no duplicates to remove.

The result set's column names are determined by the set operation's left input. Columns in corresponding positions must match in their datatypes or be implicitly convertible. Finally, an interesting aspect of set operations is that they treat NULLs as equal.

> **More Info**   You can find a more detailed discussion about set operations in Chapter 5.

Conclusion

Understanding logical query processing phases and the unique aspects of SQL is important to get into the special mindset required to program in SQL. By being familiar with those aspects of the language, you will be able to produce efficient solutions and explain your choices. Remember, the idea is to master the basics.

Chapter 2
Physical Query Processing

—By Lubor Kollar

While the previous chapter described *what* outcome a query execution result should produce, this one will explain *how* Microsoft SQL Server 2005 attains that outcome.

The SQL language is spoken by most database experts, and all relational database products include some dialect of the SQL standard. Nevertheless, each product has its own particular query-processing mechanism. Understanding the way a database engine processes queries helps software architects, designers, and programmers make good choices when designing database schemas and writing queries.

When a query reaches the database engine, the SQL Server performs two major steps to produce the desired query result. The first step is query compilation, which generates a *query plan*, and the second step is the execution of the query plan.

Query compilation in SQL Server 2005 consists of three steps: parsing, algebrization, and query optimization. After those steps are completed, the compiler stores the optimized query plan in the procedure cache. There, the execution engine copies the plan into its executable form and subsequently executes the steps in the query plan to produce the query result. If the same query or stored procedure is executed again and the plan is located in the procedure cache, the compilation step is skipped and the query or stored procedure proceeds directly to execution reusing the stored plan.

In this chapter, we will look at how the query optimizer produces the query plan and how you can get your hands on both the estimated and actual plans used when processing the query. This is a case where starting with an example of the final product, together with a description of how the product performs its desired function, helps us understand the process of building the product itself. Therefore, I will start with an example of executing a query that is similar to the one we worked with in Chapter 1. Then, once the basics are understood, I will look more closely inside the query compilation process and describe the various forms of query plans.

Flow of Data During Query Processing

If you want to make the upcoming example a hands-on experience, start SQL Server Management Studio (SSMS). Run the query shown in Listing 2-1 against the Northwind database, after clicking the Include Actual Execution Plan icon, as shown in Figure 2-1.

> **Note**   The Northwind database is not shipped with SQL Server 2005. You can download the SQL Server 2000 version (which works on SQL Server 2005 as well) from *http://www.microsoft.com/technet/prodtechnol/sql/2000/downloads/default.mspx*. The installation script will create a directory named SQL Server 2000 Sample Databases on your C: drive, and there you will find instnwnd.sql. Run this script in SSMS to create the Northwind database. Alternatively, you can use CREATE DATABASE Northwind FOR ATTACH ... to attach the NORTHWND.LDF and NORTHWND.MDF files to your instance of SQL Server 2005.

> **Note**   Remember that you can download the source code for the book from *http://www.insidetsql.com*.

Listing 2-1   Query against Northwind to demonstrate the result of optimization

```
USE Northwind;

SELECT C.CustomerID, COUNT(O.OrderID) AS NumOrders
FROM dbo.Customers AS C
  LEFT OUTER JOIN dbo.Orders AS O
    ON C.CustomerID = O.CustomerID
WHERE C.City = 'London'
GROUP BY C.CustomerID
HAVING COUNT(O.OrderID) > 5
ORDER BY NumOrders;
```

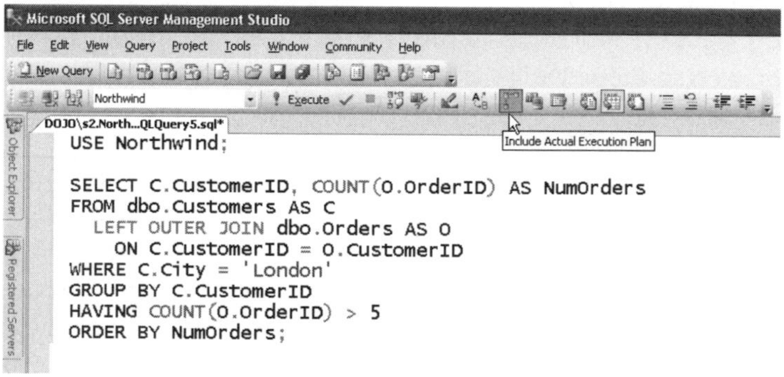

![Screenshot of Microsoft SQL Server Management Studio showing the query from Listing 2-1 with the Include Actual Execution Plan option highlighted in the toolbar.]

Figure 2-1   Include Actual Execution Plan option

You will obtain a graphical query plan similar to the one in Figure 2-2 in the Execution Plan pane of the SSMS window.

> **Note** The execution plan in Figure 2-2 contains some elements that were added for demonstration purposes, and you will not see them in the plan that you will get. For each arrow, I have added the estimated numbers of rows in parentheses and a reference number used in the following text.

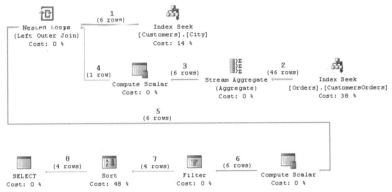

Figure 2-2 Execution plan for query in Listing 2-1

This query returns the ID (*CustomerID*) and number of orders placed (*NumOrders*) for all customers from London that placed more than five orders. The result is shown in Table 2-1.

Table 2-1   Output of Query in Listing 2-1

CustomerID	NumOrders
EASTC	8
SEVES	9
BSBEV	10
AROUT	13

How does SQL Server execute the plan shown in Figure 2-2 to produce the desired result?

The execution of the individual branches is interleaved. I will demonstrate the process in an upcoming example, where SQL Server alternates its activity between the two branches of the Nested Loops step. To start, keep in mind that all gray arrows in Figure 2-2 represent data streams—rows produced by the operator are consumed by the next operator in the direction of the arrow. The thickness of the arrows corresponds to the relative number of rows the query optimizer is estimating will flow through the connection.

The engine starts execution by performing the Index Seek at the top of Figure 2-2 on the Customers table—and it will select the first row with the customer residing in London. You can see the seek predicate *Prefix: [Northwind].[dbo].[Customers].City = N'London'* in a small pop-up window if you hover the cursor over the Index Seek on the Customer table icon, as shown in Figure 2-3. The selected row is passed to the Nested Loops operator on the arrow 1, and as soon as it reaches the Nested Loops the so-called inner side of the Nested Loops operator is activated. In our case, in Figure 2-2 the inner side of the Nested Loops operator consists of the Compute Scalar, Stream Aggregate, and Index Seek operators connected to the Nested Loops by arrows 4, 3, and 2, respectively.

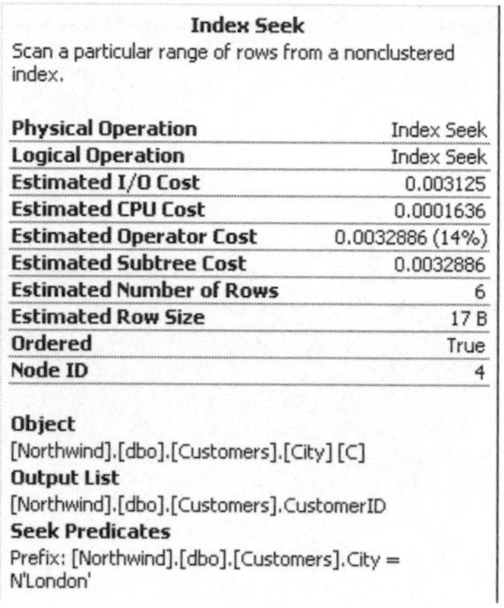

Index Seek	
Scan a particular range of rows from a nonclustered index.	
Physical Operation	Index Seek
Logical Operation	Index Seek
Estimated I/O Cost	0.003125
Estimated CPU Cost	0.0001636
Estimated Operator Cost	0.0032886 (14%)
Estimated Subtree Cost	0.0032886
Estimated Number of Rows	6
Estimated Row Size	17 B
Ordered	True
Node ID	4
Object	
[Northwind].[dbo].[Customers].[City] [C]	
Output List	
[Northwind].[dbo].[Customers].CustomerID	
Seek Predicates	
Prefix: [Northwind].[dbo].[Customers].City = N'London'	

Figure 2-3   Pop-up information window for the Index Seek operator

If we investigate the Index Seek operator on the inner side of the Nested Loops in Figure 2-2, we find out that its seek predicate is *Prefix: [Northwind].[dbo].[Orders].CustomerID = [Northwind] .[dbo].[Customers].[CustomerID] as [C].[CustomerID]*. We see that the *C.CustomerID* value is used to seek into the Orders table to retrieve all orders for the *CustomerID*. This is an example where the inner side of the Nested Loops references the value obtained in the other, so-called outer side of the Nested Loops.

After all orders for the first London customer are fetched, they are passed via the arrow marked 2 to the Stream Aggregate operator, where they are counted and the resulting count named *Expr1004* is stored in the row by the Compute Scalar operator between arrows 3 and 4. Then the row composed from the *CustomerID* and the order count is passed through arrows 5 and 6 to the Filter operator with the predicate *[Expr1004] > (5)*. *Expr1004* represents the expression *COUNT(O.OrderID)*, and the *(5)* is the constant we have used in the query to limit the result to only customers with more than five orders.

Again, you can see the predicate in a pop-up window once you position the cursor on the Filter icon. If the predicate holds (meaning the customer has more than five orders), the row is passed to the Sort operator via arrow 7. Observe that SQL Server cannot output any rows from the Sort until it collects all the rows to be sorted. This is because the last row that arrives at the Sort potentially could be the one that should be "first" in the given order (the customer with the lowest number of orders exceeding five in our case). Therefore, the rows are "waiting" in the Sort, and the above outlined process is repeated for the next London customer found in the Index Seek on the Customers table. Once all the rows to be returned reach the Sort operator, it will return them in the correct order (arrow 8).

Compilation

A batch is a group of one or more Transact-SQL statements compiled as a single unit. A stored procedure is an example of a batch. Another example is a set of statements in the Query window in the SQL Pane in SSMS. The GO command divides sets of statements into separate batches. Observe that GO is not a T-SQL statement. SQLCMD, OSQL, and SSMS use the keyword GO to signal the end of a batch.

SQL Server compiles the statements of a batch into a single executable unit called an *execution plan*. During compilation, the compiler expands the statements by including the relevant constraints, triggers, and cascading actions that have to be carried out during the statement execution. If the compiled batch contains invocations of other stored procedures or functions and their plans are not in the cache, the stored procedures and functions are recursively compiled as well. The main steps in batch compilation are shown in Figure 2-4.

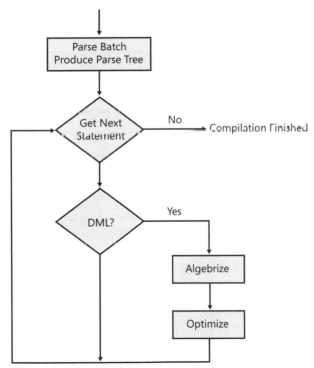

Figure 2-4   Compilation

It is important to be aware that compilation and execution are distinct phases of query processing and that the gap between when SQL Server compiles a query and when the query is executed can be as short as a few microseconds or as long as several days. An ad-hoc query usually doesn't have its plans in the cache when it is processed; therefore, it is compiled and its plan is immediately executed. On the other hand, the compiled plan for a frequently executed stored procedure might reside in the procedure cache for a very long time because SQL Server removes the infrequently used plans from the procedure cache first if the storage space is required for other purposes, including storing new query plans.

The optimizer is taking into account how many CPUs are available for SQL Server and the amount of memory that is available for query execution. However, the number of CPUs available to execute the query and the amount of available memory can change dramatically from moment to moment. You really have to think of compilation and execution as two separate activities, even when you are submitting an ad-hoc SQL statement through SSMS and executing it immediately.

When SQL Server is ready to process a batch, an execution plan for the batch might already be available in SQL Server's cache. If not, the compiler compiles the batch and produces a query plan. The compilation process encompasses a few things. First, SQL Server goes through the phases of *parsing* and *binding*. Parsing is the process of checking the syntax and transforming your SQL batch into a parse tree. Parsing is a generic operation used by compilers for almost all programming languages. The only specific thing in SQL Server's parser is its own grammar for defining valid T-SQL syntax.

Parsing includes checking, for example, whether a nondelimited table or column name starts with a digit. The parser flags an error if one is found. However, parsing does not check whether a column used in a WHERE clause really exists in any of the tables listed in the FROM clause; that issue is dealt with during binding.

The binding process determines the characteristics of the objects that you reference inside your SQL statements, and it checks whether the semantics you're asking for make sense. For example, while a query including FROM A JOIN B may be parsed successfully, binding will fail if A is a table and B is a stored procedure.

Optimization is the last step in the compilation. The optimizer has to translate the nonprocedural request of a set-based SQL statement into a procedure that can execute efficiently and return the desired results. Similar to binding, optimization is performed one statement at a time for all statements in the batch. After the compiler generates the plan for the batch and stores the plan in the procedure cache, a special copy of the plan's *execution context* is executed. SQL Server caches the execution contexts much like it does with the query plans, and if the same batch starts the second execution before the first one is finished, SQL Server will create the second execution context from the same plan. You can learn more about the SQL Server procedure cache from *Inside Microsoft SQL Server 2005: Query Tuning and Optimization* (Microsoft Press, 2006) by Kalen Delaney or from the white paper "Batch Compilation, Recompilation, and Plan Caching Issues in SQL Server 2005" at *http://www.microsoft.com/technet/prodtechnol/sql/2005/recomp.mspx#EJAA*.

SQL Server does not optimize every statement in the batch. It optimizes only certain classes of statements: those that access database tables and for which there might be multiple execution choices. SQL Server optimizes all DML (data manipulation language) statements—these are SELECT, INSERT, DELETE, and UPDATE statements. In addition to the DML, some other T-SQL statements are optimized; CREATE INDEX is one of them. Only the optimized statements will produce query plans. The following example shows that the optimizer creates a plan for CREATE INDEX:

```
CREATE TABLE dbo.T(a INT, b INT, c INT, d INT);
INSERT INTO dbo.T VALUES(1, 1, 1, 1);
SET STATISTICS PROFILE ON; -- forces producing showplan from execution
CREATE INDEX i ON dbo.T(a, b) INCLUDE(c, d);
SET STATISTICS PROFILE OFF; -- reverse showplan setting
DROP TABLE dbo.T; -- remove the table
```

It will produce this optimized query plan:

```
insert [dbo].[T] select *, %%bmk%% from [dbo].[T]
  |--Index Insert(OBJECT:([db].[dbo].[T].[i]))
    |--Sort(ORDER BY:([db].[dbo].[T].[a] ASC, [db].[dbo].[T].[b] ASC, [Bmk1000] ASC))
      |--Table Scan(OBJECT:([db].[dbo].[T]))
```

Similar to the CREATE INDEX statement, CREATE STATISTICS, UPDATE STATISTICS, and some forms of ALTER INDEX are also optimized. Several statements executed internally to perform database checking in DBCC CHECKDB are optimized as well. However, be aware that out of these non-DML optimized statements only CREATE INDEX produces a showplan with a statistics profile and none of them produces a query plan directly in SSMS. (Showplans will be explained later in the "Working with the Query Plan" section.)

Algebrizer

The *algebrizer*[*] is a new component in SQL Server 2005, and binding is its most important function. (Note that because the binding is the most significant function of the algebrizer often the whole process performed by the algebrizer is called *binding*). The algebrizer replaces the *normalizer* in SQL Server 2000. The algebrizer is a good example of the long-term focus of the SQL Server development team. With each release of SQL Server, several parts of the product are completely re-architected and rewritten to maintain a healthy code base. In the case of the algebrizer, the redesign spanned two releases of SQL Server. The development team's goals were not only to rewrite but also to completely redesign the logic to serve current and future expansions of SQL Server functionality.

The output of parsing—a parse tree—is the algebrizer's input. After performing several walks through the parse tree, the algebrizer produces its output—called a *query processor tree*—that is ready for query optimization.

---

* Thanks goes to Eugene Zabokritski for permission to include information from the patent filed for the algebrizer.

In addition to binding, which is mostly concerned with name resolution by accessing the catalog information, the algebrizer flattens some binary operators and performs type derivation. In addition to performing name resolution, the algebrizer performs special binding for aggregates and groupings.

Operator Flattening

The algebrizer performs flattening of the binary operators UNION, AND, and OR. The parser's notion of these operators is binary only, as demonstrated on the left side of the illustration in the Figure 2-5 for the expression *(A=1) OR (A=2) OR (A=3) OR (A=4) OR (A=5) OR (A=6) OR (A=7)*. On the other hand, all compilation passes following the parser prefer to assemble multiples of binary operators into single *n*-ary operator whenever possible, as shown on the right side of the same figure. This is especially important for very long IN lists that the parser converts into chains of Ors. Among other things, flattening will eliminate most of the stack-overflow problems in subsequent passes that are caused by very deep trees. The code inside SQL Server that performs the flattening is itself carefully written to use iteration rather than recursion whenever possible so that the algebrizer itself is not prone to the same problem.

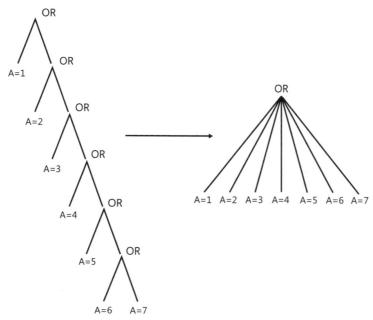

Figure 2-5   OR flattening

Name Resolution

Every table and column name in the parse tree is associated with a reference to the corresponding table or column definition object. Names representing the same object get the same reference. This is important information for the next step—query optimization. The algebrizer checks that every object name in the query actually refers to a valid table or column that exists in the system catalogs and is visible in the particular query scope. The algebrizer subsequently associates the object name with information from the catalogs.

Name resolution for views is the process of replacing a view reference by its view tree (the parse tree of the query that defines the view). Views are resolved recursively if they refer to additional views.

Type Derivation

Because T-SQL is statically typed, the algebrizer determines the type of each node of the parse tree. The algebrizer performs this in a bottom-up fashion, starting from the leaf nodes—columns (whose type information is in the catalogs) and constants. Then, for a non-leaf node, the type information is derived from the types of the children and the attributes of the node. A good example of type derivation is the process of figuring out the final data type of a UNION query, where different data types can appear in corresponding column positions. (See the "Guidelines for Using Union" chapter in the SQL Server 2005 Books Online for more details.)

Aggregate Binding

Consider the following example against table T1 with columns $c1$ and $c2$, and table T2 with column x of the same data type as $T1.c2$:

```
SELECT c1 FROM dbo.T1
GROUP BY c1
HAVING EXISTS
  (SELECT * FROM dbo.T2
   WHERE T2.x > MAX(T1.c2));
```

SQL Server computes the MAX aggregate in the outer query *SELECT c1 FROM dbo.T1 GROUP BY c1*, although it is syntactically located in the inner one. The algebrizer makes this decision based on the aggregate's argument. The bottom line is that every aggregate needs to be bound to its hosting query—the place where it is correctly evaluated. This is known as *aggregate binding*.

Grouping Binding

This is perhaps the least obvious of all activities performed by the algebrizer. Let's consider an example against table T1 with columns $c1$, $c2$, and $c3$:

```
SELECT c1 + c2, MAX(c3) FROM dbo.T1 GROUP BY c1 + c2;
```

The use of the expression $c1 + c2$ in the SELECT list is legitimate, although had we placed just $c1$ in this list, the query would have been semantically incorrect. The reason for this is that *grouped queries* (for example, those with an explicit GROUP BY or HAVING clause) have different semantics than nongrouped ones. In particular, all nonaggregated columns or expressions in the SELECT list of a query with GROUP BY must have a direct match in the GROUP BY list, and the process of verifying this fact is known as *grouping binding*.

Unfortunately, explicit clauses such as GROUP BY or HAVING aren't the only factors that might force a SELECT list to become grouped. According to SQL's rules, just the presence of an aggregate function that binds to a particular list makes that SELECT list grouped, even if it has no GROUP BY or HAVING clauses. Here is a simple example:

```
SELECT c1, MAX(c2) FROM dbo.T1;
```

This is a grouped SELECT, because there is a MAX aggregate. Because it is a grouped SELECT, the use of the nonaggregated column *c1* is illegal and the query is incorrect.

An important role of the algebrizer is to identify any semantic errors in the statement. The following example shows that this is a nontrivial task for some queries with aggregates:

```
SELECT c1, (SELECT T2.y FROM dbo.T2 WHERE T2.x = MAX(T1.c2)) FROM dbo.T1;
```

This query is incorrect for the same reason as the previous one, but it is clear that we have to complete aggregate binding for the entire query just to realize this. The *MAX(T1.c2)* in the inner query must be evaluated in the outer query much as it was in the query *SELECT c1, MAX(c2) FROM dbo.T1;* just shown, and therefore, the use of the nonaggregated column *c1* in the SELECT list is illegal and the query is incorrect.

Optimization

One of the most important and complex components involved in processing your queries is the query optimizer. The optimizer's job is to produce an efficient execution plan for each query in a batch or a stored procedure. The plan lists the steps SQL Server has to carry out to execute your query, and it includes such information as which index or indexes to use when accessing data from each table in the query. The plan also includes the strategy for processing each join operation, each aggregation, each sort, and each partitioned table access. The plan shows an intent to perform operations on parallel threads—that is, where the row streams are partitioned, repartitioned, and then merged into a single stream.

SQL Server's query optimizer is a cost-based optimizer, which means that it tries to come up with the cheapest execution plan for each SQL statement. The cost of the plan reflects the estimated time to complete the query. For each query, the optimizer must analyze the possible plans and choose the one with the lowest estimated cost. Some complex statements have millions of possible execution plans. In these cases, the query optimizer does not analyze all possible combinations. Instead, it tries to find an execution plan that has a cost reasonably close to the theoretical minimum. Later in this section, I'll explain some ways the optimizer can reduce the amount of time it spends on optimization.

The lowest estimated cost is not necessarily the lowest resource cost; the query optimizer chooses the plan that most quickly returns results to the user with a reasonable cost in resources. For example, processing a query in parallel (using multiple CPUs simultaneously for the same query) typically uses more resources than processing it serially using a single CPU, but the query completes much faster in parallel. The optimizer will propose a parallel execution plan to return results, and SQL Server will use such a parallel plan for execution if the load on the server is not adversely affected.

Optimization itself involves several steps. The *trivial plan* optimization is the first step. The idea behind trivial plan optimization is that cost-based optimization is expensive to initialize and run. The optimizer can try many possible variations in looking for the cheapest plan. If SQL Server knows by investigating the query and the relevant metadata that there is only one viable plan for a query, it can avoid a lot of the work required to initialize and perform cost-based optimization. A common example is a query that consists of an INSERT with a VALUES clause into a table that does not participate in any indexed views. There is only one possible plan. Another example is a SELECT from single table with no indexes and no GROUP BY. In these two cases, SQL Server should just generate the plan and not try to find something better. The trivial plan the optimizer finds is the obvious plan, and usually it is very inexpensive. Later in the chapter, I will show how to determine whether the optimizer produced a trivial plan for a particular query.

If the optimizer doesn't find a trivial plan, SQL Server will perform some simplifications, which are usually syntactic transformations of the query itself, to look for commutative properties and operations that can be rearranged. SQL Server can perform operations that don't require considering the cost or analyzing what indexes are available but that result in a more efficient query. An example of simplification is to evaluate simple single table where filters before the joins. As described in Chapter 1, the filters are *logically* evaluated after the joins, but evaluating the filters before the joins produces correct result as well and is always more efficient because it removes unqualified rows before the join operation.

Another example of simplification is transforming outer joins into inner joins in some cases, as shown in Figure 2-6. In general, an outer join will add rows to the result set of an inner join. These additional rows have the NULL value in all columns of the inner set if there is no inner row satisfying the join predicate. Therefore, if there is a predicate on the inner set that disqualifies these rows, the result of the outer join is the same as the inner join and it will never be cheaper to generate the outer join result. Therefore, SQL Server changes the outer join to an inner join during simplification. In the following OUTER JOIN query, the predicate *Products.UnitPrice > 10* disqualifies all additional rows that would be produced by the OUTER JOIN, and therefore, the OUTER JOIN is simplified into an INNER join:

```
USE Northwind;
SELECT
  [Order Details].OrderID,
  Products.ProductName,
  [Order Details].Quantity,
  [Order Details].UnitPrice
FROM dbo.[Order Details]
  LEFT OUTER JOIN dbo.Products
    ON [Order Details].ProductID = Products.ProductID
WHERE Products.UnitPrice > 10;
```

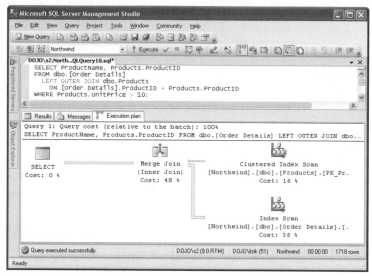

Figure 2-6 Outer join simplification

SQL Server then loads up the statistical information on the indexes and tables, and the optimizer begins the cost-based optimization process.

The cost-based optimizer is using a set of transformation rules that try various permutations of data access strategies, join orders, aggregation placement, subquery transformations, and other rules that guarantee the correct result is still produced. Usually, correct results are the same results; however, it is important to recognize that for some queries there is more than one correct result. For example, any set of 10 orders would be a correct result for the query

```
SELECT TOP (10) <select_list> FROM Orders;
```

A change to data that affects the optimizer's cost-based analysis could change the chosen plan, which in turn could change the result unexpectedly.

If the optimizer compared the cost of every valid plan and chose the least costly one, the optimization process could take a very long time—the number of valid plans can be huge. Therefore, the optimization is broken up into three *search phases*. A set of transformation rules is associated with each phase. After each phase, SQL Server evaluates the cost of the cheapest query plan to that point. If the plan is cheap enough, SQL Server ends the optimization and chooses that plan. If the plan is not cheap enough, the optimizer runs the next phase, which contains an additional set of usually more complex rules.

Many queries, even though they are complicated, have very cheap plans. If SQL Server applied many transformation rules and tried various join orders, the optimization process could take substantially longer than the query execution itself. Therefore, the first phase of the cost-based optimization, Phase 0, contains a limited set of rules and is applied to queries with at least four tables. Because join reordering alone generates many potential plan candidates, the optimizer uses a limited number of join orders in Phase 0, and it considers only Hash joins and Nested Loops. If this phase finds a plan with an estimated cost below 0.2, the optimization ends. The queries with final query plans produced by Phase 0 are typically found in transaction processing applications; therefore, this phase is also called the *Transaction Processing phase*.

The next step, Phase 1 or Quick Plan optimization, uses more transformation rules and tries different join orders. When the phase is completed, if the best plan costs less than 1.0, the optimization ends. Up to this point, the optimizer considers only nonparallel query plans. If more than one CPU is available to SQL Server and the least expensive plan produced by Phase 1 is more than the *cost threshold for parallelism* (which you can determine by using sp_configure to find the current value–the default is 5), Phase 1 is repeated with the goal of finding the best parallel plan. The costs of the serial and parallel plans obtained in Phase 1 are compared, and Phase 2, the Full Optimization phase, is executed for the cheaper of the two. Phase 2 contains additional rules–for example, it uses Outer Join reordering and automatic Indexed View substitution for multitable views. Figure 2-7 shows the phases of query optimization in SQL Server 2005.

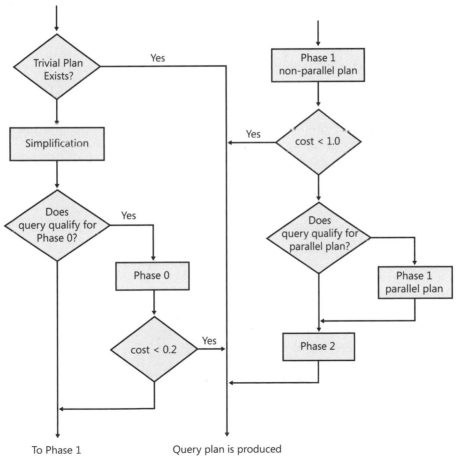

Figure 2-7   Phases of query optimization

SQL Server 2005 provides plenty of insight into its own operation. This is true also for query optimization. In the previous releases of SQL Server, the only product of query optimization was the query plan; the history of the optimization was forgotten, and only the final result was preserved. In SQL Server 2005, there exists a new peephole into the optimizer's activity—it is the dynamic management view (DMV) sys.dm_exec_query_optimizer_info. This view provides cumulative information about all the optimizations performed since the SQL Server was started.

Using this DMV, you can find out what optimizer events are happening while the optimizer is processing your batches. The sys.dm_exec_query_optimizer_info DMV returns three columns: *counter*, *occurrence*, and *value*. The column named *counter* provides the name of the optimizer event. The *occurrence* column shows the cumulative number of occurrences of the optimizer event, and some events are using the *value* column to provide additional event-specific values. For example, each time the optimizer chooses a trivial plan, the *occurrence* column value for the trivial plan counter will be increased by one. Similarly, you can find out how many times each optimization phase—Phase 0, 1, or 2—was executed by investigating the corresponding "search 0", "search 1", or "search 2" events. The *value* column is used, for example, for the "tables" event—it captures the average number of tables referenced in the optimized statements. Please refer to the sys.dm_exec_query_optimizer_info topic in the "SQL Server Language Reference" section of Books Online for a detailed description of all counters returned by the sys.dm_exec_query_optimizer_info DMV.

When using sys.dm_exec_query_optimizer_info, you should be careful about the procedure cache. If the cache already contains the plan for your query or batch, the optimization phase is skipped and there will be no optimizer events generated. You can use DBCC FREEPROCCACHE to clear up the procedure cache to ensure the compilation will take place afterwards. However, you should be careful using the DBCC FREEPROCCACHE on production servers because it will delete the contents of the procedure cache, and all statements and stored procedures will have to be compiled anew.

Because the counters of optimizer events are cumulative, you want to find their values before and after the optimization of your batch or workload if you are interested in the generated events and statistics. However, execution of 'select * from sys.dm_exec_query_optimizer_info' itself might generate optimizer events. Therefore, I have carefully constructed the code example in Listing 2-2 to avoid self-spoiling of the optimizer information provided by the sys.dm_exec_query_optimizer_info in SQL Server 2005. Your statement or batch has to be inserted in the marked place inside the example in Listing 2-2. Out of the 38 types of events in this DMV, the example will display only those that either have changed the *occurrence* or *value* column as a result of your statement or batch. After you insert your code, you should execute the whole batch once from SSMS to obtain the optimizer events triggered by your code.

Listing 2-2   Script to obtain information about your batch from sys.dm_exec_query_optimizer_info

```
SET NOCOUNT ON;
USE Northwind; -- use your database name here
DBCC FREEPROCCACHE; -- empty the procedure cache
GO
-- we will use tempdb..OptStats table to capture
-- the information from several executions
-- of sys.dm_exec_query_optimizer_info
IF (OBJECT_ID('tempdb..OptStats') IS NOT NULL)
  DROP TABLE tempdb..OptStats;
GO
-- the purpose of this statement is
-- to create the temporary table tempdb..OptStats
SELECT 0 AS Run, *
INTO tempdb..OptStats
FROM sys.dm_exec_query_optimizer_info;
GO
-- this will populate the procedure cache
-- with this statement's plan so that it will not
-- generate any optimizer events when executed
-- next time
-- the following GO is intentional to ensure
-- the query plan reuse will happen for the following
-- INSERT for its next invocation in this script
GO
INSERT INTO tempdb..OptStats
  SELECT 1 AS Run, *
  FROM sys.dm_exec_query_optimizer_info;
GO
-- same reason as above; observe the "2" replaced "1"
-- therefore, we will have a different plan
GO
INSERT INTO tempdb..OptStats
  SELECT 2 AS Run, *
  FROM sys.dm_exec_query_optimizer_info;
GO
-- empty the temporary table
TRUNCATE TABLE tempdb..OptStats;
GO
-- store the "before run" information
-- in the temporary table with the output
-- of sys.dm_exec_query_optimizer_info
-- with value "1" in the column Run
GO
INSERT INTO tempdb..OptStats
  SELECT 1 AS Run, *
  FROM sys.dm_exec_query_optimizer_info;
GO
-- your statement or batch is executed here
/*** the following is an example
SELECT C.CustomerID, COUNT(O.OrderID) AS NumOrders
FROM dbo.Customers AS C
  LEFT OUTER JOIN dbo.Orders AS O
    ON C.CustomerID = O.CustomerID
```

```
WHERE C.City = 'London'
GROUP BY C.CustomerID
HAVING COUNT(O.OrderID) > 5
ORDER BY NumOrders;
***/
GO
-- store the "after run" information
-- in the temporary table with the output
-- of sys.dm_exec_query_optimizer_info
-- with value "2" in the column Run
GO
INSERT INTO tempdb..OptStats
  SELECT 2 AS Run, *
  FROM sys.dm_exec_query_optimizer_info;
GO
-- extract all "events" that changed either
-- the Occurrence or Value column value between
-- the Runs 1 and 2 from the temporary table.
-- Display the values of Occurrence and Value
-- for all such events before (Run1Occurrence and
-- Run1Value) and after (Run2Occurrence and
-- Run2Value) executing your batch or query.
-- This is the result set generated by the script.
WITH X (Run,Counter, Occurrence, Value)
AS
(
  SELECT *
  FROM tempdb..OptStats WHERE Run=1
),
Y (Run,Counter, Occurrence, Value)
AS
(
  SELECT *
  FROM tempdb..OptStats
  WHERE Run=2
)
SELECT X.Counter, Y.Occurrence-X.Occurrence AS Occurrence,
  CASE (Y.Occurrence-X.Occurrence)
    WHEN 0 THEN (Y.Value*Y.Occurrence-X.Value*X.Occurrence)
       ELSE (Y.Value*Y.Occurrence-X.Value*X.Occurrence)/(Y.Occurrence-X.Occurrence)
  END AS Value
FROM X JOIN Y
  ON (X.Counter=Y.Counter
     AND (X.Occurrence<>Y.Occurrence OR X.Value<>Y.Value));
GO
-- drop the temporary table
DROP TABLE tempdb..OptStats;
GO
```

If we use the preceding script to investigate the compiler events and the corresponding counters and values for the statement from Listing 2-1, after we run the script with the statement embedded in the marked place (– your statement or batch is executed here), we will see the result of the statement itself followed by Table 2-2. From the counters, we see that SQL Server optimized the batch consisting of a single statement 0.008752 seconds, the cost of the final plan is 0.023881, the DOP is 0 (which means serial plan), a single optimization has been executed, only Phase 1 (same as "search 1") of optimization has been exercised using 647 search tasks in 0.00721 seconds (the "search" is almost always the most expensive part of the query compilation), and the query has 2 tables. If the batch consists of multiple statements, the *Value* column in Table 2-2 would contain average values of the counters and statistics.

Table 2-2   Counters of the Optimizer Event for the Statement from Listing 2-1

Counter	Occurrence	Value
Elapsed time	1	0.008752
Final cost	1	0.023881
Maximum DOP	1	0
Optimizations	1	1
search 1	1	1
search 1 tasks	1	647
search 1 time	1	0.00721
Tables	1	2
Tasks	1	647

Working with the Query Plan

Showplan is the term used by SQL Server users to name the textual, graphical, or XML form of a query plan produced by the query optimizer. We use it also as a verb to name the process of obtaining the query plan. A showplan shows information about how SQL Server will (or did) process the query. For each table in the query plan, a showplan tells whether indexes are used or whether a table scan is necessary. It also indicates the order of execution of the different operations in the plan. Reading showplan output is as much an art as it is a science, but it really just takes a lot of practice to get comfortable interpreting it. I hope that the description and examples in this section will be enough to give you a good start.

Note   Throughout the book, you will find discussions where query plans are analyzed; therefore, both this chapter and the next spend a fair amount of space describing how to work with query plans and how to analyze them. This chapter will teach you how to obtain various forms of the query plans, while Chapter 3 will teach you how to examine those from a query-tuning perspective. You will find some overlap of content in both chapters, but the discussions are vital to providing a thorough background for the rest of the book.

SQL Server 2005 can produce showplans in any of three different formats: graphical, text, and XML. When considering the content, SQL Server can produce plans with operators only, plans with additional cost estimates, and plans with additional run-time information. Table 2-

3 summarizes the commands and interfaces used to obtain the query plans with different content in the various formats:

Table 2-3   Commands Generating Various Formats of a Showplan

Content	Format		
	Text	XML	Graphical
Operators	SET SHOWPLAN_TEXT ON	N/A	N/A
Operators and estimated costs	SET SHOWPLAN_ALL ON	SET SHOWPLAN_XML ON	Display Estimated Execution Plan in Management Studio
Run-time info	SET STATISTICS PROFILE ON	SET STATISTICS XML ON	Include Actual Execution Plan in Management Studio

Let's start with the simplest forms of the showplan.

SET SHOWPLAN_TEXT and SHOWPLAN_ALL

Here's an example of SHOWPLAN_TEXT for a two-table join from the Northwind database:

```
SET NOCOUNT ON;
USE Northwind;
GO
SET SHOWPLAN_TEXT ON;
GO
SELECT ProductName, Products.ProductID
FROM dbo.[Order Details]
  JOIN dbo.Products
    ON [Order Details].ProductID = Products.ProductID
WHERE Products.UnitPrice > 100;
GO
SET SHOWPLAN_TEXT OFF;
GO
```

The following is the result of executing the preceding code in SQL Server Management Studio:

```
StmtText
-----------------------------------------------------------------------
SELECT ProductName, Products.ProductID
FROM dbo.[Order Details]
  JOIN dbo.Products
    ON [Order Details].ProductID = Products.ProductID
WHERE Products.UnitPrice > 100;

StmtText
-----------------------------------------------------------------------
```

```
|--Nested Loops(Inner Join, OUTER REFERENCES: ([Northwind].[dbo].[Products].[ProductID]))
     |--Clustered Index Scan(OBJECT: ([Northwind].[dbo].[Products].[PK_Products]),
WHERE:([Northwind].[dbo].[Products].[UnitPrice]>($100.0000)))
     |--Index Seek(OBJECT:([Northwind].[dbo].[Order Details].[ProductID]),
SEEK:([Northwind].[dbo].[Order Details].[ProductID]= [Northwind].[dbo].[Products]
.[ProductID]) ORDERED FORWARD)
```

The output tells us the query plan consists of three operators: Nested Loops, Clustered Index Scan, and Index Seek. The Nested Loops is performing an inner join on the two tables. The outer table (the table accessed first when performing the inner join, which is always the one on the upper branch entering the join operator) in the join is the Products table, and SQL Server is using a Clustered Index Scan to access the physical data. Because a clustered index contains all the table data, scanning the clustered index is equivalent to scanning the whole table. The inner table is the Order Details table, which has a nonclustered index on the *ProductID* column, and SQL Server is using an Index Seek to access the index rows. The Object reference after the Index Seek operator shows us the full name of the index used: [Northwind].[dbo].[Order Details].[ProductID]. In this case, it is a bit confusing because the name of the index is the same as the name of the join column. For this reason, I recommend not giving indexes the same names as the columns they will access. The Seek predicate follows the Object reference. The outer table's column value is used to perform the seek into the ProductID index.

When the plan is executed, the general flow of the rows is from the top down and from right to left. The more indented operator produces rows consumed by the less indented operator, and it produces rows for the next operator above, and so forth. In the case of a join, there are two input operators at the same level to the right of the join operator denoting the two joined row sets. The higher of the two (the Clustered Index Scan in our example) is referred to as the outer table, and the lower (Index Seek in our example) is the inner table. The operation on the outer table is initiated first; the one on the inner table is repeatedly executed for each row of the outer table that arrives to the join operator. In addition to the binary join operators, there are also *n*-ary operators with *n* input branches—for example, concatenation in the plans for queries with UNION ALL. For the *n*-ary operators, the upper branch is executed first, and then the lower branch, and so forth.

Observe that in the preceding example I used SET SHOWPLAN_TEXT OFF following the query. This is because SET SHOWPLAN_TEXT ON is not only causing the query plan to show up, it is also turning off query execution for the connection. Query execution will stay turned off until SQL Server executes SET SHOWPLAN_TEXT OFF on the same connection. You must be careful when performing a showplan of a batch that is creating or altering indexes or permanent tables and subsequently using them in queries in the same batch. Because SQL Server does not execute the batch if SHOWPLAN_TEXT is turned on, the new or altered objects in the batch are not recognized when subsequently referenced. Consequently, you will see a failure if a permanent table is created and used in the same batch, or you might incorrectly think the newly created index will not be used in the query plan. The only exceptions to this rule are temporary tables and table variables that are created to produce the showplan, but their creation is subsequently rolled back at the end of the showplan execution.

SHOWPLAN_ALL is very similar to SHOWPLAN_TEXT. The only difference is the additional information about the query plan produced by SHOWPLAN_ALL. It adds estimates of the number of rows produced by each operator in the query plan, the estimated size of the result rows, the estimated CPU time, and the total cost estimate that was used internally when comparing this plan to other possible plans. I won't show you the output from SHOWPLAN_ALL because it's too wide to fit nicely on a page of this book. But the returned information is still only a subset of the information compared to the XML format of a showplan, which I describe next.

XML Form of the Showplan

There are two different kinds of XML showplans. One, obtained through SET SHOWPLAN_XML ON, contains an estimated execution plan; the second one, the output of the SET STATISTICS XML ON, includes run-time information as well. Because the output of SET SHOWPLAN_XML is generated by a compilation of a batch, it will produce a single XML document for the whole batch. On the other hand, the output of SET STATISTICS XML is produced at runtime and you will see a separate XML document for each statement in the batch. In addition to the SET commands, there are two other ways to obtain the XML showplan—by saving the graphical showplan displayed in SSMS, and by using the SQL Server Profiler. I will describe both of them later in this chapter.

A single XML schema, showplanxml.xsd, covers both the estimated and run-time XML showplans; however, the run-time output provides additional information. Therefore, its specific elements and attributes are optional in the xsd. Installing SQL Server 2005 places the schema in the Microsoft SQL Server\90\Tools\Binn\schemas\sqlserver\2004\07\showplan directory. It is also available at *http://schemas.microsoft.com/sqlserver*.

A showplan in XML format can be saved in a file and given the extension sqlplan (for example, batch1.sqlplan). Opening a file with a .sqlplan will automatically use SQL Server Management Studio (if installed) to display a graphical showplan. There is no need to connect to the server where the showplan was produced or which holds the referenced objects. This great new feature of SQL Server 2005 enables working with the stored and shared (for example, through e-mail) showplans in graphical form without permanently storing large static images.

XML is the richest format of the showplan. It contains some unique information not available in any other textual or graphical showplan. For example, only the XML showplan contains the size of the plan (the *CachedPlanSize* attribute) and parameter values for which the plan has been optimized (the *ParameterList* element), and only the run-time XML showplan contains the number of rows processed in different threads of a parallel plan (the *ActualRows* attribute of the *RunTimeCountersPerThread* element) or the true degree of parallelism when the query was executed (the *DegreeOfParallelism* attribute of the plan).

As I explained earlier, a single XML showplan can capture information about several statements in a batch. You should have this in mind when developing software that processes the XML showplan. You should definitely think about cases of multistatement batches and include them in your tests unless you will be processing only XML showplan documents that are produced by the SET STATISTICS XML or by SQL Server Profiler.

Probably the greatest benefit of the XML format is that it can be processed using any XML technology—for example, XPath, XQuery, or XSLT.

> **More Info**   A good example of extracting data from the XML showplan can be found at *http://msdn.microsoft.com/library/default.asp?url=/library/en-us/dnsql90/html/xmlshowplans.asp*.
>
> This white paper describes an application that extracts the estimated execution cost of a query from its XML showplan. Using this technique, a user can restrict the submitting of queries to only queries that cost less than a predetermined threshold. This will ensure that long-running queries will not overload the server.

I'm convinced the XML showplan will lead to the development of numerous tools to help the administrators, programmers, and operational personnel with their daily work. New queries that help to analyze the XML showplans are appearing on the Internet with increasing frequency.

Graphical Showplan

SSMS has two options to present the graphical form of a showplan: the Display Estimated Execution Plan and Include Actual Execution Plan commands, which are available in the Query menu and as toolbar buttons as depicted in Figure 2-8.

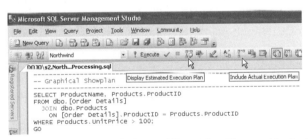

Figure 2-8   Display Estimated Execution Plan and Include Actual Execution Plan options in SSMS

There is a significant difference between the Display Estimated Execution Plan and Include Actual Execution Plan options. If you select the former, a picture showing the graphical showplan of the query or batch in the query window is shown almost immediately (with the speed depending on the compilation time and whether the plan is already cached or not) under the Execution Plan tab in the result portion of SSMS, as shown in Figure 2-9.

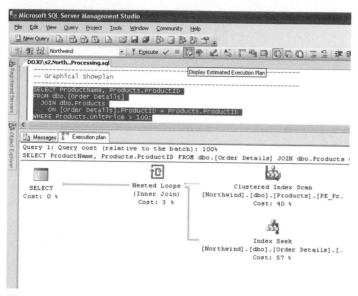

Figure 2-9 Display Estimated Execution Plan

Activating the Include Actual Execution Plan button has no immediate action associated with it. It only changes the state of SSMS to include the run-time showplan with any executed statement or batch. I activated the button, and then executed the same query as above by clicking the Execute button with the red exclamation mark. The additional Results tab appeared among the result windows alongside the Messages and Execution Plan tabs in the lower half of the SSMS window. If you select the tabs one by one, you will see that the Results window contains the query result and the Execution Plan window has a plan that is a similar plan to the one just shown in Figure 2-9. The differences in the plan become apparent only after you investigate the contents of the information inside the individual operators. In Figure 2-10, I hovered the mouse pointer over the Nested Loops operator, which brought up additional information that is not present in the Estimated Plan—fields and values for "Actual Number Of Rows," "Actual Rebinds," and "Actual Rewinds" (all of which will be explained later).

The rows flow from the right to the left, and when joining two tables, the outer table is above the inner table in the graphical showplan.

If you right-click in the Execution Plan window, you will see a pop-up window with the choices shown in Figure 2-11. I used the Zoom To Fit option to produce the pictures of the plans in Figures 2-9 and 2-10. The Properties option will display properties of the operator you select prior to the right-click, similar to the example shown for the Nested Loops operator in Figure 2-10. Probably the least obvious action is associated with the Save Execution Plan As option. If you make this choice, SSMS prompts you for a file location in which to store the XML showplan (not the graphical representation of the plan). The default extension for the file name is sqlplan.

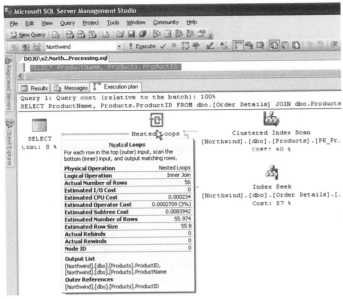

Figure 2-10   Include Actual Execution Plan

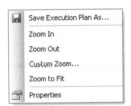

Figure 2-11   Execution plan options

Run-Time Information in Showplan

SQL Server collects the run-time information during the query execution. As I explained previously, XML showplan is the most complete form of a query plan. Therefore, we will start examining the additional run-time information returned in the XML showplan first. Then we will talk about the output of the SET STATISTICS PROFILE command, and finally, we'll discuss the SQL Server Profiler's run-time showplan information.

SET STATISTICS XML ON|OFF   There are two kinds of run-time information in the XML showplan: per SQL statement and per thread. If a statement has a parameter, the plan contains the *ParameterRuntimeValue* attribute, which shows the value for each parameter when the statement is executed. This might differ from the value used to compile the statement under the *ParameterCompiledValue* attribute, but this attribute is in the plan only if the optimizer knows the value of the parameter at the optimization time and is true only for parameters passed to stored procedures.

Next, we have the *DegreeOfParallelism* attribute, which shows the actual degree of parallelism (or DOP, which is the number of concurrent threads working on the single query) of the execution. This, again, might be different from the compile-time value. The compile-time value is not captured in the query plan, but it is always equal to half the number of processors available to SQL Server unless the number of processors is 2—in which case, the compile-time DOP value will be 2 as well. The optimizer is considering half of the CPUs because the DOP at the execution time will be adjusted based on the workload at the time the execution starts; it might end up being any number between 1 and the number of processors. Regardless of the final choice for DOP, the same parallel plan is used. If a parallel plan ends up being executed with DOP = 1, SQL Server will remove the Exchange operators from the query plan when creating the execution context. The *MemoryGrant* attribute shows actual memory given to the query for execution in kilobytes. SQL Server uses this memory to build the hash tables for hash joins or to perform a sort in the memory.

The element *RunTimeCountersPerThread* contains five attributes, each with one value per thread: *ActualRebinds*, *ActualRewinds*, *ActualRows*, *ActualEndofScans*, and *ActualExecutions*. Chapter 3 describes how SSMS shows Actual Number Of Rows and Actual Rebinds And Actual Rewinds in the Operator information ToolTip box of a graphical showplan. The ToolTip box shows cumulative (added across all executions of all threads) values for each of the *ActualRows*, *ActualRebinds*, and *ActualRewinds* values from the XML showplan. The *Actual-Executions* value tells us how many times the operator has been initialized on each of the threads. If the operator is a scan operator, the *ActualEndofScans* count shows how many times the scan reached the end of the set. Consequently, subtracting *ActualEndofScans* from *Actual-Executions* tells us how many times the operator didn't scan the whole set—this might happen, for example, if TOP in the SELECT restricts the number of returned rows and the output set is collected before the scan reaches the end of the table. Similarly, in the case of a Merge Join, if one of the sets is exhausted we don't need to continue scanning the other set because there cannot be any more matches.

The XML showplan might also contain warnings. These are events generated either during compilation or during execution. Examples of compiler-generated warnings are missing statistics and a missing join predicate. Examples of run-time warnings are a hash bailout and an exchange spill. If you encounter a warning in your query plan, you should consult the "Errors and Warnings Event Category" in Books Online to find more information.

SET STATISTICS PROFILE   SET STATISTICS PROFILE ON returns information similar to SET SHOWPLAN_ALL ON. There are two differences, however. SET STATISTICS PROFILE is active during statement execution, which is when it produces additional information alongside the actual result of the query. (The statement must finish execution before the additional output is produced.) Also, it adds two columns to the output: *Rows* and *Executes*. These values are derived from the run-time XML showplan output. The *Rows* value is the sum of the *RowCount* attribute in the element *RunTimeCountersPerThread* across all threads. (There are multiple threads only if it is a parallel plan and if it was run in parallel.) The *Executes* value is the sum of the *ActualExecutions* attribute in the same element. Table 2-4 shows an example of a trimmed portion of the SET STATISTICS PROFILE output for the same query we were working with earlier.

Table 2-4 **Output of STATISTICS PROFILE**

Rows	Executes	StmtText
56	1	SELECT ProductName, Products.ProductId
56	1	|--Nested Loops(Inner Join, OUTER REFERENCES:([Northwind]
2	1	|--Clustered Index Scan(OBJECT:([Northwind].[dbo].[Products].[
56	2	|--Index Seek(OBJECT:([Northwind].[dbo].[Order Details].[Produ

The column *Rows* contains the number of rows actually returned by each operator. The number for *Executes* tells us how many times SQL Server initialized the operator to perform work on one or more rows. Because the outer side of the join (the Clustered Index Scan of the Products table) returned two rows, we had to execute the inner side of the join (the Index Seek) two times. Therefore, the Index Seek has the number 2 in the *Executes* column in the output.

When examining the plan for a particular query, a good way to find potential problems is to find the biggest discrepancies between the optimizer's estimates and the real number of executes and returned rows. Here we must be careful because the optimizer's estimate in the column *EstimateRows* is per estimated execution, while the *Rows* in the showplan output mentioned previously is the cumulative number of rows returned by the operator from all its executions. Therefore, to assess the optimizer's discrepancy we must multiply the *EstimateRows* by *EstimateExecutions* and compare the result with the actual number of all rows returned in the *Rows* column of the SET STATISTICS PROFILE output.

In some cases, it is possible to generate plans using SET STATISTICS PROFILE and SET STATISTICS XML for statements for which the SET SHOWPLAN does not produce any output. A CREATE INDEX on a nonempty table, sp_executesql, and a batch that creates and references the same object are such examples.

Capturing Showplan with SQL Trace

SQL Server Profiler is a GUI tool that defines and captures SQL Server 2005 trace events received from a server. SQL Server displays the events in the Profiler window and optionally saves them in a trace file or a table that can later be analyzed or used to replay a specific series of steps when trying to diagnose a problem. In Chapter 3, we explain why using the T-SQL code to define the trace is more efficient than using the Profiler GUI, and why T-SQL should be used when tracing nontrivial workloads. The following information about capturing the showplan is equally applicable to using both the GUI and the T-SQL sp_trace_ group of stored procedures.

Using a trace to capture the showplan information is very accurate because you will avoid rare but possible discrepancies between the showplan you examine in the SSMS and the actual plan used during the execution of your application. Even if you are not changing the metadata (adding or dropping indexes, modifying constraints, creating or updating statistics), you might still encounter cases where you have a different plan at execution time than at the original compile time. The most common cases occur when one stored procedure is called with different parameter values, when statistics are auto-updated, and when there is a change in available resources (CPU and memory) between compile time and run time. However, monitoring with a trace is resource intensive, and it might adversely affect the performance of your server. The more events you monitor, the bigger the impact. Therefore, you should choose the events you monitor carefully and alternatively consider extracting showplans from the procedure cache, as I will describe later. The downside of using the procedure cache is its volatility (if the query is not executed, the query plan might be removed from the cache) and the lack of run-time information about individual query executions.

There are nine event classes that capture various forms of showplan information in the Performance Event Category. Table 2-5 will help you to pick the most appropriate event for your needs.

Table 2-5   Showplan-Related Trace Event Classes

Trace Event Class	Compile or Run	Includes run-time info	Includes XML showplan	Generates trace against SQL Server 2000
Showplan All	Run	No	No	Yes
Showplan All for Query Compile	Compile	No	No	No
Showplan Statistics Profile	Run	Yes[1]	No	Yes
Showplan Text	Run	No	No	Yes
Showplan Text (Unencoded)	Run	No	No	Yes[2]
Showplan XML	Run	No	Yes	No
Showplan XML for Query Compile	Compile	No	Yes	No
Showplan XML Statistics Profile	Run	Yes[3]	Yes	No
Performance Statistics	Compile and Run[4]	Yes[5]	Yes	No

[1] The generated run-time information is identical to that produced by the SET STATISTICS PROFILE ON.

[2] If the SQL Server 2005 Profiler is connected to a SQL Server 2000 server, it automatically shows only the showplan events supported by SQL Server 2000. Note that the "Showplan Text (Unencoded)" event is named "Execution plan" in SQL Server 2000.

[3] The *TextData* column in the profiler output contains the XML showplan, including all the same run-time information as in the output of SET STATISTICS XML ON.

[4] The Performance Statistics event class is a combination of several subevents. Subevents 1 and 2 produce the same showplan as the Showplan XML For Query Compile event—1 for stored procedures, and 2 for ad-hoc statements. Subevent 3 produces cumulative run-time statistics for the query when it is removed from the procedure cache.

[5] This is cumulative run-time information for all executions of this query produced for subevent 3. The captured information is the same as that produced by the sys.dm_exec_query_stats DMV, and it is stored in XML format in the *TextData* column in the trace output.

For simplicity, I will restrict further discussion to tracing against SQL Server 2005 only.

If your server is not very busy or is a development or test machine, you should use the Showplan XML Statistics Profile event. It generates all the query plan and run-time information you might need. You can also process the plans programmatically or display them in graphical form.

Even if your server is busy but the compile rate is kept low by good plan reuse, you can use the Showplan XML For Query Compile event because it produces trace records only when a stored procedure or statement is compiled or recompiled. This trace will not contain run-time information.

The Showplan Text event generates output identical to that of the Showplan Text (Unencoded) event except the showplan is stored as a character string in the *TextData* column for the latter plan and as encoded binary data in the *BinaryData* column for the former. A consequence of using the Binary Data column is that it's not human-readable—we need the Profiler or at least the Profiler's decoding DLL to read the showplan. The binary format also limits the number of levels in the XML document to 128. On the other hand, it requires less space to hold all the plan information.

You can reduce the size of the trace by selecting filter values for various columns. A good approach is to generate a small experimental trace, analyze which events and columns you don't need, and remove them from the trace. Using this process, you can also identify some missing information you might want to add to the trace. When setting up the trace filter (for example, by using sp_trace_setfilter), only the filters on the *ApplicationName*, *ClientProcessID*, *HostName*, *LoginName*, *LoginSid*, *NTDomainName*, *NTUserName*, and *SPID* columns suppress the generation of the event. The rest of the filters are applied only after the event has been generated and marshaled to the client. Therefore, you should not substitute extensive filtering for careful event selection; the filtering might potentially result in removing all records of a particular event class from the trace without helping to minimize the impact on the server. In fact, more work rather than less will be needed.

Compared to the SET STATISTICS PROFILE and SET STATISTICS XML options, the showplan trace events further enlarge the set of statements SQL Server captures the plans for. The additional classes of statements are auto- and non-auto- CREATE and UPDATE STATISTICS, as well as the INSERT INTO ... EXEC statement.

Extracting the Showplan from the Procedure Cache

After the query optimizer produces the plan for the batch or stored procedure, the plan is placed in the procedure cache. You can examine the procedure cache using several dynamic management views (DMV) and functions (DMF), DBCC PROCCACHE, and the deprecated catalog view sys.syscacheobjects. I will show how you can access a showplan in XML format for the queries currently in the procedure cache.

The sys.dm_exec_query_plan DMF returns the showplan in XML format for any query whose query execution plan currently resides in the procedure cache. The sys.dm_exec_query_plan DMF requires a plan handle as its only argument. The plan handle is a VARBINARY (64) identifier of the query plan, and the sys.dm_exec_query_stats DMV returns it for each query currently in the procedure cache. The following query returns the XML showplans for all cached query plans. If a batch or stored procedure contains multiple SQL statements with a query plan, the view will contain a separate row for each one of them.

```
SELECT qplan.query_plan AS [Query Plan]
FROM sys.dm_exec_query_stats AS qstats
 CROSS APPLY sys.dm_exec_query_plan(qstats.plan_handle) AS qplan;
```

It is difficult to find the query plan for a particular query using the preceding query because the query text is contained only deep inside the XML showplan. The following extension to the previous query extracts the sequence number (the column named No) and the query text (the Statement Text column) from the showplan using the *Xquery* value method. Each batch has a single sql_handle; therefore, specifying *ORDER BY sql_handle, [No]* ensures the output rows for the batch containing multiple SQL statements are displayed one after another in the order they appear in the batch.

```
WITH XMLNAMESPACES ('http://schemas.microsoft.com/sqlserver/2004/07/showplan' AS sql)
SELECT
  C.value('@StatementId','INT') AS [No],
  C.value('(./@StatementText)','NVARCHAR(MAX)') AS [Statement Text],
  qplan.query_plan AS [Query Plan]
FROM (SELECT DISTINCT plan_handle FROM sys.dm_exec_query_stats) AS qstats
  CROSS APPLY sys.dm_exec_query_plan(qstats.plan_handle) AS qplan
  CROSS APPLY query_plan.nodes('/sql:ShowPlanXML/sql:BatchSequence/sql:Batch/sql:Statements/
descendant::*[attribute::StatementText]')
    AS T(C)
ORDER BY plan_handle, [No];
```

Next, I will show a portion of the result returned by the preceding query. The output depends on the current contents of the procedure cache; therefore, your output will almost certainly be different than the one shown in Table 2-6.

Table 2-6   Information about Query Plans Extracted from Cache

No	Statement Text	Query Plan
1	SELECT CAST(serverproperty(N'S	<ShowPlanXML xmlns="http://sch
1	select value_in_use from sys.c	<ShowPlanXML xmlns="http://sch
1	with XMLNAMESPACES ('http://sc	<ShowPlanXML xmlns="http://sch
1	with XMLNAMESPACES ('http://sc	<ShowPlanXML xmlns="http://sch
1	IF (@@microsoftversion / 0x010	<ShowPlanXML xmlns="http://sch
2	SELECT se.is_admin_endpoint A	<ShowPlanXML xmlns="http://sch
3	ELSE	<ShowPlanXML xmlns="http://sch
1	SELECT CAST(serverproperty(N'S	<ShowPlanXML xmlns="http://sch

Update Plans

The query optimizer must take care of several specific issues when optimizing INSERT, UPDATE, and DELETE—or, in other words, *data modifying*—statements. Here I will describe the techniques employed by the SQL Server to process these statements.

The IUD (shorthand I will use for "INSERT, UPDATE, and DELETE") plans have two stages. The first stage is *read only*, and it determines which rows need to be inserted/updated/deleted by generating a data stream describing the changes to be made. For INSERTs, the data stream contains column values; for DELETEs, it has the table keys, and for UPDATEs, it has both the table keys and the values of changed columns. The second stage applies changes in the data stream to the table; additionally, it takes actions necessary to preserve data integrity by performing constraint validation, it maintains nonclustered indexes and indexed views, and it fires triggers if they exist. Usually the UPDATE and DELETE query plans contain two references to the target table: the first reference is used to identify the affected rows and the second to perform the change. The INSERT plans contain only one reference to the target table unless the same target table also participates in generating the inserted rows.

In some simple cases, SQL Server merges the read and write stages of the IUD plans together. This is the case, for example, when inserting values directly into a table (a process known as a *scalar insert*) or updating/deleting rows identified by a value of a primary key on the target table.

The Assert operator is automatically included in the query plans in the second phase if SQL Server needs to perform constraint validation. SQL Server validates the CHECK constraints for INSERTs and UPDATEs by evaluating a usually inexpensive scalar expression on each affected row and column. Foreign key constraints are enforced on INSERTs and UPDATEs to the table containing the foreign key constraint, and they're enforced on UPDATEs and DELETEs to the table containing the referenced key. The related table that is not the target of the IUD operation is scanned to verify the constraint; therefore, data access is involved. Declaring a primary key automatically creates a unique index on the key columns, but this is not the case for a foreign key. UPDATEs and DELETEs of referenced keys must access the foreign key table for each updated or deleted primary key value, either to validate nonexistence of the removed key or to propagate the change if it is a cascading referential integrity constraint. Therefore, you should ensure there is an index on the foreign key if you plan to perform UPDATEs affecting the key values or DELETEs from the primary table.

In addition to performing the IUD operation on the clustered index or heap, processing of the INSERT and DELETE queries also maintains all nonclustered indexes, and the UPDATE queries maintain indexes containing the modified columns. Because nonclustered indexes include the clustered index and partitioning keys to allow efficient access to the table row, updating columns that participate in the clustered index or in the partitioning key is expensive because it requires maintenance of all indexes. Updating the partitioning key might also cause rows to move between partitions. Therefore, when you have a choice, choose clustering and partitioning keys that you don't plan to update.

> **Note** SQL Server 2005 restricts the partitioning keys to a single column; therefore, "partitioning key" and "partitioning column" are synonyms.

In general, the performance of IUD statements is closely tied to the number of maintained indexes that include the target columns, because those must all be modified. Performing single-row INSERT and DELETE operations to an index requires a single index-tree traversal. SQL Server implements update to an index or partitioning key as a DELETE followed by an INSERT—therefore, it is roughly twice as expensive as a nonkey UPDATE.

The query optimizer considers and costs two different strategies for IUD statements: per-row and per-index maintenance. These two strategies are demonstrated in the plans for queries 1 and 2, respectively, in Figure 2-12. With per-row maintenance, SQL Server maintains the indexes and the base table together for each row affected by the query. The updates to all non-clustered indexes are performed in conjunction with each single row update on the base table (which might be a heap or a clustered index). The plan for Query 1 *DELETE FROM dbo.Orders WHERE OrderDate='2002-01-01'* (the top one in Figure 2-12) is an example of a per-row maintenance. Query 1is deleting only 24 rows in the Orders table in the Performance database that is generated by Listing 3-1 from Chapter 3. The plan for Query 1 does not show any deletes performed on the secondary indexes because they are carried out together with the deletes of the clustered index rows one row at a time.

The plan for Query 2 *DELETE FROM dbo.Orders WHERE OrderDate<'2006-01-01'* in the bottom portion of the Figure 2-12 will delete 751,216 rows against the same Orders table, and its plan is very different because it is performing per-index maintenance. At first, the plan deletes the qualifying rows from the clustered index (indicated by the Clustered Index Delete icon on the right) while at the same time building a temporary spool table containing the key values for the three nonclustered indexes that must be maintained. SQL Server reads the spooled data three times, once for each of these indexes. Between reading the spooled data and deleting the rows from the nonclustered index, SQL Server sorts the data in the order of the maintained index, thus ensuring optimal access to the index pages.

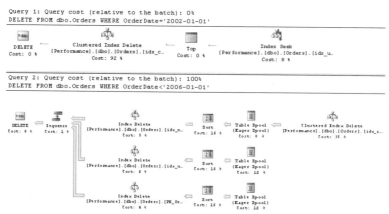

Figure 2-12   Per-row and per-index update plans

The Sequence operator enforces the execution order of its branches. SQL Server updates the indexes one after another from the top of the plan to the bottom.

The per-row update strategy is efficient in terms of CPU because there is a short code path required to update the table and all indexes together. The code for per-index maintenance is somewhat more complicated, but there might be significant savings in I/O. By updating the nonclustered indexes individually after sorting the keys, we will never visit an index page more than once even if many rows are updated on the same page. Therefore, a per-index update plan is usually chosen when many rows are updated and the optimizer estimates the same page of the maintained index would be read more than once to accomplish the maintenance using the per-row strategy.

In addition to the spools holding the keys for index maintenance, you might also encounter in the IUD plans the special spool operator that provides "Halloween protection" known also as the *Halloween spool*. (I will explain the origins of this name later in this chapter.) The query optimizer injects a spool operator into some IUD plans to ensure correctness of the produced result. I will use the following small example to demonstrate the problem. My Tiny_employees table has two columns—*name* and *salary*—and one nonclustered index on the *name* column to start with. Run the code in Listing 2-3 to create and populate the Tiny_employees table.

Listing 2-3   Script for Halloween database

```
SET NOCOUNT ON;
USE master;
GO
IF DB_ID('Halloween') IS NULL
  CREATE DATABASE Halloween;
GO
USE Halloween;
GO


-- Creating and Populating the Tiny_employees Table
IF OBJECT_ID('dbo.Tiny_employees') IS NOT NULL
  DROP TABLE dbo.Tiny_employees;
GO
CREATE TABLE dbo.Tiny_employees (name CHAR(8), salary INT);
INSERT INTO dbo.Tiny_employees VALUES ('emp_A',30000);
INSERT INTO dbo.Tiny_employees VALUES ('emp_B',20000);
INSERT INTO dbo.Tiny_employees VALUES ('emp_C',19000);
INSERT INTO dbo.Tiny_employees VALUES ('emp_D',8000);
INSERT INTO dbo.Tiny_employees VALUES ('emp_E',7500);
GO
CREATE INDEX ind_name ON dbo.Tiny_employees(name);
GO
```

Now consider implementing the following request: Increase salary by 10 percent for all employees with salary less than 25,000. The query is simple:

```
UPDATE dbo.Tiny_employees
  SET salary = salary * 1.1
WHERE salary < 25000;
```

Its query plan, shown in Figure 2-13, is using per-row maintenance. (You don't see an update node for the index ind_name anywhere in the plan.)

Figure 2-13   Execution plan for the UPDATE statement

Now let's create a clustered index on the Tiny_employees table on the *salary* column:

```
CREATE CLUSTERED INDEX ind_salary ON dbo.Tiny_employees(salary);
```

Again, let's investigate the query plan, shown in Figure 2-14, for the same query:

```
UPDATE dbo.Tiny_employees
  SET salary = salary * 1.1
WHERE salary < 25000;
```

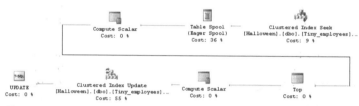

Figure 2-14   Execution plan for the UPDATE statement after creating index ind_salary

Once more, there is no update node for the index ind_name because this is a per-row maintenance plan. However, there is a Table Spool operator. I will explain why.

The clustered index seek scans the rows in the order of the clustered key values. We have the clustered index ordered on the *salary* column, and that is the same column updated in our query. Let's assume SQL Server seeks into the clustered index from the smallest value to the largest. The first value encountered in our table is 7500 for the employee emp_E. We increase it by 10 percent to 8250. By that account, the record will be placed between the emp_D and emp_C with "old" salaries of 8000 and 19,000, respectively. Next, we encounter the salary of 8000, and we will increase it to 8800. Figure 2-15 shows the update in progress.

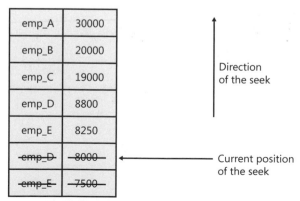

Figure 2-15   Update in progress

If the seek continues, it will reach the emp_E record *again* and update it a second time, and of course, that would be incorrect. Now observe the position of the Table Spool in the preceding query plan—it separates the Clustered Index Seek and Clustered Index Update operators. The spool consumes all records from the index seek before it proceeds with the updates against the same clustered index. The spool, not the index, is producing the updated values. Therefore, the spool prevents updating the same record twice and ensures a correct result. We call such a spool in our IUD query plans a Halloween spool.

You might be wondering what Halloween has in common with the query plans just described? We have to go back almost 30 years in the history of database technology—and query optimization in particular—for the answer. Researchers at the Almaden Research Center in California encountered the same problem when they trained their query optimizer prototype to use indexes in update plans. In fact, they used the *salary* column and salary increase update query similarly to what I just did. Moreover, to their big surprise nobody had a salary under 25,000 after they ran the update query! It was on Halloween 1977 (or maybe 1976?) when the researchers described and debated the glitch. Since then, many database texts, papers, and articles have used the "Halloween" term to name the double-update problem I just outlined.

Conclusion

Physical query processing consists of two fundamental steps: query compilation and query execution. The main link between the two steps is the query plan. Understanding how SQL Server generates the query plans and how it is using the plans to deliver the query result is vital for application developers, database designers, and administrators. Constructive use of the knowledge of how SQL Server performs its physical query processing might improve the database server's performance and the application's response time and throughput.

Acknowledgment

I received great help from several colleagues at Microsoft while I was working on this chapter. Mike Blaszczak, Alexis Boukouvalas, Milind Joshi, Stefano Stefani, Don Vilen, Umachandar Jayachandran, and Eugene Zabokritski reviewed and commented on part of the chapter or on the whole chapter and provided me with a wealth of feedback and ideas for improving the content.

Chapter 3
Query Tuning

This chapter lays the foundation of query tuning knowledge required for both this book and *Inside Microsoft SQL Server 2005: T-SQL Programming*. (For brevity, I'll refer to the programming book as *Inside T-SQL Programming*, and to both this book and *Inside T-SQL Programming* as "these books.") Here you will be introduced to a tuning methodology, acquire tools for query tuning, learn how to analyze execution plans and perform index tuning, and learn the significance of preparing good sample data and the importance of using set-based solutions.

When building the table of contents for this book, I faced quite a dilemma with regard to the query tuning chapter, a dilemma which I've also faced when teaching advanced T-SQL—should this material appear early or late? On one hand, the chapter provides important background information that is required for the rest of the book; on the other hand, some techniques used for query tuning involve advanced queries—sort of a chicken and egg quandary. I decided to incorporate the chapter early in the book, but I wrote it as an independent unit that can be used as a reference. My recommendation is that you read this chapter before the rest of the book, and when a query uses techniques that you're not familiar with yet, just focus on the conceptual elements described in text. Some queries will use techniques that are described later in the book (for example, pivoting, running aggregations, the OVER clause, CUBE, CTEs, and so on) or in *Inside T-SQL Programming* (for example, temporary tables, cursors, routines, CLR integration, compilations, and so on). Don't be concerned if the techniques are not clear. Feel free, though, to jump to the relevant chapter if you're curious about a certain technique. When you finish reading the books, I suggest that you return to this chapter and revisit any queries that were not clear at first to make sure you fully understand their mechanics.

At the end of this chapter, I'll provide pointers to resources where you can find more information about the subject.

Sample Data for This Chapter

Throughout the chapter, I will use the Performance database and its tables in my examples. Run the code in Listing 3-1 to create the database and its tables, and populate them with sample data. Note that it will take a few minutes for the code to finish.

Listing 3-1   Creation script for sample database and tables

```
SET NOCOUNT ON;
USE master;
GO
IF DB_ID('Performance') IS NULL
  CREATE DATABASE Performance;
GO
USE Performance;
GO


-- Creating and Populating the Nums Auxiliary Table
IF OBJECT_ID('dbo.Nums') IS NOT NULL
  DROP TABLE dbo.Nums;
GO
CREATE TABLE dbo.Nums(n INT NOT NULL PRIMARY KEY);
DECLARE @max AS INT, @rc AS INT;
SET @max = 1000000;
SET @rc = 1;

INSERT INTO Nums VALUES(1);
WHILE @rc * 2 <= @max
BEGIN
  INSERT INTO dbo.Nums SELECT n + @rc FROM dbo.Nums;
  SET @rc = @rc * 2;
END

INSERT INTO dbo.Nums
  SELECT n + @rc FROM dbo.Nums WHERE n + @rc <= @max;
GO


-- Drop Data Tables if Exist
IF OBJECT_ID('dbo.Orders') IS NOT NULL
  DROP TABLE dbo.Orders;
GO
IF OBJECT_ID('dbo.Customers') IS NOT NULL
  DROP TABLE dbo.Customers;
GO
IF OBJECT_ID('dbo.Employees') IS NOT NULL
  DROP TABLE dbo.Employees;
GO
IF OBJECT_ID('dbo.Shippers') IS NOT NULL
  DROP TABLE dbo.Shippers;
GO


-- Data Distribution Settings
DECLARE
  @numorders   AS INT,
```

```
  @numcusts    AS INT,
  @numemps     AS INT,
  @numshippers AS INT,
  @numyears    AS INT,
  @startdate   AS DATETIME;

SELECT
  @numorders   =   1000000,
  @numcusts    =     20000,
  @numemps     =       500,
  @numshippers =         5,
  @numyears    =         4,
  @startdate   = '20030101';

-- Creating and Populating the Customers Table
CREATE TABLE dbo.Customers
(
  custid   CHAR(11)     NOT NULL,
  custname NVARCHAR(50) NOT NULL
);

INSERT INTO dbo.Customers(custid, custname)
  SELECT
    'C' + RIGHT('000000000' + CAST(n AS VARCHAR(10)), 10) AS custid,
    N'Cust_' + CAST(n AS VARCHAR(10)) AS custname
  FROM dbo.Nums
  WHERE n <= @numcusts;

ALTER TABLE dbo.Customers ADD
  CONSTRAINT PK_Customers PRIMARY KEY(custid);

-- Creating and Populating the Employees Table
CREATE TABLE dbo.Employees
(
  empid     INT          NOT NULL,
  firstname NVARCHAR(25) NOT NULL,
  lastname  NVARCHAR(25) NOT NULL
);

INSERT INTO dbo.Employees(empid, firstname, lastname)
  SELECT n AS empid,
    N'Fname_' + CAST(n AS NVARCHAR(10)) AS firstname,
    N'Lname_' + CAST(n AS NVARCHAR(10)) AS lastname
  FROM dbo.Nums
  WHERE n <= @numemps;

ALTER TABLE dbo.Employees ADD
  CONSTRAINT PK_Employees PRIMARY KEY(empid);

-- Creating and Populating the Shippers Table
CREATE TABLE dbo.Shippers
(
  shipperid   VARCHAR(5)   NOT NULL,
  shippername NVARCHAR(50) NOT NULL
);
```

```
INSERT INTO dbo.Shippers(shipperid, shippername)
  SELECT shipperid, N'Shipper_' + shipperid AS shippername
  FROM (SELECT CHAR(ASCII('A') - 2 + 2 * n) AS shipperid
        FROM dbo.Nums
        WHERE n <= @numshippers) AS D;

ALTER TABLE dbo.Shippers ADD
  CONSTRAINT PK_Shippers PRIMARY KEY(shipperid);

-- Creating and Populating the Orders Table
CREATE TABLE dbo.Orders
(
  orderid   INT         NOT NULL,
  custid    CHAR(11)    NOT NULL,
  empid     INT         NOT NULL,
  shipperid VARCHAR(5)  NOT NULL,
  orderdate DATETIME    NOT NULL,
  filler    CHAR(155)   NOT NULL DEFAULT('a')
);

INSERT INTO dbo.Orders(orderid, custid, empid, shipperid, orderdate)
  SELECT n AS orderid,
    'C' + RIGHT('000000000'
           + CAST(
               1 + ABS(CHECKSUM(NEWID())) % @numcusts
               AS VARCHAR(10)), 10) AS custid,
    1 + ABS(CHECKSUM(NEWID())) % @numemps AS empid,
    CHAR(ASCII('A') - 2
         + 2 * (1 + ABS(CHECKSUM(NEWID())) % @numshippers)) AS shipperid,
      DATEADD(day, n / (@numorders / (@numyears * 365.25)), @startdate)
        -- late arrival with earlier date
        - CASE WHEN n % 10 = 0
            THEN THEN 1 + ABS(CHECKSUM(NEWID())) % 30
            ELSE 0
          END AS orderdate
  FROM dbo.Nums
  WHERE n <= @numorders
  ORDER BY CHECKSUM(NEWID());

CREATE CLUSTERED INDEX idx_cl_od ON dbo.Orders(orderdate);

CREATE NONCLUSTERED INDEX idx_nc_sid_od_cid
  ON dbo.Orders(shipperid, orderdate, custid);

CREATE UNIQUE INDEX idx_unc_od_oid_i_cid_eid
  ON dbo.Orders(orderdate, orderid)
  INCLUDE(custid, empid);

ALTER TABLE dbo.Orders ADD
  CONSTRAINT PK_Orders PRIMARY KEY NONCLUSTERED(orderid),
  CONSTRAINT FK_Orders_Customers
    FOREIGN KEY(custid)     REFERENCES dbo.Customers(custid),
  CONSTRAINT FK_Orders_Employees
    FOREIGN KEY(empid)      REFERENCES dbo.Employees(empid),
  CONSTRAINT FK_Orders_Shippers
    FOREIGN KEY(shipperid) REFERENCES dbo.Shippers(shipperid);
```

The Orders table is the main data table, and it's populated with 1,000,000 orders spanning four years beginning in 2003. The Customers table is populated with 20,000 customers, the Employees table with 500 employees, and the Shippers table with 5 shippers. Note that I distributed the order dates, customer IDs, employee IDs, and shipper IDs in the Orders table with random functions. You might not get the same numbers of rows that I'll be getting in my examples back from the queries, but statistically they should be fairly close.

The Nums table is an auxiliary table of numbers, containing only one column called *n*, populated with integers in the range 1 through 1,000,000.

The code in Listing 3-1 creates the following indexes on the Orders table:

- **idx_cl_od**   Clustered index on *orderdate*
- **PK_Orders**   Unique nonclustered index on *orderid*, created implicitly by the primary key
- **idx_nc_sid_od_cid**   Nonclustered index on *shipperid, orderdate, custid*
- **idx_unc_od_oid_i_cid_eid**   Unique nonclustered index on *orderdate, orderid*, with included non-key columns *custid, empid*

Index structures and their properties will be explained later in the "Index Tuning" section.

Tuning Methodology

This section describes a tuning methodology developed in the company I work for—Solid Quality Learning—and have been implementing with our customers. Credits go to the mentors within the company who took part in developing and practicing the methodology, especially to Andrew J. Kelly, Brian Moran, Fernando G. Guerrero, Eladio Rincón, Dejan Sarka, Mike Hotek, and Ron Talmage, just to name a few.

So, when your system suffers from performance problems, how do you start to solve the problems?

The answer to this question reminds me of a programmer and an IT manager at a company I worked for years ago. The programmer had to finish writing a component and deploy it, but there was a bug in his code that he couldn't find. He produced a printout of the code (which was pretty thick) and went to the IT manager, who was in a meeting. The IT manager was extremely good at detecting bugs, which is why the programmer sought him. The IT manager took the thick printout, opened it, and immediately pointed to a certain line of code. "Here's your bug," he said. "Now go." After the meeting was over, the programmer asked the IT manager how he found the bug so fast? The IT manager replied, "I knew that anywhere I pointed there would be a bug."

Back to query tuning, you can point anywhere in the database and there will be room for tuning there. The question is, is it worth it? For example, would it be worthwhile to tune the concurrency aspects of the system if blocking contributes only to 1 percent of the waits in the system as a whole? It's important to follow a path or methodology that leads you through a series of steps to the main problem areas or bottlenecks in the system—those that contribute to most of the waits. This section will introduce such a methodology.

Before you continue, drop the existing clustered index from the Orders table:

```
USE Performance;
GO
DROP INDEX dbo.Orders.idx_cl_od;
```

Suppose your system suffers from performance problems as a whole—users complain that "everything is slow." Listing 3-2 contains a sampling of queries that run regularly in your system.

Listing 3-2   Sample queries

```
SET NOCOUNT ON;
USE Performance;
GO

SELECT orderid, custid, empid, shipperid, orderdate, filler
FROM dbo.Orders
WHERE orderid = 3;

SELECT orderid, custid, empid, shipperid, orderdate, filler
FROM dbo.Orders
WHERE orderid = 5;

SELECT orderid, custid, empid, shipperid, orderdate, filler
FROM dbo.Orders
WHERE orderid = 7;

SELECT orderid, custid, empid, shipperid, orderdate, filler
FROM dbo.Orders
WHERE orderdate = '20060212';

SELECT orderid, custid, empid, shipperid, orderdate, filler
FROM dbo.Orders
WHERE orderdate = '20060118';

SELECT orderid, custid, empid, shipperid, orderdate, filler
FROM dbo.Orders
WHERE orderdate = '20060828';

SELECT orderid, custid, empid, shipperid, orderdate, filler
FROM dbo.Orders
WHERE orderdate >= '20060101'
  AND orderdate < '20060201';

SELECT orderid, custid, empid, shipperid, orderdate, filler
FROM dbo.Orders
WHERE orderdate >= '20060401'
  AND orderdate < '20060501';
```

```
SELECT orderid, custid, empid, shipperid, orderdate, filler
FROM dbo.Orders
WHERE orderdate >= '20060201'
  AND orderdate < '20070301';

SELECT orderid, custid, empid, shipperid, orderdate, filler
FROM dbo.Orders
WHERE orderdate >= '20060501'
  AND orderdate < '20060601';
```

Restart your SQL Server instance, and then run the code in Listing 3-2 several times (say, 10). SQL Server will internally record performance information you will rely on later. Restarting your instance will reset some of the counters you will rely on later.

When dealing with performance problems, database professionals tend to focus on the technical aspects of the system, such as resource queues, resource utilization, and so on. However, users perceive performance problems simply as waits—they make a request and have to wait to get the results back. A response that takes longer than three seconds to arrive after an interactive request is typically perceived by users as a performance problem. They don't really care how many commands wait on average on each disk spindle or what the cache hit ratio is, and they don't care about blocking, CPU utilization, average page life expectancy in cache, and so on. They care about waits, and that's where performance tuning should start.

The tuning methodology I recommend applies a top-down approach. It starts by investigating waits at the instance level, and then drills down through a series of steps until the processes/ components that generate the bulk of the waits in the system are identified. Once you identify the offending processes, you can focus on tuning them. Following are the main steps of the methodology:

1. Analyze waits at the instance level.

2. Correlate waits with queues.

3. Determine a course of action.

4. Drill down to the database/file level.

5. Drill down to the process level.

6. Tune indexes/queries.

The following sections describe each step in detail.

Analyze Waits at the Instance Level

The first step in the tuning methodology is to identify, at the instance level, which types of waits contribute most to the waits in the system. In SQL Server 2005, you do this by querying a dynamic management view (DMV) called *sys.dm_os_wait_stats*; in SQL Server 2000, you do this by running the command DBCC SQLPERF(WAITSTATS). The aforementioned DMV in

SQL Server 2005 is fully documented, and I urge you to read the section describing it in Books Online. I'm not sure why, but the command in SQL Server 2000 is undocumented and surfaced only several years after the product was released. However, from the documentation in SQL Server 2005 you can learn about the different types of waits that are relevant to SQL Server 2000 as well.

The sys.dm_os_wait_stats DMV contains 194 wait types, while the command in SQL Server 2000 will return 77. If you think about it, these are small manageable numbers that are convenient to work with as a starting point. Some other performance tools give you too much information to start with, and create a situation in which you can't see the forest for the trees. I'll continue the discussion assuming you're working with SQL Server 2005.

Run the following query to return the waits in your system sorted by type:

```
SELECT
  wait_type,
  waiting_tasks_count,
  wait_time_ms,
  max_wait_time_ms,
  signal_wait_time_ms
FROM sys.dm_os_wait_stats
ORDER BY wait_type;
```

Table 3-1 shows an abbreviated version of the results I got when I ran this query on my system.

Table 3-1   Contents of *sys.dm_os_wait_stats* in Abbreviated Form

wait_type	waiting_tasks_ count	wait_time_ms	max_wait_ time_ms	signal_wait_ time_ms
...				
ASYNC_IO_ COMPLETION	9	43993	40247	20
ASYNC_ NETWORK_IO	69	1682	941	110
CHKPT	1	3234	3234	0
IO_COMPLETION	29167	466270	620	1932
LATCH_EX	41	13589	2082	290
LATCH_SH	3	110	110	30
LATCH_UP	0	0	0	0
LAZYWRITER_SLEEP	284462	266925468	18236	48329
LCK_M_S	3	1882	1612	10
LCK_M_U	41	26898	1992	0
LCK_M_X	0	0	0	0
LOGBUFFER	9495	194920	751	1692
LOGMGR_ RESERVE_APPEND	200	198745	1331	50

Table 3-1   Contents of *sys.dm_os_wait_stats* in Abbreviated Form

wait_type	waiting_tasks_ count	wait_time_ms	max_wait_ time_ms	signal_wait_ time_ms
OLEDB	1451	3034	851	0
PAGELATCH_EX	123	60	20	40
PAGELATCH_SH	25300	365115	2012	54288
PAGELATCH_UP	29	7080	1041	0
PAGEIOLATCH_EX	1259	46536	721	480
PAGEIOLATCH_SH	39491	358205	1762	2733
PAGEIOLATCH_UP	382	6389	480	70
RESOURCE_QUEUE	0	0	0	0
RESOURCE_ SEMAPHORE	0	0	0	0
RESOURCE_ SEMAPHORE_MUTEX	0	0	0	0
RESOURCE_ SEMAPHORE_ QUERY_COMPILE	0	0	0	0
RESOURCE_ SEMAPHORE_ SMALL_QUERY	0	0	0	0
WRITELOG	5176	97400	781	3114
...				

Note   Of course, you shouldn't draw conclusions about production systems from the output that I got. Needless to say, my personal machine or your test machine or personal test environment would not necessarily reflect a real production environment. I'm just using the output in this table for illustration purposes. I'll mention later which types of waits we typically find to be predominant in production environments.

The DMV accumulates values since the server was last restarted. If you want to reset its values, run the following code (but don't run it now):

```
DBCC SQLPERF('sys.dm_os_wait_stats', CLEAR);
```

In SQL Server 2000, this code will reset the wait statistics:

```
DBCC SQLPERF(WAITSTATS, CLEAR);
```

The DMV *sys.dm_os_wait_stats* contains the following attributes: *wait_type*; *waiting_tasks_count*, which is the number of waits on this wait type; *wait_time_ms*, which is total wait time for this wait type in milliseconds (including *signal_wait_time*); *max_wait_time_ms*; and *signal_wait_time*, which is the difference between the time the waiting thread was signaled and when it started running.

As I mentioned earlier, you can find information about the various wait types in Books Online. At the end of this chapter, I will point you to resources that provide more detailed information about the different wait types.

Among the various types of waits, you will find ones related to locks, latches (lightweight locks), I/O (including I/O latches), the transaction log, memory, compilations, OLEDB (linked servers and other OLEDB components), and so on. Typically, you will want to ignore some types of waits—for example, those involving a sleep of a thread (meaning that a thread is simply suspended, doing nothing). Make sure you filter out irrelevant waits so that they do not skew your calculations.

In my experience with Solid Quality Learning, I/O waits are by far the most common types of waits our customers need help with. There are several reasons for this. I/O is typically the most expensive resource involved with data-manipulation activities. Also, when queries or indexes are not designed and tuned well, the result is typically excessive I/O. Also, when customers think of "strong" machines, they usually focus their attention on CPU and memory, and they don't pay adequate attention to the I/O subsystem. Database systems need strong I/O subsystems.

Of course, we also deal with other problem areas. There are systems that don't necessarily access large portions of data; instead, these systems involve processes that access small portions of data very frequently. Such is typically the case with online transaction processing (OLTP) environments, which have stored procedures and queries that access small portions of data but are invoked very frequently. In such environments, compilations and recompilations of the code might be the main cause of a bottleneck. OLTP systems also involve a lot of data modification in small portions, and the transaction log often becomes a bottleneck in such environments. The tempdb database can also be a serious bottleneck because all temporary tables, whether created implicitly by an execution plan or explicitly, are created in tempdb. SQL Server also uses tempdb's space to perform other activities. Occasionally, we also find systems with concurrency related (blocking) problems, as well as other problems.

Let's get back to the wait information that you receive from the DMV. You probably won't find it convenient to browse all wait types and try to manually figure out which are the most substantial ones. You want to isolate the top waits—those that in total accumulate to some threshold percentage of the total waits in the system. You can use numbers like 80 percent or 90 percent, because typically a small number of wait types contributes to the bulk of the waits in the system.

The following query isolates the top waits that accumulate in total to 90 percent of the wait time in the system, and it generates (on my system) the output shown in Table 3-2:

```
WITH Waits AS
(
  SELECT
    wait_type,
    wait_time_ms / 1000. AS wait_time_s,
```

```
     100. * wait_time_ms / SUM(wait_time_ms) OVER() AS pct,
       ROW_NUMBER() OVER(ORDER BY wait_time_ms DESC) AS rn
     FROM sys.dm_os_wait_stats
     WHERE wait_type NOT LIKE '%SLEEP%'
     -- filter out additional irrelevant waits
)
SELECT
     W1.wait_type,
     CAST(W1.wait_time_s AS DECIMAL(12, 2)) AS wait_time_s,
     CAST(W1.pct AS DECIMAL(12, 2)) AS pct,
     CAST(SUM(W2.pct) AS DECIMAL(12, 2)) AS running_pct
FROM Waits AS W1
     JOIN Waits AS W2
       ON W2.rn <= W1.rn
GROUP BY W1.rn, W1.wait_type, W1.wait_time_s, W1.pct
HAVING SUM(W2.pct) - W1.pct < 90 -- percentage threshold
ORDER BY W1.rn;
```

Table 3-2   Top Waits

wait_type	wait_time_s	pct	running_pct
IO_COMPLETION	466.24	23.98	23.98
PAGEIOLATCH_SH	365.08	18.78	42.76
ASYNC_NETWORK_IO	358.21	18.42	61.18
LOGMGR_RESERVE_APPEND	198.75	10.22	71.40
LOGBUFFER	194.92	10.02	81.42
WRITELOG	97.40	5.01	86.43
PAGEIOLATCH_EX	46.54	2.39	88.83
ASYNC_IO_COMPLETION	43.99	2.26	91.09

This query uses techniques to calculate running aggregates, which I'll explain later in the book. Remember, focus for now on the concepts rather than on the techniques used to achieve them. This query returns the top waits that accumulate to 90 percent of the waits in the system, after filtering out irrelevant wait types. Of course, you can adjust the threshold and filter out other irrelevant waits to your analysis. If you want to see at least *n* rows in the output (say *n = 10*), add the expression *OR W1.rn <= 10* to the HAVING clause. With each wait type, the query returns the following: the total wait time in seconds that processes waited on that wait type since the system was last restarted or the counters were cleared; the percentage of the wait time of this type out of the total; and the running percentage from the top-most wait type until the current one.

Note   In the *sys.dm_os_wait_stats* DMV, *wait_time_ms* represents the total wait time of all processes that waited on this type, even if multiple processes were waiting concurrently. Still, these numbers would typically give you a good sense of the main problem areas in the system.

Examining the top waits shown in Table 3-2, you can identify three problem areas: I/O, network, and the transaction log. With this information in hand, you are ready for the next step.

I also find it handy to collect wait information in a table and update it at regular intervals (for example, once an hour). By doing this, you can analyze the distribution of waits during the day and identify peak periods.

Run the following code to create the WaitStats table:

```
USE Performance;
GO
IF OBJECT_ID('dbo.WaitStats') IS NOT NULL
  DROP TABLE dbo.WaitStats;
GO

SELECT GETDATE() AS dt,
  wait_type, waiting_tasks_count, wait_time_ms,
  max_wait_time_ms, signal_wait_time_ms
INTO dbo.WaitStats
FROM sys.dm_os_wait_stats
WHERE 1 = 2;

ALTER TABLE dbo.WaitStats
  ADD CONSTRAINT PK_WaitStats PRIMARY KEY(dt, wait_type);
CREATE INDEX idx_type_dt ON dbo.WaitStats(wait_type, dt);
```

Define a job that runs on regular intervals and uses the following code to load the current data from the DMV:

```
INSERT INTO Performance.dbo.WaitStats
  SELECT GETDATE(),
    wait_type, waiting_tasks_count, wait_time_ms,
    max_wait_time_ms, signal_wait_time_ms
FROM sys.dm_os_wait_stats;
```

Remember that the wait information in the DMV is cumulative. To get the waits that took place within each interval, you need to apply a self-join between two instances of the table— one representing the current samples, and the other representing the previous samples. The join condition will match to each current row the row representing the previous sampling for the same wait type. Then you can subtract the cumulative wait time of the previous sampling from the current, thus producing the wait time during the interval. The following code creates the *fn_interval_waits* function, which implements this logic:

```
IF OBJECT_ID('dbo.fn_interval_waits') IS NOT NULL
  DROP FUNCTION dbo.fn_interval_waits;
GO

CREATE FUNCTION dbo.fn_interval_waits
  (@fromdt AS DATETIME, @todt AS DATETIME)
RETURNS TABLE
AS
```

```
RETURN
  WITH Waits AS
  (
    SELECT dt, wait_type, wait_time_ms,
      ROW_NUMBER() OVER(PARTITION BY wait_type
                            ORDER BY dt) AS rn
    FROM dbo.WaitStats
    WHERE dt >= @fromdt
      AND dt < @todt + 1
  )
  SELECT Prv.wait_type, Prv.dt AS start_time,
    CAST((Cur.wait_time_ms - Prv.wait_time_ms)
          / 1000. AS DECIMAL(12, 2)) AS interval_wait_s
  FROM Waits AS Cur
    JOIN Waits AS Prv
      ON Cur.wait_type = Prv.wait_type
      AND Cur.rn = Prv.rn + 1
      AND Prv.dt <= @todt;
GO
```

The function accepts the boundaries of a period that you want to analyze. For example, the following query returns the interval waits for the period '20060212' through '20060215' (inclusive), sorted by the totals for each wait type in descending order, wait type, and start time:

```
SELECT wait_type, start_time, interval_wait_s
FROM dbo.fn_interval_waits('20060212', '20060215') AS F
ORDER BY SUM(interval_wait_s) OVER(PARTITION BY wait_type) DESC,
  wait_type, start_time;
```

I find Microsoft Office Excel pivot tables or Analysis Services cubes extremely handy in analyzing such information graphically. These tools allow you to easily see the distribution of waits graphically. For example, suppose you want to analyze the waits over the period '20060212' through '20060215' using Excel pivot tables. Prepare the following VIntervalWaits view, which will be used as the external source data for the pivot table:

```
IF OBJECT_ID('dbo.VIntervalWaits') IS NOT NULL
  DROP VIEW dbo.VIntervalWaits;
GO

CREATE VIEW dbo.VIntervalWaits
AS

SELECT wait_type, start_time, interval_wait_s
FROM dbo.fn_interval_waits('20060212', '20060215') AS F;
GO
```

Create a pivot table and pivot chart in Excel, and specify the *VIntervalWaits* view as the pivot table's external source data. Figure 3-1 shows what the pivot table looks like with my sample data, after filtering only the top waits.

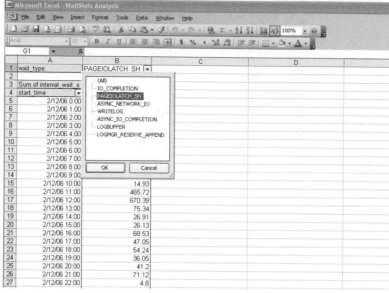

Figure 3-1   Pivot table in Excel

Figure 3-2 has a pivot chart, showing graphically the distribution of the PAGEIOLATCH_SH wait type over the input period.

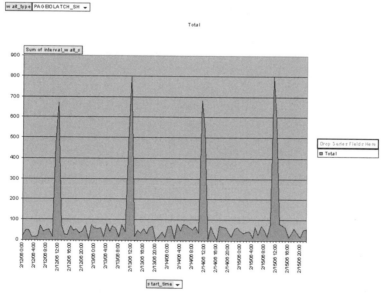

Figure 3-2   Pivot chart 1 in Excel

The PAGEIOLATCH_SH wait type indicates waits on I/O for read operations. You can clearly see that, in our case, there are dramatic peaks every day around noon.

Figure 3-3 has a pivot chart, showing graphically the distribution of all top wait types.

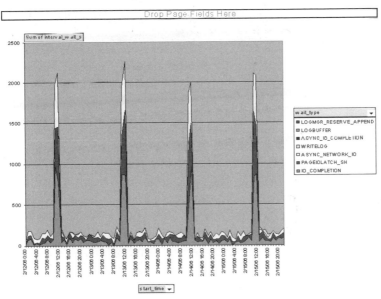

Figure 3-3   Pivot chart 2 in Excel

Again, you can see that most waits occur around noon, daily.

As an example of how handy the analysis of interval waits can be, in one of my tuning projects I found high peaks of I/O latches every four hours that lasted for quite a while (almost the whole four hours), and then dropped. Naturally, in such a case you look for activities that run on a scheduled basis. Sure enough, the "criminal" was isolated. It was a scheduled job that invoked the *sp_updatestats* stored procedure against every database every four hours and ran for almost four hours. This stored procedure is used to update statistics globally at the database level. Statistics are histograms maintained for columns that the optimizer uses to determine selectivity of queries, density of joins, and so on. Apparently, in this case some years prior a query didn't perform well because of a lack of up-to-date statistics on a particular indexed column. The customer got a recommendation back then to refresh statistics, and running the stored procedure seemed to solve the problem. Since then, the customer had been running *sp_updatestats* globally every four hours.

Note that SQL Server automatically creates and updates statistics. Typically, the automatic maintenance of statistics is sufficient, and you should intervene manually only in special cases. And if you do intervene manually, do not use *sp_updatestats* globally! The *sp_updatestats* stored procedure is useful mainly to refresh statistics globally after an upgrade of the product, or after attaching a database from an earlier version of the product or service pack level.

Ironically, when the problem was found, the query that was the trigger for creating the job was not even used anymore in the system. We simply removed the job and let SQL Server use its automatic maintenance of statistics. Naturally, the graph of I/O latches simply flattened and the performance problem was gone.

Correlate Waits with Queues

Once you identify the top waits at the instance level, you should correlate them with queues to identify the problematic resources. You mainly use System Monitor for this task. For example, if you identified I/O-related waits in the previous step, you would check the different I/O queues, cache hit ratios, and memory counters. There should be fewer than two I/O commands waiting on an I/O queue on average per spindle (disk). Cache hit ratios should be as high as possible.

As for memory, it is tightly related to I/O because the more memory you have, the more time pages (data and execution plans) can remain in cache, reducing the need for physical I/O. However, if you have I/O issues, how do you know if adding memory will really help? You need to be familiar with the tools that would help you make the right choice. For example, the counter *SQL Server:Buffer Manager – Page life expectancy* will tell you how many seconds on average a page is expected to remain in cache without reference. Low values indicate that adding memory will allow pages to remain longer in cache, while high values indicate that adding memory won't help you much in this respect. The actual numbers depend on your expectations and the frequency with which you run queries that rely on the same data/execution plans. Typically, numbers greater than several hundred indicate a good state of memory.

But let's say that you have very low values in the counter. Does this mean that you have to add memory? Adding memory in such a case would probably help, but some queries lack important indexes on the source tables and end up performing excessive I/O that could be avoided with a better index design. With less I/O and less memory pressure, the problem can be eliminated without investing in hardware. Of course, if you continue your analysis and realize that your indexes and queries are tuned well, you would then consider hardware upgrades.

Similarly, if you identified other types of waits as the top ones, you would check the relevant queues and resource utilization. For example, if the waits involve compilations/recompilations, you would check the compilations/recompilations and CPU utilization counters, and so on.

SQL Server 2005 provides you with a DMV called *sys.dm_os_performance_counters* containing all the SQL Server object-related counters that you can find in System Monitor. Unfortunately, this DMV doesn't give you the more generic counters, such as CPU utilization, I/O queues, and so on. You have to analyze those externally.

For example, when I ran the following query on my system I got the output shown (in abbreviated form) in Table 3-3:

```
SELECT
  object_name,
  counter_name,
  instance_name,
  cntr_value,
  cntr_type
FROM sys.dm_os_performance_counters;
```

Table 3-3   Contents of *sys.dm_os_performance_counters* in Abbreviated Form

object_name	counter_name	instance_name	cntr_value	cntr_type
MSSQL$S2:Buffer Manager	Buffer cache hit ratio		634	537003264
MSSQL$S2:Buffer Manager	Buffer cache hit ratio base		649	1073939712
MSSQL$S2:Buffer Manager	Page lookups/sec		62882649	272696576
MSSQL$S2:Buffer Manager	Free list stalls/sec		22370	272696576
MSSQL$S2:Buffer Manager	Free pages		43	65792
MSSQL$S2:Buffer Manager	Total pages		21330	65792
MSSQL$S2:Buffer Manager	Target pages		44306	65792
MSSQL$S2:Buffer Manager	Database pages		19134	65792
MSSQL$S2:Buffer Manager	Reserved pages		0	65792
MSSQL$S2:Buffer Manager	Stolen pages		2153	65792
...				

Note that in SQL Server 2000 you query *master.dbo.sysperfinfo* instead.

You might find the ability to query these performance counters in SQL Server useful because you can use query manipulation to analyze the data. As with wait information, you can collect performance counters in a table on regular intervals, and then use queries and tools such as pivot tables to analyze the data over time.

Determine Course of Action

This point—after you have identified the main types of waits and resources involved—is a junction in the tuning process. Based on your discoveries thus far, you will determine a course of action for further investigation. In our case, we need to identify the causes of I/O, network-related waits, and transaction log–related waits; then we will continue with a route based on our findings. But if the previous steps had identified blocking problems, compilation/recompilation problems, or others, you would need to proceed with a completely different course of action. Here I'll demonstrate tuning I/O-related performance problems, and at the end of the chapter I'll provide pointers for more information about other related performance problems, some of which are covered in these books.

Drill Down to the Database/File Level

The next step in our tuning process is to drill down to the database/file level. You want to isolate the databases that involve most of the cost. Within the database, you want to drill down to the file type (data/log), as the course of action you take depends on the file type. The tool that allows you to analyze I/O information at the database/file level is a dynamic management function (DMF) called *sys.dm_io_virtual_file_stats*. The function accepts a database ID and file ID as inputs, and returns I/O information about the input database file. You specify NULLs in both to request information about all databases and all files. Note that in SQL Server 2000 you query a function called *::fn_virtualfilestats*, providing it −1 in both parameters to get information about all databases.

The function returns the attributes: *database_id*; *file_id*; *sample_ms*, which is the number of milliseconds since the instance of SQL Server has started (and can be used to compare different outputs from this function); *num_of_reads*; *num_of_bytes_read*; *io_stall_read_ms*, which is the total time, in milliseconds, that the users waited for reads issued on the file; *num_of_writes*; *num_of_bytes_written*; *io_stall_write_ms*; *io_stall*, which is the total time, in milliseconds, that users waited for I/O to be completed on the file; *size_on_disk_bytes* (in bytes); and *file_handle*, which is the Microsoft Windows file handle for this file.

Note The measurements are reset when SQL Server starts, and they only indicate physical I/O against the files and not logical I/O.

At this point, we want to figure out which databases involve most of the I/O and I/O stalls in the system and, within the database, which file type (data/log). The following query will give you this information, sorted in descending order by the I/O stalls, and it will generate (on my system) the output shown in abbreviated form in Table 3-4:

```
WITH DBIO AS
(
  SELECT
    DB_NAME(IVFS.database_id) AS db,
    CASE WHEN MF.type = 1 THEN 'log' ELSE 'data' END AS file_type,
    SUM(IVFS.num_of_bytes_read + IVFS.num_of_bytes_written) AS io,
    SUM(IVFS.io_stall) AS io_stall
  FROM sys.dm_io_virtual_file_stats(NULL, NULL) AS IVFS
    JOIN sys.master_files AS MF
      ON IVFS.database_id = MF.database_id
      AND IVFS.file_id = MF.file_id
  GROUP BY DB_NAME(IVFS.database_id), MF.type
)
SELECT db, file_type,
  CAST(1. * io / (1024 * 1024) AS DECIMAL(12, 2)) AS io_mb,
  CAST(io_stall / 1000. AS DECIMAL(12, 2)) AS io_stall_s,
  CAST(100. * io_stall / SUM(io_stall) OVER()
       AS DECIMAL(10, 2)) AS io_stall_pct,
  ROW_NUMBER() OVER(ORDER BY io_stall DESC) AS rn
FROM DBIO
ORDER BY io_stall DESC;
```

Table 3-4   Database I/O Information in Abbreviated Form

db	file_type	io_mb	io_stall_s	io_stall_pct	rn
Performance	data	11400.81	11172.55	74.86	1
Performance	log	3732.40	2352.55	15.76	2
tempdb	data	940.08	1327.59	8.90	3
Generic	data	54.10	21.78	0.15	4
master	log	7.33	13.75	0.09	5
tempdb	log	5.24	11.20	0.08	6
master	data	13.56	6.20	0.04	7
Generic	log	1.02	3.81	0.03	8
msdb	data	5.07	2.76	0.02	9
AdventureWorks	log	0.55	1.71	0.01	10

...

The output shows the database name, file type, total I/O (reads and writes) in megabytes, I/O stalls in seconds, I/O stalls in percent of the total for the whole system, and a row number indicating a position in the sorted list based on I/O stalls. Of course, if you want, you can calculate a percentage and row number based on I/O as opposed to I/O stalls, and you can also use running aggregation techniques to calculate a running percentage, as I demonstrated earlier. You might also be interested in a separation between the reads and writes for your analysis. In this output, you can clearly identify the three main elements involving most of the system's I/O stalls—the data portion of Performance, which scores big time; the log portion of Performance; and the data portion of tempdb. Obviously, you should focus on these three elements, with special attention to data activity against the Performance database.

Regarding the bulk of our problem—I/O against the data portion of the Performance database—you now need to drill down to the process level to identify the processes that involve most of the waits.

As for the transaction log, you first need to check whether it's configured adequately. That is, whether it is placed on its own disk drive with no interference, and if so, whether the disk drive is fast enough. If the log happens to be placed on a slow disk drive, you might want to consider dedicating a faster disk for it. Once the logging activity exceeds the throughput of the disk drive, you start getting waits and stalls. You might be happy with dedicating a faster disk drive for the log, but then again, you might not have the budget or you might have already assigned the fastest disk you could for it. Keep in mind that the transaction log is written sequentially, so striping it over multiple disk drives won't help, unless you also have activities that read from the log (such as transaction log replication, or triggers in SQL Server 2000). You might also be able to optimize the processes that cause intensive logging by reducing their amount of logging. I'll elaborate on the transaction log and its optimization in Chapter 8.

As for tempdb, there are many activities—both explicit and implicit—that might cause tension in tempdb to the point where it can become a serious bottleneck in the system. In fact, internally tempdb is used more heavily in SQL Server 2005 because of the new row-versioning technology incorporated in the engine. Row versioning is used for the new snapshot-based isolations, the special inserted and deleted tables in triggers, the new online index operations, and the new multiple active result sets (MARS). The new technology maintains an older, consistent version of a row in a linked list in tempdb. Typically, there's a lot of room for optimizing tempdb, and you should definitely give that option adequate attention. I'll elaborate on tempdb and on row versioning in *Inside T-SQL Programming* in the chapters that cover temporary tables, triggers, and transactions.

For our demonstration, let's focus on solving the I/O problems related to the data portion of the Performance database.

Drill Down to the Process Level

Now that you know which databases (in our case, one) involve most of the performance problem, you want to drill down to the process level; namely, identify the processes (stored procedures, queries, and so on) that need to be tuned. For this task, you will find SQL Server's built-in tracing capabilities extremely powerful. You need to trace a workload representing the typical activities in the system against the databases you need to focus on, analyze the trace data, and isolate the processes that need to be tuned.

Before I talk about the specific trace you need to create for such tuning purposes, I'd first like to point out a few important tips regarding working with traces in SQL Server in general.

Traces have an impact on the performance of the system, and you should put effort into reducing their impact. My good friend Brian Moran once compared the problematic aspect of measuring performance to the Heisenberg Uncertainty Principle in quantum mechanics. The principle was formulated by Werner Heisenberg in 1927. Very loosely speaking, when you measure something, there's a factor of uncertainty caused by your measurement. The more precise the measure of something's position, the more uncertainty there is regarding its momentum (loosely, velocity and direction). So the more precisely you know one thing, the less precisely you can know some parallel quantity. On the scale of atoms and elementary particles, the effect of the uncertainty principle is very important. There's no proof to support the uncertainty principal (just like there's no scientific proof of God or of evolution), but the theory is mathematically sound and supported by experimentation.

Going back to our traces, you don't want your tracing activity to cause a performance problem itself. You can't avoid its effect altogether—that's impossible—but you can definitely do much to reduce it by following some important guidelines:

- Don't trace with the SQL Server Profiler GUI; instead, use the T-SQL code that defines the trace. When you trace with Profiler, you're actually running two traces—one that directs the output to the target file, and one that streams the trace information to the client running Profiler. You can define the trace graphically with Profiler, and then script the trace definition to T-SQL code using the menu item File>Export>Script Trace Definition>For SQL Server 2005... (or 2000...). You can then make slight revisions to the code depending on your needs. I like to encapsulate the code in a stored procedure, which accepts as arguments elements that I want to make variable—for example, the database ID I use as a filter in the trace definition.

■ Do not trace directly to a table, as this will have a significant performance impact. Tracing to a file on a local disk is the fastest option (tracing to a network share is bad as well). You can later load the trace data to a table for analysis using the *fn_trace_gettable* function with a SELECT INTO statement. SELECT INTO is considered a bulk operation. Bulk operations are minimally logged when the database recovery model is not set to FULL; therefore, they run much faster then when running in a fully logged mode.

■ Tracing can produce enormous amount of data and excessive I/O activity. Make sure the target trace file does not reside on disk drives that contain database files (such as data, log, and tempdb). Ideally, dedicate a separate disk drive for the target trace files, even if it means adding external disk drives.

■ Be selective in your choices of event classes and data columns—only trace what you need, removing all default and unnecessary ones. Of course, don't be too selective; make sure that all relevant event classes and data columns are included.

■ Use the trace filtering capabilities to filter only the relevant events. For example, when tuning a particular database, make sure you filter events only for the relevant database ID.

With these important guidelines in mind, let's proceed to the trace that we need for our tuning purposes.

Trace Performance Workload

You now need to define a trace that will help you identify processes that need to be tuned in the Performance database. When faced with such a need, there's a tendency to trace slow-running processes by filtering events where the Duration data column is greater than or equal to some value (say, 3000 milliseconds). This approach is problematic. Think of the following: You have a query that runs for about 30 seconds a couple of times a day, and another query that runs for a about half a second 40,000 times a day. Which would you say is more important to tune? Obviously, the latter is more important, but if you filter only events that run for at least three seconds, you'll filter out the more important query to tune.

In short, for our purposes you don't want to filter based on Duration at all. Of course, this means that you might get enormous amounts of trace data, so make sure you follow the guidelines I suggested earlier. You do want to filter only the databases that are relevant to your tuning process.

As for event classes, if most activities in your system are invoked by stored procedures and each stored procedure invokes a small or limited number of activities, trace the *SP:Completed* event class. You will then be able to aggregate the data by the procedure. However, if each procedure invokes many activities, you want to trace the *SP:StmtCompleted* event class to capture each individual statement invoked from each stored procedure. If you have activities that are submitted as ad hoc batches (as in our case), trace the *SQL:StmtCompleted* event class. Finally, if you have activities submitted as remote procedure calls, trace the *RPC:Completed* event class. Notice that all event classes are *Completed* ones as opposed to the respective *Starting* event classes. Only the *Completed* event classes carry performance information such as Duration, CPU, Reads, and Writes because, naturally, these values are unknown when the respective event starts.

As for data columns, you mainly need the TextData column that will carry the actual T-SQL code, and the relevant performance-related counters—most importantly, the Duration column. Remember that users perceive waits as the performance problem, and Duration stands for the elapsed time it took the event to run. I also like to trace the RowCounts data column, especially when looking for network-related problems. Queries returning the result set to the client with large numbers in this counter would indicate potential pressure on the network. Other than that, you might want additional data columns based on your needs. For example, if you later want to analyze the data by host, application, login, and so on, make sure you also include the corresponding data columns.

You can define a trace following these guidelines, and then script its definition to T-SQL code. I did so, and encapsulated the code in a stored procedure called *sp_perfworkload_trace_start*.

> **Note**   Microsoft doesn't recommend using the *sp_* prefix for local user stored procedures. I created the stored procedure with the *sp_* prefix in the master database because it makes the procedure "special" in the sense that you can invoke it from any database without specifying the database qualifier.

The stored procedure accepts a database ID and file name as input parameters. It defines a trace using the specified database ID as a filter, and the given file name as the target for the trace data; it starts the trace, and returns the newly generated trace ID via an output parameter. Run the code in Listing 3-3 to create the *sp_perfworkload_trace_start* stored procedure.

Listing 3-3   Creation script for the *sp_perfworkload_trace_start* stored procedure

```
SET NOCOUNT ON;
USE master;
GO

IF OBJECT_ID('dbo.sp_perfworkload_trace_start') IS NOT NULL
  DROP PROC dbo.sp_perfworkload_trace_start;
GO

CREATE PROC dbo.sp_perfworkload_trace_start
  @dbid      AS INT,
  @tracefile AS NVARCHAR(254),
  @traceid   AS INT OUTPUT
AS
```

```
-- Create a Queue
DECLARE @rc         AS INT;
DECLARE @maxfilesize AS BIGINT;

SET @maxfilesize = 5;

EXEC @rc = sp_trace_create @traceid OUTPUT, 0, @tracefile, @maxfilesize, NULL
IF (@rc != 0) GOTO error;

-- Client side File and Table cannot be scripted

-- Set the events
DECLARE @on AS BIT;
SET @on = 1;
EXEC sp_trace_setevent @traceid, 10, 15, @on;
EXEC sp_trace_setevent @traceid, 10, 8, @on;
EXEC sp_trace_setevent @traceid, 10, 16, @on;
EXEC sp_trace_setevent @traceid, 10, 48, @on;
EXEC sp_trace_setevent @traceid, 10, 1, @on;
EXEC sp_trace_setevent @traceid, 10, 17, @on;
EXEC sp_trace_setevent @traceid, 10, 10, @on;
EXEC sp_trace_setevent @traceid, 10, 18, @on;
EXEC sp_trace_setevent @traceid, 10, 11, @on;
EXEC sp_trace_setevent @traceid, 10, 12, @on;
EXEC sp_trace_setevent @traceid, 10, 13, @on;
EXEC sp_trace_setevent @traceid, 10, 14, @on;
EXEC sp_trace_setevent @traceid, 45, 8, @on;
EXEC sp_trace_setevent @traceid, 45, 16, @on;
EXEC sp_trace_setevent @traceid, 45, 48, @on;
EXEC sp_trace_setevent @traceid, 45, 1, @on;
EXEC sp_trace_setevent @traceid, 45, 17, @on;
EXEC sp_trace_setevent @traceid, 45, 10, @on;
EXEC sp_trace_setevent @traceid, 45, 18, @on;
EXEC sp_trace_setevent @traceid, 45, 11, @on;
EXEC sp_trace_setevent @traceid, 45, 12, @on;
EXEC sp_trace_setevent @traceid, 45, 13, @on;
EXEC sp_trace_setevent @traceid, 45, 14, @on;
EXEC sp_trace_setevent @traceid, 45, 15, @on;
EXEC sp_trace_setevent @traceid, 41, 15, @on;
EXEC sp_trace_setevent @traceid, 41, 8, @on;
EXEC sp_trace_setevent @traceid, 41, 16, @on;
EXEC sp_trace_setevent @traceid, 41, 48, @on;
EXEC sp_trace_setevent @traceid, 41, 1, @on;
EXEC sp_trace_setevent @traceid, 41, 17, @on;
EXEC sp_trace_setevent @traceid, 41, 10, @on;
EXEC sp_trace_setevent @traceid, 41, 18, @on;
EXEC sp_trace_setevent @traceid, 41, 11, @on;
EXEC sp_trace_setevent @traceid, 41, 12, @on;
EXEC sp_trace_setevent @traceid, 41, 13, @on;
EXEC sp_trace_setevent @traceid, 41, 14, @on;

-- Set the Filters
DECLARE @intfilter AS INT;
DECLARE @bigintfilter AS BIGINT;
```

```
-- Application name filter
EXEC sp_trace_setfilter @traceid, 10, 0, 7, N'SQL Server Profiler%';
-- Database ID filter
EXEC sp_trace_setfilter @traceid, 3, 0, 0, @dbid;

-- Set the trace status to start
EXEC sp_trace_setstatus @traceid, 1;

-- Print trace id and file name for future references
PRINT 'Trce ID: ' + CAST(@traceid AS VARCHAR(10))
  + ', Trace File: ''' + @tracefile + '''';

GOTO finish;

error:
PRINT 'Error Code: ' + CAST(@rc AS VARCHAR(10));

finish:
GO
```

Run the following code to start the trace, filtering events against the Performance database and sending the trace data to the file 'c:\temp\Perfworkload 20060828.trc':

```
DECLARE @dbid AS INT, @traceid AS INT;
SET @dbid = DB_ID('Performance');

EXEC dbo.sp_perfworkload_trace_start
  @dbid      = @dbid,
  @tracefile = 'c:\temp\Perfworkload 20060828.trc',
  @traceid   = @traceid OUTPUT;
```

If you were to assume that the newly generated trace ID is 2, you would get the following output:

```
Trace ID: 2, Trace File: 'c:\temp\perfworkload 20060828.trc'
```

You need to keep the trace ID aside, as you will use it later to stop the trace and close it.

Next, run the sample queries from Listing 3-2 several times. When done, stop the trace and close it by running the following code (assuming the trace ID is 2):

```
EXEC sp_trace_setstatus 2, 0;
EXEC sp_trace_setstatus 2, 2;
```

Of course, you should specify the actual trace ID you got for your trace. If you lost the scrap of paper you wrote the trace ID on, query the sys.traces view to get information about all running traces.

When tracing a workload in a production environment for tuning purposes, make sure you trace a sufficiently representative one. In some cases, this might mean tracing for only a couple of hours, while in other cases it can be a matter of days.

The next step is to load the trace data to a table and analyze it. Of course, you can open it with Profiler and examine it there; however, typically such traces generate a lot of data, and there's not much that you can do with Profiler to analyze the data. In our case, we have a small number of sample queries. Figure 3-4 shows what the trace data looks like when loaded in Profiler.

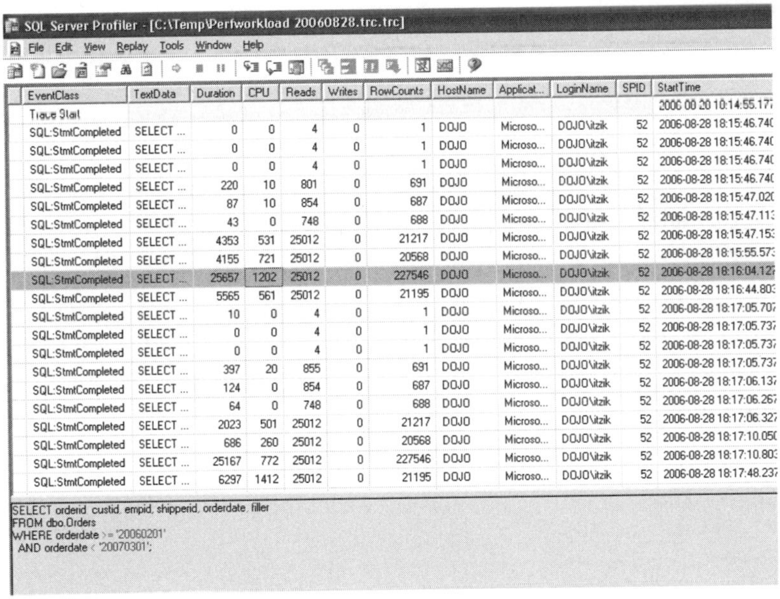

Figure 3-4   Performance workload trace data

Examining the trace data, you can clearly see some long-running queries that generate a lot of I/O. These queries use range filters based on the *orderdate* column and seem to consistently incur about 25,000 reads. The Orders table currently contains 1,000,000 rows and resides on about 25,000 pages. This tells you that these queries are causing full table scans to acquire the data and are probably missing an important index on the *orderdate* column. The missing index is probably the main cause of the excessive I/O in the system.

Also, you can find some queries that return a very large number of rows in the result set—several thousand and, in some cases, hundreds of thousands of rows. You should check whether filters and further manipulation are applied in the server when possible, rather than bringing everything to the client through the network and performing filtering and further manipulation there. These queries are probably the main cause of the network issues in the system.

Of course, such graphical analysis with Profiler is feasible only with tiny traces such as the one we're using for demonstration purposes. In production environments, it's just not realistic; you will need to load the trace data to a table and use queries to analyze the data.

Analyze Trace Data

As I mentioned earlier, you use the *fn_trace_gettable* function to return the trace data in table format. Run the following code to load the trace data from our file to the Workload table:

```
SET NOCOUNT ON;
USE Performance;
GO
IF OBJECT_ID('dbo.Workload') IS NOT NULL
  DROP TABLE dbo.Workload;
GO

SELECT CAST(TextData AS NVARCHAR(MAX)) AS tsql_code,
  Duration AS duration
INTO dbo.Workload
FROM sys.fn_trace_gettable('c:\temp\Perfworkload 20060828.trc', NULL) AS T
WHERE Duration IS NOT NULL;
```

Note that this code loads only the TextData (T-SQL code) and Duration data columns to focus particularly on query run time. Typically, you would want to also load other data columns that are relevant to your analysis—for example, the I/O and CPU counters, row counts, host name, application name, and so on.

Remember that it is important to aggregate the performance information by the query or T-SQL statement to figure out the overall performance impact of each query with its multiple invocations. The following code attempts to do just that, and it generates the output shown in abbreviated form in Table 3-5:

```
SELECT
  tsql_code,
  SUM(duration) AS total_duration
FROM dbo.Workload
GROUP BY tsql_code;
```

Table 3-5   Aggregated Duration by Query in Abbreviated Form

tsql_code	duration
SELECT orderid, custid, empid, shipperid, orderdate, filler FROM dbo.Orders WHERE orderdate = '20060118';	161055
SELECT orderid, custid, empid, shipperid, orderdate, filler FROM dbo.Orders WHERE orderdate = '20060212';	367430
SELECT orderid, custid, empid, shipperid, orderdate, filler FROM dbo.Orders WHERE orderdate = '20060828';	132466
SELECT orderid, custid, empid, shipperid, orderdate, filler FROM dbo.Orders WHERE orderdate >= '20060101' AND orderdate < '20060201';	3821240

Table 3-5   Aggregated Duration by Query in Abbreviated Form

tsql_code	duration
SELECT orderid, custid, empid, shipperid, orderdate, filler FROM dbo.Orders WHERE orderdate >= '20060201' AND orderdate < '20070301';	47881415
...	

But there's a problem. You can see in the aggregated data that some queries that are logically the same or follow the same pattern ended up in different groups. That's because they happened to be using different values in their filters. Only query strings that are completely identical were grouped together. As an aside, you wouldn't be facing this problem had you used stored procedures, each invoking an individual query or a very small number of queries. Remember that in such a case you would have traced the *SP:Completed* event class, and then you would have received aggregated data by the procedure. But that's not our case.

A simple but not very accurate way to deal with the problem is to extract a substring of the query strings and aggregate by that substring. Typically, the left portion of query strings that follow the same pattern is the same, while somewhere to the right you have the arguments that are used in the filter. You can apply trial and error, playing with the length of the substring that you will extract; hopefully, the substring will be long enough to allow grouping queries following the same pattern together, and small enough to distinguish queries of different patterns from each other. This approach, as you can see, is tricky and would not guarantee accurate results. Essentially, you pick a number that seems reasonable, close your eyes, and hope for the best.

For example, the following query aggregates the trace data by a query prefix of 100 characters and generates the output shown in Table 3-6:

```
SELECT
    SUBSTRING(tsql_code, 1, 100) AS tsql_code,
    SUM(duration) AS total_duration
FROM dbo.Workload
GROUP BY SUBSTRING(tsql_code, 1, 100);
```

Table 3-6   Aggregated Duration by Query Prefix

tsql_code	total_duration
SELECT orderid, custid, empid, shipperid, orderdate, filler FROM dbo.Orders WHERE orderdate = '200	660951
SELECT orderid, custid, empid, shipperid, orderdate, filler FROM dbo.Orders WHERE orderdate >= '20	60723155

Table 3-6   Aggregated Duration by Query Prefix

tsql_code	total_duration
SELECT orderid, custid, empid, shipperid, orderdate, filler FROM dbo.Orders WHERE orderid = 3;	17857
SELECT orderid, custid, empid, shipperid, orderdate, filler FROM dbo.Orders WHERE orderid = 5;	426
SELECT orderid, custid, empid, shipperid, orderdate, filler FROM dbo.Orders WHERE orderid = 7;	598
SET NOCOUNT ON;	7
USE Performance;	12857

In our case, this prefix length did the trick for some queries, but it wasn't very successful with others. With more realistic trace data, you won't have the privilege of looking at a tiny number of queries and being able to play with the numbers so easily. But the general idea is that you adjust the prefix length by applying trial and error.

Here's code that uses a prefix length of 94 and generates the output shown in Table 3-7:

```
SELECT
  SUBSTRING(tsql_code, 1, 94) AS tsql_code,
  SUM(duration) AS total_duration
FROM dbo.Workload
GROUP BY SUBSTRING(tsql_code, 1, 94);
```

Table 3-7   Aggregated Duration by Query Prefix, Adjusted

tsql_code	total_duration
SELECT orderid, custid, empid, shipperid, orderdate, filler FROM dbo.Orders WHERE orderdate	61384106
SELECT orderid, custid, empid, shipperid, orderdate, filler FROM dbo.Orders WHERE orderid =	18881
SET NOCOUNT ON;	7
USE Performance;	12857

Now you end up with overgrouping. In short, finding the right prefix length is a tricky process, and its accuracy and reliability is questionable.

A much more accurate approach is to parse the query strings and produce a *query signature* for each. A query signature is a query template that is the same for queries following the same pattern. After creating these, you can then aggregate the data by query signatures instead of by the query strings themselves. SQL Server 2005 provides you with the *sp_get_query_template* stored procedure, which parses an input query string and returns the query template and the definition of the arguments via output parameters.

As an example, the following code invokes the stored procedure, providing a sample query string as input, and it generates the output shown in Table 3-8:

```
DECLARE @my_templatetext AS NVARCHAR(MAX);
DECLARE @my_parameters   AS NVARCHAR(MAX);

EXEC sp_get_query_template
  N'SELECT * FROM dbo.T1 WHERE col1 = 3 AND col2 > 78',
  @my_templatetext OUTPUT,
  @my_parameters OUTPUT;

SELECT @my_templatetext AS querysig, @my_parameters AS params;
```

Table 3-8   Query Template

querysig	params
select * from dbo . T1 where col1 = @0 and col2 > @1	@0 int,@1 int

The problem with this stored procedure is that you need to use a cursor to invoke it against every query string from the trace data, and this can take quite a while with large traces. The stored procedure also (by design) returns an error in some cases (see Books Online for details), which could compromise its value. It would be much more convenient to have this logic implemented as a function, allowing you to invoke it directly against the table containing the trace data. Fortunately, such a function exists; it was written by Stuart Ozer, and its code is provided in Listing 3-4. Stuart is with the Microsoft SQL Server Customer Advisory Team, and I would like to thank him for allowing me to share the code with the readers of this book.

Listing 3-4   Creation script for the *fn_SQLSigTSQL UDF*

```
IF OBJECT_ID('dbo.fn_SQLSigTSQL') IS NOT NULL
  DROP FUNCTION dbo.fn_SQLSigTSQL;
GO

CREATE FUNCTION dbo.fn_SQLSigTSQL
  (@p1 NTEXT, @parselength INT = 4000)
RETURNS NVARCHAR(4000)


--
-- This function is provided "AS IS" with no warranties,
-- and confers no rights.
-- Use of included script samples are subject to the terms specified at
-- http://www.microsoft.com/info/cpyright.htm
--
-- Strips query strings
AS
```

```
BEGIN
  DECLARE @pos AS INT;
  DECLARE @mode AS CHAR(10);
  DECLARE @maxlength AS INT;
  DECLARE @p2 AS NCHAR(4000);
  DECLARE @currchar AS CHAR(1), @nextchar AS CHAR(1);
  DECLARE @p2len AS INT;

  SET @maxlength = LEN(RTRIM(SUBSTRING(@p1,1,4000)));
  SET @maxlength = CASE WHEN @maxlength > @parselength
                        THEN @parselength ELSE @maxlength END;
  SET @pos = 1;
  SET @p2 = '';
  SET @p2len = 0;
  SET @currchar = '';
  set @nextchar = '';
  SET @mode = 'command';

  WHILE (@pos <= @maxlength)
  BEGIN
    SET @currchar = SUBSTRING(@p1,@pos,1);
    SET @nextchar = SUBSTRING(@p1,@pos+1,1);
    IF @mode = 'command'
    BEGIN
      SET @p2 = LEFT(@p2,@p2len) + @currchar;
      SET @p2len = @p2len + 1 ;
      IF @currchar IN (',','(',' ','=','<','>','!')
         AND @nextchar BETWEEN '0' AND '9'
      BEGIN
        SET @mode = 'number';
        SET @p2 = LEFT(@p2,@p2len) + '#';
        SET @p2len = @p2len + 1;
      END
      IF @currchar = ''''
      BEGIN
        SET @mode = 'literal';
        SET @p2 = LEFT(@p2,@p2len) + '#''';
        SET @p2len = @p2len + 2;
      END
    END
    ELSE IF @mode = 'number' AND @nextchar IN (',',')',' ','=','<','>','!')
      SET @mode= 'command';
    ELSE IF @mode = 'literal' AND @currchar = ''''
      SET @mode= 'command';

    SET @pos = @pos + 1;
  END
  RETURN @p2;
END
GO
```

The function accepts as inputs a query string and the length of the code you want to parse. The function returns the query signature of the input query, with all parameters replaced by a number sign (#). Note that this is a fairly simple function and might need to be tailored to particular situations. Run the following code to test the function:

```
SELECT dbo.fn_SQLSigTSQL
  (N'SELECT * FROM dbo.T1 WHERE col1 = 3 AND col2 > 78', 4000);
```

You will get the following output:

```
SELECT * FROM dbo.T1 WHERE col1 = # AND col2 > #
```

Of course, you could now use the function and aggregate the trace data by query signature. However, keep in mind that although T-SQL is very efficient with data manipulation, it is slow in processing iterative/procedural logic. This is a classic example where a CLR implementation of the function makes more sense. The CLR is much faster than T-SQL for iterative/procedural logic and string manipulation. SQL Server 2005 introduces .NET integration within the product, allowing you to develop .NET routines based on the *common language runtime* (CLR). CLR routines are discussed in *Inside T-SQL Programming*; there you will find more thorough coverage and a comparison of the T-SQL and CLR-based implementations of the function that generates query signatures. You can also find some background information about CLR development in SQL Server in Chapter 6 of this book.

The CLR-based "enhanced" implementation of the function using C# code is provided in Listing 3-5.

Listing 3-5   *fn_SQLSigCLR* and *fn_RegexReplace* functions, C# version

```
using System.Text;
using Microsoft.SqlServer.Server;
using System.Data.SqlTypes;
using System.Text.RegularExpressions;

public partial class SQLSignature
{
    // fn_SQLSigCLR
    [SqlFunction(IsDeterministic = true, DataAccess = DataAccessKind.None)]
    public static SqlString fn_SQLSigCLR(SqlString querystring)
    {
        return (SqlString)Regex.Replace(
            querystring.Value,
            @"([\s,(=<>!](?![^\]]+[\]]))(?:(?:(?:(?#    expression coming
            )(?:([N])?(')(?:[^']|'')*('))(?#             character
            )|(?:0x[\da-fA-F]*)(?#                       binary
            )|(?:[-+]?(?:(?:[\d]*\.[\d]*|[\d]+)(?#       precise number
            )(?:[eE]?[\d]*)))(?#                         imprecise number
            )|(?:[~]?[-+]?(?:[\d]+))(?#                  integer
            ))(?:[\s]?[\+\-\*\/\%\&\|\^][\s]?)?)+(?#     operators
            ))",
            @"$1$2$3#$4");
    }
}
```

```
    // fn_RegexReplace - for generic use of RegEx-based replace
    [SqlFunction(IsDeterministic = true, DataAccess = DataAccessKind.None)]
    public static SqlString fn_RegexReplace(
        SqlString input, SqlString pattern, SqlString replacement)
    {
        return (SqlString)Regex.Replace(
            input.Value, pattern.Value, replacement.Value);
    }
}
```

The code in Listing 3-5 has the definitions of two functions: *fn_SQLSigCLR* and
fn_RegexReplace. The function *fn_SQLSigCLR* accepts a query string and returns the query
signature. This function covers cases that the T-SQL function overlooks, and it can be easily
enhanced to support more cases if you need it to. The function *fn_RegexReplace* exposes more
generic pattern-based string replacement capabilities based on regular expressions, and it is
provided for your convenience.

> **Note** I didn't bother checking for NULL inputs in the CLR code because T-SQL allows you
> to specify the option RETURNS NULL ON NULL INPUT when you register the functions, as I
> will demonstrate later. This option means that when a NULL input is provided, SQL Server
> doesn't invoke the function at all; rather, it simply returns a NULL output.

If you're familiar with developing CLR routines in SQL Server, deploy these functions in the
Performance database. If you're not, just follow these steps:

1. Create a new Microsoft Visual C#, Class Library project in Microsoft Visual Studio 2005
    (File>New>Project...>Visual C#>Class Library).

2. In the New Project dialog box, name the project and solution **SQLSignature**, specify C:\
    as the location, and confirm.

3. Rename the file Class1.cs to **SQLSignature.cs**, and within it paste the code from
    Listing 3-5, overriding its current content.

4. Build the assembly by choosing the Build>Build SQLSignature menu item. A file named
    C:\SQLSignature\SQLSignature\bin\Debug\SQLSignature.dll containing the assem-
    bly will be created.

5. At this point, you go back to SQL Server Management Studio (SSMS) and apply a cou-
    ple of additional steps to deploy the assembly in the Performance database, and then
    register the *fn_SQLSigCLR* and *fn_RegexReplace* functions. But first, you need to
    enable CLR in SQL Server (which is disabled by default) by running the following
    code:

```
EXEC sp_configure 'clr enable', 1;
RECONFIGURE;
```

6. Next, you need to load the intermediate language (IL) code from the .dll file into the Performance database by running the following code:

```
USE Performance;
CREATE ASSEMBLY SQLSignature
FROM 'C:\SQLSignature\SQLSignature\bin\Debug\SQLSignature.dll';
```

7. Finally, register the *fn_SQLSigCLR* and *fn_RegexReplace* functions by running the following code:

```
CREATE FUNCTION dbo.fn_SQLSigCLR(@querystring AS NVARCHAR(MAX))
RETURNS NVARCHAR(MAX)
WITH RETURNS NULL ON NULL INPUT
EXTERNAL NAME SQLSignature.SQLSignature.fn_SQLSigCLR;
GO

CREATE FUNCTION dbo.fn_RegexReplace(
    @input       AS NVARCHAR(MAX),
    @pattern     AS NVARCHAR(MAX),
    @replacement AS NVARCHAR(MAX))
RETURNS NVARCHAR(MAX)
WITH RETURNS NULL ON NULL INPUT
EXTERNAL NAME SQLSignature.SQLSignature.fn_RegexReplace;
GO
```

You're done. At this point, you can start using the functions like you do any other user-defined function. In case you're curious, the CLR implementation of the function runs faster than the T-SQL one by a factor of 10.

To test the *fn_SQLSigCLR* function, invoke it against the Workload table by running the following query, which will generate the output shown in abbreviated form in Table 3-9:

```
SELECT
  dbo.fn_SQLSigCLR(tsql_code) AS sig,
  duration
FROM dbo.Workload;
```

You can also use the more generic *fn_RegexReplace* function to achive the same output, like so:

```
SELECT
  dbo.fn_RegexReplace(tsql_code,
    N'([\s,(=<>!](?![^\]]+[\]]))(?:(?:(?:(?#     expression coming
    )(?:([N])?('')(?:[^'']|'''')*(''))(?#        character
    )|(?:0x[\da-fA-F]*)(?#                        binary
    )|(?:[-+]?(?:(?:[\d]*\.[\d]*|[\d]+)(?#        precise number
    )(?:[eE]?[\d]*)))(?#                          imprecise number
    )|(?:[~]?[-+]?(?:[\d]+))(?#                   integer
    ))(?:[\s]?[\+\-\*\/\%\&\|\^][\s]?)?)+(?#      operators
    ))',
    N'$1$2$3#$4') AS sig,
  duration
FROM dbo.Workload;
```

Table 3-9   Trace Data with Query Signatures in Abbreviated Form

sig	duration
...	
SELECT orderid, custid, empid, shipperid, orderdate, filler FROM dbo.Orders WHERE orderid = #;	17567
SELECT orderid, custid, empid, shipperid, orderdate, filler FROM dbo.Orders WHERE orderid = #;	72
SELECT orderid, custid, empid, shipperid, orderdate, filler FROM dbo.Orders WHERE orderid = #;	145
SELECT orderid, custid, empid, shipperid, orderdate, filler FROM dbo.Orders WHERE orderdate = '#';	99204
SELECT orderid, custid, empid, shipperid, orderdate, filler FROM dbo.Orders WHERE orderdate = '#';	56191
SELECT orderid, custid, empid, shipperid, orderdate, filler FROM dbo.Orders WHERE orderdate = '#';	38718
SELECT orderid, custid, empid, shipperid, orderdate, filler FROM dbo.Orders WHERE orderdate >= '#' AND orderdate < '#';	1689740
SELECT orderid, custid, empid, shipperid, orderdate, filler FROM dbo.Orders WHERE orderdate >= '#' AND orderdate < '#';	738292
SELECT orderid, custid, empid, shipperid, orderdate, filler FROM dbo.Orders WHERE orderdate >= '#' AND orderdate < '#';	13601583
...	

As you can see, you get back query signatures, which you can use to aggregate the trace data. Keep in mind, though, that query strings can get lengthy, and grouping the data by lengthy strings is slow and expensive. Instead, you might prefer to generate an integer checksum for each query string by using the T-SQL CHECKSUM function. For example, the following query generates a checksum value for each query string from the Workload table, and it generates the output shown in abbreviated form in Table 3-10:

```
SELECT
  CHECKSUM(dbo.fn_SQLSigCLR(tsql_code)) AS cs,
  duration
FROM dbo.Workload;
```

Table 3-10   Query Signature Checksums in Abbreviated Form

cs	duration
...	
−1872968693	17567
−1872968693	72
−1872968693	145
−184235228	99204
−184235228	56191
−184235228	38718
368623506	1689740
368623506	738292
368623506	13601583
...	

Use the following code to add a column called *cs* to the Workload table, populate it with the checksum of the query signatures, and create a clustered index on the *cs* column:

```
ALTER TABLE dbo.Workload ADD cs INT NOT NULL DEFAULT (0);
GO
UPDATE dbo.Workload
  SET cs = CHECKSUM(dbo.fn_SQLSigCLR(tsql_code));

CREATE CLUSTERED INDEX idx_cl_cs ON dbo.Workload(cs);
```

Run the following code to return the new contents of the Workload table, shown in abbreviated form in Table 3-11:

```
SELECT tsql_code, duration, cs
FROM dbo.Workload
```

Table 3-11   Contents of Table Workload

tsql_code	duration	cs
...		
SELECT orderid, custid, empid, shipperid, orderdate, filler FROM dbo.Orders WHERE orderdate = '20060118';	36094	−184235228

Table 3-11   Contents of Table Workload

tsql_code	duration	cs
SELECT orderid, custid, empid, shipperid, orderdate, filler FROM dbo.Orders WHERE orderdate = '20060828';	32662	−184235228
SELECT orderid, custid, empid, shipperid, orderdate, filler FROM dbo.Orders WHERE orderdate >= '20060101' AND orderdate < '20060201';	717757	368623506
SELECT orderid, custid, empid, shipperid, orderdate, filler FROM dbo.Orders WHERE orderdate >= '20060401' AND orderdate < '20060501';	684754	368623506
...		

At this point, you want to aggregate the data by the query signature checksum. It would also be very useful to get running aggregates of the percentage of each signature's duration of the total duration. This information can help you easily isolate the query patterns that you need to tune. Remember that typical production workloads can contain a large number of query signatures. It would make sense to populate a temporary table with the aggregate data and index it, and then run a query against the temporary table to calculate the running aggregates.

Run the following code to populate the temporary table #AggQueries with the total duration per signature checksum, including the percentage of the total, and a row number based on the duration in descending order:

```
IF OBJECT_ID('tempdb..#AggQueries') IS NOT NULL
  DROP TABLE #AggQueries;
GO

SELECT cs, SUM(duration) AS total_duration,
  100. * SUM(duration) / SUM(SUM(duration)) OVER() AS pct,
  ROW_NUMBER() OVER(ORDER BY SUM(duration) DESC) AS rn
INTO #AggQueries
FROM dbo.Workload
GROUP BY cs;

CREATE CLUSTERED INDEX idx_cl_cs ON #AggQueries(cs);
```

Run the following code, which generates the output shown in Table 3-12, to return the contents of the temporary table:

```
SELECT cs, total_duration, pct, rn
FROM #AggQueries
ORDER BY rn;
```

Table 3-12 Aggregated Duration by Query Signature Checksum

cs	total_duration	pct	rn
368623506	60723155	98.872121791489952	1
−184235228	660951	1.076189598024132	2
−1872968693	18881	0.030742877762941	3
1018047893	12857	0.020934335013936	4
1037912028	7	0.000011397709037	5

Use the following query to return the running aggregates of the percentages, filtering only those rows where the running percentage accumulates to a certain threshold that you specify:

```
SELECT AQ1.cs,
  CAST(AQ1.total_duration / 1000.
    AS DECIMAL(12, 2)) AS total_s,
  CAST(SUM(AQ2.total_duration) / 1000.
    AS DECIMAL(12, 2)) AS running_total_s,
  CAST(AQ1.pct AS DECIMAL(12, 2)) AS pct,
  CAST(SUM(AQ2.pct) AS DECIMAL(12, 2)) AS run_pct,
  AQ1.rn
FROM #AggQueries AS AQ1
  JOIN #AggQueries AS AQ2
    ON AQ2.rn <= AQ1.rn
GROUP BY AQ1.cs, AQ1.total_duration, AQ1.pct, AQ1.rn
HAVING SUM(AQ2.pct) - AQ1.pct <= 90 -- percentage threshold
--   OR AQ1.rn <= 5
ORDER BY AQ1.rn;
```

In our case, if you use 90 percent as the threshold, you would get only one row. For demonstration purposes, I uncommented the part of the expression in the HAVING clause to return at least 5 rows and got the output shown in Table 3-13.

Table 3-13 Running Aggregated Duration

cs	total_s	running_total_s	pct	running_pct	rn
368623506	60723.16	60723.16	98.87	98.87	1
−184235228	660.95	61384.11	1.08	99.95	2
−1872968693	18.88	61402.99	0.03	99.98	3
1018047893	12.86	61415.84	0.02	100.00	4
1037912028	0.01	61415.85	0.00	100.00	5

You can see at the top that there's one query pattern that accounts for 98.87 percent of the total duration. Based on my experience, typically a handful of query patterns cause most of the performance problems in a given system.

To get back the actual queries that you need to tune, you should join the result table returned from the preceding query with the Workload table, based on a match in the checksum value (*cs* column), like so:

```
WITH RunningTotals AS
(
  SELECT AQ1.cs,
    CAST(AQ1.total_duration / 1000.
      AS DECIMAL(12, 2)) AS total_s,
    CAST(SUM(AQ2.total_duration) / 1000.
      AS DECIMAL(12, 2)) AS running_total_s,
    CAST(AQ1.pct AS DECIMAL(12, 2)) AS pct,
    CAST(SUM(AQ2.pct) AS DECIMAL(12, 2)) AS run_pct,
    AQ1.rn
  FROM #AggQueries AS AQ1
    JOIN #AggQueries AS AQ2
      ON AQ2.rn <= AQ1.rn
  GROUP BY AQ1.cs, AQ1.total_duration, AQ1.pct, AQ1.rn
  HAVING SUM(AQ2.pct) - AQ1.pct <= 90 -- percentage threshold
-- OR AQ1.rn <= 5
)
SELECT RT.rn, RT.pct, W.tsql_code
FROM RunningTotals AS RT
  JOIN dbo.Workload AS W
    ON W.cs = RT.cs
ORDER BY RT.rn;
```

You will get the output shown in abbreviated form in Table 3-14.

Table 3-14   Top Slow Queries in Abbreviated Form

rn	pct	tsql_code

1	98.87	`SELECT orderid, custid, empid, shipperid, orderdate, filler`
		`FROM dbo.Orders`
		`WHERE orderdate >= '20060101'`
		`  AND orderdate < '20060201';`

1	98.87	`SELECT orderid, custid, empid, shipperid, orderdate, filler`
		`FROM dbo.Orders  WHERE orderdate >= '20060401'`
		`  AND orderdate < '20060501';`

1	98.87	`SELECT orderid, custid, empid, shipperid, orderdate, filler`
		`FROM dbo.Orders  WHERE orderdate >= '20060201'`
		`  AND orderdate < '20070301';`

...		

Of course, with a more realistic workload you might get a large number of queries back, but you're really interested in the query pattern that you need to tune. So instead of joining back to the Workload table, use the APPLY operator to return only one row for each query signature with the query pattern, and a single sample per pattern out of the actual queries like so:

```
WITH RunningTotals AS
(
  SELECT AQ1.cs,
    CAST(AQ1.total_duration / 1000.
      AS DECIMAL(12, 2)) AS total_s,
    CAST(SUM(AQ2.total_duration) / 1000.
      AS DECIMAL(12, 2)) AS running_total_s,
    CAST(AQ1.pct AS DECIMAL(12, 2)) AS pct,
    CAST(SUM(AQ2.pct) AS DECIMAL(12, 2)) AS run_pct,
    AQ1.rn
  FROM #AggQueries AS AQ1
    JOIN #AggQueries AS AQ2
      ON AQ2.rn <= AQ1.rn
  GROUP BY AQ1.cs, AQ1.total_duration, AQ1.pct, AQ1.rn
  HAVING SUM(AQ2.pct) - AQ1.pct <= 90 -- percentage threshold
)
SELECT RT.rn, RT.pct, S.sig, S.tsql_code AS sample_query
FROM RunningTotals AS RT
  CROSS APPLY
    (SELECT TOP(1) tsql_code, dbo.fn_SQLSigCLR(tsql_code) AS sig
      FROM dbo.Workload AS W
      WHERE W.cs = RT.cs) AS S
ORDER BY RT.rn;
```

You will get the output shown in Table 3-15.

Table 3-15 Signature and Sample of the Top Slow Queries

rn	pct	sig	sample_query
1	98.87	SELECT orderid, custid, empid, shipperid, orderdate, filler FROM dbo.Orders WHERE orderdate >= '#' AND orderdate < '#';	SELECT orderid, custid, empid, shipperid, orderdate, filler FROM dbo.Orders WHERE orderdate >= '20060101' AND orderdate < '20060201';

Now you can focus your tuning efforts on the query patterns that you got back—in our case, only one. Of course, in a similar manner you can identify the query patterns that generate the largest result sets, most of the I/O, and so on.

Tune Indexes/Queries

Now that you know which patterns you need to tune, you can start with a more focused query-tuning process. The process might involve index tuning or query code revisions, and we will practice it thoroughly throughout the book. Or you might realize that the queries are already tuned pretty well, in which case you would need to inspect other aspects of the system (for example, hardware, database layout, and so on).

In our case, the tuning process is fairly simple. You need to create a clustered index on the *orderdate* column:

```
CREATE CLUSTERED INDEX idx_cl_od ON dbo.Orders(orderdate);
```

Later in the chapter, I'll cover index tuning and explain why a clustered index is adequate for query patterns such as the ones that our tuning process isolated.

To see the effect of adding the index, run the following code to start a new trace:

```
DECLARE @dbid AS INT, @traceid AS INT;
SET @dbid = DB_ID('Performance');

EXEC dbo.sp_perfworkload_trace_start
  @dbid      = @dbid,
  @tracefile = 'c:\temp\Perfworkload 20060829',
  @traceid   = @traceid OUTPUT;
```

When I ran this code, I got the following output showing that the trace ID generated is 2:

```
Trace ID: 2, Trace File: 'c:\temp\Perfworkload 20060829.trc'
```

Run the sample queries from Listing 3-2 again, and then stop the trace:

```
EXEC sp_trace_setstatus 2, 0;
EXEC sp_trace_setstatus 2, 2;
```

Figure 3-5 shows the trace data loaded with Profiler.

EventClass	TextData	Duration	CPU	Reads	Writes	RowCounts	HostName	Applicati...	LoginName	SPID	StartTime
SQL:StmtCompleted	SELECT ...	0	0	6	0	1	DOJO	Microsoft...	DOJO\itzik	52	2006-08-29 21:03:42.5(
SQL:StmtCompleted	SELECT ...	0	0	6	0	1	DOJO	Microsoft...	DOJO\itzik	52	2006-08-29 21:03:42.6:
SQL:StmtCompleted	SELECT ...	0	0	6	0	1	DOJO	Microsoft...	DOJO\itzik	52	2006-08-29 21:03:42.6(
SQL:StmtCompleted	SELECT ...	113	0	21	0	691	DOJO	Microsoft...	DOJO\itzik	52	2006-08-29 21:03:42.7(
SQL:StmtCompleted	SELECT ...	27	0	22	0	687	DOJO	Microsoft...	DOJO\itzik	52	2006-08-29 21:03:42.8:
SQL:StmtCompleted	SELECT ...	31	10	21	0	688	DOJO	Microsoft...	DOJO\itzik	52	2006-08-29 21:03:42.8!
SQL:StmtCompleted	SELECT ...	687	40	536	0	21217	DOJO	Microsoft...	DOJO\itzik	52	2006-08-29 21:03:42.8!
SQL:StmtCompleted	SELECT ...	521	20	520	0	20568	DOJO	Microsoft...	DOJO\itzik	52	2006-08-29 21:03:43.5:
SQL:StmtCompleted	SELECT ...	11217	270	5710	0	227546	DOJO	Microsoft...	DOJO\itzik	52	2006-08-29 21:03:44.0!
SQL:StmtCompleted	SELECT ...	1500	20	536	0	21195	DOJO	Microsoft...	DOJO\itzik	52	2006-08-29 21:03:58.8(
SQL:StmtCompleted	SET SHO...	0	0	0	0	0	DOJO	Microsoft...	DOJO\itzik	52	2006-08-29 21:04:13.1(
SQL:StmtCompleted	SET NOC...	0	0	0	0	0	DOJO	Microsoft...	DOJO\itzik	52	2006-08-29 21:04:18.7:
SQL:StmtCompleted	USE Perf...	0	0	0	0	0	DOJO	Microsoft...	DOJO\itzik	52	2006-08-29 21:04:18.7:
SQL:StmtCompleted	SELECT ...	0	0	6	0	1	DOJO	Microsoft...	DOJO\itzik	52	2006-08-29 21:04:18.7:
SQL:StmtCompleted	SELECT ...	0	0	6	0	1	DOJO	Microsoft...	DOJO\itzik	52	2006-08-29 21:04:18.8'
SQL:StmtCompleted	SELECT ...	0	0	6	0	1	DOJO	Microsoft...	DOJO\itzik	52	2006-08-29 21:04:18.9(
SQL:StmtCompleted	SELECT ...	72	0	21	0	691	DOJO	Microsoft...	DOJO\itzik	52	2006-08-29 21:04:18.9!
SQL:StmtCompleted	SELECT ...	29	0	22	0	687	DOJO	Microsoft...	DOJO\itzik	52	2006-08-29 21:04:19.0:
SQL:StmtCompleted	SELECT ...	38	0	21	0	688	DOJO	Microsoft...	DOJO\itzik	52	2006-08-29 21:04:19.0(
SQL:StmtCompleted	SELECT ...	540	50	536	0	21217	DOJO	Microsoft...	DOJO\itzik	52	2006-08-29 21:04:19.1(
SQL:StmtCompleted	SELECT ...	688	70	520	0	20568	DOJO	Microsoft...	DOJO\itzik	52	2006-08-29 21:04:19.6‹

```
SELECT orderid, custid, empid, shipperid, orderdate, filler
FROM dbo.Orders
WHERE orderdate >= '20060201'
  AND orderdate < '20070301';
```

Figure 3-5   Performance workload trace data after adding index

You can see that the duration and I/O involved with the query pattern we tuned are greatly reduced. Still, there are queries that generate a lot of network traffic. With those, you might want to check whether some of the processing of their result sets could be achieved at the server side, thus reducing the amount of data submitted through the network.

Tools for Query Tuning

This section provides an overview of the query-tuning tools that will be used throughout these books, and it will focus on analyzing execution plans.

syscacheobjects

SQL Server 2000 provides you with a virtual system table called master.dbo.syscacheobjects, which contains information about cached execution plans. SQL Server 2005 provides you with a compatibility view called *sys.syscacheobjects*, and a new DMV and two DMFs that replace the legacy system table and compatibility view. The three new objects are: *sys.dm_exec_cached_plans*, *sys.dm_exec_plan_attributes*, and *sys.dm_exec_sql_text*. These give you extremely useful information when analyzing the caching, compilation, and recompilation behavior of execution plans. The *sys.dm_exec_cached_plans* object contains information about the cached query execution plans; *sys.dm_exec_plan_attributes* contains one row per attribute associated with the plan, whose handle is provided as input to the DMF; *sys.dm_exec_sql_text* returns the text associated with the query, whose handle is provided as input to the DMF.

Clearing the Cache

When analyzing query performance, you sometimes need to clear the cache. SQL Server provides you with tools to clear both data and execution plans from cache. To clear data from cache globally, use the following command:

```
DBCC DROPCLEANBUFFERS;
```

To clear execution plans from cache globally, use the following command:

```
DBCC FREEPROCCACHE;
```

To clear execution plans of a particular database, use the following command:

```
DBCC FLUSHPROCINDB(<db_id>);
```

Note that the DBCC FLUSHPROCINDB command is undocumented.

Caution   Be careful not to use these commands in production environments because, obviously, clearing the cache will have a performance impact on the whole system. After clearing the data cache, SQL Server will need to physically read pages accessed for the first time from disk. After clearing execution plans from cache, SQL Server will need to generate new execution plans for queries. Also, be sure that you are aware of the global impact of clearing the cache even when doing so in development or test environments.

Dynamic Management Objects

SQL Server 2005 introduces more than 70 dynamic management objects, including DMVs and DMFs. These contain extremely useful information about the server that you can use to monitor SQL Server, diagnose problems, and tune performance. Much of the information provided by these views and functions was never available in the past. It is time very well spent to study them in detail. In these books, I will make use of the ones that are relevant to my discussions, but I urge you to take a close look at others as well. You can find information about them in Books Online, and I will also give you pointers to additional information at the end of the chapter.

STATISTICS IO

STATISTICS IO is a session option that is used extensively throughout these books. It returns I/O-related information about the statements that you run. To demonstrate its use, first clear the data cache:

```
DBCC DROPCLEANBUFFERS;
```

Then run the following code to turn the session option on and invoke a query:

```
SET STATISTICS IO ON;

SELECT orderid, custid, empid, shipperid, orderdate, filler
FROM dbo.Orders
WHERE orderdate >= '20060101'
  AND orderdate < '20060201';
```

You should get output similar to the following:

```
Table 'Orders'. Scan count 1, logical reads 536, physical reads 2, read-
ahead reads 532, lob logical reads 0, lob physical reads 0, lob read-ahead reads 0.
```

The output tells you how many times the table was accessed in the plan (*Scan count*); how many reads from cache were involved (*logical reads*); how many reads from disk were involved (*physical reads* and *read-ahead reads*); and similarly, how many logical and physical reads related to large objects were involved (*lob logical reads*, *lob physical reads*, *lob read-ahead reads*).

Run the following code to turn the session option off:

```
SET STATISTICS IO OFF;
```

Measuring the Run Time of Queries

STATISTICS TIME is a session option that returns the net CPU and elapsed clock time information about the statements that you run. It returns this information for both the time it took to parse and compile the query, and the time it took to execute it. To demonstrate the use of this session option, first clear both the data and execution plans from cache:

```
DBCC DROPCLEANBUFFERS;
DBCC FREEPROCCACHE;
```

Run the following code to turn the session option on:

```
SET STATISTICS TIME ON;
```

Then invoke the following query:

```
SELECT orderid, custid, empid, shipperid, orderdate, filler
FROM dbo.Orders
WHERE orderdate >= '20060101'
  AND orderdate < '20060201';
```

You will get output similar to the following:

```
SQL Server parse and compile time:
   CPU time = 0 ms, elapsed time = 30 ms.
SQL Server parse and compile time:
   CPU time = 0 ms, elapsed time = 1 ms.

SQL Server Execution Times:
   CPU time = 30 ms,  elapsed time = 619 ms.
```

The output tells you the net CPU time and elapsed clock time for parsing and compiling the query, and also the time it took to execute it. Run the following code to turn the option off:

```
SET STATISTICS TIME OFF;
```

This tool is convenient when you want to analyze the performance of an individual query interactively. When you run benchmarks in batch mode, the way to measure the run time of queries is different. Store the value of the GETDATE function in a variable right before the query. Right after the query, issue an INSERT statement into the table where you collect performance information, subtracting the value stored in the variable from the current value of GETDATE. Note that GETDATE returns a DATETIME value, which has an accuracy level of 3.33 milliseconds. When measuring the time statistics of queries for which this accuracy level is insufficient, run the queries repeatedly in a loop and divide run time for the entire loop by the number of iterations.

Analyzing Execution Plans

An execution plan is the "work plan" the optimizer generates to determine how to process a given query. The plan contains operators that are generally applied in a specific order. Some operators can be applied while their preceding operator is still in progress. Some operators might be applied more than once. Also, some branches of the plan are invoked in parallel if the optimizer chose a parallel plan. In the plan, the optimizer determines the order in which to access the tables involved in the query, which indexes to use and which access methods to use to apply to them, which join algorithms to use, and so on. In fact, for a given query the optimizer considers multiple execution plans, and it chooses the plan with the lowest cost out of the ones that were generated. Note that SQL Server might not generate all possible execution plans for a given query. If it always did, the optimization process could take too long. SQL Server will calculate a cost threshold for the optimization process based on the sizes of the tables involved in the query, among other things. At the end of the chapter, I'll point you to a white paper that provides detailed information about this process.

Throughout these books, I'll frequently analyze execution plans of queries. This section and the one that follows ("Index Tuning") should give you the background required to follow and understand the discussions involving plan analysis. Note that the purpose of this section is not to get you familiarized with all possible operators, rather it is to familiarize you with the techniques to analyze plans. The "Index Tuning" section will familiarize you with index-related operators, and later in the book I'll elaborate on additional operators—for example, join-related operators will be described in Chapter 5.

Graphical Execution Plans

Graphical execution plans are used extensively throughout these books. SSMS allows you to get both an estimated execution plan (by pressing Ctrl+L) and to include an actual one (by pressing Ctrl+M) along with the output of the query you run. Note that both will give you the same plan; remember that an execution plan is generated before the query is run. However, when you request an estimated plan, the query is not run at all. Obviously, some measures can be collected only at run time (for example, the actual number of rows returned from each operator, and the actual number of rebinds and rewinds). In the estimated plan, you will see estimations for measures that can be collected only at run time, while the actual plan will show the actuals and also some of the same estimates.

To demonstrate a graphical execution plan analysis, I will use the following query:

```
SELECT custid, empid, shipperid, COUNT(*) AS numorders
FROM dbo.Orders
WHERE orderdate >= '20060201'
  AND orderdate < '20060301'
GROUP BY custid, empid, shipperid
WITH CUBE;
```

The query returns aggregated counts of orders for a given period, grouped by *custid*, *empid*, and *shipperid*, including the calculation of super aggregates (generated by the CUBE option). I'll discuss CUBE queries in detail in Chapter 6.

> **Note** I did some graphical manipulation on the execution plans that appear in this chapter to fit images in the printed pages and for clarity.

As an example, if you request an estimated execution plan for the preceding query, you will get the plan shown in Figure 3-6.

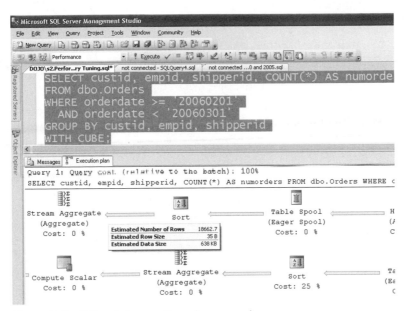

Figure 3-6   Estimated execution plan example

Notice that when you place your mouse pointer over an arrow that goes out of an operator (for example, the one going out of the first Sort operator), you get an estimated number of rows. By the way, a nice aspect of the arrows representing data flow is that their thickness is proportional to the number of rows returned by the source operator. You want to keep an eye especially on thick arrows, as these might indicate a performance issue.

Next, turn on the Include Actual Execution Plan option, and run the query. You will get both the output of the query and the actual plan, as shown in Figure 3-7.

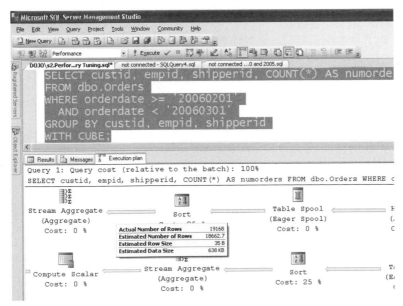

Figure 3-7   Actual execution plan example

Notice that now you get the actual number of rows returned by the source operator.

When you get elaborated plans like this one that do not fit in one screen, you can use a really cool new zooming feature. Press the + button that appears at the bottom right corner of the execution plan pane, and you will get a rectangle that allows you to navigate to a desired place in the plan, as shown in Figure 3-8.

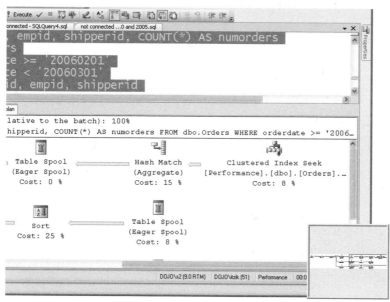

Figure 3-8   Zooming feature in graphical showplan

Figure 3-9 shows the full execution plan for our CUBE query—that's after some graphical manipulation for clarity and to make it fit in one screen.

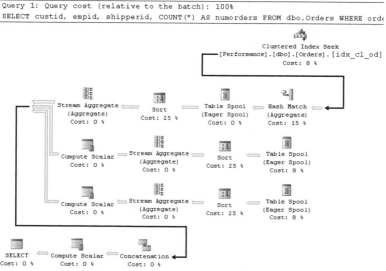

Figure 3-9   Execution plan for CUBE query

I shifted the position of some of the operators and added arrows to denote the original flow. Also, I included the full object names where relevant. In the original plan, object names are truncated if they are long.

A plan is a tree of operators. Data flows from a child operator to a parent operator. The tree order of graphical plans that you get in SSMS is expressed from right to left and from top to bottom. That's typically the order in which you should analyze a plan to figure out the flow of activity. In our case, the *Clustered Index Seek* operator is the first operator that starts the flow, yielding its output to the next operator in the tree—*Hash Match (Aggregate)*—and so on.

In computer science, tree structures are typically depicted with the root node on top and leaf nodes at the bottom; and siblings' precedence is depicted from left to right. If you're accustomed to working with algorithms related to trees (or the more generic graphs), you'd probably feel comfortable with the more common representation of trees, where the execution of the operators would flow in the order depicted in Figure 3-10.

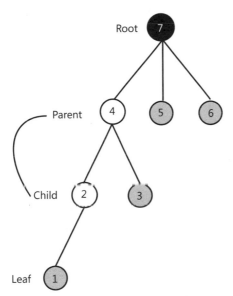

Figure 3-10   Tree

The numbers in the figure represent execution order of operators in a plan. If you feel more comfortable with the common tree representation in computer science as illustrated in Figure 3-10, you would probably appreciate the depiction shown in Figure 3-11 of our CUBE query plan.

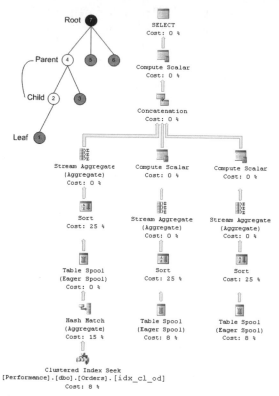

Figure 3-11   Execution plan for CUBE query (reoriented)

Logically, to produce such a plan, you need to rotate the original plan you get from SSMS 90 degrees to the left, and then flip it vertically. However, I guess that you wouldn't want to try this at home. It did take me a whole day to produce this graphic, working at the pixel level with one of my favorite tools—mspaint.exe. I did this mainly as a gesture to my mentor and friend Lubor Kollar. Lubor, this one is for you!

Go back to the original execution plan for the CUBE query shown in Figure 3-9 to examine other aspects of the plan. Notice that there's a cost percentage associated with each operator. This value is the percentage of the operator's cost out of the total cost of the query, as estimated by the optimizer. I'll explain what's behind the query's cost value shortly. You want to keep an eye especially on operators that involve high-percentage values, and focus your tuning efforts on those operators. When you place your mouse pointer over an operator, you will get a yellow information box, which I will describe shortly. One of the measures you will find there is called *Estimated Subtree Cost*. This value represents the cumulative estimated cost of the subtree, starting with the current operator (all operators in all branches leading to the current operator). The subtree cost associated with the root operator (topmost, leftmost) represents the estimated cost of the whole query, as shown in Figure 3-12.

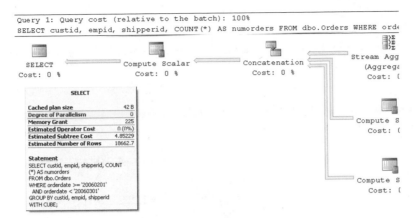

Figure 3-12   Subtree cost

The query cost value is generated by formulas that, loosely speaking, aim at reflecting the number of seconds it would take the query to run on a test machine that SQL Server's developers used in their labs. For example, our CUBE query's estimated subtree cost is a little under 5—meaning that the formulas estimate that it would roughly take the query close to 5 seconds to run on Microsoft's test machine. Of course, that's an estimate. There are so many factors involved in the costing algorithms that even on Microsoft's original test machine you would see large variations of the actual run time of a query from its estimated cost value. Additionally, in the system you're running, your hardware and database layouts can vary significantly from the system Microsoft used for calibration. Therefore, you shouldn't expect a direct correlation between a query's subtree cost and its actual run time.

Another nice feature of the graphical execution plans is that you can easily compare the costs of multiple queries. You might want to compare the costs of different queries that produce the same result, or in some cases even queries that do slightly different things. For example, suppose you want to compare the cost of our query using the CUBE option with the same query using the ROLLUP option:

```
SELECT custid, empid, shipperid, COUNT(*) AS numorders
FROM dbo.Orders
WHERE orderdate >= '20060201'
  AND orderdate < '20060301'
GROUP BY custid, empid, shipperid
WITH CUBE;

SELECT custid, empid, shipperid, COUNT(*) AS numorders
FROM dbo.Orders
WHERE orderdate >= '20060201'
  AND orderdate < '20060301'
GROUP BY custid, empid, shipperid
WITH ROLLUP;
```

You highlight the queries that you want to compare and request a graphical execution plan (estimated or actual, as needed). In our case, you will get the plans shown in Figure 3-13.

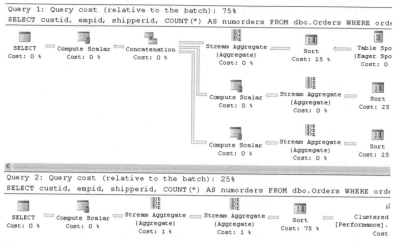

Figure 3-13   Comparing costs of execution plans

At the top of each plan, you will get the percentage of the estimated cost of the query out of the whole batch. For example, in our case, you can notice that the CUBE query is estimated to be three times as expensive than the ROLLUP query.

When placing your mouse pointer over an operator, you will get a yellow ToolTip box with information about the operator, as shown in Figure 3-14.

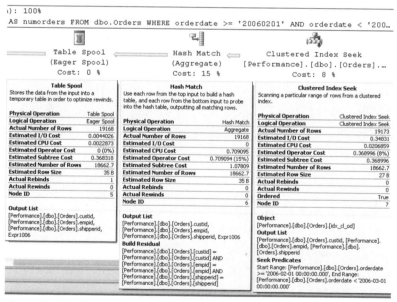

Figure 3-14   Operator info ToolTip box

The information box will give you the following information:

- The operator's name and a short description of its function.

- **Physical Operation:** The physical operation that will take place in the engine.

- **Logical Operation:** The logical operation according to Microsoft's conceptual model of query processing. For example, for a join operator you will get the join algorithm used as the physical operation (Nested Loops, Merge, Hash), and the logical join type used as the logical operation (Inner Join, Outer Join, Semi Join, and so on). When there's no logical operation associated with the operator, this measure will have the same value as shown in the physical operation.

- **Actual Number of Rows:** The actual number of rows returned from the operator (shown only for actual plans).

- **Estimated I/O Cost, and Estimated CPU Cost:** The estimated part of the operator's cost associated with that particular resource (I/O or CPU). These measures will help you identify whether the operator is I/O or CPU intensive. For example, you can see that the Clustered Index Seek operator is mainly I/O bound, while the Hash Match operator is mainly CPU bound.

- **Estimated Operator Cost:** The cost associated with the particular operator.

- **Estimated Subtree Cost:** As described earlier, the cumulative cost associated with the whole subtree up to the current node.

- **Estimated Number of Rows:** The number of rows that are estimated to be returned from this operator. In some cases, you can identify costing problems related to insufficient statistics or to other reasons by observing a discrepancy between the actual number of rows and the estimated number.

- **Estimated Row Size:** You might wonder why an actual value for this number is not shown in the actual query plan. The reason is that you might have dynamic-length attribute types in your table with rows that vary in size.

- **Actual Rebinds, and Actual Rewinds:** These measures are relevant only for operators that appear as the inner side of a Nested Loops join; otherwise, Rebinds will show 1 and Rewinds will show 0. These operators refer to the number of times that an internal *Init* method is called. The sum of the number of rebinds and rewinds should be equal to the number of rows processed on the outer side of the join. A rebind means that one or more of the correlated parameters of the join changed and the inner side must be reevaluated. A rewind means that none of the correlated parameters changed and the prior inner result set might be reused.

- **Bottom part of the info box:** Shows other aspects related to the operator, such as the associated object name, output, arguments, and so on.

In SQL Server 2005, you can get more detailed coverage of the properties of an operator in the Properties window (by pressing F4), as shown in Figure 3-15.

Coverage of graphical execution plans will continue in the "Index Tuning" section when we discuss index access methods.

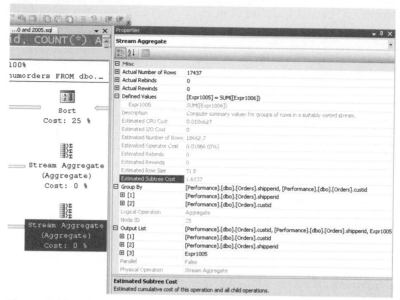

Figure 3-15 Properties window

Textual Showplans

SQL Server also gives you tools to get an execution plan as text. For example, if you turn the SHOWPLAN_TEXT session option on, when you run a query, SQL Server will not process it. Rather, it just generates an execution plan and returns it as text. To demonstrate this session option, turn it on by running the following code:

```
SET SHOWPLAN_TEXT ON;
```

Then invoke the following query:

```
SELECT orderid, custid, empid, shipperid, orderdate, filler
FROM dbo.Orders
WHERE orderid = 280885;
```

You will get the following output:

```
|--Nested Loops(Inner Join, OUTER REFERENCES:([Uniq1002],
     [Performance].[dbo].[Orders].[orderdate]))
  |--Index Seek(OBJECT:([Performance].[dbo].[Orders].[PK_Orders]),
       SEEK:([Performance].[dbo].[Orders].[orderid]=[@1])
         ORDERED FORWARD)
  |--Clustered Index Seek(OBJECT:(
       [Performance].[dbo].[Orders].[idx_cl_od]),
       SEEK:([Performance].[dbo].[Orders].[orderdate]=
       [Performance].[dbo].[Orders].[orderdate]
       AND [Uniq1002]=[Uniq1002]) LOOKUP ORDERED FORWARD)
```

To analyze the plan, you "read" or "follow" branches in inner levels before outer ones (bottom to top), and branches that appear in the same level from top to bottom. As you can see, you get only the operator names and their basic arguments. Run the following code to turn the session option off:

```
SET SHOWPLAN_TEXT OFF;
```

If you want more detailed information about the plan that is similar to what the graphical execution plan gives you, use the SHOWPLAN_ALL session option for an estimated plan and the STATISTICS PROFILE session option for the actual one. SHOWPLAN_ALL will produce a table result, with the information provided by SHOWPLAN_TEXT, and also the following measures: StmtText, StmtId, NodeId, Parent, PhysicalOp, LogicalOp, Argument, DefinedValues, EstimateRows, EstimateIO, EstimateCPU, AvgRowSize, TotalSubtreeCost, OutputList, Warnings, Type, Parallel, and EstimateExecutions.

To test this session option, turn it on:

```
SET SHOWPLAN_ALL ON;
```

Run the preceding query, and examine the result. When you're done, turn it off:

```
SET SHOWPLAN_ALL OFF;
```

The STATISTICS PROFILE option will produce an actual plan. The query will be run, and its output will be produced. You will also get the output returned by SHOWPLAN_ALL. In addition, you will get the attributes *Rows* and *Executes*, which hold actual values as opposed to estimated ones. To test this session option, turn it on:

```
SET STATISTICS PROFILE ON;
```

Run the preceding query, and examine the result. When you're done, turn it off:

```
SET STATISTICS PROFILE OFF;
```

XML Showplans

If you want to develop your own code that would parse and analyze execution plan information, you will find the information returned by SHOWPLAN_TEXT, SHOWPLAN_ALL, and STATISTICS PROFILE very hard to work with. SQL Server 2005 introduces two new session options that allow you to get estimated and actual execution plan information in XML format; XML data is much more convenient for an application code to parse and work with. The SHOWPLAN_XML session option will produce an XML value with the estimated plan information, and the STATISTICS XML session option will produce a value with actual plan information

To test SHOWPLAN_XML, turn it on by running the following code:

```
SET SHOWPLAN_XML ON;
```

Then run the following query:

```
SELECT orderid, custid, empid, shipperid, orderdate, filler
FROM dbo.Orders
WHERE orderid = 280885;
```

You will get the following XML value, shown here in abbreviated form:

```
<ShowPlanXML xmlns="http://schemas.microsoft.com/sqlserver/2004/07/
showplan" Version="1.0" Build="9.00.1399.06">
  <BatchSequence>
    <Batch>
      <Statements>
        <StmtSimple StatementText="SELECT orderid, custid, empid, shipperid, orderdate, fill
er&#xD;&#xA;FROM dbo.Orders&#xD;&#xA;WHERE orderid = 280885;" StatementId="1" StatementCompI
d="1" StatementType="SELECT" StatementSubTreeCost="0.00657038" StatementEstRows="1" Statemen
tOptmLevel="TRIVIAL">
          <StatementSetOptions QUOTED_IDENTIFIER="false" ARITHABORT="true" CONCAT_NULL_YIELD
S_NULL="false" ANSI_NULLS="false" ANSI_PADDING="false" ANSI_WARNINGS="false" NUMERIC_ROUNDAB
ORT="false" />
          <QueryPlan CachedPlanSize="14">
            <RelOp NodeId="0" PhysicalOp="Nested Loops" LogicalOp="Inner Join" EstimateRows=
"1" EstimateIO="0" EstimateCPU="4.18e-006" AvgRowSize="195" EstimatedTotalSubtreeCost=
"0.00657038" Parallel="0" EstimateRebinds="0" EstimateRewinds="0">
              <OutputList>
                <ColumnReference Database="[Performance]" Schema="[dbo]" Table="[Orders]"
Column="orderid" />
                <ColumnReference Database="[Performance]" Schema="[dbo]" Table="[Orders]"
Column="custid" />
                <ColumnReference Database="[Performance]" Schema="[dbo]" Table="[Orders]"
Column="empid" />
                <ColumnReference Database="[Performance]" Schema="[dbo]" Table="[Orders]"
Column="shipperid" />
                <ColumnReference Database="[Performance]" Schema="[dbo]" Table="[Orders]"
Column="orderdate" />
                <ColumnReference Database="[Performance]" Schema="[dbo]" Table="[Orders]"
Column="filler" />
              </OutputList>
              <NestedLoops Optimized="0">
                <OuterReferences>
                  <ColumnReference Column="Uniq1002" />
                  <ColumnReference Database="[Performance]" Schema="[dbo]" Table="[Orders]"
Column="orderdate" />
                </OuterReferences>
                <RelOp NodeId="1" PhysicalOp="Index Seek" LogicalOp="Index Seek" EstimateRow
s="1" EstimateIO="0.003125" EstimateCPU="0.0001581" AvgRowSize="23" EstimatedTotalSubtreeCos
t="0.0032831" Parallel="0" EstimateRebinds="0" EstimateRewinds="0">
...
          </QueryPlan>
        </StmtSimple>
      </Statements>
    </Batch>
  </BatchSequence>
</ShowPlanXML>
```

Note that if you save the XML value to a file with the extension .*sqlplan*, you can then open it with SSMS and get a graphical view of the execution plan, as shown in Figure 3-16.

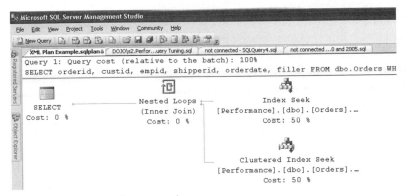

Figure 3-16   XML plan example

Run the following code to turn the session option off:

```
SET SHOWPLAN_XML OFF;
```

As I mentioned earlier, to get an XML value with information about the actual execution plan, use the STATISTICS XML session option as follows:

```
SET STATISTICS XML ON;
GO
SELECT orderid, custid, empid, shipperid, orderdate, filler
FROM dbo.Orders
WHERE orderid = 280885;
GO
SET STATISTICS XML OFF;
```

Hints

Hints allow you to override the default behavior of SQL Server in different respects, and SQL Server will comply with your request when technically possible. The term *hint* is a misnomer because it's not a kind gesture that SQL Server might or might not comply with; rather, you're forcing SQL Server to apply a certain behavior when it's technically possible. Syntactically, there are three types of hints: join hints, query hints, and table hints. Join hints are specified between the keyword representing the join type and the JOIN keyword (for example, INNER MERGE JOIN). Query hints are specified in an OPTION clause following the query itself; for example, SELECT ... OPTION (OPTIMIZE FOR (@od = '99991231')). Table hints are specified right after a table name or alias in a WITH clause (for example FROM dbo.Orders WITH (index = idx_unc_od_oid_i_cid_eid)).

Hints can be classified in different categories based on their functionality, including: index hints, join hints, parallelism, locking, compilation, and others. Some performance-related hints, such as forcing the usage of a certain index, have both negative and positive aspects.

On the negative side, a hint makes that particular aspect of the plan static. When data distribution in the queried tables changes, the optimizer would not consult statistics to determine whether it is worthwhile to use the index or not, because you forced it to always use it. You lose the benefit in cost-based optimization that SQL Server's optimizer gives you. On the positive side, by specifying hints you reduce the time it takes to optimize queries and, in some cases, you override inefficient choices that the optimizer occasionally makes as a result of the nature of cost-based optimization, which relies on statistics, or as a result of an optimizer bug. Make sure that you use performance-related hints in production code only after exhausting all other means, including query revisions, ensuring that statistics are up to date, and ensuring that statistics have a sufficient sampling rate, and so on.

You can find detailed information about the various supported hints in Books Online. I will use hints in several occasions in these books and explain them in context.

To conclude this section, I'd like to introduce a nifty new hint in SQL Server 2005 that you might consider to be the ultimate hint—USE PLAN. This hint allows you to provide an XML value holding complete execution plan information to force the optimizer to use the plan that you provided. Remember that you can use the SHOWPLAN_XML session option to generate an XML plan. To see a demonstration of what happens when you use this hint, first run the following code to generate the XML plan:

```
SET SHOWPLAN_XML ON;
GO
SELECT orderid, custid, empid, shipperid, orderdate
FROM dbo.Orders
WHERE orderid >= 2147483647;
GO
SET SHOWPLAN_XML OFF;
```

Then run the query, providing the XML plan value in the USE PLAN hint like so:

```
DECLARE @oid AS INT;
SET @oid = 1000000;

SELECT orderid, custid, empid, shipperid, orderdate
FROM dbo.Orders
WHERE orderid >= @oid
OPTION (USE PLAN
N'<ShowPlanXML xmlns="http://schemas.microsoft.com/sqlserver/2004/07/
showplan" Version="1.0" Build="9.00.1399.06">
  <BatchSequence>
    <Batch>
      <Statements>
        <StmtSimple StatementText="SELECT orderid, custid, empid, shipperid, orderdate&#xD;&
#xA;FROM dbo.Orders&#xD;&#xA;WHERE orderid &gt;= 2147483647;&#xD;&#xA;" StatementId="1" Stat
ementCompId="1" StatementType="SELECT" StatementSubTreeCost="0.00657038" StatementEstRows="1
" StatementOptmLevel="FULL" StatementOptmEarlyAbortReason="GoodEnoughPlanFound">
          <StatementSetOptions QUOTED_IDENTIFIER="false" ARITHABORT="true" CONCAT_NULL_YIELD
S_NULL="false" ANSI_NULLS="false" ANSI_PADDING="false" ANSI_WARNINGS="false" NUMERIC_ROUNDAB
ORT="false" />
```

```
        <QueryPlan CachedPlanSize="14">
            <RelOp NodeId="0" PhysicalOp="Nested Loops" LogicalOp="Inner Join" EstimateRows=
"1" EstimateIO="0" EstimateCPU="4.18e-006" AvgRowSize="40" EstimatedTotalSubtreeCost=
"0.00657038" Parallel="0" EstimateRebinds="0" EstimateRewinds="0">
...
            <ParameterList>
              <ColumnReference Column="@1" ParameterCompiledValue="(2147483647)" />
            </ParameterList>
          </QueryPlan>
        </StmtSimple>
      </Statements>
    </Batch>
  </BatchSequence>
</ShowPlanXML>');
```

Note that the XML value in the preceding code is shown in abbreviated form. Of course, you should specify the full-blown XML value. SQL Server 2005 also supports a new plan guide feature, which allows you to attach an XML plan to a query when you cannot or do not want to change the query's text directly by adding hints. You use the stored procedure *sp_create_plan_guide* to produce a plan guide for a query. You can find more details about it in Books Online.

SQL Server 2005 also introduces several other interesting hints, among them the RECOMPILE and OPTIMIZE FOR query hints. I'll discuss those in *Inside T-SQL Programming* as part of the discussion about stored procedure compilations and recompilations.

Traces/Profiler

The tracing capabilities of SQL Server give you extremely powerful tools for tuning and for other purposes as well. One of the great benefits tracing has over other external tools is that you get information about events that took place within the server in various components. Tracing allows you to troubleshoot performance problems, application behavior, deadlocks, audit information, and so much more. I demonstrated using traces for collecting performance workload data earlier in the book. Make sure you go over the guidelines for tracing that I provided earlier. I'll also demonstrate tracing to troubleshoot deadlocks in *Inside T-SQL Programming*. At the end of this chapter, I'll point you to additional resources that cover tracing and Profiler.

Database Engine Tuning Advisor

The Database Engine Tuning Advisor (DTA) is an enhanced tool that was formerly called Index Tuning Wizard in SQL Server 2000. DTA will give you index design recommendations based on an analysis of a workload that you give it as input. The input workload can be a trace file or table, and it can also be a script file containing T-SQL queries. One benefit of DTA is that it uses SQL Server's optimizer to make cost estimations—the same optimizer that generates execution plans for your queries. DTA generates statistics and hypothetical indexes, which it uses in its cost estimations. Among the new features in SQL Server 2005 available in DTA are partitioning recommendations for tables and indexes. Note that you can run DTA in batch mode by using the dta.exe command-line utility.

Index Tuning

This section covers index tuning, which is an important facet of query tuning. Indexes are sorting and searching structures. They reduce the need for I/O when looking for data and for sorting when certain elements in the plan need or can benefit from sorted data. While some aspects of tuning can improve performance by a modest percentage, index tuning can often improve query performance by orders of magnitude. Hence, if you're in charge of tuning, learning about indexes in depth is time well spent. Here I'll cover index tuning aspects that are relevant to these books, and at the end of the chapter I'll point you to other resources where you can find more information.

I'll start by describing table and index structures that are relevant for our discussions. Then I'll describe index access methods used by the optimizer and conclude the section by introducing an index optimization scale.

Table and Index Structures

Before delving into index access methods, you need to familiarize yourself with table and index structures. This section will describe pages and extents, heaps, clustered indexes, and nonclustered indexes.

Pages and Extents

A page is an 8-KB unit where SQL Server stores data. It can contain table or index data, execution plan data, bitmaps for allocation, free space information, and so on. A page is the smallest I/O unit that SQL Server can read or write. In SQL Server 2000 and earlier, a row could not span multiple pages and was limited to 8060 bytes gross (aside from large object data). The limitation was because of the page size (8192 bytes), which was reduced by the header size (96 bytes), a pointer to the row maintained at the end of the page (2 bytes), and a few additional bytes reserved for future use. SQL Server 2005 introduces a new feature called *row-overflow data*, which relaxes the limitation on row size for tables that contain VARCHAR, NVARCHAR, VARBINARY, SQL_VARIANT, or CLR user-defined type columns. Each such column can reach up to 8000 bytes, allowing the row to span multiple pages.

Keep in mind that a page is the smallest I/O unit that SQL Server can read or write. Even if SQL Server needs to access a single row, it has to load the whole page to cache and read it from there. Queries that involve primarily data manipulation are typically bound mainly by their I/O cost. Of course, a physical read of a page is much more expensive than a logical read of a page that already resides in cache. It's hard to come up with a number that would represent the performance ratio between them, as there are several factors involved in the cost of a read, including the type of access method used, the fragmentation level of the data, and other factors as well. If you really need a ballpark number, use 1/50—that is, a logical read would very roughly be 50 times faster than a physical read. But I'd strongly advise against relying on any number as a rule of thumb.

Extents are allocation units of 8 contiguous pages. When a table or index needs more space for data, SQL Server allocates a full extent to the object. There is one exception that applies to small objects: if the object is smaller than 64 KB, SQL Server typically allocates an individual page when more space is needed, not a full extent. That page can reside within a mixed extent whose eight pages belong to different objects. Some activities of data deletion—for example, dropping a table and truncating a table—deallocate full extents. Such activities are minimally logged; therefore, they are very fast compared to the fully logged DELETE statement. Also, some read activities—such as read-ahead reads, which are typically applied for large table or index scans—can read data at the extent level. The most expensive part of an I/O operation is the movement of the disk arm, while the actual magnetic read or write operation is much less expensive; therefore, reading a page can take almost as long as reading a full extent.

Heap

A *heap* is a table that has no clustered index. The structure is called a heap because the data is not organized in any order; rather, it is laid out as a bunch of extents. Figure 3-17 illustrates how our Orders table might look like when organized as a heap

The only structure that keeps track of the data belonging to a heap is a bitmap page (or a series of pages if needed) called the Index Allocation Map (IAM). This bitmap has pointers to the first 8 pages allocated from mixed extents, and a representative bit for each extent in a range of 4 GB in the file. The bit is 0 if the extent it represents does not belong to the object owning the IAM page, and 1 if it does. If one IAM is not enough to cover all the object's data, SQL Server will maintain a chain of IAM pages. SQL Server uses IAM pages to move through the object's data when the object needs to be scanned. SQL Server loads the object's first IAM page, and then directs the disk arm sequentially to fetch the extents by their physical order on disk.

As you can see in the figure, SQL Server maintains internal pointers to the first IAM page and the first data page of a heap.

Clustered Index

All indexes in SQL Server are structured as *balanced trees*. The definition of a balanced tree (adopted from *www.nist.gov*) is: "a tree where no leaf is much farther away from the root than any other leaf."

> **More Info**   If you're interested in the theoretical algorithmic background for balanced trees, please refer to *http://www.nist.gov/dads/HTML/balancedtree.html,* and to *The Art of Computer Programming, Volume 3: Sorting and Searching (2nd Edition)* by Donald E. Knuth (Addison-Wesley Professional, 1998).

A *clustered index* is structured as a balanced tree, and it maintains all the table's data in its leaf level. The clustered index is not a copy of the data; rather, it *is* the data. I'll describe the structure of a clustered index in SQL Server through the illustration shown in Figure 3-18.

The figure shows an illustration of how the Orders table might look when organized in a clustered index where the *orderdate* column is defined as the index's key column. Throughout these books, I'll refer to a table that has a clustered index as a *clustered table*. As you can see in the figure, the full data rows of the Orders table are stored in the index *leaf level*. The data rows are organized in the leaf in a sorted fashion based on the index key columns (*orderdate* in our case). A doubly linked list maintains this logical order, but note that depending on the fragmentation level of the index, the physical order of the pages on disk might not match the logical order maintained by the linked list.

Also notice that with each leaf row, the index maintains a value called a *uniquifier* (abbreviated to *unq* in the illustration). This value enumerates rows that have the same key value, and it is used together with the key value to uniquely identify rows when the index's key columns are not unique. Later, when discussing nonclustered indexes, I'll elaborate on the reasoning behind this architecture and the need to uniquely identify a row in a clustered index.

The rest of the discussion in this section is relevant to both clustered and nonclustered indexes just the same, unless explicitly stated otherwise. When SQL Server needs to perform ordered scan (or ordered partial scan) operations in the leaf level of the index, it does so by following the linked list. Note that besides the linked list, SQL Server also maintains an IAM page (or pages) to map the data stored in the index by physical order on disk. SQL Server will typically use the IAM page when it needs to perform unordered scans of the index's leaf level. The performance difference between ordered and unordered scans of the index will depend on the level of fragmentation in the index. Remember that the most expensive part of an I/O operation is the movement of the disk arm. An ordered scan in an index with no fragmentation at all will be similar in performance to an unordered scan, while the former will be substantially slower in an index with a high level of fragmentation.

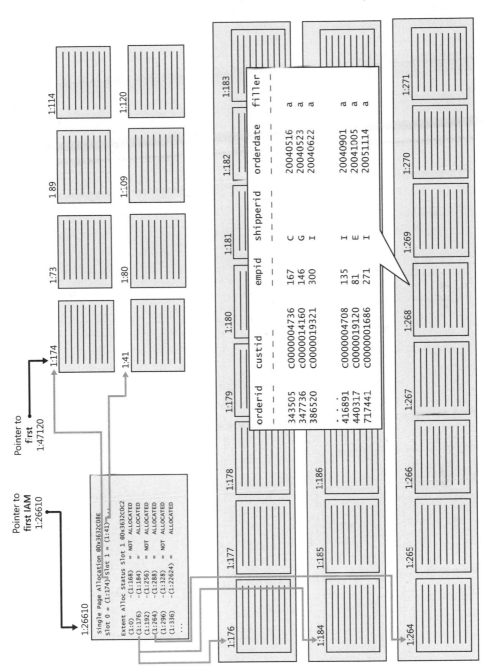

Figure 3-17   Heap

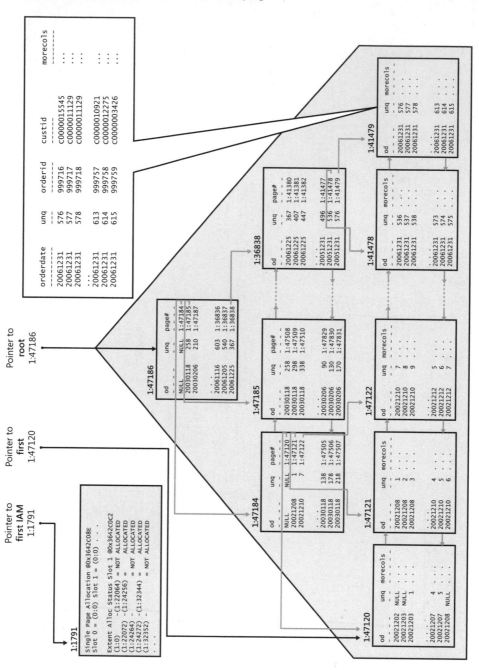

Figure 3-18   Clustered table/index

On top of the leaf level of the index, the index maintains additional levels, each summarizing the level below it. Each row in a non-leaf index page points to a whole page in the level below it. The row contains two elements: the key column value of the first row in the pointed index page, and a 6-byte pointer to that page. The pointer holds the file number in the database and the page number in the file. When SQL Server builds an index, it starts from the leaf level and adds levels on top. It stops as soon as a level contains a single page, also known as the *root* page.

SQL Server always starts with the root page when it needs to navigate to a particular key at the leaf, using an access method called an *index seek*, which I'll elaborate on later in the chapter. The seek operation will "jump" from the root to the relevant page in the next level, and it will continue jumping from one level to the next until it reaches the page containing the sought key at the leaf. Remember that all leaf pages are the same distance from the root, meaning that a seek operation will cost as many page reads as the number of levels in the index. The I/O pattern of these reads is *random I/O*, as opposed to sequential I/O, because naturally the pages read by a seek operation will seldom reside next to each other.

In terms of our performance estimations, it is crucial to know what the number of levels in an index is because that number will be the cost of a seek operation in terms of page reads, and some execution plans invoke multiple seek operations repeatedly (for example, a Nested Loops join operator). For an existing index, you can get this number by invoking the INDEX-PROPERTY function with the *IndexDepth* property. But for an index that you didn't create yet, you need to be familiar with the calculations that will allow you to estimate the number of levels that the index will contain.

The operands and steps required for calculating the number of levels in an index (call it L) are as follows (remember that these calculations apply to clustered and nonclustered indexes, unless explicitly stated otherwise):

- **The number of rows in the table (call it *num_rows*)**: This is 1,000,000 in our case.

- **The average gross leaf row size (call it *leaf_row_size*)**: In a clustered index, this is actually the data row size. By "gross," I mean that you need to take the internal overhead of the row and the 2-byte pointer—stored at the end of the page—pointing to the row. The row overhead typically involves a few bytes. In our Orders table, the gross average data row size is roughly 200 bytes.

- **The average leaf page density (call it *page_density*)**: This value is the average percentage of population of leaf pages. Reasons for pages not being completely full include: data deletion, page splits caused by insertion of rows to full pages, having very large rows, and explicit requests not to populate the pages in full by specifying a *fillfactor* value when rebuilding indexes. In our case, we created a clustered index on the Orders table after populating it with the data, we did not add rows after creating the clustered index, and we did not specify a fillfactor value. Therefore, *page_density* in our case is close to 100 percent.

- **The number of rows that fit in a leaf page (call it *rows_per_leaf_page*)**: The formula to calculate this value is: (*page_size - header_size*) * *page_density* / *leaf_row_size*. Note that if you have a good estimation of *page_density*, there's no need to floor this value, as the fact that a row cannot span pages (with the aforementioned exceptions) is already accounted for in the *page_density* value. In such a case, you want to use the result number as is even if it's not an integer. On the other hand, if you just estimate that *page_density* will be close to 100 percent, as it is in our case, omit the *page_density* operand from the calculation and floor the result. In our case, *rows_per_leaf_page* amount to *floor((8192 - 96) / 200) = 40*.

- **The number of pages maintained in the leaf (call it *num_leaf_pages*):** This is a simple formula: *num_rows / rows_per_leaf_page*. In our case, it amounts to *1,000,000 / 40 = 25,000*.

- **The average gross non-leaf row size (call it *non_leaf_row_size*):** A non-leaf row contains the key columns of the index (in our case, only *orderdate*, which is 8 bytes); the 4-byte *uniquifier* (which exists only in a clustered index that is not unique); the page pointer, which is 6 bytes; a few additional bytes of internal overhead, which total 5 bytes in our case; and the row offset pointer at the end of the page, which is 2 bytes. In our case, the gross non-leaf row size is 25 bytes.

- **The number of rows that can fit in a non-leaf page (call it *rows_per_non_leaf_page*):** The formula to calculate this value is similar to calculating *rows_per_leaf_page*. For the sake of simplicity, I'll ignore the non-leaf page density factor, and calculate the value as *floor((page_size - header_size) / non_leaf_row_size)*, which in our case amounts to *floor((8192 - 96) / 25) = 323*.

- **The number of levels above the leaf (call it *L-1*):** This value is calculated with the following formula: $ceiling(log_{rows\_per\_non\_leaf\_page}(num\_leaf\_pages))$. In our case, *L-1* amounts to $ceiling(log_{323}(25000)) = 2$. Obviously, you simply need to add 1 to get *L*, which in our case is 3.

This exercise leads me to a very important point that I will rely on in my performance discussions. You can play with the formula and see that with up to about several thousand rows, our index will have 2 levels. Three levels would have up to about 4,000,000 rows, and 4 levels would have up to about 4,000,000,000 rows. With nonclustered indexes, the formulas are identical, it's just that you can fit more rows in each leaf page, as I will describe later. So with nonclustered indexes, the upper bound for each number of levels covers even more rows in the table. The point is that in our table all indexes have 3 levels, which is the cost you have to consider in your performance estimation when measuring the cost of a seek operation. And in general, with small tables most indexes will typically have up to 2 levels, and with large tables, they will typically have 3 or 4 levels, unless the total size of the index keys is large. Keep these numbers in mind for our later discussions.

Nonclustered Index on a Heap

A nonclustered index is also structured as a balanced tree, and in many respects is similar to a clustered index. The only difference is that a leaf row in a nonclustered index contains only the index key columns and a *row locator* value pointing to a particular data row. The content of the row locator depends on whether the table is a heap or a clustered table. This section describes nonclustered indexes on a heap, and the following section will describe nonclustered indexes on a clustered table.

Figure 3-19 illustrates the nonclustered index created by our primary key constraint (*PK_Orders*) defining the *orderid* column as the key column.

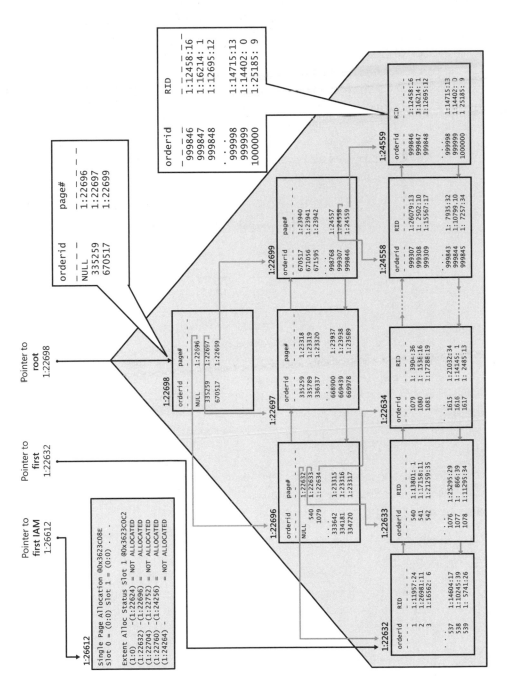

Figure 3-19   Nonclustered index on a heap

The row locator used by a nonclustered index leaf row to point to a data row is an 8-byte physical pointer called *RID*. It consists of the file number in the database, the target page number in the file, and the row number in the target page (zero-based). When looking for a particular data row through the index, SQL Server will have to follow the seek operation with an *RID lookup* operation, which translates to reading the page that contains the data row. Therefore, the cost of an RID lookup is one page read. For a single lookup or a very small number of lookups the cost is not high, but for a large number of lookups the cost can be very high because SQL Server ends up reading one whole page per sought row. For range queries that use a nonclustered index, and a series of lookups—one per qualifying key—the cumulative cost of the lookup operations typically makes up the bulk of the cost of the query. I'll demonstrate this point in the "Index Access Methods" section. As for the cost of a seek operation, remember that the formulas I provided earlier are just as relevant to nonclustered indexes. It's just that the *leaf_row_size* is smaller, and therefore the *rows_per_leaf_page* will be higher. But the formulas are the same.

Nonclustered Index on a Clustered Table

As of SQL Server 7.0, nonclustered indexes created on a clustered table are architected differently than on a heap. The only difference is that the row locator in a nonclustered index created on a clustered table is a value called a *clustering key*, as opposed to being an RID. The clustering key consists of the values of the clustered index keys from the pointed row, and the *uniquifier* (if present). The idea is to point to a row "logically" as opposed to "physically." This architecture was designed mainly for OLTP systems, where clustered indexes often suffer from many page splits upon data insertions. In a page split, half the rows from the split page are physically moved to a newly allocated page. If nonclustered indexes kept physical pointers to rows, all pointers to the data rows that moved would have to be changed to reflect their new physical locations—and that's true for all relevant pointers in all nonclustered indexes. Instead, SQL Server maintains logical pointers that don't change when data rows physically move.

Figure 3-20 illustrates what the *PK_Orders* nonclustered index might look like; the index is defined with the *orderid* as the key column, and the Orders table has a clustered index defined with the *orderdate* as the key column.

A seek operation looking for a particular key in the nonclustered index (some *orderid* value) will end up reaching the relevant leaf row and have access to the row locator. The row locator in this case is the clustering key of the pointed row. To actually grab the pointed row, a lookup operation will need to perform a whole seek within the clustered index based on the acquired clustering key. I will demonstrate this access method later in the chapter. The cost of each lookup operation here (in terms of the number of page reads) is as high as the number of levels in the clustered index (3 in our case). That's compared to a single page read for an RID lookup when the table is a heap. Of course, with range queries that use a nonclustered index and a series of lookups, the ratio between the number of logical reads in a heap case and a clustered table case will be close to *1:L*, where *L* is the number of levels in the clustered index.

Before you worry too much about this point and remove all clustered indexes from your tables, keep in mind that with all lookups going through the clustered index, the non-leaf levels of the clustered index will typically reside in cache. Typically, most of the physical reads in the clustered index will be against the leaf level. Therefore, the additional cost of lookups against a clustered table compared to a heap is usually a small portion of the total query cost. Now that the background information about table and index structures has been covered, the next section will describe index access methods.

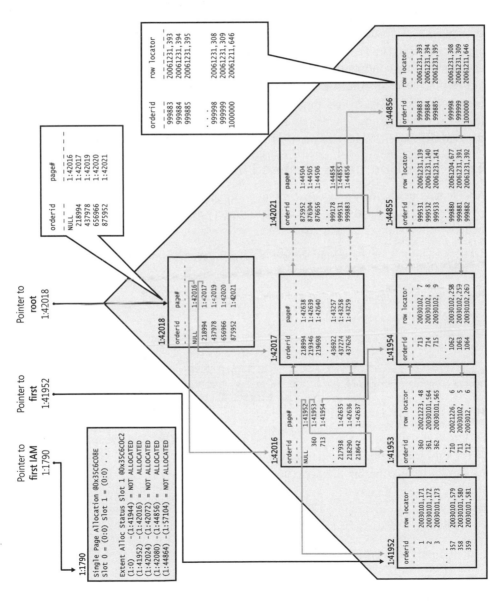

Figure 3-20   Nonclustered index on a clustered table

Index Access Methods

This section provides a technical description of the various index access methods; it is designed to be used as a reference for discussions in these books involving analysis of execution plans. Later in this chapter, I'll describe an index optimization scale that demonstrates how you can put this knowledge into action.

If you want to follow the examples in this section, rerun the code in Listing 3-1 to re-create the sample tables in our Performance database along with all the indexes. I'll be discussing some access methods to use against the Orders table that are structured as a heap and some that are structured as a clustered table. Therefore, I'd also suggest that you run the code in Listing 3-1 against another database (say, Performance2), after renaming the database name in the script accordingly, and commenting out the statement that creates the clustered index on Orders. When I discuss an access method involving a clustered table, run the code against the Performance database. When the discussion is about heaps, run it against Performance2. Also remember that Listing 3-1 uses randomization to populate the customer IDs, employee IDs, shipper Ids, and order dates in the Orders table. This means that your results will probably slightly differ from mine.

Table Scan/Unordered Clustered Index Scan

A *table scan* or an *unordered clustered index scan* simply involves a sequential scan of all data pages belonging to the table. The following query against the Orders table structured as a heap would require a table scan:

```
SELECT orderid, custid, empid, shipperid, orderdate
FROM dbo.Orders;
```

Figure 3-21 shows an illustration of this access method, and Figure 3-22 shows the graphical execution plan you would get for this query.

Figure 3-21 Table scan

SQL Server will use the table's IAM pages to direct the disk arm to scan the extents belonging to the table sequentially by their physical order on disk. The number of logical reads should be similar to the number of pages the table consumes (around 25,000 in our case). Note that in such scans SQL Server typically uses a very efficient read-ahead strategy that can read the data in larger chunks than 8 KB. When I ran this query on my system, I got the following performance measures from STATISTICS IO, STATISTICS TIME, and the execution plan:

- Logical reads: 24391
- Physical reads: 0
- Read-ahead reads: 24408

- CPU time: 971 ms

- Elapsed time: 20265 ms

- Estimated subtree cost: 19.1699

Figure 3-22   Table scan (execution plan)

Of course, the run times I got are not an indication of the run times you would get in an average production system. But I wanted to show them for illustration and comparison purposes.

If the table has a clustered index, the access method that will be applied will be an unordered clustered index scan, as illustrated in Figure 3-23. It will produce the execution plan shown in Figure 3-24.

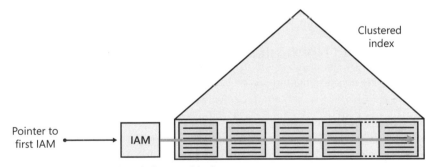

Figure 3-23   Unordered clustered index scan

Note that even though the execution plan shows a clustered index scan, the activity is no different than a table scan, and throughout the book I will often refer to it simply as a table scan. As shown in the illustration, here SQL Server will also use the index's IAM pages to scan the data sequentially. The information box of the Clustered Index Scan operator tells you that the scan was not ordered, meaning that the access method did not rely on the linked list that maintains the logical order of the index. Of course, you did get a scan of the pages by their physical order on disk. Here are the performance measures I got for this query:

- Logical reads: 25080

- Physical reads: 1

- Read-ahead reads: 25071

- CPU time: 941 ms

- Elapsed time: 22122 ms

- Estimated subtree cost: 19.6211

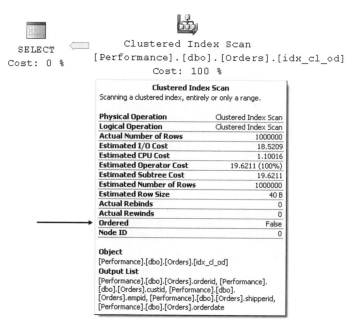

Figure 3-24   Unordered clustered index scan (execution plan)

Unordered Covering Nonclustered Index Scan

An *unordered covering nonclustered index scan* is similar in concept to an unordered clustered index scan. The concept of a *covering index* means that a nonclustered index contains all columns specified in a query. In other words, a covering index is not an index with special properties; rather, it becomes a covering index with respect to a particular query. SQL Server can find all the data it needs to satisfy the query by accessing solely the index data, without the need to access the full data rows. Other than that, the access method is the same as an unordered clustered index scan; only obviously, the leaf level of the covering nonclustered index contains fewer pages than the leaf of the clustered index, because the row size is smaller and more rows fit in each page. I explained earlier how to calculate the number of pages in the leaf level of an index (clustered or nonclustered).

As an example for this access method, the following query requests all *orderid* values from the Orders table:

```
SELECT orderid
FROM dbo.Orders;
```

Our Orders table has a nonclustered index on the *orderid* column (*PK_Orders*), meaning that all the table's order IDs reside in the index's leaf level. The index covers our query. Figure 3-25 illustrates this access method, and Figure 3-26 shows the graphical execution plan you would get for this query.

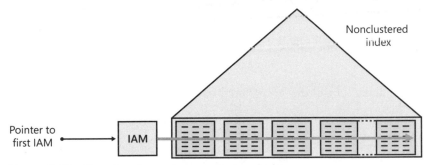

Figure 3-25   Unordered covering nonclustered index scan

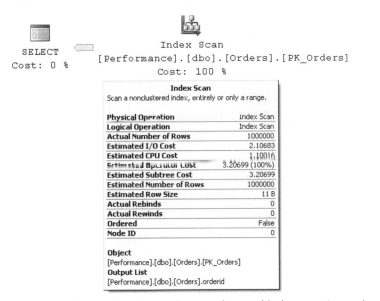

Figure 3-26   Unordered covering nonclustered index scan (execution plan)

The leaf level of the *PK_Orders* index contains fewer than 3000 pages, compared to the 25,000 data pages in the table. Here are the performance measures I got for this query:

- Logical reads: 2848

- Physical reads: 1

- Read-ahead reads: 2841

- CPU time: 340 ms

- Elapsed time: 12071 ms
- Estimated subtree cost: 3.20699

Ordered Clustered Index Scan

An *ordered clustered index scan* is a full scan of the leaf level of the clustered index following the linked list. For example, the following query, which requests all orders sorted by *orderdate*, will get such an access method in its plan:

```
SELECT orderid, custid, empid, shipperid, orderdate
FROM dbo.Orders
ORDER BY orderdate;
```

You can find an illustration of this access method in Figure 3-27, and the execution plan for this query in Figure 3-28.

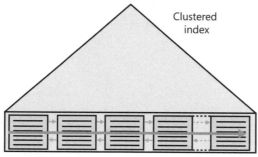

Clustered
index

Figure 3-27   Ordered clustered index scan

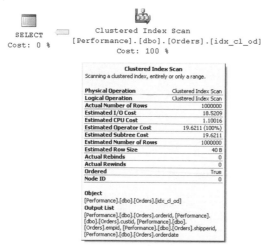

SELECT
Cost: 0 %

Clustered Index Scan
[Performance].[dbo].[Orders].[idx_cl_od]
Cost: 100 %

Clustered Index Scan	
Scanning a clustered index, entirely or only a range.	
Physical Operation	Clustered Index Scan
Logical Operation	Clustered Index Scan
Actual Number of Rows	1000000
Estimated I/O Cost	18.5209
Estimated CPU Cost	1.10016
Estimated Operator Cost	19.6211 (100%)
Estimated Subtree Cost	19.6211
Estimated Number of Rows	1000000
Estimated Row Size	40 B
Actual Rebinds	0
Actual Rewinds	0
Ordered	True
Node ID	0
Object	
[Performance].[dbo].[Orders].[idx_cl_od]	
Output List	
[Performance].[dbo].[Orders].orderid, [Performance].	
[dbo].[Orders].custid, [Performance].[dbo].	
[Orders].empid, [Performance].[dbo].[Orders].shipperid,	
[Performance].[dbo].[Orders].orderdate	

Figure 3-28   Ordered clustered index scan (execution plan)

Note that unlike an unordered scan of an index, the performance of an ordered scan will depend on the fragmentation level of the index—that is, the percentage of the out-of-order pages in the leaf level of the index with respect to the total number of pages. An out-of-order page is a page that appears logically after a certain page according to the linked list, but physically before it. With no fragmentation at all, the performance of an ordered scan of an index should be very close to the performance of an unordered scan, because both will end up reading the data physically in a sequential manner. However, as the fragmentation level grows higher, the performance difference will be more substantial, in favor of the unordered scan, of course. The natural deductions are that you shouldn't request the data sorted if you don't need it sorted, and that you should resolve fragmentation issues in indexes that incur large ordered scans. I'll elaborate on fragmentation and its treatment later. Here are the performance measures that I got for this query:

- Logical reads: 25080
- Physical reads: 1
- Read-ahead reads: 25071
- CPU time: 1191 ms
- Elapsed time: 22263 ms
- Estimated subtree cost: 19.6211

Note that the optimizer is not limited to ordered-forward activities. Remember that the linked list is a doubly linked list, where each page contains both a *next* and a *previous* pointer. Had you requested a descending sort order, you would have still gotten an ordered index scan, only ordered backwards (from tail to head) instead of ordered forward (from head to tail). SQL Server also supports descending indexes as of version 2000, but these are not needed in simple cases like getting descending sort orders. Rather, descending indexes are valuable when you create an index on multiple key columns that have opposite directions in their sort requirements—for example, sorting by col1, col2 DESC.

Ordered Covering Nonclustered Index Scan

An *ordered covering nonclustered index scan* is similar in concept to an ordered clustered index scan, with the former performing the access method in a nonclustered index—typically when covering a query. The cost is of course lower than a clustered index scan because fewer pages are involved. For example, the *PK_Orders* index on our clustered Orders table happens to cover the following query, even though it might not seem so at first glance:

```
SELECT orderid, orderdate
FROM dbo.Orders
ORDER BY orderid;
```

Keep in mind that on a clustered table, nonclustered indexes will use clustering keys as row locators. In our case, the clustering keys contain the *orderdate* values, which can be used for covering purposes as well. Also, the first (and, in our case, the only) key column in the nonclustered index is the *orderid* column, which is the column specified in the ORDER BY clause of the query; therefore, an ordered index scan is a natural access method for the optimizer to choose.

Figure 3-29 illustrates this access method, and Figure 3-30 shows the query's execution plan.

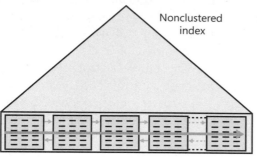

Figure 3-29   Ordered covering nonclustered index scan

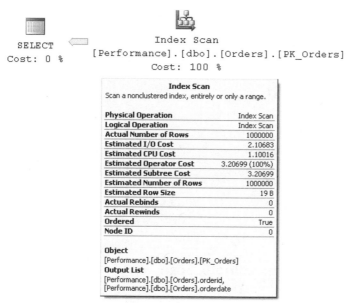

Figure 3-30   Ordered covering nonclustered index scan (execution plan 1)

Notice in the plan that the *Ordered* measure for the *Index Scan* operator in the yellow information box shows *True*.

Here are the performance measures that I got for this query:

- Logical reads: 2848

- Physical reads: 2

- Read-ahead reads: 2841

- CPU time: 370 ms

- Elapsed time: 13582 ms

- Estimated subtree cost: 3.20699

An ordered index scan is not used only when you explicitly request the data sorted; rather, it is also used when the plan uses an operator that can benefit from sorted input data. For example, check out the execution plan shown in Figure 3-31 for the following query:

```
SELECT orderid, custid, empid, orderdate
FROM dbo.Orders AS O1
WHERE orderid =
  (SELECT MAX(orderid)
   FROM dbo.Orders AS O2
   WHERE O2.orderdate = O1.orderdate);
```

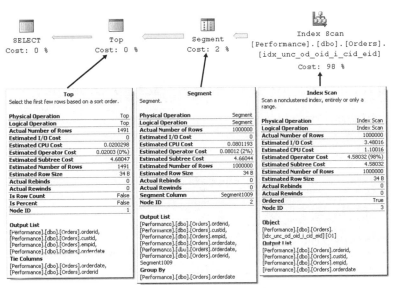

Figure 3-31 Ordered covering nonclustered index scan (execution plan 2)

The *Segment* operator arranges the data in groups and emits a group at a time to the next operator (*Top* in our case). Our query requests the orders with the maximum *orderid* per *orderdate*. Fortunately, we have a covering index for the task (*idx_unc_od_oid_i_cid_eid*), with the key columns being (*orderdate, orderid*), and included non-key columns are (*custid, empid*). I'll elaborate on included non-key columns later in the chapter. The important point for our discussion is that the segment operator organizes the data by groups of *orderdate* values and emits the data, a group at a time, where the last row in each group is the maximum *orderid* in the group; because *orderid* is the second key column right after *orderdate*. Therefore, there's no need for the plan to sort the data; rather, the plan just collects it with an ordered scan from the covering index, which is already sorted by *orderdate* and *orderid*. The *Top* operator has a simple task of just collecting the last row (TOP 1 descending), which is the row of interest for the group. The number of rows reported by the *Top* operator is 1491, which is the number of unique groups (*orderdate* values), each of which got a single row from the operator. Because our nonclustered index covers the query by including in its leaf level all other columns that are mentioned in the query (*custid, empid*), there's no need to look up the data rows; the query is satisfied by the index data alone. Here are the performance measures I got for this query:

- Logical reads: 4720
- Physical reads: 3
- Read-ahead reads: 4695
- CPU time: 781 ms
- Elapsed time: 2128 ms
- Estimated subtree cost: 4.68047

The number of logical reads that you see is similar to the number of pages that the leaf level of the index holds.

Nonclustered Index Seek + Ordered Partial Scan + Lookups

The access method *nonclustered index seek + ordered partial scan + lookups* is typically used for small-range queries (including a point query) using a nonclustered index scan that doesn't cover the query. To demonstrate this access method, I will use the following query:

```
SELECT orderid, custid, empid, shipperid, orderdate
FROM dbo.Orders
WHERE orderid BETWEEN 101 AND 120;
```

There's no covering index because the first key column is the filtered column *orderid*, but we do have a noncovering one—the *PK_Orders* index. If the query is *selective* enough, the optimizer would use the index. Selectivity is defined as the percentage of the number of rows returned by the query out of the total number of rows in the table. The term *high selectivity* refers to a small percentage, while *low selectivity* refers to a large percentage. Our access method first performs a seek within the index to find the first key in the sought range (*orderid = 101*). The second part of the access method is an ordered partial scan in the leaf level from the first key in the range until the last (*orderid = 101*). The third and last part involves lookups of the corresponding data row for each key. Note that the third part doesn't have to wait for the second part to finish. For each key that is found in the range, SQL Server can already apply a lookup. Remember that a lookup in a heap translates to a single page read, while a lookup in a clustered table translates to as many reads as the number of levels in the clustered index (3 in our case).

It is vital for making performance estimations to understand that with this access method the last part involving the lookups typically incurs most of the query's cost; this is because it involves most of the I/O activity. Remember, the lookup translates to a whole page read or one whole seek within the clustered index per sought row, and the lookups are always random I/O (as opposed to sequential ones).

To estimate the I/O cost of such a query, you can typically focus on the cost of the lookups. If you want to make more accurate estimations, also taking into consideration the seek within the index and the ordered partial scan, feel free to do so; but these parts will be negligible as the range grows larger. The I/O cost of a seek operation is 3 reads in our case (number of levels in the index). The I/O cost of the ordered partial scan depends on the number of rows in the range (20 in our case) and the number of rows that fit in an index page (more than 600 in our case). For our query, there's actually no additional read involved for the partial scan; that's because all the keys in the range we are after reside in the leaf page that the seek reached, or they might span an additional page if the first key appears close to the end of the page. The I/O cost of the lookup operations will be the number of rows in the range (20 in our case), multiplied by one if the table is a heap, or multiplied by the number of levels in the clustered index (3 in our case) if the table is clustered. So you should expect around 23 logical reads in total if you run the query against a heap, and around 63 logical reads if you run it against a clustered table. Remember that the non-leaf levels of the clustered index typically reside in cache because of all the lookup operations going through it; so you shouldn't concern yourself too much over the seemingly higher cost of the query in the clustered table scenario.

Figure 3-32 has an illustration of the access method over a heap, and Figure 3-33 shows the execution plan for the query.

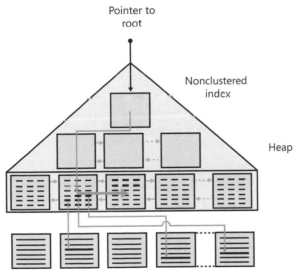

Figure 3-32   Nonclustered index seek + ordered partial scan + lookups against a heap

Note that in the execution plan you won't explicitly see the partial scan part of the access method; rather, it's hidden in the *Index Scan* operator. You can deduce it from the fact that the information box for the operator shows *True* in the *Ordered* measure.

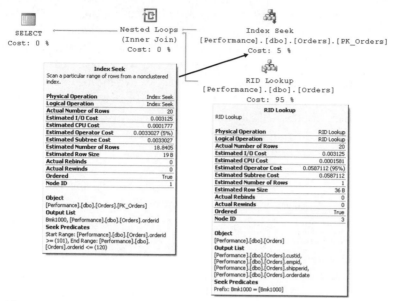

Figure 3-33   Nonclustered index seek + ordered partial scan + lookups against a heap (execution plan)

Here are the performance measures I got for the query:

- Logical reads: 23

- Physical reads: 22

- CPU time: 0 ms

- Elapsed time: 133 ms

- Estimated subtree cost: 0.0620926

Figure 3-34 has an illustration of the access method over a clustered table, and Figure 3-35 shows the execution plan for the query.

And here are the performance measures I got for the query in this case:

- Logical reads: 63

- Physical reads: 6

- CPU time: 0 ms

- Elapsed time: 136 ms

- Estimated subtree cost: 0.0620931

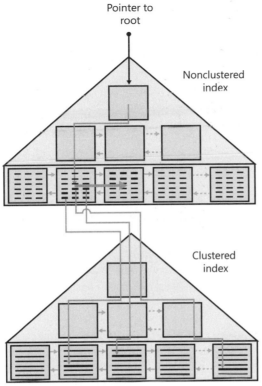

Figure 3-34   Nonclustered index seek + ordered partial scan + lookups against a clustered tale

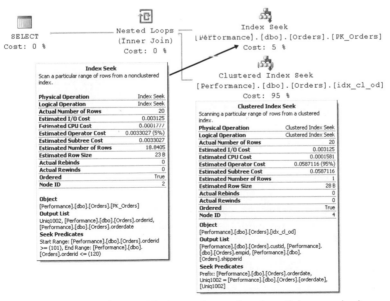

Figure 3-35   Nonclustered index seek + ordered partial scan + lookups against a clustered tale (execution plan)

Interestingly, graphical execution plans in SQL Server 2000 did not clearly distinguish between an RID lookup and a clustering key lookup, the latter in fact being a seek within the clustered index. In SQL Server 2000, both were just called Bookmark Lookup. As you can see in the plans shown in Figures 3-33 and 3-35, graphical plans in SQL Server 2005 depict the difference more accurately.

This access method is efficient only when the query is very selective (a point query or a small range). Feel free to play with the range in the filter, increasing it gradually, and see how dramatically the cost increases as the range grows larger. That will happen up to the point at which the optimizer figures that it would simply be more efficient to apply a table scan rather than using the index. I'll demonstrate such an exercise later in the chapter in the "Index Optimization Scale" section.

Remember that ordered operations, like the ordered partial scan part of this access method, can take place both in a forward or backwards manner. In our query's case, it was forward, but you can explore cases like a filter on *orderid <= 100*, and see an ordered backwards partial scan. An indication of whether the scan was ordered forward or backwards would not show up in the operator's yellow information box; rather, it would show up in the *Scan Direction* measure in the operator's Properties dialog box.

Unordered Nonclustered Index Scan + Lookups

The optimizer typically uses the *unordered nonclustered index scan + lookups* access method when the following conditions are in place:

- The query is selective enough
- The optimal index for a query does not cover it
- The index doesn't maintain the sought keys in order

For example, such is the case when you filter a column that is not the first key column in the index. The access method will involve an unordered full scan of the leaf level of the index, followed by a series of lookups. As I mentioned, the query must be selective enough to justify this access method; otherwise, with too many lookups it will be more expensive than simply scanning the whole table. To figure out the selectivity of the query, SQL Server will need statistics on the filtered column (a histogram with the distribution of values). If such statistics do not exist, SQL Server will create them.

For example, the following query will use such an access method against the index *idx_nc_sid_od_cid*, created on the key columns (*shipperid, orderdate, custid*), where *custid* is not the first key column in the list:

```
SELECT orderid, custid, empid, shipperid, orderdate
FROM dbo.Orders
WHERE custid = 'C0000000001';
```

Figure 3-36 illustrates the access method over a heap, and Figure 3-37 shows the execution plan for the query.

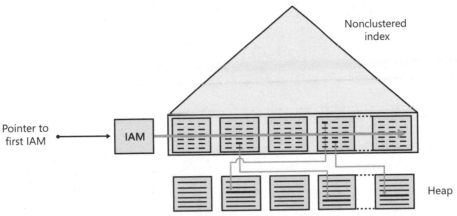

Figure 3-36   Unordered nonclustered index scan + lookups against a heap

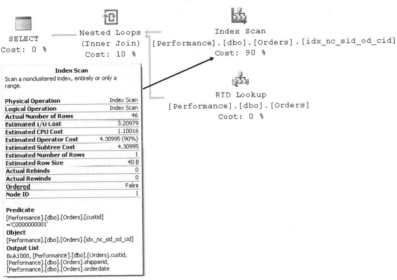

Figure 3-37   Unordered nonclustered index scan + lookups against a heap (execution plan)

The I/O cost of this query involves the cost of the unordered scan of the leaf of the index (sequential I/O using IAM pages) plus the cost of the lookups (random I/O). The scan will cost as many page reads as the number of pages in the leaf of the index. As described earlier, the cost of the lookups is the number of qualifying rows multiplied by 1 in a heap, and multiplied by the number of levels in the clustered index (3 in our case) if the table is clustered. Here are the measures I got for this query against a heap:

- Logical reads: 4400

- Physical reads: 47

- Read-ahead reads: 4345

- CPU time: 1281 ms

- Elapsed time: 2287 ms

- Estimated subtree cost: 4.479324

Figure 3-38 illustrates the access method over a clustered table, and Figure 3-39 shows the execution plan for the query.

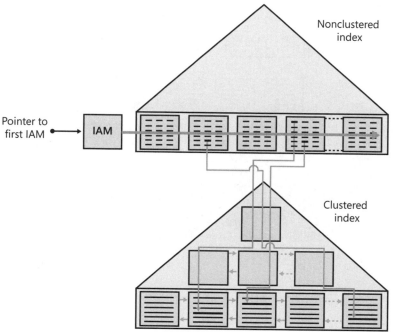

Figure 3-38 Unordered nonclustered index scan + lookups against a clustered table

Here are the measures I got for this query against a clustered table:

- Logical reads: 4252

- Physical reads: 89

- Read-ahead reads: 4090

- CPU time: 1031 ms

- Elapsed time: 3148 ms

- Estimated subtree cost: 4.60953

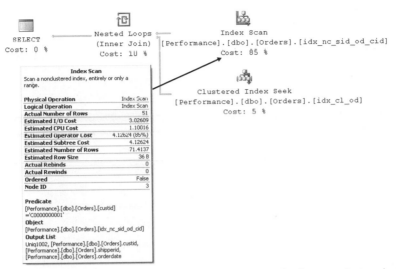

Figure 3-39   Unordered nonclustered index scan + lookups against a clustered table (execution plan 1)

Remember that SQL Server will need statistics on the *custid* column to determine the selectivity of the query. The following query will tell you which statistics SQL Server created automatically on the Orders table:

```
SELECT name
FROM sys.stats
WHERE object_id = OBJECT_ID('dbo.Orders')
  AND auto_created = 1;
```

You should get statistics with a name similar to *_WA_Sys_00000002_31B762FC*, which SQL Server created automatically for this purpose.

SQL Server 2005 introduces new optimization capabilities based on cardinality information that it maintains internally on substrings within string columns. Now it can estimate the selectivity of a query when you apply pattern-matching filters with the LIKE predicate even when the pattern starts with a wildcard. This capability was not available in earlier versions of SQL Server.

To demonstrate this capability, SQL Server will be able to estimate the selectivity of the following query, which produces the plan shown in Figure 3-40 by using the access method, which is the focus of this section's discussion:

```
SELECT orderid, custid, empid, shipperid, orderdate
FROM dbo.Orders
WHERE custid LIKE '%9999';
```

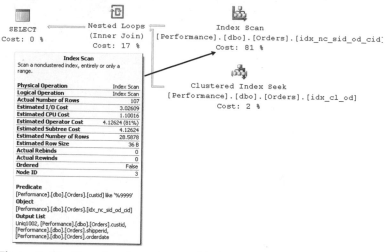

Figure 3-40 Unordered nonclustered index scan + lookups against a clustered table (execution plan 2)

Here are the performance measures that I got for this query:

- Logical reads: 4685

- Physical reads: 1

- Read-ahead reads: 3727

- CPU time: 3795 ms

- Elapsed time: 4824 ms

- Estimated subtree cost: 5.09967

Clustered Index Seek + Ordered Partial Scan

The optimizer typically uses the access method *clustered index seek + ordered partial scan* for range queries where you filter based on the first key columns of the clustered index. This access method first performs a seek operation to the first key in the range; then it applies an ordered partial scan at the leaf level from the first key in the range until the last. The main benefit of this method is that there are no lookups involved. Remember that lookups are very expensive with large ranges. The performance ratio between this access method—which doesn't involve lookups—and one that uses a nonclustered index and lookups becomes larger and larger as the range grows.

The following query, which looks for all orders placed on a given *orderdate*, uses the access method, which is the focus of this discussion:

```
SELECT orderid, custid, empid, shipperid, orderdate
FROM dbo.Orders
WHERE orderdate = '20060212';
```

Note that even though the filter uses an equality operator, it is in essence a range query because there are multiple qualifying rows. Either way, a point query can be considered a special case of a range query. The I/O cost of this access method will involve the cost of the seek operation (3 random reads in our case) and the cost of the ordered partial scan within the leaf (in our case, 18 page reads). In total, you get 21 logical reads. Note that the ordered scan typically incurs the bulk of the cost of the query because it involves most of the I/O. Remember that with ordered index scans, index fragmentation plays a crucial role. When fragmentation is at minimum (as in our case), physical reads will be close to sequential. However, as the fragmentation level grows higher, the disk arm will have to move frantically to and fro, degrading the performance of the scan.

Figure 3-41 illustrates the access method, and Figure 3-42 shows the execution plan for the query.

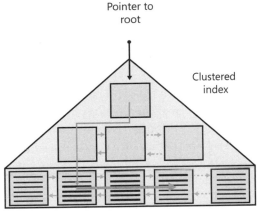

Figure 3-41   Clustered index seek + ordered partial scan

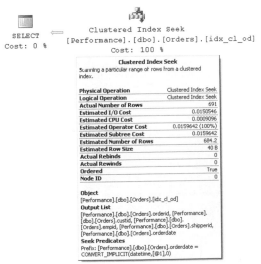

Figure 3-42   Clustered index seek + ordered partial scan (execution plan)

Here are the performance measures I got for this query:

- Logical reads: 21
- Physical reads: 0
- Read-ahead reads: 18
- CPU time: 0 ms
- Elapsed time: 73 ms
- Estimated subtree cost: 0.0159642

Note that this plan is trivial for the optimizer to generate. That is, the plan is not dependent on the selectivity of the query. Rather, it will always be used regardless of the size of the sought range. Unless, of course, you have an even better index for the query to begin with.

Covering Nonclustered Index Seek + Ordered Partial Scan

The access method *covering nonclustered index seek + ordered partial scan* is almost identical to the previously described access method, with the only difference being that the former uses a covering nonclustered index instead of the clustered index. To use this method, of course the filtered columns must be the first key columns in the index. The benefit of this access method over the previous one lies in the fact that a nonclustered index leaf page naturally can fit more rows than a clustered index one; therefore, the bulk cost of the plan, which is the partial scan cost of the leaf, is lower. The cost is lower because fewer pages need to be scanned for the same size of the range. Of course, here as well, index fragmentation plays an important performance role because the partial scan is ordered.

As an example, the following query looking for a range of *orderdate* values for a given *shipperid* uses this access method against the covering index *idx_nc_sid_od_cid*, created on (*shipperid, orderdate, custid*):

```
SELECT shipperid, orderdate, custid
FROM dbo.Orders
WHERE shipperid = 'C'
  AND orderdate >= '20060101'
  AND orderdate < '20070101';
```

Note   To have the partial scan read the minimum required pages, the first index key columns must be *shipperid, orderdate,* in that order. If you swap their order, the partial scan will end up also scanning rows that meet the date range also for other shippers, requiring more I/O.

Figure 3-43 illustrates the access method, and Figure 3-44 shows the execution plan for the query.

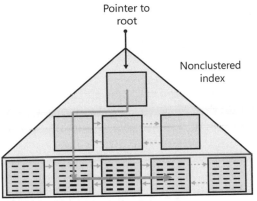

Figure 3-43   Covering nonclustered index seek + ordered partial scan

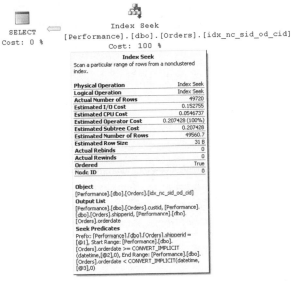

Figure 3-44   Covering nonclustered index seek + ordered partial scan (execution plan)

Here are the performance measures I got for this query:

- Logical reads: 208

- CPU time: 30 ms

- Elapsed time: 954 ms

- Estimated subtree cost: 0.207428

Note that this plan is also a trivial plan that is not based on the query's selectivity.

Remember, the main benefit of this access method is that there are no lookups involved because the index covers the query. Also, you read fewer pages than in a similar access method against a clustered index.

Also note that when you create covering indexes, the index columns serve two different functions. Columns that you filter or sort by are required as key columns that will be maintained in all levels of the balanced tree, and they will also determine the sort order at the leaf. Other index columns might be required only for covering purposes. If you include all index columns in the index's key column list, bear in mind that this has a cost. SQL Server needs to keep the tree balanced, and it will have to apply physical movement of data and adjustments in the tree when you modify key column values in the table. That's just a waste with columns that are required only for covering purposes and not for filtering or sorting.

To tackle this need, SQL Server 2005 introduces the concept of *included non-key columns* in the index. When you create an index, you separately specify which columns will make the key list and which will be included just for covering purposes—only at the leaf level of the index.

As an example, our last query relied only on *shipperid* and *orderdate* for filtering and sorting purposes, while it relied on *custid* only for covering purposes. To benefit from the new feature in SQL Server 2005, drop the index and create a new one, specifying *custid* in the INCLUDE clause like so:

```
DROP INDEX dbo.Orders.idx_nc_sid_od_cid;

CREATE NONCLUSTERED INDEX idx_nc_sid_od_i_cid
  ON dbo.Orders(shipperid, orderdate)
  INCLUDE(custid);
```

Note that the key list is limited to 16 columns and 900 bytes. This is true in both SQL Server 2000 and SQL Server 2005. An added bonus with included non-key columns is that they are not bound by the same limitations. In fact, they can even include large objects such as variable-length columns defined with the MAX specifier and XML columns.

Index Intersection

So far, I mainly focused on the performance benefit you get from indexes when reading data. Keep in mind, though, that indexes incur a cost when you modify data. Any change of data (deletes, inserts, updates) must be reflected in the indexes that hold a copy of that data, and it might cause page splits and adjustments in the balanced trees, which can be very expensive. Therefore, you cannot freely create as many indexes as you like, especially in systems that involve intensive modifications like OLTP environments. You want to prioritize and pick the more important indexes. This is especially a problem with covering indexes because different queries can benefit from completely different covering indexes, and you might end up with a very large number of indexes that your queries could benefit from.

Fortunately, the problem is somewhat reduced because the optimizer supports a technique called *index intersection*, where it intersects data obtained from two indexes and, if required, then intersects the result with data obtained from another index, and so on. As an example, the optimizer will use index intersection for the following query, producing the plan shown in Figure 3-45:

```
SELECT orderid, custid
FROM dbo.Orders
WHERE shipperid = 'A';
```

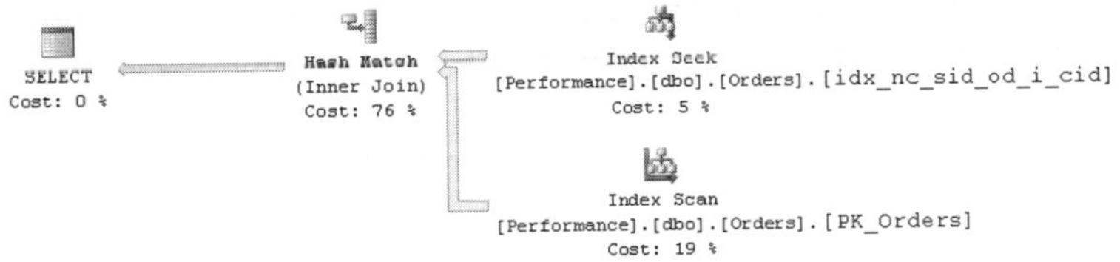

Figure 3-45   Execution plan with index intersection

I will elaborate on join operators in Chapter 5. The optimal index here would be one where *shipperid* is defined as the key column, and *orderid* and *custid* are defined as included non-key columns, but there's no such index on the table. Rather, the index *idx_nc_sid_od_i_cid* defines the *shipperid* as the key column and also contains the *custid* column, and the index *PK_Orders* contains the *orderid* column. The optimizer used the access method nonclustered index seek + ordered partial scan to obtain the relevant data from *idx_nc_sid_od_i_cid*, and it used an unordered nonclustered index scan to obtain the relevant data from *PK_Orders*. It then intersected the two sets based on the row locator values; naturally, row locator values pointing to the same rows will be matched. You can think of index intersection as an internal join based on a match in row locator values.

Here are the performance measures that I got for this query:

- Scan count: 2
- Logical reads: 3671
- Physical reads: 33
- Read-ahead reads: 2347
- CPU time: 1161 ms
- Elapsed time: 5202 ms
- Estimated subtree cost: 16.7449

Indexed Views

This section briefly describes and demonstrates the concept of *indexed views* for the sake of completeness. I won't conduct a lengthy discussion on the subject here. I'll provide a bit more details in *Inside T-SQL Programming* and point you to more resources at the end of the chapter.

As of SQL Server 2000, you can create indexes on views—not just on tables. Normally, a view is a virtual object, and a query against it ultimately queries the underlying tables. However, when you create a clustered index on a view, you materialize all of the view's contents within the clustered index on disk. After creating a clustered index, you can also create multiple non-clustered indexes on the view as well. The data in the indexes on the view will be kept in sync with the changes in the underlying tables as with any other index.

Indexed views are mainly beneficial in reducing I/O costs and expensive processing of data. Such costs are especially apparent in aggregation queries that scan large volumes of data and produce small result sets, and in expensive join queries.

As an example, the following code creates an indexed view that is designed to tune aggregate queries that group orders by *empid* and *YEAR(orderdate)*, returning the count of orders for each group:

```
IF OBJECT_ID('dbo.VEmpOrders') IS NOT NULL
  DROP VIEW dbo.VEmpOrders;
GO
CREATE VIEW dbo.VEmpOrders
  WITH SCHEMABINDING
AS

SELECT empid, YEAR(orderdate) AS orderyear, COUNT_BIG(*) AS numorders
FROM dbo.Orders
GROUP BY empid, YEAR(orderdate);
GO

CREATE UNIQUE CLUSTERED INDEX idx_ucl_eid_oy
  ON dbo.VEmpOrders(empid, orderyear);
```

Query the view, and you will get the execution plan shown in Figure 3-46, showing that the clustered index on the view was scanned:

```
SELECT empid, orderyear, numorders
FROM dbo.VEmpOrders;
```

The view contains a very small number of rows (around a couple of thousands) compared to the number of rows in the table (a million). The leaf of the index contains only about 10 pages. Hence, the I/O cost of the plan would be about 10 page reads.

Here are the performance measures I got for this query:

- Logical reads: 10
- CPU time: 0 ms
- Elapsed time: 78 ms
- Estimated subtree cost: 0.011149

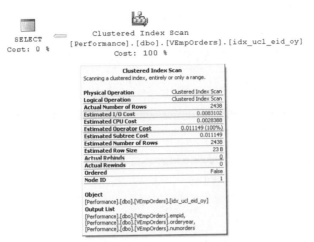

Figure 3-46   Execution plan for query against indexed view

Interestingly, if you work with an Enterprise (or Developer) edition of SQL Server, the optimizer will consider using indexes on the view even when querying the underlying tables directly. For example, the following query produces a similar plan to the one shown in Figure 3-46, with the same query cost:

```
SELECT empid, YEAR(orderdate) AS orderyear, COUNT_BIG(*) AS numorders
FROM dbo.Orders
GROUP BY empid, YEAR(orderdate);
```

If you're not working with an Enterprise edition, you have to query the view directly, and also specify that you do not want the optimizer to expand its optimization choices beyond the scope of the view. You do so by specifying the NOEXPAND table hint: *FROM <view_name> WITH (NOEXPAND)*.

SQL Server 2005 enhances the circumstances in which indexed views are used, supporting subintervals, logically equivalent filter expressions, and more. As I mentioned, I'll point you to resources that describe these in detail.

Index Optimization Scale

Recall the earlier discussion about the tuning methodology. When you perform index tuning, you do so with respect to the query patterns that incur the highest cumulative costs in the system. For a given query pattern, you can build an index optimization scale that would help you make the right design choices. I will demonstrate this process through an example. To follow the demonstrations, before you continue, drop the view created earlier and all the indexes on the Orders table, except for the clustered index. Alternatively, you can rerun the code in

Listing 3-1, after commenting or removing all index and primary key creation statements on Orders, keeping only the clustered index.

In our example, suppose that you need to tune the following query pattern:

```
SELECT orderid, custid, empid, shipperid, orderdate
FROM dbo.Orders
WHERE orderid >= value;
```

Remember that the efficiency of some access methods depends on the selectivity of the query, while the efficiency of others doesn't. For access methods that depend on selectivity, assume that the query pattern is typically fairly selective (around 0.1 percent selectivity, or around 1000 qualifying rows). Use the following query in your tuning process when aiming at such selectivity:

```
SELECT orderid, custid, empid, shipperid, orderdate
FROM dbo.Orders
WHERE orderid >= 999001;
```

I'll progress in the index optimization scale from the worst-case scenario to the best, using this query as a reference, but I'll also describe what would happen when the selectivity of the query changes.

Table Scan (Unordered Clustered Index Scan)

The worst-case scenario for our query pattern with fairly high selectivity is when you have no good index. You will get the execution plan shown in Figure 3-47, using a table scan (unordered clustered index scan).

```
    SELECT      <===      Clustered Index Scan
   Cost: 0 %            [Performance].[dbo].[Orders]. …
                               Cost: 100 %
```

Figure 3-47   Execution plan with table scan (unordered clustered index scan)

Even though you're after a fairly small number of rows (1000 in our case), the whole table is scanned. I got the following performance measures for this query:

- Logical reads: 25080

- CPU time: 1472 ms

- Elapsed time: 16399

- Estimated subtree cost: 19.6211

This plan is trivial and not dependent on selectivity—that is, you would get the same plan regardless of the selectivity of the query.

Unordered Covering Nonclustered Index Scan

The next step in the optimization scale would be to create a covering nonclustered index where the filtered column (*orderid*) is not the first index column:

```
CREATE NONCLUSTERED INDEX idx_nc_od_i_oid_cid_eid_sid
  ON dbo.Orders(orderdate)
  INCLUDE(orderid, custid, empid, shipperid);
```

This index would yield an access method that uses a full unordered scan of the leaf of the index as shown in Figure 3-48:

```
SELECT          Index Scan
Cost: 0 %    [Performance].[dbo].[Orders]...
                  Cost: 100 %
```

Figure 3-48   Execution plan with unordered covering nonclustered index scan

The row size in the covering index is about a fifth of the size of a full data row, and this would be reflected in the query's cost and run time. Here are the performance measures I got for this query:

- Logical reads: 5095
- CPU time: 170 ms
- Elapsed time: 1128 ms
- Estimated subtree cost: 4.86328

As with the previous plan, this plan is also trivial and not dependent on selectivity.

> **Note**   The run times you will get for your queries will vary based on what portion of the data is cached. If you want to make credible performance comparisons in terms of run times, make sure that the caching environment in both cases reflect what you would have in your production environment. That is, if you expect most pages to reside in cache in your production environment (warm cache), run each query twice, and measure the run time of the second run. If you expect most pages not to reside in cache (cold cache), in your tests clear the cache before you run each query.

Before you proceed, drop the index that you just created:

```
DROP INDEX dbo.Orders.idx_nc_od_i_oid_cid_eid_sid;
```

Unordered Nonclustered Index Scan + Lookups

The next step in our index optimization scale is to create a smaller nonclustered index that would not cover the query and that contains the filtered column (*orderid*), but not as the first key column:

```
CREATE NONCLUSTERED INDEX idx_nc_od_i_oid
  ON dbo.Orders(orderdate)
  INCLUDE(orderid);
```

You would get an unordered nonclustered index scan + lookups as shown in Figure 3-49:

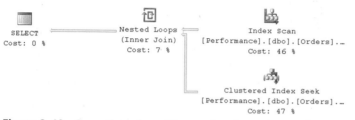

Figure 3-49   Execution plan with unordered nonclustered index scan + lookups

Note that the efficiency of this plan compared to the previous one will depend on the selectivity of the query. As the selectivity of the query grows larger, the more substantial the cost is of the lookups here. In our case, the query is fairly selective, so this plan is more efficient than the previous two; however, with low selectivity, this plan will be less efficient than the previous two.

Here are the performance measures that I got for this query:

- Logical reads: 5923
- CPU time: 100 ms
- Elapsed time: 379 ms
- Estimated subtree cost: 7.02136

Note that even though the number of logical reads and the query cost seem higher than in the previous plan, you can see that the run times are lower. Remember that the lookup operations here traverse the clustered index, and the nonleaf levels of the clustered index are most likely to reside in cache.

Before you continue, drop the new index:

```
DROP INDEX dbo.Orders.idx_nc_od_i_oid;
```

Nonclustered Index Seek + Ordered Partial Scan + Lookups

You can get the next level of optimization in the scale by creating a nonclustered noncovering index on *orderid*:

```
CREATE UNIQUE NONCLUSTERED INDEX idx_unc_oid
  ON dbo.Orders(orderid);
```

This index would yield a nonclustered index seek + ordered partial scan + lookups as shown in Figure 3-50.

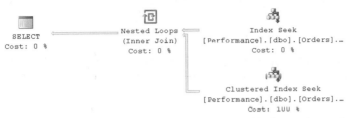

Figure 3-50   Execution plan with nonclustered index seek + ordered partial scan + lookups

Instead of performing the full index scan as the previous plan did, this plan performs a seek to the first key in the sought range, followed by an ordered partial scan of only the relevant range. Still, you get as many lookups as previously, which in our case amounts to a big chunk of the query cost. As the range grows larger, the contribution of the lookups to the query's cost becomes more substantial, and the costs of these two plans would become closer and closer.

Here are the performance measures for this query:

- Logical reads: 3077

- CPU time: 0 ms

- Elapsed time: 53 ms

- Estimated subtree cost: 3.22852

Determining the Selectivity Point

Allow me to digress a bit to expand on a subject I started discussing earlier—plans that are dependent on the selectivity of the query. The efficiency of the last plan is dependent on selectivity because you get one whole lookup per sought row. At some selectivity point, the optimizer would realize that a table scan is more efficient than using this plan. You might find it surprising, but that selectivity point is a pretty small percentage. Even if you have no clue about how to calculate this point, you can practice a trial-and-error approach, where you apply a binary algorithm, shifting the selectivity point to the left or right based on the plan that you get. Remember that *high selectivity* means a low percentage of rows, so going to the left of a selectivity point (lowering the percentage) would mean getting higher selectivity. You can invoke a range query, where you start with 50 percent selectivity by invoking the following query:

```
SELECT orderid, custid, empid, shipperid, orderdate
FROM dbo.Orders
WHERE orderid >= 500001;
```

Examine the estimated (no need for actual here) execution plan, and determine whether to proceed in the next step to the left or to the right of this point, based on whether you got a table scan (clustered index scan) or an index seek. With the median key, you get the plan shown in Figure 3-51, showing a table scan:

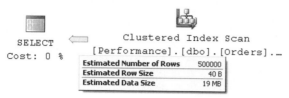

Figure 3-51   Estimated plan showing a table scan

This tells you that 50 percent is not selective enough to justify using the nonclustered index. So you go to the right, to the middle point between 50 percent and a 100 percent. Following this logic, you would end up using the following keys: 750001, 875001, 937501, 968751, 984376, 992189, 996095. The last key would yield a plan where the nonclustered index is used. So now you go to the left, to the point between the keys 992189 and 996095, which is 994142. You will find that the nonclustered index is still used, so you keep on going left, to the point between the keys 992189 and 994142. You continue this process, going left or right according to your findings, until you reach the first selectivity point where the nonclustered index is used. You will find that this point is the key 992820, producing the plan shown in Figure 3-52:

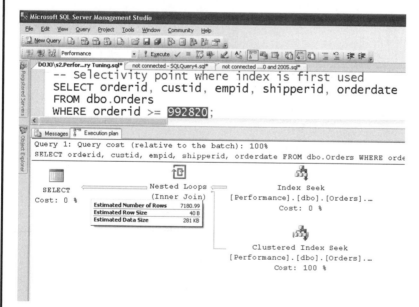

Figure 3-52   Estimated plan showing the index is used

You can now calculate the selectivity, which is the number of qualifying rows (7181) divided by the number of rows in the table (1,000,000), which amounts to 0.7181 percent.

In our query pattern's case, with this selectivity or higher (lower percentage), the optimizer will use the nonclustered index, while with a lower selectivity, it will opt for a table scan. As you can see, in our query pattern's case, the selectivity point is even lower than one percent. Some database professionals might find this number surprisingly small, but if you make performance estimations like the ones we did earlier, you will find it reasonable. Don't forget that page reads is not the only factor that you should take into consideration. You should also consider the access pattern (random/sequential) and other factors as well. Remember that random I/O is much more expensive than sequential I/O. Lookups use random I/O, while a table scan uses sequential I/O.

Before you proceed, drop the index used in the previous step:

```
DROP INDEX dbo.Orders.idx_unc_oid;
```

Clustered Index Seek + Ordered Partial Scan

You can get the next level of optimization by creating a clustered index on the *orderid* column. Because there's already a clustered index on the Orders table, drop it first and then create the desired one:

```
DROP INDEX dbo.Orders.idx_cl_od;
CREATE UNIQUE CLUSTERED INDEX idx_cl_oid ON dbo.Orders(orderid);
```

You will get a trivial plan that uses a seek to the first key matching the filter, followed by an ordered partial scan of the sought range, as shown in Figure 3-53.

```
                              Clustered Index Seek
SELECT  <===          [Performance].[dbo].[Orders].…
Cost: 0 %                         Cost: 100 %
```

Figure 3-53 Execution plan with clustered index seek + ordered partial scan

The main benefit of this plan is that there are no lookups involved. As the selectivity of the query goes lower, this plan becomes more and more efficient compared to a plan that does apply lookups. The I/O cost involved with this plan is the cost of the seek (3 in our case), plus the number of pages that hold the data rows in the filtered range (26 in our case). The main cost of such a plan is typically, for the most part, the cost of the ordered partial scan, unless the range is really tiny (for example, a point query). Remember that the performance of an ordered index scan will, to a great extent, depend on the fragmentation level of the index. Here are the performance measures that I got for this query:

- Logical reads: 29
- CPU time: 0 ms
- Elapsed time: 87 ms
- Estimated subtree cost: 0.022160

Before proceeding to the next step, restore the original clustered index:

```
DROP INDEX dbo.Orders.idx_cl_oid;
CREATE UNIQUE CLUSTERED INDEX idx_cl_od ON dbo.Orders(orderid);
```

Covering Nonclustered Index Seek + Ordered Partial Scan

The optimal level in our scale is a nonclustered covering index defined with the *orderid* column as the key and all the other columns as included non-key columns:

```
CREATE UNIQUE NONCLUSTERED INDEX idx_unc_oid_i_od_cid_eid_sid
  ON dbo.Orders(orderid)
  INCLUDE(orderdate, custid, empid, shipperid);
```

The plan's logic is similar to the previous one, only here, the ordered partial scan ends up reading fewer pages. That, of course, is because more rows fit in a leaf page of this index than data rows do in a clustered index page. You get the plan shown in Figure 3-54.

```
  SELECT         ⟸        Index Seek
  Cost: 0 %           [Performance].[dbo].[Orders]. ...
                          Cost: 100 %
```

Figure 3-54   Execution plan with covering nonclustered index seek + ordered partial scan

And here are the performance measures I got for this query:

- Logical reads: 9
- CPU time: 0 ms
- Elapsed time: 47 ms
- Estimated subtree cost: 0.008086

Again, this is a trivial plan. And also here, the performance of the ordered partial scan will vary depending on the fragmentation level of the index. As you can see, the cost of the query dropped from 19.621100 in the lowest level in the scale to 0.008086, and the elapsed time from more than 16 seconds to 47 milliseconds. Such a drop in run time is common when tuning indexes in an environment with poor index design.

When done, drop the last index you created:

```
DROP INDEX dbo.Orders.idx_unc_oid_i_od_cid_eid_sid;
```

Index Optimization Scale Summary and Analysis

Remember that the efficiency of several plans in our index optimization scale was based on the selectivity of the query. If the selectivity of a query you're tuning varies significantly between invocations of the query, make sure that in your tuning process you take this into account. For example, you can prepare tables and graphs with the performance measurements vs. selectivity, and analyze such data before you make your index design choices. For example, Table 3-16 shows a summary of logical reads vs. selectivity of the different levels in the scale for the sample query pattern under discussion against the sample Orders table.

Table 3-16   Logical Reads vs. Selectivity for Each Access Method

Access Method	1	1,000	10,000	100,000	200,000	500,000	1,000,000	rows
	0.0001%	0.1%	1%	10%	20%	50%	100%	selectivity
Table Scan/ Unordered Clustered Index Scan	25,080	25,080	25,080	25,080	25,080	25,080	25,080	
Unordered Nonclustered Index Scan	5,095	5,095	5,095	5,095	5,095	5,095	5,095	
Unordered Nonclustered Index Scan + Lookups	2,855	5,923	33,486	309,111	615,361	1,534,111	3,065,442	
Nonclustered Index Seek + Ordered Partial Scan + Lookups	6	3,078	30,667	306,547	613,082	1,532,685	3,073,741	
Clustered Index Seek + Ordered Partial Scan	4	29	249	2,447	4,890	12,219	24,433	
Covering Nonclustered Index Seek + Ordered Partial Scan	4	9	54	512	1,021	2,546	5,087	

Note   To apply a certain execution plan in a case where the optimizer would normally opt for another plan that is more efficient, I had to use a table hint to force using the relevant index.

Of course, logical reads shouldn't be the only indication you rely on. Remember that different I/O patterns have different performance, and that physical reads are much more expensive than logical reads. But when you see a significant difference in logical reads between two options, it is usually a good indication of which option is faster. Figure 3-55 has a graphical depiction of the information from Table 3-16.

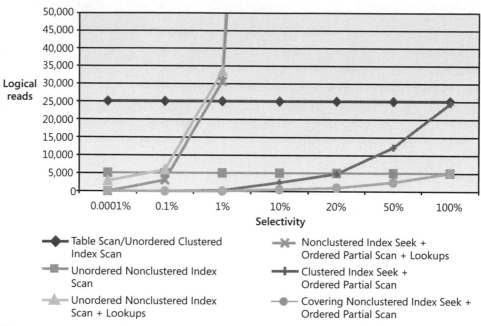

Figure 3-55   Graph of logical reads vs. selectivity

You can observe many interesting things when analyzing the graph. For example, you can clearly see which plans are based on selectivity and which aren't. And also, you can see the selectivity point at which one plan becomes better than another.

Similarly, Table 3-17 shows summary performance statistics of the query cost vs. selectivity.

Table 3-17   Estimated Subtree Costs vs. Selectivity for Each Access Method

Access Method	1	1,000	10,000	100,000	200,000	500,000	1,000,000	rows
	0.0001%	0.1%	1%	10%	20%	50%	100%	selec-tivity
Table Scan/ Unordered Clustered Index Scan	19.621100	19.621100	19.621100	19.621100	19.621100	19.621100	19.621100	
Unordered Nonclus-tered Index Scan	4.863280	4.863280	4.863280	4.863280	4.863280	4.863280	4.863280	
Unordered Nonclus-tered Index Scan + Lookups	3.690270	7.021360	30.665400	96.474000	113.966000	163.240000	244.092000	

Table 3-17   Estimated Subtree Costs vs. Selectivity for Each Access Method

Access Method	1	1,000	10,000	100,000	200,000	500,000	1,000,000	rows
	0.0001%	0.1%	1%	10%	20%	50%	100%	selectivity
Nonclustered Index Seek + Ordered Partial Scan + Lookups	0.006570	3.228520	21.921600	100.881000	127.376000	204.329000	335.109000	
Clustered Index Seek + Ordered Partial Scan	0.022160	0.022160	0.022160	0.022160	0.022160	0.022160	19.169900	
Covering Nonclustered Index Seek + Ordered Partial Scan	0.008086	0.008086	0.008086	0.008086	0.008086	0.008086	4.862540	

Figure 3-56 shows a graph based on the data in Table 3-17.

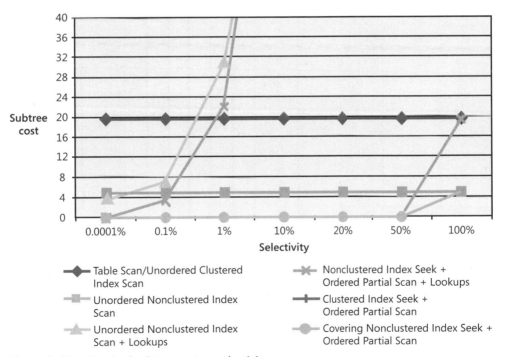

Figure 3-56   Graph of subtree cost vs. selectivity

You can observe a striking resemblance between the two graphs; but when you think about it, it makes sense because most of the cost involved with our query pattern is because of I/O.

Naturally, in plans where a more substantial portion of the cost is related to CPU, you will get different results.

Of course, you would also want to generate similar statistics and graphs for the actual run times of the queries in your benchmarks. At the end of the day, run time is what the user cares about.

I also find it valuable to visualize performance information in another graphical way as shown in Figure 3-57.

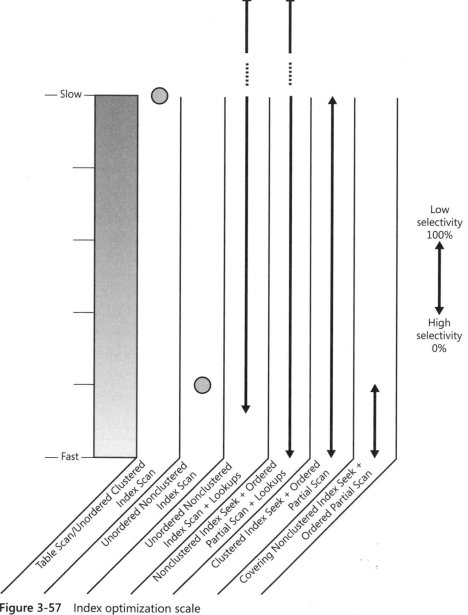

Figure 3-57   Index optimization scale

You might find it easier with this illustration to identify plans that are based on selectivity vs. plans that aren't (represented as a dot), and also to make comparisons between the performance of the different levels of optimization in the scale.

> **Note**   For simplicity's sake, all statistics and graphs shown in this section were collected against the Performance database I used in this chapter, where the level of fragmentation of indexes was minimal. When you conduct benchmarks and performance tests, make sure you introduce the appropriate levels of fragmentation in the indexes in your test system so that they reflect the fragmentation levels of the indexes in your production system adequately. The performance of ordered scans might vary significantly based on the level of fragmentation of your indexes. Similarly, you also need to examine the average page densities in your production system, and introduce similar page densities in the test system.

Besides having the ability to design good indexes, it is also important to be able to identify which indexes are used more heavily and which are rarely or never used. You don't want to keep indexes that are rarely used, as they do have negative performance effects on modifications. In SQL Server 2000, the only available techniques to determine index usage were very awkward, to say the least. For example, you could take a script that contains a representative sampling of the queries that run in the system and produce textual SHOWPLAN information for the queries in the script. You could write an application that parses the output, extracts the names of the indexes that are used, and calculates index usage statistics. Obviously, it's a problematic technique that also requires a fair amount of effort.

Another option you could use in SQL Server 2000 is to run the Index Tuning Wizard (ITW) based on a sample workload. Among the reports that ITW generates is a report that shows you usage statistics of the existing indexes for the input queries.

In SQL Server 2005, you have much more powerful and convenient tools to work with. You get a DMF called *dm_db_index_operational_stats* and a DMV called *dm_db_index_usage_stats*. The *dm_db_index_operational_stats* DMF gives you low-level I/O, locking, latching, and access method activity information. You provide the function a database ID, object ID, index ID (or 0 for a heap), and partition ID. You can also request information about multiple entities by specifying a NULL in the relevant argument. For example, to get information about all objects, indexes, and partitions in the Performance database, you would invoke the function as follows:

```
SELECT *
FROM sys.dm_db_index_operational_stats(
  DB_ID('Performance'), null, null, null);
```

The *dm_db_index_usage_stats* DMV gives you usage counts of the different index operations:

```
SELECT *
FROM sys.dm_db_index_usage_stats;
```

These dynamic management objects make the analysis of index usage much simpler and more accurate than before.

Fragmentation

I referred to index fragmentation on multiple occasions in this chapter. When I mentioned fragmentation, I referred to a type known as *logical scan fragmentation* or *average fragmentation in percent* or *external fragmentation*. As I mentioned earlier, this type reflects the percentage of out-of-order pages in the index, in terms of their physical order vs. their logical order in the linked list. Remember that this fragmentation can have a substantial impact on ordered scan operations in indexes. It has no effect on operations that do not rely on the index's linked list— for example, seek operations, lookups, unordered scans, and so on. You want to minimize the fragmentation level of indexes for queries with a substantial portion of their cost involved with ordered scans. You do so by rebuilding or reorganizing indexes.

Another type of fragmentation that you typically care about is what I referred to as average page density. Some database professionals refer to this type of fragmentation as *internal fragmentation*, but to avoid confusion I consciously didn't use this term earlier. While logical scan fragmentation is never a good thing, average scan fragmentation has two facets. A low percentage (low level of page population) has a negative impact on queries that read data, as they end up reading more pages than they could potentially if the pages were better populated. The positive impact of having some free space in index pages is that insertions of rows to such pages would not cause page splits—which are very expensive. As you can guess, free space in index pages is bad in systems that involve mostly reads (for example, data warehouses) and good for systems that involve many inserts (for example, OLTP systems). You might even want to introduce some free space in index pages by specifying a fillfactor value when you rebuild your indexes.

To determine whether you need to rebuild or reorganize your indexes, you need information about both types of fragmentation. In SQL Server 2005, you can get this information by querying the DMF *dm_db_index_physical_stats*. For example, the following query will return fragmentation information about the indexes in the Performance database:

```
SELECT *
FROM sys.dm_db_index_physical_stats(
  DB_ID('Performance'), NULL, NULL, NULL, NULL);
```

The fragmentation types I mentioned will show up in the attributes *avg_fragmentation_in_percent* and *avg_page_space_used_in_percent*, and as you can see, the attribute names are self explanatory. In SQL Server 2000, you use the DBCC SHOWCONTIG command to get similar information:

```
DBCC SHOWCONTIG WITH ALL_INDEXES, TABLERESULTS, NO_INFOMSGS;
```

The two attributes of interest to our discussion are *LogicalFragmentation* and *AveragePageDensity*.

As I mentioned earlier, to treat both types of fragmentation you need to rebuild or reorganize the index. Rebuilding an index has the optimal defragmentation effect. The operation makes its best attempt to rebuild the index in the same physical order on disk as in the linked list and to make the pages as contiguous as possible. Also, remember that you can specify a fillfactor to introduce some free space in the index leaf pages.

In SQL Server 2000, index rebuilds were offline operations. Rebuilding a clustered index acquired an exclusive lock for the whole duration of the operation, meaning that process can neither read nor write to the table. Rebuilding a nonclustered index acquired a shared lock, meaning that writes are blocked against the table, and obviously, the index can not be used during the operation. SQL Server 2005 introduces *online index operations* that allow you to create, rebuild, and drop indexes online. In addition, these operations allow users to interact with the data while the operation is in progress. Online index operations use the new row-versioning technology introduced in SQL Server 2005. When an index is rebuilt online, SQL Server actually maintains two indexes behind the scenes, and when the operation is done, the new one overrides the old one.

As an example, the following code rebuilds the *idx_cl_od* index on the Orders table online:

```
ALTER INDEX idx_cl_od ON dbo.Orders REBUILD WITH (ONLINE = ON);
```

Note that online index operations need sufficient space in the database and overall are slower than offline operations. If you can spare a maintenance window for the activity to work offline, you better do so. Even when you do perform the operations online, they will have a performance impact on the system while they are running, so it's best to run them during off-peak hours.

Instead of rebuilding an index, you can also reorganize it. Reorganizing an index involves a bubble sort algorithm to sort the index pages physically on disk according to their order in the index's linked list. The operation does not attempt to make the pages more contiguous (reduce gaps). As you can guess, the defragmentation level that you get from this operation is not as optimal as fully rebuilding an index. Also, overall, this operation performs more logging than an index rebuild and, therefore, is typically slower.

So why use this type of defragmentation? First, in SQL Server 2000 it was the only online defragmentation utility. The operation grabs short-term locks on a pair of pages at a time to determine whether they are in the correct order, and if they are not, it swaps them. Second, an index rebuild must run as a single transaction, and if it's aborted while it's in process, the whole activity is rolled back. This is unlike an index reorganize operation, which can be interrupted as it operates on a pair of pages at a time. When you later run the reorganize activity again, it will pick up where it left off earlier.

Here's how you would reorganize the *idx_cl_od* index in SQL Server 2005:

```
ALTER INDEX idx_cl_od ON dbo.Orders REORGANIZE;
```

In SQL Server 2000, you use the DBCC INDEXDEFRAG command for the same purpose.

Partitioning

SQL Server 2005 introduces native partitioning of tables and indexes. Partitioning your objects means that they are internally split into multiple physical units that together make the object (table or index). Partitioning is virtually unavoidable in medium to large environments. By partitioning your objects, you improve the manageability and maintainability of your system and you improve the performance of activities such as purging historic data, data loads, and others as well. Partitioning in SQL Server is native—that is, you have built-in tools to partition the tables and indexes, while logically, to the applications and users they appear as whole units. In SQL Server 2000, partitioning was achieved by manually creating multiple tables and a view on top that unifies the pieces. SQL Server 2005 native partitioning has many advantages over partitioned views in SQL Server 2000, including improved execution plans, a substantially relaxed set of requirements, and more.

> **More Info**   Partitioning is outside the scope of this book, but I covered it in detail in a series of articles in *SQL Server Magazine*. You can find these articles at *http://www.sqlmag.com*. (Look up instant document IDs 45153, 45533, 45877, and 46207.)

Preparing Sample Data

When conducting performance tests, it is vital that the sample data you use be well prepared so that it reflects the production system as closely as possible, especially with respect to the factors you are trying to tune. Typically, it's not realistic to just copy all the data from the production tables, at least not with the big ones. However, you should make your best effort to have an adequate representation, which will reflect similar data distribution, density of keys, cardinality, and so on. Also, you want your queries against the test system to have similar selectivity to the queries against the production system. Performance tests can be skewed when the sample data does not adequately represent the production data.

In this section, I'll provide an example of skewed performance testing results resulting from inadequate sample data. I'll also discuss the new TABLESAMPLE option.

Data Preparation

When I prepared the sample data for this chapter's demonstrations, I didn't need to reflect a specific production system, so preparing sample data was fairly simple. I mainly needed it for the "Tuning Methodology" and "Index Tuning" sections. I could express most of my points through simple random distribution of the different attributes that were relevant to our discussions. But our main data table—Orders—does not accurately reflect an average production Orders table. For example, I produced a fairly even distribution of values in the different attributes, while typically in production systems, different attributes have different types of distribution (some uniform, some standard). Some customers place many orders, and others place few. Also, some customers are more active in some periods of time and less active in others. Depending on your tuning needs, you might or might not need to reflect such things in your sample data, but you definitely need to consider them and decide whether they do matter.

When you need large tables with sample data, the easiest thing to do is to generate some small table and duplicate its content (save the key columns) many times. This can be fine if, for example, you want to test the performance of a user-defined function invoked against every row or a cursor manipulation iterating through many rows. But such sample data in some cases can yield completely different performance than what you would get with sample data that more adequately reflects your production data. To demonstrate this, I'll walk you through an example that I cover in much more depth in *Inside T-SQL Programming*. I often give this exercise in class and ask students to prepare a large amount of sample data without giving any hints.

The exercise has to do with a table called Sessions, which you create and populate by running the code in Listing 3-6.

Listing 3-6   Creating and populating the Sessions table

```
SET NOCOUNT ON;
USE Performance;
GO
IF OBJECT_ID('dbo.Sessions') IS NOT NULL
  DROP TABLE dbo.Sessions;
GO

CREATE TABLE dbo.Sessions
(
  keycol    INT          NOT NULL IDENTITY,
  app       VARCHAR(10) NOT NULL,
  usr       VARCHAR(10) NOT NULL,
  host      VARCHAR(10) NOT NULL,
  starttime DATETIME     NOT NULL,
  endtime   DATETIME     NOT NULL,
  CONSTRAINT PK_Sessions PRIMARY KEY(keycol),
  CHECK(endtime > starttime)
);

INSERT INTO dbo.Sessions
  VALUES('app1', 'user1', 'host1', '20030212 08:30', '20030212 10:30');
INSERT INTO dbo.Sessions
  VALUES('app1', 'user2', 'host1', '20030212 08:30', '20030212 08:45');
INSERT INTO dbo.Sessions
  VALUES('app1', 'user3', 'host2', '20030212 09:00', '20030212 09:30');
INSERT INTO dbo.Sessions
  VALUES('app1', 'user4', 'host2', '20030212 09:15', '20030212 10:30');
INSERT INTO dbo.Sessions
  VALUES('app1', 'user5', 'host3', '20030212 09:15', '20030212 09:30');
INSERT INTO dbo.Sessions
  VALUES('app1', 'user6', 'host3', '20030212 10:30', '20030212 14:30');
```

```
INSERT INTO dbo.Sessions
  VALUES('app1', 'user7', 'host4', '20030212 10:45', '20030212 11:30');
INSERT INTO dbo.Sessions
  VALUES('app1', 'user8', 'host4', '20030212 11:00', '20030212 12:30');
INSERT INTO dbo.Sessions
  VALUES('app2', 'user8', 'host1', '20030212 08:30', '20030212 08:45');
INSERT INTO dbo.Sessions
  VALUES('app2', 'user7', 'host1', '20030212 09:00', '20030212 09:30');
INSERT INTO dbo.Sessions
  VALUES('app2', 'user6', 'host2', '20030212 11:45', '20030212 12:00');
INSERT INTO dbo.Sessions
  VALUES('app2', 'user5', 'host2', '20030212 12:30', '20030212 14:00');
INSERT INTO dbo.Sessions
  VALUES('app2', 'user4', 'host3', '20030212 12:45', '20030212 13:30');
INSERT INTO dbo.Sessions
  VALUES('app2', 'user3', 'host3', '20030212 13:00', '20030212 14:00');
INSERT INTO dbo.Sessions
  VALUES('app2', 'user2', 'host4', '20030212 14:00', '20030212 16:30');
INSERT INTO dbo.Sessions
  VALUES('app2', 'user1', 'host4', '20030212 15:30', '20030212 17:00');

CREATE INDEX idx_nc_app_st_et ON dbo.Sessions(app, starttime, endtime);
```

The Sessions table contains information about user sessions against different applications. The request is to calculate the maximum number of concurrent sessions per application—that is, the maximum number of sessions that were active at any point in time against each application.

The following query produces the requested information, as shown in Table 3-18:

```
SELECT app, MAX(concurrent) AS mx
FROM (SELECT app,
        (SELECT COUNT(*)
          FROM dbo.Sessions AS S2
          WHERE S1.app = S2.app
            AND S1.ts >= S2.starttime
            AND S1.ts < S2.endtime) AS concurrent
      FROM (SELECT DISTINCT app, starttime AS ts
            FROM dbo.Sessions) AS S1) AS C
GROUP BY app;
```

Table 3-18   Max Concurrent Sessions per Application

app	mx
app1	4
app2	3

The derived table S1 contains the distinct application name (*app*) and session start time (*starttime as ts*) pairs. For each row of S1, a subquery counts the number of sessions that were active for the application *S1.app* at time *S1.ts*. The outer query then groups the data by *app* and returns the maximum count for each group. SQL Server's optimizer generates the execution plan shown in Figure 3-58 for this query.

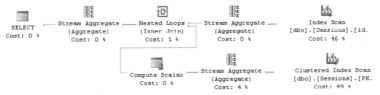

Figure 3-58 Execution plan for query against the Sessions table

In the script in Listing 3-6, I created the covering index *idx_nc_app_st_et* on (*app, starttime, endtime*), which is the optimal index for this query. In the plan, this index is scanned in order (Index Scan operator) and distinct rows are isolated (Stream Aggregate operator). As rows are streamed out from the Stream Aggregate operator, a Nested Loops operator invokes a series of activities to calculate the count of active sessions for each row. Because the Sessions table is so tiny (only one page of data), the optimizer simply decides to scan the whole table (unordered clustered index scan) to calculate each count. With a larger data set, instead of scanning the table, the plan would perform a seek and ordered partial scan of the covering index to obtain each count. Finally, another Stream Aggregate operator groups the data by *app* to calculate the maximum count for each group.

Now that you're familiar with the problem, suppose you were asked to prepare sample data with 1,000,000 rows in the source table (call it BigSessions) such that it would represent a realistic environment. Ideally, you should be thinking about the number of customers, the number of different order dates, and so on. However, people often take the most obvious approach, which is to duplicate the data from the small source table many times; in our case, such an approach would drastically skew the performance compared to a more realistic representation of production environments.

Now run the code in Listing 3-7 to generate the BigSessions table by duplicating the data from the Sessions table many times. You will get 1,000,000 rows in the BigSessions table.

Listing 3-7 Populate sessions with inadequate sample data

```
SET NOCOUNT ON;
USE Performance;
GO
IF OBJECT_ID('dbo.BigSessions') IS NOT NULL
  DROP TABLE dbo.BigSessions;
GO
SELECT IDENTITY(int, 1, 1) AS keycol,
  app, usr, host, starttime, endtime
INTO dbo.BigSessions
FROM dbo.Sessions AS S, Nums
WHERE n <= 62500;

ALTER TABLE dbo.BigSessions
  ADD CONSTRAINT PK_BigSessions PRIMARY KEY(keycol);
CREATE INDEX idx_nc_app_st_et
  ON dbo.BigSessions(app, starttime, endtime);
```

Run the following query against BigSessions:

```
SELECT app, MAX(concurrent) AS mx
FROM (SELECT app,
        (SELECT COUNT(*)
         FROM dbo.BigSessions AS S2
         WHERE S1.app = S2.app
           AND S1.ts >= S2.starttime
           AND S1.ts < S2.endtime) AS concurrent
      FROM (SELECT DISTINCT app, starttime AS ts
            FROM dbo.BigSessions) AS S1) AS C
GROUP BY app;
```

Note that this is the same query as before (but against a different table). The query will finish in a few seconds, and you will get the execution plan shown in Figure 3-59.

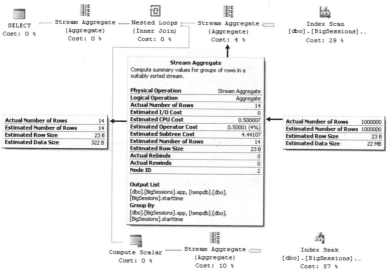

Figure 3-59   Execution plan for query against the BigSessions table with inadequate sample data

Here are the performance measures I got for this query:

- Logical reads: 20024

- CPU time: 1452 ms

- Elapsed time: 1531 ms

- Estimated subtree cost: 13.6987

Of course, after the first Stream Aggregate operator eliminated duplicate rows, it yielded only 14 distinct rows; so the Nested Loops operator that follows invoked only 14 iterations of the activity that calculates the count of active sessions. Therefore, the query finished in only a few seconds. In a production environment, there might be only a few applications, but so few distinct start times would be unlikely.

You might think it's obvious that the sample data is inadequate because the first step in the query constructing the derived table S1 isolates distinct *app* and *starttime* values—meaning that the COUNT aggregate in the subquery will be invoked only a small number of times. But in many cases, the fact that there's a performance skew due to bad sample data is much more elusive. For example, many programmers would come up with the following query solution to our problem, where they won't isolate distinct *app* and *starttime* values first:

```
SELECT app, MAX(concurrent) AS mx
FROM (SELECT app,
        (SELECT COUNT(*)
         FROM dbo.BigSessions AS S2
         WHERE S1.app = S2.app
           AND S1.starttime >= S2.starttime
           AND S1.starttime < S2.endtime) AS concurrent
      FROM dbo.BigSessions AS S1) AS C
GROUP BY app;
```

Examine the execution plan generated for this query, as shown in Figure 3-60.

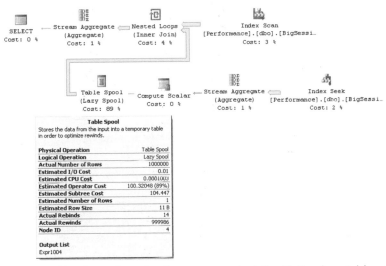

Figure 3-60   Execution plan for query against the BigSessions table with inadequate sample data

Focus on the Table Spool operator, which represents a temporary table holding the session count for each distinct combination of *app* and *starttime* values. Because you didn't isolate distinct *app* and *starttime* values, the optimizer elegantly does the job for you. Notice the number of rebinds (14) and the number of rewinds (999,986). Remember that a rebind means that one or more correlated parameters of the join operator changed and the inner side must be reevaluated. That happens 14 times, once for each distinct pair of *app* and *starttime*—meaning that the actual count activity preceding the operator took place only 14 times. A rewind means that none of the correlated parameters changed and the prior inner result set can be reused; this happened 999,986 times (1,000,000 − 14 = 999,986). Naturally, with more realistic data distribution for our scenario, the count activity will take place many more times than 14, and you will get a much slower query. It was a mistake to prepare the sample data by simply copying the rows from the small Sessions table many times. The distribution of values in the different columns should represent production environments more realistically.

Run the code in Listing 3-8 to populate BigSessions with more adequate sample data.

Listing 3-8   Populate the BigSessions table with adequate sample data

```
SET NOCOUNT ON;
USE Performance;
GO
IF OBJECT_ID('dbo.BigSessions') IS NOT NULL
  DROP TABLE dbo.BigSessions;
GO

SELECT
  IDENTITY(int, 1, 1) AS keycol,
  D.*,
  DATEADD(
    second,
    1 + ABS(CHECKSUM(NEWID())) % (20*60),
    starttime) AS endtime
INTO dbo.BigSessions
FROM
(
  SELECT
    'app' + CAST(1 + ABS(CHECKSUM(NEWID())) % 10 AS VARCHAR(10)) AS app,
    'user1' AS usr,
    'host1' AS host,
    DATEADD(
      second,
      1 + ABS(CHECKSUM(NEWID())) % (30*24*60*60),
      '20040101') AS starttime
  FROM dbo.Nums
  WHERE n <= 1000000
) AS D;

ALTER TABLE dbo.BigSessions
  ADD CONSTRAINT PK_BigSessions PRIMARY KEY(keycol);
CREATE INDEX idx_nc_app_st_et
  ON dbo.BigSessions(app, starttime, endtime);
```

I populated the table with sessions that start at random times over a period of one month and that last up to 20 minutes. I also distributed 10 different application names randomly. Now request an estimated execution plan for the original query and you will get the plan shown in Figure 3-61.

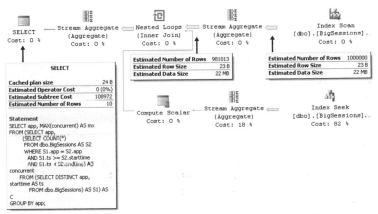

Figure 3-61   Estimated execution plan for query against the BigSessions table with adequate sample data

The cost of the query is now 108,972. Trust me; you don't want to run it to see how long it really takes. Or, if you like, you can start running it and come back the next day hoping that it finished.

Now that the sample data is more realistic, you can see that the set-based solution presented in this section is slow—unlike what you might be led to believe when using inadequate sample data. In short, you can see how vital it is to put some thought into preparing good sample data. Of course, the tuning process only starts now; you might want to consider query revisions, cursor-based solutions, revisiting the model, and so on. But here I wanted to focus the discussion on bad sample data. I'll conduct a more thorough tuning discussion related to the problem at hand in *Inside T-SQL Programming*.

TABLESAMPLE

SQL Server 2005 introduces a new feature that allows you to sample data from an existing table. The tool is a clause called TABLESAMPLE that you specify after the table name in the FROM clause along with some options. Here's an example for using TABLESAMPLE to request 1000 rows from the Orders table in the Performance database:

```
SELECT *
FROM Performance.dbo.Orders TABLESAMPLE (1000 ROWS);
```

Note that if you run this query you probably won't get exactly 1000 rows. I'll explain why shortly.

You can specify TABLESAMPLE on a table-by-table basis. Following the TABLESAMPLE keyword, you can optionally specify the sampling method to use. Currently, SQL Server supports only the SYSTEM method, which is also the default if no method is specified. In the future, we might see additional algorithms. Per ANSI, the SYSTEM keyword represents an implementation-dependent sampling method. This means that you will find different algorithms implemented in different products when using the SYSTEM method. In SQL Server, the SYSTEM method implements the same sampling algorithm used to sample pages to generate statistics.

You can use either the ROWS or the PERCENT keyword to specify how many rows you would like to get back. Based on your inputs, SQL Server will calculate random values to figure out whether or not a page should be returned. Note that the decision of whether or not to read a portion of data is done at the page level. This fact, along with the fashion in which SQL Server determines whether or not to pick a page based on a random factor, means that you won't necessarily get the exact number of rows that you asked for; rather, you'll get a fairly close value. The more rows you request, the more likely you are to get a result set size close to what you requested.

Here's an example for using the TABLESAMPLE clause in a query against the Orders table, requesting 1,000 rows:

```
SET NOCOUNT ON;
USE Performance;

SELECT *
FROM dbo.Orders TABLESAMPLE SYSTEM (1000 ROWS);
```

I ran this query three times and got a different number of rows every time: 880, 1200, and 920.

An important benefit you get with the SYSTEM sampling method is that only the chosen pages (those that SQL Server picked) will be physically scanned. So even if you query a huge table, you will get the results pretty fast—as long as you specify a fairly small number of rows. As I mentioned earlier, you can also specify a percentage of rows. Here's an example requesting 0.1 percent, which is equivalent to 1,000 rows in our table:

```
SELECT *
FROM dbo.Orders TABLESAMPLE (0.1 PERCENT);
```

When you use the ROWS option, SQL Server internally first converts the specified number of rows to a percentage. Remember that you are not guaranteed to get the exact number of rows that you requested; rather, you'll get a close value that's determined by the number of pages that were picked and the number of rows on those pages (which may vary).

To make it more likely that you'll get the exact number of rows you are after, specify a higher number of rows in the TABLESAMPLE clause and use the TOP option to limit the upper bound that you will get, like so:

```
SELECT TOP(1000) *
FROM dbo.Orders TABLESAMPLE (2000 ROWS);
```

There's still a chance that you will get fewer rows than the number you requested, but you're guaranteed not to get more. By specifying a higher value in the TABLESAMPLE clause, you increase the likelihood of getting the number of rows you are after.

If you need to get repeatable results, use a clause called REPEATABLE which was designed for this purpose, providing it with the same seed in all invocations. For example, running the following query multiple times will yield the same result, provided that the data in the table has not changed:

```
SELECT *
FROM dbo.Orders TABLESAMPLE (1000 ROWS) REPEATABLE(42);
```

Note that with small tables you might not get any rows at all. For example, run the following query multiple times, requesting a single row from the Sales.StoreContact table in the AdventureWorks database:

```
SELECT *
FROM AdventureWorks.Sales.StoreContact TABLESAMPLE (1 ROWS);
```

You will only occasionally get any rows back. I witnessed a very interesting discussion in a technical SQL Server forum. Someone presented such a query and wanted to know why he didn't get any rows back. Steve Kass, a friend of mine and the ingenious technical editor of these books, provided the following illuminating answer and kindly allowed me to quote him here:

> As documented in Books Online ("Limiting Results Sets by Using TABLESAMPLE"), the sampling algorithm can only return full data pages. Each page is selected or skipped with probability [desired number of rows]/[rows in table].

> The StoreContact table fits on 4 data pages. Three of those pages contain 179 rows, and one contains 37 rows. When you sample for 10 rows (1/75 of the table), each of the 4 pages is returned with probability 1/75 and skipped with probability 74/75. The chance that no rows are returned is about (74/75)^4, or about 87%. When rows are returned, about 3/4 of the time you will see 179 rows, and about 1/4 of the time you will see 37 rows. Very rarely, you will see more rows, if two or more pages are returned, but this is very unlikely.

> As BOL suggests, SYSTEM sampling (which is the only choice) is not recommended for small tables. I would add that if the table fits on N data pages, you should not try to sample fewer than 1/N-th of the rows, or that you should never try to sample fewer rows than fit on at least 2 or 3 data pages.

> If you were to sample roughly two data pages worth of rows, say 300 rows, the chance of seeing no rows would be about 13%. The larger (more data pages) the table, the smaller the chance of seeing no rows when at least a couple of pages worth are requested. For example, if you request 300 rows from a 1,000,000-row table that fits on 10,000 data pages, only in 5% of trials would you see no rows, even though the request is for far less than 1% of the rows.

> *By choosing the REPEATABLE option, you will get the same sample each time. For most seeds, this will be an empty sample in your case. With other seeds, it will contain 37, 179, 216, 358, 395, 537, 574, or 753 rows, depending on which pages were selected, with the larger numbers of rows returned for very few choices of seed.*
>
> *That said, I agree that the consequences of returning only full data pages results in very confusing behavior!*

With small tables, you might want to consider other sampling methods. You don't care too much about scanning the whole table because you will consider these techniques against small tables anyway. For example, the following query will scan the whole table, but it will guarantee that you get a single random row:

```
SELECT TOP(1) *
FROM AdventureWorks.Sales.StoreContact
ORDER BY NEWID();
```

Note that other database platforms, such as DB2, implement additional algorithms—for example, the Bernoulli sampling algorithm. You can implement it in SQL Server by using the following query, provided by Steve Kass:

```
SELECT *
FROM AdventureWorks.Sales.StoreContact
WHERE ABS((customerid%customerid)+CHECKSUM(NEWID()))/POWER(2.,31) < 0.01
GO
```

The constant 0.01 is the desired probability (in this case, 1%) of choosing a row. The expression *customerid%customerid* was included to make the WHERE clause correlated and force its evaluation on each row of StoreContact. Without it, the value of the WHERE condition would be calculated just once, and either the entire table would be returned or no rows would be returned. Note that this technique will require a full table scan and can take a while with large tables. You can test it against our Orders table and see for yourself.

An Examination of Set-Based vs. Iterative/Procedural Approaches, and a Tuning Exercise

Thus far in the chapter, I mainly focused on index tuning for given queries. However, in large part, query tuning involves query revisions. That is, with different queries or different T-SQL code you can sometimes get substantially different plans, with widely varying costs and run times. In a perfect world, the ideal optimizer would always figure out exactly what you are trying to achieve; and for any form of query or T-SQL code that attempts to achieve the same thing, you would get the same plan—and only the best plan, of course. But alas, we're not there yet. There are still many performance improvements to gain merely from the changing way you write your code. This will be demonstrated thoroughly throughout these books. Here, I'll demonstrate a typical tuning process based on code revisions by following an example.

Note that set-based queries are typically superior to solutions based on iterative/procedural logic—such as ones using cursors, loops, and the like. Besides the fact that set-based solutions usually require much less code, they also usually involve less overhead than cursors. There's a lot of overhead incurred with the record-by-record manipulation of cursors. You can make simple benchmarks to observe the performance differences. Run a query that simply selects all rows from a big table, discarding the results in the graphical tool so that the time it takes to display the output won't be taken into consideration. Also run cursor code that simply scans all table rows one at a time. Even if you use the fastest available cursor—FAST_FORWARD (forward only, read only)—you will find that the set-based query runs dozens of times faster. Besides the overhead involved with a cursor, there's also an issue with the execution plans. When using a cursor, you apply a very rigid physical approach to accessing the data, because your code focuses a lot on how to achieve the result. A set-based query, on the other hand, focuses logically on *what* you want to achieve rather than *how* to achieve it. Typically, set-based queries leave the optimizer with much more room for maneuvering and leeway to do what it is good at—optimization.

That's the rule of thumb. However, I'm typically very careful with adopting rules of thumb, especially with regard to query tuning—because optimization is such a dynamic world, and there are always exceptions. In fact, as far as query tuning is concerned, my main rule of thumb is to be careful about adopting rules of thumb.

You will encounter cases where it is very hard to beat cursor code, and you need to be able to identify them; but these cases are the minority. I'll discuss the subject at length in Chapter 3, "Cursors," of *Inside T-SQL Programming*.

To demonstrate a tuning process based on code revisions, I'll use our Orders and Shippers tables. The request is to return shippers that used to be active, but do not have any activity as of January 1, 2001. That is, a qualifying shipper is one for whom you cannot find an order on or after January 1, 2001. You don't care about shippers who have made no orders at all.

Before you start working, remove all indexes from the Orders table, and make sure that you have only the clustered index defined on the *orderdate* column and the primary key (nonclustered) defined on the *orderid* column.

If you rerun the code in Listing 3-1, make sure that for the Orders table, you keep only the following index and primary key definitions:

```
SET NOCOUNT ON;
USE Performance;
CREATE CLUSTERED INDEX idx_cl_od ON dbo.Orders(orderdate);
ALTER TABLE dbo.Orders ADD
  CONSTRAINT PK_Orders PRIMARY KEY NONCLUSTERED(orderid);
```

Next, run the following code to add a few shippers to the Shippers table and a few orders to the Orders table:

```
INSERT INTO dbo.Shippers(shipperid, shippername) VALUES('B', 'Shipper_B');
INSERT INTO dbo.Shippers(shipperid, shippername) VALUES('D', 'Shipper_D');
INSERT INTO dbo.Shippers(shipperid, shippername) VALUES('F', 'Shipper_F');
INSERT INTO dbo.Shippers(shipperid, shippername) VALUES('H', 'Shipper_H');
INSERT INTO dbo.Shippers(shipperid, shippername) VALUES('X', 'Shipper_X');
INSERT INTO dbo.Shippers(shipperid, shippername) VALUES('Y', 'Shipper_Y');
INSERT INTO dbo.Shippers(shipperid, shippername) VALUES('Z', 'Shipper_Z');

INSERT INTO dbo.Orders(orderid, custid, empid, shipperid, orderdate)
  VALUES(1000001, 'C0000000001', 1, 'B', '20000101');
INSERT INTO dbo.Orders(orderid, custid, empid, shipperid, orderdate)
  VALUES(1000002, 'C0000000001', 1, 'D', '20000101');
INSERT INTO dbo.Orders(orderid, custid, empid, shipperid, orderdate)
  VALUES(1000003, 'C0000000001', 1, 'F', '20000101');
INSERT INTO dbo.Orders(orderid, custid, empid, shipperid, orderdate)
  VALUES(1000004, 'C0000000001', 1, 'H', '20000101');
```

You're supposed to get the shipper IDs B, D, F, and H in the result. These are the only shippers that were active at some point, but not as of January 1, 2001.

In terms of index tuning, it's sometimes hard to figure out what the optimal indexes are without having an existing query to tune. But in our case, index tuning is rather simple and possible without having the solution code first. Obviously, you will want to search for an *orderdate* value for each *shipperid*, so naturally the optimal index would be a nonclustered covering index defined with *shipperid* and *orderdate* as the key columns, in that order:

```
CREATE NONCLUSTERED INDEX idx_nc_sid_od
  ON dbo.Orders(shipperid, orderdate);
```

I suggest that at this point you try to come up with the best performing solution that you can; then compare it with the solutions that I will demonstrate.

As the first solution, I'll start with the cursor-based code shown in Listing 3-9.

Listing 3-9   Cursor solution

```
DECLARE
  @sid     AS VARCHAR(5),
  @od      AS DATETIME,
  @prevsid AS VARCHAR(5),
  @prevod  AS DATETIME;

DECLARE ShipOrdersCursor CURSOR FAST_FORWARD FOR
  SELECT shipperid, orderdate
  FROM dbo.Orders
  ORDER BY shipperid, orderdate;

OPEN ShipOrdersCursor;
```

```
FETCH NEXT FROM ShipOrdersCursor INTO @sid, @od;

SELECT @prevsid = @sid, @prevod = @od;

WHILE @@fetch_status = 0
BEGIN
  IF @prevsid <> @sid AND @prevod < '20010101' PRINT @prevsid;
  SELECT @prevsid = @sid, @prevod = @od;
  FETCH NEXT FROM ShipOrdersCursor INTO @sid, @od;
END

IF @prevod < '20010101' PRINT @prevsid;

CLOSE ShipOrdersCursor;

DEALLOCATE ShipOrdersCursor;
```

This code implements a straightforward data-aggregation algorithm based on sorting. The cursor is defined on a query that sorts the data by *shipperid* and *orderdate*, and it scans the records in a forward-only, read-only manner—the fastest scan you can get with a cursor. For each shipper, the code inspects the last row found—which happens to hold the maximum *orderdate* for that shipper—and if that date is earlier than '20010101', the code emits the *shipperid* value. This code ran on my machine for 27 seconds. Imagine the run time in a larger Orders table that contains millions of rows.

The next solution (call it *set-based solution 1*) is a natural GROUP BY query that many programmers would come up with:

```
SELECT shipperid
FROM dbo.Orders
GROUP BY shipperid
HAVING MAX(orderdate) < '20010101';
```

You just say what you want, rather than spending most of your code describing how to get it. The query groups the data by *shipperid*, and it returns only shippers with a maximum *orderdate* that is earlier than '20010101'.

This query ran for just under one second in my machine. The optimizer produced the execution plan shown in Figure 3-62 for this query.

Figure 3-62 Execution plan for set-based solution 1

The plan shows that our covering index was fully scanned in order. The maximum *orderdate* was isolated for each *shipperid* by the Stream Aggregate operator. Then the filter operator filtered only shippers for whom the maximum *orderdate* was before '20010101'.

Here are the vital performance measures I got for this query:

- Logical reads: 2730
- CPU time: 670 ms
- Elapsed time: 732 ms

Note that you might get slightly different performance measures. At this point, you need to ask yourself if you're happy with the result, and if you're not, whether there's potential for optimization at all.

Of course, this solution is a big improvement over the cursor-based one, both in terms of performance and code readability and maintenance. However, a run time of close to one second for such a query might not be satisfactory. Keep in mind that an Orders tables in some production environments can contain far more than one million rows.

If you determine that you want to tune the solution further, you now need to figure out whether there's potential for optimization. Remember that in the execution plan for the last query, the leaf level of the index was fully scanned to obtain the latest *orderdate* for each shipper. That scan required 2730 page reads. Our Shippers table contains 12 shippers. Your gut feelings should tell you that there must be a way to obtain the data with much fewer reads. In our index, the rows are sorted by *shipperid* and *orderdate*. This means that there are groups of rows—a group for each *shipperid*—where the last row in each group contains the latest *orderdate* that you want to inspect. Alas, the optimizer currently doesn't have the logic within it to "zig-zag" between the levels of the index, jumping from one shipper's latest *orderdate* to the next. If it had, the query would have incurred substantially less I/O. By the way, such zigzagging logic can be beneficial for other types of requests—for example, requests involving filters on a non-first index column and others as well. But I won't digress.

Of course, if you request the latest *orderdate* for a particular shipper, the optimizer can use a seek directly to the last shipper's row in the index. Such a seek would cost 3 reads in our case. Then the optimizer can apply a TOP operator going one step backwards, returning the desired value—the latest *orderdate* for the given shipper—to a Stream Aggregate operator.

The following query demonstrates acquiring the latest *orderdate* for a particular shipper, producing the execution plan shown in Figure 3-63:

```
SELECT MAX(orderdate) FROM dbo.Orders WHERE shipperid = 'A';
```

Figure 3-63   Execution plan for a query handling a particular shipper

This plan incurs only 5 logical reads. Now, if you do the math for 12 shippers, you will realize that you can potentially obtain the desired result with substantially less I/O than 2730 reads.

Of course, you could scan the Shippers rows with a cursor, and then invoke such a query for each shipper; but it would be counterproductive and a bit ironic to beat a cursor solution with a set-based solution, that you then beat with another cursor.

Realizing that what you're after is invoking a seek operation for each shipper, you might come up with the following attempt (call it *set-based solution 2*):

```
SELECT shipperid
FROM (SELECT shipperid,
        (SELECT MAX(orderdate)
         FROM dbo.Orders AS O
         WHERE O.shipperid = S.shipperid) AS maxod
      FROM dbo.Shippers AS S) AS D
WHERE maxod < '20010101';
```

You query the Shippers table, and for each shipper, a subquery acquires the latest *orderdate* value (aliased as *maxod*). The outer query then filters only shippers with a *maxod* value that is earlier than '20010101'. Shippers who have never placed an order will be filtered out; for those, the subquery will yield a NULL, and a NULL compared to any value yields UNKNOWN, which in turn is filtered out.

But strangely enough, you get the plan shown in Figure 3-64, which looks surprisingly similar to the previous one.

Figure 3-64 Execution plan for set-based solution 2

And the performance measures are also similar to the previous ones. This query also incurred 2730 logical reads against the Orders table, and ran for close to one second on my machine. So what happened here?

It seems that the optimizer got "too sophisticated" this time. One guess is that it realized that for shippers who have made no orders, the subquery would return a NULL and they would be filtered out in the outer query's filter—meaning that only shippers that do appear in the Orders table are of interest. Thus, it internally "simplified" the query to one that is similar to our set-based solution 1, hence the similar plans.

The situation seems to be evolving into a battle of wits with the optimizer—not a battle to the death, of course; there won't be any iocane powder involved here, just I/O. The optimizer pulls a trick on you; now pull your best trick. You can make the optimizer believe that shippers with no orders might also be of interest, by substituting a NULL value returned from the subquery with a constant; you can do so by using the COALESCE function. Of course, you'd use a constant that will never allow the filter expression to yield TRUE, as you're not interested in shippers that have no associated orders.

You issue the following query (call it *set-based solution 3*), close your eyes, and hope for the best:

```
SELECT shipperid
FROM (SELECT shipperid,
        (SELECT MAX(orderdate)
         FROM dbo.Orders AS O
         WHERE O.shipperid = S.shipperid) AS maxod
      FROM dbo.Shippers AS S) AS D
WHERE COALESCE(maxod, '99991231') < '20010101';
```

And when you open your eyes, voilà! You see the plan you wished for, as shown in Figure 3-65.

Figure 3-65 Execution plan for set-based solution 3

The Shippers table is scanned, and for each of the 12 shippers, a Nested Loops operator invokes a similar activity to the one you got when invoking a query for a particular shipper. This plan incurs only 60 logical reads. The net CPU time is not even measurable with STATISTICS TIME (shows up as 0), and I got 26 milliseconds of elapsed time.

Once you get over the excitement of outwitting the optimizer, you start facing some troubling facts. Such a query is not very natural, and it's not the most intuitive for programmers to grasp. It uses a very artificial technique, with the sole purpose of overcoming an optimizer issue—which is similar to using a hint, but with tricky logic applied. Some other programmer who needed to maintain your code in the future might stare at the query for awhile and then ask, "What on earth was the programmer who wrote this query thinking? I can do this much more simply." The programmer would then revise the code back to set-based solution 1. Of course, you can add comments documenting the technique and the reasoning behind it. But humor aside, the point is that queries should be simple, natural, and intuitive for people to read and understand—of course, as much as that's humanly possible. A complex solution, as fast as it might be, is not a good solution. Bear in mind that our case is a simplistic scenario used for illustration purposes. Typical production queries involve several joins, more filters, and more logic. Adding such "tricks" would only add to the complexity of the queries.

In short, you shouldn't be satisfied with this solution, and you should keep looking for other alternatives.

And if you look hard enough, you will find this one (call it *set-based solution 4*):

```
SELECT shipperid
FROM dbo.Shippers AS S
WHERE NOT EXISTS
  (SELECT * FROM dbo.Orders AS O
   WHERE O.shipperid = S.shipperid
     AND O.orderdate >= '20010101')
  AND EXISTS
  (SELECT * FROM dbo.Orders AS O
   WHERE O.shipperid = S.shipperid);
```

This solution is natural. You query the Shippers table and filter shippers for whom you cannot find an order on or past '20010101' and for whom you can find at least one order.

You get the plan shown in Figure 3-66.

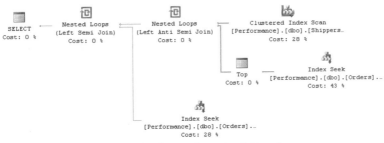

Figure 3-66   Execution plan for set-based solution 4

The Shippers table is scanned, yielding 12 rows. For each shipper, a Nested Loops operator invokes a seek against our covering index to check whether an *orderdate* of '20010101' or later exists for the shipper. If the answer is yes, another seek operation is invoked against the index to check whether an order exists at all. The I/O cost against the Orders table is 78 reads—slightly higher than the previous solution. However, in terms of simplicity and naturalness this solution wins big time! Therefore, I would stick to it.

As you probably realize, index tuning alone is not enough; there's much you can do with the way you write your queries. Being a "Matrix" fan, I'd like to believe that it's not the spoon that bends; it's only your mind.

Additional Resources

As promised, here is a list of resources where you can find more information about the subjects discussed in this chapter:

- Later in this book, you will find coverage of the querying techniques used in this chapter, including subqueries, table expressions and ranking functions, joins, aggregations, TOP, data modification, recursive queries, and others.

■ The *Inside Microsoft SQL Server 2005: T-SQL Programming* book focuses on areas related to T-SQL programming, some of which were touched on in this chapter, including datatypes, temporary tables, tempdb, row versioning, cursors, dynamic execution, T-SQL and CLR routines, compilations/recompilations, concurrency, and others.

■ The books *Inside Microsoft SQL Server 2005: The Storage Engine* and *Inside Microsoft SQL Server 2005: Query Tuning and Optimization*, both written by Kalen Delaney (Microsoft Press, 2006 and 2007), cover various internals-related subjects in great depth, including the storage engine, indexes, transaction log architecture, the query optimizer, concurrency, dynamic management objects, tracing and Profiler, and many others as well.

■ You can find more information about wait types and analyzing wait statistics at the following links:

  ❑ "Opening Microsoft's Performance-Tuning Toolbox" by Tom Davidson (*http://www.windowsitpro.com/Article/ArticleID/40925/40925.html*)

  ❑ Gert Drapers' Web site: SQLDev.Net (*http://www.sqldev.net/*)

■ You can find information about balanced trees at the following sources:

  ❑ *http://www.nist.gov/dads/HTML/balancedtree.html*

  ❑ *The Art of Computer Programming, Volume 3: Sorting and Searching* (2nd Edition) by Donald E. Knuth (Addison-Wesley Professional, 1998)

■ The following white papers elaborate on subjects touched on in this chapter:

  ❑ "Troubleshooting Performance Problems in SQL Server 2005," written by various authors (*http://www.microsoft.com/technet/prodtechnol/sql/2005/tsprfprb.mspx*)

  ❑ "Batch Compilation, Recompilation, and Plan Caching Issues in SQL Server 2005" by Arun Marathe (*http://www.microsoft.com/technet/prodtechnol/sql/2005/recomp.mspx*)

  ❑ "Statistics Used by the Query Optimizer in Microsoft SQL Server 2005" by Eric N. Hanson (*http://www.microsoft.com/technet/prodtechnol/sql/2005/qrystats.mspx*)

  ❑ "Forcing Query Plans with SQL Server 2005" by Burzin A. Patel (*http://download.microsoft.com/download/1/3/4/134644FD-05AD-4EE8-8B5A-0AED1C18A31E/Forcing_Query_Plans.doc*)

  ❑ "Improving Performance with SQL Server 2005 Indexed Views" by Eric Hanson (*http://www.microsoft.com/technet/prodtechnol/sql/2005/ipsql05iv.mspx*)

  ❑ "Database Concurrency and Row Level Versioning in SQL Server 2005" by Kalen Delaney and Fernando Guerrero (*http://www.microsoft.com/technet/prodtechnol/sql/2005/cncrrncy.mspx*)

- You can find a series of articles I wrote covering table and index partitioning at the *SQL Server Magazine* Web site (*http://www.sqlmag.com*). Look up the following instant document IDs: 45153, 45533, 45877, and 46207.

- You can find all resources related to this book at *http://www.insidetsql.com.*

Conclusion

This chapter covered a tuning methodology, index tuning, the importance of sample data, and query tuning by query revisions. There's so much involved in tuning that knowledge of the product's architecture and internals plays a big role in doing it well. But knowledge is not enough. I hope this chapter gave you the tools and guidance that will allow you to put your knowledge into action as you progress in these books—and, of course, in your production environments.

Chapter 4
Subqueries, Table Expressions, and Ranking Functions

This chapter essentially covers nesting of queries. Within an outer query, you can incorporate inner queries (also known as subqueries). You can use subqueries where a single value is expected (scalar subqueries)—for example, to the right of an equal sign in a logical expression. You can use them where multiple values are expected (multivalued subqueries)—for example, as input to the IN predicate. Or you can use them where a table is expected (table expressions)—for example, in the FROM clause of a query.

I'll refer to scalar and multivalued subqueries just as *subqueries*, and to subqueries that are used where a table is expected as *table expressions*. In this chapter, I'll cover the inline table expressions: derived tables and common table expressions (CTE).

In the last part of the chapter, I'll cover ranking calculations, including row number, rank, dense rank, and tiling. I found it appropriate to cover ranking calculations in this chapter because in Microsoft SQL Server 2000 you can use subqueries for these calculations. SQL Server 2005 introduces built-in ranking functions, which allow you to calculate these values much more simply and efficiently.

Because this book is intended for experienced programmers, I'm assuming that you're already familiar with subqueries and table expressions. I'll go over their definitions briefly, and focus on their applications and on problem solving.

Subqueries

Subqueries can be characterized in two main ways. One is by the expected number of values (either scalar or multivalued), and another is by the subquery's dependency on the outer query (either self-contained or correlated). Both scalar and multivalued subqueries can be either self-contained or correlated.

191

Self-Contained Subqueries

A self-contained subquery is a subquery that can be run independently of the outer query. Self-contained subqueries are very convenient to debug, of course, compared to correlated subqueries.

Scalar subqueries can appear anywhere in the query where an expression resulting in a scalar value is expected, while multivalued subqueries can appear anywhere in the query where a collection of multiple values is expected.

A scalar subquery is valid when it returns a single value, and also when it returns no values—in which case, the value of the subquery is NULL. However, if a scalar subquery returns more than one value, a run-time error will occur.

For example, run the following code three times: once as shown, a second time with LIKE *N'Kollar'* in place of LIKE *N'Davolio'*, and a third time with LIKE *N'D%*:

```
SET NOCOUNT ON;
USE Northwind;

SELECT OrderID
FROM dbo.Orders
WHERE EmployeeID =
  (SELECT EmployeeID FROM dbo.Employees
  -- also try with N'Kollar' and N'D%' in place of N'Davolio'
  WHERE LastName LIKE N'Davolio');
```

With *N'Davolio'*, the subquery returns a single value (1) and the outer query returns all orders with *EmployeeID* 1.

With *N'Kollar'*, the subquery returns no values, and is therefore NULL. The outer query obviously doesn't find any orders for which EmployeeID = NULL and therefore returns an empty set. Note that the query doesn't break (fail), as it's a valid query.

With *N'D%'*, the subquery returns two values (1, 9), and because the outer query expects a scalar, it breaks at run time and generates the following error:

```
Msg 512, Level 16, State 1, Line 1
Subquery returned more than 1 value. This is not permitted when the subquery follows =,
!=, <, <= , >, >= or when the subquery is used as an expression.
```

Logically, a self-contained subquery can be evaluated just once for the whole outer query. Physically, the optimizer can consider many different ways to achieve the same thing, so you shouldn't think in such strict terms.

Now that we've covered the essentials, let's move on to more sophisticated problems involving self-contained subqueries.

I'll start with a problem belonging to a group of problems called relational division. Relational division problems have many nuances and many practical applications. Logically, it's like dividing one set by another, producing a result set. For example, from the Northwind database, return all customers for whom every Northwind employee from the USA has handled at least one order. In this case, you're dividing the set of all orders by the set of all employees from the USA, and you expect the set of matching customers back. Filtering here is not that simple because for each customer you need to inspect multiple rows to figure out whether you have a match.

Here I'll show a technique using GROUP BY and DISTINCT COUNT to solve relational division problems. Later in the book, I'll show others as well.

If you knew ahead of time the list of all *EmployeeIDs* for USA employees, you could write the following query to solve the problem, generating the output shown in Table 4-1:

```
SELECT CustomerID
FROM dbo.Orders
WHERE EmployeeID IN(1, 2, 3, 4, 8)
GROUP BY CustomerID
HAVING COUNT(DISTINCT EmployeeID) = 5;
```

Table 4-1   Customers with Orders Handled by All Employees from the USA

CustomerID
BERGS
BONAP
ERNSH
FOLKO
HANAR
HILAA
HUNGO
ISLAT
KOENE
LAMAI
LILAS
LINOD
LONEP
MEREP
OLDWO
QUICK
RATTC
SAVEA
TORTU
VAFFE
VICTE
WARTH
WHITC

This query finds all orders with one of the five U.S. *EmployeeIDs*, groups those orders by *CustomerID*, and returns *CustomerIDs* that have (all) five distinct *EmployeeID* values in their group of orders.

To make the solution more dynamic and accommodate lists of *EmployeeIDs* that are unknown ahead of time and also large lists even when known, you can use subqueries instead of literals:

```
SELECT CustomerID
FROM dbo.Orders
WHERE EmployeeID IN
  (SELECT EmployeeID FROM dbo.Employees WHERE Country = N'USA')
GROUP BY CustomerID
HAVING COUNT(DISTINCT EmployeeID) =
  (SELECT COUNT(*) FROM dbo.Employees WHERE Country = N'USA');
```

Another problem involving self-contained subqueries is returning all orders placed on the last actual order date of the month. Note that the last actual order date of the month might be different than the last date of the month—for example, if a company doesn't place orders on weekends. So the last actual order date of the month has to be queried from the data. Here's the solution query producing the output (abbreviated) shown in Table 4-2:

```
SELECT OrderID, CustomerID, EmployeeID, OrderDate
FROM dbo.Orders
WHERE OrderDate IN
  (SELECT MAX(OrderDate)
   FROM dbo.Orders
   GROUP BY CONVERT(CHAR(6), OrderDate, 112));
```

Table 4-2   Orders Placed on the Last Actual Order Date of the Month

OrderID	CustomerID	EmployeeID	OrderDate
10461	LILAS	1	1997-02-28
10616	GREAL	1	1997-07-31
10916	RANCH	1	1998-02-27
11077	RATTC	1	1998-05-06
10368	ERNSH	2	1996-11-29
10553	WARTH	2	1997-05-30
10583	WARTH	2	1997-06-30
10686	PICCO	2	1997-09-30
10915	TORTU	2	1998-02-27
10989	QUEDE	2	1998-03-31
...			
11075	RICSU	8	1998-05-06
10687	HUNGO	9	1997-09-30

The self-contained subquery returns a list of values with the last actual order date of each month, as shown in Table 4-3.

Table 4-3   Last Actual Order Date of Each Month

MAX(OrderDate)
1997-04-30
1996-09-30
1996-10-31
1998-02-27
1997-06-30
1997-08-29
1997-03-31
1997-01-31
1997-09-30
1996-07-31
1997-02-28
1998-01-30
1997-11-28
1998-04-30
1997-05-30
1997-12-31
1998-05-06
1997-10-31
1996-11-29
1996-12-31
1996-08-30
1997-07-31
1998-03-31

The subquery achieves this result by grouping the orders by month and returning the *MAX(OrderDate)* for each group. I extracted the year-plus-month portion of *OrderDate* by converting it to *CHAR(6)* using the style 112 (ISO format 'YYYYMMDD'). Because the target string is shorter than the style's string length (6 characters instead of 8), the two right-most characters are truncated. You could obtain the same result by using *YEAR(OrderDate)*, *MONTH(OrderDate)* as the GROUP BY clause.

The outer query returns all orders with an *OrderDate* that appears in the list returned by the subquery.

Correlated Subqueries

Correlated subqueries are subqueries that have references to columns from the outer query. Logically, the subquery is evaluated once for each row of the outer query. Again, physically, it's a much more dynamic process and will vary from case to case. There isn't just one physical way to process a correlated subquery.

Tiebreaker

I'll start dealing with correlated subqueries through a problem that introduces a very important concept in SQL querying—a *tiebreaker*. I'll refer to this concept throughout the book. A tiebreaker is an attribute or attribute list that allows you to uniquely rank elements. For example, suppose you need the most recent order for each Northwind employee. You are supposed to return only one order for each employee, but the attributes *EmployeeID* and *OrderDate* do not necessarily identify a unique order. You need to introduce a tiebreaker to be able to identify a unique most recent order for each employee. For example, out of the multiple orders with the maximum *OrderDate* for an employee you could decide to return the one with the maximum *OrderID*. In this case, *MAX(OrderID)* is your tiebreaker. Or you could decide to return the row with the maximum *RequiredDate*, and if you still have multiple rows, return the one with the maximum *OrderID*. In this case, your tiebreaker is *MAX(RequiredDate)*, *MAX(OrderID)*. A tiebreaker is not necessarily limited to a single attribute.

Before moving on to the solutions, run the following code to create indexes that support the physical processing of the queries that will follow:

```
CREATE UNIQUE INDEX idx_eid_od_oid
  ON dbo.Orders(EmployeeID, OrderDate, OrderID);
CREATE UNIQUE INDEX idx_eid_od_rd_oid
  ON dbo.Orders(EmployeeID, OrderDate, RequiredDate, OrderID);
```

I'll explain the indexing guidelines after presenting the solution queries.

Let's start with the basic request to return the orders with the maximum *OrderDate* for each employee. Here you can get multiple rows for each employee because an employee can have multiple orders with the same order date.

You might be tempted to use this solution, which includes a self-contained subquery similar to the one used to return orders on the last actual order date of the month:

```
SELECT OrderID, CustomerID, EmployeeID, OrderDate, RequiredDate
FROM dbo.Orders
WHERE OrderDate IN
  (SELECT MAX(OrderDate) FROM dbo.Orders
   GROUP BY EmployeeID);
```

However, this solution is incorrect. The result set will include the correct orders (the ones with the maximum *OrderDate* for each employee). But you will also get any order for employee A with an *OrderDate* that happens to be the maximum for employee B, even though it's not also the maximum for employee A. This wasn't an issue with the previous problem, as an order date in month A can't be equal to the maximum order date of a different month B.

In our case, the subquery must be correlated to the outer query, matching the inner *EmployeeID* to the one in the outer row:

```
SELECT OrderID, CustomerID, EmployeeID, OrderDate, RequiredDate
FROM dbo.Orders AS O1
WHERE OrderDate =
  (SELECT MAX(OrderDate)
   FROM dbo.Orders AS O2
   WHERE O2.EmployeeID = O1.EmployeeID);
```

This query generates the correct results, shown in Table 4-4.

Table 4-4   Orders with the Maximum *OrderDate* for Each Employee

OrderID	CustomerID	EmployeeID	OrderDate	RequiredDate
11077	RATTC	1	1998-05-06	1998-06-03
11070	LEHMS	2	1998-05-05	1998-06-02
11073	PERIC	2	1998-05-05	1998-06-02
11063	HUNGO	3	1998-04-30	1998-05-28
11076	BONAP	4	1998-05-06	1998-06-03
11043	SPECD	5	1998-04-22	1998-05-20
11045	BOTTM	6	1998-04-23	1998-05-21
11074	SIMOB	7	1998-05-06	1998-06-03
11075	RICSU	8	1998-05-06	1998-06-03
11058	BLAUS	9	1998-04-29	1998-05-27

The output contains one example of multiple orders for an employee, in the case of employee 2. If you want to return only one row for each employee, you have to introduce a tiebreaker. For example, out of the multiple rows with the maximum *OrderDate*, return the one with the maximum *OrderID*. This can be achieved by adding another subquery that keeps the order only if *OrderID* is equal to the maximum among the orders with the same *EmployeeID* and *OrderDate* as in the outer row:

```
SELECT OrderID, CustomerID, EmployeeID, OrderDate, RequiredDate
FROM dbo.Orders AS O1
WHERE OrderDate =
  (SELECT MAX(OrderDate)
   FROM dbo.Orders AS O2
   WHERE O2.EmployeeID = O1.EmployeeID)
  AND OrderID =
  (SELECT MAX(OrderID)
   FROM dbo.Orders AS O2
   WHERE O2.EmployeeID = O1.EmployeeID
     AND O2.OrderDate = O1.OrderDate);
```

Notice in the output shown in Table 4-5, that of the two orders for employee 2 in the previous query's output, only the one with the maximum *OrderID* remains.

Table 4-5   Most Recent Order for Each Employee; Tiebreaker: *MAX(OrderID)*

OrderID	CustomerID	EmployeeID	OrderDate	RequiredDate
11077	RATTC	1	1998-05-06	1998-06-03
11073	PERIC	2	1998-05-05	1998-06-02
11063	HUNGO	3	1998-04-30	1998-05-28
11076	BONAP	4	1998-05-06	1998-06-03
11043	SPECD	5	1998-04-22	1998-05-20
11045	BOTTM	6	1998-04-23	1998-05-21
11074	SIMOB	7	1998-05-06	1998-06-03
11075	RICSU	8	1998-05-06	1998-06-03
11058	BLAUS	9	1998-04-29	1998-05-27

Instead of using two separate subqueries for the sort column (*OrderDate*) and the tiebreaker (*OrderID*), you can use nested subqueries:

```
SELECT OrderID, CustomerID, EmployeeID, OrderDate, RequiredDate
FROM dbo.Orders AS O1
WHERE OrderID =
  (SELECT MAX(OrderID)
   FROM dbo.Orders AS O2
   WHERE O2.EmployeeID = O1.EmployeeID
     AND O2.OrderDate =
       (SELECT MAX(OrderDate)
        FROM dbo.Orders AS O3
        WHERE O3.EmployeeID = O1.EmployeeID));
```

I compared the performance of the two and found it very similar, with a slight advantage to the latter. I find the nested approach more complex, so as long as there's no compelling performance benefit, I'd rather stick to the simpler approach. Simpler is easier to understand and maintain, and therefore less prone to errors.

Going back to the simpler approach, for each tiebreaker attribute you have, you need to add a subquery. Each such subquery must be correlated by the group column, sort column, and all preceding tiebreaker attributes. So, to use *MAX(RequiredDate), MAX(OrderID)* as the tiebreaker, you would write the following query:

```
SELECT OrderID, CustomerID, EmployeeID, OrderDate, RequiredDate
FROM dbo.Orders AS O1
WHERE OrderDate =
  (SELECT MAX(OrderDate)
   FROM dbo.Orders AS O2
   WHERE O2.EmployeeID = O1.EmployeeID)
  AND RequiredDate =
  (SELECT MAX(RequiredDate)
   FROM dbo.Orders AS O2
   WHERE O2.EmployeeID = O1.EmployeeID
     AND O2.OrderDate = O1.OrderDate)
```

```
AND OrderID =
(SELECT MAX(OrderID)
 FROM dbo.Orders AS O2
 WHERE O2.EmployeeID = O1.EmployeeID
   AND O2.OrderDate = O1.OrderDate
   AND O2.RequiredDate = O1.RequiredDate);
```

The indexing guideline for the tiebreaker queries above is to create an index on (*group_cols, sort_cols, tiebreaker_cols*). For example, when the tiebreaker is *MAX(OrderID)*, you want an index on (*EmployeeID, OrderDate, OrderID*). When the tiebreaker is *MAX(RequiredDate), MAX(OrderID)*, you want an index on (*EmployeeID, OrderDate, RequiredDate, OrderID*). Such an index would allow retrieving the relevant sort value or tiebreaker value for an employee using a seek operation within the index.

When you're done testing the tiebreaker solutions, run the following code to drop the indexes that were created just for these examples:

```
DROP INDEX dbo.Orders.idx_eid_od_oid;
DROP INDEX dbo.Orders.idx_eid_od_rd_oid;
```

I presented here only one approach to solving tiebreaker problems using ANSI correlated subqueries. This approach is neither the most efficient nor the simplest. You will find other solutions to tiebreaker problems in Chapter 6 in the "Tiebreakers" section, and in Chapter 7 in the "TOP *n* for Each Group" section.

EXISTS

EXISTS is a powerful predicate that allows you to efficiently check whether or not any rows result from a given query. The input to EXISTS is a subquery, which is typically but not necessarily correlated, and the predicate returns TRUE or FALSE, depending on whether the subquery returns at least one row or none. Unlike other predicates and logical expressions, EXISTS cannot return UNKNOWN. Either the input subquery returns rows or it doesn't. If the subquery's filter returns UNKNOWN for a certain row, the row is not returned. Remember that in a filter, UNKNOWN is treated like FALSE. In other words, when the input subquery has a filter, EXISTS will return TRUE only if the filter is TRUE for at least one row. The reason I'm stressing this subtle point will become apparent shortly.

First, let's look at an example that will demonstrate the use of EXISTS. The following query returns all customers from Spain that made orders, generating the output shown in Table 4-6:

```
SELECT CustomerID, CompanyName
FROM dbo.Customers AS C
WHERE Country = N'Spain'
  AND EXISTS
    (SELECT * FROM Orders AS O
     WHERE O.CustomerID = C.CustomerID);
```

Table 4-6 Customers from Spain that Made Orders

CustomerID	CompanyName
BOLID	Bólido Comidas preparadas
GALED	Galería del gastrónomo
GODOS	Godos Cocina Típica
ROMEY	Romero y tomillo

The outer query returns customers from Spain for whom the EXISTS predicate finds at least one order row in the Orders table with the same *CustomerID* as in the outer customer row.

> **Tip** The use of * here is perfectly safe, even though in general it's not a good practice. The optimizer ignores the SELECT list specified in the subquery because EXISTS cares only about the existence of rows and not about any specific attributes.

Examine the execution plan produced for this query, as shown in Figure 4-1.

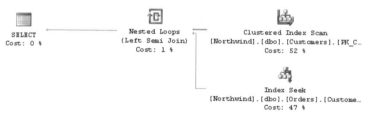

Figure 4-1 Execution plan for an EXISTS query

The plan scans the Customers table and filters customers from Spain. For each matching customer, the plan performs a seek within the index on *Orders.CustomerID* to check whether the Orders table contains an order with that customer's *CustomerID*. The index on the filtered column in the subquery (*Orders.CustomerID* in our case) is very helpful here, because it provides direct access to the rows of the Orders table with a given *CustomerID* value.

EXISTS vs. IN Programmers frequently wonder whether a query with the EXISTS predicate is more efficient than a logically equivalent query with the IN predicate. For example, the last query could be written using an IN predicate with a self-contained subquery as follows:

```
SELECT CustomerID, CompanyName
FROM dbo.Customers AS C
WHERE Country = N'Spain'
  AND CustomerID IN(SELECT CustomerID FROM dbo.Orders);
```

In versions prior to SQL Server 2000, I used to see differences between plans generated for EXISTS and for IN, and typically EXISTS performed better because of its inherent short-circuiting. However, in SQL Server 2000 and 2005 the optimizer usually generates identical plans for the two queries *when they are truly logically equivalent*, and this case qualifies.

The plan generated for the last query using IN is identical to the one shown in Figure 4-1, which was generated for the query using EXISTS.

If you're always thinking of the implications of three-valued logic, you might realize that there is a difference between IN and EXISTS. Unlike EXISTS, IN can in fact produce an UNKNOWN logical result when the input list contains a NULL. For example, *a IN(b, c, NULL)* is UNKNOWN. However, because UNKNOWN is treated like FALSE in a filter, the result of a query with the IN predicate is the same as with the EXISTS predicate, and the optimizer is aware of that, hence the identical plans.

NOT EXISTS vs. NOT IN   The logical difference between EXISTS and IN does show up if we compare NOT EXISTS and NOT IN, when the input list of NOT IN might contain a NULL.

For example, suppose you need to return customers from Spain who made no orders. Here's the solution using the NOT EXISTS predicate, which generates the output shown in Table 4-7:

```
SELECT CustomerID, CompanyName
FROM dbo.Customers AS C
WHERE Country = N'Spain'
  AND NOT EXISTS
    (SELECT * FROM Orders AS O
     WHERE O.CustomerID = C.CustomerID);
```

Table 4-7   Customers from Spain Who Made No Orders

CustomerID	CompanyName
FISSA	FISSA Fabrica Inter. Salchichas S.A.

Even if there is a NULL *CustomerID* in the Orders table, it is of no concern to us. You get all customers from Spain for which SQL Server cannot find even one row in the Orders table with the same *CustomerID*. The plan generated for this query is shown in Figure 4-2.

Figure 4-2   Execution plan for a NOT EXISTS query

The plan scans the Customers table and filters customers from Spain. For each matching customer, the plan performs a seek within the index on *Orders.CustomerID*. The *Top* operator appears because it's only necessary to see whether there's at least one matching order for the customer—that's the short-circuiting capability of EXISTS in action. This use of *Top* is particularly efficient when the *Orders.CustomerID* column has a high density (that is, a large number of duplicates). The seek takes place only once for each customer, and regardless of the number of orders the customer has, only one row is scanned at the leaf level (bottom level of the index) to look for a match, as opposed to all matching rows.

In this case, the following solution using the NOT IN predicate does yield the same output. It seems to have the same meaning, but we'll see later that it does not.

```
SELECT CustomerID, CompanyName
FROM dbo.Customers AS C
WHERE Country = N'Spain'
  AND CustomerID NOT IN(SELECT CustomerID FROM dbo.Orders);
```

If you examine the execution plan, shown in Figure 4-3, you will find that it's different from the one generated for the NOT EXISTS query.

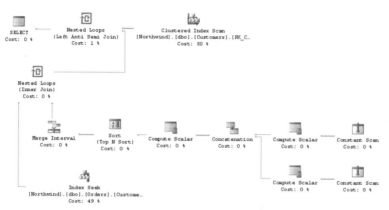

Figure 4-3   Execution plan for a NOT IN query

There are some additional operations at the beginning of this plan, compared to the previous plan—steps needed to look for NULL *CustomerIDs*. Why is this plan different than the one generated for the NOT EXISTS query? And why would SQL Server care particularly about the existence of NULLs in *Orders.CustomerID*?

The discrepancy between the plans doesn't affect the result because there's no row in the Orders table with a NULL *CustomerID*. However, because the *CustomerID* column allows NULLs, the optimizer must take this fact into consideration. Let's see what happens if we add a row with a NULL *CustomerID* to the Orders table:

```
INSERT INTO dbo.Orders DEFAULT VALUES;
```

Now rerun both the NOT EXISTS and NOT IN queries. You will find that the NOT EXISTS query still returns the same output as before, while the NOT IN query now returns an empty set. In fact, when there's a NULL in the *Orders.CustomerID* column, the NOT IN query will always return an empty set. The reason is that the predicate *val IN(val1, val2, ..., NULL)* can never return FALSE; rather, it can return only TRUE or UNKNOWN. As a result, *val **NOT** IN(val1, val2, ..., NULL)* can only return NOT TRUE or NOT UNKNOWN, neither of which is TRUE.

For example, suppose the customer list in this query is *(a, b, NULL)*. Customer *a* appears in the list, and therefore the predicate *a IN(a, b, NULL)* returns TRUE. The predicate *a NOT*

IN(a, b, NULL) returns NOT TRUE, or FALSE, and customer *a* is not returned by the query. Customer *c*, on the other hand, does *not* appear in the list *(a, b, NULL)*, but the logical result of *c IN(a, b, NULL)* is UNKNOWN, because of the NULL. The predicate *b NOT IN(a, b, NULL)* therefore returns NOT UNKNOWN, which equals UNKNOWN, and customer *c* is not returned by the query, either, even though *c* does not appear in the customer list. Whether or not a customer appears in the customer list, if the list contains NULL, the customer is not returned by the query. You realize that when NULLs are potentially involved (such as when the queried column allows NULLs), NOT EXISTS and NOT IN are not logically equivalent. This explains the discrepancy between the plans and the potential difference in results. To make the NOT IN query logically equivalent to the EXISTS query, declare the column as NOT NULL (if appropriate) or add a filter to the subquery to exclude NULLs:

```
SELECT CustomerID, CompanyName
FROM dbo.Customers AS C
WHERE Country = N'Spain'
  AND CustomerID NOT IN(SELECT CustomerID FROM dbo.Orders
                        WHERE CustomerID IS NOT NULL);
```

This query generates the same result as the NOT EXISTS query, as well as the same plan.

Once you're done testing the queries, make sure you remove the row with the NULL *CustomerID*:

```
DELETE FROM dbo.Orders WHERE CustomerID IS NULL;
```

Minimum Missing Value   To put your knowledge of the EXISTS predicate into action, try to solve the following problem. First create and populate the table T1 by running the code in Listing 4-1.

Listing 4-1   Creating and populating the table T1

```
USE tempdb;
GO
IF OBJECT_ID('dbo.T1') IS NOT NULL
  DROP TABLE dbo.T1;
GO

CREATE TABLE dbo.T1
(
  keycol  INT         NOT NULL PRIMARY KEY CHECK(keycol > 0),
  datacol VARCHAR(10) NOT NULL
);
INSERT INTO dbo.T1(keycol, datacol) VALUES(3, 'a');
INSERT INTO dbo.T1(keycol, datacol) VALUES(4, 'b');
INSERT INTO dbo.T1(keycol, datacol) VALUES(6, 'c');
INSERT INTO dbo.T1(keycol, datacol) VALUES(7, 'd');
```

Notice that *keycol* must be positive. Your task is to write a query that returns the lowest missing key, assuming that key values start at 1. For example, the table is currently populated with the keys 3, 4, 6, and 7, so your query should return the value 1. If you insert two more rows, with the keys 1 and 2, your query should return 5.

Solution:

Here's a suggested CASE expression (incomplete) that I used in my solution:

```
SELECT
  CASE
    WHEN NOT EXISTS(SELECT * FROM dbo.T1 WHERE keycol = 1) THEN 1
    ELSE (...subquery returning minimum missing value...)
  END;
```

If 1 doesn't exist in the table, the CASE expression returns 1; otherwise, it returns the result of a subquery returning the minimum missing value.

Here's the subquery that I used to return the minimum missing value:

```
SELECT MIN(A.keycol + 1) as missing
FROM dbo.T1 AS A
WHERE NOT EXISTS
  (SELECT * FROM dbo.T1 AS B
   WHERE B.keycol = A.keycol + 1);
```

The NOT EXISTS predicate returns TRUE only for values in T1 that are right before a gap (4 and 7 in our case). A value is right before a gap if the value plus one does not exist in the same table. The outer T1 table has the alias A, and the inner T1 table has the alias B. You could use the expression $B.keycol - 1 = A.keycol$ in the subquery's filter; although it might be a bit confusing to use such an expression when looking for a value in B that is greater than the value in A by one. If you think about it, for $B.keycol$ to be greater than $A.keycol$ by one, $B.keycol$ minus one must be equal to $A.keycol$. If this logic confuses you, you can use $B.keycol = A.keycol + 1$ instead, as I did. Once all points before gaps are isolated, the outer query returns the minimum plus one, which is the first missing value in the first gap. Make a mental note of the technique to identify a point before a gap, as it's a very handy key technique.

Now you can incorporate the query returning the minimum missing value in the CASE expression:

```
SELECT
  CASE
    WHEN NOT EXISTS(SELECT * FROM dbo.T1 WHERE keycol = 1) THEN 1
    ELSE (SELECT MIN(keycol + 1)
          FROM dbo.T1 AS A
          WHERE NOT EXISTS
            (SELECT *
             FROM dbo.T1 AS B
             WHERE B.keycol = A.keycol + 1))
  END;
```

If you run this query with the sample data inserted by Listing 4-1, you should get 1 as the result. If you then insert two more rows, with the keys 1 and 2 (as shown in the following code), and rerun the query, you should get 5 as the result.

```
INSERT INTO dbo.T1(keycol, datacol) VALUES(1, 'e');
INSERT INTO dbo.T1(keycol, datacol) VALUES(2, 'f');
```

Here is an example of how you might use the CASE expression for the minimum missing key in an INSERT ... SELECT statement, perhaps in a scenario where you needed to reuse deleted keys:

```
INSERT INTO dbo.T1(keycol, datacol)
  SELECT
    CASE
      WHEN NOT EXISTS(SELECT * FROM dbo.T1 WHERE keycol = 1) THEN 1
      ELSE (SELECT MIN(keycol + 1)
            FROM dbo.T1 AS A
            WHERE NOT EXISTS
              (SELECT *
               FROM dbo.T1 AS B
               WHERE B.keycol = A.keycol + 1))
    END,
    'f';
```

Query the T1 table after running this INSERT, and notice in the output shown in Table 4-8 that the insert generated the key value 5, which was the minimum missing key:

```
SELECT * FROM dbo.T1;
```

Table 4-8   Content of T1 after Insert

keycol	datacol
1	e
2	f
3	a
4	b
5	f
6	c
7	d

Note   Multiple processes running such code simultaneously might get the same key. You can overcome this issue by introducing error-handling code that traps a duplicate key error and then retries. There are other more efficient techniques to reuse deleted keys, but they are more complex and require you to maintain a table with ranges of missing values. Also note that reusing deleted keys is not often a good idea, for reasons beyond concurrency. Here I just wanted to give you a chance to practice with the EXISTS predicate.

Note that you can merge the two cases where 1 does exist in the table, and where 1 doesn't, instead of using a CASE expression. The solution requires some tricky logical manipulation:

```
SELECT COALESCE(MIN(keycol + 1), 1)
FROM dbo.T1 AS A
WHERE NOT EXISTS
  (SELECT * FROM dbo.T1 AS B
    WHERE B.keycol = A.keycol + 1)
  AND EXISTS(SELECT * FROM dbo.T1 WHERE keycol = 1);
```

The query has both logical expressions from the CASE expression in the WHERE clause. It returns the minimum missing value if 1 does exist in the table (that is, when the second EXISTS predicate is always TRUE). If 1 doesn't exist in the table (that is, the second EXISTS predicate is always FALSE), the filter generates an empty set and the expression *MIN(keycol)* + *1* yields a NULL. The value of the COALESCE expression is then 1.

Even though this solution achieves the request with a single query, I personally like the original solution better. This solution is a bit tricky and isn't as intuitive as the previous one, and simplicity and readability of code goes a long way.

Reverse Logic Applied to Relational Division Problems   Our minds are usually accustomed to think in positive terms. However, positive thinking in some cases can get you only so far. In many fields, including SQL programming, negative thinking or reverse logic can give you new insight or be used as another tool to solve problems. Applying reverse logic can in some cases lead to simpler or more efficient solutions than applying a positive approach. It's another tool in your toolbox.

Euclid, for example, was very fond of applying reverse logic in his mathematical proofs (proof by way of negation). He used reverse logic to prove that there's an infinite number of prime numbers. By contradicting a certain assumption, creating a paradox, you prove that the opposite must be true.

Before I demonstrate an application of reverse logic in SQL, I'd like to deliver the idea through an ancient puzzle. Two guards stand in front of two doors. One door leads to gold and treasures, and the other leads to sudden death, but you don't know which is which. One of the guards always tells the truth and the other always lies, but you don't know who the liar is and who's the sincere one (even though the guards do). Obviously, you want to enter the door that leads to the gold and not to sudden death. You have but one opportunity to ask one of the guards a question; what will the question be?

Any question that you ask applying positive thinking will not give you 100-percent assurance of picking the door that leads to the gold. However, applying reverse logic can give you that assurance.

Ask either guard, "If I ask the other guard where the door is that leads to the gold, which door would he point to?"

If you asked the sincere guard, he would point at the door that leads to sudden death, knowing that the other is a liar. If you asked the liar, he'd also point at the door that leads to sudden death, knowing that the other guard is sincere and would point to the door that leads to the gold. All you would have to do is enter the door that was not pointed at.

Reverse logic is sometimes a handy tool in solving problems with SQL. An example of where you can apply reverse logic is in solving relational division problems. At the beginning of the chapter, I discussed the following problem: from the Northwind database, return all customers with orders handled by all employees from the USA. I showed an example to solving the problem that used positive thinking. To apply reverse logic, you first need to be able to phrase the request in a negative way. Instead of saying, "Return customers for whom all USA employees handled orders," you can say, "Return customers for whom no USA employee handled no order." Remember that two negatives produce a positive. If for customer A you cannot find even one USA employee who did not handle any orders, then all USA employees must have handled orders for customer A.

Once you phrase the request in a negative way, the translation to SQL is intuitive using correlated subqueries:

```
SELECT * FROM dbo.Customers AS C
WHERE NOT EXISTS
  (SELECT * FROM dbo.Employees AS E
   WHERE Country = N'USA'
     AND NOT EXISTS
       (SELECT * FROM dbo.Orders AS O
        WHERE O.CustomerID = C.CustomerID
          AND O.EmployeeID = E.EmployeeID));
```

When you "read" the query, it really sounds like the English phrasing of the request:

```
Return customers
for whom you cannot find
  any employee
  from the USA
  for whom you cannot find
    any order
    placed for the subject customer
    and by the subject employee
```

You get the same 23 customers back as the ones shown in Table 4-1 returned by the query applying the positive approach. Notice, though, that the negative solution gives you access to all the customer attributes, while the positive solution gives you access only to the customer IDs. To access other customer attributes, you need to add a join between the result set and the Customers table.

When comparing the performance of the solutions in this case, the solution applying the positive approach performs better. In other cases, the negative approach might yield better performance. You now have another tool that you can use when solving problems.

Misbehaving Subqueries

There's a very tricky programming error involving subqueries that I've seen occasionally and have even had the misfortune to introduce into production code myself. I'll first describe the bug, and then make recommendations on what you can do to avoid it.

Suppose that you are asked to return the shippers from the Northwind database that did not ship orders to customer LAZYK. Examining the data, shipper 1 (Speedy Express) is the only one that qualifies. The following query is supposed to return the desired result:

```
SELECT ShipperID, CompanyName
FROM dbo.Shippers
WHERE ShipperID NOT IN
  (SELECT ShipperID FROM dbo.Orders
   WHERE CustomerID = N'LAZYK');
```

Surprisingly, this query returns an empty set. Can you tell why? Can you identify the elusive bug in my code?

Well, apparently the column in the Orders table holding the *ShipperID* is called *ShipVia* and not *ShipperID*. There is no *ShipperID* column in the Orders table. Realizing this, you'd probably expect the query to have failed because of the invalid column name. Sure enough, if you run only the part that was supposed to be a self-contained subquery, it does fail: Invalid column name 'ShipperID'. However, in the context of the outer query, apparently the subquery is valid! The name resolution process works from the inner nesting level outward. The query processor first looked for a *ShipperID* column in the Orders table, which is referenced in the current level. Not having found such a column name, it looked for one in the Shippers table—the outer level—and found it. Unintentionally, the subquery became correlated, as if it were written as the following illustrative code:

```
SELECT ShipperID, CompanyName
FROM dbo.Shippers AS S
WHERE ShipperID NOT IN
  (SELECT S.ShipperID FROM dbo.Orders AS O
   WHERE O.CustomerID = N'LAZYK');
```

Logically, the query doesn't make much sense of course; nevertheless, it is technically valid.

You can now understand why you got an empty set back. Unless there's no order for customer LAZYK anywhere in the Orders table, obviously shipper *n* is always going to be in the set (*SELECT n FROM dbo.Orders WHERE CustomerID = 'LAZYK'*). And the NOT IN predicate will always yield FALSE. This buggy query logically became a nonexistence query equivalent to the following illustrative code:

```
SELECT ShipperID, CompanyName
FROM dbo.Shippers
WHERE NOT EXISTS
  (SELECT * FROM dbo.Orders
   WHERE CustomerID = N'LAZYK');
```

To fix the problem, of course, you should use the correct name for the column from Orders that holds the *ShipperID–ShipVia*:

```
SELECT ShipperID, CompanyName
FROM dbo.Shippers AS S
WHERE ShipperID NOT IN
  (SELECT ShipVia FROM dbo.Orders AS O
   WHERE CustomerID = N'LAZYK');
```

This will generate the expected result shown in Table 4-9.

Table 4-9   Shippers that Did Not Ship Orders to Customer LAZYK

ShipperID	CompanyName
1	Speedy Express

However, to avoid such bugs in the future, it's a good practice to always include the table name or alias for all attributes in a subquery, even when the subquery is self-contained. Had I aliased the *ShipperID* column in the subquery (as shown in the following code), a name resolution error would have been generated and the bug would have been detected:

```
SELECT ShipperID, CompanyName
FROM dbo.Shippers AS S
WHERE ShipperID NOT IN
  (SELECT O.ShipperID FROM dbo.Orders AS O
   WHERE O.CustomerID = N'LAZYK');

Msg 207, Level 16, State 1, Line 4
Invalid column name 'ShipperID'
```

Finally, correcting the bug, here's how the solution query should look:

```
SELECT ShipperID, CompanyName
FROM dbo.Shippers AS S
WHERE ShipperID NOT IN
  (SELECT O.ShipVia FROM dbo.Orders AS O
   WHERE O.CustomerID = N'LAZYK');
```

Uncommon Predicates

In addition to IN and EXISTS, there are three more predicates in SQL, but they are rarely used: ANY, SOME, and ALL. You can consider them to be generalizations of the IN predicate. (ANY and SOME are synonyms, and there is no logical difference between them.)

An IN predicate is translated to a series of equality predicates separated by OR operators—for example, $v\ IN(x, y, z)$ is translated to $v = x\ OR\ v = y\ OR\ v = z$. ANY (or SOME) allows you to specify the comparison you want in each predicate, not limiting you to the equality operator. For example, $v <> ANY(x, y, z)$ is translated to $v <> x\ OR\ v <> y\ OR\ v <> z$.

ALL is similar, but it's translated to a series of logical expressions separated by AND operators. For example, $v <> ALL(x, y, z)$ is translated to $v <> x$ AND $v <> y$ AND $v <> z$.

> **Note**   IN allows as input either a list of literals or a subquery returning a single column. ANY/SOME and ALL support only a subquery as input. If you have the need to use these uncommon predicates with a list of literals as input, you must convert the list to a subquery. So, instead of $v <> ANY(x, y, z)$, you would use $v <> ANY(SELECT\ x\ UNION\ ALL\ SELECT\ y\ UNION\ ALL\ SELECT\ z)$.

To demonstrate the use of these uncommon predicates, let's suppose you were asked to return, for each employee, the order with the minimum *OrderID*. Here's how you can achieve this with the ANY operator, which would generate the result shown in Table 4-10:

```
SELECT OrderID, CustomerID, EmployeeID, OrderDate
FROM dbo.Orders AS O1
WHERE NOT OrderID >
  ANY(SELECT OrderID
       FROM dbo.Orders AS O2
       WHERE O2.EmployeeID = O1.EmployeeID);
```

Table 4-10   Row with the Minimum *OrderID* for Each Employee

OrderID	CustomerID	EmployeeID	OrderDate
10248	VINET	5	1996-07-04
10249	TOMSP	6	1996-07-05
10250	HANAR	4	1996-07-08
10251	VICTE	3	1996-07-08
10255	RICSU	9	1996-07-12
10258	ERNSH	1	1996-07-17
10262	RATTC	8	1996-07-22
10265	BLONP	2	1996-07-25
10289	BSBEV	7	1996-08-26

A row has the minimum *OrderID* for an employee if its *OrderID* is not greater than any *OrderID* for the same employee.

You can also write a query using ALL to achieve the same thing:

```
SELECT OrderID, CustomerID, EmployeeID, OrderDate
FROM dbo.Orders AS O1
WHERE OrderID <=
  ALL(SELECT OrderID
       FROM dbo.Orders AS O2
       WHERE O2.EmployeeID = O1.EmployeeID);
```

A row has the minimum *OrderID* for an employee if its *OrderID* is less than or equal to all *OrderID*s for the same employee.

None of the solutions above would fall into the category of intuitive solutions, and maybe this can explain why these predicates are not commonly used. The natural way to write the solution query would probably be as follows:

```
SELECT OrderID, CustomerID, EmployeeID, OrderDate
FROM dbo.Orders AS O1
WHERE OrderID =
  (SELECT MIN(OrderID)
   FROM dbo.Orders AS O2
   WHERE O2.EmployeeID = O1.EmployeeID);
```

Table Expressions

So far, I've covered scalar and multi-valued subqueries. This section deals with table subqueries, which are known as *Table Expressions*. In this chapter, I'll discuss derived tables and the new common table expressions (CTE).

> **More Info**   For information about the two other types of table expressions—views and user-defined functions (UDF)—please refer to *Inside Microsoft SQL Server 2005: T-SQL Programming* (Microsoft Press, 2006).

Derived Tables

A derived table is a table expression—that is, a virtual result table derived from a query expression. A derived table appears in the FROM clause of a query like any other table. The scope of existence of a derived table is the outer query's scope only.

The general form in which a derived table is used is as follows:

```
FROM (derived_table_query expression) AS derived_table_alias
```

> **Note**   A derived table is completely virtual. It's not physically materialized, nor does the optimizer generate a separate plan for it. The outer query and the inner one are merged, and one plan is generated. You shouldn't have any special concerns regarding performance when using derived tables. Merely using derived tables neither degrades nor improves performance. Their use is more a matter of simplification and clarity of code.

A derived table must be a valid table; therefore, it must follow several rules:

- All columns must have names.
- The column names must be unique.
- ORDER BY is not allowed (unless TOP is also specified).

> **Note** Unlike scalar and multivalued subqueries, derived tables cannot be correlated; they must be self-contained. There's an exception to this rule when using the new APPLY operator, which I'll cover in Chapter 7.

Result Column Aliases

One of the uses of derived tables is to enable the reuse of column aliases when expressions are so long you'd rather not repeat them. For simplicity's sake, I'll demonstrate column alias reuse with short expressions.

Remember from Chapter 1 that aliases created in the query's SELECT list cannot be used in most of the query elements. The reason for this is that the SELECT clause is logically processed almost last, just before the ORDER BY clause. For this reason, the following illustrative query fails:

```
SELECT
  YEAR(OrderDate) AS OrderYear,
  COUNT(DISTINCT CustomerID) AS NumCusts
FROM dbo.Orders
GROUP BY OrderYear;
```

The GROUP BY clause is logically processed before the SELECT clause, so at the GROUP BY phase, the *OrderYear* alias has not yet been created.

By using a derived table that contains only the SELECT and FROM elements of the original query, you can create aliases and make them available to the outer query in any element.

There are two formats of aliasing the derived table's result columns. One is inline column aliasing:

```
SELECT OrderYear, COUNT(DISTINCT CustomerID) AS NumCusts
FROM (SELECT YEAR(OrderDate) AS OrderYear, CustomerID
      FROM dbo.Orders) AS D
GROUP BY OrderYear;
```

And the other is external column aliasing following the derived table's alias:

```
SELECT OrderYear, COUNT(DISTINCT CustomerID) AS NumCusts
FROM (SELECT YEAR(OrderDate), CustomerID
      FROM dbo.Orders) AS D(OrderYear, CustomerID)
GROUP BY OrderYear;
```

These days, I typically use inline column aliasing, as I find it much more practical. You don't have to specify aliases for base columns, and it's much more convenient to troubleshoot. When you highlight and run only the derived table query, the result set you get includes all result column names. Also, it's clear which column alias belongs to which expression.

The external column aliasing format lacks all the aforementioned benefits. I can't think of even one advantage it has. Because external column aliasing is not common knowledge among SQL programmers, you might find it kind of cool, as using it could demonstrate a higher level of mastery of SQL. I know I did at some stage. Of course, it's not as noble a guideline as clarity of code and ease of troubleshooting and maintenance.

Using Arguments

Even though a derived table query cannot be correlated, it can refer to variables defined in the same batch. For example, the following code returns for each year the number of customers handled by employee 3, and it generates the output shown in Table 4-11:

```
DECLARE @EmpID AS INT;
SET @EmpID = 3;

SELECT OrderYear, COUNT(DISTINCT CustomerID) AS NumCusts
FROM (SELECT YEAR(OrderDate) AS OrderYear, CustomerID
      FROM dbo.Orders
      WHERE EmployeeID = @EmpID) AS D
GROUP BY OrderYear;
```

Table 4-11   **Yearly Count of Customers Handled by Employee 3**

OrderYear	NumCusts
1996	16
1997	46
1998	30

Nesting

Derived tables can be nested. Logical processing in a case of nested derived tables starts at the innermost level and proceeds outward.

The following query (which produces the output shown in Table 4-12) returns the order year and the number of customers for years with more than 70 active customers:

```
SELECT OrderYear, NumCusts
FROM (SELECT OrderYear, COUNT(DISTINCT CustomerID) AS NumCusts
      FROM (SELECT YEAR(OrderDate) AS OrderYear, CustomerID
            FROM dbo.Orders) AS D1
      GROUP BY OrderYear) AS D2
WHERE NumCusts > 70;
```

Table 4-12   **Order Year and Number of Customers for Years with More than 70 Active Customers**

OrderYear	NumCusts
1997	86
1998	81

Multiple References

Out of all the types of table expressions available in T-SQL, derived tables are the only type that suffers from a certain limitation related to multiple references. You can't refer to the same derived table multiple times in the same query. For example, suppose you want to compare each year's number of active customers to the previous year's. You want to join two instances of a derived table that contains the yearly aggregates. In such a case, unfortunately, you have to create two derived tables, each repeating the same derived table query:

```
SELECT Cur.OrderYear,
  Cur.NumCusts AS CurNumCusts, Prv.NumCusts AS PrvNumCusts,
  Cur.NumCusts - Prv.NumCusts AS Growth
FROM (SELECT YEAR(OrderDate) AS OrderYear,
        COUNT(DISTINCT CustomerID) AS NumCusts
      FROM dbo.Orders
      GROUP BY YEAR(OrderDate)) AS Cur
  LEFT OUTER JOIN
    (SELECT YEAR(OrderDate) AS OrderYear,
        COUNT(DISTINCT CustomerID) AS NumCusts
      FROM dbo.Orders
      GROUP BY YEAR(OrderDate)) AS Prv
  ON Cur.OrderYear = Prv.OrderYear + 1;
```

The output of this query is shown in Table 4-13.

Table 4-13 Comparing Current Year to Previous Year's Number of Customers

OrderYear	CurNumCusts	PrvNumCusts	Growth
1996	67	NULL	NULL
1997	86	67	19
1998	81	86	−5

Common Table Expressions (CTE)

A common table expression (CTE) is a new type of table expression introduced in SQL Server 2005. As for the standard, CTEs were introduced in the ANSI SQL:1999 specification. In many aspects, you will find CTEs very similar to derived tables. However, CTEs have several important advantages, which I'll describe in this section.

Remember that a derived table appears in its entirety in the FROM clause of an outer query. A CTE, however, is defined first using a WITH statement, and an outer query referring to the CTE's name follows the CTE's definition:

```
WITH cte_name
AS
(
  cte_query
)
outer_query_referring to_cte_name;
```

> **Note**   Because the WITH keyword is used in T-SQL for other purposes as well, to avoid
> ambiguity, the statement preceding the CTE's WITH clause must be terminated with a semi-
> colon. The use of a semicolon to terminate statements is supported by ANSI. It's a good
> practice, and you should start getting used to it even where T-SQL currently doesn't require it.

A CTE's scope of existence is the outer query's scope. It's not visible to other statements in the same batch.

The same rules I mentioned for the validity of a derived table's query expression apply to the CTE's as well. That is, the query must generate a valid table, so all columns must have names, all column names must be unique, and ORDER BY is not allowed (unless TOP is also specified).

Next, I'll go over aspects of CTEs, demonstrating their syntax and capabilities, and compare them to derived tables.

Result Column Aliases

Just as you can with derived tables, you can provide aliases to result columns either inline in the CTE's query or externally in parentheses following the CTE's name. The following code illustrates the first method:

```
WITH C AS
(
  SELECT YEAR(OrderDate) AS OrderYear, CustomerID
  FROM dbo.Orders
)
SELECT OrderYear, COUNT(DISTINCT CustomerID) AS NumCusts
FROM C
GROUP BY OrderYear;
```

The next bit of code illustrates how to provide aliases externally in parentheses following the CTE's name:

```
WITH C(OrderYear, CustomerID) AS
(
  SELECT YEAR(OrderDate), CustomerID
  FROM dbo.Orders
)
SELECT OrderYear, COUNT(DISTINCT CustomerID) AS NumCusts
FROM C
GROUP BY OrderYear;
```

Using Arguments

Another similarity between CTEs and derived tables is that CTEs can refer to variables declared in the same batch:

```
DECLARE @EmpID AS INT;
SET @EmpID = 3;
```

```
WITH C AS
(
  SELECT YEAR(OrderDate) AS OrderYear, CustomerID
  FROM dbo.Orders
  WHERE EmployeeID = @EmpID
)
SELECT OrderYear, COUNT(DISTINCT CustomerID) AS NumCusts
FROM C
GROUP BY OrderYear;
```

Multiple CTEs

Unlike derived tables, CTEs cannot be nested directly. That is, you cannot define a CTE within another CTE. However, you can define multiple CTEs using the same WITH statement, each of which can refer to the preceding CTEs. The outer query has access to all the CTEs. Using this capability, you can achieve the same result you would by nesting derived tables. For example, the following WITH statement defines two CTEs:

```
WITH C1 AS
(
  SELECT YEAR(OrderDate) AS OrderYear, CustomerID
  FROM dbo.Orders
),
C2 AS
(
  SELECT OrderYear, COUNT(DISTINCT CustomerID) AS NumCusts
  FROM C1
  GROUP BY OrderYear
)
SELECT OrderYear, NumCusts
FROM C2
WHERE NumCusts > 70;
```

C1 returns order years and customer IDs for each order, generating the *OrderYear* alias for the order year. C2 groups the rows returned from C1 by *OrderYear* and calculates the count of distinct *CustomerID*s (number of active customers). Finally, the outer query returns only order years with more than 70 active customers.

Multiple References

One of the advantages CTEs have over derived tables is that you can refer to the same CTE name multiple times in the outer query. You don't need to repeat the same CTE definition like you do with derived tables. For example, the following code demonstrates a CTE solution for the request to compare each year's number of active customers to the previous year's number:

```
WITH YearlyCount AS
(
  SELECT YEAR(OrderDate) AS OrderYear,
    COUNT(DISTINCT CustomerID) AS NumCusts
  FROM dbo.Orders
  GROUP BY YEAR(OrderDate)
)
```

```
SELECT Cur.OrderYear,
  Cur.NumCusts AS CurNumCusts, Prv.NumCusts AS PrvNumCusts,
  Cur.NumCusts - Prv.NumCusts AS Growth
FROM YearlyCount AS Cur
  LEFT OUTER JOIN YearlyCount AS Prv
    ON Cur.OrderYear = Prv.OrderYear + 1;
```

You can see that the outer query refers to the *YearlyCount* CTE twice—once representing the current year (*Cur*), and once representing the previous year (*Prv*).

Modifying Data

You can modify data through CTEs. To demonstrate this capability, first run the code in Listing 4-2 to create and populate the dbo.CustomersDups table with sample data.

Listing 4-2   Creating and populating the CustomersDups table

```
IF OBJECT_ID('dbo.CustomersDups') IS NOT NULL
  DROP TABLE dbo.CustomersDups;
GO

WITH CrossCustomers AS
(
  SELECT 1 AS c, C1.*
  FROM dbo.Customers AS C1, dbo.Customers AS C2
)
SELECT ROW_NUMBER() OVER(ORDER BY c) AS KeyCol,
  CustomerID, CompanyName, ContactName, ContactTitle, Address,
  City, Region, PostalCode, Country, Phone, Fax
INTO dbo.CustomersDups
FROM CrossCustomers;

CREATE UNIQUE INDEX idx_CustomerID_KeyCol
  ON dbo.CustomersDups(CustomerID, KeyCol);
```

Note that I used a new function called ROW_NUMBER here to create sequential integers that will be used as unique keys. In SQL Server 2000, you can achieve this by using the IDENTITY function in the SELECT INTO statement. I'll discuss this function in detail later in this chapter.

Basically, the code in Listing 4-2 creates a table of customers with a lot of duplicate occurrences of each customer. The following code demonstrates how you can remove duplicate customers using a CTE.

```
WITH JustDups AS
(
  SELECT * FROM dbo.CustomersDups AS C1
  WHERE KeyCol <
    (SELECT MAX(KeyCol) FROM dbo.CustomersDups AS C2
     WHERE C2.CustomerID = C1.CustomerID)
)
DELETE FROM JustDups;
```

The CTE *JustDups* has all duplicate rows for each customer, not including the row where *KeyCol* is the maximum for the customer. Notice that the code in Listing 4-2 creates an index on (*CustomerID*, *KeyCol*) to support the filter. The outer query merely deletes all rows from *JustDups*. After this code is run, the CustomersDups table contains only unique rows. At this point, you can create a primary key or a unique constraint on the *CustomerID* column to avoid duplicates in the future.

Container Objects

CTEs can be used in container objects such as views and inline UDFs. This capability provides encapsulation, which is important for modular programming. Also, I mentioned earlier that CTEs cannot be nested directly. However, you can nest CTEs indirectly by encapsulating a CTE in a container object and querying the container object from an outer CTE.

Using CTEs in views or inline UDFs is very trivial. The following example creates a view returning a yearly count of customers:

```
CREATE VIEW dbo.VYearCnt
AS
WITH YearCnt AS
(
  SELECT YEAR(OrderDate) AS OrderYear,
    COUNT(DISTINCT CustomerID) AS NumCusts
  FROM dbo.Orders
  GROUP BY YEAR(OrderDate)
)
SELECT * FROM YearCnt;
GO
```

Querying the view, as shown in the following code, returns the output shown in Table 4-14:

```
SELECT * FROM dbo.VYearCnt;
```

Table 4-14 Yearly Count of Customers

OrderYear	NumCusts
1996	67
1997	86
1998	81

If you want to pass an input argument to the container object—for example, return the yearly count of customers for the given employee—you'd create an inline UDF as follows:

```
CREATE FUNCTION dbo.fn_EmpYearCnt(@EmpID AS INT) RETURNS TABLE
AS
RETURN
  WITH EmpYearCnt AS
  (
    SELECT YEAR(OrderDate) AS OrderYear,
      COUNT(DISTINCT CustomerID) AS NumCusts
```

```
    FROM dbo.Orders
    WHERE EmployeeID = @EmpID
    GROUP BY YEAR(OrderDate)
  )
  SELECT * FROM EmpYearCnt;
GO
```

Querying the UDF and providing employee ID 3 as input returns the output shown in Table 4-15:

```
SELECT * FROM dbo.fn_EmpYearCnt(3);
```

Table 4-15   Yearly Count of Customers

OrderYear	NumCusts
1996	16
1997	46
1998	30

Recursive CTEs

Recursive CTEs represent one of the most significant T-SQL enhancements in SQL Server 2005. Finally, SQL Server supports recursive querying capabilities with pure set-based queries. The types of tasks and activities that can benefit from recursive queries include manipulation of graphs, trees, hierarchies, and many others. Here I'll just introduce you to recursive CTEs. For more information and detailed applications, you can find extensive coverage in Chapter 9.

I'll describe a recursive CTE using an example. You're given an input *EmployeeID* (for example, employee 5) from the Employees table in the Northwind database. You're supposed to return the input employee and subordinate employees in all levels, based on the hierarchical relationships maintained by the *EmployeeID* and *ReportsTo* attributes. The attributes you need to return for each employee include: *EmployeeID*, *ReportsTo*, *FirstName*, and *LastName*.

Before I demonstrate and explain the recursive CTE's code, I'll create the following covering index, which is optimal for the task:

```
CREATE UNIQUE INDEX idx_mgr_emp_ifname_ilname
  ON dbo.Employees(ReportsTo, EmployeeID)
  INCLUDE(FirstName, LastName);
```

This index will allow fetching direct subordinates of each manager by using a single seek plus a partial scan. Note the included columns (*FirstName* and *LastName*) that were added for covering purposes.

Here's the recursive CTE code that will return the desired result, which is shown in Table 4-16:

```
WITH EmpsCTE AS
(
  SELECT EmployeeID, ReportsTo, FirstName, LastName
  FROM dbo.Employees
  WHERE EmployeeID = 5
```

```
    UNION ALL

    SELECT EMP.EmployeeID, EMP.ReportsTo, EMP.FirstName, EMP.LastName
    FROM EmpsCTE AS MGR
      JOIN dbo.Employees AS EMP
        ON EMP.ReportsTo = MGR.EmployeeID
)
SELECT * FROM EmpsCTE;
```

Table 4-16   Subordinates of Employee 5

EmployeeID	ReportsTo	FirstName	LastName
5	2	Steven	Buchanan
6	5	Michael	Suyama
7	5	Robert	King
9	5	Anne	Dodsworth

A recursive CTE contains at minimum two queries (also known as *members*). The first query that appears in the preceding CTE's body is known as the *Anchor Member*. The anchor member is merely a query that returns a valid table and is used as the basis or anchor for the recursion. In our case, the anchor member simply returns the row for the input root employee (employee 5). The second query that appears in the preceding CTE's body is known as the *Recursive Member*. What makes the query a recursive member is a recursive reference to the CTE's name—EmpsCTE. Note that this reference is not the same as the reference to the CTE's name in the outer query. The reference in the outer query gets the final result table returned by the CTE, and it involves no recursion. However, the inner reference is made before the CTE's result table is finalized, and it is the key element that triggers the recursion. This inner reference to the CTE's name stands for "the previous result set," loosely speaking. In the first invocation of the recursive member, the reference to the CTE's name represents the result set returned from the anchor member. In our case, the recursive member returns subordinates of the employees returned in the previous result set—in other words, the next level of employees.

There's no explicit termination check for the recursion; rather, recursion stops as soon as the recursive member returns an empty set. Because the first invocation of the recursive member yielded a nonempty set (employees 6, 7, and 9), it is invoked again. The second time the recursive member is invoked, the reference to the CTE's name represents the result set returned by the previous invocation of the recursive member (employees 6, 7, and 9). Because these employees have no subordinates, the second invocation of the recursive member yields an empty set, and recursion stops.

The reference to the CTE's name in the outer query stands for the unified (concatenated) results sets of the invocation of the anchor member and all the invocations of the recursive member.

If you run the same code providing employee 2 as input instead of employee 5, you will get the result shown in Table 4-17.

Table 4-17   Subordinates of Employee 2

EmployeeID	ReportsTo	FirstName	LastName
2	NULL	Andrew	Fuller
1	2	Nancy	Davolio
3	2	Janet	Leverling
4	2	Margaret	Peacock
5	2	Steven	Buchanan
8	2	Laura	Callahan
6	5	Michael	Suyama
7	5	Robert	King
9	5	Anne	Dodsworth

Here, the anchor member returns the row for employee 2. The first invocation of the recursive member returns direct subordinates of employee 2: employees 1, 3, 4, 5, and 8. The second invocation of the recursive member returns direct subordinates of employees 1, 3, 4, 5, and 8: employees 6, 7, and 9. The third invocation of the recursive member returns an empty set, and recursion stops. The outer query returns the unified result sets with the rows for employees: 2, 1, 3, 4, 5, 8, 6, 7, and 9.

If you suspect that your data might contain cycles, you can specify the MAXRECURSION hint as a safety measure to limit the number of invocations of the recursive member. You specify the hint right after the outer query:

```
WITH cte_name AS (cte_body) outer_query OPTION(MAXRECURSION n);
```

In this line of code, n is the limit for the number of recursive iterations. As soon as the limit is exceeded, the query breaks and an error is generated. Note that MAXRECURSION is set to 100 by default. If you want to remove this limit, specify MAXRECURSION 0. This setting can be specified at the query level only; there's no session, database, or server-level option that you can set to change the default.

To understand how SQL Server processes the recursive CTE, examine the execution plan in Figure 4-4, which was produced for the earlier query returning subordinates of employee 5.

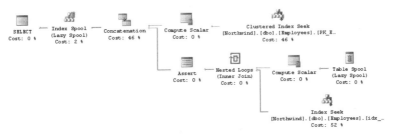

Figure 4-4   Execution plan for recursive CTE

As you can see in the plan, the result set of the anchor member (the row for employee 5) is retrieved using a clustered index seek operation (on the *EmployeeID* column). The *Compute Scalar* operator calculates an iteration counter, which is set to 0 initially (at the first occurrence of *Compute Scalar* in the plan) and incremented by one with each iteration of the recursive member (the second occurrence of *Compute Scalar* in the plan).

Each interim set generated by both the anchor member and the recursive member is spooled in a hidden temporary table (the *Table Spool* operator).

You can also notice later in the plan that a temporary index is created (indicated by the *Index Spool* operator). The index is created on the iteration counter plus the attributes retrieved (*EmployeeID*, *ReportsTo*, *FirstName*, *LastName*).

The interim set of each invocation of the recursive member is retrieved using index seek operations in the covering index I created for the query. The *Nested Loops* operator invokes a seek for each manager returned and spooled in the previous level, to fetch its direct subordinates.

The *Assert* operator checks whether the iteration counter exceeds 100 (the default MAXRE-CURSION limit). This is the operator in charge of breaking the query in case the number of recursive member invocations exceeds the MAXRECURSION limit.

The *Concatenation* operator concatenates (unifies) all interim result sets.

When you're done testing and experimenting with the recursive CTE, drop the index created for this purpose:

```
DROP INDEX dbo.Employees.idx_mgr_emp_ifname_ilname;
```

Analytical Ranking Functions

SQL Server 2005 introduces four new analytical ranking functions: ROW_NUMBER, RANK, DENSE_RANK, and NTILE. These functions provide a simple and highly efficient way to produce ranking calculations.

ROW_NUMBER is by far my favorite enhancement in SQL Server 2005. Even though it might not seem that significant on the surface compared to other enhancements (for example, recursive queries), it has an amazing number of practical applications that extend far beyond classic ranking and scoring calculations. I have been able to optimize many solutions by using the ROW_NUMBER function, as I will demonstrate throughout the book.

Even though the other ranking functions are technically calculated similarly to ROW_NUMBER underneath the covers, they have far fewer practical applications. RANK and DENSE_RANK are mainly used for ranking and scoring purposes. NTILE is used for more analytical purposes.

The need for such calculations has always existed, but the techniques to achieve them suffered from one or more limitations—they were dramatically slow, complex, or nonstandard. Because this book is intended for both SQL Server 2000 and 2005 users, I'll present the techniques for each version. Because all ranking functions are technically calculated underneath the covers in similar ways, I'll spend most of this section's space on row numbers and follow mainly with the logical aspects of the other functions. After covering the techniques for calculating row numbers, I'll present a benchmark that compares their performance with different table sizes. In my examples, I'll use a Sales table, which you should create and populate by running the code in Listing 4-3.

Listing 4-3   Creating and populating the Sales table

```
SET NOCOUNT ON;
USE tempdb;
GO
IF OBJECT_ID('dbo.Sales') IS NOT NULL
  DROP TABLE dbo.Sales;
GO

CREATE TABLE dbo.Sales
(
  empid VARCHAR(10) NOT NULL PRIMARY KEY,
  mgrid VARCHAR(10) NOT NULL,
  qty   INT         NOT NULL
);

INSERT INTO dbo.Sales(empid, mgrid, qty) VALUES('A', 'Z', 300);
INSERT INTO dbo.Sales(empid, mgrid, qty) VALUES('B', 'X', 100);
INSERT INTO dbo.Sales(empid, mgrid, qty) VALUES('C', 'X', 200);
INSERT INTO dbo.Sales(empid, mgrid, qty) VALUES('D', 'Y', 200);
INSERT INTO dbo.Sales(empid, mgrid, qty) VALUES('E', 'Z', 250);
INSERT INTO dbo.Sales(empid, mgrid, qty) VALUES('F', 'Z', 300);
INSERT INTO dbo.Sales(empid, mgrid, qty) VALUES('G', 'X', 100);
INSERT INTO dbo.Sales(empid, mgrid, qty) VALUES('H', 'Y', 150);
INSERT INTO dbo.Sales(empid, mgrid, qty) VALUES('I', 'X', 250);
INSERT INTO dbo.Sales(empid, mgrid, qty) VALUES('J', 'Z', 100);
INSERT INTO dbo.Sales(empid, mgrid, qty) VALUES('K', 'Y', 200);

CREATE INDEX idx_qty_empid ON dbo.Sales(qty, empid);
CREATE INDEX idx_mgrid_qty_empid ON dbo.Sales(mgrid, qty, empid);
```

The content of the Sales table returned by the following query is shown in Table 4-18:

```
SELECT * FROM dbo.Sales;
```

Table 4-18   Content of Sales Table

empid	mgrid	qty
A	Z	300
B	X	100
C	X	200
D	Y	200
E	Z	250
F	Z	300

Table 4-18   Content of Sales Table

empid	mgrid	qty
G	X	100
H	Y	150
I	X	250
J	Z	100
K	Y	200

The SQL Server 2005 ranking functions can appear only in the SELECT and ORDER BY clauses of a query. The general form of a ranking function is as follows:

```
ranking_function OVER([PARTITION BY col_list] ORDER BY col_list)
```

The optional PARTITION BY clause allows you to request that the ranking values will be calculated for each partition (or group) of rows separately. For example, if you specify *mgrid* in the PARTITION BY clause, the ranking values will be calculated independently for each manager's rows. In the ORDER BY clause, you specify the column list that determines the order of assignment of the ranking values.

The optimal index for ranking calculations (regardless of the method you use) is one created on *partitioning_columns*, *sort_columns*, *covered_cols*. I created optimal indexes on the Sales table for several ranking calculation requests.

Row Number

Row numbers are sequential integers assigned to rows of a query's result set based on a specified ordering. In the following sections, I'll describe the tools and techniques to calculate row numbers in both SQL Server 2005 and in earlier versions.

The ROW_NUMBER Function in SQL Server 2005

The ROW_NUMBER function assigns sequential integers to rows of a query's result set based on a specified order, optionally within partitions. For example, the following query (which produces the output shown in Table 4-19) returns employee sales rows and assigns row numbers in order of *qty*:

```
SELECT empid, qty,
  ROW_NUMBER() OVER(ORDER BY qty) AS rownum
FROM dbo.Sales
ORDER BY qty;
```

Table 4-19   Row Numbers in Order of *qty*

empid	qty	rownum
B	100	1
G	100	2
J	100	3

Table 4-19   Row Numbers in Order of *qty*

empid	qty	rownum
H	150	4
K	200	5
C	200	6
D	200	7
E	250	8
I	250	9
F	300	10
A	300	11

To understand the efficiency of the ranking functions in SQL Server 2005, examine the execution plan shown in Figure 4-5, which was generated for this query.

Figure 4-5   Execution plan for ROW_NUMBER

To calculate ranking values, the optimizer needs the data to be sorted first on the partitioning column or columns and then on the sort column or columns.

If you have an index that already maintains the data in the required order, the leaf level of the index is simply scanned in an ordered fashion (as in our case). Otherwise, the data will be scanned and then sorted with a sort operator. The *Sequence Project* operator is the operator in charge of calculating the ranking values. For each input row, it needs two "flags":

1.   Is the row the first in the partition? If it is, the *Sequence Project* operator will reset the ranking value.

2.   Is the sorting value in this row different than in the previous one? If it is, the *Sequence Project* operator will increment the ranking value as dictated by the specific ranking function.

For all ranking functions, a *Segment* operator will produce the first flag value.

The *Segment* operator basically determines grouping boundaries. It keeps one row in memory and compares it with the next. If they are different, it emits one value. If they are the same, it emits a different value.

To generate the first flag, which indicates whether the row is the first in the partition, the *Segment* operator compares the PARTITON BY column values of the current and previous rows. Obviously, it emits "true" for the first row read. From the second row on, its output depends on whether the PARTITION BY column value changed. In our example, I didn't specify a PARTITION BY clause, so the whole table is treated as one partition. In this case, *Segment* will emit "true" for the first row and "false" for all others.

As for the second flag (which answers, "Is the value different than the previous value?"), the operator that will calculate it depends on which ranking function you requested. For ROW_NUMBER, the ranking value must be incremented for each row regardless of whether the sort value changes. So in our case, a plain *Compute Scalar* operator simply emits "true" (1) all the time. In other cases (for example, with the RANK and DENSE_RANK functions), another *Segment* operator will be used to tell the *Sequence Project* operator whether the sort value changed in order to determine whether to increment the ranking value or not.

The brilliance of this plan and the techniques the optimizer uses to calculate ranking values might not be apparent yet. For now, it suffices to say that the data is scanned only once, and if it's not already sorted within an index, it is also sorted. This is much faster than any technique that was available to calculate ranking values in SQL Server 2000, as I will demonstrate in detail shortly.

Determinism   As you probably noticed in the output of the previous query, row numbers keep incrementing regardless of whether the sort value changes or not. Row numbers must be unique within the partition. This means that for a nonunique sort list, the query is nondeterministic. That is, there are different result sets that are correct and not just one. For example, in Table 4-19 you can see that employees B, G, and J, all having a quantity of 100, got the row numbers 1, 2, and 3, respectively. However, the result would also be valid if these three employees received the row numbers 1, 2, and 3 in a different order.

For some applications determinism is mandatory. To guarantee determinism, you simply need to add a tiebreaker that makes the values of *partitioning column(s) + sort column(s)* unique.

For example, the following query (which generates the output shown in Table 4-20) demonstrates both a nondeterministic row number based on the *qty* column alone and also a deterministic one based on the order of *qty* and *empid*:

```
SELECT empid, qty,
  ROW_NUMBER() OVER(ORDER BY qty)        AS nd_rownum,
  ROW_NUMBER() OVER(ORDER BY qty, empid) AS d_rownum
FROM dbo.Sales
ORDER BY qty, empid;
```

Table 4-20   Row Numbers, Determinism

empid	qty	nd_rownum	d_rownum
B	100	1	1
G	100	2	2
J	100	3	3
H	150	4	4
C	200	6	5
D	200	7	6

Table 4-20   Row Numbers, Determinism

empid	qty	nd_rownum	d_rownum
K	200	5	7
E	250	8	8
I	250	9	9
A	300	11	10
F	300	10	11

Partitioning   As I mentioned earlier, you can also calculate ranking values within partitions (groups of rows). The following example (which generates the output shown in Table 4-21) calculates row numbers based on the order of *qty* and *empid*, for each manager separately:

```
SELECT mgrid, empid, qty,
  ROW_NUMBER() OVER(PARTITION BY mgrid ORDER BY qty, empid) AS rownum
FROM dbo.Sales
ORDER BY mgrid, qty, empid;
```

Table 4-21   Row Numbers, Partitioned

mgrid	empid	qty	rownum
X	B	100	1
X	G	100	2
X	C	200	3
X	I	250	4
Y	H	150	1
Y	D	200	2
Y	K	200	3
Z	J	100	1
Z	E	250	2
Z	A	300	3
Z	F	300	4

The Set-Based Technique prior to SQL Server 2005

There are several techniques for calculating ranking values using a version of SQL Server prior to SQL Server 2005, and all of them suffer from some limitation. Before I start describing these techniques, keep in mind that you can also calculate ranking values at the client. Whatever way you choose, your client will iterate through the records in the recordset returned from SQL Server. The client can simply request the rows sorted and, in a loop, increment a counter. Of course, if you need the ranking values for further server-side manipulation before results are sent to the client, client-side ranking is not an option.

I'll start with the standard and set-based technique. Unfortunately, it is usually the slowest of all.

Unique Sort Column   Prior to SQL Server 2005, reasonably simple set-based calculations of row numbers were possible, given a unique *partitioning + sort column(s)* combination. As I will describe later, set-based row number calculations without this unique combination also exist, but they are substantially more complex.

All ranking value calculations can be achieved by counting rows. To calculate row numbers, you can employ the following fundamental technique. You simply use a subquery to count the number of rows with a smaller or equal sort value. This count corresponds to the desired row number. For example, the following query produces row numbers based on *empid*, generating the output in Table 4-22:

```
SELECT empid,
  (SELECT COUNT(*)
   FROM dbo.Sales AS S2
   WHERE S2.empid <= S1.empid) AS rownum
FROM dbo.Sales AS S1
ORDER BY empid;
```

Table 4-22   Row Numbers, Unique Sort Column

empid	rownum
A	1
B	2
C	3
D	4
E	5
F	6
G	7
H	8
I	9
J	10
K	11

This technique to calculate row numbers, though fairly simple, is extremely slow. To understand why, examine the execution plan shown in Figure 4-6 created for the query.

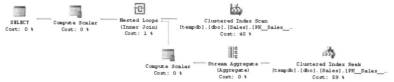

Figure 4-6   Execution plan for pre–SQL Server 2005, set-based, row number query

There is an index on the sort column (*empid*) that happens to be the Sales table's clustered index. The table is first fully scanned (*Clustered Index Scan* operator) to return all rows.

For each row returned from the initial full scan, the *Nested Loops* operator invokes the activity that generates the row number by counting rows. Each row number calculation involves a seek operation within the clustered index, followed by a partial scan operation (from the head of the leaf level's linked list to the last point where *inner_empid* is smaller than or equal to *outer_empid*).

Note that there are two different operators that use the clustered index—first, a full scan to return all rows; second, a seek followed by a partial scan for each outer row to achieve the count.

Remember that the primary factor affecting the performance of queries that do data manipulation will usually be I/O. A rough estimate of the number or rows accessed here will show how inefficient this execution plan is. To calculate *rownum* for the first row of the table, SQL Server needs to scan 1 row in the index. For the second row, it needs to scan 2 rows. For the third row, it needs to scan 3 rows, and so on, and for the nth row of the table, it needs to scan n rows. For a table with n rows, having an index based on the sort column in place, the total number of rows scanned is $1 + 2 + 3 + ... + n$. You may not grasp immediately the large number of rows that are going to be scanned. To give you a sense, for a table with 100,000 rows, you're looking at 5,000,050,000 rows that are going to be scanned in total.

As an aside, there's a story told about the mathematician Gauss. When he was a child, he and his classmates got an assignment from their teacher to find the sum of all the integers from 1 through 100. Gauss gave the answer almost instantly. When the teacher asked him how he came up with the answer so fast, he said that he added the first and the last values (1+100 = 101), and then multiplied that total by half the number of integers (50), which is the number of pairs. Sure enough, the result of *first_val* + *last_val* is equal to the *second_val* + *next_to_last val*, and so on. In short, the formula for the sum of the first n positive integers is $(n + n^2) / 2$. That's the number of rows that need to be scanned in total to calculate row numbers using this technique when there is an index based on the sort column. You're looking at an n^2 graph of I/O cost and run time based on the number of rows in the table. You can play with the numbers in the formula and see that the cost gets humongous pretty quickly.

When there's no index on the table, matters are even worse. To calculate each row number, the entire table needs to be scanned. The total number of rows scanned by the query is then n^2. For example, given a table with 100,000 rows, the query will end up scanning 10,000,000,000 rows in total.

Nonunique Sort Column and Tiebreaker   When the sort column is not unique, you can make it unique by introducing a tiebreaker, to allow a solution that keeps a reasonable level of simplicity. Let *sortcol* be the sort column, and let *tiebreaker* be the tiebreaker column. To count rows with the same or smaller values of the sort list (*sortcol+tiebreaker*), use the following expression in the subquery:

```
inner_sortcol < outer_sortcol
OR inner_sortcol = outer_sortcol
   AND inner_tiebreaker <= outer_tiebreaker
```

Note that operator precedence dictates that AND would be evaluated prior to OR. For clarity, manageability, and readability you might want to use parentheses.

The following query (which generates the output shown in Table 4-23) produces row numbers based on *qty* and *empid*, in that order:

```
SELECT empid, qty,
  (SELECT COUNT(*)
   FROM dbo.Sales AS S2
   WHERE S2.qty < S1.qty
     OR (S2.qty = S1.qty AND S2.empid <= S1.empid)) AS rownum
FROM dbo.Sales AS S1
ORDER BY qty, empid;
```

Table 4-23 Row Numbers, Nonunique Sort Column, and Tiebreaker

empid	qty	rownum
B	100	1
G	100	2
J	100	3
H	150	4
C	200	5
D	200	6
K	200	7
E	250	8
I	250	9
A	300	10
F	300	11

Nonunique Sort Column without a Tiebreaker   The problem becomes substantially more complex when you need to assign row numbers according to a nonunique sort column and using no tiebreaker, with a pre–SQL Server 2005 set-based technique. For example, given the table T1, which you create and populate by running the code in Listing 4-4, say you are supposed to produce row numbers based on *col1* ordering.

Listing 4-4   Creating and populating the T1 table

```
IF OBJECT_ID('dbo.T1') IS NOT NULL
  DROP TABLE dbo.T1;
GO
CREATE TABLE dbo.T1(col1 VARCHAR(5));
INSERT INTO dbo.T1(col1) VALUES('A');
INSERT INTO dbo.T1(col1) VALUES('A');
INSERT INTO dbo.T1(col1) VALUES('A');
INSERT INTO dbo.T1(col1) VALUES('B');
INSERT INTO dbo.T1(col1) VALUES('B');
INSERT INTO dbo.T1(col1) VALUES('C');
```

```
INSERT INTO dbo.T1(col1) VALUES('C');
INSERT INTO dbo.T1(col1) VALUES('C');
INSERT INTO dbo.T1(col1) VALUES('C');
INSERT INTO dbo.T1(col1) VALUES('C');
```

The solution must be compatible with SQL Server 2000, so you can't simply use the ROW_NUMBER function. Also, the solution must be standard.

In the solution for this problem, I'll make first use of a very important key technique—generating duplicate rows using an auxiliary table of numbers. More accurately, the technique generates sequentially numbered copies of each row, but for simplicity's sake, I'll refer to it throughout the book as "generating duplicates."

I'll explain the concept of the auxiliary table of numbers and how to create one later in the chapter in the section "Auxiliary Table of Numbers." For now, simply run the code in Listing 4-8, which creates the Nums table and populates it with the 1,000,000 integers in the range $1 <= n <= 1,000,000$.

The technique that I'm talking about is "generating duplicates" or "expanding" the number of rows. For example, given a table T1, say you want to generate 5 copies of each row. To achieve this, you can use the Nums table as follows:

```
SELECT ... FROM dbo.T1, dbo.Nums WHERE n <= 5;
```

I will provide more details on the "generating duplicates" technique and its uses in Chapter 5.

Going back to our original problem, you're supposed to generate row numbers for the rows of T1, based on *col1* order. The first step in the solution is "collapsing" the rows by grouping them by *col1*. For each group, you return the number of duplicates (a count of rows in the group). You also return, using a subquery, the number of rows in the base table that have a smaller sort value. Here's the query that accomplishes the first step, and its output is shown in Table 4-24:

```
SELECT col1, COUNT(*) AS dups,
  (SELECT COUNT(*) FROM dbo.T1 AS B
   WHERE B.col1 < A.col1) AS smaller
FROM dbo.T1 AS A
GROUP BY col1;
```

Table 4-24 Row Numbers, Nonunique Sort Column, No Tiebreaker, Step 1's Output

col1	dups	smaller
A	3	0
B	2	3
C	5	5

For example, A appears 3 times, and there are 0 rows with a *col1* value smaller than A. B appears 2 times, and there are 3 rows with a *col1* value smaller than B. And so on.

The next step (which produces the output shown in Table 4-25) is to expand the number of rows or create sequentially numbered copies of each row. You achieve this by creating a derived table out of the previous query and joining it to the Nums table as follows, based on $n \le dups$:

```
SELECT col1, dups, smaller, n
FROM (SELECT col1, COUNT(*) AS dups,
        (SELECT COUNT(*) FROM dbo.T1 AS B
          WHERE B.col1 < A.col1) AS smaller
      FROM dbo.T1 AS A
      GROUP BY col1) AS D, Nums
WHERE n <= dups;
```

Table 4-25 Row Numbers, Nonunique Sort Column, No Tiebreaker, Step 2's Output

col1	dups	smaller	n
A	3	0	1
A	3	0	2
A	3	0	3
B	2	3	1
B	2	3	2
C	5	5	1
C	5	5	2
C	5	5	3
C	5	5	4
C	5	5	5

Now look carefully at the output in Table 4-25, and see whether you can figure out how to produce the row numbers.

The row number can be expressed as the number of rows with a smaller sort value, plus the row number within the same sort value group—in other words, $n + smaller$. The following query is the final solution, and it generates the output shown in Table 4-26:

```
SELECT n + smaller AS rownum, col1
FROM (SELECT col1, COUNT(*) AS dups,
        (SELECT COUNT(*) FROM dbo.T1 AS B
          WHERE B.col1 < A.col1) AS smaller
      FROM dbo.T1 AS A
      GROUP BY col1) AS D, Nums
WHERE n <= dups;
```

Table 4-26   Row Numbers, Nonunique Sort Column, No Tiebreaker, Final Output

rownum	col1
1	A
2	A
3	A
4	B
5	B
6	C
7	C
8	C
9	C
10	C

Partitioning   Partitioning is achieved by simply adding a correlation in the subquery based on a match between the partitioning column or columns in the inner and outer tables. For example, the following query against the Orders table (which generates the output shown in Table 4-27) calculates row numbers that are partitioned by *mgrid*, ordered by *qty*, and use *empid* as a tiebreaker:

```
SELECT mgrid, empid, qty,
  (SELECT COUNT(*)
   FROM dbo.Sales AS S2
   WHERE S2.mgrid = S1.mgrid
     AND (S2.qty < S1.qty
          OR (S2.qty = S1.qty AND S2.empid <= S1.empid))) AS rownum
FROM dbo.Sales AS S1
ORDER BY mgrid, qty, empid;
```

Table 4-27   Row Numbers, Partitioned

mgrid	empid	qty	rownum
X	B	100	1
X	G	100	2
X	C	200	3
X	I	250	4
Y	H	150	1
Y	D	200	2
Y	K	200	3
Z	J	100	1
Z	E	250	2
Z	A	300	3
Z	F	300	4

> **Note** As I mentioned earlier, the pre–SQL Server 2005 set-based technique to calculate row numbers has a num_rows^2 cost. However, for a fairly small number of rows (in the area of dozens), it's pretty fast. Note that the performance problem has more to do with the partition size rather than the table's size. If you create the recommended index based on *partitioning_cols*, *sort_cols*, *tiebreaker_cols*, the number of rows scanned within the index is equivalent to the row number generated. The row number is reset (starts from 1) with every new partition. So even for very large tables, when the partition size is fairly small and you have a proper index in place, the solution is pretty fast. If you have *p* partitions and *r* rows in each partition, the number of rows scanned in total is: $p * (r + r^2) / 2$. For example, if you have 100,000 partitions, and 10 rows in each partition, you get 5,500,000 rows scanned in total. Though this number might seem large, it's nowhere near the number you get without partitioning. And as long as the partition size remains constant, the graph of query cost compared with the number of rows in the table is linear.

Cursor-Based Solution

You can use a cursor to calculate row numbers. A cursor-based solution for any of the aforementioned variations is pretty straightforward. You create a fast-forward (read-only, forward-only) cursor based on a query that orders the data by *partitioning_cols*, *sort_cols*, *tiebreaker_cols*. As you fetch rows from the cursor, you simply increment a counter, resetting it every time a new partition is detected. You can store the result rows along with the row numbers in a temporary table or a table variable.

As an example, the code in Listing 4-5 (which generates the output shown in Table 4-28) uses a cursor to calculate row numbers based on the order of *qty* and *empid*:

Listing 4-5 Calculating row numbers with a cursor

```
DECLARE @SalesRN TABLE(empid VARCHAR(5), qty INT, rn INT);
DECLARE @empid AS VARCHAR(5), @qty AS INT, @rn AS INT;

BEGIN TRAN

DECLARE rncursor CURSOR FAST_FORWARD FOR
  SELECT empid, qty FROM dbo.Sales ORDER BY qty, empid;
OPEN rncursor;

SET @rn = 0;

FETCH NEXT FROM rncursor INTO @empid, @qty;
WHILE @@fetch_status = 0
BEGIN
  SET @rn = @rn + 1;
  INSERT INTO @SalesRN(empid, qty, rn) VALUES(@empid, @qty, @rn);
  FETCH NEXT FROM rncursor INTO @empid, @qty;
END
```

```
CLOSE rncursor;
DEALLOCATE rncursor;

COMMIT TRAN

SELECT empid, qty, rn FROM @SalesRN;
```

Table 4-28   Output of Cursor Calculating Row Numbers

empid	qty	rn
B	100	1
G	100	2
J	100	3
H	150	4
C	200	5
D	200	6
K	200	7
E	250	8
I	250	9
A	300	10
F	300	11

Generally, working with cursors should be avoided, as cursors have a lot of overhead that is a drag on performance. However, in this case, unless the partition size is really tiny, the cursor-based solution performs much better than the pre–SQL Server 2005 set-based technique, as it scans the data only once. This means that as the table grows larger, the cursor-based solution has a linear performance degradation, as opposed to the n^2 one that the pre–SQL Server 2005 set-based solution has.

IDENTITY-Based Solution

In versions prior to SQL Server 2005, you can also rely on the IDENTITY function and IDENTITY column property to calculate row numbers. As such, calculating row numbers with IDENTITY is a useful technique to know. Before you proceed, though, you should be aware that when you use the IDENTITY function, you cannot guarantee the order of assignment of IDENTITY values. You can, however, guarantee the order of assignment by using an IDENTITY column instead of the IDENTITY function: first create a table with an IDENTITY column, and then load the data using an INSERT SELECT statement with an ORDER BY clause.

More Info   You can find a detailed discussion of IDENTITY and ORDER BY in Knowledge Base article 273586 (*http://support.microsoft.com/default.aspx?scid=kb;en-us;273586*), which I strongly recommend that you read.

Nonpartitioned   Using the IDENTITY function in a SELECT INTO statement is by far the fastest way to calculate row numbers at the server prior to SQL Server 2005. The first reason for this is that you scan the data only once, without the overhead involved with cursor manipulation. The second reason is that SELECT INTO is a minimally logged operation when the database recovery model is not FULL. However, keep in mind that you can trust it only when you don't care about the order of assignment of the row numbers.

For example, the following code demonstrates how to use the IDENTITY function to create and populate a temporary table with row numbers, in no particular order:

```
SELECT empid, qty, IDENTITY(int, 1, 1) AS rn
INTO #SalesRN FROM dbo.Sales;

SELECT * FROM #SalesRN;

DROP TABLE #SalesRN;
```

This technique is handy when you need to generate integer identifiers to distinguish rows for some processing need.

Don't let the fact that you can technically specify an ORDER BY clause in the SELECT INTO query mislead you. In SQL Server 2000, there's no guarantee that in the execution plan the assignment of IDENTITY values will take place after the sort. In SQL Server 2005, it's irrelevant because you will use the ROW_NUMBER function anyway.

As mentioned earlier, when you do care about the order of assignment of the IDENTITY values—in other words, when the row numbers should be based on a given order—first create the table, and then load the data. This technique is not as fast as the SELECT INTO approach because INSERT SELECT is always fully logged; however, it's still much faster than the other techniques available prior to SQL Server 2005.

Here's an example for calculating row numbers based on the order of *qty* and *empid*:

```
CREATE TABLE #SalesRN(empid VARCHAR(5), qty INT, rn INT IDENTITY);

INSERT INTO #SalesRN(empid, qty)
  SELECT empid, qty FROM dbo.Sales ORDER BY qty, empid;

SELECT * FROM #SalesRN;

DROP TABLE #SalesRN;
```

Partitioned   Using the IDENTITY approach to create partitioned row numbers requires an additional step. As with the nonpartitioned solution, you insert the data into a table with an IDENTITY column, only this time it is sorted by *partitioning_cols, sort_cols, tiebreaker_cols*.

The additional step is a query that calculates the row number within the partition using the following formula: *general_row_number – min_row_number_within_partition* + 1. The minimum row number within the partition can be obtained by either a correlated subquery or a join.

As an example, the code in Listing 4-6 generates row numbers partitioned by *mgrid*, sorted by *qty* and *empid*. The code presents both the subquery approach and the join approach to obtaining the minimum row number within the partition.

Listing 4-6   Calculating partitioned row numbers with an IDENTITY

```
CREATE TABLE #SalesRN
  (mgrid VARCHAR(5), empid VARCHAR(5), qty INT, rn INT IDENTITY);
CRFATF UNIQUE CLUSTERED INDEX idx_mgrid_rn ON #SalesRN(mgrid, rn);

INSERT INTO #SalesRN(mgrid, empid, qty)
  SELECT mgrid, empid, qty FROM dbo.Sales ORDER BY mgrid, qty, empid;

-- Option 1 - using a subquery
SELECT mgrid, empid, qty,
  rn - (SELECT MIN(rn) FROM #SalesRN AS S2
        WHERE S2.mgrid = S1.mgrid) + 1 AS rn
FROM #SalesRN AS S1;

-- Option 2 - using a join
SELECT S.mgrid, empid, qty, rn - minrn + 1 AS rn
FROM #SalesRN AS S
  JOIN (SELECT mgrid, MIN(rn) AS minrn
        FROM #SalesRN
        GROUP BY mgrid) AS M
  ON S.mgrid = M.mgrid;

DROP TABLE #SalesRN;
```

Performance Comparisons

I presented four different techniques to calculate row numbers server-side. One is available only in SQL Server 2005 (using the ROW_NUMBER function), and three (set-based using subqueries, cursor-based, and IDENTITY-based) are available in both versions. As I mentioned earlier, the other three ranking calculations that I'll describe later in this chapter are technically calculated using very similar access methods. So the performance aspects that I discussed and the following benchmark that I'll present are relevant to all ranking calculations.

I ran the benchmark shown in Listing 4-7 on my laptop (single CPU: Intel Centrino 1.7 Mhz; RAM: 1GB, single disk drive). Even though my laptop is not exactly the best model for a production server, you can get a good sense of the performance differences between the techniques. The benchmark populates a table with increasing numbers of rows, starting with 10,000 and progressing up to 100,000 in steps of 10,000 rows. The benchmark calculates row numbers using all four techniques, with the Discard Results option turned on in SQL Server Management Studio (SSMS) to remove the effect of generating the output. The benchmark records the run times in milliseconds in the RNBenchmark table.

Listing 4-7 Benchmark comparing techniques to calculate row numbers

```
-- Change Tool's Options to Discard Query Results
SET NOCOUNT ON;
USE tempdb;
GO
IF OBJECT_ID('dbo.RNBenchmark') IS NOT NULL
  DROP TABLE dbo.RNBenchmark;
GO
IF OBJECT_ID('dbo.RNTechniques') IS NOT NULL
  DROP TABLE dbo.RNTechniques;
GO
IF OBJECT_ID('dbo.SalesBM') IS NOT NULL
  DROP TABLE dbo.SalesBM;
GO
IF OBJECT_ID('dbo.SalesBMIdentity') IS NOT NULL
  DROP TABLE dbo.SalesBMIdentity;
GO
IF OBJECT_ID('dbo.SalesBMCursor') IS NOT NULL
  DROP TABLE dbo.SalesBMCursor;
GO

CREATE TABLE dbo.RNTechniques
(
  tid INT NOT NULL PRIMARY KEY,
  technique VARCHAR(25) NOT NULL
);
INSERT INTO RNTechniques(tid, technique) VALUES(1, 'Set-Based 2000');
INSERT INTO RNTechniques(tid, technique) VALUES(2, 'IDENTITY');
INSERT INTO RNTechniques(tid, technique) VALUES(3, 'Cursor');
INSERT INTO RNTechniques(tid, technique) VALUES(4, 'ROW_NUMBER 2005');
GO

CREATE TABLE dbo.RNBenchmark
(
  tid       INT    NOT NULL REFERENCES dbo.RNTechniques(tid),
  numrows   INT    NOT NULL,
  runtimems BIGINT NOT NULL,
  PRIMARY KEY(tid, numrows)
);
GO

CREATE TABLE dbo.SalesBM
(
  empid INT NOT NULL IDENTITY PRIMARY KEY,
  qty   INT NOT NULL
);
CREATE INDEX idx_qty_empid ON dbo.SalesBM(qty, empid);
GO
CREATE TABLE dbo.SalesBMIdentity(empid INT, qty INT, rn INT IDENTITY);
GO
CREATE TABLE dbo.SalesBMCursor(empid INT, qty INT, rn INT);
GO
```

```
DECLARE
  @maxnumrows    AS INT,
  @steprows      AS INT,
  @curnumrows    AS INT,
  @dt            AS DATETIME;

SET @maxnumrows    = 100000;
SET @steprows      = 10000;
SET @curnumrows    = 10000;

WHILE @curnumrows <= @maxnumrows
BEGIN

  TRUNCATE TABLE dbo.SalesBM;
  INSERT INTO dbo.SalesBM(qty)
    SELECT CAST(1+999.9999999999*RAND(CHECKSUM(NEWID())) AS INT)
    FROM dbo.Nums
    WHERE n <= @curnumrows;

  -- 'Set-Based 2000'

  DBCC FREEPROCCACHE WITH NO_INFOMSGS;
  DBCC DROPCLEANBUFFERS WITH NO_INFOMSGS;

  SET @dt = GETDATE();

  SELECT empid, qty,
    (SELECT COUNT(*)
     FROM dbo.SalesBM AS S2
     WHERE S2.qty < S1.qty
        OR (S2.qty = S1.qty AND S2.empid <= S1.empid)) AS rn
  FROM dbo.SalesBM AS S1
  ORDER BY qty, empid;

  INSERT INTO dbo.RNBenchmark(tid, numrows, runtimems)
    VALUES(1, @curnumrows, DATEDIFF(ms, @dt, GETDATE()));

  -- 'IDENTITY'

  TRUNCATE TABLE dbo.SalesBMIdentity;

  DBCC FREEPROCCACHE WITH NO_INFOMSGS;
  DBCC DROPCLEANBUFFERS WITH NO_INFOMSGS;

  SET @dt = GETDATE();

  INSERT INTO dbo.SalesBMIdentity(empid, qty)
    SELECT empid, qty FROM dbo.SalesBM ORDER BY qty, empid;

  SELECT empid, qty, rn FROM dbo.SalesBMIdentity;

  INSERT INTO dbo.RNBenchmark(tid, numrows, runtimems)
    VALUES(2, @curnumrows, DATEDIFF(ms, @dt, GETDATE()));
```

```
-- 'Cursor'

TRUNCATE TABLE dbo.SalesBMCursor;

DBCC FREEPROCCACHE WITH NO_INFOMSGS;
DBCC DROPCLEANBUFFERS WITH NO_INFOMSGS;

SET @dt = GETDATE();

DECLARE @empid AS INT, @qty AS INT, @rn AS INT;

BEGIN TRAN

DECLARE rncursor CURSOR FAST_FORWARD FOR
  SELECT empid, qty FROM dbo.SalesBM ORDER BY qty, empid;
OPEN rncursor;

SET @rn = 0;

FETCH NEXT FROM rncursor INTO @empid, @qty;
WHILE @@fetch_status = 0
BEGIN
  SET @rn = @rn + 1;
  INSERT INTO dbo.SalesBMCursor(empid, qty, rn)
    VALUES(@empid, @qty, @rn);
  FETCH NEXT FROM rncursor INTO @empid, @qty;
END

CLOSE rncursor;
DEALLOCATE rncursor;

COMMIT TRAN

SELECT empid, qty, rn FROM dbo.SalesBMCursor;

INSERT INTO dbo.RNBenchmark(tid, numrows, runtimems)
  VALUES(3, @curnumrows, DATEDIFF(ms, @dt, GETDATE()));

-- 'ROW_NUMBER 2005'

DBCC FREEPROCCACHE WITH NO_INFOMSGS;
DBCC DROPCLEANBUFFERS WITH NO_INFOMSGS;

SET @dt = GETDATE();

SELECT empid, qty, ROW_NUMBER() OVER(ORDER BY qty, empid) AS rn
FROM dbo.SalesBM;

INSERT INTO dbo.RNBenchmark(tid, numrows, runtimems)
  VALUES(4, @curnumrows, DATEDIFF(ms, @dt, GETDATE()));

SET @curnumrows = @curnumrows + @steprows;

END
```

The following query returns the benchmark's results in a conveniently readable format, which is shown in Table 4-29:

```
SELECT numrows,
  [Set-Based 2000], [IDENTITY], [Cursor], [ROW_NUMBER 2005]
FROM (SELECT technique, numrows, runtimems
      FROM dbo.RNBenchmark AS B
        JOIN dbo.RNTechniques AS T
          ON B.tid = T.tid) AS D
PIVOT(MAX(runtimems) FOR technique IN(
  [Set-Based 2000], [IDENTITY], [Cursor], [ROW_NUMBER 2005])) AS P
ORDER BY numrows;
```

Table 4-29   Benchmark Results

numrows	Set-Based 2000	IDENTITY	Cursor	ROW_NUMBER 2005
10000	11960	80	550	30
20000	33260	160	1343	40
30000	72646	660	1613	30
40000	127033	893	2110	60
50000	199740	870	2873	70
60000	283616	990	3043	63
70000	382130	900	3913	103
80000	499580	1123	4276	80
90000	634653	1040	4766	100
100000	796806	1060	5280	140

The query uses a pivoting technique that I'll describe in Chapter 6, so don't try to squeeze your brains if you're not familiar with it. For our discussion, the important thing is the benchmark's results. You can immediately see that the pre–SQL Server 2005 set-based technique is dramatically slower than all the rest, and I explained why earlier. You will also notice that the ROW_NUMBER function is dramatically faster than all the rest. I wanted to present a graph with all results, but the run times of the pre–SQL Server 2005 set-based techniques were so great that the lines for the other solutions were simply flat. So I decided to present two separate graphs. Figure 4-7 shows the graph of run times for the IDENTITY-based, cursor-based, and ROW_NUMBER function-based techniques. Figure 4-8 shows the graph for the set-based pre–SQL Server 2005 technique.

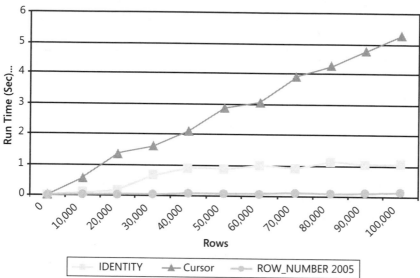

Figure 4-7   Row Numbers benchmark graph I

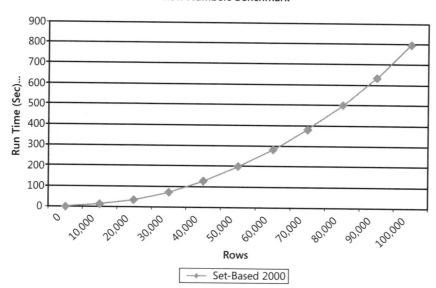

Figure 4-8   Row Numbers benchmark graph II

You can see in Figure 4-7 that all three techniques have a fairly linear performance graph, while Figure 4-8 shows a beautifully curved n^2 graph.

The obvious conclusion is that in SQL Server 2005 you should always use the new ranking functions. In SQL Server 2000, if it's important to you to use a standard set-based technique, only use that technique when the partition size is fairly small (measured in dozens). Otherwise, use the IDENTITY-based technique, first creating the table, and then loading the data.

Paging

As I mentioned earlier, row numbers have many practical applications that I'll demonstrate throughout the book. Here I'd like to show one example where I use row numbers to achieve paging—accessing rows of a result set in chunks. Paging is a common need in applications, allowing the user to navigate through chunks or portions of a result set. Paging with row numbers is also a handy technique. This example will also allow me to demonstrate additional optimization techniques that the optimizer applies when using the ROW_NUMBER function. Of course, in SQL Server 2000 you can use the less efficient techniques to calculate row numbers to achieve paging.

Ad Hoc Paging   Ad hoc paging is a request for a single page, where the input is the page number and page size (the number of rows in a page). When the user needs a particular single page and won't request additional pages, you implement a different solution than the one you would for multiple page requests. First you have to realize that there's no way to access page *n* without physically accessing pages 1 through *n*−1. Bearing this in mind, the following code returns a page of rows from the Sales table ordered by *qty* and *empid*, given the page size and page number as inputs:

```
DECLARE @pagesize AS INT, @pagenum AS INT;
SET @pagesize = 5;
SET @pagenum = 2;

WITH SalesCTE AS
(
  SELECT ROW_NUMBER() OVER(ORDER BY qty, empid) AS rownum,
    empid, mgrid, qty
  FROM dbo.Sales
)
SELECT rownum, empid, mgrid, qty
FROM SalesCTE
WHERE rownum > @pagesize * (@pagenum-1)
  AND rownum <= @pagesize * @pagenum
ORDER BY rownum;
```

This code generates the output shown in Table 4-30.

Table 4-30   Second Page of Sales Ordered by *qty*, *empid* with a Page Size of 5 Rows

rownum	empid	mgrid	qty
6	D	Y	200
7	K	Y	200
8	E	Z	250
9	I	X	250
10	A	Z	300

The CTE called SalesCTE assigns row numbers to the sales rows based on the order of *qty* and *empid*. The outer query filters only the target page's rows using a formula based on the input page size and page number.

You might be concerned that the query appears to calculate row numbers for all rows and then filter only the requested page's rows. This might seem to require a full table scan. With very large tables this, of course, would be a serious performance issue. However, before getting concerned, examine the execution plan for this query, which is shown in Figure 4-9.

Figure 4-9   Execution plan for the ad hoc paging solution

The figure shows only the left part of the plan starting with the Sequence Project, which assigns the row numbers. If you look at the properties of the *Top* operator, you will see that the plan scans only the first 10 rows of the table. Because the code requests the second page of five rows, only the first two pages are scanned. Then the *Filter* operator filters only the second page (rows 6 through 10).

Another way to demonstrate that the whole table is not scanned is by populating the table with a large number of rows and running the query with the SET STATISTICS IO option turned on. You will notice by the number of reads reported that when you request page *n*, regardless of the size of the table, only the first *n* pages of rows are scanned.

This solution can perform well even when there are multiple page requests that usually "move forward"—that is, page 1 is requested, then page 2, then page 3, and so on. When the first page of rows is requested, the relevant data/index pages are physically scanned and loaded into cache (if they're not there already). When the second page of rows is requested, the data pages for the first request already reside in cache, and only the data pages for the second page of rows need to be physically scanned. This requires mostly logical reads (reads from cache), and physical reads are only needed for the requested page. Logical reads are much faster than physical reads, but keep in mind that they also have a cost that accumulates.

Multipage Access   There's another solution for paging that will typically perform better overall than the previous solution when there are multiple page requests that do not move forward, if the result set is not very large. First materialize all pages in a table along with row numbers, and create a clustered index on the row number column:

```
SELECT ROW_NUMBER() OVER(ORDER BY qty, empid) AS rownum,
  empid, mgrid, qty
INTO #SalesRN
FROM dbo.Sales;

CREATE UNIQUE CLUSTERED INDEX idx_rn ON #SalesRN(rownum);
```

Now you can satisfy any page request with a query like the following:

```
DECLARE @pagesize AS INT, @pagenum AS INT;
SET @pagesize = 5;
SET @pagenum = 2;
```

```
SELECT rownum, empid, mgrid, qty
FROM #SalesRN
WHERE rownum BETWEEN @pagesize * (@pagenum-1) + 1
                 AND @pagesize * @pagenum
ORDER BY rownum;
```

The execution plan for this query is shown in Figure 4-10 (abbreviated by removing the operators that calculate boundaries up to the *Merge Interval* operator, to focus on the actual data access).

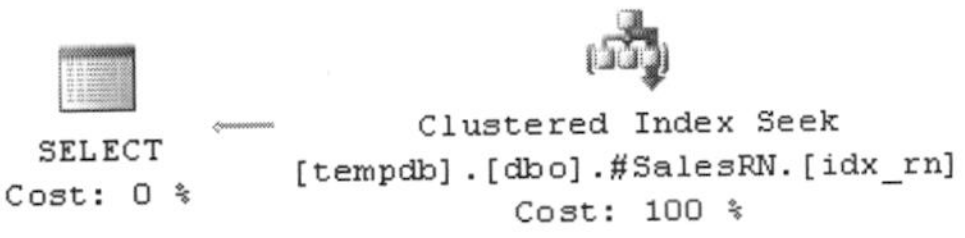

Figure 4-10   Execution plan for multipaging solution

This is a very efficient plan that performs a seek within the index to reach the low boundary row (row number 6 in this case), followed by a partial scan (not visible in the plan), until it reaches the high boundary row (row number 10). Only the rows of the requested page of results are scanned within the index.

If your application design is such that it disconnects after each request, obviously the temporary table will be gone as soon as the creating session disconnects. In such a case, you might want to create a permanent table that is logically "temporary." You can achieve this by naming the table *some_name<some_identifier>*—for example, T<guid> (Global Unique Identifier).

You will also need to develop a garbage-collection (cleanup) process that gets rid of tables that the application didn't have a chance to drop explicitly in cases where it terminated in a disorderly way.

In cases where you need to support large result sets or a high level of concurrency, you will have scalability issues related to tempdb resources. You can develop a partitioned solution that materializes only a certain number of pages and not all of them—for example, 1000 rows at a time. Typically, users don't request more than the first few pages anyway. If a user ends up requesting pages beyond the first batch, you can materialize the next partition (that is, the next 1000 rows).

When you don't care about materializing the result set in a temporary table for multipage access, you might want to consider using a table variable where you materialize only the first batch of pages (for example, 1000 rows). Table variables don't involve recompilations, and they suffer less from logging and locking issues. The optimizer doesn't collect statistics for table variables, so you should be very cautious and selective in choosing the cases to use them for. But when all you need to do is store a small result set and scan it entirely anyway, that's fine.

Once you're done using this table, you can drop it:

```
DROP TABLE #SalesRN;
```

Rank and Dense Rank

Rank and dense rank are calculations similar to row number. But unlike row number, which has a large variety of practical applications, rank and dense rank are typically used for ranking and scoring applications.

RANK and DENSE_RANK Functions in SQL Server 2005

SQL Server 2005 provides you with built-in RANK and DENSE_RANK functions that are similar to the ROW_NUMBER function. The difference between these functions and ROW_NUMBER is that, as I described earlier, ROW_NUMBER is not deterministic when the ORDER BY list is not unique. RANK and DENSE_RANK are always deterministic—that is, the same ranking values are assigned to rows with the same sort values. The difference between RANK and DENSE_RANK is that RANK might have gaps in the ranking values, but allows you to know how many rows have lower sort values. DENSE_RANK values have no gaps.

As an example, the following query (which produces the output shown in Table 4-31) returns both rank and dense rank values for the sales rows based on an ordering by quantity:

```
SELECT empid, qty,
  RANK() OVER(ORDER BY qty) AS rnk,
  DENSE_RANK() OVER(ORDER BY qty) AS drnk
FROM dbo.Sales
ORDER BY qty;
```

Table 4-31   Rank and Dense Rank

empid	qty	rnk	drnk
B	100	1	1
G	100	1	1
J	100	1	1
H	150	4	2
C	200	5	3
D	200	5	3
K	200	5	3
E	250	8	4
I	250	8	4
A	300	10	5
F	300	10	5

Here's a short quiz: what's the difference between the results of ROW_NUMBER, RANK and DENSE_RANK given a unique ORDER BY list?

For the answer, run the following code:

```
SELECT REVERSE('!gnihton yletulosbA');
```

Set-Based Solutions prior to SQL Server 2005

Rank and dense rank calculations using a set-based technique from pre–SQL Server 2005 are very similar to row number calculations. To calculate rank, use a subquery that counts the number of rows with a smaller sort value, and add one. To calculate dense rank, use a subquery that counts the distinct number of smaller sort values, and add one.

```
SELECT empid, qty,
  (SELECT COUNT(*) FROM dbo.Sales AS S2
   WHERE S2.qty < S1.qty) + 1 AS rnk,
  (SELECT COUNT(DISTINCT qty) FROM dbo.Sales AS S2
   WHERE S2.qty < S1.qty) + 1 AS drnk
FROM dbo.Sales AS S1
ORDER BY qty;
```

Of course, you can add a correlation to return partitioned calculations just like you did with row numbers.

NTILE

The NTILE function distributes rows into a specified number of tiles (or groups). The tiles are numbered 1 and on. Each row is assigned with the tile number to which it belongs. NTILE is based on row number calculation–namely, it is based on a requested order and can optionally be partitioned. Based on the number of rows in the table (or partition), the number of requested tiles, and the row number, you can determine the tile number for each row. For example, for a table with 10 rows, the value of NTILE(2) OVER (ORDER BY c) would be 1 for the first 5 rows in column c order, and 2 for the 6th through 10th rows.

Typically, NTILE calculations are used for analytical purposes such as calculating percentiles or arranging items in groups.

The task of "tiling" has more than one solution, and SQL Server 2005 implements a specific solution, called ANSI NTILE. I will describe the NTILE function implementation in SQL Server 2005, and then cover other solutions.

NTILE Function in SQL Server 2005

Calculating NTILE in SQL Server 2005 is as simple as calculating any of the other ranking values–in this case, using the NTILE function. The only difference is that NTILE accepts an input, the number of tiles, while the other ranking functions have no input. Because NTILE calculations are based on row numbers, NTILE has exactly the same issues regarding determinism that I described in the row numbers section.

As an example, the following query calculates NTILE values for the rows from the Sales table, producing three tiles, based on the order of *qty* and *empid*:

```
SELECT empid, qty,
  NTILE(3) OVER(ORDER BY qty, empid) AS tile
FROM dbo.Sales
ORDER BY qty, empid;
```

The output of this query is shown in Table 4-32.

Table 4-32   NTILE Query Output

empid	qty	tile
B	100	1
G	100	1
J	100	1
H	150	1
C	200	2
D	200	2
K	200	2
E	250	2
I	250	3
A	300	3
F	300	3

Note that when the number of tiles (*num_tiles*) does not evenly divide the count of rows in the table (*cnt*), the first *r* tiles (where *r* is *cnt* % *num_tiles*) get one more row than the others. In other words, the remainder is assigned to the first tiles first. In our example, the table has eleven rows, and three tiles were requested. The base tile size is 11 / 3 = 3 (integer division). The remainder is 11 % 3 = 2. The % (modulo) operator provides the integer remainder after dividing the first integer by the second one. So the first two tiles get an additional row beyond the base tile size and end up with four rows.

As a more meaningful example, suppose you need to split the sales rows into three categories based on quantities: low, medium, and high. You want each category to have about the same number of rows. You can calculate NTILE(3) values based on *qty* order (using *empid* as a tiebreaker just to assure deterministic and reproducible results) and use a CASE expression to convert the tile numbers to more meaningful descriptions:

```
SELECT empid, qty,
  CASE NTILE(3) OVER(ORDER BY qty, empid)
    WHEN 1 THEN 'low'
    WHEN 2 THEN 'medium'
    WHEN 3 THEN 'high'
  END AS lvl
FROM dbo.Sales
ORDER BY qty, empid;
```

The output of this query is shown in Table 4-33.

Table 4-33   **Descriptive Tiles**

empid	qty	lvl
B	100	low
G	100	low
J	100	low
H	150	low
C	200	medium
D	200	medium
K	200	medium
E	250	medium
I	250	high
A	300	high
F	300	high

To calculate the range of quantities corresponding to each category as shown in Table 4-34, simply group the data by the tile number, returning the minimum and maximum sort values for each group:

```
WITH Tiles AS
(
  SELECT empid, qty,
    NTILE(3) OVER(ORDER BY qty, empid) AS tile
  FROM dbo.Sales
)
SELECT tile, MIN(qty) AS lb, MAX(qty) AS hb
FROM Tiles
GROUP BY tile
ORDER BY tile;
```

Table 4-34   **Ranges of Quantities Corresponding to Each Category**

tile	lb	hb
1	100	150
2	200	250
3	250	300

Other Set-Based Solutions to NTILE

Calculating ANSI NTILE prior to SQL Server 2005 using set-based techniques is more difficult, and obviously far more expensive. Calculating other types of tiling is not trivial even in SQL Server 2005.

The formula you use to calculate NTILE depends on what exactly you want to do with the remainder in case the number of rows in the table doesn't divide evenly by the number of tiles. You might want to use the ANSI NTILE function's approach, which says, "Just assign the remainder to the first tiles, one to each until it's all consumed." Another approach, which is probably more correct statistically is to more evenly distribute the remainder among the tiles instead of putting them into the initial tiles only.

I'll start with the latter approach, calculating NTILE values with even distribution, because it's simpler. You need two inputs to calculate the tile number for a row: the row number and the tile size. You already know how to calculate row numbers. To calculate the tile size, you divide the number of rows in the table by the requested number of tiles. The formula that calculates the target tile number is

```
(row_number - 1) / tile_size + 1
```

The trick that would allow you to distribute the remainder evenly is to use a decimal calculation when calculating the *tile_size* value, instead of an integer one. That is, instead of using an integer calculation of the tile size (*num_rows/num_tiles*), which will truncate the fraction, use *1.*numrows/numtiles*, which will return a more accurate decimal result. Finally, to get rid of the fraction in the tile number, convert the result back to an integer value.

Here's the complete query that produces tile numbers using the even-distribution approach and generates the output shown in Table 4-35:

```
DECLARE @numtiles AS INT;
SET @numtiles = 3;

SELECT empid, qty,
  CAST((rn - 1) / tilesize + 1 AS INT) AS tile
FROM (SELECT empid, qty, rn,
        1.*numrows/@numtiles AS tilesize
      FROM (SELECT empid, qty,
              (SELECT COUNT(*) FROM dbo.Sales AS S2
               WHERE S2.qty < S1.qty
                  OR S2.qty = S1.qty
                    AND S2.empid <= S1.empid) AS rn,
              (SELECT COUNT(*) FROM dbo.Sales) AS numrows
            FROM dbo.Sales AS S1) AS D1) AS D2
ORDER BY qty, empid;
```

Table 4-35 NTILE, Even Distribution of Remainder, 3 Tiles

empid	qty	tile
B	100	1
G	100	1
J	100	1
H	150	1
C	200	2
D	200	2
K	200	2
E	250	2
I	250	3
A	300	3
F	300	3

With three tiles, you can't see the even distribution of the remaining rows. If you run this code using nine tiles as input, you get the output shown in Table 4-36 where the even distribution is clearer.

Table 4-36   NTILE, Even Distribution of Remainder, 9 Tiles

empid	qty	tile
B	100	1
G	100	1
J	100	2
H	150	3
C	200	4
D	200	5
K	200	5
E	250	6
I	250	7
A	300	8
F	300	9

You can see in the result that the first tile contains two rows, the next three tiles contain one row each, the next tile contains two rows, and the last four tiles contain one row each. You can experiment with the input number of tiles to get a clearer picture of the even-distribution algorithm.

To get the same result as the ANSI NTILE function, where the remainder is distributed to the lowest-numbered tiles, you need a different formula. First, the calculations involve only integers. The inputs you need for the formula in this case include the row number, tile size, and remainder (*number of rows in the table % number of requested tiles*). These inputs are used in calculating NTILE with non-even distribution.

The formula for the target tile number is as follows:

```
if row_number <= (tilesize + 1) * remainder then
  tile_number = (row_number - 1) / (tile_size + 1) + 1
else
  tile_number = (row_number - remainder - 1) / tile_size + 1
```

Translated to T-SQL, the query (which produces the output shown in Table 4-37) looks like this:

```
DECLARE @numtiles AS INT;
SET @numtiles = 9;

SELECT empid, qty,
  CASE
    WHEN rn <= (tilesize+1) * remainder
      THEN (rn-1) / (tilesize+1) + 1
    ELSE (rn - remainder - 1) / tilesize + 1
  END AS tile
```

```
FROM (SELECT empid, qty, rn,
         numrows/@numtiles AS tilesize,
         numrows%@numtiles AS remainder
      FROM (SELECT empid, qty,
              (SELECT COUNT(*) FROM dbo.Sales AS S2
                WHERE S2.qty < S1.qty
                  OR S2.qty = S1.qty
                      AND S2.empid <= S1.empid) AS rn,
              (SELECT COUNT(*) FROM dbo.Sales) AS numrows
           FROM dbo.Sales AS S1) AS D1) AS D2
ORDER BY qty, empid;
```

Table 4-37   NTILE, Remainder Added to First Groups

empid	qty	tile
B	100	1
G	100	1
J	100	2
H	150	2
C	200	3
D	200	4
K	200	5
E	250	6
I	250	7
A	300	8
F	300	9

The output is the same as the one you would get using the SQL Server 2005 NTILE function; the first tiles get an additional row until the remainder is consumed.

Auxiliary Table of Numbers

An auxiliary table of numbers is a very powerful tool that I often use in my solutions. So I decided to dedicate a section in this chapter to it. In this section, I'll simply describe the concept and the methods used to generate such a table. I'll refer to this auxiliary table throughout the book and demonstrate many of its applications.

An auxiliary table of numbers (call it Nums) is simply a table that contains the integers between 1 and N for some (typically large) value of N. I recommend that you create a permanent Nums table and populate it with as many values as you might need for your solutions.

The code in Listing 4-8 demonstrates how to create such a table containing 1,000,000 rows. Of course, you might want a different number of rows, depending on your needs.

Listing 4-8   Creating and populating auxiliary table of numbers

```
SET NOCOUNT ON;
USE AdventureWorks;
GO
IF OBJECT_ID('dbo.Nums') IS NOT NULL
  DROP TABLE dbo.Nums;
GO
CRFATE TABLE dbo.Nums(n INT NOT NULL PRIMARY KEY);
DECLARE @max AS INT, @rc AS INT;
SET @max = 1000000;
SET @rc = 1;

INSERT INTO Nums VALUES(1);
WHILE @rc * 2 <= @max
BEGIN
  INSERT INTO dbo.Nums SELECT n + @rc FROM dbo.Nums;
  SET @rc = @rc * 2;
END

INSERT INTO dbo.Nums
  SELECT n + @rc FROM dbo.Nums WHERE n + @rc <= @max;
```

Tip   Because there are so many practical uses for a Nums table, you'll probably end up needing to access it from various databases. To avoid the need to refer to it using the fully qualified name AdventureWorks.dbo.Nums, you can create a synonym in the model database pointing to Nums in AdventureWorks like this:

```
USE model;
CREATE SYNONYM dbo.Nums FOR AdventureWorks.dbo.Nums;
```

Creating the synonym in *model* will make it available in all newly created databases from that point on, including tempdb after SQL Server is restarted. For existing databases, you will just need to explicitly run the CREATE SYNONYM command once.

In practice, it doesn't really matter how you populate the Nums table because you run this process only once. Nevertheless, I used an optimized process that populates the table in a very fast manner. The process demonstrates the technique of creating Nums with a multiplying INSERT loop.

The code keeps track of the number of rows already inserted into the table in a variable called @rc. It first inserts into Nums the row where *n = 1*. It then enters a loop while @rc * 2 <= @max (@max is the desired number of rows). In each iteration, the process inserts into Nums the result of a query that selects all rows from Nums after adding @rc to each *n* value. This technique doubles the number of rows in Nums in each iteration—that is, first {1} is inserted, then {2}, then {3, 4}, then {5, 6, 7, 8}, then {9, 10, 11, 12, 13, 14, 15, 16}, and so on.

As soon as the table is populated with more than half the target number of rows, the loop ends. Another INSERT statement after the loop inserts the remaining rows using the same INSERT statement as within the loop, but this time with a filter to ensures that only values <= @max will be loaded.

The main reason that this process runs fast is that it minimizes writes to the transaction log compared to other available solutions. This is achieved by minimizing the number of INSERT statements (the number of INSERT statements is *CEILING(LOG2(@max)) + 1*). This code populated the Nums table with 1,000,000 rows in 6 seconds on my laptop. As an exercise, you can try populating the Nums table using a simple loop of individual inserts and see how long it takes.

Whenever you need the first @n numbers from Nums, simply query it, specifying *WHERE n <= @n* as the filter. An index on the n column will ensure that the query will scan only the required rows and no others.

If you're not allowed to add permanent tables in the database, you can create a table-valued UDF with a parameter for the number of rows needed. You use the same logic as used above to generate the required number of values.

In SQL Server 2005, you can use the new recursive CTEs and ROW_NUMBER function to create extremely efficient solutions that generate a table of numbers on the fly.

I'll start with a naïve solution that is fairly slow (about 20 seconds, with results discarded). The following solution uses a simple recursive CTE, where the anchor member generates a row with *n = 1*, and the recursive member adds a row in each iteration with *n = prev n + 1*:

```
DECLARE @n AS BIGINT;
SET @n = 1000000;

WITH Nums AS
(
  SELECT 1 AS n
  UNION ALL
  SELECT n + 1 FROM Nums WHERE n < @n
)
SELECT n FROM Nums
OPTION(MAXRECURSION 0);
```

> **Note**   If you're running the code to test it, remember to turn on the Discard Results After Execution option in SSMS; otherwise, you will get an output with a million rows.

You have to use a hint that removes the default recursion limit of 100. This solution runs for about 20 seconds.

You can optimize the solution significantly by using a CTE (call it *Base*) that generates as many rows as the square root of the target number of rows. Take the cross join of two instances of *Base* to get the target number of rows, and finally, generate row numbers for the result to serve as the sequence of numbers.

Here's the code that implements this approach:

```
DECLARE @n AS BIGINT;
SET @n = 1000000;

WITH Base AS
(
  SELFCT 1 AS n
  UNION ALL
  SELECT n + 1 FROM Base WHERE n < CEILING(SQRT(@n))
),
Expand AS
(
  SELECT 1 AS c
  FROM Base AS B1, Base AS B2
),
Nums AS
(
  SELECT ROW_NUMBER() OVER(ORDER BY c) AS n
  FROM Expand
)
SELECT n FROM Nums WHERE n <= @n
OPTION(MAXRECURSION 0);
```

This solution runs for only 0.8 seconds (results discarded).

Next, I'll describe the third approach to generate Nums. You start with a CTE that has only two rows, and multiply the number of rows with each following CTE by cross-joining two instances of the previous CTE. With n levels of CTEs (0-based), you reach 2^{2n} rows. For example, with 5 levels, you get 4,294,967,296 rows.

Another CTE generates row numbers, and finally the outer query filters the desired number of values (where *row number column* <= *input*). Remember that when you filter a *row number* <= *some* value, SQL Server doesn't bother to generate row numbers beyond that point. So you shouldn't be concerned about performance. It's not the case that your code will really generate more than four billion rows every time and then filter.

Here's the code that implements this approach:

```
DECLARE @n AS BIGINT;
SET @n = 1000000;

WITH
L0   AS(SELECT 1 AS c UNION ALL SELECT 1),
L1   AS(SELECT 1 AS c FROM L0 AS A, L0 AS B),
L2   AS(SELECT 1 AS c FROM L1 AS A, L1 AS B),
L3   AS(SELECT 1 AS c FROM L2 AS A, L2 AS B),
L4   AS(SELECT 1 AS c FROM L3 AS A, L3 AS B),
L5   AS(SELECT 1 AS c FROM L4 AS A, L4 AS B),
Nums AS(SELECT ROW_NUMBER() OVER(ORDER BY c) AS n FROM L5)
SELECT n FROM Nums WHERE n <= @n;
```

It runs for about 0.9 seconds to generate a sequence of 1,000,000 numbers.

As I mentioned earlier, you can wrap the logic in a UDF. The value of this solution is that it will never near the MAXRECURSION limit, and that limit cannot be modified in a UDF definition. The code in Listing 4-9 encapsulates the last solution's logic in a UDF.

Listing 4-9   UDF returning an auxiliary table of numbers

```
CREATE FUNCTION dbo.fn_nums(@n AS BIGINT) RETURNS TABLE
AS
RETURN
  WITH
  L0   AS(SELECT 1 AS c UNION ALL SELECT 1),
  L1   AS(SELECT 1 AS c FROM L0 AS A, L0 AS B),
  L2   AS(SELECT 1 AS c FROM L1 AS A, L1 AS B),
  L3   AS(SELECT 1 AS c FROM L2 AS A, L2 AS B),
  L4   AS(SELECT 1 AS c FROM L3 AS A, L3 AS B),
  L5   AS(SELECT 1 AS c FROM L4 AS A, L4 AS B),
  Nums AS(SELECT ROW_NUMBER() OVER(ORDER BY c) AS n FROM L5)
  SELECT n FROM Nums WHERE n <= @n;
GO
```

To test the function, run the following code, which returns an auxiliary table with 10 numbers:

```
SELECT * FROM dbo.fn_nums(10) AS F;
```

Existing and Missing Ranges (Also Known as Islands and Gaps)

To put your knowledge of subqueries, table expressions, and ranking calculations into action, I'll provide a couple of problems that have many applications in production environments. I'll present a generic form of the problem, though, so you can focus on the techniques and not the data.

Create and populate a table named T1 by running the code in Listing 4-10.

Listing 4-10   Creating and populating the T1 table

```
USE tempdb;
GO
IF OBJECT_ID('dbo.T1') IS NOT NULL
  DROP TABLE dbo.T1
GO
CREATE TABLE dbo.T1(col1 INT NOT NULL PRIMARY KEY);
INSERT INTO dbo.T1(col1) VALUES(1);
INSERT INTO dbo.T1(col1) VALUES(2);
INSERT INTO dbo.T1(col1) VALUES(3);
INSERT INTO dbo.T1(col1) VALUES(100);
INSERT INTO dbo.T1(col1) VALUES(101);
INSERT INTO dbo.T1(col1) VALUES(103);
INSERT INTO dbo.T1(col1) VALUES(104);
INSERT INTO dbo.T1(col1) VALUES(105);
INSERT INTO dbo.T1(col1) VALUES(106);
```

You have two tasks. The first task is to return the missing ranges of keys within the data, generating the output shown in Table 4-38.

Table 4-38   Missing Ranges

start_range	end_range
4	99
102	102

The second task is to return ranges of consecutive keys in the data, generating the output shown in Table 4-39.

Table 4-39   Existing Ranges

start_range	end_range
1	3
100	101
103	106

These problems manifest in production systems in many forms—for example, availability or nonavailability reports. In some cases, the values appear as integers, such as in our case. In other cases, they appear as *datetime* values. The techniques that are needed to solve the problem with integers apply to *datetime* values with very minor revisions.

Missing Ranges (Also Known as Gaps)

There are several approaches you can use to solve the problem of missing ranges (gaps), but first it's important to identify the steps in the solution before you start coding.

One approach can be described by the following steps:

- Find the points before the gaps, and add one to each.
- For each starting point of a gap, find the next existing value in the table and subtract one.

Having the logical aspects of the steps resolved, you can start coding. You will find in the preceding logical steps that the chapter covered all the fundamental techniques that are mentioned—namely, finding "points before gaps" and finding the "next" existing value.

The following query returns the points before the gaps shown in Table 4-40:

```
SELECT col1
FROM dbo.T1 AS A
WHERE NOT EXISTS
  (SELECT * FROM dbo.T1 AS B
  WHERE B.col1 = A.col1 + 1);
```

Table 4-40 Points Before Gaps

col1
3
101
106

Remember a point before a gap is a value after which the next doesn't exist.

Notice in the output that the last row is of no interest to us because it's before infinity. The following query returns the starting points of the gaps, and its output is shown in Table 4-41. It achieves this by adding one to the points before the gaps to get the first values in the gaps, filtering out the point before infinity.

```
SELECT col1 + 1 AS start_range
FROM dbo.T1 AS A
WHERE NOT EXISTS
  (SELECT * FROM dbo.T1 AS B
   WHERE B.col1 = A.col1 + 1)
  AND col1 < (SELECT MAX(col1) FROM dbo.T1);
```

Table 4-41 Starting Points of Gaps

start_range
4
102

Finally, for each starting point in the gap, you use a subquery to return the next value in the table minus 1—in other words, the end of the gap:

```
SELECT col1 + 1 AS start_range,
  (SELECT MIN(col1) FROM dbo.T1 AS B
   WHERE B.col1 > A.col1) - 1 AS end_range
FROM dbo.T1 AS A
WHERE NOT EXISTS
  (SELECT * FROM dbo.T1 AS B
   WHERE B.col1 = A.col1 + 1)
  AND col1 < (SELECT MAX(col1) FROM dbo.T1);
```

That's one approach to solving the problem. Another approach, which I find much simpler and more intuitive is the following one:

- To each existing value, match the next existing value, generating current, next pairs.

- Keep only pairs where next minus current is greater than one.

- With the remaining pairs, add one to the current and subtract one from the next.

This approach relies on the fact that adjacent values with a distance greater than one represent the boundaries of a gap. Identifying a gap based on identification of the next existing value is another useful technique.

To translate the preceding steps to T-SQL, the following query simply returns the next value for each current value, generating the output shown in Table 4-42:

```
SELECT col1 AS cur,
  (SELECT MIN(col1) FROM dbo.T1 AS B
   WHERE B.col1 > A.col1) AS nxt
FROM dbo.T1 AS A;
```

Table 4-42   Current, Next Pairs

cur	nxt
1	2
2	3
3	100
100	101
101	103
103	104
104	105
105	106
106	NULL

Finally, you create a derived table out of the previous step's query, and you keep only pairs where *nxt* − *cur* is greater than one. You add one to *cur* to get the actual start of the gap, and subtract one from *nxt* to get the actual end of the gap:

```
SELECT cur + 1 AS start_range, nxt - 1 AS end_range
FROM (SELECT col1 AS cur,
        (SELECT MIN(col1) FROM dbo.T1 AS B
         WHERE B.col1 > A.col1) AS nxt
      FROM dbo.T1 AS A) AS D
WHERE nxt - cur > 1;
```

Note that this solution got rid of the point before infinity with no special treatment, because the *nxt* value for it was NULL.

I compared the performance of the two solutions and found them to be similar. However, the second solution is doubtless simpler and more intuitive, and that's a big advantage in terms of readability and maintenance.

By the way, if you need to return the list of individual missing values as opposed to missing ranges, using the Nums table, the task is very simple:

```
SELECT n FROM dbo.Nums
WHERE n BETWEEN (SELECT MIN(col1) FROM dbo.T1)
           AND (SELECT MAX(col1) FROM dbo.T1)
   AND NOT EXISTS(SELECT * FROM dbo.T1 WHERE col1 = n);
```

Existing Ranges (Also Known as Islands)

Returning ranges of existing values or collapsing ranges with consecutive values involves a concept I haven't discussed yet—a grouping factor. You basically need to group data by a factor that does not exist in the data as a base attribute. In our case, you need to calculate some x value for all members of the first subset of consecutive values {1, 2, 3}, some y value for the second {100, 101}, some z value for the third {104, 105, 106}, and so on. Once you have this grouping factor available, you can group the data by this factor and return the minimum and maximum $col1$ values in each group.

One approach to calculating this grouping factor brings me to another technique: calculating the min or max value of a group of consecutive values. Take the group {1, 2, 3} as an example. If you will manage to calculate for each of the members the max value in the group (3), you will be able to use it as your grouping factor.

The logic behind the technique to calculating the maximum within a group of consecutive values is: return the minimum value that is greater than or equal to the current, after which there's a gap. Here's the translation to T-SQL, yielding the output shown in Table 4-43:

```
SELECT col1,
  (SELECT MIN(col1) FROM dbo.T1 AS B
   WHERE B.col1 >= A.col1
     AND NOT EXISTS
       (SELECT * FROM dbo.T1 AS C
        WHERE B.col1 = C.col1 - 1)) AS grp
FROM dbo.T1 AS A;
```

Table 4-43   Grouping Factor

col1	grp
1	3
2	3
3	3
100	101
101	101
103	106
104	106
105	106
106	106

The rest is really easy: create a derived table out of the previous step's query, group the data by the grouping factor, and return the minimum and maximum values for each group:

```
SELECT MIN(col1) AS start_range, MAX(col1) AS end_range
FROM (SELECT col1,
        (SELECT MIN(col1) FROM dbo.T1 AS B
        WHERE B.col1 >= A.col1
          AND NOT EXISTS
            (SELECT * FROM dbo.T1 AS C
              WHERE B.col1 = C.col1 - 1)) AS grp
      FROM dbo.T1 AS A) AS D
GROUP BY grp;
```

This solution solves the problem, but I'm not sure I'd qualify it as a very simple and intuitive solution with satisfactory performance.

In search for a simpler and faster way to calculate the grouping factor, check out the output shown in Table 4-44 of the following query that simply produces row numbers based on *col1* order.

```
SELECT col1, ROW_NUMBER() OVER(ORDER BY col1) AS rn
FROM dbo.T1;
```

Table 4-44   Row Numbers Based on *col1* Order

col1	rn
1	1
2	2
3	3
100	4
101	5
103	6
104	7
105	8
106	9

If you're working with SQL Server 2000, you'd probably want to use the IDENTITY-based technique I described earlier for calculating row numbers.

See if you can identify a relationship between the way the *col1* values increment and the way row numbers do.

Well, their difference remains constant within the same group of consecutive values, because it has no gaps. As soon as you get to a new group, the difference between *col1* and the row number increases.

To make this idea more tangible, calculate the difference between *col1* and the row number and examine the result shown in Table 4-45. This key technique shows one way to calculate the group factor with ROW_NUMBER.

```
SELECT col1, col1 - ROW_NUMBER() OVER(ORDER BY col1) AS diff
FROM dbo.T1;
```

Table 4-45   Difference between *col1* and Row Number

col1	diff
1	0
2	0
3	0
100	96
101	96
103	97
104	97
105	97
106	97

Now it's crystal clear. You have created a grouping factor with close to zero effort. Simple and fast!

Now simply replace in the previous solution the derived table query with the preceding query to get the desired result:

```
SELECT MIN(col1) AS start_range, MAX(col1) AS end_range
FROM (SELECT col1, col1 - ROW_NUMBER() OVER(ORDER BY col1) AS grp
      FROM dbo.T1) AS D
GROUP BY grp;
```

Conclusion

This chapter covered many subjects, all related to subqueries. I discussed scalar and list subqueries, self-contained and correlated subqueries, table expressions, and ranking calculations.

It's important to make mental notes of the fundamental techniques that I point out here and throughout the book, such as generating duplicates using an auxiliary table of numbers, introducing a tiebreaker, finding points before gaps, returning the next or previous value, calculating a grouping factor, and so on. This builds your T-SQL vocabulary and enhances your skills. As you progress with this approach, you'll see that it becomes easier and easier to identify fundamental elements in a problem. Having already resolved and polished key techniques separately in a focused manner, you will use them naturally to solve problems.

Chapter 5
Joins and Set Operations

This chapter covers joins and set operations—their logical aspects as well as their physical/performance aspects. I'll demonstrate practical applications for each type of join and set operation. I have used the ANSI SQL terminology to categorize the elements of the language that I'll cover here. *Joins* (CROSS, INNER, OUTER) refer to *horizontal* operations (loosely speaking) between tables, while *set operations* (UNION, EXCEPT, INTERSECT) refer to *vertical* operations between tables.

Joins

Joins are operations that allow you to match rows between tables. I informally referred to these operations as horizontal ones because the virtual table resulting from a join operation between two tables contains all columns from both tables.

I'll first describe the different syntaxes for joins supported by the standard, and I'll also mention the proprietary elements in T-SQL. I'll then describe the fundamental join types and their applications followed by other categorizations of joins. I'll also have a focused discussion on the internal processing of joins—namely, join algorithms.

You'll have a couple of chances to practice what you've learned by trying to solve a problem that encompasses previously discussed aspects of joins.

Old Style vs. New Style

T-SQL supports two different syntaxes for joins. There's a lot of confusion surrounding the two. When do you use each? Which performs better? Which is standard and which is proprietary? Is the older syntax going to be deprecated soon? And so on. Hopefully, this chapter will clear the fog.

I'll start by saying there are two different syntaxes for joins supported by the ANSI standard, and neither is in a process of deprecation yet. The join elements of the older standard are a complete part of the newer. This means that you can use either one without worrying that it will not be supported by Microsoft SQL Server sometime soon. SQL Server will not remove support for implemented features that were not deprecated by the standard.

The older of the two syntaxes was introduced in ANSI SQL:1989. What distinguishes it from the newer one is the use of commas to separate table names that appear in the FROM clause, and the absence of the JOIN keyword and the ON clause:

```
FROM T1, T2
WHERE where_filter
```

The ANSI SQL:1989 syntax had support only for cross and inner join types. It did not have support for outer joins.

The newer syntax was introduced in ANSI SQL:1992, and what distinguishes it from the older syntax is the removal of the commas and the introduction of the JOIN keyword and the ON clause:

```
FROM T1 <join_type> JOIN T2 ON <on_filter>
WHERE where_filter
```

ANSI SQL:1992 introduced support for outer joins, and this drove the need for a separation of filters—the ON filter and the WHERE filter. I'll explain this in detail in the outer joins section.

Part of the confusion surrounding the two syntaxes has to do with the fact that T-SQL supported a proprietary syntax for outer joins before SQL Server added support for the ANSI SQL:1992 syntax. There was a practical need for outer joins, and SQL Server provided an answer to that need. Particularly, I'm talking about the old-style proprietary outer join syntax using *= and =* for left outer and right outer joins, respectively.

For backward compatibility reasons, SQL Server has not removed support for the proprietary outer join syntax thus far. However, these syntax elements were deprecated in SQL Server 2005 and will work only under a backward-compatibility flag. All other join syntax elements are standard and are not being considered for deprecation—neither by the standard, nor by SQL Server.

As I describe the different fundamental join types, I'll discuss both syntaxes and give you my opinion regarding which one I find more convenient to use and why.

Fundamental Join Types

As I describe the different fundamental join types—cross, inner, and outer—keep in mind the phases in query logical processing that I described in detail in the Chapter 1. In particular, keep in mind the logical phases involved in join processing.

Each fundamental join type takes place only between two tables. Even if you have more than two tables in the FROM clause, the first three query logical processing phases will take place between two tables at a time. Each join will result in a virtual table, which in turn will be joined with the next table in the FROM clause. This process will continue until all tables in the FROM clause are processed.

The fundamental join types differ in the logical phases that they apply. Cross join applies only the first (Cartesian product), inner join applies the first and the second (Cartesian product, ON filter), and outer join applies all three (Cartesian product, ON filter, add outer rows).

CROSS

A cross join performs a Cartesian product between two tables. In other words, it returns a row for each possible combination of a row from the left table and a row from the right table. If the left table has n rows and the right table has m rows, a cross join will return a table with $n \times m$ rows.

There are many practical applications to cross joins, but I'll start with a very simple example—a plain cross.

The following query produces all possible pairs of employees from the Employees table in the Northwind database:

```
USE Northwind;

SELECT E1.FirstName, E1.LastName AS emp1,
  E2.FirstName, E2.LastName AS emp2
FROM dbo.Employees AS E1
  CROSS JOIN dbo.Employees AS E2;
```

Because the Employees table contains nine rows, the result set will contain 81 rows

And here's the ANSI SQL:1989 syntax you would use for the same task:

```
SELECT E1.FirstName, E1.LastName AS emp1,
  E2.FirstName, E2.LastName AS emp2
FROM dbo.Employees AS E1, dbo.Employees AS E2;
```

For cross joins only, I prefer using a comma (as opposed to using the CROSS JOIN keywords) because it allows for shorter code. I also find the older syntax to be more natural and readable. The optimizer will produce the same plan for both, so you shouldn't have any concerns about performance.

As you will see later on, I will give a different recommendation for inner joins. Now let's look at more sophisticated uses of cross joins.

In Chapter 4, I presented a powerful key technique to generate duplicates. Recall that I used an auxiliary table of numbers (Nums) as follows to generate the requested number of duplicates of each row:

```
SELECT ...
FROM T1, Nums
WHERE n <= <num_of_dups>
```

The preceding technique will generate in the result set *num_of_dups* duplicates of each row in T1. As a practical example, suppose you need to fill an Orders table with sample data for testing. You have a Customers table with sample customer information and an Employees table with sample employee information. You want to generate, for each combination of a customer and an employee, an order for each day in January 2006.

I will demonstrate this technique, generating test data based on duplicates, in the Northwind database. The Customers table contains 91 rows, the Employees table contains 9 rows, and for each customer-employee combination, you need an order for each day in January 2006—that is, for 31 days. The result set should contain 25,389 rows ($91 \times 9 \times 31 = 25,389$). Naturally, you will want to store the result set in a target table and generate an order ID for each order.

You already have tables with customers and employees, but there's a missing table—you need a table to represent the days. You probably guessed already that the Nums table will assume the role of the missing table:

```
SELECT CustomerID, EmployeeID,
  DATEADD(day, n-1, '20060101') AS OrderDate
FROM dbo.Customers, dbo.Employees, dbo.Nums
WHERE n <= 31;
```

You cross Customers, Employees, and Nums, filtering the first 31 values of *n* from the Nums table for the 31 days of the month. In the SELECT list, you calculate the specific target dates by adding *n* − *1* days to the first date of the month, January 1, 2006.

The last missing element is the order ID. But you can easily generate it using the ROW_NUMBER function in SQL Server 2005, or the IDENTITY function or property in SQL Server 2000.

In practice, you'd probably want to encapsulate this logic in a stored procedure that accepts the date range as input. Instead of using a literal for the number of days in the filter, you will use the following expression:

```
DATEDIFF(day, @fromdate, @todate) + 1
```

Similarly, the DATEADD function in the SELECT list will refer to *@fromdate* instead of a literal base date:

```
DATEADD(day, n-1, @fromdate) AS OrderDate
```

Here's the code that you would need in SQL Server 2000 to generate the test data to populate a target table. I'm using the IDENTITY function to generate the order IDs and the date range boundaries as input arguments:

```
DECLARE @fromdate AS DATETIME, @todate AS DATETIME;
SET @fromdate = '20060101';
SET @todate = '20060131';

SELECT IDENTITY(int, 1, 1) AS OrderID,
  CustomerID, EmployeeID,
  DATEADD(day, n-1, @fromdate) AS OrderDate
```

```
INTO dbo.MyOrders
FROM dbo.Customers, dbo.Employees, dbo.Nums
WHERE n <= DATEDIFF(day, @fromdate, @todate) + 1;
```

In SQL Server 2005, you can use the ROW_NUMBER function instead of the IDENTITY function, and assign the row numbers based on a desired ordering column (for example, *OrderDate*):

```
IF OBJECT_ID('dbo.MyOrders') IS NOT NULL
  DROP TABLE dbo.MyOrders;
GO

DECLARE @fromdate AS DATETIME, @todate AS DATETIME;
SET @fromdate = '20060101';
SET @todate = '20060131';

WITH Orders
AS
(
  SELECT CustomerID, EmployeeID,
    DATEADD(day, n-1, @fromdate) AS OrderDate
  FROM dbo.Customers, dbo.Employees, dbo.Nums
  WHERE n <= DATEDIFF(day, @fromdate, @todate) + 1
)
SELECT ROW_NUMBER() OVER(ORDER BY OrderDate) AS OrderID,
  CustomerID, EmployeeID, OrderDate
INTO dbo.MyOrders
FROM Orders;
```

When you're done experimenting with this code, don't forget to drop the MyOrders table:

```
DROP TABLE dbo.MyOrders;
```

Another application of cross joins allows you to improve performance of queries that apply calculations between row attributes and aggregates over rows. To demonstrate this fundamental key technique, I'll use the sales table in the *pubs* database. First, create an index on the *qty* column, which is important for our task:

```
USE pubs;
CREATE INDEX idx_qty ON dbo.sales(qty);
```

The task at hand is to calculate for each sale that sale's percentage of total quantity sold, and the difference between the sale quantity and the average quantity for all sales. The intuitive way for programmers to write calculations between row attributes and aggregates over rows is to use subqueries. The following code (which produces the output shown in Table 5-1) demonstrates the subquery approach:

```
SELECT stor_id, ord_num, title_id,
  CONVERT(VARCHAR(10), ord_date, 120) AS ord_date, qty,
  CAST(1.*qty / (SELECT SUM(qty) FROM dbo.sales) * 100
      AS DECIMAL(5, 2)) AS per,
  qty - (SELECT AVG(qty) FROM dbo.sales) as diff
FROM dbo.sales;
```

Table 5-1   Sales Information, Including Percentage of Total and Difference from Average

stor_id	ord_num	title_id	ord_date	qty	per	diff
6380	6871	BU1032	1994-09-14	5	1.01	−18
6380	722a	PS2091	1994-09-13	3	0.61	−20
7066	A2976	PC8888	1993-05-24	50	10.14	27
7066	QA7442.3	PS2091	1994-09-13	75	15.21	52
7067	D4482	PS2091	1994-09-14	10	2.03	−13
7067	P2121	TC3218	1992-06-15	40	8.11	17
7067	P2121	TC4203	1992-06-15	20	4.06	−3
7067	P2121	TC7777	1992-06-15	20	4.06	−3
7131	N914008	PS2091	1994-09-14	20	4.06	−3
7131	N914014	MC3021	1994-09-14	25	5.07	2
7131	P3087a	PS1372	1993-05-29	20	4.06	−3
7131	P3087a	PS2106	1993-05-29	25	5.07	2
7131	P3087a	PS3333	1993-05-29	15	3.04	−8
7131	P3087a	PS7777	1993-05-29	25	5.07	2
7896	QQ2299	BU7832	1993-10-28	15	3.04	−8
7896	TQ456	MC2222	1993-12-12	10	2.03	−13
7896	X999	BU2075	1993-02-21	35	7.10	12
8042	423LL922	MC3021	1994-09-14	15	3.04	−8
8042	423LL930	BU1032	1994-09-14	10	2.03	−13
8042	P723	BU1111	1993-03-11	25	5.07	2
8042	QA879.1	PC1035	1993-05-22	30	6.09	7

Before I get into the performance aspects of the query, I first want to discuss some of its logical aspects. As you can see, both the total quantity and the average quantity are obtained using self-contained subqueries. The expression calculating the percentage takes into account the way expressions are processed in T-SQL. The datatype of an expression is determined by the datatype with the higher precedence among the participating operands. This means that *qty / totalqty* (where *totalqty* stands for the subquery returning the total quantity) will yield an integer result—because both operands are integers, and the / operator will be integer division. Because *qty* is a portion of *totalqty*, you'd always get a zero as the result, because the remainder is truncated. To get an accurate decimal calculation, you need to convert the operands to decimals. This can be achieved by using either explicit conversion or implicit conversion, as I did. *1. * qty* will implicitly convert the *qty* value to a decimal because a decimal is higher in precedence than an integer. Consequently, *totalqty* will also be converted to a decimal, and so will the integer literal 100. Finally, I used an explicit conversion to DECIMAL(5, 2) for the *per* result column to maintain an accuracy of only two decimal places. Three digits to the left of the decimal point are sufficient for the percentages here because the highest possible value is 100.

As for performance, examine this query's execution plan, which is shown in Figure 5-1.

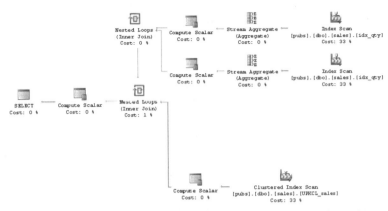

Figure 5-1   Execution plan for obtaining aggregates with subqueries

You will notice that the index I created on the *qty* column is scanned twice—once to calculate the sum, and once to calculate the average. In other words, provided that you have an index on the aggregated column, the index will be scanned once for each subquery that returns an aggregate. If you don't have an index containing the aggregated column, matters are even worse, as you'll get a table scan for each subquery.

This query can be optimized using a key technique that utilizes a cross join. You can calculate all needed aggregates in one query that will require only a single index or table scan. Such a query will produce a single result row with all aggregates. You create a derived table defined by this query and cross it with the base table. Now you have access to both attributes and aggregates. Here's the solution query, which produces the more optimal plan shown in Figure 5-2:

```
SELECT stor_id, ord_num, title_id,
  CONVERT(VARCHAR(10), ord_date, 120) AS ord_date, qty,
  CAST(1.*qty / sumqty * 100 AS DECIMAL(5, 2)) AS per,
  qty - avgqty as diff
FROM dbo.sales,
  (SELECT SUM(qty) AS sumqty, AVG(qty) AS avgqty
   FROM dbo.sales) AS AGG;
```

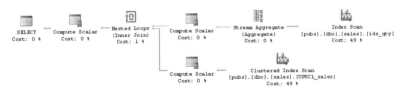

Figure 5-2   Execution plan for obtaining aggregates with a cross join

As you can see in the plan, the index on the *qty* column is scanned only once, and both aggregates are calculated with the same scan. Of course, in SQL Server 2005 you can use a common table expression (CTE), which you might find easier to read:

```
WITH Agg AS
(
  SELECT SUM(qty) AS sumqty, AVG(qty) AS avgqty
  FROM dbo.sales
)
SELECT stor_id, ord_num, title_id,
  CONVERT(VARCHAR(10), ord_date, 120) AS ord_date, qty,
  CAST(1.*qty / sumqty * 100 AS DECIMAL(5, 2)) AS per,
  qty - avgqty as diff
FROM dbo.sales, Agg;
```

You will find that both queries generate the same plan. In Chapter 6, I'll demonstrate how to use the new OVER clause in SQL Server 2005 to tackle similar problems.

Once you're done experimenting with this technique, drop the index on the *qty* column:

```
DROP INDEX dbo.sales.idx_qty;
```

INNER

Inner joins are used to match rows between two tables based on some criterion. Out of the first three query logical processing phases, inner joins apply the first two—namely, Cartesian product and ON filter. There's no phase that adds outer rows. Consequently, if an INNER JOIN query contains both an ON clause and a WHERE clause, logically they are applied one after the other. With one exception, there's no difference between specifying a logical expression in the ON clause or in the WHERE clause of an INNER JOIN, because there's no intermediate step that adds outer rows between the two.

The one exception is when you specify GROUP BY ALL. Remember that GROUP BY ALL adds back groups that were filtered out by the WHERE clause, but it does not add back groups that were filtered out by the ON clause. Remember also that this is a nonstandard legacy feature that you should avoid using.

As for performance, when not using the GROUP BY ALL option, you will typically get the same plan regardless of where you place the filter expression. That's because the optimizer is aware that there's no difference. I should always be cautious when saying such things related to optimization choices because the process is so dynamic.

As for the two supported join syntaxes, using the ANSI SQL:1992 syntax, you have more flexibility in choosing which clause you will use to specify a filter expression. Because logically it makes no difference where you place your filters, and typically there's also no performance difference, your guideline should be natural and intuitive writing. Write in a way that feels more natural to you and to the programmers who need to maintain your code. For example, to me a filter that matches attributes between the tables should appear in the ON clause, while a filter on an attribute from only one table should appear in the WHERE clause. I'll use the following query to return orders placed by U.S. customers:

```
USE Northwind;

SELECT C.CustomerID, CompanyName, OrderID
FROM dbo.Customers AS C
  JOIN dbo.Orders AS O
    ON C.CustomerID = O.CustomerID
WHERE Country = 'USA';
```

Using the ANSI SQL:1989 syntax, you have no choice but to specify all filter expressions in the WHERE clause:

```
SELECT C.CustomerID, CompanyName, OrderID
FROM dbo.Customers AS C, dbo.Orders AS O
WHERE C.CustomerID = O.CustomerID
  AND Country = 'USA';
```

Remember that the discussion here is about inner joins; with outer joins, there are logical differences between specifying a filter expression in the ON clause and specifying it in the WHERE clause.

I mentioned earlier that I like using the ANSI SQL:1989 syntax for cross joins. However, with inner joins, my recommendation is different. The reason for this is that there's a risk in using the ANSI SQL:1989 syntax. If you forget to specify the join condition, unintentionally you get a cross join, as demonstrated in the following code:

```
SELECT C.CustomerID, CompanyName, OrderID
FROM dbo.Customers AS C, dbo.Orders AS O;
```

In SQL Server Management Studio (SSMS), the query plan for a cross join will include a join operator marked with a yellow warning symbol, and the pop-up details will say "No Join Predicate" in the Warnings section. This warning is designed to alert you that you might have forgotten to specify a join predicate.

However, if you explicitly specify INNER JOIN when you write an inner join query, an ON clause is required. If you forget to specify any join condition, the parser traps the error and the query is not run:

```
SELECT C.CustomerID, CompanyName, OrderID
FROM dbo.Customers AS C JOIN dbo.Orders AS O;

Msg 102, Level 15, State 1, Line 2
Incorrect syntax near ';'.
```

The parser finds a semicolon after dbo.Orders AS O, even though it expects something else (an ON clause or other options), so it generates an error saying that there's incorrect syntax near ';'.

> **Note**   If you have a composite join (a join based on multiple attributes), and you specify at least one expression but forget the others, neither syntax will trap the error. Similarly, other logical errors won't be trapped—for example, if you mistakenly type **ON C.OrderID = C.OrderID**.

OUTER

Outer joins are used to return matching rows from both tables based on some criterion, plus rows from the "preserved" table or tables for which there was no match.

You identify preserved tables with the LEFT, RIGHT, or FULL keywords. LEFT marks the left table as preserved, RIGHT marks the right table, and FULL marks both.

Outer joins apply all three query logical processing phases—namely, Cartesian product, ON filter, and adding outer rows. Outer rows added for rows from the preserved table with no match have NULLs for the attributes of the nonpreserved table.

The following query returns customers with their order IDs (just as would an inner join with the same ON clause), but it also returns a row for each customer with no orders because the keyword LEFT identifies the Customers table as preserved:

```
SELECT C.CustomerID, CompanyName, OrderID
FROM dbo.Customers AS C
  LEFT OUTER JOIN dbo.Orders AS O
    ON C.CustomerID = O.CustomerID;
```

The keyword OUTER is optional because the mention of one of the keywords LEFT, RIGHT, or FULL implies an outer join. However, unlike inner joins, where most programmers typically don't specify the optional INNER keyword, most programmers (including me) typically do specify the OUTER keyword. I guess it *feels* more natural.

As I mentioned earlier, SQL Server 2005 will support the nonstandard proprietary syntax for outer joins only under a backward-compatibility flag. To enable the older syntax, change the Northwind database's compatibility mode to 80 (SQL Server 2000):

```
EXEC sp_dbcmptlevel Northwind, 80;
```

> **Note**   Changing the compatibility mode of a database to an earlier version will prevent you from using the new language elements (for example, PIVOT, UNPIVOT, and so on). I'm just changing the compatibility mode to demonstrate the code. Once I'm done, I'll instruct you to turn it back to 90 (SQL Server 2005).

The old-style outer join was indicated in the WHERE clause, not the FROM clause. Instead of =, it used *= to represent a left outer join and =* to represent a right outer join. There was no support for a full outer join. For example, the following query returns customers with their order IDs, and customers with no orders:

```
SELECT C.CustomerID, CompanyName, OrderID
FROM dbo.Customers AS C, dbo.Orders AS O
WHERE C.CustomerID *= O.CustomerID;
```

This syntax is very problematic because of the lack of separation between an ON filter and a WHERE filter. For example, if you want to return only customers with no orders, using ANSI syntax it's very simple:

```
SELECT C.CustomerID, CompanyName, OrderID
FROM dbo.Customers AS C
  LEFT OUTER JOIN dbo.Orders AS O
    ON C.CustomerID = O.CustomerID
WHERE O.CustomerID IS NULL;
```

You get customers FISSA and PARIS back. The query initially applies the first three steps in query logical processing, yielding an intermediate virtual table containing customers with their orders (inner rows) and also customers with no orders (outer rows). For the outer rows, the attributes from the Orders table are NULL. The WHERE filter is subsequently applied to this intermediate result. Only the rows with a NULL in the join column from the nonpre-served side, which represent the customers with no orders, satisfy the condition in the WHERE clause.

If you attempt to write the query using the old-style syntax, you will get surprising results:

```
SELECT C.CustomerID, CompanyName, OrderID
FROM dbo.Customers AS C, dbo.Orders AS O
WHERE C.CustomerID *= O.CustomerID
  AND O.CustomerID IS NULL;
```

The query returns all 91 customers. Because there's no distinction between an ON clause and a WHERE clause, I specified both expressions in the WHERE clause separated by the logical operator AND. You have no control over which part of the filter will take place before adding the outer rows and which part will take place afterwards. That's at the sole discretion of SQL Server. By looking at the result, you can guess what SQL Server did. Logically, it applied the whole expression before adding outer rows. Obviously, there's no row in the Cartesian prod-uct for which `C.CustomerID = O.CustomerID` and `O.CustomerID IS NULL`. So the second phase in query logical processing yields an empty set. The third phase adds outer rows for rows from the preserved table (Customers) with no match. Because none of the rows matched the join condition, all customers are added back as outer rows. That's why this query returned all 91 customers.

Bearing in mind that you got this surprising result because both expressions were applied before adding the outer rows, and being familiar with query logical processing, there is a way to "fix" the problem. Remember that there's another filter available to you in a query—the

HAVING filter. First write a join query without the filter to isolate outer rows. Even though the rows in the result of the join are unique, group them by all columns to allow the query to include a HAVING clause. Then put the filter that isolates the outer rows into the HAVING clause:

```
SELECT C.CustomerID, CompanyName, OrderID
FROM dbo.Customers AS C, dbo.Orders AS O
WHERE C.CustomerID *= O.CustomerID
GROUP BY C.CustomerID, CompanyName, OrderID
HAVING OrderID IS NULL;
```

In this manner, you control which filter will be applied before adding outer rows and which will be applied after.

Important   Keep in mind that I demonstrated the older proprietary syntax just to make you aware of its issues. It is of course strongly recommended that you refrain from using it and revise all code that does use it to the ANSI syntax. In short, don't try this at home!

When you're done experimenting with the old-style syntax, change the database's compatibility level back to 90 (SQL Server 2005):

```
EXEC sp_dbcmptlevel Northwind, 90;
```

In the previous chapter, I provided a solution using subqueries for the minimum missing value problem. As a reminder, you begin with the table T1, which you create and populate by running the code in Listing 5-1.

Listing 5-1   Creating and populating the table T1

```
USE tempdb;
GO
IF OBJECT_ID('dbo.T1') IS NOT NULL
  DROP TABLE dbo.T1;
GO

CREATE TABLE dbo.T1
(
  keycol  INT         NOT NULL PRIMARY KEY,
  datacol VARCHAR(10) NOT NULL
);
INSERT INTO dbo.T1(keycol, datacol) VALUES(1, 'e');
INSERT INTO dbo.T1(keycol, datacol) VALUES(2, 'f');
INSERT INTO dbo.T1(keycol, datacol) VALUES(3, 'a');
INSERT INTO dbo.T1(keycol, datacol) VALUES(4, 'b');
INSERT INTO dbo.T1(keycol, datacol) VALUES(6, 'c');
INSERT INTO dbo.T1(keycol, datacol) VALUES(7, 'd');
```

Your task is to find the minimum missing key (in this case, 5) assuming the key starts at 1. I provided the following solution based on subqueries:

```
SELECT MIN(A.keycol + 1)
FROM dbo.T1 AS A
WHERE NOT EXISTS
  (SELECT * FROM dbo.T1 AS B
   WHERE B.keycol = A.keycol + 1);
```

Remember that I provided a CASE expression that returns the value 1 if it is missing; otherwise, it returns the result of the preceding query. You can solve the same problem—returning the minimum missing key when 1 exists in the table—by using the following outer join query between two instances of T1:

```
SELECT MIN(A.keycol + 1)
FROM dbo.T1 AS A
  LEFT OUTER JOIN dbo.T1 AS B
    ON B.keycol = A.keycol + 1
WHERE B.keycol IS NULL;
```

The first step in the solution is applying the left outer join between two instances of T1, called A and B, based on the join condition *B.keycol = A.keycol + 1*. This step involves the first three query logical processing phases I described in Chapter 1 (Cartesian product, ON filter, and adding outer rows). For now, ignore the WHERE filter and the SELECT clause. The join condition matches each row in A with a row from B whose key value is 1 greater than A's key value. Because it's an outer join, rows from A that have no match in B are added as outer rows, producing the virtual table shown in Table 5-2.

Table 5-2 Output of Step 1 in Minimum Missing Value Solution

A.keycol	A.datacol	B.keycol	B.datacol
1	e	2	f
2	f	3	a
3	a	4	b
4	b	NULL	NULL
6	c	7	d
7	d	NULL	NULL

Note that the outer rows represent the points before the gaps because the next key value is missing. The second step in the solution is to isolate only the points before the gaps, the WHERE clause filters only rows where *B.keycol* is NULL, producing the virtual table shown in Table 5-3.

Table 5-3 Output of Step 2 in Minimum Missing Value Solution

A.keycol	A.datacol	B.keycol	B.datacol
4	b	NULL	NULL
7	d	NULL	NULL

Finally, the last step in the solution is to isolate the minimum *A.keycol* value, which is the minimum key value before a gap, and adds 1. The result is the requested minimum missing value.

The optimizer generates very similar plans for both queries, with identical costs. So you can use the solution that you feel more comfortable with. To me, the solution based on subqueries seems more intuitive.

Nonsupported Join Types

ANSI SQL supports a couple of join types that are not supported by T-SQL—natural join and union join. I haven't found practical applications for a union join, so I won't bother to describe or demonstrate it in this book.

A natural join is an inner join where the join condition is implicitly based on equating columns that share the same names in both tables. The syntax for a natural join, not surprisingly, is NATURAL JOIN. For example, the two queries shown next are logically equivalent, but only the second is recognized by SQL Server:

```
SELECT C.CustomerID, CompanyName, OrderID
FROM dbo.Customers AS C NATURAL JOIN dbo.Orders AS O;
```

and

```
SELECT C.CustomerID, CompanyName, OrderID
FROM dbo.Customers AS C
  JOIN dbo.Orders AS O
    ON O.CustomerID = O.CustomerID;
```

Further Examples of Joins

So far, I have demonstrated fundamental join types. There are other ways to categorize joins besides their fundamental type. In this section, I'll describe self joins, nonequijoins, queries with multiple joins, and semi joins.

Self Joins

A self join is simply a join between two instances of the same table. I've already shown examples of self joins without classifying them explicitly as such.

Here's a simple example of a self join between two instances of the Employees table, one representing employees (E), and the other representing managers (M):

```
USE Northwind;

SELECT E.FirstName, E.LastName AS emp,
  M.FirstName, M.LastName AS mgr
FROM dbo.Employees AS E
  LEFT OUTER JOIN dbo.Employees AS M
    ON E.ReportsTo = M.EmployeeID;
```

The query produces the output shown in Table 5-4, where the employees' names are returned along with their managers' names.

Table 5-4   Employees and Their Managers

emp	mgr
Nancy Davolio	Andrew Fuller
Andrew Fuller	NULL
Janet Leverling	Andrew Fuller
Margaret Peacock	Andrew Fuller
Steven Buchanan	Andrew Fuller
Michael Suyama	Steven Buchanan
Robert King	Steven Buchanan
Laura Callahan	Andrew Fuller
Anne Dodsworth	Steven Buchanan

I used a left outer join to include Andrew—the Vice President of Sales—in the result. He has a NULL in the ReportsTo column because he has no manager.

> **Note**   When joining two instances of the same table, you must alias at least one of the tables. This provides a unique name or alias to each instance so that there is no ambiguity in the result column names and in the column names in the intermediate virtual tables.

Nonequijoins

Equijoins are joins with a join condition based on an equality operator. Nonequijoins have operators other than equality in their join condition.

As an example, suppose that you need to generate all pairs of two different employees from an Employees table. Assume that currently the table contains employee IDs A, B, and C. A cross join would generate the following nine pairs:

A, A

A, B

A, C

B, A

B, B

B, C

C, A

C, B

C, C

Obviously, a "self" pair (x, x) that has the same employee ID twice is not a pair of two different employees. Also, for each pair (x, y), you will find its "mirror" pair (y, x) in the result. You need to return only one of the two. To take care of both issues, you can specify a join condition that filters pairs where the key from the left table is smaller than the key from the right table. Pairs where the same employee appears twice will be removed. Also, one of the mirror pairs (x, y) and (y, x) will be removed because only one will have a left key smaller than the right key.

The following query returns the required result, without mirror pairs and without self pairs:

```
SELECT E1.EmployeeID, E1.LastName, E1.FirstName,
  E2.EmployeeID, E2.LastName, E2.FirstName
FROM dbo.Employees AS E1
  JOIN dbo.Employees AS E2
    ON E1.EmployeeID < E2.EmployeeID;
```

You can also calculate row numbers using a nonequijoin. As an example, the following query calculates row numbers for orders from the Orders table, based on increasing *OrderID*:

```
SELECT O1.OrderID, O1.CustomerID, O1.EmployeeID, COUNT(*) AS rn
FROM dbo.Orders AS O1
  JOIN dbo.Orders AS O2
    ON O2.OrderID <= O1.OrderID
GROUP BY O1.OrderID, O1.CustomerID, O1.EmployeeID;
```

You can find similarities between this solution and the pre–SQL Server 2005 set-based solution I showed in the previous chapter using subqueries. The join condition here contains the same logical expression I used in a subquery before. After applying the first two phases in query logical processing (Cartesian product and ON filter), each order from O1 is matched with all orders from O2 that have a smaller or equal *OrderID*. This means that a row from O1 with a target row number *n* will be matched with *n* rows from O2. Each row from O1 will be duplicated in the result of the join *n* times. If this is confusing, bear with me as I try to demonstrate this logic with an example. Say you have orders with the following IDs (in order): x, y, and z. The result of the join would be the following:

x, x

y, x

y, y

z, x

z, y

z, z

The join created duplicates out of each row from O1—as many as the target row number. The next step is to collapse each group of rows back to one row, returning the count of rows as the row number:

x, 1

y, 2

z, 3

Note that you must include in the GROUP BY clause all attributes from O1 that you want to return. Remember that in an aggregate query, an attribute that you want to return in the SELECT list must appear in the GROUP BY clause. This query suffers from the same N^2 performance issues I described with the subquery solution. This query also demonstrates an "expand-collapse" technique, where the join achieves the expansion of the number of rows by generating duplicates, and the grouping achieves the collapsing of the rows allowing you to calculate aggregates.

I find the subquery technique more appealing because it's so much more intuitive. I find the "expand-collapse" technique to be artificial and nonintuitive.

Remember that in both solutions to generating row numbers you used an aggregate function—a count of rows. Very similar logic can be used to calculate other aggregates either with a subquery or with a join (expand-collapse technique). I will elaborate on this technique in Chapter 6 in the "Running Aggregations" section. I'll also describe there scenarios in which I'd still consider using the "expand-collapse" technique even though I find it less intuitive than the subquery technique.

Multiple Joins

A query with multiple joins involves three or more tables. In this section, I'll describe both physical and logical aspects of multi-join queries.

Controlling the Physical Join Evaluation Order   In a multi-join query with no outer joins, you can rearrange the order in which the tables are specified without affecting the result. The optimizer is aware of that and will determine the order in which it accesses the tables based on cost estimations. In the query's execution plan, you might find that the optimizer chose to access the tables in a different order than the one you specified in the query.

For example, the following query returns customer company name and supplier company name, where the supplier supplied products to the customer:

```
SELECT DISTINCT C.CompanyName AS customer, S.CompanyName AS supplier
FROM dbo.Customers AS C
  JOIN dbo.Orders AS O
    ON O.CustomerID = C.CustomerID
```

```
    JOIN dbo.[Order Details] AS OD
      ON OD.OrderID = O.OrderID
    JOIN dbo.Products AS P
      ON P.ProductID = OD.ProductID
    JOIN dbo.Suppliers AS S
      ON S.SupplierID = P.SupplierID;
```

Examine the execution plan shown in Figure 5-3, and you will find that the tables are accessed physically in a different order than the logical order specified in the query.

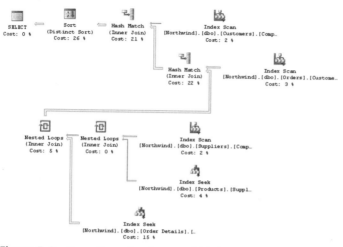

Figure 5-3 Execution plan for a multi-join query

If you suspect that a plan that accesses the tables in a different order than the one chosen by the optimizer will be more efficient, you can force the order of join processing by using one of two options. You can use the FORCE ORDER hint as follows, forcing the optimizer to process the joins physically in the same order as the logical one:

```
SELECT DISTINCT C.CompanyName AS customer, S.CompanyName AS supplier
FROM dbo.Customers AS C
  JOIN dbo.Orders AS O
    ON O.CustomerID = C.CustomerID
  JOIN dbo.[Order Details] AS OD
    ON OD.OrderID = O.OrderID
  JOIN dbo.Products AS P
    ON P.ProductID = OD.ProductID
  JOIN dbo.Suppliers AS S
    ON S.SupplierID = P.SupplierID
OPTION (FORCE ORDER);
```

This query generates the execution plan shown in Figure 5-4, where you can see that tables are accessed in the order they appear in the query.

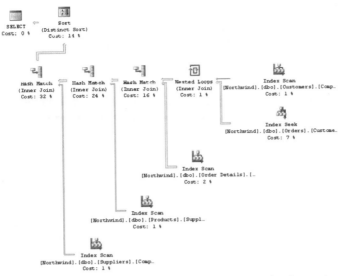

Figure 5-4   Execution plan for a multi-join query, forcing order

Another option to force order of join processing is to turn on the session option SET FORCE-
PLAN. This will affect all queries in the session.

Hints

Note that, in general, using hints to override the optimizer's choice of plan should be the
last resort when dealing with performance issues. A hint is not a kind gesture; rather, you
force the optimizer to use a particular route in optimization. If you introduce a hint in
production code, that aspect of the plan becomes static (for example, the use of a particular index or a certain join algorithm). The optimizer will not make dynamic choices to
accommodate changes in data volume and distribution.

There are several reasons that the optimizer might not produce an optimal plan and why
a hint can improve performance.

First, the optimizer doesn't necessarily generate all possible execution plans for a query.
If it did, the optimization phase could simply take too long. The optimizer calculates a
threshold for optimization based on the input table sizes, and it will stop optimizing
when that threshold is reached, yielding the plan with the lowest cost among the ones
it did generate. This means that you won't necessarily get the optimal plan.

Second, optimization in many cases is based on data selectivity and density information,
especially with regard to the choice of indexes and access methods. If statistics are not
up to date or don't have a sufficient sampling rate, the optimizer might make inaccurate
estimates.

> Third, the key distribution histograms SQL Server maintains for indexed columns (and in some cases, nonindexed ones as well) have at most 200 steps. With many join conditions and filters, the difference between the selectivity/density information that the optimizer estimates and the actual information can be substantial in some cases, leading to inefficient plans.
>
> Keep in mind though that you're not guaranteed to get the optimal plan. You should do everything in your power to avoid using hints in production code—for example, making sure that statistics are up to date, increasing the sampling rate if needed, and in some cases revising the query to help the optimizer make better choices. Use a hint only as a last resort if all other means fail. And if you do end up using a hint, revisit the code from time to time after doing more research or opening a support case with Microsoft.

Controlling the Logical Join Evaluation Order   There are also cases where you might want to be able to control the logical order of join processing beyond the observable order in which the tables are specified in the FROM clause. For example, consider the previous request to return all pairs of customer company name and supplier company name, where the supplier supplied products to the customer. Suppose you were also asked to return customers that made no orders. By intuition, you'd probably make the following attempt, using a left outer join between Customers and Orders:

```
SELECT DISTINCT C.CompanyName AS customer, S.CompanyName AS supplier
FROM dbo.Customers AS C
  LEFT OUTER JOIN dbo.Orders AS O
    ON O.CustomerID = C.CustomerID
  JOIN dbo.[Order Details] AS OD
    ON OD.OrderID = O.OrderID
  JOIN dbo.Products AS P
    ON P.ProductID = OD.ProductID
  JOIN dbo.Suppliers AS S
    ON S.SupplierID = P.SupplierID;
```

The previous query returned 1,236 pairs of customer-supplier, and you expected this query to return 1,238 rows (because there are two customers that made no orders). However, this query returns the same result set as the previous one without the outer customers. Remember that the first join takes place only between the first two tables (Customers and Orders), applying the first three phases of query logical processing, and results in a virtual table. The resulting virtual table is then joined with the third table ([Order Details]), and so on.

The first join did in fact generate outer rows for customers with no orders, but the *OrderID* in those outer rows was NULL, of course. The second join—between the result virtual table and [Order Details]—removed those outer rows because an equijoin will never find a match based on a comparison to a NULL.

There are several ways to make sure that those outer customers will not disappear. One technique is to use a left outer join in all joins, even though logically you want inner joins between Orders, [Order Details], Products, and Suppliers:

```
SELECT DISTINCT C.CompanyName AS customer, S.CompanyName AS supplier
FROM dbo.Customers AS C
  LEFT OUTER JOIN dbo.Orders AS O
    ON O.CustomerID = C.CustomerID
  LEFT OUTER JOIN dbo.[Order Details] AS OD
    ON OD.OrderID = O.OrderID
  LEFT OUTER JOIN dbo.Products AS P
    ON P.ProductID = OD.ProductID
  LEFT OUTER JOIN dbo.Suppliers AS S
    ON S.SupplierID = P.SupplierID;
```

The left outer joins will keep the outer customers in the intermediate virtual tables. This query correctly produces 1,238 rows, including the two customers that made no orders. However, if you had orders with no related order details, order details with no related products, or products with no related suppliers, this query would have produced incorrect results. That is, you would have received outer rows for them that you didn't want to get.

Another option is to make sure the join with the Customers table is logically last. This can be achieved by using inner joins between all other tables, and finally a right outer join with Customers:

```
SELECT DISTINCT C.CompanyName AS customer, S.CompanyName AS supplier
FROM dbo.Orders AS O
  JOIN dbo.[Order Details] AS OD
    ON OD.OrderID = O.OrderID
  JOIN dbo.Products AS P
    ON P.ProductID = OD.ProductID
  JOIN dbo.Suppliers AS S
    ON S.SupplierID = P.SupplierID
  RIGHT OUTER JOIN dbo.Customers AS C
    ON O.CustomerID = C.CustomerID;
```

This scenario was fairly simple, but in cases where you mix different types of joins—not to mention new table operators that were added in SQL Server 2005 (for example, APPLY, PIVOT, UNPIVOT)—it might not be that simple. Furthermore, using left outer joins all along the way is very artificial. It's more intuitive to think of the query as a single left outer join, where the left table is the Customers table and the right table is the result of inner joins between all the other tables. Both ANSI SQL and T-SQL allow you to control the logical order of join processing:

```
SELECT DISTINCT C.CompanyName AS customer, S.CompanyName AS supplier
FROM dbo.Customers AS C
  LEFT OUTER JOIN
    (dbo.Orders AS O
      JOIN dbo.[Order Details] AS OD
        ON OD.OrderID = O.OrderID
```

```
        JOIN dbo.Products AS P
          ON P.ProductID = OD.ProductID
        JOIN dbo.Suppliers AS S
          ON S.SupplierID = P.SupplierID)
  ON O.CustomerID = C.CustomerID;
```

Technically, the parentheses are ignored here, but I recommend you use them because they will help you write the query correctly. Using parentheses caused you to change another aspect of the query, which is the one that the language really uses to determine the logical order of processing. If you haven't guessed yet, it's the ON clause order. Specifying the ON clause *ON O.CustomerID = C.CustomerID* last causes the other joins to be logically processed first; the left outer join occurs logically between Customers and the inner join of the rest of the tables. You could write the query without parentheses, and it would mean the same thing:

```
SELECT DISTINCT C.CompanyName AS customer, S.CompanyName AS supplier
FROM dbo.Customers AS C
  LEFT OUTER JOIN
    dbo.Orders AS O
      JOIN dbo.[Order Details] AS OD
        ON OD.OrderID = O.OrderID
      JOIN dbo.Products AS P
        ON P.ProductID = OD.ProductID
      JOIN dbo.Suppliers AS S
        ON S.SupplierID = P.SupplierID
    ON O.CustomerID = C.CustomerID;
```

Other variations that specify the ON clause that refers to *C.CustomerID* last include the following two:

```
SELECT DISTINCT C.CompanyName AS customer, S.CompanyName AS supplier
FROM dbo.Customers AS C
  LEFT OUTER JOIN dbo.Orders AS O
  JOIN dbo.Products AS P
  JOIN dbo.[Order Details] AS OD
    ON P.ProductID = OD.ProductID
    ON OD.OrderID = O.OrderID
  JOIN dbo.Suppliers AS S
    ON S.SupplierID = P.SupplierID
    ON O.CustomerID = C.CustomerID;

SELECT DISTINCT C.CompanyName AS customer, S.CompanyName AS supplier
FROM dbo.Customers AS C
  LEFT OUTER JOIN dbo.Orders AS O
  JOIN dbo.[Order Details] AS OD
  JOIN dbo.Products AS P
  JOIN dbo.Suppliers AS S
    ON S.SupplierID = P.SupplierID
    ON P.ProductID = OD.ProductID
    ON OD.OrderID = O.OrderID
    ON O.CustomerID = C.CustomerID;
```

There's an obvious disadvantage to not using parentheses—a decrease in the readability and clarity of code. Without parentheses, the queries are far from intuitive. But there's another issue, too.

> **Important**   You cannot play with the ON clause's order any way you'd like. There's a certain relationship that must be maintained between the order of the specified tables and the order of the specified ON clauses for the query to be valid. The relationship is called a *chiastic* relationship. A chiastic relationship is neither unique to SQL nor to computer science; rather, it appears in many fields, including poetry, linguistics, mathematics, and others. In an ordered series of items, this relationship correlates the first item with the last, the second with the next to last, and so on. For example, the word ABBA has a chiastic relationship between the letters. As an example for a chiastic relationship in mathematics, recall the arithmetic sequence I described in the last chapter: 1, 2, 3, ..., n. To calculate the sum of the elements, you make *n/2* pairs based on a chiastic relationship ($1 + n$, $2 + n - 1$, $3 + n - 2$, and so on). The sum of each pair is always $1 + n$; therefore, the total sum of the arithmetic sequence is $(1 + n) * n / 2 = (n + n^2) / 2$.
>
> Similarly, the relationship between the tables specified in the FROM clause and the ON clauses must be chiastic for the query to be valid. That is, the first ON clause can refer only to the immediate two tables right above it. The second ON clause can refer to the previously referenced tables and to an additional one right above them, and so on. Figure 5-5 illustrates the chiastic relationship maintained in the last query. The code in the figure was slightly rearranged for readability.

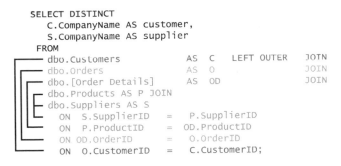

Figure 5-5   Chiastic relationship in a multi-join query

Without using parentheses, the queries are not very readable and you need to be aware of the chiastic relationship in order to write a valid query. Conversely, if you do use parentheses, the queries are more readable and intuitive and you don't need to concern yourself with chiastic relationships, as parentheses force you to write correctly.

Semi Joins

Semi joins are joins that return rows from one table based on the existence of related rows in the other table. If you return attributes from the left table, the join is called a left semi join. If you return attributes from the right table, it's called a right semi join.

There are several ways to achieve a semi join: using inner joins, subqueries, and set operations (which I'll demonstrate later in the chapter). Using an inner join, you select attributes from only one of the tables and apply DISTINCT. For example, the following query returns customers from Spain that made orders:

```
SELECT DISTINCT C.CustomerID, C.CompanyName
FROM dbo.Customers AS C
  JOIN dbo.Orders AS O
    ON O.CustomerID = C.CustomerID
WHERE Country = N'Spain';
```

You can also use the EXISTS predicate as follows:

```
SELECT CustomerID, CompanyName
FROM dbo.Customers AS C
WHERE Country = N'Spain'
  AND EXISTS
    (SELECT * FROM dbo.Orders AS O
     WHERE O.CustomerID = C.CustomerID);
```

If you're wondering whether there's any performance difference between the two, in this case the optimizer generates an identical plan for both. This plan is shown in Figure 5-6.

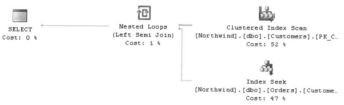

Figure 5-6 Execution plan for a left semi join

The inverse of a semi join is an anti–semi join, where you're looking for rows in one table based on their nonexistence in the other. You can achieve an anti–semi join (left or right) using an outer join, filtering only outer rows. For example, the following query returns customers from Spain that made no orders. The anti-semi join is achieved using an outer join:

```
SELECT C.CustomerID, C.CompanyName
FROM dbo.Customers AS C
  LEFT OUTER JOIN dbo.Orders AS O
    ON O.CustomerID = C.CustomerID
WHERE Country = N'Spain'
  AND O.CustomerID IS NULL;
```

You can also use the NOT EXISTS predicate as follows:

```
SELECT CustomerID, CompanyName
FROM dbo.Customers AS C
WHERE Country = N'Spain'
  AND NOT EXISTS
    (SELECT * FROM dbo.Orders AS O
     WHERE O.CustomerID = C.CustomerID);
```

As you can see in the execution plans shown in Figure 5-7 for the two query variations, the solution using the NOT EXISTS predicate performs better.

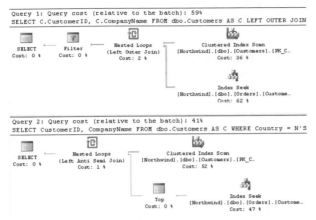

Figure 5-7 Execution plan for a left anti–semi join

The plan for the outer join solution shows that all orders for customers from Spain were actually processed. Let *c* equal the number of customers from Spain, and *o* equal the average number of orders per customer. You get *c* × *o* orders accessed. Then only the outer rows are filtered.

The plan for the NOT EXISTS solution is more efficient. Like the plan for the LEFT OUTER JOIN solution, this plan performs a seek within the index on *Orders.CustomerID* for each customer. However, the NOT EXISTS plan only checks whether or not a row with that customer ID was found (shown by the TOP operator) while the plan for the outer join actually scans all index rows for each customer.

Sliding Total of Previous Year

The following exercise demonstrates a mix of several join categories: a self join, non-equijoin, and multi-join query. First create and populate the MonthlyOrders table by running the code in Listing 5-2.

Listing 5-2 Creating and populating the MonthlyOrders table

```
IF OBJECT_ID('dbo.MonthlyOrders') IS NOT NULL
  DROP TABLE dbo.MonthlyOrders;
GO

SELECT
  CAST(CONVERT(CHAR(6), OrderDate, 112) + '01' AS DATETIME)
    AS ordermonth,
  COUNT(*) AS numorders
INTO dbo.MonthlyOrders
FROM dbo.Orders
GROUP BY CAST(CONVERT(CHAR(6), OrderDate, 112) + '01' AS DATETIME);

CREATE UNIQUE CLUSTERED INDEX idx_ordermonth ON dbo.MonthlyOrders(ordermonth);
```

The table stores the total number of orders for each month as shown in Table 5-5.

Table 5-5 Contents of the MonthlyOrders Table

ordermonth	numorders
1996-07-01 00:00:00.000	22
1996-08-01 00:00:00.000	25
1996-09-01 00:00:00.000	23
1996-10-01 00:00:00.000	26
1996-11-01 00:00:00.000	25
1996-12-01 00:00:00.000	31
1997-01-01 00:00:00.000	33
1997-02-01 00:00:00.000	29
1997-03-01 00:00:00.000	30
1997-04-01 00:00:00.000	31
1997-05-01 00:00:00.000	32
1997-06-01 00:00:00.000	30
1997-07-01 00:00:00.000	33
1997-08-01 00:00:00.000	33
1997-09-01 00:00:00.000	37
1997-10-01 00:00:00.000	38
1997-11-01 00:00:00.000	34
1997-12-01 00:00:00.000	48
1998-01-01 00:00:00.000	55
1998-02-01 00:00:00.000	54
1998-03-01 00:00:00.000	73
1998-04-01 00:00:00.000	74
1998-05-01 00:00:00.000	14

Notice that I used the DATETIME datatype for the *ordermonth* column. A valid date must include a day portion, so I just used the 1st of the month. When I'll need to present data, I'll get rid of the day portion. Storing the order month in a DATETIME datatype allows more flexible manipulations using DATETIME related functions.

The request is to return, for each month, a sliding total of the previous year. In other words, for each month n, return the total number of orders from month n minus 11 through month n.

The solution I will show is not the most efficient technique to achieve this task. I'm showing it here as an example of a mix between different join types and categories. Also, I'm assuming that there are no gaps in the sequence of months. In Chapter 6, you will find a focused discussion on running aggregates, including performance issues.

The following query returns the sliding total of the previous year for each month, generating the output shown in Table 5-6:

```
SELECT
  CONVERT(CHAR(6), O1.ordermonth, 112) AS frommonth,
  CONVERT(CHAR(6), O2.ordermonth, 112) AS tomonth,
  SUM(O3.numorders) AS numorders
FROM dbo.MonthlyOrders AS O1
  JOIN dbo.MonthlyOrders AS O2
    ON DATEADD(month, -11, O2.ordermonth) = O1.ordermonth
  JOIN dbo.MonthlyOrders AS O3
    ON O3.ordermonth BETWEEN O1.ordermonth AND O2.ordermonth
GROUP BY O1.ordermonth, O2.ordermonth;
```

Table 5-6   Sliding Total of Previous Year

frommonth	tomonth	numorders
199607	199706	337
199608	199707	348
199609	199708	356
199610	199709	370
199611	199710	382
199612	199711	391
199701	199712	408
199702	199801	430
199703	199802	455
199704	199803	498
199705	199804	541
199706	199805	523

The query first joins two instances of MonthlyOrders, O1 and O2. The two instances supply the boundary dates of the sliding year, O1 for the lower boundaries (*frommonth*), and O2 for the upper boundaries (*tomonth*). Therefore, the join condition is as follows: *ordermonth in O1 = ordermonth in O2 – 11 months*. For example, July 1996 in O1 will match June 1997 in O2.

Once the boundaries are fixed, another join, to a third instance of MonthlyOrders (O3), matches to each boundary-pair row that falls within that range. In other words, each boundary-pair will find 12 matches, one for each month, assuming there were orders in all 12 months. The logic here is similar to the expand technique I was talking about earlier. Now that each boundary pair has been duplicated 12 times, once for each qualifying month from O3, you want to collapse the group back to a single row, returning the total number of orders for each group.

Note that this solution will return only pairs in which both boundaries exist in the data and are 11 months apart. It will not return high-bound months for which a low-bound month does not exist in the data. July 1996 is currently the earliest month that exists in the table. Therefore, June 1997 is the first high-bound month that appears in the result set. If you also want to get results with *tomonth* before June 1997, you need to change the first join to a right outer join. The right outer join will yield a NULL in the *frommonth* column for the outer rows. In order not to lose those outer rows in the second join, in the join condition you convert a NULL *frommonth* to the date January 1, 1900, ensuring that *frommonth* <= *tomonth*. Another option would be to use the minimum month within the 12-month range over which the total is calculated. For simplicity's sake, I'll use the former option.

Similarly, in the SELECT list you convert a NULL in the *frommonth* column to the minimum existing month.

To note that some ranges do not cover a whole year, return also the count of months involved in the aggregation.

Here's the complete solution, which returns the output shown in Table 5-7:

```
SELECT
  CONVERT(VARCHAR(6),
    COALESCE(O1.ordermonth,
      (SELECT MIN(ordermonth) FROM dbo.MonthlyOrders)),
    112) AS frommonth,
  CONVERT(VARCHAR(6), O2.ordermonth, 112) AS tomonth,
  SUM(O3.numorders) AS numorders,
  DATEDIFF(month,
    COALESCE(O1.ordermonth,
      (SELECT MIN(ordermonth) FROM dbo.MonthlyOrders)),
    O2.ordermonth) + 1 AS nummonths
FROM dbo.MonthlyOrders AS O1
  RIGHT JOIN dbo.MonthlyOrders AS O2
    ON DATEADD(month, -11, O2.ordermonth) = O1.ordermonth
  JOIN dbo.MonthlyOrders AS O3
    ON O3.ordermonth BETWEEN COALESCE(O1.ordermonth, '19000101')
                         AND O2.ordermonth
GROUP BY O1.ordermonth, O2.ordermonth;
```

Table 5-7   Sliding Total of Previous Year, Including All Months

frommonth	tomonth	numorders	nummonths
199607	199607	22	1
199607	199608	47	2
199607	199609	70	3
199607	199610	96	4
199607	199611	121	5
199607	199612	152	6
199607	199701	185	7
199607	199702	214	8
199607	199703	244	9

Table 5-7   Sliding Total of Previous Year, Including All Months

frommonth	tomonth	numorders	nummonths
199607	199704	275	10
199607	199705	307	11
199607	199706	337	12
199608	199707	348	12
199609	199708	356	12
199610	199709	370	12
199611	199710	382	12
199612	199711	391	12
199701	199712	408	12
199702	199801	430	12
199703	199802	455	12
199704	199803	498	12
199705	199804	541	12
199706	199805	523	12

To clean up, drop the MonthlyOrders table:

```
DROP TABLE dbo.MonthlyOrders;
```

Join Algorithms

Join algorithms are the physical strategies SQL Server can use to process joins. Prior to SQL Server 7.0, only one join algorithm (called nested loops or loop join) was supported. Since version 7.0, SQL Server supports Merge and Hash join algorithms also.

Loop Join

A loop join scans one of the joined tables (the upper table in the graphical query plan), and for each row it searches the matching rows in the other joined table (the lower table in the plan).

> **Note**   The presence of a loop join operator in the execution plan does not indicate whether it's an efficient plan or not. A loop join is a default algorithm that can always be applied. The other algorithms have requirements—for example, the join must be an equijoin.

Using a loop join is efficient when there's an index on the join column in the larger table, allowing a seek followed by a partial scan. How efficient it is depends on where the index is positioned in this index optimization scale:

Worse Performance←no index (table scan per outer row)→nonclustered noncovering (seek + partial ordered scan + lookups)→clustered(seek + partial scan)→nonclustered covering (seek + partial scan)→nonclustered covering with included nonkey columns(seek + partial scan)→Best Performance.

The following query, which produces the plan shown in Figure 5-8, is an example of a query for which the optimizer chooses the loop join operator:

```
SELECT C.CustomerID, C.CompanyName, O.OrderID, O.OrderDate
FROM dbo.Customers AS C
  JOIN dbo.Orders AS O
    ON O.CustomerID = C.CustomerID
WHERE C.CustomerID = N'ALFKI';
```

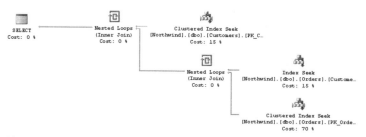

Figure 5-8   Execution plan for a loop join

The plan performs a seek within the clustered index on Customers to return the filtered customers. For each customer (in our case, there's only one), a loop join operator initiates a seek within the index on *Orders.CustomerID*. The seek is followed by a partial scan to get the row locators to all the customer's orders. For each row locator, another loop join operator (below and to the right of the first one) initiates a lookup of the data row. Note that this loop join operator does not correspond to a join in the query; rather, it is used to initiate the physical lookup operations. Try to think of it as an internal join between indexes on the Orders table. In the plan, the lookup shows up as a seek within the clustered index on Orders, because the table is clustered and the row locator is the clustering key.

> **Important**   With regard to joins and indexing, remember that joins are often based on foreign key/primary key relationships. While an index (to enforce uniqueness) is automatically created when a primary key is declared, a foreign key declaration doesn't automatically create an index. Remember that for loop joins, typically an index on the join column in the larger table is preferable. So it's your responsibility to create that index explicitly.

Merge

A merge join is a very efficient join algorithm, which relies on two inputs that are sorted on the join columns. With a one-to-many join, a merge join operator scans each input only once—hence, the superiority over the other operators. To have two sorted inputs, the optimizer can use clustered, or better yet, nonclustered covering indexes with the first column or columns being the join column(s). SQL Server will start scanning both sides, moving forward first through the "many" side (say, "one" side is *x* and "many" is *x*, *x*, *x*, *x*, *y*). SQL Server will step through the "one" side when the join column value on the "many" side changes (the "one" side steps through *y*, and then the "many" side steps through *y*, *y*, *y*, *z*). Ultimately, each side is scanned only once, in an ordered fashion. Things become more complicated when you have a many-to-many join, where the optimizer might still use a merge join operator with rewind logic.

When you see a merge join in the plan, it's usually a good sign.

As an example, the following query joins Orders and [Order Details] on equal *OrderID* values:

```
SELECT O.OrderID, O.OrderDate, OD.ProductID, OD.Quantity
FROM dbo.Orders AS O
  JOIN dbo.[Order Details] AS OD
    ON O.OrderID = OD.OrderID;
```

Both tables have a clustered index on *OrderID*, so the optimizer chooses a merge join. The merge join operator appears in the plan for this query, shown in Figure 5-9.

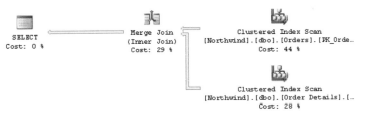

Figure 5-9   Execution plan for a merge join

In some cases, the optimizer might decide to use a merge join even when one of the inputs is not presorted by an index, especially if that input is fairly small. In such a case, you will see that input scanned and then sorted, as in the execution plan of the following query. Figure 5-10 shows the execution plan for this query:

```
SELECT C.CustomerID, CompanyName, ContactName, ContactTitle,
  OrderID, OrderDate
FROM dbo.Customers AS C
 JOIN dbo.Orders AS O
    ON O.CustomerID = C.CustomerID;
```

Figure 5-10   Execution plan for a merge join with sort

Hash

The hash join operator is typically chosen by the optimizer when good indexes on the join columns are missing. If you don't create appropriate indexes for the join, the optimizer creates a hash table as an alternative searching structure to balanced trees. Balanced trees are usually more efficient to use as a searching structure than hash tables, but they are more expensive to create. Occasionally, you see execution plans where the optimizer decides that it's worthwhile to create a temporary index (an Index Spool operator). But usually, for ad-hoc queries, it's more expensive to create a temporary index (balanced tree), use it, and drop it than to create a hash table and use it.

The optimizer uses the smaller input of the two as the build input for the hash table. It distributes the rows (relevant attributes for query) from the build input into buckets, based on a hash function applied to the join column values. The hash function is chosen to create a predetermined number of buckets of fairly equal size. Say you have a garage with a large number of tools and items. If you don't organize them in a particular manner, every time you look for an item you need to scan all of them. This is similar to a table scan. Of course, you will want to organize the items in groups and shelves by some criteria—for example, by functionality, size, color, and so on. You'd probably choose a criterion that would result in fairly equal sized, manageable groups.

The criterion you would use is analogous to the hash function, and a shelf or group of items is analogous to the hash bucket. Once the items in the garage are organized, every time you need to look for one, you apply to it the same criterion as the one you used to organize the items, go directly to the relevant shelf, and scan it.

> **Tip** When you see a hash join operator in the execution plan, it should be a warning to you that your data might be missing an important index. Of course, if you're running an ad-hoc query that is not repeated frequently, you might be happy with the hash join. However, if it's a production query that is invoked frequently, you might want to create the missing indexes.

To demonstrate a hash join, first create copies of the tables Orders and Order Details without indexes on the join columns:

```
SELECT * INTO dbo.MyOrders FROM dbo.Orders;
SELECT * INTO dbo.MyOrderDetails FROM dbo.[Order Details];
```

Next, run the following query:

```
SELECT O.OrderID, O.OrderDate, OD.ProductID, OD.Quantity
FROM dbo.MyOrders AS O
  JOIN dbo.MyOrderDetails AS OD
    ON O.OrderID = OD.OrderID;
```

You will see the Hash Match operator in the execution plan generated for the query as shown in Figure 5-11:

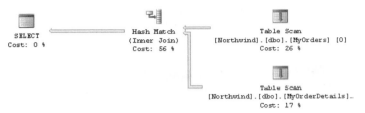

Figure 5-11   Execution plan for a hash join

When you're done, drop the tables you just created:

```
DROP TABLE dbo.MyOrders;
DROP TABLE dbo.MyOrderDetails;
```

Forcing a Join Strategy

You can force the optimizer to use a particular join algorithm, provided that it's technically supported for the given query. You do so by specifying a hint between the keyword or keywords representing the join type (for example, INNER, LEFT OUTER) and the JOIN keyword. For example, the following query forces a loop join:

```
SELECT C.CustomerID, C.CompanyName, O.OrderID
FROM dbo.Customers AS C
 INNER LOOP JOIN dbo.Orders AS O
    ON O.CustomerID = C.CustomerID;
```

 Note   With inner joins, when forcing a join algorithm, the keyword INNER is not optional. With outer joins, the OUTER keyword is still optional. For example, you can use LEFT LOOP JOIN or LEFT OUTER LOOP JOIN.

Using the older join syntax, you can't specify a different join algorithm for each join; rather, one algorithm will be used for all joins in the query. You do so by using the OPTION clause, like so:

```
SELECT C.CustomerID, C.CompanyName, O.OrderID
FROM dbo.Customers AS C, dbo.Orders AS O
WHERE O.CustomerID = C.CustomerID
OPTION (LOOP JOIN);
```

 Tip   Keep in mind the discussion held earlier in the chapter regarding using hints to override the optimizer's choices. Limit their use, and try to exhaust all other means before you introduce such a hint in production code.

Separating Elements

At this point, you have a chance to put your knowledge of joins and the key techniques you learned so far into action. Here I'll present a generic form of a fairly tough problem that has many practical applications in production. Create and populate a table called Arrays by running the code in Listing 5-3.

Listing 5-3   Creating and populating the table Arrays

```
USE tempdb;
GO
IF OBJECT_ID('dbo.Arrays') IS NOT NULL
  DROP TABLE dbo.Arrays;
GO

CREATE TABLE dbo.Arrays
(
  arrid VARCHAR(10)   NOT NULL PRIMARY KEY,
  array VARCHAR(8000) NOT NULL
)

INSERT INTO Arrays(arrid, array) VALUES('A', '20,22,25,25,14');
INSERT INTO Arrays(arrid, array) VALUES('B', '30,33,28');
INSERT INTO Arrays(arrid, array) VALUES('C', '12,10,8,12,12,13,12,14,10,9');
INSERT INTO Arrays(arrid, array) VALUES('D', '-4,-6,-4,-2');
```

The table contains arrays of elements separated by commas. Your task is to write a query that generates the result shown in Table 5-8.

Table 5-8   Arrays Split to Elements

arrid	pos	val
A	1	20
A	2	22
A	3	25
A	4	25
A	5	14
B	1	30
B	2	33
B	3	28
C	1	12
C	2	10
C	3	8
C	4	12
C	5	12
C	6	13

Table 5-8   Arrays Split to Elements

arrid	pos	val
C	7	12
C	8	14
C	9	10
D	1	−4
D	2	−6
D	3	−4
D	4	−2

The request is to normalize data that is not in first normal form—no multivalued attributes. The result set should have a row for each array element, including the array ID, the element's position within the array, and the element value. The solution is presented in the following paragraphs.

Before you even start coding, it's always a good idea to identify the steps in the solution and resolve them logically. It's often a good starting point to think in terms of the number of rows in the target and consider how that is related to the number of rows in the source. Obviously, here you need to generate multiple rows in the result from each row in Arrays. In other words, as the first step, you need to generate duplicates.

You already know that to generate duplicates, you can join the Arrays table with an auxiliary table of numbers. Here the join is not a simple cross join and a filter on a fixed number of rows. The number of duplicates here should equal the number of elements in the array. Each element is identified by a preceding comma (except for the first element, which we must not forget). So the join condition can be based on the existence of a comma in the *n*th character position in the array, where *n* comes from the Nums table.

Obviously, you wouldn't want to check characters beyond the length of the array, so you can limit *n* to the array's length. The following query implements the first step of the solution, generating the output shown in Table 5-9:

```
SELECT arrid, array, n
FROM dbo.Arrays
  JOIN dbo.Nums
    ON n <= LEN(array)
    AND SUBSTRING(array, n, 1) = ',';
```

Table 5-9   Solution to Separating Elements Problem, Step 1

arrid	array	n
A	20,22,25,25,14	3
A	20,22,25,25,14	6
A	20,22,25,25,14	9
A	20,22,25,25,14	12

Table 5-9   Solution to Separating Elements Problem, Step 1

arrid	array	n
B	30,33,28	3
B	30,33,28	6
C	12,10,8,12,12,13,12,14,10,9	3
C	12,10,8,12,12,13,12,14,10,9	6
C	12,10,8,12,12,13,12,14,10,9	8
C	12,10,8,12,12,13,12,14,10,9	11
C	12,10,8,12,12,13,12,14,10,9	14
C	12,10,8,12,12,13,12,14,10,9	17
C	12,10,8,12,12,13,12,14,10,9	20
C	12,10,8,12,12,13,12,14,10,9	23
C	12,10,8,12,12,13,12,14,10,9	26
D	–4,–6,–4,–2	3
D	–4,–6,–4,–2	6
D	–4,–6,–4,–2	9

You have almost generated the correct number of duplicates for each array, along with the *n* value representing the matching comma's position. You have one fewer duplicate than the desired number of duplicates for each array. For example, array A has five elements but you have only four rows. The reason that a row is missing for each array is that there's no comma preceding the first element in the array. To fix this small problem, concatenate a comma and the array to generate the first input of the SUBSTRING function:

```
SELECT arrid, array, n
FROM dbo.Arrays
  JOIN dbo.Nums
    ON n <= LEN(array)
    AND SUBSTRING(',' + array, n, 1) = ',';
```

As you can see in the output shown in Table 5-10, each array now produces an additional row in the result with *n = 1*.

Table 5-10   Solution to Separating Elements Problem, Step 2

arrid	array	N
A	20,22,25,25,14	1
A	20,22,25,25,14	4
A	20,22,25,25,14	7
A	20,22,25,25,14	10
A	20,22,25,25,14	13
B	30,33,28	1

Table 5-10   Solution to Separating Elements Problem, Step 2

arrid	array	N
B	30,33,28	4
B	30,33,28	7
C	12,10,8,12,12,13,12,14,10,9	1
C	12,10,8,12,12,13,12,14,10,9	4
C	12,10,8,12,12,13,12,14,10,9	7
C	12,10,8,12,12,13,12,14,10,9	9
C	12,10,8,12,12,13,12,14,10,9	12
C	12,10,8,12,12,13,12,14,10,9	15
C	12,10,8,12,12,13,12,14,10,9	18
C	12,10,8,12,12,13,12,14,10,9	21
C	12,10,8,12,12,13,12,14,10,9	24
C	12,10,8,12,12,13,12,14,10,9	27
D	–4,–6,–4,–2	1
D	–4,–6,–4,–2	4
D	–4,–6,–4,–2	7
D	–4,–6,–4,–2	10

Also, because all characters in ',' + *array* are one character to the right than in the original array, all *n* values are greater than before by one. That's actually even better for us because now *n* represents the starting position of the corresponding element within the array.

The third step is to extract from each row the element starting at the *n*th character. You know where the element starts—at the *n*th character—but you need to figure out its length. The length of the element is the position of the next comma minus the element's starting position (*n*). You use the CHARINDEX function to find the position of the next comma. You will need to provide the function with the *n* value as the third argument to tell it to start looking for the comma at or after the *n*th character, and not from the beginning of the string. Just keep in mind that you'll face a very similar problem here to the one that caused you to get one less duplicate than the number of elements. Here, there's no comma after the last element. Just as you added a comma before the first element earlier, you can now add one at the end. The following query shows the third step in the solution and generates the output shown in Table 5-11:

```
SELECT arrid,
  SUBSTRING(array, n, CHARINDEX(',', array + ',', n) - n) AS element
FROM dbo.Arrays
  JOIN dbo.Nums
    ON n <= LEN(array)
    AND SUBSTRING(',' + array, n, 1) = ',';
```

Table 5-11   Solution to Separating Elements Problem, Step 3

arrid	element
A	20
A	22
A	25
A	25
A	14
B	30
B	33
B	28
C	12
C	10
C	8
C	12
C	12
C	13
C	12
C	14
C	10
C	9
D	−4
D	−6
D	−4
D	−2

Note that the element result column is currently a character string. You might want to convert it to a more appropriate datatype (for example, an integer in this case).

Finally, the last step in the solution is to calculate the position of each element within the array. This is a tricky step.

You first need to figure out what determines the position of an element within an array. The position is the number of commas in the original array up to the nth character, plus one. Once you figure this out, you need to come up with an expression that will calculate this. You want to avoid writing a T-SQL user-defined function, as it will slow the query down. If you come up with an inline expression that uses only built-in functions, you will get a very fast solution. To phrase the problem more technically, you need to take the first n characters (*LEFT(array, n)*) and count the number of commas within that substring. The problem is that most string functions have no notion of repetitions or multiple occurrences of a substring within a string. There is one built-in function, though, that does—REPLACE. This function replaces each occurrence of a certain substring (call it *oldsubstr*) within a string (call it *str*) with another substring (call it *newsubstr*). You invoke the function with the aforementioned arguments in the following order: *REPLACE(str, oldsubstr, newsubstr)*. Here's an interesting way we can use the REPLACE function: *REPLACE(LEFT(array, n), ',', '')*. Here *str* is the first *n* characters within the array (*LEFT(array, n)*), *oldsubstr* is a comma, and *newsubstr* is an empty string. We replace each occurrence of a comma within the substring with an empty string. Now, what can you say about the difference in length between the original substring (*n*) and the new one? The new one will obviously be *n – num_commas*, where *num_commas* is the number of commas in *str*. In other words, *n – (n – num_commas)* will give you the number of commas. Add one, and you have the position of the element within the array. Use the LEN function to return the number of characters in *str* after removing the commas. Here's the complete expression that calculates *pos*:

```
n - LEN(REPLACE(LEFT(array, n), ',', '')) + 1 AS pos
```

Using the REPLACE function to count occurrences of a string within a string is a trick that can come in handy.

> **Tip**   In SQL Server 2005, you can use the ROW_NUMBER() function to calculate *pos*:
>
> ```
> ROW_NUMBER() OVER(PARTITION BY arrid ORDER BY n) AS pos
> ```

The following query shows the final solution to the problem, including the position calculation:

```
SELECT arrid,
  n - LEN(REPLACE(LEFT(array, n), ',', '')) + 1 AS pos,
  CAST(SUBSTRING(array, n, CHARINDEX(',', array + ',', n) - n)
      AS INT) AS element
FROM dbo.Arrays
  JOIN dbo.Nums
    ON n <= LEN(array)
    AND SUBSTRING(',' + array, n, 1) = ',';
```

In SQL Server 2005, you can use a recursive CTE to separate elements without the need to use an auxiliary table of numbers.

```
WITH SplitCTE AS
(
  SELECT arrid, 1 AS pos, 1 AS startpos,
    CHARINDEX(',', array + ',') - 1 AS endpos
  FROM dbo.Arrays
  WHERE LEN(array) > 0

  UNION ALL

  SELECT Prv.arrid, Prv.pos + 1, Prv.endpos + 2,
    CHARINDEX(',', Cur.array + ',', Prv.endpos + 2) - 1
  FROM SplitCTE AS Prv
    JOIN dbo.Arrays AS Cur
      ON Cur.arrid = Prv.arrid
      AND CHARINDEX(',', Cur.array + ',', Prv.endpos + 2) > 0
)
```

```
SELECT A.arrid, pos,
  CAST(SUBSTRING(array, startpos, endpos-startpos+1) AS INT) AS element
FROM dbo.Arrays AS A
  JOIN SplitCTE AS S
    ON S.arrid = A.arrid
ORDER BY arrid, pos;
```

The CTE calculates the start and end position of each element. The anchor member calculates the values for the first element within each array. The recursive member calculates the values of the "next" elements, terminating when no "next" elements are found. The *pos* column is initialized with the constant 1, and incremented by 1 in each iteration. The outer query joins the Arrays table with the CTE, and it extracts the individual elements of the arrays based on the start and end positions calculated by the CTE. This solution is a bit slower than the previous one, but it has the advantage of not requiring an auxiliary table of numbers.

Once I posted this puzzle in a private SQL trainer's forum. One of the trainers posted a very witty solution that one of his colleagues came up with. Here it is:

```
SELECT CAST(arrid AS VARCHAR(10)) AS arrid,
  REPLACE(array, ',', CHAR(10)+CHAR(13)
    + CAST(arrid AS VARCHAR(10)) + SPACE(10)) AS value
FROM dbo.Arrays;
```

First examine the solution to see whether you can figure it out, and then run it with Results To Text output mode. You will get the output shown in Table 5-12, which "seems" correct.

Table 5-12   Output of Solution to Separating Elements Problem that "Seems" Correct

arrid	value
A	20
A	22
A	25
A	25
A	14
B	30
B	33
B	28
C	12
C	10
C	8
C	12
C	12
C	13
C	12
C	14
C	10

Table 5-12   Output of Solution to Separating Elements Problem that "Seems" Correct

arrid	value
C	9
D	–4
D	–6
D	–4
D	2

This solution replaces each comma with a newline $(CHAR(10)+CHAR(13))$ + array id + 10 spaces. It seems correct when you run it in text mode, but it isn't. If you run it in grid output mode, you will see that the output really contains only one row for each array.

Set Operations

You can think of joins as *horizontal* operations between tables, generating a virtual table that contains columns from both tables. This section covers *vertical* operations between tables, including UNION, EXCEPT, and INTERSECT. Any mention of *set operations* in this section refers to these vertical operations.

A set operation accepts two tables as inputs, each resulting from a query specification. For simplicity's sake, I'll just use the term *inputs* in this section to describe the input tables of the set operations.

UNION returns the unified set of rows from both inputs, EXCEPT returns the rows that appear in the first input but not the second, and INTERSECT returns rows that are common to both inputs.

ANSI SQL:1999 defines native operators for all three set operations, each with two nuances: one optionally followed by DISTINCT (the default) and one followed by ALL. SQL Server 2000 supported only two of these set operators, UNION and UNION ALL. SQL Server 2005 added native support for the set operators EXCEPT and INTERSECT. Currently, SQL Server does not support the optional use of DISTINCT for set operations. This is not a functional limitation because DISTINCT is implied when you don't specify ALL. I will discuss solutions to all set operations, with both nuances, in both versions.

Like joins, these set operations always operate on only two inputs, generating a virtual table as the result. You might feel comfortable calling the input tables *left* and *right* as with joins, or you might feel more comfortable referring to them as the *first* and *second* input tables.

Before I describe each set operation in detail, let's get a few technicalities regarding how set operations work out of the way.

The two inputs must have the same number of columns, and corresponding columns must have the same datatype, or at least be implicitly convertible. The column names of the result are determined by the first input.

An ORDER BY clause is not allowed in the individual table expressions. All other logical processing phases (joins, filtering, grouping, and so on) are supported on the individual queries except the TOP option.

Conversely, ORDER BY is the only logical processing phase supported directly on the final result of a set operation. If you specify an ORDER BY clause at the end of the query, it will be applied to the final result set. None of the other logical processing phases are allowed directly on the result of a set operation. I will provide alternatives later in the chapter.

Set operations work on complete rows from the two input tables. Note that when comparing rows between the inputs, set operations treat NULLs as equal, just like identical known values. In this regard, set operations are not like query filters (ON, WHERE, HAVING), which as you recall do not treat NULLs as equal.

UNION

UNION generates a result set combining the rows from both inputs. The following sections describe the differences between UNION (implicit DISTINCT) and UNION ALL.

UNION DISTINCT

Specifying UNION without the ALL option combines the rows from both inputs and applies a DISTINCT on top (in other words, removes duplicate rows).

For example, the following query returns all occurrences of *Country, Region, City* that appear in either the Employees table or the Customers table, with duplicate rows removed:

```
USE Northwind;

SELECT Country, Region, City FROM dbo.Employees
UNION
SELECT Country, Region, City FROM dbo.Customers;
```

The query returns 71 unique rows.

UNION ALL

You can think of UNION ALL as UNION without duplicate removal. That is, you get one result set containing all rows from both inputs, including duplicates. For example, the following query returns all occurrences of Customer, Region, City from both tables:

```
SELECT Country, Region, City FROM dbo.Employees
UNION ALL
SELECT Country, Region, City FROM dbo.Customers;
```

Because the Employees table has 9 rows and the Customers table has 91 rows, you get a result set with 100 rows.

EXCEPT

EXCEPT allows you to identify rows that appear in the first input but not in the second.

EXCEPT DISTINCT

EXCEPT DISTINCT returns distinct rows that appear in the first input but not in the second input. To achieve EXCEPT, programmers usually use the NOT EXISTS predicate, or an outer join filtering only outer rows, as I demonstrated earlier in the "Semi Joins" section. However, those solutions treat two NULLs as different from each other. For example, (UK, NULL, London) will not be considered equal to (UK, NULL, London). If both tables contain such a row, `input1 EXCEPT input2` is not supposed to return it, yet the NOT EXISTS and outer join solutions will.

SQL Server versions prior to 2005 did not have support for the EXCEPT operator. The following code has a solution that is compatible with versions of SQL Server prior to SQL Server 2005 and that is logically equivalent to EXCEPT DISTINCT:

```
SELECT Country, Region, City
FROM (SELECT DISTINCT 'E' AS Source, Country, Region, City
      FROM dbo.Employees
      UNION ALL
      SELECT DISTINCT 'C', Country, Region, City
      FROM dbo.Customers) AS UA
GROUP BY Country, Region, City
HAVING COUNT(*) = 1 AND MAX(Source) = 'E';
```

The derived table query unifies the distinct rows from both inputs, assigning an identifier of the source input to each row (a result column called source). Rows from Employees are assigned the identifier E, and rows from Customers are assigned C. The outer query groups the rows by *Country, Region, City*. The HAVING clause keeps only groups that have one row (meaning that the row appeared only in one of the inputs) and a maximum source identifier of E (meaning that the row was from Employees). Logically, that's EXCEPT DISTINCT.

In SQL Server 2005, things are a bit simpler:

```
SELECT Country, Region, City FROM dbo.Employees
EXCEPT
SELECT Country, Region, City FROM dbo.Customers;
```

Note that of the three set operations, only EXCEPT is asymmetrical. That is, `input1 EXCEPT input2` is not the same as `input2 EXCEPT input1`.

For example, the query just shown returned the two cities that appear in Employees but not in Customers. The following query returns 66 cities that appear in Customers but not in Employees:

```
SELECT Country, Region, City FROM dbo.Customers
EXCEPT
SELECT Country, Region, City FROM dbo.Employees;
```

EXCEPT ALL

EXCEPT ALL is trickier than EXCEPT DISTINCT and has not yet been implemented in SQL Server. Besides caring about the existence of a row, it also cares about the number of occurrences of each row. Say you request the result of `input1 EXCEPT ALL input2`. If a row appears n times in *input1* and m times in *input2* (both n and m can be $>= 0$), it will appear $MAX(0, n - m)$ times in the output. That is, if n is greater than m, the row will appear $n - m$ times in the result; otherwise, it won't appear in the result at all.

The following query demonstrates how you can achieve EXCEPT ALL using a solution compatible with versions of SQL Server prior to SQL Server 2005:

```
SELECT Country, Region, City
FROM (SELECT Country, Region, City,
        MAX(CASE WHEN Source = 'E' THEN Cnt ELSE 0 END) ECnt,
        MAX(CASE WHEN Source = 'C' THEN Cnt ELSE 0 END) CCnt
     FROM (SELECT 'E' AS Source,
             Country, Region, City, COUNT(*) AS Cnt
          FROM dbo.Employees
          GROUP BY Country, Region, City

          UNION ALL

          SELECT 'C', Country, Region, City, COUNT(*)
          FROM dbo.Customers
          GROUP BY Country, Region, City) AS UA
     GROUP BY Country, Region, City) AS P
  JOIN dbo.Nums
    ON n <= ECnt - CCnt;
```

The derived table UA has a row for each distinct source row from each input, along with the source identifier (E for Employees, C for Customers) and the number of times (*Cnt*) it appears in the source.

The query generating the derived table P groups the rows from UA by *Country*, *Region*, and *City*. It uses a couple of MAX(CASE...) expressions to return the counts of duplicates from both sources in the same result row, calling them *ECnt* and *CCnt*. This is a technique to pivot data, and I'll talk about it in detail in Chapter 6. At this point, each distinct occurrence of *Country, Region, City* has a single row in P, along with the count of duplicates it had in each input. Finally, the outer query joins P with Nums to generate duplicates. The join condition is $n <= ECnt - CCnt$. If you think about it, you will get the exact number of duplicates dictated by EXCEPT ALL. That is, if *ECnt - CCnt* is greater than 0, you will get that many duplicates; otherwise, you'll get none.

Even though you don't have a native operator for EXCEPT ALL in SQL Server 2005, you can easily generate the logical equivalent using EXCEPT and the ROW_NUMBER function. Here's the solution:

```
WITH EXCEPT_ALL
AS
(
  SELECT
```

```
    ROW_NUMBER()
      OVER(PARTITION BY Country, Region, City
            ORDER      BY Country, Region, City) AS rn,
      Country, Region, City
      FROM dbo.Employees

  EXCEPT

  SELECT
    ROW_NUMBER()
      OVER(PARTITION BY Country, Region, City
            ORDER      BY Country, Region, City) AS rn,
      Country, Region, City
    FROM dbo.Customers
)
SELECT Country, Region, City
FROM EXCEPT_ALL;
```

To understand the solution, I suggest that you first highlight sections (queries) within it and run them separately. This will allow you to examine the intermediate result sets and get a better idea of what the following paragraph tries to explain.

The code first assigns row numbers to the rows of each of the inputs, partitioned by the whole attribute list. The row numbers will number the duplicate rows within the input. For example, a row that appears five times in Employees and three times in Customers will get row numbers 1 through 5 in the first input, and row numbers 1 through 3 in the second input. You then apply `input1 EXCEPT input2`, and get rows (including the *rn* attribute) that appear in *input1* but not in *input2*. If row R appears 5 times in *input1* and 3 times in *input2*, you get the following result:

$\{(R, 1), (R, 2), (R, 3), (R, 4), (R, 5)\}$

EXCEPT

$\{(R, 1), (R, 2), (R, 3)\}$

And this produces the following result:

$\{(R, 4), (R, 5)\}$

In other words, R will appear in the result exactly the number of times mandated by EXCEPT ALL. I encapsulated this logic in a CTE to return only the original attribute list without the row number, which is what EXCEPT ALL would do.

INTERSECT

INTERSECT returns rows that appear in both inputs.

To achieve INTERSECT, programmers usually use the EXISTS predicate or an inner join, as I demonstrated earlier in the "Semi Joins" section. However, as I explained earlier, those solutions treat two NULLs as different from each other, and set operations are supposed to treat them as equal.

Support for the INTERSECT operator was introduced in SQL Server 2005, but only in the variation with the implicit DISTINCT.

INTERSECT DISTINCT

To achieve the logical equivalent of INTERSECT DISTINCT pre–SQL Server 2005 versions, you can use the following solution:

```
SELECT Country, Region, City
FROM (SELECT DISTINCT Country, Region, City FROM dbo.Employees
      UNION ALL
      SELECT DISTINCT Country, Region, City FROM dbo.Customers) AS UA
GROUP BY Country, Region, City
HAVING COUNT(*) = 2;
```

The derived table query performs a UNION ALL between distinct rows from both inputs. The outer query groups the unified result by *Country, Region* and *City*, and it returns only groups that have two occurrences. In other words, the query returns only distinct rows that appear in both inputs, which is how INTERSECT DISTINCT is defined.

In SQL Server 2005, you simply use the INTERSECT operator as follows:

```
SELECT Country, Region, City FROM dbo.Employees
INTERSECT
SELECT Country, Region, City FROM dbo.Customers;
```

INTERSECT ALL

Like EXCEPT ALL, INTERSECT ALL also considers multiple occurrences of rows. If a row R appears *n* times in one input table and *m* times in the other, it should appear *MIN(n, m)* times in the result.

The techniques to achieve INTERSECT ALL have many similarities to the techniques used to achieve EXCEPT ALL. For example, here's a pre–SQL Server 2005 solution to achieve INTERSECT ALL:

```
SELECT Country, Region, City
FROM (SELECT Country, Region, City, MIN(Cnt) AS MinCnt
      FROM (SELECT Country, Region, City, COUNT(*) AS Cnt
            FROM dbo.Employees
            GROUP BY Country, Region, City

            UNION ALL

            SELECT Country, Region, City, COUNT(*)
            FROM dbo.Customers
            GROUP BY Country, Region, City) AS UA
      GROUP BY Country, Region, City
      HAVING COUNT(*) > 1) AS D
  JOIN dbo.Nums
    ON n <= MinCnt;
```

UA has the UNION ALL of distinct rows from each input along with the number of occurrences they had in the source. The query against UA that generates the derived table D groups the rows by *Country, Region*, and *City*. The HAVING clause filters only rows that appeared in both inputs (*COUNT(*) > 1*), returning their minimum count (*MinCnt*). This is the number of times the row should appear in the output. To generate that many copies, the outer query joins D with Nums based on *n <= MinCnt*.

The solution to INTERSECT ALL in SQL Server 2005 is identical to the one for EXCEPT ALL except for one obvious difference—the use of the INTERSECT operator instead of EXCEPT:

```
WITH INTERSECT_ALL
AS
(
  SELECT
    ROW_NUMBER()
      OVER(PARTITION BY Country, Region, City
           ORDER     BY Country, Region, City) AS rn,
    Country, Region, City
  FROM dbo.Employees

  INTERSECT

  SELECT
    ROW_NUMBER()
      OVER(PARTITION BY Country, Region, City
           ORDER     BY Country, Region, City) AS rn,
    Country, Region, City
    FROM dbo.Customers
)
SELECT Country, Region, City
FROM INTERSECT_ALL;
```

Precedence of Set Operations

The INTERSECT set operation has a higher precedence than the others. In a query that mixes multiple set operations, INTERSECT is evaluated first. Other than that, set operations are evaluated from left to right. The exception is that parentheses are always first in precedence, so by using parentheses you have full control of the logical order of evaluation of set operations.

For example, in the following query INTERSECT is evaluated first even though it appears second:

```
SELECT Country, Region, City FROM dbo.Suppliers
EXCEPT
SELECT Country, Region, City FROM dbo.Employees
INTERSECT
SELECT Country, Region, City FROM dbo.Customers;
```

The meaning of the query is: return supplier cities that do not appear in the intersection of employee cities and customer cities.

However, if you use parentheses, you can change the evaluation order:

```
(SELECT Country, Region, City FROM dbo. Suppliers
 EXCEPT
 SELECT Country, Region, City FROM dbo.Employees)
INTERSECT
SELECT Country, Region, City FROM dbo.Customers;
```

This query means: return supplier cities that are not employee cities and are also customer cities.

Using INTO with Set Operations

If you want to write a SELECT INTO statement where you use set operations, specify the INTO clause just before the FROM clause of the first input. For example, here's how you populate a temporary table #T with the result of one of the previous queries:

```
SELECT Country, Region, City INTO #T FROM dbo.Suppliers
EXCEPT
SELECT Country, Region, City FROM dbo.Employees
INTERSECT
SELECT Country, Region, City FROM dbo.Customers;
```

Circumventing Unsupported Logical Phases

As I mentioned earlier, logical processing phases other than sorting (joins, filtering, grouping, TOP, and so on) are not allowed directly on the result of a set operation. This limitation can easily be circumvented by using a derived table or a CTE like so:

```
SELECT DISTINCT TOP ...
FROM (<set operation query>) AS D
JOIN | PIVOT | APPLY ...
WHERE ...
GROUP BY ...
HAVING ...
ORDER BY ...
```

For example, the following query (which generates the output shown in Table 5-13) tells you how many cities there are in each country covered by customers or employees:

```
SELECT Country, COUNT(*) AS NumCities
FROM (SELECT Country, Region, City FROM dbo.Employees
      UNION
      SELECT Country, Region, City FROM dbo.Customers) AS U
GROUP BY Country;
```

Table 5-13   Number of Cities per Country Covered by Customers or Employees

Country	NumCities
Argentina	1
Austria	2
Belgium	2
Brazil	4
Canada	3
Denmark	2
Finland	2
France	9
Germany	11
Ireland	1
Italy	3
Mexico	1
Norway	1
Poland	1
Portugal	1
Spain	3
Sweden	2
Switzerland	2
UK	2
USA	14
Venezuela	4

In a similar manner, you can circumvent the limitations on the individual queries used as inputs to the set operation. Each input can be written as a simple SELECT query from a derived table or a CTE, where you use the disallowed elements in the derived table or CTE expression..

For example, the following query returns the two most recent orders for employees 3 and 5, generating the output shown in Table 5-14:

```
SELECT EmployeeID, OrderID, OrderDate
FROM (SELECT TOP 2 EmployeeID, OrderID, OrderDate
      FROM dbo.Orders
      WHERE EmployeeID = 3
      ORDER BY OrderDate DESC, OrderID DESC) AS D1

UNION ALL

SELECT EmployeeID, OrderID, OrderDate
FROM (SELECT TOP 2 EmployeeID, OrderID, OrderDate
      FROM dbo.Orders
      WHERE EmployeeID = 5
      ORDER BY OrderDate DESC, OrderID DESC) AS D2;
```

Table 5-14   Two Most Recent Orders for Employees 3 and 5

EmployeeID	OrderID	OrderDate
3	11063	1998-04-30 00:00:00.000
3	11057	1998-04-29 00:00:00.000
5	11043	1998-04-22 00:00:00.000
5	10954	1998-03-17 00:00:00.000

As for the limitation on sorting the individual inputs, suppose you need to sort each input independently. For example, you want to return orders placed by customer ALFKI and also orders handled by employee 3. As for sorting the rows in the output, you want customer ALFKI's orders to appear first, sorted by *OrderDate* descending, and then orders handled by employee 3, sorted by *OrderID* ascending. To achieve this, you create a column (*SortCol*) with the constant 1 for the first input (customer ALFKI), and 2 for the second (employee 3). Create a derived table (call it U) out of the UNION ALL between the two. In the outer query, first sort by *SortCol*, and then by a CASE expression for each set. The CASE expression will return the relevant value based on the source set; otherwise, it returns a NULL, which won't affect sorting. Here's the solution query generating the output (abbreviated) shown in Table 5-15:

```
SELECT EmployeeID, CustomerID, OrderID, OrderDate
FROM (SELECT 1 AS SortCol, CustomerID, EmployeeID, OrderID, OrderDate
      FROM dbo.Orders
      WHERE CustomerID = N'ALFKI'

      UNION ALL

      SELECT 2 AS SortCol, CustomerID, EmployeeID, OrderID, OrderDate
      FROM dbo.Orders
      WHERE EmployeeID = 3) AS U
ORDER BY SortCol,
  CASE WHEN SortCol = 1 THEN OrderID END,
  CASE WHEN SortCol = 2 THEN OrderDate END DESC;
```

Table 5-15   Sorting Each Input Independently (Abbreviated)

EmployeeID	CustomerID	OrderID	OrderDate
6	ALFKI	10643	1997-08-25 00:00:00.000
4	ALFKI	10692	1997-10-03 00:00:00.000
4	ALFKI	10702	1997-10-13 00:00:00.000
1	ALFKI	10835	1998-01-15 00:00:00.000
1	ALFKI	10952	1998-03-16 00:00:00.000
3	ALFKI	11011	1998-04-09 00:00:00.000
3	HUNGO	11063	1998-04-30 00:00:00.000
3	NORTS	11057	1998-04-29 00:00:00.000
3	HANAR	11052	1998-04-27 00:00:00.000

Table 5-15   Sorting Each Input Independently (Abbreviated)

EmployeeID	CustomerID	OrderID	OrderDate
3	GOURL	11049	1998-04-24 00:00:00.000
3	CHOPS	11041	1998-04-22 00:00:00.000
3	QUICK	11021	1998-04-14 00:00:00.000
...			

Conclusion

I covered many aspects of joins and set operations and demonstrated new techniques that you might find handy.

Remember that the old-style proprietary syntax for outer joins is not supported any more and will work only under a backward compatibility mode. At the same time, other types of joins that use the ANSI SQL:1989 syntax are fully supported, as this syntax is still part of the standard—although when using the older syntax for inner joins, there's a risk of getting a Cartesian product when you forget to specify a WHERE clause.

SQL Server 2005 introduces native operators for EXCEPT and INTERSECT. It also provides other tools that allow simple solutions for achieving EXCEPT ALL and INTERSECT ALL.

Chapter 6
Aggregating and Pivoting Data

This chapter covers various data-aggregation techniques, including the new OVER clause, tiebreakers, running aggregates, pivoting, unpivoting, custom aggregations, histograms, grouping factors, and the CUBE and ROLLUP options.

Throughout this chapter, in my solutions I'll reuse techniques that I introduced earlier. I'll also introduce new techniques for you to familiarize yourself with.

Logic will naturally be an integral element in the solutions. Remember that at the heart of every querying problem lies a logical puzzle.

OVER Clause

The OVER clause allows you to request window-based calculations—that is, the calculation is performed on a whole window of values. In Chapter 4, I described in detail how you use the OVER clause with the new analytical ranking functions. Microsoft SQL Server 2005 also introduces support for the OVER clause with scalar aggregate functions; however, currently it can be used only with the PARTITION BY clause. Hopefully, future versions of SQL Server will also support the other ANSI elements of aggregate window functions, including the ORDER BY and ROWS clauses.

The purpose of using the OVER clause with scalar aggregates is to calculate, for each row, an aggregate based on a window of values that extends beyond the scope of the row—and to do all this without using a GROUP BY clause in the query. In other words, the OVER clause allows you to add aggregate calculations to the results of an ungrouped query. This capability provides an alternative to requesting aggregates with subqueries, in case you need to include both base row attributes and aggregates in your results.

As a reminder, in Chapter 5 I presented a problem in which you were required to calculate two aggregates for each sales row: the percentage the row contributed to the total sales quantity and the difference between the row's sales quantity and the average quantity over all sales. I showed the following optimized query in which I used a cross join between the base table and a derived table of aggregates, instead of using multiple subqueries:

```
SET NOCOUNT ON;
USE pubs;

SELECT stor_id, ord_num, title_id,
  CONVERT(VARCHAR(10), ord_date, 120) AS ord_date, qty,
  CAST(1.*qty / sumqty * 100 AS DECIMAL(5, 2)) AS per,
  CAST(qty - avgqty AS DECIMAL(9, 2)) as diff
FROM dbo.sales,
  (SELECT SUM(qty) AS sumqty, AVG(1.*qty) AS avgqty
   FROM dbo.sales) AS AGG;
```

This query produces the output shown in Table 6-1.

Table 6-1   Sales Percentage of Total and Diff from Average

stor_id	ord_num	title_id	ord_date	qty	per	diff
6380	6871	BU1032	1994-09-14	5	1.01	-18.48
6380	722a	PS2091	1994-09-13	3	0.61	-20.48
7066	A2976	PC8888	1993-05-24	50	10.14	26.52
7066	QA7442.3	PS2091	1994-09-13	75	15.21	51.52
7067	D4482	PS2091	1994-09-14	10	2.03	-13.48
7067	P2121	TC3218	1992-06-15	40	8.11	16.52
7067	P2121	TC4203	1992-06-15	20	4.06	-3.48
7067	P2121	TC7777	1992-06-15	20	4.06	-3.48
7131	N914008	PS2091	1994-09-14	20	4.06	-3.48
7131	N914014	MC3021	1994-09-14	25	5.07	1.52
7131	P3087a	PS1372	1993-05-29	20	4.06	-3.48
7131	P3087a	PS2106	1993-05-29	25	5.07	1.52
7131	P3087a	PS3333	1993-05-29	15	3.04	-8.48
7131	P3087a	PS7777	1993-05-29	25	5.07	1.52
7896	QQ2299	BU7832	1993-10-28	15	3.04	-8.48
7896	TQ456	MC2222	1993-12-12	10	2.03	-13.48
7896	X999	BU2075	1993-02-21	35	7.10	11.52
8042	423LL922	MC3021	1994-09-14	15	3.04	-8.48
8042	423LL930	BU1032	1994-09-14	10	2.03	-13.48
8042	P723	BU1111	1993-03-11	25	5.07	1.52
8042	QA879.1	PC1035	1993-05-22	30	6.09	6.52

The motivation for calculating the two aggregates in a single derived table instead of as two separate subqueries stemmed from the fact that each subquery accessed the table/index, while the derived table calculated the aggregates using a single scan of the data.

Similarly, you can calculate multiple aggregates using the same OVER clause, and SQL Server will scan the required source data only once for all. Here's how you use the OVER clause to answer the same request:

```
SELECT stor_id, ord_num, title_id,
  CONVERT(VARCHAR(10), ord_date, 120) AS ord_date, qty,
  CAST(1.*qty / SUM(qty) OVER() * 100 AS DECIMAL(5, 2)) AS per,
  CAST(qty - AVG(1.*qty) OVER() AS DECIMAL(9, 2)) AS diff
FROM dbo.sales;
```

> **Note**   In Chapter 4, I described the PARTITION BY clause, which is used with window functions, including aggregate window functions. This clause is optional. When not specified, the aggregate is based on the whole input rather than being calculated per partition.

Here, because I didn't specify a PARTITION BY clause, the aggregates were calculated based on the whole input. Logically, *SUM(qty) OVER()* is equivalent here to the subquery (*SELECT SUM(qty) FROM dbo.sales*). Physically, it's a different story. As an exercise, you can compare the execution plans of the following two queries, each requesting a different number of aggregates using the same OVER clause:

```
SELECT stor_id, ord_num, title_id,
  SUM(qty) OVER() AS sumqty
FROM dbo.sales;

SELECT stor_id, ord_num, title_id,
  SUM(qty)   OVER() AS sumqty,
  COUNT(qty) OVER() AS cntqty,
  AVG(qty)   OVER() AS avgqty,
  MIN(qty)   OVER() AS minqty,
  MAX(qty)   OVER() AS maxqty
FROM dbo.sales;
```

You'll find the two plans nearly identical, with the only difference being that the single *Stream Aggregate* operator calculates a different number of aggregates for each. The query costs are identical. On the other hand, compare the execution plans of the following two queries, each requesting a different number of aggregates using subqueries:

```
SELECT stor_id, ord_num, title_id,
  (SELECT SUM(qty) FROM dbo.sales) AS sumqty
FROM dbo.sales;

SELECT stor_id, ord_num, title_id,
  (SELECT SUM(qty)   FROM dbo.sales) AS sumqty,
  (SELECT COUNT(qty) FROM dbo.sales) AS cntqty,
  (SELECT AVG(qty)   FROM dbo.sales) AS avgqty,
```

```
  (SELECT MIN(qty)    FROM dbo.sales) AS minqty,
  (SELECT MAX(qty)    FROM dbo.sales) AS maxqty
FROM dbo.sales;
```

You'll find that they have different plans, with the latter being more expensive, as it rescans the source data for each aggregate.

Another benefit of the OVER clause is that it allows for shorter and simpler code. This is especially apparent when you need to calculate partitioned aggregates. Using OVER, you simply specify a PARTITION BY clause. Using subqueries, you have to correlate the inner query to the outer, making the query longer and more complex.

As an example for using the PARTITION BY clause, the following query calculates the percentage of the quantity out of the store total and the difference from the store average, yielding the output shown in Table 6-2:

```
SELECT stor_id, ord_num, title_id,
  CONVERT(VARCHAR(10), ord_date, 120) AS ord_date, qty,
  CAST(1.*qty / SUM(qty) OVER(PARTITION BY stor_id) * 100
    AS DECIMAL(5, 2)) AS per,
  CAST(qty - AVG(1.*qty) OVER(PARTITION BY stor_id)
    AS DECIMAL(9, 2)) AS diff
FROM dbo.sales
ORDER BY stor_id;
```

Table 6-2   Sales Percentage of Store Total and Diff from Store Average

stor_id	ord_num	title_id	ord_date	qty	per	diff
6380	6871	BU1032	1994-09-14	5	62.50	1.00
6380	722a	PS2091	1994-09-13	3	37.50	-1.00
7066	A2976	PC8888	1993-05-24	50	40.00	-12.50
7066	QA7442.3	PS2091	1994-09-13	75	60.00	12.50
7067	D4482	PS2091	1994-09-14	10	11.11	-12.50
7067	P2121	TC3218	1992-06-15	40	44.44	17.50
7067	P2121	TC4203	1992-06-15	20	22.22	-2.50
7067	P2121	TC7777	1992-06-15	20	22.22	-2.50
7131	N914008	PS2091	1994-09-14	20	15.38	-1.67
7131	N914014	MC3021	1994-09-14	25	19.23	3.33
7131	P3087a	PS1372	1993-05-29	20	15.38	-1.67
7131	P3087a	PS2106	1993-05-29	25	19.23	3.33
7131	P3087a	PS3333	1993-05-29	15	11.54	-6.67
7131	P3087a	PS7777	1993-05-29	25	19.23	3.33
7896	QQ2299	BU7832	1993-10-28	15	25.00	-5.00
7896	TQ456	MC2222	1993-12-12	10	16.67	-10.00
7896	X999	BU2075	1993-02-21	35	58.33	15.00

Table 6-2   Sales Percentage of Store Total and Diff from Store Average

stor_id	ord_num	title_id	ord_date	qty	per	diff
8042	423LL922	MC3021	1994-09-14	15	18.75	-5.00
8042	423LL930	BU1032	1994-09-14	10	12.50	-10.00
8042	P723	BU1111	1993-03-11	25	31.25	5.00
8042	QA879.1	PC1035	1993-05-22	30	37.50	10.00

In short, the OVER clause allows for shorter and faster queries.

Tiebreakers

In this section, I want to introduce a new technique based on aggregates to solve tiebreaker problems, which I started discussing in Chapter 4. I'll use the same example as I used there—returning the most recent order for each employee—using different combinations of tiebreaker attributes that uniquely identify an order for each employee. Keep in mind that the performance of the solutions that use subqueries very strongly depends on indexing. That is, you need an index on the partitioning column, sort column, and tiebreaker attributes. But in practice, you don't always have the option to add as many indexes as you like. The subquery-based solutions will greatly suffer in performance from a lack of appropriate indexes. Using aggregation techniques, you'll see that the solution will yield good performance even when an optimal index is not in place—in fact, even when no good index is in place.

Let's start with using the *MAX(OrderID)* as the tiebreaker. To recap, you're after the most recent order for each employee, using the *MAX(OrderID)* as the tiebreaker. For each order, you're supposed to return the *EmployeeID*, *OrderDate*, *OrderID*, *CustomerID*, and *RequiredDate*.

The aggregate technique to solve the problem applies the following logical idea in pseudocode:

```
SELECT EmployeeID, MAX(OrderDate, OrderID, CustomerID, RequiredDate)
FROM dbo.Orders
GROUP BY EmployeeID;
```

There's no such ability in T-SQL, so don't try to run this query. The idea here is to generate a row for each employee, with the *MAX(OrderDate)* (most recent) and the *MAX(OrderID)*—the tiebreaker—among orders on the most recent *OrderDate*. Because the combination *EmployeeID*, *OrderDate*, *OrderID* is already unique, all other attributes (*CustomerID*, *RequiredDate*) are simply returned from the selected row. Because a MAX of more than one attribute does not exist in T-SQL, you must mimic it somehow, and you can do so by concatenating all attributes to provide a scalar input value to the MAX function, and then in an outer query, extract back the individual elements.

The question is this: what technique should you use to concatenate the attributes? The trick is to use a fixed-width string for each attribute and to convert the attributes in a way that will not change the sorting behavior. When dealing exclusively with positive numbers, you can use an arithmetic calculation to merge values. For example, say you have the numbers m and n, each with a valid range of 1 through 999. To merge m and n, use the following formula: $m*1000 + n$ AS r. To later extract the individual pieces, use r divided by 1000 to get m, and use r modulo 1000 to get n. However, in many cases you'll probably have non-numeric data to concatenate, so arithmetic concatenation would be out of the question. You might want to consider converting all values to fixed-width character strings ($CHAR(n)/NCHAR(n)$) or to fixed-width binary strings ($BINARY(n)$).

Here's an example for returning the order with the *MAX(OrderDate)* for each employee, using *MAX(OrderID)* as the tiebreaker, using binary concatenation:

```
USE Northwind;

SELECT EmployeeID,
  CAST(SUBSTRING(binstr, 1, 8)   AS DATETIME) AS OrderDate,
  CAST(SUBSTRING(binstr, 9, 4)   AS INT)      AS OrderID,
  CAST(SUBSTRING(binstr, 13, 10) AS NCHAR(5)) AS CustomerID,
  CAST(SUBSTRING(binstr, 23, 8)  AS DATETIME) AS RequiredDate
FROM (SELECT EmployeeID,
        MAX(CAST(OrderDate       AS BINARY(8))
            + CAST(OrderID       AS BINARY(4))
            + CAST(CustomerID    AS BINARY(10))
            + CAST(RequiredDate  AS BINARY(8))) AS binstr
    FROM dbo.Orders
    GROUP BY EmployeeID) AS D;
```

The derived table D contains the maximum concatenated string for each employee. Notice that each value was converted to the appropriate fixed-size string before concatenation based on its datatype (DATETIME—8 bytes, INT—4 bytes, and so on).

> **Note**   When converting numbers to binary strings, only nonnegative values will preserve their original sort behavior. As for character strings, converting them to binary values makes them use similar sort behavior to a binary sort order.

The outer query uses SUBSTRING functions to extract the individual elements, and it converts them back to their original datatypes.

The real benefit in this solution is that it scans the data only once regardless of whether you have a good index or not. If you do, you'll probably get an ordered scan of the index and a sort-based aggregate. If you don't—as is the case here—you'll probably get a hash-based aggregate, as you can see in Figure 6-1.

Figure 6-1   Execution plan for a tiebreaker query

Things get trickier when the sort columns and tiebreaker attributes have different sort directions within them. For example, suppose the tiebreaker was *MIN(OrderID)*. In that case, you would need to apply a MAX to *OrderDate*, and MIN to *OrderID*. There is a logical solution when the attribute with the opposite direction is numeric. Say you need to calculate the MIN value of a nonnegative integer column *n*, using only MAX. This can be achieved by using *<maxint> - MAX(<maxint> - n)*.

The following query incorporates this logical technique:

```
SELECT EmployeeID,
  CAST(SUBSTRING(binstr, 1, 8)   AS DATETIME) AS OrderDate,
  2147483647 - CAST(SUBSTRING(binstr, 9, 4) AS INT) AS OrderID,
  CAST(SUBSTRING(binstr, 13, 10) AS NCHAR(5)) AS CustomerID,
  CAST(SUBSTRING(binstr, 23, 8)  AS DATETIME) AS RequiredDate
FROM (SELECT EmployeeID,
        MAX(CAST(OrderDate        AS BINARY(8))
            + CAST(2147483647 - OrderID AS BINARY(4))
            + CAST(CustomerID    AS BINARY(10))
            + CAST(RequiredDate AS BINARY(8))) AS binstr
      FROM dbo.Orders
      GROUP BY EmployeeID) AS D;
```

Of course, you can play with the tiebreakers you're using in any way you like. For example, here's the query that will return the most recent order for each employee, using *MAX(RequiredDate), MAX(OrderID)* as the tiebreaker:

```
SELECT EmployeeID,
  CAST(SUBSTRING(binstr, 1, 8)   AS DATETIME) AS OrderDate,
  CAST(SUBSTRING(binstr, 9, 8)   AS DATETIME) AS RequiredDate,
  CAST(SUBSTRING(binstr, 17, 4)  AS INT)      AS OrderID,
  CAST(SUBSTRING(binstr, 21, 10) AS NCHAR(5)) AS CustomerID
FROM (SELECT EmployeeID,
        MAX(CAST(OrderDate        AS BINARY(8))
            + CAST(RequiredDate AS BINARY(8))
            + CAST(OrderID       AS BINARY(4))
            + CAST(CustomerID    AS BINARY(10))
            ) AS binstr
      FROM dbo.Orders
      GROUP BY EmployeeID) AS D;
```

Running Aggregations

Running aggregations are aggregations of data over a sequence (typically temporal). There are many variations of running aggregate problems, and I'll describe several important ones here.

In my examples, I'll use a summary table called EmpOrders that contains one row for each employee and month, with the total quantity of orders made by that employee in that month. Run the code in Listing 6-1 to create the EmpOrders table, and populate the table with sample data.

Listing 6-1 Creating and populating the EmpOrders table

```
USE tempdb;
GO

IF OBJECT_ID('dbo.EmpOrders') IS NOT NULL
  DROP TABLE dbo.EmpOrders;
GO

CREATE TABLE dbo.EmpOrders
(
  empid    INT      NOT NULL,
  ordmonth DATETIME NOT NULL,
  qty      INT      NOT NULL,
  PRIMARY KEY(empid, ordmonth)
);

INSERT INTO dbo.EmpOrders(empid, ordmonth, qty)
  SELECT O.EmployeeID,
    CAST(CONVERT(CHAR(6), O.OrderDate, 112) + '01'
      AS DATETIME) AS ordmonth,
    SUM(Quantity) AS qty
  FROM Northwind.dbo.Orders AS O
    JOIN Northwind.dbo.[Order Details] AS OD
      ON O.OrderID = OD.OrderID
  GROUP BY EmployeeID,
    CAST(CONVERT(CHAR(6), O.OrderDate, 112) + '01'
      AS DATETIME);
```

Tip I will represent each month by its start date stored as a DATETIME. This will allow flexible manipulation of the data using date-related functions. To ensure the value would be valid in the datatype, I stored the first day of the month as the day portion. Of course, I'll ignore it in my calculations.

Run the following query to get the contents of the EmpOrders table, which is shown in abbreviated form in Table 6-3:

```
SELECT empid, CONVERT(VARCHAR(7), ordmonth, 121) AS ordmonth, qty
FROM dbo.EmpOrders
ORDER BY empid, ordmonth;
```

Table 6-3 Contents of EmpOrders Table (Abbreviated)

empid	ordmonth	qty
1	1996-07	121
1	1996-08	247
1	1996-09	255
1	1996-10	143
1	1996-11	318

Table 6-3   Contents of EmpOrders Table (Abbreviated)

empid	ordmonth	qty
1	1996-12	536
1	1997-01	304
1	1997-02	168
1	1997-03	275
1	1997-04	20
...	...	...
2	1996-07	50
2	1996-08	94
2	1996-09	137
2	1996-10	248
2	1996-11	237
2	1996-12	319
2	1997-01	230
2	1997-02	36
2	1997-03	151
2	1997-04	468
...	...	...

I'll discuss three types of running aggregation problems: cumulative, sliding, and year-to-date (YTD).

Cumulative Aggregations

Cumulative aggregations accumulate data from the first element within the sequence up to the current point. For example, imagine the following request: for each employee and month, return the total quantity and average monthly quantity from the beginning of the employee's activity to the month in question.

Recall the pre–SQL Server 2005 set-based techniques for calculating row numbers; using these techniques, you scan the same rows we need to scan now to calculate the total quantities. The difference is that for row numbers you used the aggregate COUNT, and here you're asked for the SUM and the AVG. I demonstrated two solutions to calculate row numbers—one using subqueries and one using joins. In the solution using joins, I applied what I called an *expand-collapse technique*. To me, the subquery solution is much more intuitive than the join solution, with its artificial expand-collapse technique. So, when there's no performance difference, I'd rather use subqueries. Typically, you won't see a performance difference when only one aggregate is involved, as the plans would be similar. However, when you request multiple aggregates, the subquery solution might result in a plan that scans the data separately for each aggregate. Compare this to the plan for the join solution, which typically calculates all aggregates during a single scan of the source data.

So my choice is usually simple—use a subquery for one aggregate, and a join for multiple aggregates. The following query applies the expand-collapse approach to produce the desired result, which is shown in abbreviated form in Table 6-4:

```
SELECT O1.empid, CONVERT(VARCHAR(7), O1.ordmonth, 121) AS ordmonth,
  O1.qty AS qtythismonth, SUM(O2.qty) AS totalqty,
  CAST(AVG(1.*O2.qty) AS DECIMAL(12, 2)) AS avgqty
FROM dbo.EmpOrders AS O1
  JOIN dbo.EmpOrders AS O2
    ON O2.empid = O1.empid
    AND O2.ordmonth <= O1.ordmonth
GROUP BY O1.empid, O1.ordmonth, O1.qty
ORDER BY O1.empid, O1.ordmonth;
```

Table 6-4   Cumulative Aggregates Per Employee, Month (Abbreviated)

empid	ordmonth	qtythismonth	totalqty	avgqty
1	1996-07	121	121	121.00
1	1996-08	247	368	184.00
1	1996-09	255	623	207.67
1	1996-10	143	766	191.50
1	1996-11	318	1084	216.80
1	1996-12	536	1620	270.00
1	1997-01	304	1924	274.86
1	1997-02	168	2092	261.50
1	1997-03	275	2367	263.00
1	1997-04	20	2387	238.70
...	...	...	...	...
2	1996-07	50	50	50.00
2	1996-08	94	144	72.00
2	1996-09	137	281	93.67
2	1996-10	248	529	132.25
2	1996-11	237	766	153.20
2	1996-12	319	1085	180.83
2	1997-01	230	1315	187.86
2	1997-02	36	1351	168.88
2	1997-03	151	1502	166.89
2	1997-04	468	1970	197.00
...	...	...	...	...

Now let's say that you were asked to return only one aggregate (say, total quantity). You can safely use the subquery approach:

```
SELECT O1.empid, CONVERT(VARCHAR(7), O1.ordmonth, 121) AS ordmonth,
  O1.qty AS qtythismonth,
```

```
    (SELECT SUM(O2.qty)
     FROM dbo.EmpOrders AS O2
     WHERE O2.empid = O1.empid
       AND O2.ordmonth <= O1.ordmonth) AS totalqty
FROM dbo.EmpOrders AS O1
GROUP BY O1.empid, O1.ordmonth, O1.qty;
```

> **Note**   In both cases, the same N^2 performance issues I discussed with regard to row numbers apply here as well. Because running aggregates typically are calculated on a fairly small number of rows per group, you won't be adversely affected by performance issues, assuming you have appropriate indexes (grouping_columns, sort_columns, covering_columns).
>
> ANSI SQL:2003 and OLAP extensions to ANSI SQL:1999 provide support for running aggregates by means of aggregate window functions. As I mentioned earlier, SQL Server 2005 implemented the OVER clause for aggregate functions only with the PARTITION BY clause. Per ANSI, you could provide a solution relying exclusively on window functions like so:
>
> ```
> SELECT empid, CONVERT(VARCHAR(7), ordmonth, 121) AS ordmonth, qty,
>   SUM(O2.qty) OVER(PARTITION BY empid ORDER BY ordmonth) AS totalqty,
>   CAST(AVG(1.*O2.qty) OVER(PARTITION BY empid ORDER BY ordmonth)
>   AS DECIMAL(12, 2)) AS avgqty
> FROM dbo.EmpOrders;
> ```
>
> When this code is finally supported in SQL Server, you can expect dramatic performance improvements, and obviously much simpler queries.

You might also be requested to filter the data—for example, return monthly aggregates for each employee only for months before the employee reached a certain target. Typically, you'll have a target for each employee stored in a Targets table that you'll need to join to. To make this example simple, I'll assume that all employees have the same target total quantity—1000. In practice, you'll use the target attribute from the Targets table. Because you need to filter an aggregate, not an attribute, you must specify the filter expression (in this case, *SUM(O2.qty) < 1000*) in the HAVING clause, not the WHERE clause. The solution is as follows and will yield the output shown in abbreviated form in Table 6-5:

```
SELECT O1.empid, CONVERT(VARCHAR(7), O1.ordmonth, 121) AS ordmonth,
  O1.qty AS qtythismonth, SUM(O2.qty) AS totalqty,
  CAST(AVG(1.*O2.qty) AS DECIMAL(12, 2)) AS avgqty
FROM dbo.EmpOrders AS O1
  JOIN dbo.EmpOrders AS O2
    ON O2.empid = O1.empid
    AND O2.ordmonth <= O1.ordmonth
GROUP BY O1.empid, O1.ordmonth, O1.qty
HAVING SUM(O2.qty) < 1000
ORDER BY O1.empid, O1.ordmonth;
```

Table 6-5   Cumulative Aggregates, Where totalqty < 1000 (Abbreviated)

empid	ordmonth	qtythismonth	totalqty	avgqty
1	1996-07	121	121	121.00
1	1996-08	247	368	184.00
1	1996-09	255	623	207.67
1	1996-10	143	766	191.50
2	1996-07	50	50	50.00
2	1996-08	94	144	72.00
2	1996-09	137	281	93.67
2	1996-10	248	529	132.25
2	1996-11	237	766	153.20
3	...	...	...	...

Things get a bit tricky if you also need to include the rows for those months in which the employees reached their target. If you specify $SUM(O2.qty) <= 1000$ (that is, write <= instead of <), you still won't get the row in which the employee reached the target unless the total through that month is exactly 1000. But remember that you have access to both the cumulative total and the current month's quantity, and using these two values together, you can solve this problem. If you change the HAVING filter to $SUM(O2.qty) - O1.qty < 1000$, you will get the months in which the employee's total quantity, *excluding the current month's orders*, had not reached the target. In particular, the first month in which an employee reached or exceeded the target satisfies this new criterion, and that month will appear in the results. The complete solution follows, and it yields the output shown in abbreviated form in Table 6-6:

```
SELECT O1.empid, CONVERT(VARCHAR(7), O1.ordmonth, 121) AS ordmonth,
  O1.qty AS qtythismonth, SUM(O2.qty) AS totalqty,
  CAST(AVG(1.*O2.qty) AS DECIMAL(12, 2)) AS avgqty
FROM dbo.EmpOrders AS O1
  JOIN dbo.EmpOrders AS O2
    ON O2.empid = O1.empid
    AND O2.ordmonth <= O1.ordmonth
GROUP BY O1.empid, O1.ordmonth, O1.qty
HAVING SUM(O2.qty) - O1.qty < 1000
ORDER BY O1.empid, O1.ordmonth;
```

Table 6-6   Cumulative Aggregates, Until totalqty First Reaches or Exceeds 1000 (Abbreviated)

empid	ordmonth	qtythismonth	totalqty	avgqty
1	1996-07	121	121	121.00
1	1996-08	247	368	184.00
1	1996-09	255	623	207.67
1	1996-10	143	766	191.50
1	1996-11	318	1084	216.80

Table 6-6   Cumulative Aggregates, Until totalqty First Reaches or Exceeds 1000 (Abbreviated)

empid	ordmonth	qtythismonth	totalqty	avgqty
2	1996-07	50	50	50.00
2	1996-08	94	144	72.00
2	1996-09	137	281	93.67
2	1996-10	248	529	132.25
2	1996-11	237	766	153.20
2	1996-12	319	1085	180.83
3	...	...	...	...

Note   You might have another solution in mind that would seem like a plausible and simpler alternative—to leave the SUM condition alone but change the join condition to *O2.ordmonth < O1.ordmonth*. This way, the query would select rows where the total through the previous month did not meet the target. However, in the end, this solution is not any easier (the AVG is hard to generate, for example); and worse, you might come up with a solution that does not work for employees who reach the target in their first month.

Suppose you were interested in seeing results only for the specific month in which the employee reached the target of 1000, without seeing results for preceding months. What's true for only those rows of Table 6-6? What you're looking for are rows from Table 6-6 where the total quantity is greater than or equal to 1000. Simply add this criterion to the HAVING filter. Here's the query, which will yield the output shown in Table 6-7:

```
SELECT O1.empid, CONVERT(VARCHAR(7), O1.ordmonth, 121) AS ordmonth,
   O1.qty AS qtythismonth, SUM(O2.qty) AS totalqty,
   CAST(AVG(1.*O2.qty) AS DECIMAL(12, 2)) AS avgqty
FROM dbo.EmpOrders AS O1
   JOIN dbo.EmpOrders AS O2
     ON O2.empid = O1.empid
     AND O2.ordmonth <= O1.ordmonth
GROUP BY O1.empid, O1.ordmonth, O1.qty
HAVING SUM(O2.qty) - O1.qty < 1000
   AND SUM(O2.qty) >= 1000
ORDER BY O1.empid, O1.ordmonth;
```

Table 6-7   Cumulative Aggregates only for Months in Which totalqty First Reaches or Exceeds 1000

empid	ordmonth	qtythismonth	totalqty	avgqty
1	1996-11	318	1084	216.80
2	1996-12	319	1085	180.83
3	1997-01	364	1304	186.29
4	1996-10	613	1439	359.75
5	1997-05	247	1213	173.29

Table 6-7 **Cumulative Aggregates only for Months in Which totalqty First Reaches or Exceeds 1000**

empid	ordmonth	qtythismonth	totalqty	avgqty
6	1997-01	64	1027	171.17
7	1997-03	191	1069	152.71
8	1997-01	305	1228	175.43
9	1997-06	161	1007	125.88

Sliding Aggregations

Sliding aggregates are calculated over a sliding window in a sequence (again, typically temporal), as opposed to being calculated from the beginning of the sequence until the current point. A *moving average*—such as the employee's average quantity over the last three months—is one example of a sliding aggregate.

> **Note** Without clarification, expressions like "last three months" are ambiguous. The last three months could mean the previous three months (*not including this month*), or it could mean the previous two months *along with this month*. When you get a problem like this, be sure you know precisely what window of time you are using for aggregation—for a particular row, exactly when does the window begin and end?
>
> In our example, the window of time is: greater than the point in time starting three months ago and smaller than or equal to the current point in time. Note that this definition will work well even in cases where you track finer time granularities than a month (including day, hour, minute, second, and millisecond). This definition also addresses implicit conversion issues due to the accuracy level supported by SQL Server for the DATETIME datatype—3.33 milliseconds. It's wiser to use > and <= predicates than the BETWEEN predicate to avoid implicit conversion issues.

The main difference between the solution for cumulative aggregates and the solution for running aggregates is in the join condition (or in the subquery's filter, in the case of the alternate solution using subqueries). Instead of using *O2.ordmonth <= O1.current_month*, you use *O2.ordmonth > three_months_before_current AND O2.ordmonth <= current_month*. In T-SQL, this translates to the following query, yielding the output shown in abbreviated form in Table 6-8:

```
SELECT O1.empid,
  CONVERT(VARCHAR(7), O1.ordmonth, 121) AS ordmonth,
  O1.qty AS qtythismonth,
  SUM(O2.qty) AS totalqty,
  CAST(AVG(1.*O2.qty) AS DECIMAL(12, 2)) AS avgqty
FROM dbo.EmpOrders AS O1
  JOIN dbo.EmpOrders AS O2
    ON O2.empid = O1.empid
    AND (O2.ordmonth > DATEADD(month, -3, O1.ordmonth)
    AND O2.ordmonth <= O1.ordmonth)
GROUP BY O1.empid, O1.ordmonth, O1.qty
ORDER BY O1.empid, O1.ordmonth;
```

Table 6-8   Sliding Aggregates Per Employee over Three Months Leading to Current (Abbreviated)

empid	ordmonth	qtythismonth	totalqty	avgqty
1	1996-07	121	121	121.00
1	1996-08	247	368	184.00
1	1996-09	255	623	207.67
1	1996-10	143	645	215.00
1	1996-11	318	716	238.67
1	1996-12	536	997	332.33
1	1997-01	304	1158	386.00
1	1997-02	168	1008	336.00
1	1997-03	275	747	249.00
1	1997-04	20	463	154.33
...	...	...	...	...
2	1996-07	50	50	50.00
2	1996-08	94	144	72.00
2	1996-09	137	281	93.67
2	1996-10	248	479	159.67
2	1996-11	237	622	207.33
2	1996-12	319	804	268.00
2	1997-01	230	786	262.00
2	1997-02	36	585	195.00
2	1997-03	151	417	139.00
2	1997-04	468	655	218.33
...	...	...	...	...

Note that this solution includes aggregates for three-month periods that don't include three months of actual data. If you want to return only periods with three full months accumulated, without the first two periods which do not cover three months, you can add the criterion *MIN(O2.ordmonth) = DATEADD(month, -2, O1.ordmonth)* to the HAVING filter.

Note   In addition to supporting both the PARTITION BY and ORDER BY elements in the OVER clause for window-based aggregations, ANSI also supports a ROWS clause that allows you to request sliding aggregates. For example, here's the query that would return the desired result for the last sliding aggregates request (assuming the data has exactly one row per month):

```
SELECT empid, CONVERT(VARCHAR(7), ordmonth, 121) AS ordmonth,
  qty AS qtythismonth,
  SUM(O2.qty) OVER(PARTITION BY empid ORDER BY ordmonth
                ROWS 2 PRECEDING) AS totalqty,
  CAST(AVG(1.*O2.qty) OVER(PARTITION BY empid ORDER BY ordmonth
                    ROWS 2 PRECEDING)
    AS DECIMAL(12, 2)) AS avgqty
FROM dbo.EmpOrders;
```

Year-To-Date (YTD)

YTD aggregates accumulate values from the beginning of a period based on some DATETIME unit (say, a year) until the current point. The calculation is very similar to the sliding aggregates solution. The only difference is the low bound provided in the query's filter, which is the calculation of the beginning of the year. For example, the following query returns YTD aggregates for each employee and month, yielding the output shown in abbreviated form in Table 6-9:

```
SELECT O1.empid,
  CONVERT(VARCHAR(7), O1.ordmonth, 121) AS ordmonth,
  O1.qty AS qtythismonth,
  SUM(O2.qty) AS totalqty,
  CAST(AVG(1.*O2.qty) AS DECIMAL(12, 2)) AS avgqty
FROM dbo.EmpOrders AS O1
  JOIN dbo.EmpOrders AS O2
    ON O2.empid = O1.empid
    AND (O2.ordmonth >= CAST(CAST(YEAR(O1.ordmonth) AS CHAR(4))
                            + '0101' AS DATETIME)
        AND O2.ordmonth <= O1.ordmonth)
GROUP BY O1.empid, O1.ordmonth, O1.qty
ORDER BY O1.empid, O1.ordmonth;
```

Table 6-9   YTD Aggregates Per Employee, Month (Abbreviated)

empid	ordmonth	qtythismonth	totalqty	avgqty
1	1996-07	121	121	121.00
1	1996-08	247	368	184.00
1	1996-09	255	623	207.67
1	1996-10	143	766	191.50
1	1996-11	318	1084	216.80
1	1996-12	536	1620	270.00
1	1997-01	304	304	304.00
1	1997-02	168	472	236.00
1	1997-03	275	747	249.00
1	1997-04	20	767	191.75
...	...	...	...	...
2	1996-07	50	50	50.00
2	1996-08	94	144	72.00
2	1996-09	137	281	93.67
2	1996-10	248	529	132.25
2	1996-11	237	766	153.20
2	1996-12	319	1085	180.83
2	1997-01	230	230	230.00
2	1997-02	36	266	133.00

Table 6-9   YTD Aggregates Per Employee, Month (Abbreviated)

empid	ordmonth	qtythismonth	totalqty	avgqty
2	1997-03	151	417	139.00
2	1997-04	468	885	221.25
...	...	...	...	...

Pivoting

Pivoting is a technique that allows you to rotate rows to columns, possibly performing aggregations along the way. The number of applications for pivoting is simply astounding. In this section, I'll present a few, including pivoting attributes in an Open Schema environment, solving relational division problems, and formatting aggregated data. Later in the chapter and also in other chapters in the book, I'll show additional applications. As usual for this book, I'll present solutions that apply to versions earlier than SQL Server 2005 as well as solutions that use newly introduced specialized operators and therefore work only in SQL Server 2005.

Pivoting Attributes

I'll use *open schema* as the scenario for pivoting attributes. Open schema is a schema design you create to deal with frequent schema changes. The relational model and SQL do a very good job with data manipulation (DML), which includes changing and querying data. However, SQL's data definition language (DDL) does not make it easy to deal with frequent schema changes. Whenever you need to add new entities, you must create new tables; whenever existing entities change their structures, you must add, alter, or drop columns. Such changes usually require downtime of the affected objects, and they also bring about substantial revisions to the application.

In a scenario with frequent schema changes, you can store all data in a single table, where each attribute value resides in its own row along with the entity or object ID and the attribute name or ID. You represent the attribute values using the datatype SQL_VARIANT to accommodate multiple attribute types in a single column.

In my examples, I'll use the OpenSchema table, which you can create and populate by running the code in Listing 6-2.

Listing 6-2   Creating and populating the OpenSchema table

```
SET NOCOUNT ON;
USE tempdb;
GO

IF OBJECT_ID('dbo.OpenSchema') IS NOT NULL
  DROP TABLE dbo.OpenSchema;
GO
```

```
CREATE TABLE dbo.OpenSchema
(
  objectid  INT          NOT NULL,
  attribute NVARCHAR(30) NOT NULL,
  value     SQL_VARIANT  NOT NULL,
  PRIMARY KEY (objectid, attribute)
);

INSERT INTO dbo.OpenSchema(objectid, attribute, value)
  VALUES(1, N'attr1', CAST('ABC'      AS VARCHAR(10))  );
INSERT INTO dbo.OpenSchema(objectid, attribute, value)
  VALUES(1, N'attr2', CAST(10         AS INT)          );
INSERT INTO dbo.OpenSchema(objectid, attribute, value)
  VALUES(1, N'attr3', CAST('20040101' AS SMALLDATETIME));
INSERT INTO dbo.OpenSchema(objectid, attribute, value)
  VALUES(2, N'attr2', CAST(12         AS INT)          );
INSERT INTO dbo.OpenSchema(objectid, attribute, value)
  VALUES(2, N'attr3', CAST('20060101' AS SMALLDATETIME));
INSERT INTO dbo.OpenSchema(objectid, attribute, value)
  VALUES(2, N'attr4', CAST('Y'        AS CHAR(1))      );
INSERT INTO dbo.OpenSchema(objectid, attribute, value)
  VALUES(2, N'attr5', CAST(13.7       AS DECIMAL(9,3)) );
INSERT INTO dbo.OpenSchema(objectid, attribute, value)
  VALUES(3, N'attr1', CAST('XYZ'      AS VARCHAR(10))  );
INSERT INTO dbo.OpenSchema(objectid, attribute, value)
  VALUES(3, N'attr2', CAST(20         AS INT)          );
INSERT INTO dbo.OpenSchema(objectid, attribute, value)
  VALUES(3, N'attr3', CAST('20050101' AS SMALLDATETIME));
```

The contents of the OpenSchema table are shown in Table 6-10.

Table 6-10   Contents of OpenSchema Table

objectid	attribute	value
1	attr1	ABC
1	attr2	10
1	attr3	2004-01-01 00:00:00.000
2	attr2	12
2	attr3	2006-01-01 00:00:00.000
2	attr4	Y
2	attr5	13.700
3	attr1	XYZ
3	attr2	20
3	attr3	2005-01-01 00:00:00.000

Representing data this way allows logical schema changes to be implemented without adding, altering, or dropping tables and columns, but by using DML INSERTs, UPDATEs, and DELETEs instead. Of course, other aspects of working with the data (such as enforcing integrity, tuning, and querying) become more complex and expensive with such a representation.

There are other approaches to deal with frequent data definition changes—for example, storing the data in XML format. However, when you weigh the advantages and disadvantages of each representation, you might find the open schema representation demonstrated here more favorable in some scenarios—for example, representing auction data.

Keep in mind that this representation of the data requires very complex queries even for simple requests, because different attributes of the same entity instance are spread over multiple rows. Before you query such data, you might want to rotate it to a traditional form with one column for each attribute—perhaps store the result in a temporary table, index it, query it, and then get rid of the temporary table. To rotate the data from its open schema form into a traditional form, you need to use a pivoting technique.

In the following section, I'll describe the steps involved in solving pivoting problems. I'd like to point out that to understand the steps of the solution, it can be very helpful if you think about query logical processing phases, which I described in detail in Chapter 1. I discussed the query processing phases involved with the PIVOT table operator in SQL Server 2005, but those phases apply just as well to the solution in SQL Server 2000. Moreover, in SQL 2000 the phases are more apparent in the code, while in SQL Server 2005 they are implicit.

The first step you might want to try when solving pivoting problems is to figure out how the number of rows in the result correlates to the number of rows in the source data. Here, you need to create a single result row out of the multiple base rows for each object. This can mean creating a GROUP BY *objectid*.

As the next step in a pivoting problem, you can think in terms of the result columns. You need a result column for each unique attribute. Because the data contains five unique attributes (attr1, attr2, attr3, attr4, and attr5), you need five expressions in the SELECT list. Each expression is supposed to extract, out of the rows belonging to the grouped object, the value corresponding to a specific attribute. This can be done with the following MAX(CASE...) expression, which in this example is applied to the attribute attr2:

```
MAX(CASE WHEN attribute = 'attr2' THEN value END) AS attr2
```

Remember that with no ELSE clause CASE assumes an implicit ELSE NULL. The CASE expression just shown will yield NULL for rows where *attribute* does not equal 'attr2' and yield *value* when *attribute* does equal 'attr2'. This means that among the rows with a given value of *objectid* (say, 1), the CASE expression would yield several NULLs and, at most, one known value (10 in our example), which represents the value of the target attribute (*attr2* in our example) for the given *objectid*. The trick to extracting the one known value is to use MAX or MIN. Both ignore NULLs and will return the one non-NULL value present, because both the minimum and the maximum of a set containing one value is that value. Here's the complete query that pivots the attributes from OpenSchema, yielding the output shown in Table 6-11:

```
SELECT objectid,
  MAX(CASE WHEN attribute = 'attr1' THEN value END) AS attr1,
  MAX(CASE WHEN attribute = 'attr2' THEN value END) AS attr2,
```

```
      MAX(CASE WHEN attribute = 'attr3' THEN value END) AS attr3,
      MAX(CASE WHEN attribute = 'attr4' THEN value END) AS attr4,
      MAX(CASE WHEN attribute = 'attr5' THEN value END) AS attr5
FROM dbo.OpenSchema
GROUP BY objectid;
```

Table 6-11   Pivoted OpenSchema

objectid	attr1	attr2	attr3	attr4	attr5
1	ABC	10	2004-01-01 00:00:00.000	NULL	NULL
2	NULL	12	2006-01-01 00:00:00.000	Y	13.700
3	XYZ	20	2005-01-01 00:00:00.000	NULL	NULL

Note   To write this query, you have to know the names of the attributes. If you don't, you'll need to construct the query string dynamically.

More Info   For details about dynamic pivoting (and unpivoting), please refer to *Inside Microsoft SQL Server 2005: T-SQL Programming* (Microsoft Press, 2006).

This technique for pivoting data is very efficient because it scans the base table only once.

SQL Server 2005 introduces PIVOT, a native specialized operator for pivoting. I have to say that I find it very confusing and nonintuitive. I don't see much advantage in using it, except that it allows for shorter code. It doesn't support dynamic pivoting, and underneath the covers, it applies very similar logic to the one I presented in the last solution. So you probably won't even find noticeable performance differences. At any rate, here's how you would pivot the OpenSchema data using the PIVOT operator:

```
SELECT objectid, attr1, attr2, attr3, attr4, attr5
FROM dbo.OpenSchema
  PIVOT(MAX(value) FOR attribute
    IN([attr1],[attr2],[attr3],[attr4],[attr5])) AS P;
```

Within this solution, you can identify all the elements I used in the previous solution. The inputs to the PIVOT operator are as follows:

- The aggregate that will apply to the values in the group. In our case, it's *MAX(value)*, which extracts the single non-NULL value corresponding to the target attribute. In other cases, you might have more than one non-NULL value per group and want a different aggregate (for example, SUM or AVG).

- Following the FOR keyword, the source column holding the target column names (*attribute*, in our case).

- The list of actual target column names in parentheses following the keyword IN.

The tricky bit here is that there's no explicit GROUP BY clause, but implicit grouping does take place. It's as if the pivoting activity is based on groups defined by the list of all columns that were not mentioned in PIVOT's inputs (in the parentheses) following the PIVOT keyword). In our case, *objectid* is the column that defines the groups.

Caution   Because all unspecified columns define the groups, unintentionally, you might end up with undesired grouping. To solve this, use a derived table or a common table expression (CTE) that returns only the columns of interest, and apply PIVOT to that table expression and not to the base table. I'll demonstrate this shortly.

Tip   The input to the aggregate function must be a base column with no manipulation—it cannot be an expression (for example: *SUM(qty * price)*). If you want to provide the aggregate function with an expression as input, create a derived table or CTE where you assign the expression with a column alias (*qty * price AS value*), and in the outer query use that column as input to PIVOT's aggregate function (*SUM(value)*).

Also, you cannot rotate attributes from more than one column (the column that appears after the FOR keyword. If you need to pivot more that one column's attributes (say, *empid* and *YEAR(orderdate)*), you can use a similar approach to the previous suggestion; create a derived table or a CTE where you concatenate the values from all columns you want to rotate and assign the expression with a column alias (*CAST(empid AS VARCHAR(10)) + '_' + CAST(YEAR(orderdate) AS CHAR(4)) AS empyear*). Then, in the outer query, specify that column after PIVOT's FOR keyword (*FOR empyear IN([1_2004], [1_2005], [1_2006], [2_2004], ...)*).

Relational Division

Pivoting can also be used to solve relational division problems when the number of elements in the divisor set is fairly small. In my examples, I'll use the OrderDetails table, which you create and populate by running the code in Listing 6-3.

Listing 6-3   Creating and populating the OrderDetails table

```
USE tempdb;
GO

IF OBJECT_ID('dbo.OrderDetails') IS NOT NULL
  DROP TABLE dbo.OrderDetails;
GO

CREATE TABLE dbo.OrderDetails
(
  orderid   VARCHAR(10) NOT NULL,
  productid INT         NOT NULL,
  PRIMARY KEY(orderid, productid)
  /* other columns */
);
```

```
INSERT INTO dbo.OrderDetails(orderid, productid) VALUES('A', 1);
INSERT INTO dbo.OrderDetails(orderid, productid) VALUES('A', 2);
INSERT INTO dbo.OrderDetails(orderid, productid) VALUES('A', 3);
INSERT INTO dbo.OrderDetails(orderid, productid) VALUES('A', 4);
INSERT INTO dbo.OrderDetails(orderid, productid) VALUES('B', 2);
INSERT INTO dbo.OrderDetails(orderid, productid) VALUES('B', 3);
INSERT INTO dbo.OrderDetails(orderid, productid) VALUES('B', 4);
INSERT INTO dbo.OrderDetails(orderid, productid) VALUES('C', 3);
INSERT INTO dbo.OrderDetails(orderid, productid) VALUES('C', 4);
INSERT INTO dbo.OrderDetails(orderid, productid) VALUES('D', 4);
```

A classic relational division problem is to return orders that contain a certain basket of products—say, products 2, 3, and 4. You use a pivoting technique to rotate only the relevant products into separate columns for each order. Instead of returning an actual attribute value, you produce a 1 if the product exists in the order and a 0 otherwise. Create a derived table out of the pivot query, and in the outer query filter only orders that contain a 1 in all product columns. Here's the full query, which correctly returns orders A and B:

```
SELECT orderid
FROM (SELECT
        orderid,
        MAX(CASE WHEN productid = 2 THEN 1 END) AS P2,
        MAX(CASE WHEN productid = 3 THEN 1 END) AS P3,
        MAX(CASE WHEN productid = 4 THEN 1 END) AS P4
      FROM dbo.OrderDetails
      GROUP BY orderid) AS P
WHERE P2 = 1 AND P3 = 1 AND P4 = 1;
```

If you run only the derived table query, you get the pivoted products for each order as shown in Table 6-12.

Table 6-12   Contents of Derived Table P

orderid	P2	P3	P4
A	1	1	1
B	1	1	1
C	NULL	1	1
D	NULL	NULL	1

To answer the request at hand using the new PIVOT operator, use the following query:

```
SELECT orderid
FROM (SELECT *
      FROM dbo.OrderDetails
        PIVOT(MAX(productid) FOR productid IN([2],[3],[4])) AS P) AS T
WHERE [2] = 2 AND [3] = 3 AND [4] = 4;
```

The aggregate function must accept a column as input, so I provided the *productid* itself. This means that if the product exists within an order, the corresponding value will contain the actual *productid* and not 1. That's why the filter looks a bit different here.

Note that you can make both queries more intuitive and similar to each other in their logic by using the COUNT aggregate instead of MAX. This way, both queries would produce a 1 where the product exists and a 0 where it doesn't (instead of NULL). Here's what the SQL Server 2000 query would look like:

```
SELECT orderid
FROM (SELECT
        orderid,
        COUNT(CASE WHEN productid = 2 THEN 1 END) AS P2,
        COUNT(CASE WHEN productid = 3 THEN 1 END) AS P3,
        COUNT(CASE WHEN productid = 4 THEN 1 END) AS P4
      FROM dbo.OrderDetails
      GROUP BY orderid) AS P
WHERE P2 = 1 AND P3 = 1 AND P4 = 1;
```

And here's the query you would use in SQL Server 2005:

```
SELECT orderid
FROM (SELECT *
      FROM dbo.OrderDetails
        PIVOT(COUNT(productid) FOR productid IN([2],[3],[4])) AS P) AS T
WHERE [2] = 1 AND [3] = 1 AND [4] = 1;
```

Aggregating Data

You can also use a pivoting technique to format aggregated data, typically for reporting purposes. In my examples, I'll use the Orders table, which you create and populate by running the code in Listing 6-4.

Listing 6-4   Creating and populating the Orders table

```
USE tempdb;
GO

IF OBJECT_ID('dbo.Orders') IS NOT NULL
  DROP TABLE dbo.Orders;
GO

CREATE TABLE dbo.Orders
(
  orderid   int         NOT NULL PRIMARY KEY NONCLUSTERED,
  orderdate datetime    NOT NULL,
  empid     int         NOT NULL,
  custid    varchar(5)  NOT NULL,
  qty       int         NOT NULL
);

CREATE UNIQUE CLUSTERED INDEX idx_orderdate_orderid
  ON dbo.Orders(orderdate, orderid);

INSERT INTO dbo.Orders(orderid, orderdate, empid, custid, qty)
  VALUES(30001, '20020802', 3, 'A', 10);
```

```
INSERT INTO dbo.Orders(orderid, orderdate, empid, custid, qty)
  VALUES(10001, '20021224', 1, 'A', 12);
INSERT INTO dbo.Orders(orderid, orderdate, empid, custid, qty)
  VALUES(10005, '20021224', 1, 'B', 20);
INSERT INTO dbo.Orders(orderid, orderdate, empid, custid, qty)
  VALUES(40001, '20030109', 4, 'A', 40);
INSERT INTO dbo.Orders(orderid, orderdate, empid, custid, qty)
  VALUES(10006, '20030118', 1, 'C', 14);
INSERT INTO dbo.Orders(orderid, orderdate, empid, custid, qty)
  VALUES(20001, '20030212', 2, 'B', 12);
INSERT INTO dbo.Orders(orderid, orderdate, empid, custid, qty)
  VALUES(40005, '20040212', 4, 'A', 10);
INSERT INTO dbo.Orders(orderid, orderdate, empid, custid, qty)
  VALUES(20002, '20040216', 2, 'C', 20);
INSERT INTO dbo.Orders(orderid, orderdate, empid, custid, qty)
  VALUES(30003, '20040418', 3, 'B', 15);
INSERT INTO dbo.Orders(orderid, orderdate, empid, custid, qty)
  VALUES(30004, '20020418', 3, 'C', 22);
INSERT INTO dbo.Orders(orderid, orderdate, empid, custid, qty)
  VALUES(30007, '20020907', 3, 'D', 30);
```

The contents of the Orders table are shown in Table 6-13.

Table 6-13   Contents of Orders Table

orderid	orderdate	empid	custid	qty
30004	2002-04-18 00:00:00.000	3	C	22
30001	2002-08-02 00:00:00.000	3	A	10
30007	2002-09-07 00:00:00.000	3	D	30
10001	2002-12-24 00:00:00.000	1	A	12
10005	2002-12-24 00:00:00.000	1	B	20
40001	2003-01-09 00:00:00.000	4	A	40
10006	2003-01-18 00:00:00.000	1	C	14
20001	2003-02-12 00:00:00.000	2	B	12
40005	2004-02-12 00:00:00.000	4	A	10
20002	2004-02-16 00:00:00.000	2	C	20
30003	2004-04-18 00:00:00.000	3	B	15

Suppose you want to return a row for each customer, with the total yearly quantities in a different column for each year. You use a pivoting technique very similar to the previous ones I showed, only this time instead of using a MAX, you use a SUM aggregate, which will return the output shown in Table 6-14:

```
SELECT custid,
  SUM(CASE WHEN orderyear = 2002 THEN qty END) AS [2002],
  SUM(CASE WHEN orderyear = 2003 THEN qty END) AS [2003],
  SUM(CASE WHEN orderyear = 2004 THEN qty END) AS [2004]
FROM (SELECT custid, YEAR(orderdate) AS orderyear, qty
      FROM dbo.Orders) AS D
GROUP BY custid;
```

Table 6-14   Total Yearly Quantities per Customer

custid	2002	2003	2004
A	22	40	10
B	20	12	15
C	22	14	20
D	30	NULL	NULL

Here you can see the use of a derived table to isolate only the relevant elements for the pivoting activity (*custid, orderyear, qty*).

One of the main issues with this pivoting solution is that you might end up with lengthy query strings when the number of elements you need to rotate is large. In an effort to shorten the query string, you can use a matrix table that contains a column and a row for each attribute that you need to rotate (*orderyear*, in this case). Only column values in the intersections of corresponding rows and columns contain the value 1, and the other column values are populated with a NULL or a 0, depending on your needs. Run the code in Listing 6-5 to create and populate the Matrix table.

Listing 6-5   Creating and populating the Matrix table

```
USE tempdb;
GO

IF OBJECTPROPERTY(OBJECT_ID('dbo.Matrix'), 'IsUserTable') = 1
  DROP TABLE dbo.Matrix;
GO

CREATE TABLE dbo.Matrix
(
  orderyear INT NOT NULL PRIMARY KEY,
  y2002 INT NULL,
  y2003 INT NULL,
  y2004 INT NULL
);

INSERT INTO dbo.Matrix(orderyear, y2002) VALUES(2002, 1);
INSERT INTO dbo.Matrix(orderyear, y2003) VALUES(2003, 1);
INSERT INTO dbo.Matrix(orderyear, y2004) VALUES(2004, 1);
```

The contents of the Matrix table are shown in Table 6-15.

Table 6-15   Contents of Matrix Table

orderyear	y2002	y2003	y2004
2002	1	NULL	NULL
2003	NULL	1	NULL
2004	NULL	NULL	1

You join the base table (or table expression) with the Matrix table based on a match in *orderyear*. This means that each row from the base table will be matched with one row from Matrix—the one with the same *orderyear*. In that row, only the corresponding *orderyear's* column value will contain a 1. So you can substitute the expression

```
SUM(CASE WHEN orderyear = <some_year> THEN qty END) AS [<some_year>]
```

with the logically equivalent expression

```
SUM(qty*y<some_year>) AS [<some_year>]
```

Here's what the full query looks like:

```
SELECT custid,
  SUM(qty*y2002) AS [2002],
  SUM(qty*y2003) AS [2003],
  SUM(qty*y2004) AS [2004]
FROM (SELECT custid, YEAR(orderdate) AS orderyear, qty
      FROM dbo.Orders) AS D
  JOIN dbo.Matrix AS M ON D.orderyear = M.orderyear
GROUP BY custid;
```

If you need the number of orders instead of the sum of *qty*, in the original solution you produce a 1 instead of the *qty* column for each order, and use the COUNT aggregate function, which will produce the output shown in Table 6-16:

```
SELECT custid,
  COUNT(CASE WHEN orderyear = 2002 THEN 1 END) AS [2002],
  COUNT(CASE WHEN orderyear = 2003 THEN 1 END) AS [2003],
  COUNT(CASE WHEN orderyear = 2004 THEN 1 END) AS [2004]
FROM (SELECT custid, YEAR(orderdate) AS orderyear
      FROM dbo.Orders) AS D
GROUP BY custid;
```

Table 6-16   Count of Yearly Orders per Customer

custid	2002	2003	2004
A	2	1	1
B	1	1	1
C	1	1	1
D	1	0	0

With the Matrix table, simply specify the column corresponding to the target year:

```
SELECT custid,
  COUNT(y2002) AS [2002],
  COUNT(y2003) AS [2003],
  COUNT(y2004) AS [2004]
FROM (SELECT custid, YEAR(orderdate) AS orderyear
      FROM dbo.Orders) AS D
  JOIN dbo.Matrix AS M ON D.orderyear = M.orderyear
GROUP BY custid;
```

Of course, using the PIVOT operator in SQL Server 2005, the query strings are short to begin with. Here's the query using the PIVOT operator to calculate total yearly quantities per customer:

```
SELECT *
FROM (SELECT custid, YEAR(orderdate) AS orderyear, qty
      FROM dbo.Orders) AS D
  PIVOT(SUM(qty) FOR orderyear IN([2002],[2003],[2004])) AS P;
```

And here's a query that counts the orders:

```
SELECT *
FROM (SELECT custid, YEAR(orderdate) AS orderyear
      FROM dbo.Orders) AS D
  PIVOT(COUNT(orderyear) FOR orderyear IN([2002],[2003],[2004])) AS P;
```

Remember that static queries performing pivoting require you to know ahead of time the list of attributes you're going to rotate. For dynamic pivoting, you need to construct the query string dynamically.

Unpivoting

Unpivoting is the opposite of pivoting—namely, rotating columns to rows. Unpivoting is usually used to normalize data, but it has other applications as well.

 Note   Unpivoting is not an exact inverse of pivoting, as it won't necessarily allow you to regenerate source rows that were pivoted. However, for the sake of simplicity, think of it as the opposite of pivoting.

In my examples, I'll use the PvtCustOrders table, which you create and populate by running the code in Listing 6-6.

Listing 6-6   Creating and populating the PvtCustOrders table

```
USE tempdb;
GO
IF OBJECT_ID('dbo.PvtCustOrders') IS NOT NULL
  DROP TABLE dbo.PvtCustOrders;
GO

SELECT *
INTO dbo.PvtCustOrders
FROM (SELECT custid, YEAR(orderdate) AS orderyear, qty
      FROM dbo.Orders) AS D
  PIVOT(SUM(qty) FOR orderyear IN([2002],[2003],[2004])) AS P;
```

The contents of the PvtCustOrders table are shown in Table 6-17.

Table 6-17   Contents of PvtCustOrders Table

custid	2002	2003	2004
A	22	40	10
B	20	12	15
C	22	14	20
D	30	NULL	NULL

The goal in this case will be to generate a result row for each customer and year, containing the customer ID (*custid*), order year (*orderyear*), and quantity (*qty*).

I'll start with a solution that applies to versions earlier than SQL Server 2005. Here as well, try to think in terms of query logical processing as described in Chapter 1.

The first and most important step in the solution is to generate three copies of each base row—one for each year. This can be achieved by performing a cross join between the base table and a virtual auxiliary table that has one row per year. The SELECT list can then return the *custid* and *orderyear*, and also calculate the target year's *qty* with the following CASE expression:

```
CASE orderyear
  WHEN 2002 THEN [2002]
  WHEN 2003 THEN [2003]
  WHEN 2004 THEN [2004]
END AS qty
```

You achieve unpivoting this way, but you'll also get rows corresponding to NULL values in the source table (for example, for customer D in years 2003 and 2004). To eliminate those rows, create a derived table out of the solution query and, in the outer query, eliminate the rows with the NULL in the *qty* column.

Note   In practice, you'd typically store a *0* and not a NULL as the quantity for a customer with no orders in a certain year; the order quantity is known to be zero, and not unknown. However, I used NULLs here to demonstrate the treatment of NULLs, which is a very common need in unpivoting problems.

Here's the complete solution, which returns the desired output as shown in Table 6-18:

```
SELECT custid, orderyear, qty
FROM (SELECT custid, orderyear,
        CASE orderyear
          WHEN 2002 THEN [2002]
          WHEN 2003 THEN [2003]
          WHEN 2004 THEN [2004]
        END AS qty
```

```
FROM dbo.PvtCustOrders,
   (SELECT 2002 AS orderyear
    UNION ALL SELECT 2003
    UNION ALL SELECT 2004) AS OrderYears) AS D
WHERE qty IS NOT NULL;
```

Table 6-18   Unpivoted Total Quantities per Customer and Order Year

custid	orderyear	qty
A	2002	22
B	2002	20
C	2002	22
D	2002	30
A	2003	40
B	2003	12
C	2003	14
A	2004	10
B	2004	15
C	2004	20

In SQL Server 2005, things are dramatically simpler. You use the UNPIVOT table operator as follows:

```
SELECT custid, orderyear, qty
FROM dbo.PvtCustOrders
  UNPIVOT(qty FOR orderyear IN([2002],[2003],[2004])) AS U
```

Unlike the PIVOT operator, I find the UNPIVOT operator simple and intuitive, and obviously it requires significantly less code. UNPIVOT's first input is the target column name to hold the rotated attribute values (*qty*). Then, following the FOR keyword, you specify the target column name to hold the rotated column names (*orderyear*). Finally, in the parentheses of the IN clause, you specify the source column names that you want to rotate (*[2002],[2003],[2004]*).

Tip   All source attributes that are unpivoted must share the same datatype. If you want to unpivot attributes defined with different datatypes, create a derived table or CTE where you first convert all those attributes to SQL_VARIANT. The target column that will hold unpivoted values will also be defined as SQL_VARIANT, and within that column, the values will preserve their original types.

Note   Like PIVOT, UNPIVOT requires a static list of column names to be rotated.

Custom Aggregations

Custom aggregations are aggregations that are not provided as built-in aggregate functions—for example, concatenating strings, calculating products, performing bitwise manipulations, calculating medians, and many others. In this section, I'll provide solutions to several custom aggregate requests. Some techniques that I'll cover are generic—in the sense that you can use similar logic for other aggregate requests—while others are specific to one kind of aggregate request.

More Info   One of the generic custom aggregate techniques uses cursors. For details about cursors, including handling of custom aggregates with cursors, please refer to *Inside Microsoft SQL Server 2005: T-SQL Programming*.

In my examples, I'll use the generic Groups table, which you create and populate by running the code in Listing 6-7.

Listing 6-7   Creating and populating the Groups table

```
USE tempdb;
GO
IF OBJECT_ID('dbo.Groups') IS NOT NULL
  DROP TABLE dbo.Groups;
GO

CREATE TABLE dbo.Groups
(
  groupid  VARCHAR(10) NOT NULL,
  memberid INT         NOT NULL,
  string   VARCHAR(10) NOT NULL,
  val      INT         NOT NULL,
  PRIMARY KEY (groupid, memberid)
);

INSERT INTO dbo.Groups(groupid, memberid, string, val)
  VALUES('a', 3, 'stra1', 6);
INSERT INTO dbo.Groups(groupid, memberid, string, val)
  VALUES('a', 9, 'stra2', 7);
INSERT INTO dbo.Groups(groupid, memberid, string, val)
  VALUES('b', 2, 'strb1', 3);
INSERT INTO dbo.Groups(groupid, memberid, string, val)
  VALUES('b', 4, 'strb2', 7);
INSERT INTO dbo.Groups(groupid, memberid, string, val)
  VALUES('b', 5, 'strb3', 3);
INSERT INTO dbo.Groups(groupid, memberid, string, val)
  VALUES('b', 9, 'strb4', 11);
INSERT INTO dbo.Groups(groupid, memberid, string, val)
  VALUES('c', 3, 'strc1', 8);
INSERT INTO dbo.Groups(groupid, memberid, string, val)
  VALUES('c', 7, 'strc2', 10);
INSERT INTO dbo.Groups(groupid, memberid, string, val)
  VALUES('c', 9, 'strc3', 12);
```

The contents of the Groups table are shown in Table 6-19.

Table 6-19   Contents of Groups Table

groupid	memberid	string	val
a	3	stra1	6
a	9	stra2	7
b	2	strb1	3
b	4	strb2	7
b	5	strb3	3
b	9	strb4	11
c	3	strc1	8
c	7	strc2	10
c	9	strc3	12

The Groups table has a column representing the group (*groupid*), a column representing a unique identifier within the group (*memberid*), and some value columns (*string* and *val*) that will need to be aggregated. I like to use such a generic form of data because it allows you to focus on the techniques and not on the data. Note that this is merely a generic form of a table containing data that you want to aggregate. For example, it could represent a Sales table where *groupid* stands for *empid*, *val* stands for *qty*, and so on.

Custom Aggregations Using Pivoting

One key technique for solving custom aggregate problems is pivoting. You basically pivot the values that need to participate in the aggregate calculation; when they all appear in the same result row, you perform the calculation as a linear one across the columns. For two reasons, this pivoting technique is limited to situations where there is a small number of elements per group. First, with a large number of elements you'll end up with very lengthy query strings, which is not realistic. Second, unless you have a sequencing column within the group, you'll need to calculate row numbers that will be used to identify the position of elements within the group. For example, if you need to concatenate all values from the *string* column per group, what will you specify as the pivoted attribute list? The values in the *memberid* column are not known ahead of time, plus they differ in each group. Row numbers representing positions within the group solve your problem. Remember that in versions prior to SQL Server 2005, the calculation of row numbers is expensive for large groups.

String Concatenation Using Pivoting

As the first example, the following query calculates an aggregate string concatenation over the column *string* for each group with a pivoting technique, which generates the output shown in Table 6-20:

```
SELECT groupid,
    MAX(CASE WHEN rn = 1 THEN string ELSE '' END)
  + MAX(CASE WHEN rn = 2 THEN ',' + string ELSE '' END)
  + MAX(CASE WHEN rn = 3 THEN ',' + string ELSE '' END)
  + MAX(CASE WHEN rn = 4 THEN ',' + string ELSE '' END) AS string
```

```
FROM (SELECT groupid, string,
        (SELECT COUNT(*)
          FROM dbo.Groups AS B
         WHERE B.groupid = A.groupid
           AND B.memberid <= A.memberid) AS rn
      FROM dbo.Groups AS A) AS D
GROUP BY groupid;
```

Table 6-20 Concatenated Strings

groupid	string
a	stra1,stra2
b	strb1,strb2,strb3,strb4
c	strc1,strc2,strc3

The query that generates the derived table D calculates a row number within the group based on *memberid* order. The outer query pivots the values based on the row numbers, and it performs linear concatenation. I'm assuming here that there are at most four rows per group, so I specified four MAX(CASE...) expressions. You need as many MAX(CASE...) expressions as the maximum number of elements you anticipate.

Note It's important to return an empty string rather than a NULL in the ELSE clause of the CASE expressions. Remember that a concatenation between a known value and a NULL yields a NULL.

Aggregate Product Using Pivoting

In a similar manner, you can calculate the product of the values in the *val* column for each group, yielding the output shown in Table 6-21:

```
SELECT groupid,
     MAX(CASE WHEN rn = 1 THEN val ELSE 1 END)
   * MAX(CASE WHEN rn = 2 THEN val ELSE 1 END)
   * MAX(CASE WHEN rn = 3 THEN val ELSE 1 END)
   * MAX(CASE WHEN rn = 4 THEN val ELSE 1 END) AS product
FROM (SELECT groupid, val,
        (SELECT COUNT(*)
          FROM dbo.Groups AS B
         WHERE B.groupid = A.groupid
           AND B.memberid <= A.memberid) AS rn
      FROM dbo.Groups AS A) AS D
GROUP BY groupid;
```

Table 6-21 Aggregate Product

groupid	product
a	42
b	693
c	960

The need for an aggregate product is common in financial applications—for example, to calculate compound interest rates.

User Defined Aggregates (UDA)

SQL Server 2005 introduces the ability to create your own user defined aggregates (UDA). You write UDAs in a .NET language of your choice (for example, C# or Microsoft Visual Basic .NET), and you use them in T-SQL. This book is dedicated to T-SQL and not to common language runtime (CLR), so it won't conduct lengthy discussions explaining CLR UDAs. Rather, you'll be provided with a couple of examples with step-by-step instructions and, of course, the T-SQL interfaces involved. Examples will be provided in both C# and Visual Basic.

CLR Code in a Database

This section discusses .NET common language runtime (CLR) integration in SQL Server 2005; therefore, it's appropriate to spend a couple of words explaining the reasoning behind CLR integration in a database. It is also important to identify the scenarios where using CLR objects is more appropriate than using T-SQL.

Developing in .NET languages such as C# and Visual Basic .NET gives you an incredibly rich programming model. The .NET Framework includes literally thousands of prepared classes, and it is up to you to make astute use of them. .NET languages are not just data-oriented like SQL, so you are not as limited. For example, regular expressions are extremely useful for validating data, and they are fully supported in .NET. SQL languages are set-oriented and slow to perform row-oriented (row-by-row or one-row-at-a-time) operations. Sometimes you need row-oriented operations inside the database; moving away from cursors to CLR code should improve the performance. Another benefit of CLR code is that it can be much faster than T-SQL code in computationally intensive calculations.

Although SQL Server supported programmatic extensions even before CLR integration was introduced, CLR integration in .NET code is superior in a number of ways.

For example, you could add functionality to earlier versions of SQL Server using extended stored procedures. However, such procedures can compromise the integrity of SQL Server processes because their memory and thread management is not integrated well enough with SQL Server's resource management. .NET code is managed by the CLR inside SQL Server, and because the CLR itself is managed by SQL Server, it is much safer to use than extended procedure code.

T-SQL—a set-oriented language—was designed mainly to deal with data and is optimized for data manipulation. You should not rush to translate all your T-SQL code to CLR code. T-SQL is still SQL Server's primary language. Data access can be achieved through T-SQL only. If an operation can be expressed as a set-oriented one, you should program it in T-SQL.

There's another important decision that you need to make before you start using CLR code inside SQL Server. You need to decide where your CLR code is going to run—at the server or at the client. CLR code is typically faster and more flexible than T-SQL for computations, and thus it extends the opportunities for server-side computations. However, the server side is typically a single working box, and load balancing at the data tier is still in its infancy. Therefore, you should consider whether it would be more sensible to process those computations at the client side.

With CLR code, you can write stored procedures, triggers, user-defined functions, user-defined types, and user-defined aggregate functions. The last two objects can't be written with declarative T-SQL; rather, they can be written only with CLR code. A User-Defined Type (UDT) is the most complex CLR object type and demands extensive coverage.

> **More Info** For details about programming CLR UDTs, as well as programming CLR routines, please refer to *Inside Microsoft SQL Server 2005: T-SQL Programming*.

Let's start with a concrete implementation of two UDAs. The steps involved in creating a CLR-based UDA are as follows:

- Define the UDA as a class in a .NET language.
- Compile the class you defined to build a CLR assembly.
- Register the assembly in SQL Server using the CREATE ASSEMBLY command.
- Use the CREATE AGGREGATE command in T-SQL to create the UDA that references the registered assembly.

> **Note** You can register an assembly and create a CLR object from Microsoft Visual Studio 2005 directly, using the project deployment option (Build>Deploy menu item). This section will show you how to deploy CLR objects directly from Visual Studio. Also be aware that direct deployment from Visual Studio is supported only with the Professional edition or higher; if you're using the Standard edition, your only option is explicit deployment in SQL Server.

This section will provide examples for creating aggregate string concatenation and aggregate product functions in both C# and Visual Basic .NET. You can find the code for the C# classes in Listing 6-8 and the code for the Visual Basic .NET classes in Listing 6-9. You'll be provided with the requirements for a CLR UDA alongside the development of a UDA.

Listing 6-8 C# UDAs Code

```
using System;
using System.Data;
using System.Data.SqlClient;
using System.Data.SqlTypes;
using Microsoft.SqlServer.Server;
using System.Text;
using System.IO;
using System.Runtime.InteropServices;
```

```csharp
[Serializable]
[SqlUserDefinedAggregate(
    Format.UserDefined,             // use user-defined serialization
    IsInvariantToDuplicates = false, // duplicates make difference
     // for the result
    IsInvariantToNulls = true,      // don't care about NULLs
    IsInvariantToOrder = false,     // whether order makes difference
    IsNullIfEmpty = false,          // do not yield a NULL
     // for a set of zero strings
    MaxByteSize = 8000)]            // maximum size in bytes of persisted value
public struct CSStrAgg : IBinarySerialize
{
    private StringBuilder sb;
    private bool firstConcat;

    public void Init()
    {
        this.sb = new StringBuilder();
        this.firstConcat = true;
    }

    public void Accumulate(SqlString s)
    {
        if (s.IsNull)
        {
            return;                 // simply skip Nulls approach
        }
        if (this.firstConcat)
        {
            this.sb.Append(s.Value);
            this.firstConcat = false;
        }
        else
        {
            this.sb.Append(",");
            this.sb.Append(s.Value);
        }
    }

    public void Merge(CSStrAgg Group)
    {
        this.sb.Append(Group.sb);
    }

    public SqlString Terminate()
    {
        return new SqlString(this.sb.ToString());
    }

    public void Read(BinaryReader r)
    {
        sb = new StringBuilder(r.ReadString());
    }
```

```
    public void Write(BinaryWriter w)
    {
        if (this.sb.Length > 4000)  // check we don't
                                    // go over 8000 bytes

                                        // simply return first 8000 bytes
            w.Write(this.sb.ToString().Substring(0, 4000));
        else
            w.Write(this.sb.ToString());
    }

}   // end CSStrAgg

[Serializable]
[StructLayout(LayoutKind.Sequential)]
[SqlUserDefinedAggregate(
    Format.Native,                      // use native serialization
    IsInvariantToDuplicates = false,  // duplicates make difference
    // for the result
    IsInvariantToNulls = true,          // don't care about NULLs
    IsInvariantToOrder = false)]        // whether order makes difference
public class CSProdAgg
{
    private SqlInt64 si;

    public void Init()
    {
        si = 1;
    }


    public void Accumulate(SqlInt64 v)
    {
        if (v.IsNull || si.IsNull) // Null input = Null output approach
        {
            si = SqlInt64.Null;
            return;
        }
        if (v == 0 || si == 0)      // to prevent an exception in next if
        {
            si = 0;
            return;
        }
                                    // stop before we reach max value
        if (Math.Abs(v.Value) <= SqlInt64.MaxValue / Math.Abs(si.Value))
        {
            si = si * v;
        }
        else
        {
            si = 0;                 // if we reach too big value, return 0
        }

    }
```

```
        public void Merge(CSProdAgg Group)
        {
            Accumulate(Group.Terminate());
        }

        public SqlInt64 Terminate()
        {
            return (si);
        }

} // end CSProdAgg
```

Listing 6-9   Visual Basic .NET UDAs Code

```
Imports System
Imports System.Data
Imports System.Data.SqlTypes
Imports Microsoft.SqlServer.Server
Imports System.Text
Imports System.IO
Imports System.Runtime.InteropServices


<Serializable(), _
 SqlUserDefinedAggregate( _
             Format.UserDefined, _
             IsInvariantToDuplicates:=True, _
             IsInvariantToNulls:=True, _
             IsInvariantToOrder:=False, _
             IsNullIfEmpty:=False, _
             MaxByteSize:=8000)> _
Public Class VBStrAgg
    Implements IBinarySerialize

    Private sb As StringBuilder
    Private firstConcat As Boolean = True

    Public Sub Init()
        Me.sb = New StringBuilder()
        Me.firstConcat = True
    End Sub


    Public Sub Accumulate(ByVal s As SqlString)
        If s.IsNull Then
            Return
        End If
        If Me.firstConcat = True Then
            Me.sb.Append(s.Value)
            Me.firstConcat = False
        Else
```

```vb
                Me.sb.Append(",")
                Me.sb.Append(s.Value)
        End If
    End Sub

    Public Sub Merge(ByVal Group As VBStrAgg)
        Me.sb.Append(Group.sb)
    End Sub

    Public Function Terminate() As SqlString
        Return New SqlString(sb.ToString())
    End Function

    Public Sub Read(ByVal r As BinaryReader) _
      Implements IBinarySerialize.Read
        sb = New StringBuilder(r.ReadString())
    End Sub

    Public Sub Write(ByVal w As BinaryWriter) _
      Implements IBinarySerialize.Write
        If Me.sb.Length > 4000 Then
            w.Write(Me.sb.ToString().Substring(0, 4000))
        Else
            w.Write(Me.sb.ToString())
        End If
    End Sub

End Class


<Serializable(), _
 StructLayout(LayoutKind.Sequential), _
 SqlUserDefinedAggregate( _
                Format.Native, _
                IsInvariantToOrder:=False, _
                IsInvariantToNulls:=True, _
                IsInvariantToDuplicates:=True)> _
Public Class VBProdAgg

    Private si As SqlInt64

    Public Sub Init()
        si = 1
    End Sub

    Public Sub Accumulate(ByVal v As SqlInt64)
        If v.IsNull = True Or si.IsNull = True Then
            si = SqlInt64.Null
            Return
        End If
        If v = 0 Or si = 0 Then
            si = 0
            Return
        End If
```

```
        If (Math.Abs(v.Value) <= SqlInt64.MaxValue / Math.Abs(si.Value)) _
            Then
                si = si * v
            Else
                si = 0
            End If
    End Sub

    Public Sub Merge(ByVal Group As VBProdAgg)
        Accumulate(Group.Terminate())
    End Sub

    Public Function Terminate() As SqlInt64
        If si.IsNull = True Then
            Return SqlInt64.Null
        Else
            Return si
        End If
    End Function

End Class
```

Here are the step-by-step instructions you need to follow to create the assemblies in Visual Studio 2005:

Creating an Assembly in Visual Studio 2005

1. In Visual Studio 2005, create a new C# project. Use the Database folder and the SQL Server Project template.

> **Note**   This template is not available in Visual Studio 2005, Standard edition. If you're working with the Standard edition, use the Class Library template and manually write all the code.

2. In the New Project dialog box, specify the following information:

   ❑ Name: CSUDAs

   ❑ Location: C:\

   ❑ Solution Name: UDAs

   When you're done entering the information, confirm that it is correct.

3. At this point, you'll be requested to specify a database reference. Create a new database reference to the tempdb database in the SQL Server instance you're working with, and choose it. The database reference you choose tells Visual Studio where to deploy the UDAs that you develop.

4. After confirming the choice of database reference, a question box will pop up asking you whether you want to enable SQL/CLR debugging on this connection. Choose No. The sample UDAs you'll build in this chapter are quite simple, and there won't be a need for debugging.

5. In the Solution Explorer window, right-click the CSUDAs project, select the menu items Add and Aggregate, and then choose the Aggregate template. Rename the class Aggregate1.cs to **CSUDAs_Classes.cs**, and confirm.

6. Examine the code of the template. You'll find that a UDA is implemented as a structure (*struct* in C#, *Structure* in Visual Basic .NET). It can be implemented as a class as well. The first block of code in the template includes namespaces that are used in the assembly (lines of code starting with "using"). Add three more statements to include the following namespaces: *System.Text*, *System.IO*, and *System.Runtime.InteropServices*. (You can copy those from Listing 6-8.) You are going to use the *StringBuilder* class from the *System.Text* namespace, the *BinaryReader* and *BinaryWriter* classes from the *System.IO* namespace, and finally the *StructLayout* attribute from the *System.Runtime.InteropServices* namespace (in the second UDA).

7. Rename the default name of the UDA—which is currently the same name as the name of the class (*CSUDAs_Classes*)—to **CSStrAgg**.

8. You'll find four methods that are already provided by the template. These are the methods that every UDA must implement. However, if you use the Class Library template for your project, you have to write them manually. Using the Aggregate template, all you have to do is fill them with your code. Following is a description of the four methods:

   ❑ *Init*: This method is used to initialize the computation. It is invoked once for each group that the query processor is aggregating.

   ❑ *Accumulate*: The name of the method gives you a hint of its purpose—accumulating the aggregate values, of course. This method is invoked once for each value (that is, for every single row) in the group that is being aggregated. It uses an input parameter, and the parameter has to be of the datatype corresponding to the native SQL Server datatype of the column you are going to aggregate. The datatype of the input can also be a CLR UDT.

   ❑ *Merge*: You'll notice that this method uses an input parameter with the type that is the aggregate class. The method is used to merge multiple partial computations of an aggregation.

   ❑ *Terminate*: This method finishes the aggregation and returns the result.

9. Add two internal (private) variables—*sb* and *firstConcat*—to the class just before the *Init* method. You can do so by simply copying the code that declares them from Listing 6-8. The variable *sb* is of type *StringBuilder* and will hold the intermediate aggregate value. The *firstConcat* variable is of type *Boolean* and is used to tell whether the input string is

the first you are concatenating in the group. For all input values except the first, you are going to add a comma in front of the value you are concatenating.

10. Override the current code for the four methods with the code implementing them from Listing 6-8. Keep in mind the following points for each method:

 ❑ In the *Init* method, you initialize *sb* with an empty string and *firstConcat* with true.

 ❑ In the *Accumulate* method, note that if the value of the parameter is NULL, the accumulated value will be NULL as well. Also, notice the different treatment of the first value, which is just appended, and the following values, which are appended with the addition of a leading comma.

 ❑ In the *Merge* method, you are simply adding a partial aggregation to the current one. You do so by calling the *Accumulate* method of the current aggregation, and adding the termination (final value) of the other partial aggregation. The input of the *Merge* function refers to the class name, which you revised earlier to *CSStrAgg*.

 ❑ The *Terminate* method is very simple as well; it just returns the string representation of the aggregated value.

11. Delete the last two rows of the code in the class from the template; these are a placeholder for a member field. You already defined all member fields you need at the beginning of the UDA.

12. Next, go back to the top of the UDA, right after the inclusion of the namespaces. You'll find attribute names that you want to include. Attributes help Visual Studio in deployment, and they help SQL Server to optimize the usage of the UDA. UDAs have to include the *Serializable* attribute. Serialization in .NET means saving the values of the fields of a class persistently. UDAs need serialization for intermediate results. The format of the serialization can be native, meaning they are left to SQL Server or defined by the user. Serialization can be native if you use only .NET value types; it has to be user-defined if you use .NET reference types. Unfortunately, the *string* type is a reference type in .NET. Therefore, you have to prepare your own serialization. You have to implement the *IBinarySerialize* interface, which defines just two methods: *Read* and *Write*. The implementation of these methods in our UDA is very simple. The *Read* method uses the *ReadString* method of the *StringBuilder* class. The *Write* method uses the default *ToString* method. The *ToString* method is inherited by all .NET classes from the topmost class, called *System.Object*.

Continue implementing the UDA by following these steps:

 a. Specify that you are going to implement the *IBinarySerialize* interface in the structure. You do so by adding a colon and the name of the interface right after the name of the structure (the UDA name).

 b. Copy the *Read* and *Write* methods from Listing 6-8 to the end of your UDA.

c. Change the *Format.Native* property of the *SqlUserDefinedAggregate* attribute to **Format.UserDefined**. With user-defined serialization, your aggregate is limited to 8000 bytes only. You have to specify how many bytes your UDA can return at maximum with the *MaxByteSize* property of the *SqlUserDefinedAggregate* attribute. To get the maximum possible string length, specify *MaxByteSize = 8000*.

13. You'll find some other interesting properties of the *SqlUserDefinedAggregate* attribute in Listing 6-8. Let's explore them:

   ❑ *IsInvariantToDuplicates*: This is an optional property. For example, the MAX aggregate is invariant to duplicates, while SUM is not.

   ❑ *IsInvariantToNulls*: This is another optional property. It specifies whether the aggregate is invariant to NULLs.

   ❑ *IsInvariantToOrder*: This property is reserved for future use. It is currently ignored by the query processor. Therefore, order is currently not guaranteed.

   ❑ *IsNullIfEmpty*: This property indicates whether the aggregate will return a NULL if no values have been accumulated.

14. Add the aforementioned properties to your UDA by copying them from Listing 6-8. Your first UDA is now complete!

15. Listing 6-8 also has the code to implement a product UDA (*CSProdAgg*). Copy the complete code implementing *CSProgAgg* to your script. Note that this UDA involves handling of big integers only. Because the UDA internally deals only with value types, it can use native serialization. Native serialization requires that the *StructLayoutAttribute* be specified as *StructLayout.LayoutKindSequential* if the UDA is defined in a class and not a structure. Otherwise, the UDA implements the same four methods as your previous UDA. There is an additional check in the *Accumulate* method that prevents out-of-range values.

16. Finally, add the Visual Basic .NET version of both UDAs created so far:

   a. From the File menu, choose the menu items Add and New Project to load the Add New Project dialog box. Navigate through the Visual Basic project type and the Database folder, and choose SQL Server Project. Don't confirm yet.

   b. In the Add New Project dialog box, specify Name as **VBUDAs** and Location as **C:**. Then confirm that the information is correct.

   c. Use the same database connection you created for the C# project (the connection to tempdb). The name of the database connection you created earlier should be *instancename.tempdb.dbo*.

   d. In the Solution Explorer window, right-click the VBUDAs project, select Add, and choose the Aggregate template. Before confirming, rename the class Aggregate1.vb to **VBUDAs_Classes.vb**.

   e. Replace all code in *VBUDAs_Classes.vb* with the Visual Basic .NET code implementing the UDAs from Listing 6-9.

17. Save all files by choosing the File menu item and then Save All.

18. Create the assemblies by building the solution. You do this by choosing the Build menu item and then Build Solution.

19. Finally, deploy the solution by choosing the Build menu item and then Deploy Solution.

Both assemblies should be cataloged at this point, and all four UDAs should be created. All these steps are done if you deploy the assembly from Visual Studio .NET.

> **Note**   To work with CLR based functions in SQL Server, you need to enable the server configuration option 'clr enabled' (which is disabled by default).

You can check whether the deployment was successful by browsing the *sys.assemblies* and *sys.assembly_modules* catalog views, which are in the tempdb database in our case. To enable CLR and query these views, run the code in Listing 6-10.

Listing 6-10   Enabling CLR and querying catalog views

```
EXEC sp_configure 'clr enabled', 1;
RECONFIGURE WITH OVERRIDE;
GO
USE tempdb;
GO
SELECT * FROM sys.assemblies;
SELECT * FROM sys.assembly_modules;
```

That's basically it. You use UDAs just like you use any other built-in aggregate function. To test the new functions, run the following code, and you'll get the same results returned by the other solutions to custom aggregates I presented earlier.

Testing UDAs

```
SELECT groupid, dbo.CSStrAgg(string) AS string
FROM tempdb.dbo.Groups
GROUP BY groupid;

SELECT groupid, dbo.VBStrAgg(string) AS string
FROM tempdb.dbo.Groups
GROUP BY groupid;

SELECT groupid, dbo.CSProdAgg(val) AS product
FROM tempdb.dbo.Groups
GROUP BY groupid;

SELECT groupid, dbo.VBProdAgg(val) AS product
FROM tempdb.dbo.Groups
GROUP BY groupid;
```

When you're done experimenting with the UDAs, run the following code to disable CLR support:

```
EXEC sp_configure 'clr enabled', 0;
RECONFIGURE WITH OVERRIDE;
```

Specialized Solutions

Another type of solution for custom aggregates is developing a specialized, optimized solution for each aggregate. The advantage is usually the improved performance of the solution. The disadvantage is that you probably won't be able to use similar logic for other aggregate calculations.

Specialized Solution for Aggregate String Concatenation

A specialized solution for aggregate string concatenation uses the PATH mode of the FOR XML query option. This beautiful (and extremely fast) technique was devised by Michael Rys, a program manager with the Microsoft SQL Server development team in charge of SQL Server XML technologies, and Eugene Kogan, a technical lead on the Microsoft SQL Server Engine team. The PATH mode provides an easier way to mix elements and attributes than the EXPLICIT directive. Here's the specialized solution for aggregate string concatenation:

```
SELECT groupid,
  STUFF((SELECT ',' + string AS [text()]
         FROM dbo.Groups AS G2
         WHERE G2.groupid = G1.groupid
         ORDER BY memberid
         FOR XML PATH('')), 1, 1, '') AS string
FROM dbo.Groups AS G1
GROUP BY groupid;
```

The subquery basically returns an ordered path of all strings within the current group. Because an empty string is provided to the PATH clause as input, a wrapper element is not generated. An expression with no alias (for example, ',' + *string*) or one aliased as *[text()]* is inlined, and its contents are inserted as a text node. The purpose of the STUFF function is simply to remove the first comma (by substituting it with an empty string).

Specialized Solution for Aggregate Product

Keep in mind that to calculate an aggregate product you have to scan all values in the group. So the performance potential your solution can reach is to achieve the calculation by scanning the data only once, using a set-based query. In the case of an aggregate product, this can be achieved using mathematical manipulation based on logarithms. I'll rely on the following logarithmic equations:

Equation 1: $\log_a(b) = x$ if and only if $a^x = b$

Equation 2: $\log_a(v1 * v2 * ... * vn) = \log_a(v1) + \log_a(v2) + ... + \log_a(vn)$

Basically, what you're going to do here is a transformation of calculations. You have support in T-SQL for LOG, POWER, and SUM functions. Using those, you can generate the missing product. Group the data by the *groupid* column, as you would with any built-in aggregate. The expression *SUM(LOG10(val))* corresponds to the right side of Equation 2, where the base *a* is equal to 10 in our case, because you used the LOG10 function. To get the product of the elements, all you have left to do is raise the base (10) to the power of the right side of the equation. In other words, the expression *POWER(10., SUM(LOG10(val)))* gives you the product of elements within the group. Here's what the full query looks like:

```
SELECT groupid, POWER(10., SUM(LOG10(val))) AS product
FROM dbo.Groups
GROUP BY groupid;
```

This is the final solution if you're dealing only with positive values. However, the logarithm function is undefined for zero and negative numbers. You can use pivoting techniques to identify and deal with zeros and negatives as follows:

```
SELECT groupid,
  CASE
    WHEN MAX(CASE WHEN val = 0 THEN 1 END) = 1 THEN 0
    ELSE
      CASE WHEN COUNT(CASE WHEN val < 0 THEN 1 END) % 2 = 0
        THEN 1 ELSE -1
      END * POWER(10., SUM(LOG10(NULLIF(ABS(val), 0))))
  END AS product
FROM dbo.Groups
GROUP BY groupid;
```

The outer CASE expression first uses a pivoting technique to check whether a 0 value appears in the group, in which case it returns a 0 as the result. The ELSE clause invokes another CASE expression, which also uses a pivoting technique to count the number of negative values in the group. If that number is even, it produces a +1; if it's odd, it produces a −1. The purpose of this calculation is to determine the numerical sign of the result. The sign (−1 or +1) is then multiplied by the product of the absolute values of the numbers in the group to give the desired product.

Note that NULLIF is used here to substitute zeros with NULLs. You might expect this part of the expression not to be evaluated at all if a zero is found. But remember that the optimizer can consider many different physical plans to execute your query. As a result, you can't be certain of the actual order in which parts of an expression will be evaluated. By substituting zeros with NULLs, you ensure that you'll never get a domain error if the LOG10 function ends up being invoked with a zero as an input. This use of NULLIF, together with the use of ABS, allow this solution to accommodate inputs of any sign (negative, zero, and positive).

You could also use a pure mathematical approach to handle zeros and negative values using the following query:

```
SELECT groupid,
  CAST(ROUND(EXP(SUM(LOG(ABS(NULLIF(val,0)))))*
    (1-SUM(1-SIGN(val))%4)*(1-SUM(1-SQUARE(SIGN(val)))),0) AS INT)
 AS product
FROM dbo.Groups
GROUP BY groupid;
```

This example shows that you should never lose hope when searching for an efficient solution. If you invest the time and think outside the box, in most cases you'll find a solution.

Specialized Solutions for Aggregate Bitwise Operations

Next, I'll introduce specialized solutions for aggregating the T-SQL bitwise operations—bitwise OR (|), bitwise AND (&), and bitwise XOR (^). I'll assume that you're familiar with the basics of bitwise operators and their uses, and provide only a brief overview. If you're not, please refer first to the section "Bitwise Operators" in Books Online.

Bitwise operations are operations performed on the individual bits of integer data. Each bit has two possible values, 1 and 0. Integers can be used to store *bitmaps* or strings of bits, and in fact they are used internally by SQL Server to store metadata information—for example, properties of indexes (clustered, unique, and so on) and properties of databases (read only, restrict access, auto shrink, and so on). You might also choose to store bitmaps yourself to represent sets of binary attributes—for example, a set of permissions where each bit represents a different permission.

Some experts advise against using such a design because it violates 1NF (first normal form—no repeating groups). You might well prefer to design your data in a more normalized form, where attributes like this are stored in separate columns. I don't want to get into a debate about which design is better. Here I'll assume a given design that does store bitmaps with sets of flags, and I'll assume that you need to perform aggregate bitwise activities on these bitmaps. I just want to introduce the techniques for cases where you do find the need to use them.

Bitwise OR (|) is usually used to construct bitmaps or to generate a result bitmap that accumulates all bits that are turned on. In the result of bitwise OR, bits are turned on (that is, have value 1) if they are turned on in at least one of the separate bitmaps.

Bitwise AND (&) is usually used to check whether a certain bit (or a set of bits) are turned on by ANDing the source bitmap and a mask. It's also used to accumulate only bits that are turned on in all bitmaps. It generates a result bit that is turned on if that bit is turned on in all the individual bitmaps.

Bitwise XOR (^) is usually used to calculate parity or as part of a scheme to encrypt data. For each bit position, the result bit is turned on if it is on in an odd number of the individual bitmaps.

Note   Bitwise XOR is the only bitwise operator that is reversible. That's why it's used for parity calculations and encryption.

Aggregate versions of the bitwise operators are not provided in SQL Server, and I'll provide solutions here to perform aggregate bitwise operations. I'll use the same Groups table that I used in my other custom aggregate examples. Assume that the integer column *val* represents a bitmap. To see the bit representation of each integer, first create the function *fn_dectobase* by running the code in Listing 6-11.

Listing 6-11   Creation script for the *fn_dectobase* function

```
IF OBJECT_ID('dbo.fn_dectobase') IS NOT NULL
  DROP FUNCTION dbo.fn_dectobase;
GO
CREATE FUNCTION dbo.fn_dectobase(@val AS BIGINT, @base AS INT)
  RETURNS VARCHAR(63)
AS
BEGIN
  IF @val < 0 OR @base < 2 OR @base > 36 RETURN NULL;
  DECLARE @r AS VARCHAR(63), @alldigits AS VARCHAR(36);

  SET @alldigits = '0123456789ABCDEFGHIJKLMNOPQRSTUVWXYZ';

  SET @r = '';
  WHILE @val > 0
  BEGIN
    SET @r = SUBSTRING(@alldigits, @val % @base + 1, 1) + @r;
    SET @val = @val / @base;
  END

  RETURN @r;
END
GO
```

The function accepts two inputs: a 64-bit integer holding the source bitmap, and a base in which you want to represent the data. Use the following query to return the bit representation of the integers in the *val* column of Groups. An abbreviated form of the result (only the 10 rightmost digits of *binval*) is shown in Table 6-22:

```
SELECT groupid, val,
  RIGHT(REPLICATE('0', 32) + CAST(dbo.fn_dectobase(val, 2) AS VARCHAR(64)),
        32) AS binval
FROM dbo.Groups;
```

Table 6-22   Binary Representation of Values

groupid	val	binval
a	6	0000000110
a	7	0000000111
b	3	0000000011
b	7	0000000111
b	3	0000000011

Table 6-22 Binary Representation of Values

groupid	val	binval
b	11	0000001011
c	8	0000001000
c	10	0000001010
c	12	0000001100

The *binval* column shows the *val* column in base 2 representation, with leading zeros to create a string with a fixed number of digits. Of course, you can adjust the number of leading zeros according to your needs. In my code samples, I did not incorporate the invocation of this function to avoid distracting you from the techniques I want to focus on. But I did invoke it to generate the bit representations in all the outputs that I'll show.

Aggregate Bitwise OR   With no further ado, let's start with calculating an aggregate bitwise OR. To give tangible context to the problem, imagine that you're maintaining application security in the database. The *groupid* column represents a user, and the *val* column represents a bitmap with permission states (either 1 for granted or 0 for not granted) of a role the user is a member of. You're after the effective permissions bitmap for each user (group), which should be calculated as the aggregate bitwise OR between all bitmaps of roles the user is a member of.

The main aspect of a bitwise OR operation that I'll rely on in my solutions is the fact that it's equivalent to the arithmetic sum of the values represented by each distinct bit value that is turned on in the individual bitmaps. Within an integer, a bit represents the value $2^{(bit\_pos-1)}$. For example, the bit value of the third bit is $2^2 = 4$. Take for example the bitmaps for user c: 8 (1000), 10 (1010), and 12 (1100). The bitmap 8 has only one bit turned on—the bit value representing 8, 10 has the bits representing 8 and 2 turned on, and 12 has the 8 and 4 bits turned on. The distinct bits turned on in any of the integers 8, 10, and 12 are the 2, 4, and 8 bits, so the aggregate bitwise OR of 8, 10, and 12 is equal to *2 + 4 + 8 = 14 (1110)*.

The following solution relies on the aforementioned logic by extracting the individual bit values that are turned on in any of the participating bitmaps. The extraction is achieved using the expression *MAX(val & <bitval>)*. The query then performs an arithmetic sum of the individual bit values:

```
SELECT groupid,
    MAX(val & 1)
  + MAX(val & 2)
  + MAX(val & 4)
  + MAX(val & 8)
-- ...
  + MAX(val & 1073741824) AS agg_or
FROM dbo.Groups
GROUP BY groupid;
```

The result of the aggregate bitwise OR operation is shown in Table 6-23, including the 10 rightmost digits of the binary representation of the result value.

Table 6-23   Aggregate Bitwise OR

groupid	agg_or	agg_or_binval
a	7	0000000111
b	15	0000001111
c	14	0000001110

Similarly, you can use *SUM(DISTINCT val & <bitval>)* instead of *MAX(val & <bitval>)*, because the only possible results are *<bitval>* and *0*:

```
SELECT groupid,
    SUM(DISTINCT val & 1)
  + SUM(DISTINCT val & 2)
  + SUM(DISTINCT val & 4)
  + SUM(DISTINCT val & 8)
-- ...
  + SUM(DISTINCT val & 1073741824) AS agg_or
FROM dbo.Groups
GROUP BY groupid;
```

Both solutions suffer from the same limitation—lengthy query strings—because of the need for a different expression for each bit value. In an effort to shorten the query strings, you can use an auxiliary table. You join the Groups table with an auxiliary table that contains all relevant bit values, using *val & bitval = bitval* as the join condition. The result of the join will include all bit values that are turned on in any of the bitmaps. You can then find *SUM(DISTINCT <bitval>)* for each group. The auxiliary table of bit values can be easily generated from the Nums table used earlier. Filter as many numbers as the bits that you might need, and raise 2 to the power *n−1*. Here's the complete solution:

```
SELECT groupid, SUM(DISTINCT bitval) AS agg_or
FROM dbo.Groups
  JOIN (SELECT POWER(2, n-1) AS bitval
        FROM dbo.Nums
        WHERE n <= 31) AS Bits
    ON val & bitval = bitval
GROUP BY groupid;
```

Aggregate Bitwise AND   In a similar manner, you can calculate an aggregate bitwise AND. In the permissions scenario, an aggregate bitwise AND would represent the most restrictive permission set. Just keep in mind that a bit value should be added to the arithmetic sum only if it's turned on in all bitmaps. So first group the data by *groupid* and *bitval*, and filter only the groups where *MIN(val & bitval) > 0*, meaning that the bit value was turned on in all bitmaps. In an outer query, group the data by *groupid* and perform the arithmetic sum of the bit values from the inner query:

```
SELECT groupid, SUM(bitval) AS agg_and
FROM (SELECT groupid, bitval
      FROM dbo.Groups,
        (SELECT POWER(2, n-1) AS bitval
         FROM dbo.Nums
         WHERE n <= 31) AS Bits
      GROUP BY groupid, bitval
      HAVING MIN(val & bitval) > 0) AS D
GROUP BY groupid;
```

The result of the aggregate bitwise AND operation is shown in Table 6-24.

Table 6-24   Aggregate Bitwise AND

groupid	agg_and	agg_and_binval
a	6	0000000110
b	3	0000000011
c	8	0000001000

Aggregate Bitwise XOR   To calculate an aggregate bitwise XOR operation, filter only the *groupid, bitval* groups that have an odd number of bits that are turned on as shown in the following code, which illustrates an aggregate bitwise XOR using *Nums* and generates the output shown in Table 6-25:

```
SELECT groupid, SUM(bitval) AS agg_xor
FROM (SELECT groupid, bitval
      FROM dbo.Groups,
        (SELECT POWER(2, n-1) AS bitval
         FROM dbo.Nums
         WHERE n <= 31) AS Bits
      GROUP BY groupid, bitval
      HAVING SUM(SIGN(val & bitval)) % 2 = 1) AS D
GROUP BY groupid;
```

Table 6-25   Aggregate Bitwise XOR

groupid	agg_xor	agg_xor_binval
a	1	0000000001
b	12	0000001100
c	14	0000001110

Median

As the last example for a specialized custom aggregate solution, I'll use the statistical median calculation. Suppose that you need to calculate the median of the *val* column for each group. There are two different definitions of median. Here we will return the middle value in case there's an odd number of elements, and the average of the two middle values in case there's an even number of elements.

The following code shows a technique for calculating the median, producing the output shown in Table 6-26:

```
WITH Tiles AS
(
  SELECT groupid, val,
    NTILE(2) OVER(PARTITION BY groupid ORDER BY val) AS tile
  FROM dbo.Groups
),
GroupedTiles AS
(
  SELECT groupid, tile, COUNT(*) AS cnt,
    CASE WHEN tile = 1 THEN MAX(val) ELSE MIN(val) END AS val
  FROM Tiles
  GROUP BY groupid, tile
)
SELECT groupid,
  CASE WHEN MIN(cnt) = MAX(cnt) THEN AVG(1.*val)
       ELSE MIN(val) END AS median
FROM GroupedTiles
GROUP BY groupid;
```

Table 6-26 Median

groupid	median
a	6.500000
b	5.000000
c	10.000000

The Tiles CTE calculates the *NTILE(2)* value within the group, based on *val* order. When there's an even number of elements, the first half of the values will get tile number 1 and the second half will get tile number 2. In an even case, the median is supposed to be the average of the highest value within the first tile and the lowest in the second. When there's an odd number of elements, remember that an additional row is added to the first group. This means that the highest value in the first tile is the median.

The second CTE (GroupedTiles) groups the data by group and tile number, returning the row count for each group and tile as well as the *val* column, which for the first tile is the maximum value within the tile and for the second tile the minimum value within the tile.

The outer query groups the two rows in each group (one representing each tile). A CASE expression in the SELECT list determines what to return based on the parity of the group's row count. When the group has an even number of rows (that is, the group's two tiles have the same row count), you get the average of the maximum in the first tile and the minimum in the second. When the group has an odd number of elements (that is, the group's two tiles have different row counts), you get the minimum of the two values, which happens to be the maximum within the first tile, which in turn, happens to be the median.

Using the ROW_NUMBER function, you can come up with additional solutions to finding the median that are more elegant and somewhat simpler. Here's the first example:

```
WITH RN AS
(
  SELECT groupid, val,
    ROW_NUMBER()
      OVER(PARTITION BY groupid ORDER BY val, memberid) AS rna,
    ROW_NUMBER()
      OVER(PARTITION BY groupid ORDER BY val DESC, memberid DESC) AS rnd
  FROM dbo.Groups
)
SELECT groupid, AVG(1.*val) AS median
FROM RN
WHERE ABS(rna - rnd) <= 1
GROUP BY groupid;
```

The idea is to calculate two row numbers for each row: one based on *val, memberid* (the tie-breaker) in ascending order (*rna*), and the other based on the same attributes in descending order (*rnd*). There's an interesting mathematical relationship between two sequences sorted in opposite directions that you can use to your advantage. The absolute difference between the two is smaller than or equal to 1 only for the elements that need to participate in the median calculation. Take, for example, a group with an odd number of elements; *ABS(rna − rnd)* is equal to 0 only for the middle row. For all other rows, it is greater than 1. Given an even number of elements, the difference is 1 for the two middle rows and greater than 1 for all others.

The reason for using *memberid* as a tiebreaker is to guarantee determinism of the row number calculations. Because you're calculating two different row numbers, you want to make sure that a value that appears at the *n*th position from the beginning in ascending order will appear at the *n*th position from the end in descending order.

Once the values that need to participate in the median calculation are isolated, you just need to group them by *groupid* and calculate the average per group.

You can avoid the need to calculate two separate row numbers by deriving the second from the first. The descending row numbers can be calculated by subtracting the ascending row numbers from the count of rows in the group and adding one. For example, in a group of four elements, the row that got an ascending row number 1, would get the descending row number *4−1+1 = 4*. Ascending row number 2, would get the descending row number *4−2+1 = 3*, and so on. Deriving the descending row number from the ascending one eliminates the need for a tie-breaker. You're not dealing with two separate calculations; therefore, nondeterminism is not an issue anymore.

So the calculation $rna - rnd$ becomes the following: $rn - (cnt-rn+1) = 2*rn - cnt - 1$. Here's a query that implements this logic:

```
WITH RN AS
(
  SELECT groupid, val,
    ROW_NUMBER() OVER(PARTITION BY groupid ORDER BY val) AS rn,
    COUNT(*) OVER(PARTITION BY groupid) AS cnt
  FROM dbo.Groups
)
SELECT groupid, AVG(1.*val) AS median
FROM RN
WHERE ABS(2*rn - cnt - 1) <= 1
GROUP BY groupid;
```

There's another way to figure out which rows participate in the median calculation based on the row number and the count of rows in the group: $rn\ IN((cnt+1)/2, (cnt+2)/2)$. For an odd number of elements, both expressions yield the middle row number. For example, if you have 7 rows, both $(7+1)/2$ and $(7+2)/2$ equal 4. For an even number of elements, the first expression yields the row number just before the middle point and the second yields the row number just after it. If you have 8 rows, $(8+1)/2$ yields 4 and $(8+2)/2$ yields 5. Here's the query that implements this logic:

```
WITH RN AS
(
  SELECT groupid, val,
    ROW_NUMBER() OVER(PARTITION BY groupid ORDER BY val) AS rn,
    COUNT(*) OVER(PARTITION BY groupid) AS cnt
  FROM dbo.Groups
)
SELECT groupid, AVG(1.*val) AS median
FROM RN
WHERE rn IN((cnt+1)/2, (cnt+2)/2)
GROUP BY groupid;
```

Histograms

Histograms are powerful analytical tools that express the distribution of items. For example, suppose you need to figure out from the order information in the Orders table how many small, medium, and large orders you have, based on the order quantities. In other words, you need a histogram with three steps. What defines quantities as small, medium, or large are the extreme quantities (the minimum and maximum quantities). In our Orders table, the minimum order quantity is 10 and the maximum is 40. Take the difference between the two extremes $(40 - 10 = 30)$, and divide it by the number of steps (3) to get the step size. In our case, it's 30 divided by 3 is 10. So the boundaries of step 1 (small) would be 10 and 20; for step 2 (medium), they would be 20 and 30; and for step 3 (large), they would be 30 and 40.

To generalize this, let $mn = MIN(qty)$ and $mx = MAX(qty)$, and let $stepsize = (mx - mn) / @numsteps$. Given a step number n, the lower bound of the step (lb) is $mn + (n - 1) * stepsize$ and the higher bound (*hb*) is *mn + n * stepsize*. There's a tricky bit here. What predicate will you use to bracket the elements that belong in a specific step? You can't use *qty BETWEEN lb and hb* because a value that is equal to *hb* will appear in this step, and also in the next step, where it will equal the lower bound. Remember that the same calculation yielded the higher bound of one step and the lower bound of the next step. One approach to deal with this problem is to increase each of the lower bounds by one, so they exceed the previous step's higher bounds. With integers that's fine, but with another data type it won't work because there will be potential values in between two steps, but not inside either one—between the cracks, so to speak.

What I like to do to solve the problem is keep the same value in both bounds, and instead of using BETWEEN I use *qty >= lb* and *qty < hb*. This technique has its own issues, but I find it easier to deal with than the previous technique. The issue here is that the item with the highest quantity (40, in our case) is left out of the histogram. To solve this, I add a very small number to the maximum value before calculating the step size: *stepsize = ((1E0*mx + 0.0000000001) − mn) / @numsteps*. This is a technique that allows the item with the highest value to be included, and the effect on the histogram will otherwise be negligible. I multiplied *mx* by the float value *1E0* to protect against the loss of the upper data point when *qty* is typed as MONEY or SMALLMONEY.

So the ingredients you need to generate the lower and higher bounds of the histogram's steps are these: *@numsteps* (given as input), step number (the *n* column from the Nums auxiliary table), *mn*, and *stepsize*, which I described earlier.

Here's the T-SQL code required to produce the step number, lower bound, and higher bound for each step of the histogram, generating the output shown in Table 6-27:

```
DECLARE @numsteps AS INT;
SET @numsteps = 3;

SELECT n AS step,
  mn + (n - 1) * stepsize AS lb,
  mn + n * stepsize AS hb
FROM dbo.Nums,
  (SELECT MIN(qty) AS mn,
    ((1E0*MAX(qty) + 0.0000000001) - MIN(qty))
    / @numsteps AS stepsize
   FROM dbo.Orders) AS D
WHERE n <= @numsteps;
```

Table 6-27 Histogram Steps Table

Step	lb	hb
1	10	20.0000000000333
2	20.0000000000333	30.0000000000667
3	30.0000000000667	40.0000000001

You might want to encapsulate this code in a user-defined function to simplify the queries that return the actual histograms. Run the code in Listing 6-12 to do just that.

Listing 6-12   Creation script for *fn_histsteps* function

```
CREATE FUNCTION dbo.fn_histsteps(@numsteps AS INT) RETURNS TABLE
AS
RETURN
  SELECT n AS step,
    mn + (n - 1) * stepsize AS lb,
    mn + n * stepsize AS hb
  FROM dbo.Nums,
    (SELECT MIN(qty) AS mn,
      ((1E0*MAX(qty) + 0.0000000001) - MIN(qty))
      / @numsteps AS stepsize
    FROM dbo.Orders) AS D
  WHERE n <= @numsteps;
GO
```

To test the function, run the following query, which will give you a three-row histogram steps table:

```
SELECT * FROM dbo.fn_histsteps(3) AS S;
```

To return the actual histogram, simply join the steps table and the Orders table on the predicate I described earlier (*qty >= lb AND qty < hb*), group the data by step number, and return the step number and row count:

```
SELECT step, COUNT(*) AS numorders
FROM dbo.fn_histsteps(3) AS S
  JOIN dbo.Orders AS O
    ON qty >= lb AND qty < hb
GROUP BY step;
```

This query generates the histogram shown in Table 6-28.

Table 6-28   Histogram with Three Steps

step	numorders
1	8
2	2
3	1

You can see that there are eight small orders, two medium orders, and one large order. To return a histogram with ten steps, simply provide 10 as the input to the *fn_histsteps* function, and the query will yield the histogram shown in Table 6-29:

```
SELECT step, COUNT(*) AS numorders
FROM dbo.fn_histsteps(10) AS S
  JOIN dbo.Orders AS O
    ON qty >= lb AND qty < hb
GROUP BY step;
```

Table 6-29   Histogram with Ten Steps

step	numorders
1	4
2	2
4	3
7	1
10	1

Note that because you're using an inner join, empty steps are not returned. To return empty steps also, you can use the following outer join query, which generates the output shown in Table 6-30:

```
SELECT step, COUNT(qty) AS numorders
FROM dbo.fn_histsteps(10) AS S
  LEFT OUTER JOIN dbo.Orders AS O
    ON qty >= lb AND qty < hb
GROUP BY step;
```

Table 6-30   Histogram with Ten Steps, Including Empty Steps

step	numorders
1	4
2	2
3	0
4	3
5	0
6	0
7	1
8	0
9	0
10	1

Note   Notice that *COUNT(qty)* is used here and not *COUNT(*)*. *COUNT(*)* would incorrectly return 1 for empty steps because there's an outer row in the group. You have to provide the COUNT function an attribute from the nonpreserved side (*Orders*) to get the correct count.

Instead of using an outer join query, you can use a cross join, with a filter that matches orders to steps, and the GROUP BY ALL option which insures that also empty steps will also be returned:

```
SELECT step, COUNT(qty) AS numcusts
FROM dbo.fn_histsteps(10) AS S, dbo.Orders AS O
WHERE qty >= lb AND qty < hb
GROUP BY ALL step;
```

I just wanted to show that you can write a simpler solution using the GROUP BY ALL option. But remember that it is advisable to refrain from using this non standard legacy feature, as it will probably be removed from the product in some future version.

There's another alternative to taking care of the issue with the step boundaries and the predicate used to identify a match. You can simply check whether the step number is 1, in which case you subtract 1 from the lower bound. Then, in the query generating the actual histogram, you use the predicate $qty > lb$ AND $qty <= hb$.

Another approach is to check whether the step is the last, and if it is, add 1 to the higher bound. Then use the predicate $qty >= lb$ AND $qty < hb$.

Listing 6-13 has the revised function implementing the latter approach:

Listing 6-13   Altering the implementation of the *fn_histsteps* function

```
ALTER FUNCTION dbo.fn_histsteps(@numsteps AS INT) RETURNS TABLE
AS
RETURN
  SELECT n AS step,
    mn + (n - 1) * stepsize AS lb,
    mn + n * stepsize + CASE WHEN n = @numsteps THEN 1 ELSE 0 END AS hb
  FROM dbo.Nums,
    (SELECT MIN(qty) AS mn,
       (1E0*MAX(qty) - MIN(qty)) / @numsteps AS stepsize
     FROM dbo.Orders) AS D
  WHERE n < = @numsteps;
GO
```

And the following query generates the actual histogram:

```
SELECT step, COUNT(qty) AS numorders
FROM dbo.fn_histsteps(10) AS S
  LEFT OUTER JOIN dbo.Orders AS O
    ON qty >= lb AND qty < hb
GROUP BY step;
```

Grouping Factor

In earlier chapters, in particular in Chapter 4, I described a concept called a *grouping factor*. In particular, I used it in a problem to isolate islands, or ranges of consecutive elements in a sequence. Recall that the grouping factor is the factor you end up using in your GROUP BY clause to identify the group. In the earlier problem, I demonstrated two techniques to calculate the grouping factor. One method was calculating the maximum value within the group (specifically, the smallest value that is both greater than or equal to the current value and followed by a gap). The other method used row numbers.

Because this chapter covers aggregates, it is appropriate to revisit this very practical problem. In my examples here, I'll use the Stocks table, which you create and populate by running the code in Listing 6-14.

Listing 6-14   Creating and populating the Stocks table

```
USE tempdb;
GO
IF OBJECT_ID('Stocks') IS NOT NULL
  DROP TABLE Stocks;
GO

CREATE TABLE dbo.Stocks
(
  dt     DATETIME NOT NULL PRIMARY KEY,
  price INT      NOT NULL
);

INSERT INTO dbo.Stocks(dt, price) VALUES('20060801', 13);
INSERT INTO dbo.Stocks(dt, price) VALUES('20060802', 14);
INSERT INTO dbo.Stocks(dt, price) VALUES('20060803', 17);
INSERT INTO dbo.Stocks(dt, price) VALUES('20060804', 40);
INSERT INTO dbo.Stocks(dt, price) VALUES('20060805', 40);
INSERT INTO dbo.Stocks(dt, price) VALUES('20060806', 52);
INSERT INTO dbo.Stocks(dt, price) VALUES('20060807', 56);
INSERT INTO dbo.Stocks(dt, price) VALUES('20060808', 60);
INSERT INTO dbo.Stocks(dt, price) VALUES('20060809', 70);
INSERT INTO dbo.Stocks(dt, price) VALUES('20060810', 30);
INSERT INTO dbo.Stocks(dt, price) VALUES('20060811', 29);
INSERT INTO dbo.Stocks(dt, price) VALUES('20060812', 29);
INSERT INTO dbo.Stocks(dt, price) VALUES('20060813', 40);
INSERT INTO dbo.Stocks(dt, price) VALUES('20060814', 45);
INSERT INTO dbo.Stocks(dt, price) VALUES('20060815', 60);
INSERT INTO dbo.Stocks(dt, price) VALUES('20060816', 60);
INSERT INTO dbo.Stocks(dt, price) VALUES('20060817', 55);
INSERT INTO dbo.Stocks(dt, price) VALUES('20060818', 60);
INSERT INTO dbo.Stocks(dt, price) VALUES('20060819', 60);
INSERT INTO dbo.Stocks(dt, price) VALUES('20060820', 15);
INSERT INTO dbo.Stocks(dt, price) VALUES('20060821', 20);
INSERT INTO dbo.Stocks(dt, price) VALUES('20060822', 30);
INSERT INTO dbo.Stocks(dt, price) VALUES('20060823', 40);
INSERT INTO dbo.Stocks(dt, price) VALUES('20060824', 20);
INSERT INTO dbo.Stocks(dt, price) VALUES('20060825', 60);
INSERT INTO dbo.Stocks(dt, price) VALUES('20060826', 60);
INSERT INTO dbo.Stocks(dt, price) VALUES('20060827', 70);
INSERT INTO dbo.Stocks(dt, price) VALUES('20060828', 70);
INSERT INTO dbo.Stocks(dt, price) VALUES('20060829', 40);
INSERT INTO dbo.Stocks(dt, price) VALUES('20060830', 30);
INSERT INTO dbo.Stocks(dt, price) VALUES('20060831', 10);

CREATE UNIQUE INDEX idx_price_dt ON Stocks(price, dt);
```

The Stocks table contains daily stock prices.

> **Note**   Stock prices are rarely restricted to integers, and there is usually more than one stock, but I'll use integers and a single stock for simplification purposes. Also, stock markets usually don't have activity on Saturdays; because I want to demonstrate a technique over a sequence with no gaps, I introduced rows for Saturdays as well, with the same value that was stored in the preceding Friday.

The request is to isolate consecutive periods where the stock price was greater than or equal to 50. Figure 6-2 has a graphical depiction of the stock prices over time, and the arrows represent the periods you're supposed to return.

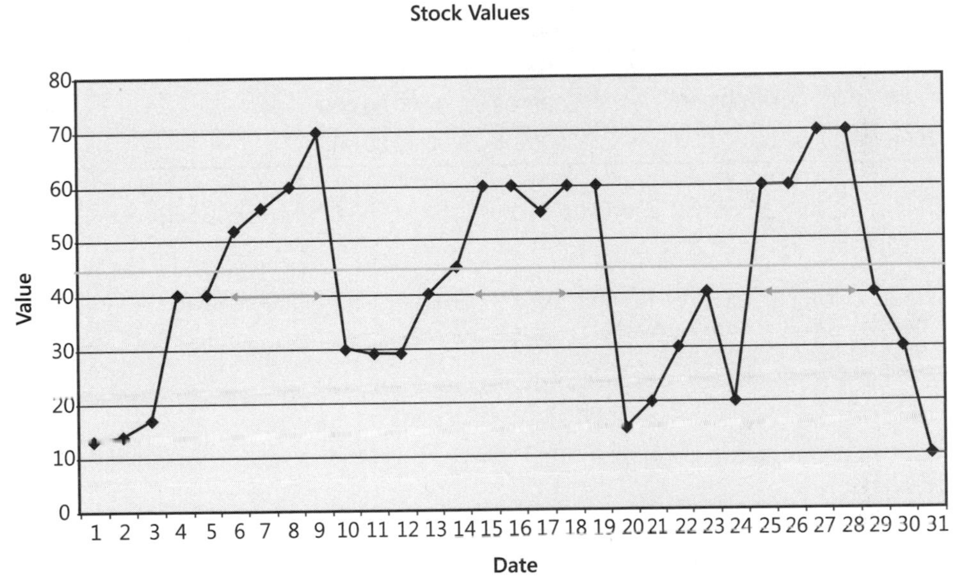

Stock Values

Figure 6-2   Periods in which stock values were greater than or equal to 50

For each such period, you need to return the starting date, ending date, duration in days, and the peak (maximum) price.

Let's start with a solution that does not use row numbers. The first step here is to filter only the rows where the price is greater than or equal to 50. Unlike the traditional problem where you really have gaps in the data, here the gaps appear only after filtering. The whole sequence still appears in the Stocks table. You can use this fact to your advantage. Of course, you could take the long route of calculating the maximum date within the group (the first date that is both later than or equal to the current date and followed by a gap). However, a much simpler and faster technique to calculate the grouping factor would be to return the first date that is greater than the current, on which the stock's price is less than 50. Here, you still get the same grouping factor for all elements of the same target group, yet you need only one nesting level of subqueries instead of two.

Here's the query that generates the desired result shown in Table 6-31:

```
SELECT MIN(dt) AS startrange, MAX(dt) AS endrange,
  DATEDIFF(day, MIN(dt), MAX(dt)) + 1 AS numdays,
  MAX(price) AS maxprice
FROM (SELECT dt, price,
        (SELECT MIN(dt)
          FROM dbo.Stocks AS S2
          WHERE S2.dt > S1.dt
            AND price < 50) AS grp
      FROM dbo.Stocks AS S1
      WHERE price >= 50) AS D
GROUP BY grp;
```

Table 6-31   Ranges Where Stock Values Were >= 50

startrange	endrange	numdays	maxprice
2006-08-06 00:00:00.000	2006-08-10 00:00:00.000	4	70
2006-08-15 00:00:00.000	2006-08-20 00:00:00.000	5	60
2006-08-25 00:00:00.000	2006-08-29 00:00:00.000	4	70

Of course, in SQL Server 2005 you can use the ROW_NUMBER function as I described in Chapter 4:

```
SELECT MIN(dt) AS startrange, MAX(dt) AS endrange,
  DATEDIFF(day, MIN(dt), MAX(dt)) + 1 AS numdays,
  MAX(price) AS maxprice
FROM (SELECT dt, price,
        dt - ROW_NUMBER() OVER(ORDER BY dt) AS grp
      FROM dbo.Stocks AS S1
      WHERE price >= 50) AS D
GROUP BY grp;
```

CUBE and ROLLUP

CUBE and ROLLUP are options available to queries that contain a GROUP BY clause. They are useful for applications that need to provide a changing variety of data aggregations based on varying sets of attributes or *dimensions*. (In the context of cubes, the word *dimension* is often used, either as a synonym for *attribute* or to describe a domain of values for an attribute.) I'll first describe the CUBE option, and then follow with a description of the ROLLUP option, which is a special case of CUBE.

CUBE

Imagine that your application needs to provide the users with the ability to request custom aggregates based on various sets of dimensions. Say, for example, that your base data is the Orders table that I used earlier in the chapter, and that the users need to analyze the data based on three dimensions: employee, customer, and order year. If you group the data by all three dimensions, you've covered only one of the possibilities the users might be interested in. However, the users might request any set of dimensions (for example, employee alone, customer alone, order year alone, employee and customer, and so on). For each request, you would need to construct a different GROUP BY query and submit it to SQL Server, returning the result set to the client. That's a lot of roundtrips and a lot of network traffic.

As the number of dimensions grows, the number of possible GROUP BY queries increases dramatically. For n dimensions, there are 2^n different queries. With 3 dimensions, you're looking at 8 possible requests; with 4 dimensions, there are 16. With 10 dimensions (the maximum number of grouping expressions we will be able to use with CUBE), users could request any one of 1024 different GROUP BY queries.

Simply put, adding the option WITH CUBE to a query with all dimensions specified in the GROUP BY clause generates one unified result set out of the result sets of all the different GROUP BY queries over subsets of the dimensions. If you think about it, Analysis Services cubes give you similar functionality, but on a much larger scale and with substantially more sophisticated options. However, when you don't need to support dynamic analysis on such a scale and at such a level of sophistication, the option WITH CUBE allows you to achieve this within the relational database.

Because each set of dimensions generates a result set with a different subset of all possible result columns, the designers who implemented CUBE and ROLLUP had to come up with a placeholder for the values in the unneeded columns. The designers chose NULL. So, for example, all rows from the result set of a GROUP BY *empid, custid* would have NULL in the *orderyear* result column. This allows all result sets to be unified into one result set with one schema.

As an example, the following CUBE query returns all possible aggregations (total quantities) of orders based on the dimensions *empid*, *custid*, and *orderyear*, generating the output shown in Table 6-32:

```
SELECT empid, custid,
  YEAR(orderdate) AS orderyear, SUM(qty) AS totalqty
FROM dbo.Orders
GROUP BY empid, custid, YEAR(orderdate)
WITH CUBE;
```

Table 6-32   Cube's Result

empid	custid	orderyear	totalqty
1	A	2002	12
1	A	NULL	12
1	B	2002	20
1	B	NULL	20

Table 6-32 Cube's Result

empid	custid	orderyear	totalqty
1	C	2003	14
1	C	NULL	14
1	NULL	NULL	46
2	B	2003	12
2	B	NULL	12
2	C	2004	20
2	C	NULL	20
2	NULL	NULL	32
3	A	2002	10
3	A	NULL	10
3	B	2004	15
3	B	NULL	15
3	C	2002	22
3	C	NULL	22
3	D	2002	30
3	D	NULL	30
3	NULL	NULL	77
4	A	2003	40
4	A	2004	10
4	A	NULL	50
4	NULL	NULL	50
NULL	NULL	NULL	205
NULL	A	2002	22
NULL	A	2003	40
NULL	A	2004	10
NULL	A	NULL	72
NULL	B	2002	20
NULL	B	2003	12
NULL	B	2004	15
NULL	B	NULL	47
NULL	C	2002	22
NULL	C	2003	14
NULL	C	2004	20
NULL	C	NULL	56
NULL	D	2002	30
NULL	D	NULL	30

Table 6-32   Cube's Result

empid	custid	orderyear	totalqty
1	NULL	2002	32
3	NULL	2002	62
NULL	NULL	2002	94
1	NULL	2003	14
2	NULL	2003	12
4	NULL	2003	40
NULL	NULL	2003	66
2	NULL	2004	20
3	NULL	2004	15
4	NULL	2004	10
NULL	NULL	2004	45

As long as the dimension columns in the table don't have NULLs, wherever you see a NULL in the result of the CUBE query, it logically means all. Later I'll discuss how to deal with NULLs in the queried table. For example, the row containing NULL, NULL, 2004, 45 shows the total quantity (45) for the orders of all employees and all customers for the order year 2004. You might want to cache the result set from a CUBE query in the client or middle tier, or you might want to save it in a temporary table and index it. The code in Listing 6-15 selects the result set into the temporary table #Cube and then creates a clustered index on all dimensions.

Listing 6-15   Populating a #Cube with CUBE query's result set

```
SELECT empid, custid,
  YEAR(orderdate) AS orderyear, SUM(qty) AS totalqty
INTO #Cube
FROM dbo.Orders
GROUP BY empid, custid, YEAR(orderdate)
WITH CUBE;

CREATE CLUSTERED INDEX idx_emp_cust_year
  ON #Cube(empid, custid, orderyear);
```

Any request for an aggregate can be satisfied using a seek operation within the clustered index. For example, the following query returns the total quantity for employee 1, generating the execution plan shown in Figure 6-3:

```
SELECT totalqty
FROM #Cube
WHERE empid = 1
  AND custid IS NULL
  AND orderyear IS NULL;
```

Figure 6-3 Execution plan for a query against the #Cube table

Once you're done querying the #Cube table, drop it:

```
DROP TABLE #Cube;
```

An issue might arise if dimension columns allow NULLs. For example, run the following code to allow NULLs in the *empid* column and introduce some actual NULL values:

```
ALTER TABLE dbo.Orders ALTER COLUMN empid INT NULL;
UPDATE dbo.Orders SET empid = NULL WHERE orderid IN(10001, 20001);
```

You should realize that when you run a CUBE query now, a NULL in the *empid* column is ambiguous. When it results from NULL in the *empid* column, it represents the group of unknown employees. When it is generated by the CUBE option, it represents all employees. However, without any specific treatment of the NULLs, you won't be able to tell which it is. I like to simply substitute for NULL a value that I know can't be used in the data—for example, –1 as the *empid*. I use the COALESCE or ISNULL function for this purpose. After this substitution, the value –1 would represent unknown employees, and NULL can only mean all employees. Here's a query that incorporates this logic:

```
SELECT COALESCE(empid, -1) AS empid, custid,
  YEAR(orderdate) AS orderyear, SUM(qty) AS totalqty
FROM dbo.Orders
GROUP BY COALESCE(empid, -1), custid, YEAR(orderdate)
WITH CUBE;
```

Another option is to use the T-SQL function GROUPING, which was designed to address the ambiguity of NULL in the result set. You supply the function with the dimension column name as input. The value of GROUPING(<dimension>) indicates whether or not the value of <dimension> in the row represents the value for a group (in this case, GROUPING returns 0) or is a placeholder that represents all values (in this case, GROUPING returns 1). Specifically for the dimension value NULL, GROUPING returns 1 if the NULL is a result of the CUBE option (meaning all) and 0 if it represents the group of source NULLs. Here's a query that uses the function GROUPING:

```
SELECT empid, GROUPING(empid) AS grp_empid, custid,
  YEAR(orderdate) AS orderyear, SUM(qty) AS totalqty
FROM dbo.Orders
GROUP BY empid, custid, YEAR(orderdate)
WITH CUBE;
```

If you're spooling the result set of a CUBE query to a temporary table, don't forget to include the grouping columns in the index, and also be sure to include them in your filters. For example, assume you spooled the result set of the preceding query to a temporary table called #Cube. The following query would return the total quantity for customer A:

```
SELECT totalqty
FROM #Cube
WHERE empid IS NULL AND grp_empid = 1
  AND custid = 'A'
  AND orderyear IS NULL;
```

ROLLUP

ROLLUP is a special case of CUBE that you can use when there's a hierarchy on the dimensions. For example, suppose you want to analyze order quantities based on the dimensions order year, order month, and order day. Assume you don't really care about totals of an item in one level of granularity across all values in a higher level of granularity—for example, the totals of the third day in all months and all years. You care only about the totals of an item in one level of granularity for all lower level values—for example, the total for year 2004, all months, all days. ROLLUP gives you just that. It eliminates all "noninteresting" aggregations in a hierarchical case. More accurately, it doesn't even bother to calculate them at all, so you should expect better performance from a ROLLUP query than a CUBE query based on the same dimensions.

As an example for using ROLLUP, the following query returns the total order quantities for the dimensions order year, order month, and order day, and it returns the output shown in Table 6-33:

```
SELECT
  YEAR(orderdate)  AS orderyear,
  MONTH(orderdate) AS ordermonth,
  DAY(orderdate)   AS orderday,
  SUM(qty) AS totalqty
FROM dbo.Orders
GROUP BY YEAR(orderdate), MONTH(orderdate), DAY(orderdate)
WITH ROLLUP;
```

Table 6-33   Rollup's Result

orderyear	ordermonth	orderday	totalqty
2002	4	18	22
2002	4	NULL	22
2002	8	2	10
2002	8	NULL	10
2002	9	7	30
2002	9	NULL	30

Table 6-33   Rollup's Result

orderyear	ordermonth	orderday	totalqty
2002	12	24	32
2002	12	NULL	32
2002	NULL	NULL	94
2003	1	9	40
2003	1	18	14
2003	1	NULL	54
2003	2	12	12
2003	2	NULL	12
2003	NULL	NULL	66
2004	2	12	10
2004	2	16	20
2004	2	NULL	30
2004	4	18	15
2004	4	NULL	15
2004	NULL	NULL	45
NULL	NULL	NULL	205

Conclusion

This chapter covered various solutions to data-aggregation problems that reused key querying techniques I introduced earlier in the book. It also introduced new techniques, such as dealing with tiebreakers by using concatenation, calculating a minimum using the MAX function, pivoting, unpivoting, calculating custom aggregates by using specialized techniques, and others.

As you probably noticed, data-aggregation techniques involve a lot of logical manipulation. If you're looking for ways to improve your logic, you can practice pure logical puzzles, as they have a lot in common with querying problems in terms of the thought processes involved. You can find pure logic puzzles in Appendix A.

Chapter 7
TOP and APPLY

This chapter covers two query elements that might seem unrelated to each other. One element is the TOP option, which allows you to limit the number of rows affected by a query. The other is the new APPLY table operator, which allows you to apply a table expression to each row of another table expression—basically creating a correlated join. I decided to cover both in the same chapter because I find that quite often you can use them together to solve querying problems.

I'll first describe the fundamentals of TOP and APPLY, and then follow with solutions to common problems using these elements.

SELECT TOP

In a SELECT query or table expression, TOP is used with an ORDER BY clause to limit the result to rows that come first in the ORDER BY ordering. You can specify the quantity of rows you want in one of two ways: as an exact number of rows, from TOP(0) to TOP(9223372036854775807) (the largest BIGINT value), or as a percentage of rows, from TOP(0E0) PERCENT to TOP(100E0) PERCENT, using a FLOAT value. In Microsoft SQL Server 2000, you could only use a constant to specify the limit. SQL Server 2005 supports any self-contained expression, not just constants, with TOP.

To make it clear which rows are the "top" rows affected by a TOP query, you must indicate an ordering of the rows. Just as you can't tell top from bottom unless you know which way is up, you won't know which rows TOP affects unless you specify an ORDER BY clause. You should think of TOP and ORDER BY together as a logical filter rather than a sorting mechanism. That's why a query with both a TOP clause and an ORDER BY clause returns a well-defined table and is allowed in table expressions. In a query without TOP, an ORDER BY clause has a different purpose—it simply specifies the order in which results are returned. Using ORDER BY without TOP is not allowed in table expressions.

> **Note** Interestingly, you can specify the TOP option in a query without an ORDER BY clause, but the logical meaning of TOP in such a query is not completely defined. I'll explain this aspect of TOP shortly.

Let's start with a basic example. The following query returns the three most recent orders, producing the output shown in Table 7-1:

```
USE Northwind;
SELECT TOP(3) OrderID, CustomerID, OrderDate
FROM dbo.Orders
ORDER BY OrderDate DESC, OrderID DESC;
```

Table 7-1   Three Most Recent Orders

OrderID	CustomerID	OrderDate
11077	RATTC	1998-05-06 00:00:00.000
11076	BONAP	1998-05-06 00:00:00.000
11075	RICSU	1998-05-06 00:00:00.000

Sorting first by *OrderDate* DESC guarantees that you will get the most recent orders. Because *OrderDate* is not unique, I added *OrderID* DESC to the ORDER BY list as a tiebreaker. Among orders with the same *OrderDate*, the tiebreaker will give precedence to orders with higher *OrderID* values.

> **Note** Notice the usage of parentheses here for the input expression to the TOP option. Because SQL Server 2005 supports any self-contained expression as input, the expression must reside within parentheses. For backward-compatibility reasons, SQL Server 2005 still supports SELECT TOP queries that use a constant without parentheses. However, it's good practice to put TOP constants in parentheses to conform to the new requirements.

As an example of the PERCENT option, the following query returns the most recent one percent of orders, generating the output shown in Table 7-2:

```
SELECT TOP(1) PERCENT OrderID, CustomerID, OrderDate
FROM dbo.Orders
ORDER BY OrderDate DESC, OrderID DESC;
```

Table 7-2   Most Recent One Percent of Orders

OrderID	CustomerID	OrderDate
11077	RATTC	1998-05-06 00:00:00.000
11076	BONAP	1998-05-06 00:00:00.000
11075	RICSU	1998-05-06 00:00:00.000
11074	SIMOB	1998-05-06 00:00:00.000
11073	PERIC	1998-05-05 00:00:00.000
11072	ERNSH	1998-05-05 00:00:00.000

Table 7-2 Most Recent One Percent of Orders

OrderID	CustomerID	OrderDate
11071	LILAS	1998-05-05 00:00:00.000
11070	LEHMS	1998-05-05 00:00:00.000
11069	TORTU	1998-05-04 00:00:00.000

The Orders table has 830 rows, and one percent of 830 is 8.3. Because only whole rows can be returned and 8.3 were requested, the actual number of rows returned is 9. When TOP ... PERCENT is used, and the specified percent includes a fractional row, the exact number of rows requested is rounded up.

TOP and Determinism

As I mentioned earlier, a TOP query doesn't require an ORDER BY clause. However, such a query is nondeterministic. That is, running the same query twice against the same data might yield different result sets, and both would be correct. The following query returns three orders, with no rule governing which three are returned:

```
SELECT TOP(3) OrderID, CustomerID, OrderDate
FROM dbo.Orders;
```

When I ran this query, I got the output shown in Table 7-3, but you might get a different output. SQL Server will return the first three rows it happened to access first.

Table 7-3 Result of TOP Query with No ORDER BY

OrderID	CustomerID	OrderDate
10248	VINET	1996-07-04 00:00:00.000
10249	TOMSP	1996-07-05 00:00:00.000
10250	HANAR	1996-07-08 00:00:00.000

> **Note** I can think of only two good reasons to use SELECT TOP without ORDER BY, and I don't recommend it otherwise. One reason to use SELECT TOP is to serve as a quick reminder of the structure or column names of a table, or to find out if the table contains any data at all. The other reason to use SELECT TOP—specifically SELECT TOP(0)—is to create an empty table with the same structure as another table or query. In this case, you can use *SELECT TOP(0) <column list> INTO <table name> FROM ... .* Obviously, you don't need an ORDER BY clause to indicate "which zero rows" you want to select!

A TOP query can be nondeterministic even when an ORDER BY clause is specified, if the ORDER BY list is nonunique. For example, the following query returns the first three orders in order of increasing *CustomerID*, generating the output shown in Table 7-4:

```
SELECT TOP(3) OrderID, CustomerID, OrderDate
FROM dbo.Orders
ORDER BY CustomerID;
```

Table 7-4   Result of TOP Query with Nonunique ORDER BY

OrderID	CustomerID	OrderDate
10643	ALFKI	1997-08-25 00:00:00.000
10692	ALFKI	1997-10-03 00:00:00.000
10702	ALFKI	1997-10-13 00:00:00.000

You are guaranteed to get the orders with the lowest *CustomerID* values. However, because the *CustomerID* column is not unique, you cannot guarantee which rows among the ones with the same *CustomerID* values will be returned in case of ties. Again, you will get the ones that SQL Server happened to access first. One way to guarantee determinism is to add a tiebreaker that makes the ORDER BY list unique—for example, the primary key:

```
SELECT TOP(3) OrderID, CustomerID, OrderDate
FROM dbo.Orders
ORDER BY CustomerID, OrderID;
```

Another way to guarantee determinism is to use the WITH TIES option. When you use WITH TIES, the query will generate a result set including any additional rows that have the same values in the sort column or columns as the last row returned. For example, the following query specifies TOP(3), yet it returns the seven rows shown in Table 7-5. Four additional orders are returned because they have the same *CustomerID* value (ALFKI) as the third row:

```
SELECT TOP(3) WITH TIES OrderID, CustomerID, OrderDate
FROM dbo.Orders
ORDER BY CustomerID;
```

Table 7-5   Result of TOP Query Using the WITH TIES Option

OrderID	CustomerID	OrderDate
10643	ALFKI	1997-08-25 00:00:00.000
10692	ALFKI	1997-10-03 00:00:00.000
10702	ALFKI	1997-10-13 00:00:00.000
10835	ALFKI	1998-01-15 00:00:00.000
10952	ALFKI	1998-03-16 00:00:00.000
11011	ALFKI	1998-04-09 00:00:00.000
10643	ALFKI	1997-08-25 00:00:00.000

Note   Some applications must guarantee determinism. For example, if you're using the TOP option to implement paging, you don't want the same row to end up on two successive pages just because the query was nondeterministic. Remember that you can always add the primary key as a tiebreaker to guarantee determinism in case the ORDER BY list is not unique.

TOP and Input Expressions

As the input to TOP, SQL Server 2005 supports any self-contained expression yielding a scalar result. An expression that is independent of the outer query can be used—a variable, an arithmetic expression, or even the result of a subquery. For example, the following query returns the @n most recent orders, where @n is a variable:

```
DECLARE @n AS INT;
SET @n = 2;

SELECT TOP(@n) OrderID, OrderDate, CustomerID, EmployeeID
FROM dbo.Orders
ORDER BY OrderDate DESC, OrderID DESC;
```

The following query shows the use of a subquery as the input to TOP. As always, the input to TOP specifies the number of rows the query returns—for this example, the number of rows returned is the monthly average number of orders. The ORDER BY clause in this example specifies that the rows returned are the most recent ones, where *OrderID* is the tiebreaker (higher ID wins):

```
SELECT TOP(SELECT COUNT(*)/(DATEDIFF(month,
             MIN(OrderDate), MAX(OrderDate))+1)
          FROM dbo.Orders)
  OrderID, OrderDate, CustomerID, EmployeeID
FROM dbo.Orders
ORDER BY OrderDate DESC, OrderID DESC;
```

The average number of monthly orders is the count of orders divided by one more than the difference in months between the maximum and minimum order dates. Because there are 830 orders in the table that were placed during a period of 23 months, the output has the most recent 36 orders.

TOP and Modifications

SQL Server 2005 provides a TOP option for data modification statements (INSERT, UPDATE, and DELETE).

> **Note**   Before SQL Server 2005, the SET ROWCOUNT option provided the same capability as some of TOP's new features. SET ROWCOUNT accepted a variable as input, and it affected both data modification statements and SELECT statements. Microsoft no longer recommends SET ROWCOUNT as a way to affect INSERT, UPDATE, and DELETE state-ments—in fact, in Katmai, the next release of SQL Server, SET ROWCOUNT will not affect data modification statements at all. Use TOP to limit the number of rows affected by data modification statements.

SQL Server 2005 introduces support for the TOP option with modification statements, allowing you to limit the number or percentage of affected rows. A TOP specification can follow the keyword DELETE, UPDATE, or INSERT.

An ORDER BY clause is not supported with modification statements, even when using TOP, so none of them can rely on ordering. SQL Server will simply affect the specified number of rows that it happens to access first.

In the following statement, SQL Server does not guarantee which rows will be inserted from the source table:

```
INSERT TOP(10) INTO target_table
  SELECT col1, col2, col3
  FROM source_table;
```

> **Note** Although you cannot use ORDER BY with INSERT TOP, you can guarantee which rows will be inserted if you specify TOP and ORDER BY in the SELECT statement, like so:
>
> ```
> INSERT INTO target_table
>   SELECT TOP(10) col1, col2, col3
>   FROM source_table
>   ORDER BY col1;
> ```

An INSERT TOP is handy when you want to load a subset of rows from a large table or result set into a target table and you don't care which subset will be chosen; instead, you care only about the number of rows.

> **Note** Although ORDER BY cannot be used with UPDATE TOP and DELETE TOP, you can overcome the limitation by creating a CTE from a SELECT TOP query that has an ORDER BY clause and then issue your UPDATE or DELETE against the CTE:
>
> ```
> WITH CTE_DEL AS
> (
>   SELECT TOP(10) * FROM some_table ORDER BY col1
> )
> DELETE FROM CTE_DEL;
>
> WITH CTE_UPD AS
> (
>   SELECT TOP(10) * FROM some_table ORDER BY col1
> )
> UPDATE CTE_UPD SET col2 = col2 + 1;
> ```

One such situation is when you need to insert or modify large volumes of data and, for practical reasons, you split it into batches, modifying one subset of the data at a time. For example, purging historic data might involve deleting millions of rows of data. Unless the target table is partitioned and you can simply drop a partition, the purging process requires a DELETE statement. Deleting such a large set of rows in a single transaction has several drawbacks. A DELETE statement is fully logged, and it will require enough space in the transaction log to accommodate the whole transaction. During the delete operation, which could take a long time, no part of the log from the oldest open transaction up to the current point can be overwritten. Furthermore, if the transaction breaks in the middle for some reason, all the activity that took place to that point will be rolled back, and this will take a while. Finally, when very many rows are deleted at once, SQL Server might escalate the individual locks held on the deleted rows to an exclusive table lock, preventing both read and write access to the target table until the DELETE is completed.

It makes sense to break the single large DELETE transaction into several smaller ones—small enough not to cause lock escalation (typically, a few thousand rows per transaction), and allowing recycling of the transaction log. You can easily verify that the number you chose doesn't cause lock escalation by testing a DELETE with the TOP option while monitoring Lock Escalation events with Profiler. Splitting the large DELETE will also allow overwriting the inactive section of the log that was already backed up.

To demonstrate purging data in multiple transactions, run the following code, which creates the LargeOrders table and populates it with sample data:

```
IF OBJECT_ID('dbo.LargeOrders') IS NOT NULL
  DROP TABLE dbo.LargeOrders;
GO
SELECT IDENTITY(int, 1, 1) AS OrderID,
  O1.CustomerID, O1.EmployeeID, O1.OrderDate, O1.RequiredDate,
  O1.ShippedDate, O1.ShipVia, O1.Freight, O1.ShipName, O1.ShipAddress,
  O1.ShipCity, O1.ShipRegion, O1.ShipPostalCode, O1.ShipCountry
INTO dbo.LargeOrders
FROM dbo.Orders AS O1, dbo.Orders AS O2;

CREATE UNIQUE CLUSTERED INDEX idx_od_oid
  ON dbo.LargeOrders(OrderDate, OrderID);
```

In versions prior to SQL Server 2005, use the SET ROWCOUNT option to split a large DELETE, as the following solution shows:

```
SET ROWCOUNT 5000;
WHILE 1 = 1
BEGIN
  DELETE FROM dbo.LargeOrders
  WHERE OrderDate < '19970101';

  IF @@rowcount < 5000 BREAK;
END
SET ROWCOUNT 0;
```

The code sets the ROWCOUNT option to 5000, limiting the number of rows affected by any DML to 5000. An endless loop attempts to delete 5000 rows in each iteration, where each 5000-row deletion resides in a separate transaction. The loop breaks as soon as the last batch is handled (that is, when the number of affected rows is less than 5000).

In SQL Server 2005, you don't need the SET ROWCOUNT option anymore. Simply specify DELETE TOP(5000):

```
WHILE 1 = 1
BEGIN
  DELETE TOP(5000) FROM dbo.LargeOrders
  WHERE OrderDate < '19970101';

  IF @@rowcount < 5000 BREAK;
END
```

In a similar manner, you can split large updates into batches. For example, say you need to change the *CustomerID* OLDWO to ABCDE wherever it appears in the LargeOrders table. Here's the solution you would use in SQL Server 2000 when relying on the SET ROWCOUNT option:

```
SET ROWCOUNT 5000;
WHILE 1 = 1
BEGIN
  UPDATE dbo.LargeOrders
    SET CustomerID = N'ABCDE'
  WHERE CustomerID = N'OLDWO';

  IF @@rowcount < 5000 BREAK;
END
SET ROWCOUNT 0;
```

And here's the solution in SQL Server 2005 using UPDATE TOP:

```
WHILE 1 = 1
BEGIN
  UPDATE TOP(5000) dbo.LargeOrders
    SET CustomerID = N'ABCDE'
  WHERE CustomerID = N'OLDWO';

  IF @@rowcount < 5000 BREAK;
END
```

When you're done experimenting with the batch modifications, drop the LargeOrders table:

```
IF OBJECT_ID('dbo.LargeOrders') IS NOT NULL
  DROP TABLE dbo.LargeOrders;
```

APPLY

The new APPLY table operator applies the right-hand table expression to every row of the left-hand table expression. Unlike a join, where there's no importance to the order in which each of the table expressions is evaluated, APPLY must logically evaluate the left table expression first. This logical evaluation order of the inputs allows the right table expression to be correlated with the left one—something that was not possible prior to SQL Server 2005. The concept can probably be made clearer with an example.

Run the following code to create an inline table-valued function called *fn_top_products*:

```
IF OBJECT_ID('dbo.fn_top_products') IS NOT NULL
  DROP FUNCTION dbo.fn_top_products;
GO
CREATE FUNCTION dbo.fn_top_products
  (@supid AS INT, @catid INT, @n AS INT)
  RETURNS TABLE
AS
RETURN
  SELECT TOP(@n) WITH TIES ProductID, ProductName, UnitPrice
  FROM dbo.Products
  WHERE SupplierID = @supid
    AND CategoryID = @catid
  ORDER BY UnitPrice DESC;
GO
```

The function accepts three inputs: a supplier ID (*@supid*), a category ID (*@catid*), and a requested number of products (*@n*). The function returns the requested number of products of the given category, supplied by the given supplier, with the highest unit prices. The query uses the TOP option WITH TIES to ensure a deterministic result set by including all products that have the same unit price as the least expensive product returned.

The following query uses the APPLY operator in conjunction with *fn_top_products* to return, for each supplier, the two most expensive beverages. The Category ID for beverages is 1, so 1 is supplied for the parameter *@catid*. This query generates the output shown in Table 7-6:

```
SELECT S.SupplierID, CompanyName, ProductID, ProductName, UnitPrice
FROM dbo.Suppliers AS S
  CROSS APPLY dbo.fn_top_products(S.SupplierID, 1, 2) AS P;
```

Table 7-6   Two Most Expensive Beverages for Each Supplier

SupplierID	CompanyName	ProductID	ProductName	UnitPrice
18	Aux joyeux ecclésiastiques	38	Côte de Blaye	263.50
18	Aux joyeux ecclésiastiques	39	Chartreuse verte	18.00
16	Bigfoot Breweries	35	Steeleye Stout	18.00
16	Bigfoot Breweries	67	Laughing Lumberjack Lager	14.00
16	Bigfoot Breweries	34	Sasquatch Ale	14.00
1	Exotic Liquids	2	Chang	19.00
1	Exotic Liquids	1	Chai	18.00
23	Karkki Oy	76	Lakkalikööri	18.00
20	Leka Trading	43	Ipoh Coffee	46.00

Table 7-6   Two Most Expensive Beverages for Each Supplier

SupplierID	CompanyName	ProductID	ProductName	UnitPrice
7	Pavlova, Ltd.	70	Outback Lager	15.00
12	Plutzer Lebensmittel-großmärkte AG	75	Rhönbräu Klosterbier	7.75
10	Refrescos Americanas LTDA	24	Guaraná Fantástica	4.50

Specifying CROSS with the APPLY operator means that there will be nothing in the result set for a row in the left table expression for which the right table expression *dbo.fn_top_products(S.SupplierID, 1, 2)* is empty. Such is the case here, for example, for suppliers that don't supply beverages. To include results for those suppliers as well, use the OUTER keyword instead of CROSS, as the following query shows:

```
SELECT S.SupplierID, CompanyName, ProductID, ProductName, UnitPrice
FROM dbo.Suppliers AS S
  OUTER APPLY dbo.fn_top_products(S.SupplierID, 1, 2) AS P;
```

This query returns 33 rows. The result set with OUTER APPLY includes left rows for which the right table expression yielded an empty set, and for these rows the right table expression's attributes are NULL.

There's a nice side-effect that resulted from the technology added to SQL Server's engine to support the APPLY operator. Now you are allowed to pass a column reference parameter from an outer query to a table-valued function. As an example of this capability, the following query returns, for each supplier, the lower of the two most expensive beverage prices (assuming there are at least two), generating the output shown in Table 7-7:

```
SELECT S.SupplierID, CompanyName,
  (SELECT MIN(UnitPrice)
    FROM dbo.fn_top_products(S.SupplierID, 1, 2) AS P) AS Price
FROM dbo.Suppliers AS S;
```

Table 7-7   The Lower of the Two Most Expensive Beverages per Supplier

SupplierID	CompanyName	Price
18	Aux joyeux ecclésiastiques	18.00
16	Bigfoot Breweries	14.00
5	Cooperativa de Quesos 'Las Cabras'	NULL
27	Escargots Nouveaux	NULL
1	Exotic Liquids	18.00
29	Forêts d'érables	NULL
14	Formaggi Fortini s.r.l.	NULL
28	Gai pâturage	NULL
24	G'day, Mate	NULL
3	Grandma Kelly's Homestead	NULL

Table 7-7   The Lower of the Two Most Expensive Beverages per Supplier

SupplierID	CompanyName	Price
11	Heli Süßwaren GmbH & Co. KG	NULL
23	Karkki Oy	18.00
20	Leka Trading	46.00
21	Lyngbysild	NULL
25	Ma Maison	NULL
6	Mayumi's	NULL
19	New England Seafood Cannery	NULL
2	New Orleans Cajun Delights	NULL
13	Nord-Ost-Fisch Handelsgesellschaft mbH	NULL
15	Norske Meierier	NULL
26	Pasta Buttini s.r.l.	NULL
7	Pavlova, Ltd.	15.00
9	PB Knäckebröd AB	NULL
12	Plutzer Lebensmittelgroßmärkte AG	7.75
10	Refrescos Americanas LTDA	4.50
8	Specialty Biscuits, Ltd.	NULL
17	Svensk Sjöföda AB	NULL
4	Tokyo Traders	NULL
22	Zaanse Snoepfabriek	NULL

Solutions to Common Problems Using TOP and APPLY

Now that the fundamentals of TOP and APPLY have been covered, I'll present common problems and solutions that use TOP and APPLY.

TOP *n* for Each Group

In Chapter 4 and Chapter 6, I discussed a problem involving tiebreakers where you were asked to return the most recent order for each employee. This problem is actually a special case of a more generic problem where you are after the top *n* rows for each group—for example, returning the three most recent orders for each employee. Again, orders with higher *OrderDate* values have precedence, but you need to introduce a tiebreaker to determine precedence in case of ties. Here I'll use the maximum *OrderID* as the tiebreaker. I'll present solutions to this class of problems using TOP and APPLY. You will find that these solutions are dramatically simpler than the ones I presented previously, and in some cases they are substantially faster. Indexing guidelines, though, remain the same. That is, you want an index with the key list being the partitioning columns (*EmployeeID*), sort columns (*OrderDate*), tiebreaker columns (*OrderID*), and for covering purposes, the other columns mentioned in the query as the included column list (*CustomerID* and *RequiredDate*). Of course, in SQL

Server 2000, which doesn't support included nonkey columns (INCLUDE clause), you need to add those to the key list.

Before going over the different solutions, run the following code to create the desired indexes on the Orders and [Order Details] tables that participate in my examples:

```
CREATE UNIQUE INDEX idx_eid_od_oid_i_cid_rd
  ON dbo.Orders(EmployeeID, OrderDate, OrderID)
    INCLUDE(CustomerID, RequiredDate);

CREATE UNIQUE INDEX idx_oid_qtyd_pid
  ON dbo.[Order Details](OrderID, Quantity DESC, ProductID);
```

The first solution that I'll present will find the most recent order for each employee. The solution queries the Orders table, filtering only orders that have an *OrderID* value that is equal to the result of a subquery. The subquery returns the *OrderID* value of the most recent order for the current employee by using a simple TOP(1) logic. Listing 7-1 has the solution query, generating the output shown in Table 7-8 and the execution plan shown in Figure 7-1.

Listing 7-1 Solution 1 to the Most Recent Order for Each Employee problem

```
SELECT OrderID, CustomerID, EmployeeID, OrderDate, RequiredDate
FROM dbo.Orders AS O1
WHERE OrderID =
  (SELECT TOP(1) OrderID
   FROM dbo.Orders AS O2
   WHERE O2.EmployeeID = O1.EmployeeID
   ORDER BY OrderDate DESC, OrderID DESC);
```

Table 7-8 Most Recent Order for Each Employee

OrderID	CustomerID	EmployeeID	OrderDate	RequiredDate
11077	RATTC	1	1998-05-06 00:00:00.000	1998-06-03 00:00:00.000
11073	PERIC	2	1998-05-05 00:00:00.000	1998-06-02 00:00:00.000
11063	HUNGO	3	1998-04-30 00:00:00.000	1998-05-28 00:00:00.000
11076	BONAP	4	1998-05-06 00:00:00.000	1998-06-03 00:00:00.000
11043	SPECD	5	1998-04-22 00:00:00.000	1998-05-20 00:00:00.000
11045	BOTTM	6	1998-04-23 00:00:00.000	1998-05-21 00:00:00.000
11074	SIMOB	7	1998-05-06 00:00:00.000	1998-06-03 00:00:00.000
11075	RICSU	8	1998-05-06 00:00:00.000	1998-06-03 00:00:00.000
11058	BLAUS	9	1998-04-29 00:00:00.000	1998-05-27 00:00:00.000

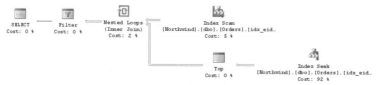

Figure 7-1 Execution plan for the query in Listing 7-1

This solution has several advantages over the solutions I presented earlier in the book. Compared to the ANSI subqueries solution I presented in Chapter 4, this one is faster and much simpler, especially when you have multiple sort/tiebreaker columns; you simply extend the ORDER BY list in the subquery to include the additional columns. Compared to the solution based on aggregations I presented in Chapter 6, this solution is slower but substantially simpler.

Examine the query's execution plan, which is shown in Figure 7-1. The Index Scan operator shows that the covering index idx_eid_od_oid_i_cid_rd is scanned once. The bottom branch of the Nested Loops operator represents the work done for each row of the Index Scan. Here you see that for each row of the Index Scan, an Index Seek and a Top operation take place to find the given employee's most recent order. Remember that the index leaf level holds the data sorted by *EmployeeID, OrderDate, OrderID*, in that order; this means that the last row within each group of rows per employee represents the sought row. The Index Seek operation reaches the end of the group of rows for the current employee, and the Top operator goes one step backwards to return the key of most recent order. A filter operator then keeps only orders where the outer *OrderID* value matches the one returned by the subquery.

The I/O cost of this query is 1,787 logical reads, and this number breaks down as follows: the full scan of the covering index requires 7 logical reads, because the index spans 7 data pages; each of the 830 index seeks requires at least 2 logical reads, because the index has 2 levels, and some of the index seeks require 3 logical reads in all, since the seek might lead to the beginning of one data page and the most recent *OrderID* might be at the end of the preceding page.

Realizing that a separate seek operation within the index was invoked for each outer order, you can figure out that there's room for optimization here. The performance potential is to invoke only a single seek per employee, not order, because ultimately you are after the most recent order for each employee. I'll describe how to achieve such optimization shortly. But before that, I'd like to point out another advantage of this solution over the ones I presented earlier in the book. Previous solutions were limited to returning only a single order per employee. This solution, however, can be easily extended to support any number of orders per employee, by converting the equality operator to an IN predicate. The solution query is shown in Listing 7-2.

Listing 7-2   Solution 1 to the Most Recent Orders for Each Employee problem

```
SELECT OrderID, CustomerID, EmployeeID, OrderDate, RequiredDate
FROM dbo.Orders AS O1
WHERE OrderID IN
  (SELECT TOP(3) OrderID
   FROM dbo.Orders AS O2
   WHERE O2.EmployeeID = O1.EmployeeID
   ORDER BY OrderDate DESC, OrderID DESC);
```

Now, let's go to the optimization technique. Remember you are attempting to give the optimizer a hint that you want one index seek operation per employee, not one per order. You can achieve this by querying the Employees table and retrieving the most recent *OrderID* for each employee. Create a derived table out of this query against Employees, and join the derived table to the Orders table on matching *OrderID* values. Listing 7-3 has the solution query, generating the execution plan shown in Figure 7-2.

Listing 7-3 Solution 2 to the Most Recent Order for Each Employee problem

```
SELECT O.OrderID, CustomerID, O.EmployeeID, OrderDate, RequiredDate
FROM (SELECT EmployeeID,
        (SELECT TOP(1) OrderID
         FROM dbo.Orders AS O2
         WHERE O2.EmployeeID = E.EmployeeID
         ORDER BY OrderDate DESC, OrderID DESC) AS TopOrder
      FROM dbo.Employees AS E) AS EO
  JOIN dbo.Orders AS O
    ON O.OrderID = EO.TopOrder;
```

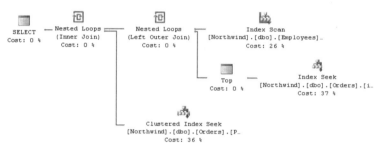

Figure 7-2 Execution plan for the query in Listing 7-3

You can see in the plan that one of the indexes on the Employees table is scanned to access the *EmployeeID*s. The next operator that appears in the plan (Nested Loops) drives a seek in the index on Orders to retrieve the ID of the employee's most recent order. With 9 employees, only 9 seek operations will be performed, compared to the previous 830 that were driven by the number of orders. Finally, another Nested Loops operator drives one seek per employee in the clustered index on *Orders.OrderID* to look up the attributes of the order from the *OrderID*. If the index on *OrderID* wasn't clustered, you would have seen an additional lookup to access the full data row. The I/O cost of this query is only 36 logical reads.

An attempt to regenerate the same success when you're after more than one order per employee is disappointing. Because you are not able to return more than one key in the SELECT list using a subquery, you might attempt to do something similar in a join condition between Employees and Orders. The solution query is shown in Listing 7-4.

Listing 7-4 Solution 3 to the Most Recent Orders for Each Employee problem

```
SELECT OrderID, CustomerID, E.EmployeeID, OrderDate, RequiredDate
FROM dbo.Employees AS E
  JOIN dbo.Orders AS O1
    ON OrderID IN
      (SELECT TOP(3) OrderID
       FROM dbo.Orders AS O2
       WHERE O2.EmployeeID = E.EmployeeID
       ORDER BY OrderDate DESC, OrderID DESC);
```

However, this solution yields the poor plan shown in Figure 7-3, generating 15,897 logical reads against the Orders table and 1661 logical reads against the Employees table. In this case, you'd be better off using the solution I showed earlier that supports returning multiple orders per employee.

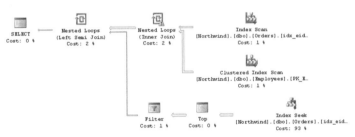

Figure 7-3 Execution plan for the query in Listing 7-4

So far, all solutions were SQL Server 2000 compatible (aside from the fact that in SQL Server 2000 you don't use parentheses with TOP, of course). In SQL Server 2005, you can use the APPLY operator in a solution that outperforms all other solutions I've shown thus far, and that also supports returning multiple orders per employee. You apply to the Employees table a table expression that returns, for a given row of the Employees table, the *n* most recent orders for the employee in that row. Listing 7-5 has the solution query, generating the execution plan shown in Figure 7-4.

Listing 7-5 Solution 4 to the Most Recent Orders for Each Employee problem

```
SELECT OrderID, CustomerID, EmployeeID, OrderDate, RequiredDate
FROM dbo.Employees AS E
  CROSS APPLY
    (SELECT TOP(3) OrderID, CustomerID, OrderDate, RequiredDate
     FROM dbo.Orders AS O
     WHERE O.EmployeeID = E.EmployeeID
     ORDER BY OrderDate DESC, OrderID DESC) AS A;
```

Figure 7-4 Execution plan for the query in Listing 7-5

The plan scans an index on the Employees table for the *EmployeeID* values. Each *EmployeeID* value drives a single seek within the covering index on Orders to return the requested most recent 3 orders for that employee. The interesting part here is that you don't get only the keys of the rows found; rather, this plan allows for returning multiple attributes. So there's no need for any additional activities to return the non-key attributes. The I/O cost of this query is only 18 logical reads.

Surprisingly, there's a solution that can be even faster than the one using the APPLY operator in certain circumstances that I'll describe shortly. The solution uses the ROW_NUMBER function. You calculate the row number of each order, partitioned by *EmployeeID*, and based on *OrderDate* DESC, *OrderID* DESC order. Then, in an outer query, you filter only results with a row number less than or equal to 3. The optimal index for this solution is similar to the covering index created earlier, but with the *OrderDate* and *OrderID* columns defined in descending order:

```
CREATE UNIQUE INDEX idx_eid_odD_oidD_i_cid_rd
  ON dbo.Orders(EmployeeID, OrderDate DESC, OrderID DESC)
    INCLUDE(CustomerID, RequiredDate);
```

Listing 7-6 has the solution query, generating the execution plan shown in Figure 7-5.

Listing 7-6 Solution 5 to the Most Recent Orders for Each Employee Problem

```
SELECT OrderID, CustomerID, OrderDate, RequiredDate
FROM (SELECT OrderID, CustomerID, OrderDate, RequiredDate,
        ROW_NUMBER() OVER(PARTITION BY EmployeeID
                          ORDER BY OrderDate DESC, OrderID DESC) AS RowNum
      FROM dbo.Orders) AS D
WHERE RowNum <= 3;
```

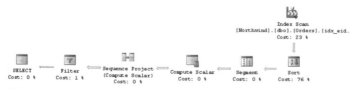

Figure 7-5 Execution plan for the query in Listing 7-6

I already described the execution plans generated for ranking functions in Chapter 4, and this one is very similar. The I/O cost here is only 7 logical reads caused by the single full scan of the covering index. Note that to calculate the row numbers here, the index must be fully scanned. With large tables, when you're seeking a small percentage of rows per group, the APPLY operator will be faster because the total cost of the multiple seek operations, one per group, will be lower than a full scan of the covering index.

There's an important advantage that the solutions using the APPLY operator and the ROW_NUMBER function have over the SQL Server 2000–compatible solutions using TOP. The SQL Server 2000–compatible solutions are supported only when the table at hand has a single column key because they rely on a subquery returning a scalar. The new solutions, on the other hand, are just as applicable with composite keys. For example, say you were after the top 3 order details for each order, with precedence determined by *Quantity* DESC, and where *ProductID* ASC is used as the tiebreaker ordering. The [Order Details] table has a composite primary key, (*OrderID*,*ProductID*), so you can't return a key for this table from a subquery. On the other hand, the APPLY operator doesn't rely on having a single-column key. It cares only about the correlation of the inner [Order Details] table to the outer Orders table based on *OrderID* match and on a sort based on *Quantity* DESC and *ProductID* ASC:

```
SELECT D.OrderID, ProductID, Quantity
FROM dbo.Orders AS O
  CROSS APPLY
    (SELECT TOP(3) OD.OrderID, ProductID, Quantity
     FROM [Order Details] AS OD
     WHERE OD.OrderID = O.OrderID
     ORDER BY Quantity DESC, ProductID) AS D;
```

Similarly, the ROW_NUMBER–based solution doesn't rely on having a single-column key. It simply calculates row numbers partitioned by *OrderID*, sorted by *Quantity* DESC and *ProductID* ASC:

```
SELECT OrderID, ProductID, Quantity
FROM (SELECT ROW_NUMBER() OVER(PARTITION BY OrderID
                               ORDER BY Quantity DESC, ProductID) AS RowNum,
          OrderID, ProductID, Quantity
       FROM dbo.[Order Details]) AS D
WHERE RowNum <= 3;
```

Matching Current and Previous Occurrences

Matching current and previous occurrences is yet another problem for which you can use the TOP option. The problem is matching to each "current" row, a row from the same table that is considered the "previous" row based on some ordering criteria—typically, time based. Such a request serves the need to make calculations involving measurements from both a "current" row and a "previous" row. Examples for such requests are calculating trends, differences, ratios, and so on. When you need to include only one value from the previous row for your calculation, use a simple TOP(1) subquery to get that value. But when you need multiple measurements from the previous row, it makes more sense in terms of performance to use a join, rather than multiple subqueries.

Suppose you need to match each employee's order with her previous order, using *OrderDate* to determine the previous order and using *OrderID* as a tiebreaker. Once the employee's orders are matched, you can request calculations involving attributes from both sides—for example, calculating differences between the current and previous order dates, required dates, and so on. For brevity's sake, I won't be showing the actual calculations of differences; rather, I'll just focus on the matching techniques. One solution is to join two instances of the Orders table: one representing the current rows (*Cur*), and the other representing the previous row (*Prv*). The join condition will match *Prv.OrderID* with the *OrderID* representing the previous order, which you return from a TOP(1) subquery. You use a LEFT OUTER join to keep the "first" order for each employee. An inner join would eliminate such orders because a match will not be found for them. Listing 7-7 has the solution query to the matching problem.

Listing 7-7 Query Solution 1 to the Matching Current and Previous Occurrences problem

```
SELECT Cur.EmployeeID,
  Cur.OrderID AS CurOrderID, Prv.OrderID AS PrvOrderID,
  Cur.OrderDate AS CurOrderDate, Prv.OrderDate AS PrvOrderDate,
  Cur.RequiredDate AS CurReqDate, Prv.RequiredDate AS PrvReqDate
FROM dbo.Orders AS Cur
  LEFT OUTER JOIN dbo.Orders AS Prv
    ON Prv.OrderID =
       (SELECT TOP(1) OrderID
        FROM dbo.Orders AS O
        WHERE O.EmployeeID = Cur.EmployeeID
          AND (O.OrderDate < Cur.OrderDate
               OR (O.OrderDate = Cur.OrderDate
                   AND O.OrderID < Cur.OrderID))
        ORDER BY OrderDate DESC, OrderID DESC)
ORDER BY Cur.EmployeeID, Cur.OrderDate, Cur.OrderID;
```

The subquery's filter is a bit tricky because ordering/precedence is determined by two attributes: *OrderDate* (ordering column) and *OrderID* (tiebreaker). Had the request been for precedence based on a single column—say, *OrderID* alone—the filter would have been much simpler—*O.OrderID* < *Cur.OrderID*. Because two attributes are involved, "previous" rows are identified with a logical expression that says: *inner_sort_col* < *outer_sort_col or (inner_sort_col = outer_sort_col and inner_tiebreaker < outer_tiebreaker*).

This query generates the execution plan shown in Figure 7-6, with an I/O cost of 3,533 logical reads.

Figure 7-6 Execution plan for the query in Listing 7-7

The plan first scans the covering index I created earlier on the key list (*EmployeeID*, *OrderDate*, *OrderID*), with the covered columns (*CustomerID*, *RequiredDate*) specified as included columns. This scan's purpose is to return the "current" rows. For each current row, a Nested Loops operator initiates an Index Seek operation in the same index, driven by the subquery to fetch the key (*OrderID*) of the "previous" row. For each returned previous *OrderID*, another Nested Loops operator retrieves the requested list of attributes of the previous row. You realize that one of the two seek operations is superfluous and there's potential for a revised query that would issue only one seek per current order.

In SQL Server 2000, you can try various query revisions that might improve performance. But because per outer row, a request with the TOP option can be initiated only in a subquery and not in a table expression, it is not simple to avoid two different activities per current order using TOP. Listing 7-8 has an example of a query revision that allows for the optimized plan shown in Figure 7-7, when the query is run in SQL Server 2005.

Listing 7-8   Query Solution 2 to the Matching Current and Previous Occurrences problem

```
SELECT Cur.EmployeeID,
  Cur.OrderID AS CurOrderID, Prv.OrderID AS PrvOrderID,
  Cur.OrderDate AS CurOrderDate, Prv.OrderDate AS PrvOrderDate,
  Cur.RequiredDate AS CurReqDate, Prv.RequiredDate AS PrvReqDate
FROM (SELECT EmployeeID, OrderID, OrderDate, RequiredDate,
        (SELECT TOP(1) OrderID
         FROM dbo.Orders AS O2
         WHERE O2.EmployeeID = O1.EmployeeID
           AND (O2.OrderDate < O1.OrderDate
               OR O2.OrderDate = O1.OrderDate
                   AND O2.OrderID < O1.OrderID)
           ORDER BY OrderDate DESC, OrderID DESC) AS PrvOrderID
      FROM dbo.Orders AS O1) AS Cur
  LEFT OUTER JOIN dbo.Orders AS Prv
    ON Cur.PrvOrderID = Prv.OrderID
ORDER BY Cur.EmployeeID, Cur.OrderDate, Cur.OrderID;
```

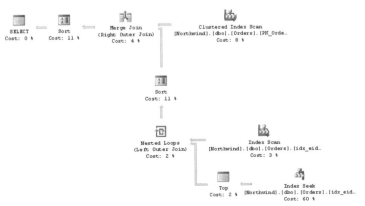

Figure 7-7   Execution plan for the query in Listing 7-8

This plan incurs an I/O cost of 2,033 logical reads (though in SQL Server 2000 you get a different plan with a higher I/O cost). The solution creates a derived table called *Cur* that contains current orders, with an additional column (*PrvOrderID*) holding the *OrderID* of the previous order as obtained by a correlated subquery. The outer query then joins *Cur* with another instance of Orders, aliased as *Prv*, which supplies the full list of attributes from the previous order. The performance improvement and the lower I/O cost is mainly the result of the Merge join algorithm that the plan uses. In the graphical query plan, the upper input to the Merge Join operator is the result of an ordered scan of the clustered index on *OrderID*, representing the "previous" orders, and this is the nonpreserved side of the outer join. The lower input is the result of scanning the covering index and fetching each previous *OrderID* with a seek operation followed by a Top 1. To prepare this input for a merge, the plan sorts the rows by *OrderID*.

A merge join turned out to be cost-effective here because the rows of the Orders table were presorted on the clustered index key column *OrderID* and it was not too much work to sort the other input in preparation for the merge. In larger production systems, things will most likely be different. With a much larger number of rows and a different clustered index—on a column that frequently appears in range queries, perhaps—you shouldn't expect to see the same query plan.

> **Note**   Keep in mind that the value of the performance discussions that I'm conducting in the book is in understanding how to read plans and how to write queries in more than one way. You might get different execution plans in different versions of SQL Server—as is the case with the query in Listing 7-8. The last paragraph described the plan that you get in SQL Server 2005, which is different than the one you would get in SQL Server 2000. Similarly, execution plans can change between service pack levels of the product. Also, remember that execution plans might vary when data distribution changes.

This is where the APPLY operator comes in handy. It often leads to simple and efficient plans that perform well even with large volumes of data. Using the APPLY operator in this case leads to a plan that scans the data once to get the current orders and performs a single index seek for each current order to fetch from the covering index all the attributes of the previous order at once.

Listing 7-9 has the solution query, which generates the plan shown in Figure 7-8, with an I/O cost of 2,011 logical reads.

Listing 7-9   Query Solution 3 to the Matching Current and Previous Occurrences problem

```
SELECT Cur.EmployeeID,
  Cur.OrderID AS CurOrderID, Prv.OrderID AS PrvOrderID,
  Cur.OrderDate AS CurOrderDate, Prv.OrderDate AS PrvOrderDate,
  Cur.RequiredDate AS CurReqDate, Prv.RequiredDate AS PrvReqDate
```

```
FROM dbo.Orders AS Cur
  OUTER APPLY
    (SELECT TOP(1) OrderID, OrderDate, RequiredDate
     FROM dbo.Orders AS O
     WHERE O.EmployeeID = Cur.EmployeeID
       AND (O.OrderDate < Cur.OrderDate
            OR (O.OrderDate = Cur.OrderDate
                AND O.OrderID < Cur.OrderID))
       ORDER BY OrderDate DESC, OrderID DESC) AS Prv
ORDER BY Cur.EmployeeID, Cur.OrderDate, Cur.OrderID;
```

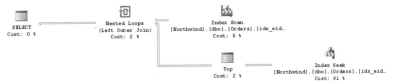

Figure 7-8   Execution plan for the query in Listing 7-9

But if you're not satisfied with "reasonable" performance and want a solution that really rocks, you will need the ROW_NUMBER function. You can create a CTE that calculates row numbers for orders partitioned by *EmployeeID* and based on *OrderDate, OrderID* ordering. Join two instances of the CTE, one representing the current orders and the other representing the previous orders. The join condition will be based on matching *EmployeeID* values and row numbers that differ by one. Listing 7-10 has the solution query, generating the execution plan shown in Figure 7-9.

Listing 7-10   Query Solution 4 to the Matching Current and Previous Occurrences problem

```
WITH OrdersRN AS
(
  SELECT EmployeeID, OrderID, OrderDate, RequiredDate,
    ROW_NUMBER() OVER(PARTITION BY EmployeeID
                      ORDER BY OrderDate, OrderID) AS rn
  FROM dbo.Orders
)
SELECT Cur.EmployeeID,
  Cur.OrderID AS CurOrderID, Prv.OrderID AS PrvOrderID,
  Cur.OrderDate AS CurOrderDate, Prv.OrderDate AS PrvOrderDate,
  Cur.RequiredDate AS CurReqDate, Prv.RequiredDate AS PrvReqDate
FROM OrdersRN AS Cur
  LEFT OUTER JOIN OrdersRN AS Prv
    ON Cur.EmployeeID = Prv.EmployeeID
    AND Cur.rn = Prv.rn + 1
ORDER BY Cur.EmployeeID, Cur.OrderDate, Cur.OrderID;
```

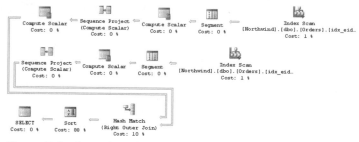

Figure 7-9   Execution plan for the query in Listing 7-10

Because the plan only scans the covering index twice to access the order attributes and calculate the row numbers, it incurs a total I/O cost of 14 logical reads, leaving all other solutions lagging far behind in terms of performance.

To clean up, run the following code, which drops indexes used for the solutions presented here:

```
DROP INDEX dbo.Orders.idx_eid_od_oid_i_cid_rd;
DROP INDEX dbo.Orders.idx_eid_odD_oidD_i_cid_rd;
DROP INDEX dbo.[Order Details].idx_oid_qtyd_pid;
```

Paging

I started talking about paging in Chapter 4, where I presented solutions based on row numbers. As a reminder, you're looking to return rows from the result set of a query in pages or chunks, allowing the user to navigate through the pages. In my examples, I used the Orders table in the Northwind database.

In production environments, paging typically involves dynamic filters and sorting based on user requests. To focus on the paging techniques, I'll assume no filters here and a desired order of *OrderDate* with *OrderID* as a tiebreaker.

The optimal index for the paging solutions that I'll present follows similar guidelines to other TOP solutions I presented—that is, an index on the sort column or columns and the tiebreaker column or columns. If you can afford to, make the index a covering index, either by making it the table's clustered index, or if it is nonclustered, by including the other columns mentioned in the query. Remember from Chapter 3 that in SQL Server 2005 an index can contain non-key columns, which are specified in the INCLUDE clause of the CREATE INDEX command. The non-key columns of an index appear only in the leaf level of the index. In SQL Server 2000, nonclustered indexes cannot include non-key columns. You must add additional columns to the key list if you want the index to cover the query, or you must make the index the table's clustered index. If you cannot afford a covering index, at least make sure that you create one on the *sort+tiebreaker* columns. The plans will be less efficient than with a covering one because lookups will be involved to obtain the data row, but at least you won't get a table scan for each page request.

For sorting by *OrderDate* and *OrderID*, and to cover the columns *CustomerID* and *EmployeeID*, create the following index:

```
CREATE INDEX idx_od_oid_i_cid_eid
  ON dbo.Orders(OrderDate, OrderID) INCLUDE(CustomerID, EmployeeID);
```

> **Note** In SQL Server 2000, remember to make all columns part of the key list, as the INCLUDE clause was introduced in SQL Server 2005.

The solution I'll present here supports paging through consecutive pages. That is, you request the first page and then proceed to the next. You might also want to provide the option to request a previous page. It is strongly recommended to implement the first, next, and previous page requests as stored procedures for both performance and encapsulation reasons. This way you can get efficient plan reuse, and you can always alter the implementation of the stored procedures if you find more efficient techniques, without affecting the users of the stored procedures.

First Page

Implementing the stored procedure that returns the first page is really simple because you don't need an anchor to mark the starting point. You simply return the number of rows requested from the top, like so:

```
CREATE PROC dbo.usp_firstpage
  @n AS INT = 10
AS
SELECT TOP(@n) OrderID, OrderDate, CustomerID, EmployeeID
FROM dbo.Orders
ORDER BY OrderDate, OrderID;
GO
```

> **Note** In this example, ORDER BY has two purposes: to specify what TOP means, and to control the order of rows in the result set.

Having an index on the sort columns, especially if it's a covering one like I created for this purpose, allows for an optimal plan where only the relevant page of rows is scanned within the index in order. You can see this by running the following stored procedure and examining the plan shown in Figure 7-10:

```
EXEC dbo.usp_firstpage;
```

Figure 7-10 Execution plan for stored procedure dbo.usp_firstpage

Rows are scanned within the index, starting with the head of the linked list and moving forward in an ordered fashion. The Top operator stops the scan as soon as the requested number of rows was accessed.

Next Page

The request for a "next" page has to rely on some anchor row that marks where the page should start. This anchor should be provided to the stored procedure as input. The anchor could be the sort column values of the last row on the previous page because, as you might remember, for determinism purposes the sort values must be unique. In the client application, you already retrieved the previous page. So you can simply set aside the sort column values from the last row in the previous page. When you get a request for the next page, you can provide those as an input to the stored procedure.

Bearing in mind that, in practice, filters and sorting are usually dynamic, you can't rely on any particular number or type of columns as input parameters. So a smarter design, which would accommodate later enhancement of the procedure to support dynamic execution, would be to provide the primary key as input, and not the sort column values. The client application would set aside the primary key value from the last row it retrieved and use it as input to the next invocation of the stored procedure.

Here's the implementation of the usp_nextpage stored procedure:

```
CREATE PROC dbo.usp_nextpage
  @anchor AS INT, -- key of last row in prev page
  @n AS INT = 10
AS
SELECT TOP(@n) O.OrderID, O.OrderDate, O.CustomerID, O.EmployeeID
FROM dbo.Orders AS O
  JOIN dbo.Orders AS A
    ON A.OrderID = @anchor
    AND (O.OrderDate > A.OrderDate
        OR (O.OrderDate = A.OrderDate
            AND O.OrderID > A.OrderID))
ORDER BY O.OrderDate, O.OrderID;
GO
```

The procedure joins the two instances of the orders table: one called O, representing the next page, and one called A, representing the anchor. The join condition first filters the anchor instance with the input key, and then it filters the instance representing the next page so that only rows following the anchor will be returned. The columns *OrderDate* and *OrderID* determine precedence both in terms of the logical expression in the ON clause that filters rows following the anchor, and in terms of the ORDER BY clause that TOP relies on. To test the stored procedure, first execute it with the *OrderID* from the last row returned from the first page (10257) as the anchor. Then execute it again with the *OrderID* of the last row in the second page (10267) as the anchor:

```
EXEC dbo.usp_nextpage @anchor = 10257;
EXEC dbo.usp_nextpage @anchor = 10267;
```

Remember that the client application iterates through the rows it got back from SQL Server, so naturally it can pick up the key from the last row and use it as input to the next invocation of the stored procedure.

Both procedure calls yield the same execution plan, which is shown in Figure 7-11.

Figure 7-11   Execution plan for the stored procedure usp_nextpage

You will see a single seek operation within the clustered index to fetch the anchor row, followed by an ordered scan within the covering index to fetch the next page of rows. That's not a very efficient plan. Ideally, the optimizer would have performed a seek within the covering index to the first row from the desired page of orders; then it would have followed with a partial ordered scan to grab the rest of the rows in the desired page of orders, physically accessing only the relevant rows. The reason for getting an inefficient plan is because the filter has an OR operator between the expression *O.OrderDate > A.OrderDate*, and the expression *O.OrderDate = A.OrderDate AND O.OrderID > A.OrderID*. See the sidebar "Logical Transformations" for details about OR optimization vs. AND optimization. Following the sidebar, I'll provide the optimized implementation of the stored procedure using AND logic.

Logical Transformations

In several solutions I've presented, I used logical expressions with an OR operator to deal with precedence based on multiple attributes. Such was the case in the recent solutions for paging, matching current and previous occurrences, and other problems. I used OR logic because this is how human minds are accustomed to thinking. The logical expressions using OR logic are fairly intuitive for the purpose of determining precedence and identifying rows that follow a certain anchor.

However, because of the way SQL Server's optimizer works, OR logic is problematic in terms of performance, especially when some of the filtered columns are not indexed. Consider for example a filter such as *col1 = 5 OR col2 = 10*. If you have individual indexes on *col1* and *col2*, the optimizer can filter the rows in each index and then perform an index intersection between the two. However, if you have an index on only one of the columns, even when the filter is very selective, the index is useless. SQL Server would still need to scan the whole table to see whether rows that didn't match the first filter qualify for the second condition.

On the other hand, AND logic has much better performance potential. With each expression, you narrow down the result set. Rows filtered by one index are already a superset of the rows you'll end up returning. So an index on any of the filtered columns can potentially be used to advantage. Whether or not it is worthwhile to use the existing index is a matter of selectivity, but the potential is there. For example, consider the filter *col1 = 5 AND col2 = 10*. The optimal index here is a composite one created on both columns. However, if you have an index on only one of them, and it's selective enough, that's sufficient already. SQL Server can filter the data through that index, and then look up the rows and examine whether they also meet the second condition.

In this chapter, the logical expressions I used in my solutions used OR logic to identify rows following a given anchor. For example, say you're looking at the row with an *OrderID* of 11075, and you're supposed to identify the rows that follow, where precedence is based on *OrderDate* and *OrderID* is the tiebreaker. The *OrderDate* of the anchor is '19980506'. A query returning the rows that come after this anchor row is very selective. I used the following logic to filter these rows:

```
OrderDate > '19980506' OR (OrderDate = '19980506' AND OrderID > 11075)
```

Say that you could afford creating only one index, on *OrderDate*. Such an index is not sufficient in the eyes of the optimizer to filter the relevant rows because the logical expression referring to *OrderDate* is followed by an OR operator, with the right side of the operator referring to other columns (*OrderID*, in this case). Such a filter would yield a table scan. You can perform a logical transformation here and end up with an equivalent expression that uses AND logic. Here's the transformed expression:

```
OrderDate >= '19980506' AND (OrderDate > '19980506' OR OrderID > 11075)
```

Instead of specifying *OrderDate > '19980506'*, you specify *OrderDate >= '19980506'*. Now you can use an AND operator and request either rows where the *OrderDate* is greater than the anchor's *OrderDate* (meaning the *OrderDate* is not equal to the anchor's *OrderDate*, in which case you don't care about the value of *OrderID*); or the *OrderID* is greater than the anchor's *OrderID* (meaning the *OrderDate* is equal to the anchor's *OrderDate*). The logical expressions are equivalent. However, the transformed one has the form *OrderDate_comparison* AND *other_logical_expression*—meaning that now an index on *OrderDate* alone can be considered. To put these words into action, first create a table called MyOrders containing the same data as the Orders table, and an index only on *OrderDate*:

```
IF OBJECT_ID('dbo.MyOrders') IS NOT NULL
  DROP TABLE dbo.MyOrders;
GO
SELECT * INTO dbo.MyOrders FROM dbo.Orders
CREATE INDEX idx_dt ON dbo.MyOrders(OrderDate);
```

Next, run the query in Listing 7-11, which uses OR logic, and examine the plan shown in Figure 7-12.

Listing 7-11   Query using OR logic

```
SELECT OrderID, OrderDate, CustomerID, EmployeeID
FROM dbo.MyOrders
WHERE OrderDate > '19980506'
    OR (OrderDate = '19980506' AND OrderID > 11075);
```

Figure 7-12   Execution plan for the query in Listing 7-11

You will see a table scan, which in the case of this table costs 21 logical reads. Of course, with more realistic table sizes you will see substantially more I/O.

Next, run the query in Listing 7-12, which uses AND logic, and examine the plan shown in Figure 7-13.

Listing 7-12   Query using AND logic

```
SELECT OrderID, OrderDate, CustomerID, EmployeeID
FROM dbo.MyOrders
WHERE OrderDate >= '19980506'
    AND (OrderDate > '19980506' OR OrderID > 11075);
```

Figure 7-13   Execution plan for the query in Listing 7-12

You will see that the index on *OrderDate* is used, and the I/O cost of this query is 6 logical reads. Creating an index on both columns (*OrderDate, OrderID*) is even better:

```
CREATE INDEX idx_dt_oid ON dbo.MyOrders(OrderDate, OrderID);
```

Run the query in Listing 7-11, which uses the OR logic. You will see in the plan, shown in Figure 7-14, that the new index is used. The I/O cost for this plan is 6 logical reads.

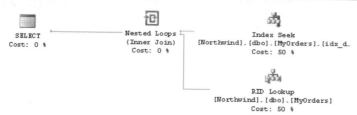

Figure 7-14   Execution plan for the query in Listing 7-11, with the new index in place

Run the query in Listing 7-12, which uses the AND logic. You will see the plan shown in Figure 7-15, which might seem similar, but it yields even a lower I/O cost of only 4 logical reads.

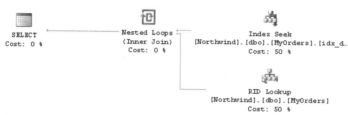

Figure 7-15   Execution plan for the query in Listing 7-12, with the new index in place

The conclusion is, of course, that SQL server can optimize AND logic better than OR logic. All the solutions I presented in this chapter would be better off in terms of performance if you transformed their OR logic to AND logic. Similarly, you might be able to achieve such transformations with other logical expressions.

Another conclusion is that it's better to have an index on all columns determining precedence. The problem is that in production environments you can't always afford it.

> **Note**   When discussing subjects that involve logic, I like to use small tables such as those in Northwind, with simple and recognizable data. With such tables, the differences in logical reads that you see when testing your solutions are small. In real performance tests and benchmarks, you should use more realistic table sizes as your test data, such as the test data I used in Chapter 3. For example, using the usp_nextpage procedure, which returns the next page of orders, you will see very small I/O differences between OR logic and the AND logic, as I'll present shortly. But when I tested the solution against an Orders table with about a million rows, the OR implementation costs more than a thousand logical reads, while the AND implementation costs only 11 logical reads, physically accessing only the relevant page of orders.

When you're done, don't forget to get rid of the MyOrders table created for these examples:

```
IF OBJECT_ID('dbo.MyOrders') IS NOT NULL
  DROP TABLE dbo.MyOrders;
```

Back to our usp_nextpage procedure, here's the optimized implementation that transforms the OR logic to AND logic:

```
ALTER PROC dbo.usp_nextpage
  @anchor AS INT, -- key of last row in prev page
  @n AS INT = 10
AS
SELECT TOP(@n) O.OrderID, O.OrderDate, O.CustomerID, O.EmployeeID
FROM dbo.Orders AS O
  JOIN dbo.Orders AS A
    ON A.OrderID = @anchor
    AND (O.OrderDate >= A.OrderDate
        AND (O.OrderDate > A.OrderDate
            OR O.OrderID > A.OrderID))
ORDER BY O.OrderDate, O.OrderID;
GO
```

Notice that the AND expression within the parentheses is logically equivalent to the previous OR expression; I just implemented the techniques described in the Logical Transformations sidebar. To show that the AND implementation is really optimized better, run the following code and examine the execution plan shown in Figure 7-16:

```
EXEC dbo.usp_nextpage @anchor = 10257;
```

Figure 7-16   Execution plan for the stored procedure usp_nextpage—second version

Now you get the desired plan. You see a single seek operation within the clustered index to fetch the anchor row, followed by a seek within the covering index and a partial ordered scan, physically accessing only the relevant rows in the desired page of orders.

Previous Page

There are two approaches to dealing with requests for previous pages. One is to locally cache pages already retrieved to the client. This means that you need to develop a caching mechanism in the client. A simpler approach is to implement another stored procedure that works like the usp_nextpage procedure in reverse. The anchor parameter will be the key of the first row after the page you want. The comparisons within the procedure will use < instead of >, and the TOP clause will use an ORDER BY list that defines the opposite sorting direction. If these were the only changes, you would get the correct page, but in reverse order from normal. To fix the ordering of the result set, encapsulate the query as a derived table, and apply SELECT ... ORDER BY to this derived table, with the desired ordering.

Here's the implementation of the usp_prevpage procedure:

```
CREATE PROC dbo.usp_prevpage
  @anchor AS INT, -- key of first row in next page
  @n AS INT = 10
AS
SELECT OrderID, OrderDate, CustomerID, EmployeeID
FROM (SELECT TOP(@n) O.OrderID, O.OrderDate, O.CustomerID, O.EmployeeID
      FROM dbo.Orders AS O
        JOIN dbo.Orders AS A
          ON A.OrderID = @anchor
          AND (O.OrderDate <= A.OrderDate
              AND (O.OrderDate < A.OrderDate
                  OR O.OrderID < A.OrderID))
      ORDER BY O.OrderDate DESC, O.OrderID DESC) AS D
ORDER BY OrderDate, OrderID;
GO
```

To test the procedure, run it with *OrderID* values from the first rows on the pages you already got:

```
EXEC dbo.usp_prevpage @anchor = 10268;
EXEC dbo.usp_prevpage @anchor = 10258;
```

Examine the execution plan shown in Figure 7-17, produced for the execution of the usp_prevpage procedure.

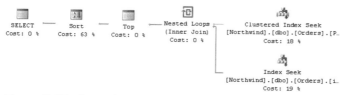

Figure 7-17 Execution plan for the previous page

You will find an almost identical plan to the one produced for the usp_nextpage procedure, with an additional Sort operator, which is a result of the extra ORDER BY clause in the usp_prevpage procedure.

Here I wanted to focus on paging techniques using the TOP option. Remember that the topic is also covered in Chapter 4, where I show paging solutions based on row numbers.

When you're finished, drop the covered index created for the paging solutions:

```
DROP INDEX dbo.Orders.idx_od_oid_i_cid_eid;
```

Tip When using solutions such as the ones in this section, changes in the underlying data will be reflected in requests for new pages. That is, if rows are added, deleted, or updated, new page requests will be submitted against the current version of the data—not to mention the possible failure of the procedure altogether, if the anchor key is gone. If this behavior is undesirable to you and you'd rather iterate through pages against a static view of the data, you can create a database snapshot right before answering page requests. Submit your paging queries against the snapshot, and get rid of the snapshot as soon as the user finishes.

For details about database snapshots please refer to *Inside Microsoft SQL Server 2005: The Storage Engine* by Kalen Delaney (Microsoft Press, 2006).

Random Rows

This section covers another class of problems that you can solve with the TOP option—returning rows in a random fashion. Dealing with randomness in T-SQL is quite tricky. Typical requests for randomness involve returning a random row from a table, sorting rows in random order, and the like. The first attempt you might make when asked to return a random row might be to use the RAND function as follows:

```
SELECT TOP(1) OrderID, OrderDate, CustomerID, EmployeeID
FROM dbo.Orders
ORDER BY RAND();
```

However, if you try running this query several times, you will probably be disappointed to find that you're not really getting a random row. RAND, as well as most other nondeterministic functions (for example, GETDATE) are invoked once per query, not once per row. So you end up getting the same value of RAND for every row, and the ORDER BY clause does not affect the ordering of the query's result set.

Tip You might be surprised to find that the RAND function—when given an integer seed as input—is not really nondeterministic; rather, it's sort of a hash function. Given the same seed, RAND(<seed>) will always yield the same result. For example, run the following code multiple times:

```
SELECT RAND (5);
```

You will always get back 0.713666525097956. And if that's not enough, when you don't specify a seed, SQL Server doesn't really choose a random seed. Rather, the new seed is based on the previous invocation of RAND. Hence, running the following code multiple times will always yield the same two results (0.713666525097956 and 0.454560299686459):

```
SELECT RAND(5);
SELECT RAND();
```

The most important use of RAND(<seed>) is probably to create reproducible sample data, because you can seed it once and then call it repeatedly without a seed to get a well-distributed sequence of values.

If you're seeking a random value, you will have much better success with the following expression:

```
SELECT CHECKSUM(NEWID());
```

> **Note** The NEWID function appears to have good distribution properties; however, to date, I haven't found any documentation from Microsoft that specifies that this is guaranteed or supported.

An interesting behavior of the NEWID function is that unlike other nondeterministic functions, NEWID is evaluated separately for each row if you invoke it in a query. Bearing this in mind, you can get a random row by using the preceding expression in the ORDER BY clause as follows:

```
SELECT TOP(1) OrderID, OrderDate, CustomerID, EmployeeID
FROM dbo.Orders
ORDER BY CHECKSUM(NEWID());
```

This gives me an opportunity to present another example for using the new functionality of TOP, which allows you to specify a self-contained expression as an input. The following query also returns a random row:

```
SELECT TOP(1) OrderID, OrderDate, CustomerID, EmployeeID
FROM (SELECT TOP(100e0*(CHECKSUM(NEWID()) + 2147483649)/4294967296e0) PERCENT
        OrderID, OrderDate, CustomerID, EmployeeID
      FROM dbo.Orders
      ORDER BY OrderID) AS D
ORDER BY OrderID DESC;
```

CHECKSUM returns an integer between 2147483648 and 2147483647. Adding 2147483649 and then dividing by the float value 4294967296e0 yields a random number in the range 0 through 1 (excluding 0). Multiplying this random number by 100 returns a random float value greater than 0 and less than or equal to 100. Remember that the TOP PERCENT option accepts a float percentage in the range 0 through 100, and it rounds up the number of returned rows. A percentage greater than 0 guarantees that at least one row will be returned. The query creating the derived table D thus returns a random number of rows from the table based on *OrderID* (primary key) sort. The outer query then simply returns the last row from the derived table—that is, the one with the greatest *OrderID* values. This solution is not necessarily more efficient than the previous one I presented, but it was a good opportunity to show how the new features of TOP can be used.

With the new APPLY operator, you can now answer other randomness requests easily and efficiently, without the need to explicitly apply iterative logic. For example, the following query returns three random orders for each employee:

```
SELECT OrderID, CustomerID, EmployeeID, OrderDate, RequiredDate
FROM dbo.Employees AS E
```

```
CROSS APPLY
  (SELECT TOP(3) OrderID, CustomerID, OrderDate, RequiredDate
   FROM dbo.Orders AS O
   WHERE O.EmployeeID = E.EmployeeID
   ORDER BY CHECKSUM(NEWID())) AS A;
```

Median

In Chapter 6 in the "Custom Aggregations" section, I discussed techniques to calculate the median value for each group based on the ROW_NUMBER function. Here I'll present techniques relying on TOP that on one hand are slower, but on the other hand are applicable in SQL Server 2000 as well. First run the code in Listing 7-13 to create the Groups table that I used in my previous solutions to obtain a median.

Listing 7-13   Creating and populating the Groups table

```
USE tempdb;
GO
IF OBJECT_ID('dbo.Groups') IS NOT NULL
  DROP TABLE dbo.Groups;
GO

CREATE TABLE dbo.Groups
(
  groupid  VARCHAR(10) NOT NULL,
  memberid INT         NOT NULL,
  string   VARCHAR(10) NOT NULL,
  val      INT         NOT NULL,
  PRIMARY KEY (groupid, memberid)
);

INSERT INTO dbo.Groups(groupid, memberid, string, val)
  VALUES('a', 3, 'stra1', 6);
INSERT INTO dbo.Groups(groupid, memberid, string, val)
  VALUES('a', 9, 'stra2', 7);
INSERT INTO dbo.Groups(groupid, memberid, string, val)
  VALUES('b', 2, 'strb1', 3);
INSERT INTO dbo.Groups(groupid, memberid, string, val)
  VALUES('b', 4, 'strb2', 7);
INSERT INTO dbo.Groups(groupid, memberid, string, val)
  VALUES('b', 5, 'strb3', 3);
INSERT INTO dbo.Groups(groupid, memberid, string, val)
  VALUES('b', 9, 'strb4', 11);
INSERT INTO dbo.Groups(groupid, memberid, string, val)
  VALUES('c', 3, 'strc1', 8);
INSERT INTO dbo.Groups(groupid, memberid, string, val)
  VALUES('c', 7, 'strc2', 10);
INSERT INTO dbo.Groups(groupid, memberid, string, val)
  VALUES('c', 9, 'strc3', 12);
GO
```

Remember that median is the middle value (assuming a sorted list) when the group has an odd number of elements, and it's the average of the two middle values when it has an even number.

It's always a good idea to handle each case separately, and then try to figure out whether the solutions can be merged. So first, assume there's an odd number of elements. You can use a TOP(50) PERCENT query to access the first half of the elements, including the middle one. Remember that the PERCENT option rounds up. Then simply query the maximum value from the returned result set.

Now handle the even case. The same query you use to get the middle value from an odd number of rows will produce the largest value of the first half of an even number of rows. You can then write a similar query to return the smallest value of the second half. Sum the two values, divide by two, and you have the median in the even case.

Now try to figure out whether the two solutions can be merged. Interestingly, running the solution for the even case against an odd number of elements yields the correct result, because both subqueries used in the even case solution will end up returning the same row when there is an odd number of rows. The average of two values that are equal is obviously the same value.

Here's what the solution looks like when you want to return the median of the *val* column for the whole table:

```
SELECT
  ((SELECT MAX(val)
    FROM (SELECT TOP(50) PERCENT val
          FROM dbo.Groups
          ORDER BY val) AS M1)
   +
   (SELECT MIN(val)
    FROM (SELECT TOP(50) PERCENT val
          FROM dbo.Groups
          ORDER BY val DESC) AS M2))
  /2. AS median;
```

To return the median for each group, you need an outer query that groups the data by *groupid*. For each group, you invoke the calculation of the median in a subquery like so:

```
SELECT groupid,
  ((SELECT MAX(val)
    FROM (SELECT TOP(50) PERCENT val
          FROM dbo.Groups AS H1
          WHERE H1.groupid = G.groupid
          ORDER BY val) AS M1)
   +
```

```
        (SELECT MIN(val)
          FROM (SELECT TOP(50) PERCENT val
                FROM dbo.Groups AS H2
                WHERE H2.groupid = G.groupid
                ORDER BY val DESC) AS M2))
    /2. AS median
FROM dbo.Groups AS G
GROUP BY groupid;
```

This query works in SQL Server 2000 with two small modifications: first, you must write TOP
50 PERCENT instead of TOP(50) PERCENT, and second, to work around an unexpected
behavior of queries that use GROUP BY together with subqueries, you must use SELECT DIS-
TINCT instead of GROUP BY to produce just one result row per group. Here is the solution
for SQL Server 2000:

```
SELECT DISTINCT groupid,
  ((SELECT MAX(val)
      FROM (SELECT TOP 50 PERCENT val
            FROM dbo.Groups AS H1
            WHERE H1.groupid = G.groupid
            ORDER BY val) AS M1)
    +
    (SELECT MIN(val)
      FROM (SELECT TOP 50 PERCENT val
            FROM dbo.Groups AS H2
            WHERE H2.groupid = G.groupid
            ORDER BY val DESC) AS M2))
    /2. AS median
FROM dbo.Groups AS G;
```

Conclusion

As you probably realized from this chapter, TOP and APPLY are two features that in many
ways complement each other. TOP with its new capabilities now allows expressions as input
and is supported with modification statements. The new TOP functionality replaces the older
SET ROWCOUNT option. The new APPLY operator allows for very simple and fast queries,
compared to the previous alternatives, whenever you need to apply a table expression to each
row of an outer query.

Chapter 8
Data Modification

This chapter covers different facets of data modification. I'll discuss logical aspects such as inserting new rows and removing rows with duplicate data and performance aspects such as dealing with large volumes of data. Note that I covered some aspects of data modification in other chapters where they fit the subject matter better. You can find coverage of modifications with TOP in Chapter 7 and of the BULK rowset provider, tempdb, and transactions in *Inside Microsoft SQL Server 2005: T-SQL Programming* (Microsoft Press, 2006). I organized this chapter in sections based on the three main types of data modification activities: inserting data, deleting data, and updating data. As usual for this book, I'll cover solutions in Microsoft SQL Server 2000 as well as enhancements in SQL Server 2005.

Inserting Data

In this section, I'll cover several subjects related to inserting data, including: SELECT INTO, INSERT EXEC, inserting new rows, INSERT with OUTPUT, and sequence mechanisms.

SELECT INTO

SELECT INTO is a statement that creates a new table containing the result set of a query, instead of returning the result set to the caller. For example, the following statement creates a temporary table called #MyShippers and populates it with all rows from the Shippers table in the Northwind database:

```
SELECT ShipperID, CompanyName, Phone
INTO #MyShippers
FROM Northwind.dbo.Shippers;
```

SELECT INTO is a BULK operation. (See the "Other Performance Considerations" section at the end of the chapter for details.) Therefore, when the database recovery model is not FULL, it's very fast compared to the alternative of creating a table and then using INSERT INTO.

The columns of the new table inherit their names, datatypes, nullability, and IDENTITY property from the query's result set. SELECT INTO doesn't copy constraints, indexes, or triggers from the query's source. If you need the results in a table with the same indexes, constraints, and triggers as the source, you have to add them afterwards.

If you need a "fast and dirty" empty copy of some table, SELECT INTO allows you to obtain such a copy very simply. You don't have to script the CREATE TABLE statement and change the table's name. All you need to do is issue the following statement:

```
SELECT * INTO target_table FROM source_table WHERE 1 = 2;
```

The optimizer is smart enough to realize that no source row will satisfy the filter $1 = 2$. Therefore, SQL Server won't bother to physically access the source data; rather, it will create the target table based on the schema of the source. Here's an example that creates a table called MyOrders in tempdb, based on the schema of the Orders table in Northwind:

```
SET NOCOUNT ON;
USE tempdb;
GO
IF OBJECT_ID('dbo.MyOrders') IS NOT NULL
  DROP TABLE dbo.MyOrders;
GO

SELECT *
INTO dbo.MyOrders
FROM Northwind.dbo.Orders
WHERE 1 = 2;
```

Keep in mind that if a source column has the IDENTITY property, the target will have it as well. For example, the *OrderID* column in the Orders table has the IDENTITY property. If you don't want the IDENTITY property to be copied to the target column, simply apply any type of manipulation to the source column. For example, you can use the expression *OrderID + 0 AS OrderID* as follows:

```
IF OBJECT_ID('dbo.MyOrders') IS NOT NULL
  DROP TABLE dbo.MyOrders;
GO

SELECT OrderID+0 AS OrderID, CustomerID, EmployeeID, OrderDate,
  RequiredDate, ShippedDate, ShipVia, Freight, ShipName,
  ShipAddress, ShipCity, ShipRegion, ShipPostalCode, ShipCountry
INTO dbo.MyOrders
FROM Northwind.dbo.Orders
WHERE 1 = 2;
```

In this case, the *OrderID* column in the target MyOrders table doesn't have the IDENTITY property.

> **Tip**   Suppose you want to insert the result set of a stored procedure or a dynamic batch into a new table, but you don't know what the schema is that you need to create. You can use a SELECT INTO statement, specifying OPENQUERY in the FROM clause, referring to your own server as if it were a linked server:
>
> ```
> EXEC sp_serveroption <your_server>, 'data access', true;
> SELECT * INTO <target_table>
> FROM OPENQUERY(<your_server>,
>   'EXEC {<proc_name> | (<dynamic_batch>)}') AS O;
> ```

INSERT EXEC

The INSERT EXEC statement allows you to direct a table result set returned from a stored procedure or dynamic batch to an existing table:

```
INSERT INTO <target_table> EXEC {<proc_name> | (<dynamic_batch>)};
```

This statement is very handy when you need to set aside the result set of a stored procedure or dynamic batch for further processing at the server, as opposed to just returning the result set back to the client.

I'll demonstrate practical uses of the INSERT EXEC statement through an example. Recall the discussion about paging techniques in Chapter 7. I provided a stored procedure called *usp_firstpage*, which returns the first page of orders based on *OrderDate, OrderID* ordering. I also provided a stored procedure called *usp_nextpage*, which returns the next page of orders based on an input key (*@anchor*) representing the last row in the previous page. In this section, I will use slightly revised forms of the stored procedures, which I'll call *usp_firstrows* and *usp_nextrows*. Run the code in Listing 8-1 to create both procedures.

Listing 8-1   Creation script for paging stored procedures

```
USE Northwind;
GO


-- Index for paging problem
IF INDEXPROPERTY(OBJECT_ID('dbo.Orders'),
    'idx_od_oid_i_cid_eid', 'IndexID') IS NOT NULL
  DROP INDEX dbo.Orders.idx_od_oid_i_cid_eid;
GO
CREATE INDEX idx_od_oid_i_cid_eid
  ON dbo.Orders(OrderDate, OrderID, CustomerID, EmployeeID);
GO


-- First Rows
IF OBJECT_ID('dbo.usp_firstrows') IS NOT NULL
  DROP PROC dbo.usp_firstrows;
GO
CREATE PROC dbo.usp_firstrows
  @n AS INT = 10 -- num rows
AS
```

```
SELECT TOP(@n) ROW_NUMBER() OVER(ORDER BY OrderDate, OrderID) AS RowNum,
  OrderID, OrderDate, CustomerID, EmployeeID
FROM dbo.Orders
ORDER BY OrderDate, OrderID;
GO


-- Next Rows
IF OBJECT_ID('dbo.usp_nextrows') IS NOT NULL
  DROP PROC dbo.usp_nextrows;
GO
CREATE PROC dbo.usp_nextrows
  @anchor_rownum  AS INT = 0, -- row number of last row in prev page
  @anchor_key     AS INT,     -- key of last row in prev page,
  @n              AS INT = 10 -- num rows
AS
SELECT TOP(@n)
  @anchor_rownum
    + ROW_NUMBER() OVER(ORDER BY O.OrderDate, O.OrderID) AS RowNum,
  O.OrderID, O.OrderDate, O.CustomerID, O.EmployeeID
FROM dbo.Orders AS O
  JOIN dbo.Orders AS A
    ON A.OrderID = @anchor_key
    AND (O.OrderDate >= A.OrderDate
        AND (O.OrderDate > A.OrderDate
              OR O.OrderID > A.OrderID))
ORDER BY O.OrderDate, O.OrderID;
GO
```

> **Note** The stored procedures use new features in SQL Server 2005, so you won't be able to create them in SQL Server 2000.

The stored procedure *usp_firstrows* returns the first @n rows of Orders, based on *OrderDate* and *OrderID* ordering. In addition to the columns that *usp_firstpage* returned, *usp_firstrows* (as well as *usp_nextrows*) also returns *RowNum*, a column representing the global logical position of the row in the full Orders table under the aforementioned ordering. Because *usp_firstrows* returns the first page of rows, *RowNum* is just the row number within the result set.

The stored procedure *usp_nextrows* returns the @n rows following an anchor row, whose key is provided as input (*@anchor_key*). For a row in the result set of *usp_nextrows*, *RowNum* equals the anchor's global row number (*@anchor_rownum*) plus the result row's logical position within the qualifying set. If you don't want the stored procedure to return a global row number—rather, just the row number within the qualifying set—don't specify a value in the input parameter. In such a case, the default 0 will be used as the anchor row number, and the minimum row number that will be assigned will be 1.

Suppose you want to allow the user to request any range of rows without limiting the solution to forward-only paging. You also want to avoid rescanning large portions of data from the

Orders table. You need to develop some caching mechanism where you set aside a copy of the rows you already scanned, along with row numbers representing their global logical position throughout the pages. Upon a request for a range of rows (a page), you first check whether rows are missing from the cache. In such a case, you insert the missing rows into the cache. You then query the cache to return the requested page. Here's an example of how you can implement a server-side solution of such a mechanism.

Run the following code to create the #CachedPages temporary table:

```
IF OBJECT_ID('tempdb..#CachedPages') IS NOT NULL
  DROP TABLE #CachedPages;
GO
CREATE TABLE #CachedPages
(
  RowNum     INT NOT NULL PRIMARY KEY,
  OrderID    INT NOT NULL UNIQUE,
  OrderDate  DATETIME,
  CustomerID NCHAR(5),
  EmployeeID INT
);
```

The caching logic is encapsulated in the stored procedure *usp_getpage*, which you create by running the code in Listing 8-2.

Listing 8-2   Creation script for the stored procedure *usp_getpage*

```
IF OBJECT_ID('dbo.usp_getpage') IS NOT NULL
  DROP PROC dbo.usp_getpage;
GO
CREATE PROC dbo.usp_getpage
  @from_rownum AS INT,        -- row number of first row in requested page
  @to_rownum   AS INT,        -- row number of last row in requested page
  @rc          AS INT OUTPUT  -- number of rows returned
AS

SET NOCOUNT ON;

DECLARE
  @last_key    AS INT, -- key of last row in #CachedPages
  @last_rownum AS INT, -- row number of last row in #CachedPages
  @numrows     AS INT; -- number of missing rows in #CachedPages

-- Get anchor values from last cached row
SELECT @last_rownum = RowNum, @last_key = OrderID
FROM (SELECT TOP(1) RowNum, OrderID
      FROM #CachedPages ORDER BY RowNum DESC) AS D;

-- If temporary table is empty insert first rows to #CachedPages
IF @last_rownum IS NULL
  INSERT INTO #CachedPages
    EXEC dbo.usp_firstrows
      @n = @to_rownum;
ELSE
```

```
  BEGIN
    SET @numrows = @to_rownum - @last_rownum;

    IF @numrows > 0
      INSERT INTO #CachedPages
        EXEC dbo.usp_nextrows
          @anchor_rownum = @last_rownum,
          @anchor_key    = @last_key,
          @n             = @numrows;
  END

  -- Return requested page
  SELECT *
  FROM #CachedPages
  WHERE RowNum BETWEEN @from_rownum AND @to_rownum
  ORDER BY RowNum;

  SET @rc = @@rowcount;
  GO
```

The stored procedure accepts the row numbers representing the first row in the requested page (*@from_rownum*) and the last (*@to_rownum*) as inputs. Besides returning the requested page of rows, the stored procedure also returns an output parameter holding the number of rows returned (*@rc*). You can inspect the output parameter to determine whether you've reached the last page.

The stored procedure's code first queries the #CachedPages temporary table in order to store aside in the local variables *@last_rownum* and *@last_key* the row number and key of the last cached row, respectively. If the temporary table is empty (*@last_rownum IS NULL*), the code invokes the *usp_firstrows* procedure with an INSERT EXEC statement to populate #CachedPages with the first rows up to the requested high boundary row number. If the temporary table already contains rows, the code checks whether rows from the requested page are missing from it (*@to_rownum - @last_rownum > 0*). In such a case, the code invokes the *usp_nextrows* procedure to insert all missing rows up to the requested high boundary row number to the temporary table.

Finally, the code queries the #CachedPages temporary table to return the requested range of rows, and it stores the number of returned rows in the output parameter *@rc*.

To get the first page of rows, assuming a page size of 10, run the following code:

```
DECLARE @rc AS INT;

EXEC dbo.usp_getpage
  @from_rownum = 1,
  @to_rownum   = 10,
  @rc          = @rc OUTPUT;
```

```
IF @rc = 0
  PRINT 'No more pages.'
ELSE IF @rc < 10
  PRINT 'Reached last page.';
```

You will get back the first 10 rows based on *OrderDate* and *OrderID* ordering. Notice in the code that you can inspect the output parameter to determine whether there are no more pages (*@rc = 0*), or whether you've reached the last page (*@rc < 10*).

Query the #CachedPages temporary table, and you will find that 10 rows were cached:

```
SELECT * FROM #CachedPages;
```

Further requests for rows that were already cached will be satisfied from #CachedPages without the need to access the Orders table. Querying #CachedPages is very efficient because the table contains a clustered index on the *RowNum* column. Only the requested rows are physically accessed.

If you now run the preceding code specifying row numbers 21 to 30 as inputs, the *usp_getpage* procedure will add rows 11 through 30 to the temporary table, and return rows 21 through 30. Following requests for rows up to row 30 will be satisfied solely from the temporary table.

Once you're done experimenting with this paging technique, run the following code for cleanup:

```
IF OBJECT_ID('tempdb..#CachedPages') IS NOT NULL
  DROP TABLE #CachedPages;
GO
IF INDEXPROPERTY(OBJECT_ID('dbo.Orders'),
    'idx_od_oid_i_cid_eid', 'IndexID') IS NOT NULL
  DROP INDEX dbo.Orders.idx_od_oid_i_cid_eid;
GO
IF OBJECT_ID('dbo.usp_firstrows') IS NOT NULL
  DROP PROC dbo.usp_firstrows;
GO
IF OBJECT_ID('dbo.usp_nextrows') IS NOT NULL
  DROP PROC dbo.usp_nextrows;
GO
IF OBJECT_ID('dbo.usp_getpage') IS NOT NULL
  DROP PROC dbo.usp_getpage;
GO
```

Inserting New Rows

The problem that is the focus of this section involves inserting rows from some source table into a target table, but filtering only rows whose keys do not exist yet in the target. You might face this problem when you need to update a master table from a table of additions and changes—for example, updating a central data warehouse with information from regional centers. In this section, I'll focus on the part of the problem involving inserting new rows.

There are several techniques you can choose from. The appropriate technique for a given task, in terms of simplicity and performance, will depend on several factors. Does the source table contain rows with duplicate values in attributes that correspond to the target table's key? If so, what is their density? And are the rows with the duplicate values guaranteed to be completely identical, or are the identical parts only the attributes making the target key? The different scenarios that I mentioned might not be clear at the moment, but I'll provide more details as I explain the scenarios in context.

To demonstrate different techniques for solving the task at hand, first run the code in Listing 8-3, which creates and populates the tables MyOrders, MyCustomers, StageCusts, and StageOrders.

Listing 8-3   Create and populate sample tables

```
USE tempdb;
GO
IF OBJECT_ID('dbo.MyOrders') IS NOT NULL
  DROP TABLE dbo.MyOrders;
GO
IF OBJECT_ID('dbo.MyCustomers') IS NOT NULL
  DROP TABLE dbo.MyCustomers;
GO
IF OBJECT_ID('dbo.StageCusts') IS NOT NULL
  DROP TABLE dbo.StageCusts;
GO
IF OBJECT_ID('dbo.StageOrders') IS NOT NULL
  DROP TABLE dbo.StageOrders;
GO

SELECT *
INTO dbo.MyCustomers
FROM Northwind.dbo.Customers
WHERE CustomerID < N'M';

ALTER TABLE dbo.MyCustomers ADD PRIMARY KEY(CustomerID);

SELECT *
INTO dbo.MyOrders
FROM Northwind.dbo.Orders
WHERE CustomerID < N'M';

ALTER TABLE dbo.MyOrders ADD
  PRIMARY KEY(OrderID),
  FOREIGN KEY(CustomerID) REFERENCES dbo.MyCustomers;

SELECT *
INTO dbo.StageCusts
FROM Northwind.dbo.Customers;

ALTER TABLE dbo.StageCusts ADD PRIMARY KEY(CustomerID);
```

```
SELECT C.CustomerID, CompanyName, ContactName, ContactTitle,
  Address, City, Region, PostalCode, Country, Phone, Fax,
  OrderID, EmployeeID, OrderDate, RequiredDate, ShippedDate,
  ShipVia, Freight, ShipName, ShipAddress, ShipCity, ShipRegion,
  ShipPostalCode, ShipCountry
INTO dbo.StageOrders
FROM Northwind.dbo.Customers AS C
  JOIN Northwind.dbo.Orders AS O
    ON O.CustomerID = C.CustomerID;

CREATE UNIQUE CLUSTERED INDEX idx_cid_oid
  ON dbo.StageOrders(CustomerID, OrderID);
ALTER TABLE dbo.StageOrders ADD PRIMARY KEY NONCLUSTERED(OrderID);
```

Let's start with the simplest scenario. You just imported some updated and new customer data into the staging table StageCusts. You now need to add to MyCustomers any customers in StageCusts that are not already in MyCustomers. There are no duplicate customers in the source data. The solution is to simply use the NOT EXISTS predicate to verify that you're inserting rows from StageCusts with keys that do not yet exist in MyCustomers as follows:

```
INSERT INTO dbo.MyCustomers(CustomerID, CompanyName, ContactName,
    ContactTitle, Address, City, Region, PostalCode, Country, Phone, Fax)
  SELECT CustomerID, CompanyName, ContactName,
    ContactTitle, Address, City, Region, PostalCode, Country, Phone, Fax
  FROM dbo.StageCusts AS S
  WHERE NOT EXISTS
    (SELECT * FROM dbo.MyCustomers AS T
    WHERE T.CustomerID = S.CustomerID);
```

Now suppose you're not given the StageCusts table; rather, you're given a StageOrders table that contains both order and customer data in a denormalized form. A new customer might appear in many StageOrders rows but must be inserted only once to MyCustomers. The techniques available to you to isolate only one row for each customer depend on whether all customer attributes are guaranteed to be duplicated identically, or whether there might be differences in the non-key attributes (for example, the format of phone numbers). If rows with the same *CustomerID* are guaranteed to have the same values in all other customer attributes, you can use a NOT EXISTS query similar to the one I showed earlier, adding a DISTINCT clause to the customer attributes you query from the StageOrders table:

```
INSERT INTO dbo.MyCustomers(CustomerID, CompanyName, ContactName,
    ContactTitle, Address, City, Region, PostalCode, Country, Phone, Fax)
  SELECT DISTINCT CustomerID, CompanyName, ContactName,
    ContactTitle, Address, City, Region, PostalCode, Country, Phone, Fax
  FROM dbo.StageOrders AS S
  WHERE NOT EXISTS
    (SELECT * FROM dbo.MyCustomers AS T
    WHERE T.CustomerID = S.CustomerID);
```

If customer attributes other than *CustomerID* might vary among rows with the same *CustomerID*, you will need to isolate only one row per customer. Naturally, DISTINCT won't work in such a case because it eliminates only completely identical row duplicates. Furthermore, the technique using DISTINCT requires a full scan of the source table, so it's slow. You can use the source table's key (*OrderID* in our case) to identify a single row per customer, because the key is unique. For example, you can use a subquery returning the minimum *OrderID* for the outer customer:

```
INSERT INTO dbo.MyCustomers(CustomerID, CompanyName, ContactName,
   ContactTitle, Address, City, Region, PostalCode, Country, Phone, Fax)
  SELECT CustomerID, CompanyName, ContactName,
   ContactTitle, Address, City, Region, PostalCode, Country, Phone, Fax
  FROM dbo.StageOrders AS S
  WHERE NOT EXISTS
    (SELECT * FROM dbo.MyCustomers AS T
     WHERE T.CustomerID = S.CustomerID)
    AND S.OrderID = (SELECT MIN(OrderID) FROM dbo.StageOrders AS S2
                      WHERE S2.CustomerID = S.CustomerID);
```

In SQL Server 2005, you can rely on the ROW_NUMBER function to get the fastest solution available among the ones that I demonstrated:

```
INSERT INTO dbo.MyCustomers(CustomerID, CompanyName, ContactName,
   ContactTitle, Address, City, Region, PostalCode, Country, Phone, Fax)
  SELECT CustomerID, CompanyName, ContactName,
   ContactTitle, Address, City, Region, PostalCode, Country, Phone, Fax
  FROM (SELECT
          ROW_NUMBER() OVER(PARTITION BY CustomerID ORDER BY OrderID) AS rn,
          CustomerID, CompanyName, ContactName, ContactTitle, Address, City,
          Region, PostalCode, Country, Phone, Fax
        FROM dbo.StageOrders) AS S
  WHERE NOT EXISTS
    (SELECT * FROM dbo.MyCustomers AS T
     WHERE T.CustomerID = S.CustomerID)
    AND rn = 1;
```

The query calculates row numbers partitioned by *CustomerID*, based on *OrderID* ordering, and isolates only rows for new customers, with a row number that is equal to 1. This way you isolate for each new customer only the row with the minimum *OrderID*.

INSERT with OUTPUT

SQL Server 2005 introduces support for returning output from a data modification statement via a new OUTPUT clause. I like to think of this feature as "DML with Results." The OUTPUT clause is supported for INSERT, DELETE, and UPDATE statements. In the OUTPUT clause, you can refer to the special tables *inserted* and *deleted*. These special tables contain the rows affected by the data modification statement—in their new, or after-modification and old, or before-modification versions, respectively. You use the inserted and deleted tables here much like you do in triggers. I will cover triggers at length in *Inside T-SQL Programming*; for now, it suffices to say that the inserted and deleted tables in a trigger hold the new and old images of the rows modified by the statement that fired the trigger. With INSERTs, you refer to the inserted table to identify attributes from the new rows. With DELETEs, you refer to the deleted table to identify attributes from the old rows. With UPDATEs, you refer to the deleted table to identify the attributes from the updated rows before the change, and you refer to the inserted table to identify the attributes from the updated rows after the change. The target of the output can be the caller (client application), a table, or even both. The feature is probably best explained through examples. In this section, I'll give an INSERT example, and later in the chapter I'll also provide DELETE and UPDATE examples.

An example of an INSERT statement in which the OUTPUT clause can be very handy is when you issue a multirow INSERT into a table with an identity column and want to know what the new identity values are. With single-row INSERTs, it's not a problem: the SCOPE_IDENTITY function provides the last identity value generated by your session in the current scope. But for a multirow INSERT statement, how do you find the new identity values? You use the OUTPUT clause and direct the new identity values back to the caller or into some target (for example, a table variable).

To demonstrate this technique, first run the following code, which generates the Customers-Dim table:

```
USE tempdb;
GO
IF OBJECT_ID('dbo.CustomersDim') IS NOT NULL
  DROP TABLE dbo.CustomersDim;
GO

CREATE TABLE dbo.CustomersDim
(
  KeyCol      INT          NOT NULL IDENTITY PRIMARY KEY,
  CustomerID  NCHAR(5)     NOT NULL,
  CompanyName NVARCHAR(40) NOT NULL
  /* ... other columns ... */
);
```

Imagine that this table represents a customer dimension in your data warehouse. You now need to insert into the CustomersDim table the UK customers from the Customers table in the Northwind database. Notice that the target has an identity column called *KeyCol* that contains surrogate keys for customers. I won't get into the reasoning behind the common use of surrogate keys in dimension tables in data warehouses (as opposed to relying on natural keys only); that's not the focus of my discussion here. I just want to demonstrate a technique that uses the OUTPUT clause. Suppose that after each insert you need to do some processing of the newly added customers and identify which surrogate key was assigned to each customer.

The following code declares a table variable (*@NewCusts*), issues an INSERT statement inserting UK customers into *CustomersDim* and directing the new *CustomerID* and *KeyCol* values into *@NewCusts*, and queries the table variable:

```
DECLARE @NewCusts TABLE
(
  CustomerID NCHAR(5) NOT NULL PRIMARY KEY,
  KeyCol     INT      NOT NULL UNIQUE
);

INSERT INTO dbo.CustomersDim(CustomerID, CompanyName)
    OUTPUT inserted.CustomerID, inserted.KeyCol
    INTO @NewCusts
    -- OUTPUT inserted.CustomerID, inserted.KeyCol
  SELECT CustomerID, CompanyName
  FROM Northwind.dbo.Customers
  WHERE Country = N'UK';

SELECT CustomerID, KeyCol FROM @NewCusts;
```

This code generates the output shown in Table 8-1, where you can see the new identity values in the column *KeyCol*.

Table 8-1   Contents of @NewCusts Table Variable

CustomerID	KeyCol
AROUT	1
BSBEV	2
CONSH	3
EASTC	4
ISLAT	5
NORTS	6
SEVES	7

Notice the commented second OUTPUT clause in the code, which isn't followed by an INTO clause. Uncomment it if you also want to send the output to the caller; you will have two OUTPUT clauses in the INSERT statement.

Sequence Mechanisms

Sequence mechanisms produce numbers that you usually use as keys. SQL Server provides a sequencing mechanism via the IDENTITY column property. The IDENTITY property has several limitations that might cause you to look for an alternative sequencing mechanism. In this section, I'll describe some of these limitations and alternative mechanisms to generate keys—some that use built-in features, such as global unique identifiers (GUIDs), and some that you can develop yourself.

Identity Columns

The IDENTITY property can be convenient when you want SQL Server to generate single column keys in a table. To guarantee uniqueness, create a PRIMARY KEY or UNIQUE constraint on the identity column. Upon INSERT, SQL Server increments the table's identity value and stores it in the new row.

However, the IDENTITY property has several limitations that might make it an impractical sequencing mechanism for some applications.

One limitation is that the IDENTITY property is table dependent. It's not an independent sequencing mechanism that assigns new values that you can then use in any manner you like. Imagine that you need to generate sequence values that will be used as keys that cannot conflict across tables.

Another limitation is that an identity value is generated when an INSERT statement is issued, not before. There might be cases where you need to generate the new sequence value and then use it in an INSERT statement, and not the other way around.

Another aspect of the IDENTITY property that can be considered a limitation in some cases is that identity values are assigned in an asynchronous manner. This means that multiple sessions issuing multirow inserts might end up getting nonsequential identity values. Moreover, the assignment of a new identity value is not part of the transaction in which the INSERT was issued. These facts have several implications. SQL Server will increment the table's identity value regardless of whether the insert succeeds or fails. You might end up with gaps in the sequence that were not generated by deletions. Some systems cannot allow missing values that cannot be accounted for (for example, invoicing systems). Try telling the Internal Revenue Service (IRS) that some of the missing invoice IDs in your system are a result of the asynchronous manner in which identity values are managed.

Custom Sequences

I'll suggest a couple of solutions to the problem of maintaining a custom sequencing mechanism. I'll show both synchronous and asynchronous solutions.

Synchronous Sequence Generation   You need a synchronous sequence generator when you must account for all values in the sequence. The classic scenario for such a sequence is generating invoice numbers. The way to guarantee that no gaps occur is to lock the sequence resource when you need to increment it and release the lock only when the transaction is finished. If you think about it, that's exactly how exclusive locks behave when you modify data in a transaction—that is, a lock is acquired to modify data, and it's released when the transaction is finished (committed or rolled back). To maintain such a sequence, create a table with a single row and a single column holding the last sequence value used. Initially, populate it with a zero if you want the first value in the sequence to be 1:

```
USE tempdb;
GO
IF OBJECT_ID('dbo.SyncSeq') IS NOT NULL
  DROP TABLE dbo.SyncSeq;
GO

CREATE TABLE dbo.SyncSeq(val INT);
INSERT INTO dbo.SyncSeq VALUES(0);
```

Now that the sequence table is in place, I'll describe how you get a single sequence value or a block of sequence values at once.

Single Sequence Value To get a single sequence value, you increment the sequence value by 1 and return the resulting value. You can achieve this by beginning a transaction, modifying the sequence value, and then retrieving it. Or you can both increment and retrieve the new sequence value in a single atomic operation using a specialized UPDATE syntax. Run the following code to create a stored procedure that uses the specialized T-SQL UPDATE syntax, increments the sequence value, and returns the new value as an output parameter:

```
IF OBJECT_ID('dbo.usp_SyncSeq') IS NOT NULL
  DROP PROC dbo.usp_SyncSeq;
GO

CREATE PROC dbo.usp_SyncSeq
  @val AS INT OUTPUT
AS
UPDATE dbo.SyncSeq
  SET @val = val = val + 1;
GO
```

The assignment *SET @val = val = val + 1* is equivalent to *SET val = val + 1, @val = val + 1*. Note that SQL Server will first lock the row exclusively and then increment *val*, retrieve it, and release the lock only when the transaction is completed.

Whenever you need a new sequence value, use the following code:

```
DECLARE @key AS INT;
EXEC dbo.usp_SyncSeq @val = @key OUTPUT;
SELECT @key;
```

To reset the sequence—for example, when the sequence value is about to overflow—set its value to zero:

```
UPDATE dbo.SyncSeq SET val = 0;
```

Block of Sequence Values   If you want a mechanism to allocate a block of sequence values all at once, you need to slightly alter the stored procedure's implementation as follows:

```
ALTER PROC dbo.usp_SyncSeq
  @val AS INT OUTPUT,
  @n   AS INT = 1
AS
UPDATE dbo.SyncSeq
  SET @val = val + 1, val = val + @n;
GO
```

In the additional argument (*@n*) you specify the block size (how many sequence values you need). The stored procedure increments the current sequence value by *@n* and returns the first value in the block via the *@val* output parameter. This procedure allocates the block of sequence values from *@val* to *@val + @n − 1*.

The following code provides an example of acquiring and using a whole block of sequence values:

```
IF OBJECT_ID('tempdb..#CustsStage') IS NOT NULL
  DROP TABLE #CustsStage
GO

DECLARE @key AS INT, @rc AS INT;

SELECT CustomerID, 0 AS KeyCol
INTO #CustsStage
FROM Northwind.dbo.Customers
WHERE Country = N'UK';

SET @rc = @@rowcount;
EXEC dbo.usp_SyncSeq @val = @key OUTPUT, @n = @rc;

SET @key = @key -1;
UPDATE #CustsStage SET @key = KeyCol = @key + 1;

SELECT CustomerID, KeyCol FROM #CustsStage;
```

This technique is an alternative to the one shown earlier that used the IDENTITY property to generate surrogate keys for UK customers. This code uses a SELECT INTO statement to insert UK customers into a temporary table called #CustsStage, temporarily assigning 0 as the *Key-Col* value in all target rows. The code then stores the number of affected rows (*@@rowcount*) in the variable *@rc*. Next, the code invokes the *usp_SyncSeq* procedure to request a block of a size *@rc* of new sequence values. The stored procedure stores the first sequence value from the block in the variable *@key* through the output parameter *@val*. Next, the code subtracts 1 from *@key* and invokes a specialized T-SQL UPDATE statement to assign the block of sequence values. The UPDATE makes a single pass over the rows in #CustsStage. With every row that the UPDATE visits, it stores the value of *@key + 1* in *KeyCol* and in *@key*. This means that with every new row visited, *@key* is incremented by one and stored in *KeyCol*. You basically distribute the new block of sequence values among the rows in #CustsStage. If you run this code after resetting the sequence value to 0, as instructed earlier, #CustsStage will contain seven UK customers, with *KeyCol* values ranging from 1 through 7. Run this code multiple times to see how you get a new block of sequence values every time (1 through 7, 8 through 14, 15 through 21, and so on).

The specialized T-SQL UPDATE statement is not standard and doesn't guarantee it will access the rows in #CustsStage in any particular order. Therefore, by using it, you cannot control the order in which SQL Server will assign the block of sequence values. There's a technique for assigning the block of sequence values where you can control the order of assignment, but it is new to SQL Server 2005. Substitute the specialized UPDATE statement just shown with an UPDATE against a CTE that calculates row numbers based on a desired order (for example, *CustomerID*) as follows:

```
WITH CustsStageRN AS
(
  SELECT KeyCol, ROW_NUMBER() OVER(ORDER BY CustomerID) AS RowNum
  FROM #CustsStage
)
UPDATE CustsStageRN SET KeyCol = RowNum + @key;
```

You can use similar techniques when you just want to assign a sequence of unique values starting with 1 (and increasing by 1 from there) that is unrelated to any existing sequence. I will describe such techniques later in the chapter in the "Assignment UPDATE" section.

So far, I demonstrated inserting a result set into a target table and modifying the rows with new sequence values. Instead, you can use a SELECT INTO statement to populate a temporary table with the target rows, and also to assign row numbers starting with 1 and increasing by 1 from there. (Let's call the column *rn*.) To generate the row numbers, you can use the IDENTITY function in SQL Server 2000 and the ROW_NUMBER function in SQL Server 2005. Right after the insert, store the *@@rowcount* value in a local variable (*@rc*) and invoke the procedure *usp_SyncSeq* to increment the sequence by *@rc* and assign the first sequence value in the new block to your variable (*@key*). Finally, query the temporary table, calculating the new sequence values as *rn* + *@key* − 1. Here's the complete code sample demonstrating this technique:

```
IF OBJECT_ID('tempdb..#CustsStage') IS NOT NULL
  DROP TABLE #CustsStage
GO

DECLARE @key AS INT, @rc AS INT;

SELECT CustomerID, IDENTITY(int, 1, 1) AS rn
  -- In 2005 can use ROW_NUMBER() OVER(ORDER BY CustomerID)
INTO #CustsStage
FROM Northwind.dbo.Customers
WHERE Country = N'UK';

SET @rc = @@rowcount;
EXEC dbo.usp_SyncSeq @val = @key OUTPUT, @n = @rc;

SELECT CustomerID, rn + @key - 1 AS KeyCol FROM #CustsStage;
```

Run the code several times to see how you get a new block of sequence values every time.

Asynchronous Sequence Generation   The synchronous sequencing mechanism doesn't allow gaps, but it might cause concurrency problems. Remember that you must exclusively lock the sequence to increment it, and then you must maintain the lock until the transaction finishes. The longer the transaction is, the longer you lock the sequence. Obviously, this solution can cause queues of processes waiting for the sequence resource to be released. But there's not much you can do if you want to maintain a synchronous sequence.

However, there are cases where you might not care about having gaps. For example, suppose that all you need is a key generator that will guarantee that you will not generate the same key twice. Say that you need those keys to uniquely identify rows across tables. You don't want the sequence resource to be locked for the duration of the transaction. Rather, you want the sequence to be locked for a fraction of a second while incrementing it, just to prevent multiple processes from getting the same value. In other words, you need an asynchronous sequence, one that will work much faster than the synchronous one, allowing better concurrency.

One option that would address these requirements is to use built-in functions that SQL Server provides you to generate GUIDs. I'll discuss this option shortly. However, GUIDs are long (16 bytes). You might prefer to use integer sequence values, which are substantially smaller (4 bytes). To achieve such an asynchronous sequencing mechanism, you create a table (AsyncSeq) with an identity column as follows:

```
USE tempdb;
GO
IF OBJECT_ID('dbo.AsyncSeq') IS NOT NULL
  DROP TABLE dbo.AsyncSeq;
GO

CREATE TABLE dbo.AsyncSeq(val INT IDENTITY(1,1));
```

Create the following *usp_AsyncSeq* procedure to generate a new sequence value and return it through the *@val* output parameter:

```
IF OBJECT_ID('dbo.usp_AsyncSeq') IS NOT NULL
  DROP PROC dbo.usp_AsyncSeq;
GO

CREATE PROC dbo.usp_AsyncSeq
  @val AS INT OUTPUT
AS
BEGIN TRAN
  SAVE TRAN S1;
  INSERT INTO dbo.AsyncSeq DEFAULT VALUES;
  SET @val = SCOPE_IDENTITY()
  ROLLBACK TRAN S1;
COMMIT TRAN
GO
```

The procedure opens a transaction just for the sake of creating a save point called S1. It inserts a new row to AsyncSeq, which generates a new identity value in the AsyncSeq table and stores it in the @*val* output parameter. The procedure then rolls back the INSERT. But a rollback doesn't undo a variable assignment, nor does it undo incrementing the identity value. Plus, the identity resource is not locked for the duration of an outer transaction; rather, it's locked only for a fraction of a second to increment. This behavior of the IDENTITY property is crucial for maintaining an asynchronous sequence.

> **Note** As of the date of writing this, I haven't found any official documentation from Microsoft that describes this behavior of the IDENTITY property.

Rolling back to a save point ensures that the rollback will not have any effect on an external transaction. The rollback prevents the AsyncSeq table from growing. In fact, it will never contain any rows from calls to *usp_AsyncSeq*.

Whenever you need the next sequence value, run the *usp_AsyncSeq*, just like you did with the synchronous one:

```
DECLARE @key AS INT;
EXEC dbo.usp_AsyncSeq @val = @key OUTPUT;
SELECT @key;
```

Only this time, the sequence will not block if you increment it within an external transaction. This asynchronous sequence solution can generate only one sequence value at a time.

If you want to reset the sequence value, you can do one of two things. You can truncate the table, which resets the identity value:

```
TRUNCATE TABLE dbo.AsyncSeq;
```

Or you can issue the DBCC CHECKIDENT statement with the RESEED option, as follows:

```
DBCC CHECKIDENT('dbo.AsyncSeq', RESEED, 0);
```

Globally Unique Identifiers

SQL Server provides you with the NEWID function, which generates a new globally unique identifier (GUID) every time it is invoked. The function returns a 16-byte value typed as UNIQUEIDENTIFIER. If you need an automatic mechanism that assigns unique keys in a table, or even across different tables, you can create a UNIQUEIDENTIFIER column with the default value *NEWID*. The downside of a UNIQUEIDENTIFIER column used as a key is that it's pretty big—16 bytes. This, of course, has an impact on index sizes, join performance, and so on.

Note that the NEWID function does not guarantee that a newly generated GUID will be greater than any previously generated one in the same computer. If you need such a guarantee, use the new NEWSEQUENTIALID function, introduced in SQL Server 2005 particularly for this purpose.

Deleting Data

In this section, I'll cover different aspects of deleting data, including TRUNCATE vs. DELETE, removing rows with duplicate data, DELETE using joins, large DELETEs, and DELETE with OUTPUT.

TRUNCATE vs. DELETE

If you need to remove all rows from a table, use TRUNCATE TABLE and not DELETE without a WHERE clause. DELETE is always fully logged, and with large tables it can take a while to complete. TRUNCATE TABLE is always minimally logged, regardless of the recovery model of the database, and therefore, it is always significantly faster than a DELETE. Note though, that TRUNCATE TABLE will not fire any DELETE triggers on the table. To give you a sense of the difference, using TRUNCATE TABLE to clear a table with millions of rows can take a matter of seconds, while clearing the table with DELETE can take a few hours.

> **Tip** SQL Server will reject DROP TABLE attempts if there's a schema-bound object pointing to the target table. It will reject both DROP TABLE and TRUNCATE TABLE attempts if there's a foreign key pointing to the target table. This limitation applies even when the foreign table is empty, and even when the foreign key is disabled. If you want to prevent accidental TRUNCATE TABLE and DROP TABLE attempts against sensitive production tables, simply create dummy tables with foreign keys pointing to them.

In addition to the substantial performance difference between TRUNCATE TABLE and DELETE, there's also a difference in the way they handle the IDENTITY property. TRUNCATE TABLE resets the IDENTITY property to its original seed, while DELETE doesn't.

Removing Rows with Duplicate Data

Duplicates typically arise from inadequate data-integrity enforcement. If you don't create a PRIMARY KEY or UNIQUE constraint where you need one, you can expect to end up with unwanted duplicate data. Data integrity is important; enforce it through constraints and design applications to protect your data.

Having said that, if you have duplicates in your data and need to get rid of them, there are a number of techniques that you can use. Your options and the efficiency of the techniques depend on several factors. One is the number of duplicates with respect to unique rows (density). Another is whether the whole row is guaranteed to be duplicated, or whether you can rely only on the set of attributes that will form the key once duplicates are removed. For example, suppose you have a table containing information about orders. A primary key was not created on the *OrderID* column, and several *OrderID* values appear more than once. You need to keep only one row per each unique *OrderID* value.

To demonstrate techniques to remove duplicates, run the following code, which creates the OrdersDups table and populates it with 83,000 rows containing many duplicates:

```
USE tempdb;
GO
IF OBJECT_ID('dbo.OrdersDups') IS NOT NULL
  DROP TABLE dbo.OrdersDups
GO

SELECT OrderID+0 AS OrderID, CustomerID, EmployeeID, OrderDate,
  RequiredDate, ShippedDate, ShipVia, Freight, ShipName, ShipAddress,
  ShipCity, ShipRegion, ShipPostalCode, ShipCountry
INTO dbo.OrdersDups
FROM Northwind.dbo.Orders, dbo.Nums
WHERE n <= 100;
```

Remember that the Nums table is an auxiliary table of numbers. I discussed it in detail in Chapter 4.

Rerun this code before testing each technique so that you have common base data in all your tests.

Before I cover set-based techniques, I should first mention that you could use a cursor, scanning the rows in the order of the attributes that determine duplicates (*OrderID* in the Orders-Dups case) and deleting all rows that you identify as duplicates. Just remember that such a cursor involves a lot of overhead and will typically be slower than set-based solutions, especially when the density of duplicates is high (a lot of duplicates). Though, with a low density of duplicates, it might be worthwhile to compare the cursor-based solution to the set-based ones, especially when there's no way to uniquely identify a row.

Let's start with a technique that you can apply when complete rows are duplicated and you have a high density of duplicates. Use a SELECT DISTINCT ... INTO statement to copy distinct rows to a new table. Drop the original table, rename the new one to the original table's name, and then create all constraints, indexes, and triggers:

```
SELECT DISTINCT * INTO dbo.OrdersTmp FROM dbo.OrdersDups;
DROP TABLE dbo.OrdersDups;
EXEC sp_rename 'dbo.OrdersTmp', 'OrdersDups';
-- Add constraints, indexes, triggers
```

This code runs for about 5 seconds on my system against the sample data I provided. The nice thing about this technique is that it doesn't require an existing unique identifier in the table.

Some other techniques require an existing unique identifier. If you already have one, your solution will not incur the cost involved with adding such a column. If you don't, you can add an identity column for this purpose, but adding such a column can take a while. If you have an existing numeric column that you can overwrite, you can use one of the techniques that I will show later to assign a sequence of values to an existing column. The process of overwriting an existing numeric column is substantially faster because it doesn't involve the restructuring and expansion of rows.

To allow a fast duplicate removal process, you want an index on the attributes that determine duplicates (*OrderID*) plus the unique identifier (call it *KeyCol*). Here's the code you need to run to add an identity column to the OrdersDups table and create the desired index:

```
ALTER TABLE dbo.OrdersDups
  ADD KeyCol INT NOT NULL IDENTITY;
CREATE UNIQUE INDEX idx_OrderID_KeyCol
  ON dbo.OrdersDups(OrderID, KeyCol);
```

Then use the following DELETE statement to get rid of the duplicates:

```
DELETE FROM dbo.OrdersDups
WHERE EXISTS
  (SELECT *
   FROM dbo.OrdersDups AS O2
   WHERE O2.OrderID = dbo.OrdersDups.OrderID
     AND O2.KeyCol > dbo.OrdersDups.KeyCol);
```

This statement deletes all orders for which another order can be found with the same *OrderID* and a higher *KeyCol*. If you think about it, you will end up with one row for each *OrderID*—the one with the highest *KeyCol*. This technique runs for 14 seconds on my system, including adding the identity column and creating the index.

One advantage this technique has over the previous DISTINCT technique is that you rely only on the attributes that determine duplicates (*OrderID*) and the surrogate key (*KeyCol*). It works even when other attributes among the redundant rows with the same *OrderID* value are not equal. However, this technique can be very slow when there's a high density of duplicates. To optimize the solution in a high-density scenario, you can use similar logic to the last solution; that is, keep rows with the maximum *KeyCol* per *OrderID*. But insert those unique rows into a new table using a SELECT INTO statement. You can then get rid of the original table; rename the new table to the original table name; and re-create all indexes, constraints, and triggers. Here's the code that applies this approach, which ran for 2 seconds on my system in total:

```
ALTER TABLE dbo.OrdersDups
  ADD KeyCol INT NOT NULL IDENTITY;
CREATE UNIQUE INDEX idx_OrderID_KeyCol
  ON dbo.OrdersDups(OrderID, KeyCol);
GO

SELECT O.OrderID, CustomerID, EmployeeID, OrderDate, RequiredDate,
  ShippedDate, ShipVia, Freight, ShipName, ShipAddress, ShipCity,
  ShipRegion, ShipPostalCode, ShipCountry
INTO dbo.OrdersTmp
```

```
FROM dbo.OrdersDups AS O
  JOIN (SELECT OrderID, MAX(KeyCol) AS mx
        FROM dbo.OrdersDups
        GROUP BY OrderID) AS U
    ON O.OrderID = O.OrderID
   AND O.KeyCol = U.mx;

DROP TABLE dbo.OrdersDups;
EXEC sp_rename 'dbo.OrdersTmp', 'OrdersDups';
-- Recreate constraints, indexes
```

You've seen several solutions to deleting rows with duplicate values, and I recommended the scenarios where I find that each is adequate. But all of them were limited in one way or another. The DISTINCT technique requires equivalence of complete rows among duplicates, and the other two techniques require a unique identifier in the table. In SQL Server 2005, you can use a CTE and the ROW_NUMBER function to generate a fast solution without these shortcomings:

```
WITH Dups AS
(
  SELECT *,
    ROW_NUMBER() OVER(PARTITION BY OrderID ORDER BY OrderID) AS rn
  FROM dbo.OrdersDups
)
DELETE FROM Dups WHERE rn > 1;
```

The query defining the CTE Dups generates row numbers starting with 1 for each partition of rows with the same *OrderID*, meaning that each set of rows with the same *OrderID* value will be assigned row numbers starting with 1 independently. Each row number here represents the duplicate number. The ROW_NUMBER function requires you to specify an ORDER BY clause, even when you don't really care how row numbers are assigned within each partition. You can specify the same column you use in the PARTITION BY clause (*OrderID*) also in the ORDER BY clause. Such an ORDER BY clause will have no effect on the assignment of row numbers within each partition. More importantly, while the row numbering is nondeterministic, there will be exactly one row within each partition with *rn* equal to 1.

Finally, the outer query simply deletes rows that have a duplicate number greater than 1 through the CTE, leaving only one row for each *OrderID* value.

This solution runs for only 1 second on my system; it doesn't require a unique identifier in the table; and it allows you to identify duplicates based on any attribute or attributes that you like.

DELETE Using Joins

T-SQL supports a proprietary syntax for DELETE and UPDATE based on joins. Here I'll cover DELETEs based on joins, and later, in the UPDATE section, I'll cover UPDATEs based on joins.

> **Note**   This syntax is not standard and should be avoided unless there's a compelling benefit over the standard syntax, as I will describe in this section.

I'll first describe the syntax, and then show examples where it provides functionality not available with standard syntax.

You write a DELETE based on a join in a similar manner to writing a SELECT based on a join. You substitute the SELECT clause with a DELETE FROM <*target_table*>, where <*target_table*> is the table from which you want to delete rows. Note that you should specify the table alias if one was provided.

The typical use of this feature is to make it easier to delete rows that meet an EXISTS or NOT EXISTS condition, to avoid having to specify a subquery for the matching condition twice. Some people also like the fact that it allows you to write a SELECT query first, and then change SELECT to DELETE.

As an example of how a SELECT join query and a DELETE join query are similar, here's a query that returns order details for orders placed on or after May 6, 1998:

```
USE Northwind;

SELECT OD.*
FROM dbo.[Order Details] AS OD
  JOIN dbo.Orders AS O
    ON OD.OrderID = O.OrderID
WHERE O.OrderDate >= '19980506';
```

If you want to delete order details for orders placed on or after May 6, 1998, simply replace *SELECT OD.** in the preceding query with *DELETE FROM OD*:

```
BEGIN TRAN

DELETE FROM OD
FROM dbo.[Order Details] AS OD
  JOIN dbo.Orders AS O
    ON OD.OrderID = O.OrderID
WHERE O.OrderDate >= '19980506';

ROLLBACK TRAN
```

In some of my examples, I use a transaction and roll back the modification so that you can try out the examples without permanently modifying the sample tables. This particular nonstandard DELETE query can be rewritten as a standard one using a subquery:

```
BEGIN TRAN

DELETE FROM dbo.[Order Details]
WHERE EXISTS
```

```
(SELECT *
 FROM dbo.Orders AS O
 WHERE O.OrderID = dbo.[Order Details].OrderID
   AND O.OrderDate >= '19980506');

ROLLBACK TRAN
```

In this case, the nonstandard DELETE has no advantage over the standard one—neither in performance nor in simplicity, so I don't see any point in using it. However, you will find cases in which it is hard to get by without using the proprietary syntax. For example, suppose you need to delete from a table variable, and you must refer to the table variable from a subquery. T-SQL doesn't support qualifying a column name with a table variable name.

The following code declares a table variable called *@MyOD* and populates it with some order details, identified by (*OrderID, ProductID*). The code then attempts to delete all rows from *@MyOD* with keys that already appear in the Order Details table:

```
DECLARE @MyOD TABLE
(
  OrderID   INT NOT NULL,
  ProductID INT NOT NULL,
  PRIMARY KEY(OrderID, ProductID)
);

INSERT INTO @MyOD VALUES(10001, 14);
INSERT INTO @MyOD VALUES(10001, 51);
INSERT INTO @MyOD VALUES(10001, 65);
INSERT INTO @MyOD VALUES(10248, 11);
INSERT INTO @MyOD VALUES(10248, 42);

DELETE FROM @MyOD
WHERE EXISTS
  (SELECT * FROM dbo.[Order Details] AS OD
   WHERE OD.OrderID = @MyOD.OrderID
     AND OD.ProductID = @MyOD.ProductID);
```

This code fails with the following error:

```
Msg 137, Level 15, State 2, Line 17
Must declare the scalar variable "@MyOD".
```

Essentially, the reason for the failure is that T-SQL doesn't support qualifying a column name with a table variable name. Moreover, T-SQL doesn't allow you to alias the target table directly; rather, it requires you to do so via a second FROM clause like so:

```
DELETE FROM MyOD
FROM @MyOD AS MyOD
WHERE EXISTS
  (SELECT * FROM dbo.[Order Details] AS OD
   WHERE OD.OrderID = MyOD.OrderID
     AND OD.ProductID = MyOD.ProductID);
```

> **Note**   If you want to test this code, make sure you run it right after declaring and populating
> the table variable in the same batch. Otherwise, you will get an error saying that the variable
> @*MyOD* was not declared. Like any other variable, the scope of a table variable is the local
> batch.

Another solution is to use a join instead of the subquery, where you can also alias tables:

```
DELETE FROM MyOD
FROM @MyOD AS MyOD
  JOIN dbo.[Order Details] AS OD
    ON OD.OrderID = MyOD.OrderID
    AND OD.ProductID = MyOD.ProductID;
```

In SQL Server 2005, you can use a CTE as an alternative to aliasing the table variable, allowing
a simpler solution:

```
WITH MyOD AS (SELECT * FROM @MyOD)
DELETE FROM MyOD
WHERE EXISTS
  (SELECT * FROM dbo.[Order Details] AS OD
   WHERE OD.OrderID = MyOD.OrderID
     AND OD.ProductID = MyOD.ProductID);
```

CTEs are extremely useful in other scenarios where you need to modify data in one table
based on data that you inspect in another. It allows you to simplify your code and, in many
cases, avoid relying on modification statements that use joins.

DELETE with OUTPUT

In Chapter 7, I described a technique to delete large volumes of data from an existing table in
batches to avoid log explosion and lock escalation problems. Here I will show how you can
use the new OUTPUT clause to archive the data that you purge. To demonstrate the technique, first run the following code, which creates the LargeOrders tables and populates it with
a little over two million orders placed in years 2000 through 2006:

```
SET NOCOUNT ON;
USE tempdb;
GO
IF OBJECT_ID('dbo.LargeOrders') IS NOT NULL
  DROP TABLE dbo.LargeOrders;
GO
SELECT IDENTITY(int, 1, 1) AS OrderID, CustomerID, EmployeeID,
  DATEADD(day, n-1, '20000101') AS OrderDate,
  CAST('a' AS CHAR(200)) AS Filler
INTO dbo.LargeOrders
FROM Northwind.dbo.Customers AS C,
  Northwind.dbo.Employees AS E,
  dbo.Nums
WHERE n <= DATEDIFF(day, '20000101', '20061231') + 1;
```

```
CREATE UNIQUE CLUSTERED INDEX idx_od_oid
  ON dbo.LargeOrders(OrderDate, OrderID);

ALTER TABLE dbo.LargeOrders ADD PRIMARY KEY NONCLUSTERED(OrderID);
```

> **Note**   It should take the code a few minutes to run, and it will require about a gigabyte of space in your tempdb database. Also, the code refers to the Nums auxiliary table, which was covered in Chapter 4.

As a reminder, you would use the following technique to delete all rows with an *OrderDate* older than 2001 in batches of 5000 rows (but don't run it yet):

```
WHILE 1 = 1
BEGIN
  DELETE TOP (5000) FROM dbo.LargeOrders WHERE OrderDate < '20010101';
  IF @@rowcount < 5000 BREAK;
END
```

Remember that in SQL Server 2005 you use DELETE TOP instead of the older SET ROWCOUNT option. Earlier in the chapter, I introduced the SQL Server 2005 support for the new OUTPUT clause, which allows you to return output from a statement that modifies data. Remember that you can direct the output to a temporary or permanent table, to a table variable, or back to the caller. I showed an example using an INSERT statement, and here I will show one using a DELETE statement. Suppose you wanted to enhance the solution that purges historic data in batches by also archiving the data that you purge. Run the following code to create the OrdersArchive table, where you will store the archived orders:

```
CREATE TABLE dbo.OrdersArchive
(
  OrderID    INT       NOT NULL PRIMARY KEY NONCLUSTERED,
  CustomerID NCHAR(5)  NOT NULL,
  EmployeeID INT       NOT NULL,
  OrderDate  DATETIME  NOT NULL,
  Filler     CHAR(200) NOT NULL
);

CREATE UNIQUE CLUSTERED INDEX idx_od_oid
  ON dbo.OrdersArchive(OrderDate, OrderID);
GO
```

Using the new OUTPUT clause, you can direct the deleted rows from each batch into the OrdersArchive table. For example, the following code is the enhanced solution, which purges orders with an *OrderDate* before 2001 in batches and also archives them:

```
WHILE 1=1
BEGIN
  BEGIN TRAN
    DELETE TOP(5000) FROM dbo.LargeOrders
      OUTPUT deleted.* INTO dbo.OrdersArchive
    WHERE OrderDate < '20010101';
```

```
      IF @@rowcount < 5000
      BEGIN
        COMMIT TRAN
        BREAK;
      END
    COMMIT TRAN
END
```

> **Note**   It should take this code a few minutes to run.

The OrdersArchive table now holds archived orders placed before 2001.

> **Note**   When using the OUTPUT clause to direct the output to a table, the table cannot have enabled triggers or CHECK constraints, nor can it participate on either side of a foreign key constraint. If the target table doesn't meet these requirements, you can direct the output to a temporary table or a table variable, and then copy the rows from there to the target table.

There are important benefits to using the OUTPUT clause when you want to archive data that you delete. Without the OUTPUT clause, you need to first query the data to archive it, and then delete it. Such a technique is slower and more complex. To guarantee that new rows matching the filter will not be added between the SELECT and the DELETE (also known as *phantoms*), you must lock the data you archive using a serializable isolation level. With the OUTPUT clause, you will not only get better performance, you won't need to worry about phantoms, as you are guaranteed to get exactly what you deleted back from the OUTPUT clause.

Updating Data

This section covers several aspects of updating data, including UPDATEs using joins, UPDATE with OUTPUT, and SELECT and UPDATE statements that perform assignments to variables.

UPDATE Using Joins

Earlier in this chapter, I mentioned that T-SQL supports a nonstandard syntax for modifying data based on a join, and I showed DELETE examples. Here I'll cover UPDATEs based on joins, focusing on cases where the nonstandard syntax has advantages over the supported standard syntax. I'll show that SQL Server 2005 introduces simpler alternatives that practically eliminate the need for the older UPDATE syntax that uses joins.

I'll start with one of the cases where an UPDATE based on a join had a performance advantages over the standard UPDATE supported by T-SQL. Suppose you wanted to update the shipping information for orders placed by USA customers, overwriting the *ShipCountry*, *ShipRegion*, and *ShipCity* attributes with the customer's *Country*, *Region*, and *City* attributes from the Customers table. You could use one subquery for each of the new attribute values, plus one in the WHERE clause to filter orders placed by USA customers as follows:

```
USE Northwind;

BEGIN TRAN

  UPDATE dbo.Orders
    SET ShipCountry = (SELECT C.Country FROM dbo.Customers AS C
                        WHERE C.CustomerID = dbo.Orders.CustomerID),
        ShipRegion =  (SELECT C.Region FROM dbo.Customers AS C
                        WHERE C.CustomerID = dbo.Orders.CustomerID),
        ShipCity =    (SELECT C.City FROM dbo.Customers AS C
                        WHERE C.CustomerID = dbo.Orders.CustomerID)
  WHERE CustomerID IN
    (SELECT CustomerID FROM dbo.Customers WHERE Country = 'USA');

ROLLBACK TRAN
```

Again, I'm rolling back the transaction so that the change will not take effect in the Northwind database. Though standard, this technique is very slow. Each such subquery involves separate access to return the requested attribute from the Customers table. I wanted to provide a figure with the graphical execution plan for this UPDATE, but it's just too big! Request a graphical execution plan in SSMS to see for yourself.

You can write an UPDATE based on a join to perform the same task as follows:

```
BEGIN TRAN

  UPDATE O
    SET ShipCountry = C.Country,
        ShipRegion = C.Region,
        ShipCity = C.City
  FROM dbo.Orders AS O
    JOIN dbo.Customers AS C
      ON O.CustomerID = C.CustomerID
  WHERE C.Country = 'USA';

ROLLBACK TRAN
```

This code is shorter and simpler, and the optimizer generates a more efficient plan for it, as you will notice if you request the graphical execution plan in SSMS. You will find in the execution plan that the Customers table is scanned only once, and through that scan, the query processor accesses all the customer attributes it needs. This plan reports half the estimated execution cost of the previous one. In practice, if you compare the two solutions against larger tables, you will find that the performance difference is substantially higher. Alas, the UPDATE with a join technique is nonstandard.

ANSI supports syntax called *row value constructors* that allows you to simplify queries like the one just shown. This syntax allows you to specify vectors of attributes and expressions and eliminates the need to issue a subquery for each attribute separately. The following example shows this syntax:

```
UPDATE dbo.Orders
  SET (ShipCountry, ShipRegion, ShipCity) =
    (SELECT Country, Region, City
     FROM dbo.Customers AS C
     WHERE C.CustomerID = dbo.Orders.CustomerID);
WHERE CustomerID IN
  (SELECT CustomerID FROM dbo.Customers WHERE Country = 'USA';
```

However, T-SQL doesn't yet support row value constructors. Such support would allow for simple standard solutions and naturally also lend itself to good optimization. However, hope is not lost. By using a CTE, you can come up with a simple solution yielding an efficient plan very similar to the one that uses a join UPDATE. Simply create a CTE out of the join, and then UPDATE the CTE like so:

```
BEGIN TRAN;

WITH UPD_CTE AS
(
  SELECT
    O.ShipCountry AS set_Country, C.Country AS get_Country,
    O.ShipRegion  AS set_Region,  C.Region AS get_Region,
    O.ShipCity    AS set_City,    C.City   AS get_City
  FROM dbo.Orders AS O
    JOIN dbo.Customers AS C
      ON O.CustomerID = C.CustomerID
  WHERE C.Country = 'USA'
)
UPDATE UPD_CTE
  SET set_Country = get_Country,
      set_Region  = get_Country,
      set_City    = get_City;

ROLLBACK TRAN
```

> **Note**   Even though CTEs are defined by ANSI SQL:1999, the DELETE and UPDATE syntax against CTEs implemented in SQL Server 2005 is not standard.

This UPDATE generates an identical plan to the one generated for the UPDATE based on a join.

There's another issue you should be aware of when using the join-based UPDATE. When you modify the table on the "many" side of a one-to-many join, you might end up with a nondeterministic update. To demonstrate the problem, run the following code, which creates the tables Customers and Orders and populates them with sample data:

```
USE tempdb;
GO
IF OBJECT_ID('dbo.Orders') IS NOT NULL
  DROP TABLE dbo.Orders;
```

```
IF OBJECT_ID('dbo.Customers') IS NOT NULL
  DROP TABLE dbo.Customers;
GO

CREATE TABLE dbo.Customers
(
  custid VARCHAR(5) NOT NULL PRIMARY KEY,
  qty    INT        NULL
);

INSERT INTO dbo.Customers(custid) VALUES('A');
INSERT INTO dbo.Customers(custid) VALUES('B');

CREATE TABLE dbo.Orders
(
  orderid INT        NOT NULL PRIMARY KEY,
  custid  VARCHAR(5) NOT NULL REFERENCES dbo.Customers,
  qty     INT        NOT NULL
);

INSERT INTO dbo.Orders(orderid, custid, qty) VALUES(1, 'A', 20);
INSERT INTO dbo.Orders(orderid, custid, qty) VALUES(2, 'A', 10);
INSERT INTO dbo.Orders(orderid, custid, qty) VALUES(3, 'A', 30);
INSERT INTO dbo.Orders(orderid, custid, qty) VALUES(4, 'B', 35);
INSERT INTO dbo.Orders(orderid, custid, qty) VALUES(5, 'B', 45);
INSERT INTO dbo.Orders(orderid, custid, qty) VALUES(6, 'B', 15);
```

There's a one-to-many relationship between Customers and Orders. Notice that each row in Customers currently has three related rows in Orders. Now, examine the following UPDATE and see if you can guess how Customers would look after the UPDATE:

```
UPDATE Customers
  SET qty = O.qty
FROM dbo.Customers AS C
  JOIN dbo.Orders AS O
    ON C.custid = O.custid;
```

The truth is that the UPDATE is nondeterministic. You can't guarantee which of the values from the related Orders rows will be used to update the *qty* value in Customers. Remember that you cannot assume or rely on any physical order of the data. For example, run the following query against Customers after running the preceding UPDATE:

```
SELECT custid, qty FROM dbo.Customers;
```

You might get the output shown in Table 8-2.

Table 8-2 Possible Contents of Customers After Nondeterministic UPDATE

custid	qty
A	20
B	35

But just the same, you might get the output shown in Table 8-3.

Table 8-3   Another Possible Contents of Customers After Nondeterministic UPDATE

custid	qty
A	10
B	15

Once you're done experimenting with nondeterministic UPDATEs, run the following code to drop Orders and Customers:

```
IF OBJECT_ID('dbo.Orders') IS NOT NULL
  DROP TABLE dbo.Orders;
IF OBJECT_ID('dbo.Customers') IS NOT NULL
  DROP TABLE dbo.Customers;
```

UPDATE with OUTPUT

As with INSERT and DELETE statements, UPDATE statements also support an OUTPUT clause, allowing you to return output when you update data. UPDATE is the only statement out of the three where there are both new and old versions of rows, so you can refer to both deleted and inserted. UPDATEs with the OUTPUT clause have many interesting applications. I will give an example of managing a message or event queue.

SQL Server 2005 introduces a whole new queuing infrastructure and a platform called Service Broker that is based on that infrastructure.

> **More Info**   For details about programming with Service Broker please refer to *Inside Microsoft SQL Server 2005: T-SQL Programming*.

You can use Service Broker to develop applications that manage queues in your database. However, when you need to manage queues on a much smaller scale, without delving into the new queuing infrastructure and platform, you can do so by using the new OUTPUT clause. To demonstrate managing a queue, run the following code, which creates the Messages table:

```
USE tempdb;
GO
IF OBJECT_ID('dbo.Messages') IS NOT NULL
  DROP TABLE dbo.Messages;
GO

CREATE TABLE dbo.Messages
(
  msgid    INT          NOT NULL IDENTITY ,
  msgdate  DATETIME     NOT NULL DEFAULT(GETDATE()),
  msg      VARCHAR(MAX) NOT NULL,
```

```
  status  VARCHAR(20)  NOT NULL DEFAULT('new'),
  CONSTRAINT PK_Messages
    PRIMARY KEY NONCLUSTERED(msgid),
  CONSTRAINT UNQ_Messages_status_msgid
    UNIQUE CLUSTERED(status, msgid),
  CONSTRAINT CHK_Messages_status
    CHECK (status IN('new', 'open', 'done'))
);
```

For each message, you store a message ID, an entry date, message text, and a status indicating whether the message wasn't processed yet (*'new'*), is being processed (*'open'*), or has already been processed (*'done'*).

The following code simulates a session that generates messages by using a loop that inserts a message with random text every second. The status of newly inserted messages is *'new'* because the status column was assigned with the default value *'new'*. Run this code from multiple sessions at the same time:

```
SET NOCOUNT ON;
USE tempdb;
GO
DECLARE @msg AS VARCHAR(MAX);
WHILE 1=1
BEGIN
  SET @msg = 'msg' + RIGHT('000000000'
    + CAST(CAST(RAND()*2000000000 AS INT)+1 AS VARCHAR(10)), 10);
  INSERT INTO dbo.Messages(msg) VALUES(@msg);
  WAITFOR DELAY '00:00:01';
END
```

Of course, you can play with the delay period as you like.

The following code simulates a session that processes messages using the following steps:

1. Form an endless loop that constantly processes messages.

2. Lock @n available new messages using an UPDATE TOP(@n) statement with the READPAST hint to skip locked rows, and change their status to *'open'*. @n represents a configurable input that determines the maximum number of messages to process in each iteration.

3. Store the attributes of the messages in the *@Msgs* table variable using the OUTPUT clause.

4. Process the messages.

5. Set the status of the messages to *'done'* by joining the Messages table and the *@Msgs* table variable.

6. If no new message was found in the Messages table, wait for one second.

```
SET NOCOUNT ON;
USE tempdb;
```

```
SET NOCOUNT ON;
USE tempdb;
GO

DECLARE @Msgs TABLE(msgid INT, msgdate DATETIME, msg VARCHAR(MAX));
DECLARE @n AS INT;
SET @n = 3;

WHILE 1 = 1
BEGIN
  UPDATE TOP(@n) dbo.Messages WITH(READPAST) SET status = 'open'
    OUTPUT inserted.msgid, inserted.msgdate, inserted.msg INTO @Msgs
    OUTPUT inserted.msgid, inserted.msgdate, inserted.msg
  WHERE status = 'new';

  IF @@rowcount > 0
  BEGIN
    PRINT 'Processing messages...';
    /* ...process messages here... */

    WITH UPD_CTE AS
    (
      SELECT M.status
      FROM dbo.Messages AS M
        JOIN @Msgs AS N
          ON M.msgid = N.msgid
    )
    UPDATE UPD_CTE
      SET status = 'done';

    DELETE FROM @Msgs;
  END
  ELSE
  BEGIN
    PRINT 'No messages to process.';
    WAITFOR DELAY '00:00:01';
  END
END
```

You can run this code from multiple sessions at the same time. You can increase the number of sessions that would run this code based on the processing throughput that you need to accommodate.

Note that just for demonstration purposes, I included in the first UPDATE statement a second OUTPUT clause, which returns the messages back to the caller. I find this UPDATE statement particularly beautiful because it encompasses four different T-SQL enhancements in SQL Server 2005: UPDATE TOP, TOP with an input expression, the OUTPUT clause, and the READPAST hint in data modification statements. The READPAST hint was available in SQL Server 2000, but only to SELECT queries.

SELECT and UPDATE Statement Assignments

This section covers statements that assign values to variables and, in the case of UPDATE, can modify data at the same time. There are some tricky issues with such assignments that you might want to be aware of. Being familiar with the way assignments work in T-SQL is important to program correctly—that is, to program what you intended to.

Assignment SELECT

I'll start with assignment SELECT statements. T-SQL supports assigning values to variables using a SELECT statement, but the ANSI form of assignment, which is also supported by T-SQL, is to use a SET statement. So, as a rule, unless there's a compelling reason to do otherwise, it's a good practice to stick to using SET. I'll describe cases where you might want to use SELECT because it has advantages over SET in those cases. However, as I will demonstrate shortly, you should be aware that when using SELECT, your code is more prone to errors.

As an example of the way an assignment SELECT works, suppose you need to assign the employee ID whose last name matches a given pattern (*@pattern*) to the *@EmpID* variable. You assume that only one employee will match the pattern. The following code, which uses an assignment SELECT, doesn't accomplish the requirement:

```
USE Northwind;

DECLARE @EmpID AS INT, @Pattern AS NVARCHAR(100);

SET @Pattern = N'Davolio'; -- Try also N'Ben-Gan', N'D%';
SET @EmpID = 999;

SELECT @EmpID = EmployeeID
FROM dbo.Employees
WHERE LastName LIKE @Pattern;

SELECT @EmpID;
```

Given *N'Davolio'* as the input pattern, you get the employee ID 1 in the *@EmpID* variable. In this case, only one employee matched the filter. However, if you're given a pattern that does not apply to any existing last name in the Employees table (for example, *N'Ben-Gan'*), the assignment doesn't take place even once. The content of the *@EmpID* variable remains as it was before the assignment—999. (This value is used for demonstration purposes.) If you're given a pattern that matches more than one last name (for example, *N'D%'*), this code will issue multiple assignments, overwriting the previous value in *@EmpID* with each assignment. The final value of *@EmpID* will be the employee ID from the qualifying row that SQL Server happened to access last.

A much safer way to assign the qualifying employee ID to the *@EmpID* variable is to use a SET statement as follows:

```
DECLARE @EmpID AS INT, @Pattern AS NVARCHAR(100);

SET @Pattern = N'Davolio'; -- Try also N'Ben-Gan', N'D%';
SET @EmpID = 999;

SET @EmpID = (SELECT EmployeeID
              FROM dbo.Employees
              WHERE LastName LIKE @Pattern);

SELECT @EmpID;
```

If only one employee qualifies, you will get the employee ID in the *@EmpID* variable. If no employee qualifies, the subquery will set *@EmpID* to NULL. When you get a NULL, you know that you had no matches. If multiple employees qualify, you will get an error saying that the subquery returned more than one value. In such a case, you will realize that there's something wrong with your assumptions or with the design of your code. But the problem will surface as opposed to eluding you.

When you understand how an assignment SELECT works, you can use it to your advantage. For example, a SET statement can assign only one variable at a time. An assignment SELECT can assign values to multiple variables within the same statement. With well-designed code, this capability can give you performance benefits. For example, the following code assigns the first name and last name of a given employee to variables:

```
DECLARE @FirstName AS NVARCHAR(10), @LastName AS NVARCHAR(20);

SELECT @FirstName = NULL, @LastName = NULL;

SELECT @FirstName = FirstName, @LastName = LastName
FROM dbo.Employees
WHERE EmployeeID = 3;

SELECT @FirstName, @LastName;
```

Notice that this code uses the primary key to filter an employee, meaning that you cannot get more than one row back. The code also initializes the *@FirstName* and *@LastName* variables with NULLs. If no employee qualifies, the variables will simply retain the NULLs. This type of assignment is especially useful in triggers when you want to read attributes from the special tables inserted and deleted into your own variables, after you verify that only one row was affected.

Technically, you could rely on the fact that an assignment SELECT performs multiple assignments when multiple rows qualify. For example, you could do aggregate calculations, such as concatenating all order IDs for a given customer:

```
DECLARE @Orders AS VARCHAR(8000), @CustomerID AS NCHAR(5);
SET @CustomerID = N'ALFKI';
SET @Orders = '';
```

```
SELECT @Orders = @Orders + CAST(OrderID AS VARCHAR(10)) + ';'
FROM dbo.Orders
WHERE CustomerID = @CustomerID;

SELECT @Orders;
```

However, this code is far from being standard, and you can't guarantee the order of assignment. I've seen attempts programmers made to control the order of assignment by introducing an ORDER BY clause like so:

```
DECLARE @Orders AS VARCHAR(8000), @CustomerID AS NCHAR(5);
SET @CustomerID = N'ALFKI';
SET @Orders = '';

SELECT @Orders = @Orders + CAST(OrderID AS VARCHAR(10)) + ';'
FROM dbo.Orders
WHERE CustomerID = @CustomerID
ORDER BY OrderDate, OrderID;

SELECT @Orders;
```

But you cannot force the optimizer to sort before applying the assignments. If the optimizer chooses to sort after the assignments, the ORDER BY clause here fails to have the desired effect. You realize that when you specify an ORDER BY clause you might get an intermediate state of the variable. In short, it's better to not rely on such techniques. There are enough supported and guaranteed techniques that you can choose from for such calculations, many of which I covered in Chapter 6.

Assignment UPDATE

T-SQL also supports a nonstandard UPDATE syntax that can assign values to variables in addition to modifying data. To demonstrate the technique, first run the following code, which creates the table T1 and populates it with sample data:

```
USE tempdb;
GO
IF OBJECT_ID('dbo.T1') IS NOT NULL
  DROP TABLE dbo.T1;
GO

CREATE TABLE dbo.T1
(
  col1 INT        NOT NULL,
  col2 VARCHAR(5) NOT NULL
);

INSERT INTO dbo.T1(col1, col2) VALUES(0, 'A');
INSERT INTO dbo.T1(col1, col2) VALUES(0, 'B');
INSERT INTO dbo.T1(col1, col2) VALUES(0, 'C');
INSERT INTO dbo.T1(col1, col2) VALUES(0, 'C');
INSERT INTO dbo.T1(col1, col2) VALUES(0, 'C');
INSERT INTO dbo.T1(col1, col2) VALUES(0, 'B');
```

```
INSERT INTO dbo.T1(col1, col2) VALUES(0, 'A');
INSERT INTO dbo.T1(col1, col2) VALUES(0, 'A');
INSERT INTO dbo.T1(col1, col2) VALUES(0, 'C');
INSERT INTO dbo.T1(col1, col2) VALUES(0, 'C');
```

Currently, the T1 table has no primary key and there's no way to uniquely identify the rows. Suppose that you wanted to assign unique integers to *col1* and then make it the primary key. You can use the following assignment UPDATE to achieve this task:

```
DECLARE @i AS INT;
SET @i = 0;
UPDATE dbo.T1 SET @i = col1 = @i + 1;
```

This code declares the variable @i and initializes it with 0. The UPDATE statement then scans the data and, for each row, sets the current *col1* value to @i + 1, and then sets @i's value to *col1*'s new value. Logically, the SET clause is equivalent to *SET col1 = @i + 1, @i = @i + 1*. However, in such an UPDATE statement, there's no way for you to control the order in which the rows in T1 will be scanned and modified. For example, Table 8-4 shows how the contents of T1 might look after the assignment.

Table 8-4   Contents of T1 After Applying Assignment UPDATE

col1	col2
1	A
2	B
3	C
4	C
5	C
6	B
7	A
8	A
9	C
10	C

But keep in mind that it might be different. As long as you don't care about the order in which the data is scanned and modified, you might be happy with this technique. It is very fast, as it scans the data only once.

SQL Server 2005 allows you to achieve the task in an elegant manner, where you can guarantee the result row numbers will be based on a requested ordering. To do so, issue an UPDATE against a CTE that calculates row numbers based on any desired order:

```
WITH T1RN AS
(
  SELECT col1, ROW_NUMBER() OVER(ORDER BY col2) AS RowNum
  FROM dbo.T1
)
UPDATE T1RN SET col1 = RowNum;
```

Table 8-5 shows the contents of T1 after the UPDATE.

Table 8-5   Contents of T1 After Applying UPDATE Against CTE

col1	col2
1	A
4	B
6	C
7	C
8	C
5	B
2	A
3	A
9	C
10	C

By now, you have probably figured out why my favorite features in SQL Server 2005 are the ROW_NUMBER function and CTEs.

Other Performance Considerations

In this section, I'll provide a brief background about designing and architecting write-intensive systems. I thought that such background might be interesting for programmers, particularly in terms of realizing that there's a lot involved in designing systems when aiming for good modification performance. If you're not familiar with the terms described in this section, feel free to skip it.

> **More Info**   You can find more thorough coverage of the subject and more detailed explanations about the terms discussed here in *Inside Microsoft SQL Server 2005: The Storage Engine* (Microsoft Press, 2006) by Kalen Delaney.

You need to take several important things into consideration when designing write-intensive systems. Unless I explicitly mention otherwise, the discussion here applies to any type of data modification (inserting, deleting, and updating data).

In terms of physical design of your database system, remember that modifications affect two sections of the database: the data and the transaction log. When a modification takes place, SQL Server first looks for the pages that need to be modified in cache. If the target pages are already in cache, SQL Server modifies them there. If not, SQL Server will first load the target pages from the data portion of the database into cache, and then modify them there. SQL Server writes the change to the transaction log. (I'll discuss aspects of logging shortly.) SQL Server periodically runs a checkpoint process, which flushes dirty (changed) pages from cache to the data portion of the database on disk. However, SQL Server will flush only dirty pages for which the change was already written to the transaction log. The transaction log essentially provides the durability facet of transactions (the D part of the ACID facets of a transaction), allowing rollback and roll-forward capabilities.

Multiple write activities to the data portion of the database can be done simultaneously by using multiple disk drives. Therefore, striping the data over multiple disk drives is a key performance factor. The more spindles, the better. RAID 10 is typically the optimal type of RAID system for write-intensive environments. RAID 10 both stripes the data and mirrors every drive. It doesn't involve any parity calculations. Its main downside is that it's expensive because half the drives in the array are used to mirror the other half. RAID 5 is usually a poor choice for write-intensive systems because it involves parity calculations with every write. Its main advantage is its low cost, because for an array with n drives, only $1/n$ is used for parity. However, in many cases RAID 10 can yield more than a 50 percent write performance improvement over RAID 5, so its higher cost is usually worthwhile. For systems that mainly read data (for example, data warehouses), RAID 5 is fine for the data portion as long as the extract, transform, and load (ETL) process has a sufficient window of time (typically during the night). While during the day, applications only read data from the data warehouse.

As for the transaction log, its architecture is such that it can be written only synchronously— that is, only in a sequential manner. Therefore, striping the log over multiple disk drives provides no benefit unless you also have processes that read from the transaction log. One example of a process that reads from the transaction log is transaction log replication. Another example is accessing the deleted and inserted views in triggers in SQL Server 2000.

These views in SQL Server 2000 reflect the portion of the log containing the change that fired the trigger. In SQL Server 2005, deleted and inserted rows are based on the new row-versioning technology, which maintains row versions in the tempdb database. This means that when you access the inserted and deleted views, SQL Server 2005 will scan data in tempdb and not the transaction log. At any rate, it's a good practice to separate the transaction log into its own drive to avoid interfering with its activity. Any interference with the transaction log activity ultimately postpones writes to the data portion of the database. Unless you have processes reading from the transaction log, RAID 1 is sufficient. RAID 1 just mirrors a drive and doesn't stripe data. But if you also have intensive processes reading from the log, RAID 10 would be a better choice.

As for tempdb, it's always a good idea to stripe it using RAID 10. That's true for both online transaction processing (OLTP) and data warehouse systems, because SQL Server spools data in tempdb for many background activities related to both reads and writes. Tuning tempdb becomes even more important in SQL Server 2005 because the new row-versioning technology that is used by several activities stores and reads row versions from tempdb. Activities that use row-versioning include online index operations, constructing the deleted and inserted tables in triggers, new snapshot isolations, and multiple active result sets (MARS).

The synchronous manner in which SQL Server writes to the transaction log has a significant performance impact on data modification. The performance of fully logged modifications is often bound by the time it takes to write to the log. Furthermore, once the capacity of writes reaches the throughput of the disk drive on which the log resides, modification will start waiting for log writes. When the transaction log becomes the bottleneck, you should consider splitting the database into multiple ones, each with its own transaction log residing on separate disk drives.

With this background, you can see that in many cases the performance of data modifications in general—and data insertions in particular—will be strongly related to the amount of logging. When designing insert processes, one of your main considerations should be the amount of logging.

SQL Server will always fully log a modification unless two conditions are met: the database recovery model is not FULL, and the operation is considered a BULK operation. A BULK operation issued against a database with a non-FULL recovery model is minimally logged. Minimal logging means recording only the addresses of the extents that were allocated during the operation to support rollback capabilities, as opposed to logging the whole change. BULK operations include creation or rebuilding of an index, inserts that use the BULK engine (for example, BULK INSERT), SELECT INTO, Large Object (LOB) manipulation. Examples for LOB manipulation in SQL Server 2000 include WRITETEXT and UPDATETEXT. SQL Server 2005 also supports new LOB manipulation techniques, including using the BULK rowset provider and the WRITE method. A minimally logged modification is typically dramatically faster than a fully logged modification.

So, when designing insert processes, your first choice should be to use a BULK operation. The second choice should be to use a set-based multirow INSERT (INSERT SELECT), and the last choice should be individual INSERTs. The basic rule is the amount of logging. Individual INSERTs incur substantially more logging than multirow INSERTs, which in turn incur more logging than BULK operations that are run in a database with a non-FULL recovery model.

Another factor that will affect the performance of your inserts is the transaction size. This is a tricky issue.

The worst-case scenario is inserting individual rows, each in its own transaction. In such a case, not only is the INSERT fully logged, each INSERT causes the writing of three records to the transaction log: BEGIN TRAN, the INSERT itself, and a COMMIT TRAN. Besides the excessive writes to the log, you need to consider the overhead involved with maintaining each transaction (for example, acquiring locks, releasing locks, and so on). To improve insert performance, you want to encapsulate each batch of multiple rows into a single transaction.

The question is, what's the optimal transaction size? That's the tricky part. Things are not black and white in the sense that single-row transactions would be the worst-case scenario and one big transaction would be the best-case scenario. In practice, as the transaction grows larger, the insert performance improves up to a point. The point at which insert performance starts degrading is when maintaining the huge transaction involves too much overhead for SQL Server. Many factors affect the transaction size that would give you the optimal insert performance. These include the hardware, layout of your database (data, log), index design, and so on. So, in practical terms, the best way to figure out the optimal transaction size for a given table is to use a benchmark. Just test your insert process with different transaction sizes, increasing or decreasing the number of rows you encapsulate in a single transaction based on the performance that you get. After tweaking the transaction size several times like this, you will find the optimal one.

When tuning single row inserts, in your test environment you can form a loop that inserts a row in each iteration, and maintain a counter in your INSERT loop. Open a new transaction before every n iterations, where n is the number of rows you want to test inserting in a single transaction, and commit the transaction after every n iterations. I've seen production environments that collect the data for insertion from the source environments, and form such a loop to insert data to the target tables. Of course, not every system is designed to accommodate such a looping logic.

This process (controlling the insert transaction size) is relevant to any type of insert—that is, single-row INSERTs, multiple row set–based INSERTs (INSERT SELECT), and bulk inserts. With bulk inserts (for example, using BULK INSERT), by default, the whole insert is considered a single transaction. But you can control the number of rows per transaction and the way the insert will be optimized by setting the BATCHSIZE and ROWS_PER_BATCH options.

Conclusion

Data modifications involve many challenges. You need to be familiar with SQL Server's architecture and internals to design systems that can cope with large volumes of data, and large-scale modifications. There are also many challenging logical problems related to data modifications, such as maintaining your own custom sequence, deleting rows with duplicate data, and assigning unique values to existing rows. In this chapter, I covered performance aspects of data modifications as well as logical ones. I introduced quite a few key techniques that you will likely find useful.

Chapter 9
Graphs, Trees, Hierarchies, and Recursive Queries

This chapter covers treatment of specialized data structures called graphs, trees, and hierarchies in Microsoft SQL Server using T-SQL. Of the three, probably the most commonly used among T-SQL programmers is *hierarchy*, and this term is sometimes used even when the data structure involved is not really a hierarchy. I'll start with a terminology section describing each data structure to clear the confusion.

Treatment (representation, maintenance, and manipulation) of graphs, trees, and hierarchies in an RDBMS is far from trivial. I'll discuss two main approaches, one based on iterative/recursive logic, and another based on materializing extra information in the database that describes the data structure.

Interestingly, even though these data structures have been and still are commonly implemented in relational database management systems (RDBMSs), support for recursive queries was only introduced in the standard ANSI SQL:1999. SQL Server 2005 for the first time adopted to some extent the ANSI SQL:1999 recursive querying extensions in T-SQL.

In this chapter, I'll cover solutions that use the new recursive queries in SQL Server 2005, as well as solutions that are applicable in earlier versions of SQL Server.

Tip I also urge you to look up Vadim Tropashko's Nested Intervals model at *http://www. dbazine.com*. It is a beautiful model, very interesting intellectually, and Vadim covers practical issues such as implementation and performance. However, I find Vadim's model to be substantially more complex than most mere mortals (including me) can grasp in full, so I won't cover it here. The solutions I will cover here, on the other hand, will be fairly simple to understand and implement by experienced T-SQL programmers. Before you make an attempt at reading Vadim's stuff, make sure you have enough coffee and enough hours of sleep.

As promised, I'll start with a terminology section describing graphs, trees, and hierarchies.

Terminology

> **Note**   The explanations in this section are based on definitions from the National Institute of Standards and Technology (NIST). I made some revisions and added narrative to the original definitions to make them less formal and keep relevance to the subject area (T-SQL).
>
> For more complete and formal definitions of graphs, trees, and related terms, please refer to: *http://www.nist.gov/dads/*

Graphs

A graph is a set of items connected by *edges*. Each item is called a *vertex* or *node*. An edge is a connection between two vertices of a graph.

A *graph* is a catch-all term for a data structure, and many scenarios can be represented as graphs—for example, employee organizational charts, bills of materials (BOMs), road systems, and so on. To narrow down the type of graph to a more specific case, you need to identify its properties:

- **Directed/Undirected**   In a directed graph (also known as a *digraph*), there's a direction or order to the two vertices of an edge. For example, in a BOM graph for coffee-shop products, Latte contains Milk and not the other way around. There's an edge (containment relationship) in the graph for the pair of vertices/items (Latte, Milk), but no edge for the pair (Milk, Latte).

  In an undirected graph, each edge simply connects two vertices, with no particular order. For example, in a road system graph there's a road between Los Angeles and San Francisco. The edge (road) between the vertices (cities) Los Angeles and San Francisco can be expressed as either of the following: {Los Angeles, San Francisco} or {San Francisco, Los Angeles}.

- **Acyclic**   An acyclic graph is a graph with no cycle—that is, no *path* that starts and ends at the same vertex—for example, employee organizational charts and BOMs. A directed acyclic graph is also known as a *DAG*.

  If there are paths that start and end at the same vertex—as there usually are in road systems—the graph is not acyclic.

- **Connected**   A connected graph is a graph where there's a path between every pair of vertices—for example, employee organizational charts.

Trees

A tree is a special case of a graph—a connected, acyclic graph.

A *rooted tree* is accessed beginning at the *root* node. Each node is either a *leaf* or an *internal node*. An internal node has one or more *child* nodes and is called the *parent* of its child nodes. All children of the same node are *siblings*. Contrary to the appearance in a physical tree, the root is usually depicted at the top of the structure and the leaves are depicted at the bottom. (See Figure 9-1.)

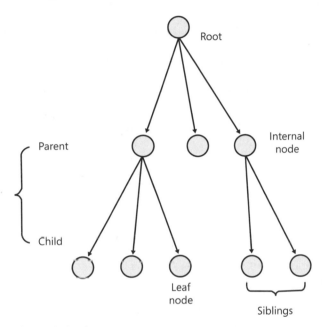

Figure 9-1   A tree

A *forest* is a collection of one or more trees—for example, forum discussions can be represented as a forest where each thread is a tree.

Hierarchies

Some scenarios can be described as a *hierarchy* and modeled as an directed acyclic graph—for example, inheritance among types/classes in object-oriented programming and reports-to relationships in an employee organizational chart. In the former, the edges of the graph locate the inheritance. Classes can inherit methods and properties from other classes (and possibly from multiple classes). In the latter, the edges represent the reports-to relationship between employees. Notice the acyclic, directed nature of these scenarios. The management chain of responsibility in a company cannot go around in circles, for example.

Scenarios

Throughout the chapter, I will use three scenarios: Employee Organizational Chart (tree, hierarchy), Bill Of Materials or BOM (DAG), and Road System (undirected cyclic graph). Note what distinguishes a (directed) tree from a DAG. All trees are DAGs, but not all DAGs are trees. In a tree, an item can have at most one parent; in some management hierarchies, an employee can have more than one manager.

Employee Organizational Chart

The employee organizational chart that I will use is depicted graphically in Figure 9-2.

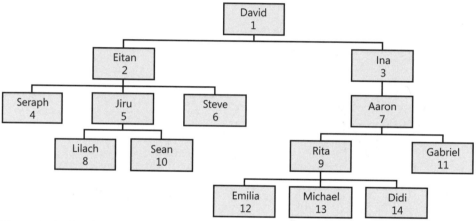

Figure 9-2 Employee Organizational Chart

To create the Employees table and populate it with sample data, run the code in Listing 9-1. The contents of the Employees table are shown in Table 9-1.

Listing 9-1 Data definition language and sample data for the Employees table

```
SET NOCOUNT ON;
USE tempdb;
GO
IF OBJECT_ID('dbo.Employees') IS NOT NULL
  DROP TABLE dbo.Employees;
GO
CREATE TABLE dbo.Employees
(
  empid   INT        NOT NULL PRIMARY KEY,
  mgrid   INT        NULL     REFERENCES dbo.Employees,
  empname VARCHAR(25) NOT NULL,
  salary  MONEY      NOT NULL,
  CHECK (empid <> mgrid)
);
```

```
INSERT INTO dbo.Employees(empid, mgrid, empname, salary)
  VALUES(1, NULL, 'David', $10000.00);
INSERT INTO dbo.Employees(empid, mgrid, empname, salary)
  VALUES(2, 1, 'Eitan', $7000.00);
INSERT INTO dbo.Employees(empid, mgrid, empname, salary)
  VALUES(3, 1, 'Ina', $7500.00);
INSERT INTO dbo.Employees(empid, mgrid, empname, salary)
  VALUES(4, 2, 'Seraph', $5000.00);
INSERT INTO dbo.Employees(empid, mgrid, empname, salary)
  VALUES(5, 2, 'Jiru', $5500.00);
INSERT INTO dbo.Employees(empid, mgrid, empname, salary)
  VALUES(6, 2, 'Steve', $4500.00);
INSERT INTO dbo.Employees(empid, mgrid, empname, salary)
  VALUES(7, 3, 'Aaron', $5000.00);
INSERT INTO dbo.Employees(empid, mgrid, empname, salary)
  VALUES(8, 5, 'Lilach', $3500.00);
INSERT INTO dbo.Employees(empid, mgrid, empname, salary)
  VALUES(9, 7, 'Rita', $3000.00);
INSERT INTO dbo.Employees(empid, mgrid, empname, salary)
  VALUES(10, 5, 'Sean', $3000.00);
INSERT INTO dbo.Employees(empid, mgrid, empname, salary)
  VALUES(11, 7, 'Gabriel', $3000.00);
INSERT INTO dbo.Employees(empid, mgrid, empname, salary)
  VALUES(12, 9, 'Emilia' , $2000.00);
INSERT INTO dbo.Employees(empid, mgrid, empname, salary)
  VALUES(13, 9, 'Michael', $2000.00);
INSERT INTO dbo.Employees(empid, mgrid, empname, salary)
  VALUES(14, 9, 'Didi', $1500.00);

CREATE UNIQUE INDEX idx_unc_mgrid_empid ON dbo.Employees(mgrid, empid);
```

Table 9-1   **Contents of Employees Table**

empid	mgrid	empname	salary
1	NULL	David	10000.0000
2	1	Eitan	7000.0000
3	1	Ina	7500.0000
4	2	Seraph	5000.0000
5	2	Jiru	5500.0000
6	2	Steve	4500.0000
7	3	Aaron	5000.0000
8	5	Lilach	3500.0000
9	7	Rita	3000.0000
10	5	Sean	3000.0000
11	7	Gabriel	3000.0000
12	9	Emilia	2000.0000
13	9	Michael	2000.0000
14	9	Didi	1500.0000

The Employees table represents a management hierarchy as an adjacency list, where the manager and employee represent the parent and child nodes, respectively.

Bill of Materials (BOM)

I will use a BOM of coffee shop products, which is depicted graphically in Figure 9-3.

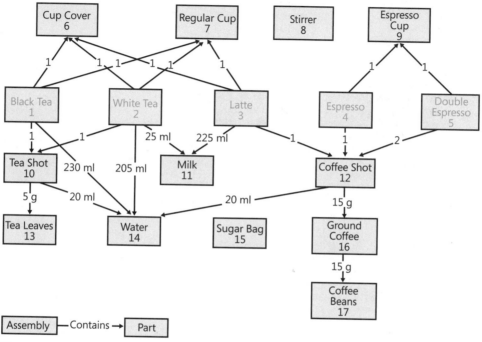

Figure 9-3   Bill of Materials (BOM)

To create the Parts and BOM tables and populate them with sample data, run the code in Listing 9-2. The contents of the Parts and BOM tables are shown in Tables 9-2 and 9-3.

Notice that the first scenario (employee organizational chart) requires only one table because it is modeled as a tree; both an edge (manager, employee) and a vertex (employee) can be represented by the same row. The BOM scenario requires two tables because it is modeled as a DAG, where multiple paths can lead to each node; an edge (assembly, part) is represented by a row in the BOM table, and a vertex (part) is represented by a row in the Parts table.

Listing 9-2   Data definition language and sample data for the Parts and BOM tables

```
SET NOCOUNT ON;
USE tempdb;
GO
IF OBJECT_ID('dbo.BOM') IS NOT NULL
  DROP TABLE dbo.BOM;
GO
IF OBJECT_ID('dbo.Parts') IS NOT NULL
  DROP TABLE dbo.Parts;
```

```
GO
CREATE TABLE dbo.Parts
(
  partid   INT         NOT NULL PRIMARY KEY,
  partname VARCHAR(25) NOT NULL
);

INSERT INTO dbo.Parts(partid, partname) VALUES( 1, 'Black Tea');
INSERT INTO dbo.Parts(partid, partname) VALUES( 2, 'White Tea');
INSERT INTO dbo.Parts(partid, partname) VALUES( 3, 'Latte');
INSERT INTO dbo.Parts(partid, partname) VALUES( 4, 'Espresso');
INSERT INTO dbo.Parts(partid, partname) VALUES( 5, 'Double Espresso');
INSERT INTO dbo.Parts(partid, partname) VALUES( 6, 'Cup Cover');
INSERT INTO dbo.Parts(partid, partname) VALUES( 7, 'Regular Cup');
INSERT INTO dbo.Parts(partid, partname) VALUES( 8, 'Stirrer');
INSERT INTO dbo.Parts(partid, partname) VALUES( 9, 'Espresso Cup');
INSERT INTO dbo.Parts(partid, partname) VALUES(10, 'Tea Shot');
INSERT INTO dbo.Parts(partid, partname) VALUES(11, 'Milk');
INSERT INTO dbo.Parts(partid, partname) VALUES(12, 'Coffee Shot');
INSERT INTO dbo.Parts(partid, partname) VALUES(13, 'Tea Leaves');
INSERT INTO dbo.Parts(partid, partname) VALUES(14, 'Water');
INSERT INTO dbo.Parts(partid, partname) VALUES(15, 'Sugar Bag');
INSERT INTO dbo.Parts(partid, partname) VALUES(16, 'Ground Coffee');
INSERT INTO dbo.Parts(partid, partname) VALUES(17, 'Coffee Beans');


CREATE TABLE dbo.BOM
(
  partid     INT         NOT NULL REFERENCES dbo.Parts,
  assemblyid INT         NULL     REFERENCES dbo.Parts,
  unit       VARCHAR(3)  NOT NULL,
  qty        DECIMAL(8, 2) NOT NULL,
  UNIQUE(partid, assemblyid),
  CHECK (partid <> assemblyid)
);

INSERT INTO dbo.BOM(partid, assemblyid, unit, qty)
  VALUES( 1, NULL, 'EA',    1.00);
INSERT INTO dbo.BOM(partid, assemblyid, unit, qty)
  VALUES( 2, NULL, 'EA',    1.00);
INSERT INTO dbo.BOM(partid, assemblyid, unit, qty)
  VALUES( 3, NULL, 'EA',    1.00);
INSERT INTO dbo.BOM(partid, assemblyid, unit, qty)
  VALUES( 4, NULL, 'EA',    1.00);
INSERT INTO dbo.BOM(partid, assemblyid, unit, qty)
  VALUES( 5, NULL, 'EA',    1.00);
INSERT INTO dbo.BOM(partid, assemblyid, unit, qty)
  VALUES( 6,    1, 'EA',    1.00);
INSERT INTO dbo.BOM(partid, assemblyid, unit, qty)
  VALUES( 7,    1, 'EA',    1.00);
INSERT INTO dbo.BOM(partid, assemblyid, unit, qty)
  VALUES(10,    1, 'EA',    1.00);
INSERT INTO dbo.BOM(partid, assemblyid, unit, qty)
  VALUES(14,    1, 'mL', 230.00);
INSERT INTO dbo.BOM(partid, assemblyid, unit, qty)
  VALUES( 6,    2, 'EA',    1.00);
```

```
INSERT INTO dbo.BOM(partid, assemblyid, unit, qty)
  VALUES( 7,    2, 'EA',   1.00);
INSERT INTO dbo.BOM(partid, assemblyid, unit, qty)
  VALUES(10,    2, 'EA',   1.00);
INSERT INTO dbo.BOM(partid, assemblyid, unit, qty)
  VALUES(14,    2, 'mL', 205.00);
INSERT INTO dbo.BOM(partid, assemblyid, unit, qty)
  VALUES(11,    2, 'mL',  25.00);
INSERT INTO dbo.BOM(partid, assemblyid, unit, qty)
  VALUES( 6,    3, 'EA',   1.00);
INSERT INTO dbo.BOM(partid, assemblyid, unit, qty)
  VALUES( 7,    3, 'EA',   1.00);
INSERT INTO dbo.BOM(partid, assemblyid, unit, qty)
  VALUES(11,    3, 'mL', 225.00);
INSERT INTO dbo.BOM(partid, assemblyid, unit, qty)
  VALUES(12,    3, 'EA',   1.00);
INSERT INTO dbo.BOM(partid, assemblyid, unit, qty)
  VALUES( 9,    4, 'EA',   1.00);
INSERT INTO dbo.BOM(partid, assemblyid, unit, qty)
  VALUES(12,    4, 'EA',   1.00);
INSERT INTO dbo.BOM(partid, assemblyid, unit, qty)
  VALUES( 9,    5, 'EA',   1.00);
INSERT INTO dbo.BOM(partid, assemblyid, unit, qty)
  VALUES(12,    5, 'EA',   2.00);
INSERT INTO dbo.BOM(partid, assemblyid, unit, qty)
  VALUES(13,   10, 'g'  ,  5.00);
INSERT INTO dbo.BOM(partid, assemblyid, unit, qty)
  VALUES(14,   10, 'mL',  20.00);
INSERT INTO dbo.BOM(partid, assemblyid, unit, qty)
  VALUES(14,   12, 'mL',  20.00);
INSERT INTO dbo.BOM(partid, assemblyid, unit, qty)
  VALUES(16,   12, 'g'  , 15.00);
INSERT INTO dbo.BOM(partid, assemblyid, unit, qty)
  VALUES(17,   16, 'g'  , 15.00);
```

Table 9-2   Contents of Parts Table

partid	partname
1	Black Tea
2	White Tea
3	Latte
4	Espresso
5	Double Espresso
6	Cup Cover
7	Regular Cup
8	Stirrer
9	Espresso Cup
10	Tea Shot

Table 9-2   **Contents of Parts Table**

partid	partname
11	Milk
12	Coffee Shot
13	Tea Leaves
14	Water
15	Sugar Bag
16	Ground Coffee
17	Coffee Beans

Table 9-3   **Contents of BOM Table**

partid	assemblyid	unit	qty
1	NULL	EA	1.00
2	NULL	EA	1.00
3	NULL	EA	1.00
4	NULL	EA	1.00
5	NULL	EA	1.00
6	1	EA	1.00
7	1	EA	1.00
10	1	EA	1.00
14	1	mL	230.00
6	2	EA	1.00
7	2	EA	1.00
10	2	EA	1.00
14	2	mL	205.00
11	2	mL	25.00
6	3	EA	1.00
7	3	EA	1.00
11	3	mL	225.00
12	3	EA	1.00
9	4	EA	1.00
12	4	EA	1.00
9	5	EA	1.00
12	5	EA	2.00
13	10	g	5.00
14	10	mL	20.00
14	12	mL	20.00
16	12	g	15.00
17	16	g	15.00

BOM represents a directed acyclic graph (DAG). It holds the parent and child node IDs in the *assemblyid* and *partid* attributes, respectively. BOM also represents a *weighted* graph, where a weight/number is associated with each edge. In our case, that weight is the *qty* attribute that holds the quantity of the part within the assembly (assembly of sub-parts). The unit attribute holds the unit of the *qty* (EA for each, g for gram, mL for milliliter, and so on).

Road System

The Road System that I will use is that of several major cities in the United States, and it is depicted graphically in Figure 9-4.

Figure 9-4   Road System

To create the Cities and Roads tables and populate them with sample data, run the code in Listing 9-3. The contents of the Cities and Roads tables are shown in Tables 9-4 and 9-5.

Listing 9-3   Data definition language and sample data for the Cities and Roads tables

```
SET NOCOUNT ON;
USE tempdb;
GO
IF OBJECT_ID('dbo.Roads') IS NOT NULL
  DROP TABLE dbo.Roads;
```

```
GO
IF OBJECT_ID('dbo.Cities') IS NOT NULL
  DROP TABLE dbo.Cities;
GO

CREATE TABLE dbo.Cities
(
  cityid  CHAR(3)     NOT NULL PRIMARY KEY,
  city    VARCHAR(30) NOT NULL,
  region  VARCHAR(30) NULL,
  country VARCHAR(30) NOT NULL
);

INSERT INTO dbo.Cities(cityid, city, region, country)
  VALUES('ATL', 'Atlanta', 'GA', 'USA');
INSERT INTO dbo.Cities(cityid, city, region, country)
  VALUES('ORD', 'Chicago', 'IL', 'USA');
INSERT INTO dbo.Cities(cityid, city, region, country)
  VALUES('DEN', 'Denver', 'CO', 'USA');
INSERT INTO dbo.Cities(cityid, city, region, country)
  VALUES('IAH', 'Houston', 'TX', 'USA');
INSERT INTO dbo.Cities(cityid, city, region, country)
  VALUES('MCI', 'Kansas City', 'KS', 'USA');
INSERT INTO dbo.Cities(cityid, city, region, country)
  VALUES('LAX', 'Los Angeles', 'CA', 'USA');
INSERT INTO dbo.Cities(cityid, city, region, country)
  VALUES('MIA', 'Miami', 'FL', 'USA');
INSERT INTO dbo.Cities(cityid, city, region, country)
  VALUES('MSP', 'Minneapolis', 'MN', 'USA');
INSERT INTO dbo.Cities(cityid, city, region, country)
  VALUES('JFK', 'New York', 'NY', 'USA');
INSERT INTO dbo.Cities(cityid, city, region, country)
  VALUES('SEA', 'Seattle', 'WA', 'USA');
INSERT INTO dbo.Cities(cityid, city, region, country)
  VALUES('SFO', 'San Francisco', 'CA', 'USA');
INSERT INTO dbo.Cities(cityid, city, region, country)
  VALUES('ANC', 'Anchorage', 'AK', 'USA');
INSERT INTO dbo.Cities(cityid, city, region, country)
  VALUES('FAI', 'Fairbanks', 'AK', 'USA');

CREATE TABLE dbo.Roads
(
  city1    CHAR(3) NOT NULL REFERENCES dbo.Cities,
  city2    CHAR(3) NOT NULL REFERENCES dbo.Cities,
  distance INT     NOT NULL,
  PRIMARY KEY(city1, city2),
  CHECK(city1 < city2),
  CHECK(distance > 0)
);

INSERT INTO dbo.Roads(city1, city2, distance) VALUES('ANC', 'FAI', 359);
INSERT INTO dbo.Roads(city1, city2, distance) VALUES('ATL', 'ORD', 715);
INSERT INTO dbo.Roads(city1, city2, distance) VALUES('ATL', 'IAH', 800);
INSERT INTO dbo.Roads(city1, city2, distance) VALUES('ATL', 'MCI', 805);
```

```
INSERT INTO dbo.Roads(city1, city2, distance) VALUES('ATL', 'MIA', 665);
INSERT INTO dbo.Roads(city1, city2, distance) VALUES('ATL', 'JFK', 865);
INSERT INTO dbo.Roads(city1, city2, distance) VALUES('DEN', 'IAH', 1120);
INSERT INTO dbo.Roads(city1, city2, distance) VALUES('DEN', 'MCI', 600);
INSERT INTO dbo.Roads(city1, city2, distance) VALUES('DEN', 'LAX', 1025);
INSERT INTO dbo.Roads(city1, city2, distance) VALUES('DEN', 'MSP', 915);
INSERT INTO dbo.Roads(city1, city2, distance) VALUES('DEN', 'SEA', 1335);
INSERT INTO dbo.Roads(city1, city2, distance) VALUES('DEN', 'SFO', 1270);
INSERT INTO dbo.Roads(city1, city2, distance) VALUES('IAH', 'MCI', 795);
INSERT INTO dbo.Roads(city1, city2, distance) VALUES('IAH', 'LAX', 1550);
INSERT INTO dbo.Roads(city1, city2, distance) VALUES('IAH', 'MIA', 1190);
INSERT INTO dbo.Roads(city1, city2, distance) VALUES('JFK', 'ORD', 795);
INSERT INTO dbo.Roads(city1, city2, distance) VALUES('LAX', 'SFO', 385);
INSERT INTO dbo.Roads(city1, city2, distance) VALUES('MCI', 'ORD', 525);
INSERT INTO dbo.Roads(city1, city2, distance) VALUES('MCI', 'MSP', 440);
INSERT INTO dbo.Roads(city1, city2, distance) VALUES('MSP', 'ORD', 410);
INSERT INTO dbo.Roads(city1, city2, distance) VALUES('MSP', 'SEA', 2015);
INSERT INTO dbo.Roads(city1, city2, distance) VALUES('SEA', 'SFO', 815);
```

Table 9-4   Contents of Cities Table

cityid	city	region	country
ANC	Anchorage	AK	USA
ATL	Atlanta	GA	USA
DEN	Denver	CO	USA
FAI	Fairbanks	AK	USA
IAH	Houston	TX	USA
JFK	New York	NY	USA
LAX	Los Angeles	CA	USA
MCI	Kansas City	KS	USA
MIA	Miami	FL	USA
MSP	Minneapolis	MN	USA
ORD	Chicago	IL	USA
SEA	Seattle	WA	USA
SFO	San Francisco	CA	USA

Table 9-5   Contents of Roads Table

city1	city2	distance
ANC	FAI	359
ATL	IAH	800
ATL	JFK	865
ATL	MCI	805
ATL	MIA	665
ATL	ORD	715

Table 9-5   Contents of Roads Table

city1	city2	distance
DEN	IAH	1120
DEN	LAX	1025
DEN	MCI	600
DEN	MSP	915
DEN	SEA	1335
DEN	SFO	1270
IAH	LAX	1550
IAH	MCI	795
IAH	MIA	1190
JFK	ORD	795
LAX	SFO	385
MCI	MSP	440
MCI	ORD	525
MSP	ORD	410
MSP	SEA	2015
SEA	SFO	815

The Roads table represents an undirected cyclic weighted graph. Each edge (road) is represented by a row in the table. The attributes *city1 and city2* are two city IDs representing the nodes of the edge. The weight in this case is the distance attribute, which holds the distance between the cities in miles. Note that the Roads table has a CHECK constraint (*city1 < city2*) as part of its schema definition to reject attempts to enter the same edge twice (for example, {SEA, SFO} and {SFO, SEA}).

Having all the scenarios and sample data in place, let's go over the approaches to treatment of graphs, trees, and hierarchies. I'll cover three main approaches: iterative/recursive, materialized path, and nested sets.

Iteration/Recursion

Iterative approaches apply some form of loops or recursion. There are many iterative algorithms that traverse graphs. Some traverse graphs a node at a time and are usually implemented with cursors, but these are typically very slow. I will focus on algorithms that traverse graphs a level at a time using a combination of iterative or recursive logic and set-based queries. Given a set of nodes U, the *next level of subordinates* refers to the set V, which consists of the direct subordinates (children) of the nodes in U. In my experience, implementations of iterative algorithms that traverse a graph a level at a time perform much better than the ones that traverse a graph a node at a time.

There are several advantages to using iterative solutions rather than the other methods. First, you don't need to materialize any extra information describing the graph to the database besides the node IDs in the edges. In other words, there's no need to redesign your tables. The solutions traverse the graph by relying solely on the stored edge information—for example, (*mgrid, empid*), (*assemblyid, partid*), (*city1, city2*), and so on.

Second, most of the solutions that apply to trees also apply to the more generic digraphs. In other words, most solutions that apply to graphs where only one path can lead to a given node also apply to graphs where multiple paths may lead to a given node.

Finally, most of the solutions that I will describe in this section support a virtually unlimited number of levels.

I will use two main tools to implement solutions in my examples: user defined functions (UDFs) and recursive common table expressions (CTEs). UDFs have been available since SQL Server 2000, while CTEs were introduced in SQL Server 2005. When using UDFs, I'll rely on SQL Server 2000–compatible features only so that you will be able to implement the solutions in SQL Server 2000. Because CTEs are new to SQL Server 2005, I felt free to rely on other new T-SQL features (for example, using the ROW_NUMBER function). The core algorithms will be similar in both versions.

In my solutions, I focused on UDFs and CTEs, but note that in some cases when performance of a UDF or CTE is not satisfactory, you might get better performance by implementing a solution with a stored procedure. Stored procedures give you more control—for example, you can materialize and index interim sets in temporary tables, and so on.

However, I used UDFs and CTEs because I wanted to focus on the algorithms and the clarity of the solutions.

Subordinates

Let's start with a classical request to return subordinates; for example, return all subordinates of a given employee. More technically, you're after a subgraph/subtree of a given root in a directed graph (digraph). The iterative algorithm is very simple:

Input: *@root*

Algorithm:

- set *@lvl* = 0; insert into table @Subs row for *@root*

- while there were rows in the previous level of employees:

- set *@lvl* = *@lvl* + 1; insert into table @Subs rows for the next level (*mgrid* in (*empid* values in previous level))

- return @Subs

Run the code in Listing 9-4 to create the *fn_subordinates1* function, which implements this algorithm as a UDF.

Listing 9-4   Creation script for the *fn_subordinates1* function

```
----------------------------------------------------------------
-- Function: fn_subordinates1, Descendants
--
-- Input    : @root INT: Manager id
--
-- Output   : @Subs Table: id and level of subordinates of
--                         input manager (empid = @root) in all levels
--
-- Process : * Insert into @Subs row of input manager
--            * In a loop, while previous insert loaded more than 0 rows
--              insert into @Subs next level of subordinates
----------------------------------------------------------------
USE tempdb;
GO
IF OBJECT_ID('dbo.fn_subordinates1') IS NOT NULL
  DROP FUNCTION dbo.fn_subordinates1;
GO
CREATE FUNCTION dbo.fn_subordinates1(@root AS INT) RETURNS @Subs TABLE
(
  empid INT NOT NULL PRIMARY KEY NONCLUSTERED,
  lvl   INT NOT NULL,
  UNIQUE CLUSTERED(lvl, empid)  -- Index will be used to filter level
)
AS
BEGIN
  DECLARE @lvl AS INT;
  SET @lvl = 0;                 -- Initialize level counter with 0

  -- Insert root node into @Subs
  INSERT INTO @Subs(empid, lvl)
    SELECT empid, @lvl FROM dbo.Employees WHERE empid = @root;

  WHILE @@rowcount > 0          -- while previous level had rows
  BEGIN
    SET @lvl = @lvl + 1;        -- Increment level counter

    -- Insert next level of subordinates to @Subs
    INSERT INTO @Subs(empid, lvl)
      SELECT C.empid, @lvl
      FROM @Subs AS P           -- P = Parent
        JOIN dbo.Employees AS C -- C = Child
          ON P.lvl = @lvl - 1   -- Filter parents from previous level
          AND C.mgrid = P.empid;
  END

  RETURN;
END
GO
```

The function accepts the *@root* input parameter, which is the ID of the requested subtree's root employee. The function returns the @Subs table variable, with all subordinates of employee with ID = *@root* in all levels. Besides containing the employee attributes, @Subs also has a column called *lvl* that keeps track of the level in the subtree (0 for the subtree's root, and increasing from there by 1 in each iteration).

The function's code keeps track of the current level being handled in the @*lvl* local variable, which is initialized with zero.

The function's code first inserts into @Subs the row from Employees where *empid* = @*root*.

Then in a loop, while the last insert affects more than zero rows, the code increments the @*lvl* variable's value by one and loads to @Subs the next level of employees—in other words, direct subordinates of the managers loaded in the previous level.

To load the next level of employees to @Subs, the query in the loop joins @Subs (representing managers) with Employees (representing subordinates).

The *lvl* column is important because it allows you to isolate the managers that were inserted into @Subs in the last iteration. To return only subordinates of the previously inserted managers, the join condition filters from @Subs only rows where the *lvl* column is equal to the previous level (@*lvl* − 1).

To test the function, run the following code, which returns the subordinates of employee 3, as shown in Table 9-6:

```
SELECT empid, lvl FROM dbo.fn_subordinates1(3) AS S;
```

Table 9-6   Subtree of Employee 3, IDs Only

empid	lvl
3	0
7	1
9	2
11	2
12	3
13	3
14	3

You can verify that the output is correct by examining Figure 9-2 and following the subtree of the root employee (ID = 3).

To get other attributes of the employees besides just the employee ID, you can either rewrite the function and add those attributes to the @Subs table, or simply join the function with the Employees table like so:

```
SELECT E.empid, E.empname, S.lvl
FROM dbo.fn_subordinates1(3) AS S
  JOIN dbo.Employees AS E
    ON E.empid = S.empid;
```

You will get the output shown in Table 9-7.

Table 9-7   Subordinates of Employee 3, Including Employee Names

empid	empname	lvl
3	Ina	0
7	Aaron	1
9	Rita	2
11	Gabriel	2
12	Emilia	3
13	Michael	3
14	Didi	3

To limit the result set to leaf employees under the given root, simply add a filter with a NOT EXISTS predicate to select only employees that are not managers of other employees:

```
SELECT empid
FROM dbo.fn_subordinates1(3) AS P
WHERE NOT EXISTS
  (SELECT * FROM dbo.Employees AS C
   WHERE c.mgrid = P.empid);
```

This query returns employee IDs 11, 12, 13, and 14.

So far, you've seen the UDF implementation of a subtree under a given root. Listing 9-5 has the CTE solution (SQL Server 2005 only).

Listing 9-5   Subtree of a given root, CTE solution

```
DECLARE @root AS INT;
SET @root = 3;

WITH SubsCTE
AS
(
  -- Anchor member returns root node
  SELECT empid, empname, 0 AS lvl
  FROM dbo.Employees
  WHERE empid = @root

  UNION ALL

  -- Recursive member returns next level of children
  SELECT C.empid, C.empname, P.lvl + 1
  FROM SubsCTE AS P
    JOIN dbo.Employees AS C
      ON C.mgrid = P.empid
)
SELECT * FROM SubsCTE;
```

Running the code in Listing 9-5 gives the same results shown in Table 9-7.

The solution applies very similar logic to the UDF implementation. It's simpler in the sense that you don't need to explicitly define the returned table or to filter the previous level's managers.

The first query in the CTE's body returns the row from Employees for the given root employee. It also returns zero as the level of the root employee. In a recursive CTE, a query that doesn't have any recursive references is known as an *anchor member*.

The second query in the CTE's body (following the UNION ALL set operation) has a recursive reference to the CTE's name. This makes it a *recursive member*, and it is treated in a special manner. The recursive reference to the CTE's name (SubsCTE) represents the result set returned previously. The recursive member query joins the previous result set, which represents the managers in the previous level, with the Employees table to return the next level of employees. The recursive query also calculates the level value as the employee's manager level plus one. The first time that the recursive member is invoked, SubsCTE stands for the result set returned by the anchor member (root employee). There's no explicit termination check for the recursive member; rather, it is invoked repeatedly until it returns an empty set. Thus, the first time it is invoked, it returns direct subordinates of the subtree's root employee. The second time it is invoked, SubsCTE represents the result set of the first invocation of the recursive member (first level of subordinates), so it returns the second level of subordinates. The recursive member is invoked repeatedly until there are no more subordinates, in which case it will return an empty set and recursion will stop.

The reference to the CTE name in the outer query represents the UNION ALL of all the result sets returned by the invocation of the anchor member and all the invocations of the recursive member.

As I mentioned earlier, using iterative logic to return a subgraph of a digraph where multiple paths might exist to a node is similar to returning a subtree. Run the code in Listing 9-6 to create the *fn_partsexplosion* function. The function accepts a part ID representing an assembly in a BOM, and it returns the parts explosion (direct and indirect subitems) of the assembly.

Listing 9-6 Creation script for the *fn_partsexplosion* function

```
---------------------------------------------------------------------
-- Function: fn_partsexplosion, Parts Explosion
--
-- Input    : @root INT: assembly id
--
-- Output   : @PartsExplosion Table:
--                id and level of contained parts of input part
--                in all levels
--
-- Process  : * Insert into @PartsExplosion row of input root part
--            * In a loop, while previous insert loaded more than 0 rows
--              insert into @PartsExplosion next level of parts
---------------------------------------------------------------------
```

```
USE tempdb;
GO
IF OBJECT_ID('dbo.fn_partsexplosion') IS NOT NULL
  DROP FUNCTION dbo.fn_partsexplosion;
GO
CREATE FUNCTION dbo.fn_partsexplosion(@root AS INT)
  RETURNS @PartsExplosion Table
(
  partid INT           NOT NULL,
  qty    DECIMAL(8, 2) NOT NULL,
  unit   VARCHAR(3)    NOT NULL,
  lvl    INT           NOT NULL,
  n      INT           NOT NULL IDENTITY, -- surrogate key
  UNIQUE CLUSTERED(lvl, n)  -- Index will be used to filter lvl
)
AS
BEGIN
  DECLARE @lvl AS INT;
  SET @lvl = 0;                   -- Initialize level counter with 0

  -- Insert root node to @PartsExplosion
  INSERT INTO @PartsExplosion(partid, qty, unit, lvl)
    SELECT partid, qty, unit, @lvl
    FROM dbo.BOM
    WHERE partid = @root;

  WHILE @@rowcount > 0            -- while previous level had rows
  BEGIN
    SET @lvl = @lvl + 1;          -- Increment level counter

    -- Insert next level of subordinates to @PartsExplosion
    INSERT INTO @PartsExplosion(partid, qty, unit, lvl)
      SELECT C.partid, P.qty * C.qty, C.unit, @lvl
      FROM @PartsExplosion AS P  -- P = Parent
        JOIN dbo.BOM AS C          -- C = Child
          ON P.lvl = @lvl - 1    -- Filter parents from previous level
          AND C.assemblyid = P.partid;
  END

  RETURN;
END
GO
```

The implementation of the *fn_partsexplosion* function is similar to the implementation of the function *fn_subordinates1*. The row for the root part is loaded to the @PartsExplosion table variable (the function's output parameter). And then in a loop, while the previous insert loaded more than zero rows, the next level parts are loaded into @PartsExplosion. There is a small addition here that is specific to a BOM—calculating the quantity. The root part's quantity is simply the one stored in the part's row. The contained (child) part's quantity is the quantity of its containing (parent) item multiplied by its own quantity.

Run the following code to test the function, returning the part explosion of *partid* 2 (White Tea):

```
SELECT P.partid, P.partname, PE.qty, PE.unit, PE.lvl
FROM dbo.fn_partsexplosion(2) AS PE
  JOIN dbo.Parts AS P
    ON P.partid = PE.partid;
```

You can check the correctness of the output shown in Table 9-8 by examining Figure 9-3.

Table 9-8   Explosion of Part 2

partid	partname	qty	unit	lvl
2	White Tea	1.00	EA	0
6	Cup Cover	1.00	EA	1
7	Regular Cup	1.00	EA	1
10	Tea Shot	1.00	EA	1
11	Milk	25.00	mL	1
14	Water	205.00	mL	1
13	Tea Leaves	5.00	g	2
14	Water	20.00	mL	2

Listing 9-7 has the CTE solution for the parts explosion, which, again, is similar to the subtree solution with the addition of the quantity calculation.

Listing 9-7   CTE solution for the parts explosion

```
DECLARE @root AS INT;
SET @root = 2;

WITH PartsExplosionCTE
AS
(
  -- Anchor member returns root part
  SELECT partid, qty, unit, 0 AS lvl
  FROM dbo.BOM
  WHERE partid = @root

  UNION ALL

  -- Recursive member returns next level of parts
  SELECT C.partid, CAST(P.qty * C.qty AS DECIMAL(8, 2)),
    C.unit, P.lvl + 1
  FROM PartsExplosionCTE AS P
    JOIN dbo.BOM AS C
      ON C.assemblyid = P.partid
)
SELECT P.partid, P.partname, PE.qty, PE.unit, PE.lvl
FROM PartsExplosionCTE AS PE
  JOIN dbo.Parts AS P
    ON P.partid = PE.partid;
```

A parts explosion might contain more than one occurrence of the same part because different parts in the assembly might contain the same subpart. For example, you can notice in Table 9-8 that water appears twice because white tea contains 205 milliliters of water directly, and it also contains a tea shot, which in turn contains 20 milliliters of water. You might want to aggregate the result set by part and unit as follows, generating the output shown in Table 9-9:

```
SELECT P.partid, P.partname, PES.qty, PES.unit
FROM (SELECT partid, unit, SUM(qty) AS qty
      FROM dbo.fn_partsexplosion(2) AS PE
      GROUP BY partid, unit) AS PES
  JOIN dbo.Parts AS P
    ON P.partid = PES.partid;
```

Table 9-9   Explosion of Part 2, with Aggregated Parts

partid	partname	qty	unit
2	White Tea	1.00	EA
6	Cup Cover	1.00	EA
7	Regular Cup	1.00	EA
10	Tea Shot	1.00	EA
13	Tea Leaves	5.00	g
11	Milk	25.00	mL
14	Water	225.00	mL

I won't get into issues with grouping of parts that might contain different units of measurements here. Obviously, you'll need to deal with those by applying conversion factors.

As another example, the following code explodes part 5 (Double Espresso), returning the output shown in Table 9-10:

```
SELECT P.partid, P.partname, PES.qty, PES.unit
FROM (SELECT partid, unit, SUM(qty) AS qty
      FROM dbo.fn_partsexplosion(5) AS PE
      GROUP BY partid, unit) AS PES
  JOIN dbo.Parts AS P
    ON P.partid = PES.partid;
```

Table 9-10   Explosion of Part 5, with Aggregated Parts

partid	partname	qty	unit
5	Double Espresso	1.00	EA
9	Espresso Cup	1.00	EA
12	Coffee Shot	2.00	EA
16	Ground Coffee	30.00	g
17	Coffee Beans	450.00	g
14	Water	40.00	mL

Going back to returning a subtree of a given employee, you might need in some cases to limit the number of returned levels. To achieve this, there's a minor addition you need to make to the original algorithm:

Input: @root, @maxlevels (besides root)

Algorithm:

- set @lvl = 0; insert into table @Subs row for @root

- while there were rows in the previous level, and @lvl < @maxlevels:

- set @lvl = @lvl + 1; insert into table @Subs rows for the next level (mgrid in (empid values in previous level))

- return @Subs

Run the code in Listing 9-8 to create the fn_subordinates2 function, which is a revision of fn_subordinates1 that also supports a level limit.

Listing 9-8   Creation script for the fn_subordinates2 function

```
---------------------------------------------------------------------
-- Function: fn_subordinates2,
--           Descendants with optional level limit
--
-- Input    : @root       INT: Manager id
--            @maxlevels INT: Max number of levels to return
--
-- Output   : @Subs TABLE: id and level of subordinates of
--                         input manager in all levels <= @maxlevels
--
-- Process  : * Insert into @Subs row of input manager
--            * In a loop, while previous insert loaded more than 0 rows
--              and previous level is smaller than @maxlevels
--              insert into @Subs next level of subordinates
---------------------------------------------------------------------
USE tempdb;
GO
IF OBJECT_ID('dbo.fn_subordinates2') IS NOT NULL
  DROP FUNCTION dbo.fn_subordinates2;
GO
CREATE FUNCTION dbo.fn_subordinates2
  (@root AS INT, @maxlevels AS INT = NULL) RETURNS @Subs TABLE
(
  empid INT NOT NULL PRIMARY KEY NONCLUSTERED,
  lvl   INT NOT NULL,
  UNIQUE CLUSTERED(lvl, empid)  -- Index will be used to filter level
)
AS
BEGIN
  DECLARE @lvl AS INT;
  SET @lvl = 0;                 -- Initialize level counter with 0
  -- If input @maxlevels is NULL, set it to maximum integer
```

```
-- to virtually have no limit on levels
SET @maxlevels = COALESCE(@maxlevels, 2147483647);

-- Insert root node to @Subs
INSERT INTO @Subs(empid, lvl)
  SELECT empid, @lvl FROM dbo.Employees WHERE empid = @root;

WHILE @@rowcount > 0              -- while previous level had rows
  AND @lvl < @maxlevels          -- and previous level < @maxlevels
BEGIN
  SET @lvl = @lvl + 1;           -- Increment level counter

  -- Insert next level of subordinates to @Subs
  INSERT INTO @Subs(empid, lvl)
    SELECT C.empid, @lvl
    FROM @Subs AS P              -- P = Parent
      JOIN dbo.Employees AS C -- C = Child
        ON P.lvl = @lvl - 1   -- Filter parents from previous level
        AND C.mgrid = P.empid;
END

RETURN;
END
GO
```

In addition to the original input, *fn_subordinates2* also accepts the *@maxlevels* input that indicates the maximum number of requested levels under *@root* to return. For no limit on levels, a NULL should be specified in *@maxlevels*. Notice that if *@maxlevels* is NULL, the function substitutes the NULL with the maximum possible integer value to practically have no limit.

The loop's condition, besides checking that the previous insert affected more than zero rows, also checks that the *@lvl* variable is smaller than *@maxlevels*. Except for these minor revisions, the function's implementation is the same as *fn_subordinates1*.

To test the function, run the following code that requests the subordinates of employee 3 in all levels (*@maxlevels* is NULL) and generates the output shown in Table 9-11:

```
SELECT empid, lvl
FROM dbo.fn_subordinates2(3, NULL) AS S;
```

Table 9-11   Subtree of Employee 3, with No Level Limit

empid	lvl
3	0
7	1
9	2
11	2
12	3
13	3
14	3

To get only two levels of subordinates under employee 3, run the following code, which generates the output shown in Table 9-12:

```
SELECT empid, lvl
FROM dbo.fn_subordinates2(3, 2) AS S;
```

Table 9-12   Subtree of Employee 3, up to 2 Levels

empid	lvl
3	0
7	1
9	2
11	2

To get only the second level employees under employee 3, add a filter on the level, which will generate the output shown in Table 9-13:

```
SELECT empid
FROM dbo.fn_subordinates2(3, 2) AS S
WHERE lvl = 2;
```

Table 9-13   Subtree of Employee 3, Only Level 2

empid
9
11

Caution   To limit levels using a CTE, you might be tempted to use the hint called MAXRECURSION, which raises an error and aborts when the number of invocations of the recursive member exceeds the input. However, MAXRECURSION was designed as a safety measure to avoid infinite recursion in cases of problems in the data or bugs in the code. When not specified, MAXRECURSION defaults to 100. You can specify MAXRECURSION 0 to have no limit, but be aware of the implications.

To test this approach, run the code in Listing 9-9, which generates the output shown in Table 9-14. It's the same subtree CTE shown earlier, with the addition of the MAXRECURSION hint, limiting recursive invocations to 2.

Listing 9-9   Subtree with level limit, CTE solution with MAXRECURSION

```
DECLARE @root AS INT;
SET @root = 3;

WITH SubsCTE
AS
(
```

```
    SELECT empid, empname, 0 AS lvl
    FROM dbo.Employees
    WHERE empid = @root

    UNION ALL

    SELECT C.empid, C.empname, P.lvl + 1
    FROM SubsCTE AS P
      JOIN dbo.Employees AS C
        ON C.mgrid = P.empid
)
SELECT * FROM SubsCTE
OPTION (MAXRECURSION 2);
```

Table 9-14   Subtree of Employee 3, Levels Limited with MAXRECURSION

empid	empname	lvl
3	Ina	0
7	Aaron	1
11	Gabriel	2
9	Rita	2

```
Server: Msg 530, Level 16, State 1, Line 4
```

Caution   The statement terminated. The maximum recursion 2 has been exhausted before statement completion.

The code breaks as soon as the recursive member is invoked the third time. It's not recommended to use the MAXRECURSION hint to logically limit the number of levels for two reasons. First, an error is generated even though there's no logical error here. Second, SQL Server does not guarantee to return any result set if an error is generated. In this particular case, a result set was returned, but there's no guarantee that will happen in other cases.

To logically limit the number of levels, simply add a filter on the parent's level column in the recursive member's join condition, as shown in Listing 9-10.

Listing 9-10   Subtree with level limit, CTE solution, with level column

```
DECLARE @root AS INT, @maxlevels AS INT;
SET @root = 3;
SET @maxlevels = 2;

WITH SubsCTE
AS
(
  SELECT empid, empname, 0 AS lvl
  FROM dbo.Employees
  WHERE empid = @root
```

```
    UNION ALL

    SELECT C.empid, C.empname, P.lvl + 1
    FROM SubsCTE AS P
      JOIN dbo.Employees AS C
        ON C.mgrid = P.empid
        AND P.lvl < @maxlevels -- limit parent's level
  )
  SELECT * FROM SubsCTE;
```

Ancestors

Requests for ancestors of a given node are also common—for example, returning the chain of management for a given employee. Not surprisingly, the algorithms for returning ancestors using iterative logic are similar to those for returning subordinates. Simply, instead of traversing the graph starting with a given node and proceeding "downwards" to child nodes, you start with a given node and proceed "upwards" to parent nodes.

Run the code in Listing 9-11 to create the *fn_managers* function. The function accepts an input employee ID (*@empid*) and, optionally, a level limit (*@maxlevels*), and it returns managers up to the requested number of levels away from the input employee (if a limit was specified).

Listing 9-11 Creation script for the *fn_managers* function

```
---------------------------------------------------------------------
-- Function: fn_managers, Ancestors with optional level limit
--
-- Input    : @empid INT : Employee id
--            @maxlevels : Max number of levels to return
--
-- Output   : @Mgrs Table: id and level of managers of
--                         input employee in all levels <= @maxlevels
--
-- Process  : * In a loop, while current manager is not null
--              and previous level is smaller than @maxlevels
--              insert into @Mgrs current manager,
--              and get next level manager
---------------------------------------------------------------------
USE tempdb;
GO
IF OBJECT_ID('dbo.fn_managers') IS NOT NULL
  DROP FUNCTION dbo.fn_managers;
GO
CREATE FUNCTION dbo.fn_managers
  (@empid AS INT, @maxlevels AS INT = NULL) RETURNS @Mgrs TABLE
(
  empid INT NOT NULL PRIMARY KEY,
  lvl   INT NOT NULL
)
AS
```

```
BEGIN
  IF NOT EXISTS(SELECT * FROM dbo.Employees WHERE empid = @empid)
    RETURN;

  DECLARE @lvl AS INT;
  SET @lvl = 0;                  -- Initialize level counter with 0
  -- If input @maxlevels is NULL, set it to maximum integer
  -- to virtually have no limit on levels
  SET @maxlevels = COALESCE(@maxlevels, 2147483647);

  WHILE @empid IS NOT NULL       -- while current employee has a manager
    AND @lvl <= @maxlevels       -- and previous level < @maxlevels
  BEGIN
    -- Insert current manager to @Mgrs
    INSERT INTO @Mgrs(empid, lvl) VALUES(@empid, @lvl);
    SET @lvl = @lvl + 1;         -- Increment level counter
    -- Get next level manager
    SET @empid = (SELECT mgrid FROM dbo.Employees
                  WHERE empid = @empid);
  END

  RETURN;
END
GO
```

The function first checks whether the input node ID exists, and then breaks if it doesn't. It then initializes the *@lvl* counter to zero, and it assigns the maximum possible integer to the *@maxlevels* variable if a NULL was specified in it to practically have no level limit.

The function then enters a loop that iterates as long as *@empid* is not null (because null represents the root's manager ID) and the current level is smaller than or equal to the requested number of levels. The loop's body inserts the current employee ID along with the level counter into the @Mgrs output table variable, increments the level counter, and assigns the current employee's manager's ID to the *@empid* variable.

I should point out a couple of differences between this function and the subordinates function. This function uses a scalar subquery to get the manager ID in the next level, unlike the subordinates function, which used a join to get the next level of subordinates. The reason for the difference is that there can be only one manager for a given employee, while there can be multiple subordinates for a given manager. Also, this function uses the expression *@lvl <= @maxlevels* to limit the number of levels, while the subordinates function used the expression *@lvl < @maxlevels*. The reason for the discrepancy is that this function doesn't have a separate INSERT statement to get the root employee and a separate one to get the next level of employees; rather, it has only one INSERT statement in the loop. Consequently the *@lvl* counter here is incremented after the INSERT, while in the subordinates function it was incremented before the INSERT.

To test the function, run the following code, which returns managers in all levels of employee 8 and generates the output shown in Table 9-15:

```
SELECT empid, lvl
FROM dbo.fn_managers(8, NULL) AS M;
```

Table 9-15 Management Chain of Employee 8, No Level Limit

empid	lvl
1	3
2	2
5	1
8	0

The CTE solution to returning ancestors is almost identical to the CTE solution returning a subtree. The minor difference is that here the recursive member treats the CTE as the child part of the join and the Employees table as the parent part, while in the subtree solution the roles were opposite. Run the code in Listing 9-12 to get the management chain of employee 8 using a CTE and generate the output shown in Table 9-16.

Listing 9-12 Management chain of employee 8, CTE solution

```
DECLARE @empid AS INT;
SET @empid = 8;

WITH MgrsCTE
AS
(
  SELECT empid, mgrid, empname, 0 AS lvl
  FROM dbo.Employees
  WHERE empid = @empid

  UNION ALL

  SELECT P.empid, P.mgrid, P.empname, C.lvl + 1
  FROM MgrsCTE AS C
    JOIN dbo.Employees AS P
      ON C.mgrid = P.empid
)
SELECT * FROM MgrsCTE;
```

Table 9-16 CTE Output for Management Chain of Employee 8

empid	mgrid	empname	lvl
8	5	Lilach	0
5	2	Jiru	1
2	1	Eitan	2
1	NULL	David	3

To get only two levels of managers of employee 8 using the *fn_managers* function, run the following code, which generates the output shown in Table 9-17:

```
SELECT empid, lvl
FROM dbo.fn_managers(8, 2) AS M;
```

Table 9-17   Management Chain of Employee 8, 2 Level Limit, CTE Solution

empid	lvl
2	2
5	1
8	0

And to return only the second-level manager, simply add a filter in the outer query, returning employee ID 2:

```
SELECT empid
FROM dbo.fn_managers(8, 2) AS M
WHERE lvl = 2;
```

To return two levels of managers of employee 8 with a CTE, simply add a filter on the child's level in the join condition of the recursive member as shown in Listing 9-13.

Listing 9-13   Ancestors with level limit, CTE solution

```
DECLARE @empid AS INT, @maxlevels AS INT;
SET @empid = 8;
SET @maxlevels = 2;

WITH MgrsCTE
AS
(
  SELECT empid, mgrid, empname, 0 AS lvl
  FROM dbo.Employees
  WHERE empid = @empid

  UNION ALL

  SELECT P.empid, P.mgrid, P.empname, C.lvl + 1
  FROM MgrsCTE AS C
    JOIN dbo.Employees AS P
      ON C.mgrid = P.empid
      AND C.lvl < @maxlevels -- limit child's level
)
SELECT * FROM MgrsCTE;
```

Subgraph/Subtree with Path Enumeration

In the subgraph/subtree solutions, you might also want to generate for each node an enumerated path consisting of all node IDs in the path leading to the node with some separator (for example, '.'). For example, the enumerated path for employee 8 in the Organization Chart scenario is '.1.2.5.8.' because employee 5 is the manager of employee 8, employee 2 is the manager of 5, employee 1 is the manager of 2, and employee 1 is the root employee.

The enumerated path has many uses—for example, to sort the nodes from the hierarchy in the output, to detect cycles, and other uses that I'll describe later in the "Materialized Path" section.

Fortunately, you can make minor additions to the solutions I provided for returning a subgraph/subtree to calculate the enumerated path without any additional I/O.

The algorithm starts with the subtree's root node, and in a loop or recursive call returns the next level. For the root node, the path is simply: '.' + *node id* + '.'. For successive level nodes, the path is: *parent's path* + *node id* + '.'.

Run the code in Listing 9-14 to create the *fn_subordinates3* function, which is the same as *fn_subordinates2* except for the addition of the enumerated path calculation.

Listing 9-14 Creation script for the *fn_subordinates3* function

```
-------------------------------------------------------------------
-- Function: fn_subordinates3,
--           Descendants with optional level limit,
--           and path enumeration
--
-- Input    : @root       INT: Manager id
--            @maxlevels INT: Max number of levels to return
--
-- Output   : @Subs TABLE: id, level and materialized ancestors path
--                         of subordinates of input manager
--                         in all levels <= @maxlevels
--
-- Process  : * Insert into @Subs row of input manager
--            * In a loop, while previous insert loaded more than 0 rows
--              and previous level is smaller than @maxlevels:
--              - insert into @Subs next level of subordinates
--              - calculate a materialized ancestors path for each
--                by concatenating current node id to parent's path
-------------------------------------------------------------------
USE tempdb;
GO
IF OBJECT_ID('dbo.fn_subordinates3') IS NOT NULL
  DROP FUNCTION dbo.fn_subordinates3;
GO
CREATE FUNCTION dbo.fn_subordinates3
  (@root AS INT, @maxlevels AS INT = NULL) RETURNS @Subs TABLE
(
  empid INT         NOT NULL PRIMARY KEY NONCLUSTERED,
  lvl   INT         NOT NULL,
  path  VARCHAR(900) NOT NULL
  UNIQUE CLUSTERED(lvl, empid)  -- Index will be used to filter level
)
AS
BEGIN
  DECLARE @lvl AS INT;
  SET @lvl = 0;                 -- Initialize level counter with 0
  -- If input @maxlevels is NULL, set it to maximum integer
  -- to virtually have no limit on levels
  SET @maxlevels = COALESCE(@maxlevels, 2147483647);

  -- Insert root node to @Subs
  INSERT INTO @Subs(empid, lvl, path)
```

```
      SELECT empid, @lvl, '.' + CAST(empid AS VARCHAR(10)) + '.'
      FROM dbo.Employees WHERE empid = @root;

  WHILE @@rowcount > 0              -- while previous level had rows
    AND @lvl < @maxlevels          -- and previous level < @maxlevels
  BEGIN
    SET @lvl = @lvl + 1;           -- Increment level counter

    -- Insert next level of subordinates to @Subs
    INSERT INTO @Subs(empid, lvl, path)
      SELECT C.empid, @lvl,
        P.path + CAST(C.empid AS VARCHAR(10)) + '.'
      FROM @Subs AS P              -- P = Parent
        JOIN dbo.Employees AS C -- C = Child
          ON P.lvl = @lvl - 1   -- Filter parents from previous level
          AND C.mgrid = P.empid;
  END

  RETURN;
END
GO
```

To test the function, run the following code, which returns all subordinates of employee 1 and their paths, as shown in Table 9-18:

```
SELECT empid, lvl, path
FROM dbo.fn_subordinates3(1, NULL) AS S;
```

Table 9-18   Subtree with Enumerated Path

empid	lvl	path
1	0	.1.
2	1	.1.2.
3	1	.1.3.
4	2	.1.2.4.
5	2	.1.2.5.
6	2	.1.2.6.
7	2	.1.3.7.
8	3	.1.2.5.8.
9	3	.1.3.7.9.
10	3	.1.2.5.10.
11	3	.1.3.7.11.
12	4	.1.3.7.9.12.
13	4	.1.3.7.9.13.
14	4	.1.3.7.9.14.

With both the *lvl* and *path* values, you can easily return output that graphically shows the hierarchical relationships of the employees in the subtree:

```
SELECT E.empid, REPLICATE(' | ', lvl) + empname AS empname
FROM dbo.fn_subordinates3(1, NULL) AS S
  JOIN dbo.Employees AS E
    ON E.empid = S.empid
ORDER BY path;
```

The query joins the subtree returned from the *fn_subordinates3* function with the Employees table based on employee ID match. From the function, you get the *lvl* and *path* values, and from the table you get other employee attributes of interest, such as the employee name. You generate indentation before the employee name by replicating a string (in this case, ' | ') *lvl* times and concatenating the employee name to it. Sorting the employees by the *path* column produces a correct hierarchical sort, which requires that a child node will appear later than its parent node—or in other words, that a child node will have a higher sort value than its parent node. By definition, a child's path is greater than a parent's path because it's prefixed with the parent's path. The output of this query is shown in Table 9-19.

Table 9-19   Subtree, Sorted by Path and Indented by Level

empid	empname
1	David
2	| Eitan
4	| | Seraph
5	| | Jiru
10	| | | Sean
8	| | | Lilach
6	| | Steve
3	| Ina
7	| | Aaron
11	| | | Gabriel
9	| | | Rita
12	| | | | Emilia
13	| | | | Michael
14	| | | | Didi

Similarly, you can add path calculation to the subtree CTE as shown in Listing 9-15.

Listing 9-15   Subtree with path enumeration, CTE solution

```
DECLARE @root AS INT;
SET @root = 1;

WITH SubsCTE
AS
```

```
(
  SELECT empid, empname, 0 AS lvl,
    -- Path of root = '.' + empid + '.'
    CAST('.' + CAST(empid AS VARCHAR(10)) + '.'
       AS VARCHAR(MAX)) AS path
  FROM dbo.Employees
  WHERE empid = @root

  UNION ALL

  SELECT C.empid, C.empname, P.lvl + 1,
    -- Path of child = parent's path + child empid + '.'
    CAST(P.path + CAST(C.empid AS VARCHAR(10)) + '.'
       AS VARCHAR(MAX)) AS path
  FROM SubsCTE AS P
    JOIN dbo.Employees AS C
      ON C.mgrid = P.empid
)
SELECT empid, REPLICATE(' | ', lvl) + empname AS empname
FROM SubsCTE
ORDER BY path;
```

 Note   Corresponding columns between an anchor member and a recursive member of a CTE must match in both data type and size. That's the reason I converted the path strings in both to the same datatype and size—VARCHAR(MAX).

Sorting

Sorting is a presentation request and usually is used by the client rather than the server. This means that you might want the sorting of hierarchies to take place on the client. In this section, however, I'll present server-side sorting techniques with T-SQL that you can use when you prefer to handle sorting on the server.

A *topological sort* of a DAG is defined as one that provides a child with a higher sort value than its parent. Occasionally, I will refer to a topological sort informally as "correct hierarchical sort." More than one way of ordering the items in a DAG may qualify as correct. You might or might not care about the order among siblings. If the order among siblings doesn't matter to you, you can achieve sorting by constructing an enumerated path for each node, as described in the previous section, and sort the nodes by that path.

Remember that the enumerated path is a character string made of the IDs of the ancestors leading to the node, using some separator. This means that siblings are sorted by their node IDs. Because the path is character based, you get character-based sorting of IDs, which might be different than the integer sorting. For example, employee ID 11 will sort lower than its sibling with ID 9 ('.1.3.7.11.' < '.1.3.7.9.'), even though 9 < 11. You can guarantee that sorting by the enumerated path will produce a correct hierarchical sort, but it will not guarantee the order of siblings. If you need such a guarantee, you need a different solution.

For optimal sorting flexibility, you might want to guarantee the following:

1. A correct topological sort—that is, a sort in which a child will have a higher sort value than its parent's.

2. Siblings are sorted in a requested order (for example, by *empname* or by *salary*).

3. Integer sort values are generated, as opposed to lengthy strings.

In the enumerated path solution, requirement 1 is met. Requirement 2 is not met because the path is made of node IDs and is character based; comparison and sorting among characters is based on collation properties, yielding different comparison and sorting behavior than with integers. Requirement 3 is not met because the solution orders the results by the path, which is lengthy compared to an integer value. To meet all three requirements, we can still make use of a path for each node, but with several differences:

- Instead of node IDs, the path will be constructed from values that represent a position (row number) among nodes based on a requested order (for example, *empname* or *salary*).

- Instead of using a character string with varying lengths for each level in the path, use a binary string with a fixed length for each level.

- Once the binary paths are constructed, calculate integer values representing path order (row numbers) and ultimately use those to sort the hierarchy.

The core algorithm to traverse the subtree is maintained. It's just that the paths are constructed differently, and you need to figure out how to calculate row numbers. In SQL Server 2000, to calculate row numbers based on a requested order you can insert the rows into a table with an identity column using INSERT...SELECT...ORDER BY. (See Knowledge Base article 273586 at *http://support.microsoft.com/default.aspx?scid=kb;en-us;273586*.)

In SQL Server 2005, you can use the ROW_NUMBER function, which is much simpler and faster than the SQL Server 2000 alternative.

Run the code in Listing 9-16 to create the SQL Server 2000–compatible stored procedure usp_sortsubs, which implements this logic.

Listing 9-16   Creation script for the usp_sortsubs procedure

```
---------------------------------------------------------------------
-- Stored Procedure: usp_sortsubs,
--   Descendants with optional level limit and sort values
--
-- Input    : @root      INT: Manager id
--            @maxlevels INT: Max number of levels to return
--            @orderby   sysname: determines sort order
--
-- Output   : Rowset: id, level and sort values
--                    of subordinates of input manager
--                    in all levels <= @maxlevels
--
```

```
-- Process : * Use a loop to load the desired subtree into #SubsPath
--           * For each node, construct a binary sort path
--           * The row number represents the node's position among
--             its siblings based on the input ORDER BY list
--           * Insert the contents of #SubPath into #SubsSort sorted
--             by the binary sortpath
--           * IDENTITY values representing the global sort value
--             in the subtree will be generated in the target
--             #SubsSort table
--           * Return all rows from #SubsSort sorted by the
--             sort value
---------------------------------------------------------------------
USE tempdb;
GO
IF OBJECT_ID('dbo.usp_sortsubs') IS NOT NULL
  DROP PROC dbo.usp_sortsubs;
GO
CREATE PROC dbo.usp_sortsubs
  @root     AS INT     = NULL,
  @maxlevels AS INT     = NULL,
  @orderby   AS sysname = N'empid'
AS

SET NOCOUNT ON;

-- #SubsPath is a temp table that will hold binary sort paths
CREATE TABLE #SubsPath
(
  rownum   INT NOT NULL IDENTITY,
  nodeid   INT NOT NULL,
  lvl      INT NOT NULL,
  sortpath VARBINARY(900) NULL
);
CREATE UNIQUE CLUSTERED INDEX idx_uc_lvl_empid ON #SubsPath(lvl, nodeid);

-- #SubsPath is a temp table that will hold the final
-- integer sort values
CREATE TABLE #SubsSort
(
  nodeid   INT NOT NULL,
  lvl      INT NOT NULL,
  sortval  INT NOT NULL IDENTITY
);
CREATE UNIQUE CLUSTERED INDEX idx_uc_sortval ON #SubsSort(sortval);

-- If @root is not specified, set it to root of the tree
IF @root IS NULL
  SET @root = (SELECT empid FROM dbo.Employees WHERE mgrid IS NULL);
-- If @maxlevels is not specified, set it maximum integer
IF @maxlevels IS NULL
  SET @maxlevels = 2147483647;

DECLARE @lvl AS INT, @sql AS NVARCHAR(4000);
SET @lvl = 0;
```

```
-- Load row for input root to #SubsPath
-- The root's sort path is simply 1 converted to binary
INSERT INTO #SubsPath(nodeid, lvl, sortpath)
  SELECT empid, @lvl, CAST(1 AS BINARY(4))
  FROM dbo.Employees
  WHERE empid = @root;

-- Form a loop to load the next level of subordinates
-- to #SubsPath in each iteration
WHILE @@rowcount > 0 AND @lvl < @maxlevels
BEGIN
  SET @lvl = @lvl + 1;

  -- Insert next level of subordinates
  -- Initially, just copy parent's path to child
  -- Note that IDENTITY values will be generated in #SubsPath
  -- based on input order by list
  --
  -- Then update the path of the employees in the current level
  -- to their parent's path + their rownum converted to binary
  INSERT INTO #SubsPath(nodeid, lvl, sortpath)
    SELECT C.empid, @lvl, P.sortpath
    FROM #SubsPath AS P
      JOIN dbo.Employees AS C
        ON P.lvl = @lvl - 1
        AND C.mgrid = P.nodeid
    ORDER BY -- determines order of siblings
      CASE WHEN @orderby = N'empid'   THEN empid   END,
      CASE WHEN @orderby = N'empname' THEN empname END,
      CASE WHEN @orderby = N'salary'  THEN salary  END;

  UPDATE #SubsPath
    SET sortpath = sortpath + CAST(rownum AS BINARY(4))
  WHERE lvl = @lvl;
END

-- Load the rows from #SubsPath to @SubsSort sorted by the binary
-- sort path
-- The target identity values in the sortval column will represent
-- the global sort value of the nodes within the result subtree
INSERT INTO #SubsSort(nodeid, lvl)
  SELECT nodeid, lvl FROM #SubsPath ORDER BY sortpath;

-- Return for each node the id, level and sort value
SELECT nodeid AS empid, lvl, sortval FROM #SubsSort
ORDER BY sortval;
GO
```

The input parameters *@root* and *@maxlevels* are similar to the ones used in the previous sub-tree routines I discussed. In addition, the stored procedure accepts the *@orderby* parameter, where you specify a column name by which you want siblings sorted. The stored procedure uses a series of CASE expressions to determine which column's values to sort by. The stored procedure returns a result set with the node IDs in the requested subtree, along with a level and an integer sort value for each node.

The stored procedure traverses the subtree in a similar fashion to the previous iterative implementations I discussed—that is, a level at a time.

First, the root employee is loaded into the #SubsPath temporary table. Then, in each iteration of the loop, the next level of employees is inserted into #SubsPath.

The #SubsPath table has an identity column (*rownum*) that will represent the position of an employee among siblings based on the desired sort (the ORDER BY section of the INSERT SELECT statement). The root's path is set to 1 converted to BINARY(4). For each level of employees that is inserted into the #SubsPath table, the parent's path is copied to the child's path, and then an UPDATE statement concatenates to the child's path the *rownum* value converted to BINARY(4).

At the end of the loop, #SubsPath contains the complete binary sort path for each node.

This process will probably be better explained by following an example. Say you're after the subtree of employee 1 (David) with no level limit, sorting siblings by *empname*. Table 9-20 shows the identity values that are generated for the employees in each level.

Table 9-20   Identity Values Generated for Employees in Each Level

Level 0	Level 1	Level 2	Level 3	Level 4
1 – David	2 – Eitan	4 – Aaron	8 – Gabriel	12 – Didi
	3 – Ina	5 – Jiru	9 – Lilach	13 – Emilia
		6 – Seraph	10 – Rita	14 – Michael
		7 – Steve	11 – Sean	

Table 9-21 shows the binary sort paths constructed for each employee, made of the position values of the ancestors leading to the node.

Table 9-21   Binary Sort Paths Constructed for Each Employee

Lvl	Manager	Employee	Sort Path				
0	NULL	David (1)	1				
1	David	Eitan (2)	1	2			
1	David	Ina (3)	1	3			
2	Eitan	Jiru (5)	1	2	5		
2	Eitan	Seraph (6)	1	2	6		
2	Eitan	Steve (7)	1	2	7		
2	Ina	Aaron (4)	1	3	4		
3	Jiru	Lilach (9)	1	2	5	9	
3	Jiru	Sean (11)	1	2	5	11	
3	Aaron	Gabriel (8)	1	3	4	8	
3	Aaron	Rita (10)	1	3	4	10	
4	Rita	Didi (12)	1	3	4	10	12
4	Rita	Emilia (13)	1	3	4	10	13
4	Rita	Michael (14)	1	3	4	10	14

The next step in the stored procedure is to insert the contents of #SubsPath into #SubsSort in *sortpath* order. #SubsSort also has an identity column (*sortval*), which will represent the employees' final sort values. Table 9-22 will help you visualize how the sort values are calculated in #SubsSort based on *sortpath* order.

Table 9-22   Integer Sort Values Calculated Based on *sortpath* Order

sortval	lvl	Manager	Employee	sortpath				
1	0	NULL	David (1)	1				
2	1	David	Eitan (2)	1	2			
3	2	Eitan	Jiru (5)	1	2	5		
4	3	Jiru	Lilach (9)	1	2	5	9	
5	3	Jiru	Sean (11)	1	2	5	11	
6	2	Eitan	Seraph (6)	1	2	6		
7	2	Eitan	Steve (7)	1	2	7		
8	1	David	Ina (3)	1	3			
9	2	Ina	Aaron (4)	1	3	4		
10	3	Aaron	Gabriel (8)	1	3	4	8	
11	3	Aaron	Rita (10)	1	3	4	10	
12	4	Rita	Didi (12)	1	3	4	10	12
13	4	Rita	Emilia (13)	1	3	4	10	13
14	4	Rita	Michael (14)	1	3	4	10	14

Finally, the stored procedure returns for each node the node ID, level, and integer sort value. To test the procedure, run the following code, specifying *empname* as the sort columns. The code generates the output shown in Table 9-23.

```
EXEC dbo.usp_sortsubs @orderby = N'empname';
```

Table 9-23   All Employee IDs with Sort Values Based on *empname*

empid	lvl	sortval
1	0	1
2	1	2
5	2	3
8	3	4
10	3	5
4	2	6
6	2	7
3	1	8
7	2	9
11	3	10

Table 9-23   All Employee IDs with Sort Values Based on *empname*

empid	lvl	sortval
9	3	11
14	4	12
12	4	13
13	4	14

To get three levels of subordinates underneath employee 1 having siblings sorted by *empname*, run the following code, which generates the output shown in Table 9-24:

```
EXEC dbo.usp_sortsubs
  @root = 1,
  @maxlevels = 3,
  @orderby = N'empname';
```

Table 9-24   Subtree with Levels Limit, and Sort Based on *empname*

empid	lvl	sortval
1	0	1
2	1	2
5	2	3
8	3	4
10	3	5
4	2	6
6	2	7
3	1	8
7	2	9
11	3	10
9	3	11

To return attributes other than the employee ID (for example, the employee name), you need to first produce the result set of the stored procedure, and then join it with the Employees table. For example, the code in Listing 9-17 returns all employees, having siblings sorted by *empname*, with indentation, and generates the output shown in Table 9-25:

Listing 9-17   Script returning all employees, having siblings sorted by *empname*

```
CREATE TABLE #Subs
(
  empid   INT NULL,
  lvl     INT NULL,
  sortval INT NULL
);
CREATE UNIQUE CLUSTERED INDEX idx_uc_sortval ON #Subs(sortval);
```

```
-- By empname
INSERT INTO #Subs(empid, lvl, sortval)
  EXEC dbo.usp_sortsubs
    @orderby = N'empname';

SELECT E.empid, REPLICATE(' | ', lvl) + E.empname AS empname
FROM #Subs AS S
  JOIN dbo.Employees AS E
    ON S.empid = E.empid
ORDER BY sortval;
```

Table 9-25 **All Employees with Sort of Siblings Based on** *empname*

empid	empname
1	David
2	| Eitan
5	| | Jiru
8	| | | Lilach
10	| | | Sean
4	| | Seraph
6	| | Steve
3	| Ina
7	| | Aaron
11	| | | Gabriel
9	| | | Rita
14	| | | | Didi
12	| | | | Emilia
13	| | | | Michael

Similarly, the code in Listing 9-18 returns all employees, having siblings sorted by *salary*, with indentation, and generates the output shown in Table 9-26:

Listing 9-18 Script returning all employees, with siblings sorted by *salary*

```
TRUNCATE TABLE #Subs;

INSERT INTO #Subs(empid, lvl, sortval)
  EXEC dbo.usp_sortsubs
    @orderby = N'salary';

SELECT E.empid, salary, REPLICATE(' | ', lvl) + E.empname AS empname
FROM #Subs AS S
  JOIN dbo.Employees AS E
    ON S.empid = E.empid
ORDER BY sortval;
```

Table 9-26 **All Employees with Siblings Sorted by** *salary*

empid	salary	empname
1	10000.00	David
2	7000.00	| Eitan
6	4500.00	| | Steve
4	5000.00	| | Seraph
5	5500.00	| | Jiru
10	3000.00	| | | Sean
8	3500.00	| | | Lilach
3	7500.00	| Ina
7	5000.00	| | Aaron
9	3000.00	| | Rita
14	1500.00	| | | Didi
12	2000.00	| | | Emilia
13	2000.00	| | | Michael
11	3000.00	| | Gabriel

Make sure you drop the temporary table #Subs once you're finished:

```
DROP TABLE #Subs
```

The implementation of a similar algorithm in SQL Server 2005 is dramatically simpler and faster, mainly because it uses CTEs and the ROW_NUMBER function.

Run the code in Listing 9-19 to return the subtree of employee 1, with siblings sorted by *empname* with indentation, and generate the output shown in Table 9-27.

Listing 9-19 Returning all employees in the hierarchy with siblings sorted by *empname*, CTE solution

```
DECLARE @root AS INT;
SET @root = 1;

WITH SubsCTE
AS
(
  SELECT empid, empname, 0 AS lvl,
    -- Path of root is 1 (binary)
    CAST(1 AS VARBINARY(MAX)) AS sortpath
  FROM dbo.Employees
  WHERE empid = @root

  UNION ALL
```

```
SELECT C.empid, C.empname, P.lvl + 1,
  -- Path of child = parent's path + child row number (binary)
  P.sortpath + CAST(
    ROW_NUMBER() OVER(PARTITION BY C.mgrid
                      ORDER BY C.empname) -- sort col(s)
    AS BINARY(4))
  FROM SubsCTE AS P
    JOIN dbo.Employees AS C
      ON C.mgrid = P.empid
)
SELECT empid, ROW_NUMBER() OVER(ORDER BY sortpath) AS sortval,
  REPLICATE(' | ', lvl) + empname AS empname
FROM SubsCTE
ORDER BY sortval;
```

Table 9-27 Employees with Sort Based on *empname*, CTE Output

empid	sortval	empname
1	1	David
2	2	| Eitan
5	3	| | Jiru
8	4	| | | Lilach
10	5	| | | Sean
4	6	| | Seraph
6	7	| | Steve
3	8	| Ina
7	9	| | Aaron
11	10	| | | Gabriel
9	11	| | | Rita
14	12	| | | | Didi
12	13	| | | | Emilia
13	14	| | | | Michael

The anchor member query returns the root, with 1 as the binary path. The recursive member query calculates the row number of an employee among siblings based on *empname* ordering and concatenates that row number converted to binary(4) to the parent's path.

The outer query simply calculates row numbers to generate the sort values based on the binary path order, and it sorts the subtree by those sort values, adding indentation based on the calculated level.

If you want siblings sorted in a different way, you need to change only the ORDER BY list of the ROW_NUMBER function in the recursive member query. Listing 9-20 has the revision that sorts siblings by *salary*, generating the output shown in Table 9-28.

Listing 9-20   Returning all employees in the hierarchy with siblings sorted by *salary*, CTE solution

```
DECLARE @root AS INT;
SET @root = 1;

WITH SubsCTE
AS
(
  SELECT empid, empname, salary, 0 AS lvl,
    -- Path of root = 1 (binary)
    CAST(1 AS VARBINARY(MAX)) AS sortpath
  FROM dbo.Employees
  WHERE empid = @root

  UNION ALL

  SELECT C.empid, C.empname, C.salary, P.lvl + 1,
    -- Path of child = parent's path + child row number (binary)
    P.sortpath + CAST(
      ROW_NUMBER() OVER(PARTITION BY C.mgrid
                        ORDER BY C.salary) -- sort col(s)
      AS BINARY(4))
  FROM SubsCTE AS P
    JOIN dbo.Employees AS C
      ON C.mgrid = P.empid
)
SELECT empid, salary, ROW_NUMBER() OVER(ORDER BY sortpath) AS sortval,
  REPLICATE(' | ', lvl) + empname AS empname
FROM SubsCTE
ORDER BY sortval;
```

Table 9-28   Employees with Sort Based on *salary*, CTE Output

empid	salary	sortval	empname
1	10000.00	1	David
2	7000.00	2	| Eitan
6	4500.00	3	| | Steve
4	5000.00	4	| | Seraph
5	5500.00	5	| | Jiru
10	3000.00	6	| | | Sean
8	3500.00	7	| | | Lilach
3	7500.00	8	| Ina
7	5000.00	9	| | Aaron
9	3000.00	10	| | Rita
14	1500.00	11	| | | Didi
12	2000.00	12	| | | Emilia
13	2000.00	13	| | | Michael
11	3000.00	14	| | | Gabriel

> **Note**   If you need to sort siblings by a single integer sort column (for example, by *empid*), you can construct the binary sort path from the sort column values themselves instead of row numbers based on that column.

Cycles

Cycles in graphs are paths that begin and end at the same node. In some scenarios, cycles are natural (for example, road systems). If you have a cycle in what's supposed to be an acyclic graph, it might indicate that there's a problem in your data. Either way, you need a way to identify them. If a cycle indicates a problem in the data, you need to identify the problem and fix it. If cycles are natural, while traversing the graph you don't want to endlessly keep returning to the same point.

Cycle detection with T-SQL can be a very complex and expensive task. However, I'll show you how to detect cycles with a fairly simple technique with reasonable performance, relying on path enumeration, which I discussed earlier. For demonstration purposes, I'll use this technique to detect cycles in the tree represented by the Employees table, but you can apply this technique to forests as well and also to more generic graphs, as I will demonstrate later.

Suppose that Didi (*empid* 14) is unhappy with her location in the company's management hierarchy. Didi also happens to be the database administrator and has full access to the Employees table. Didi runs the following code, making her the manager of the CEO and introducing a cycle:

```
UPDATE dbo.Employees SET mgrid = 14 WHERE empid = 1;
```

The Employees table currently contains the following cycle of employee IDs:

$1 \rightarrow 3 \rightarrow 7 \rightarrow 9 \rightarrow 14 \rightarrow 1$.

As a baseline, I'll use one of the solutions I covered earlier, which constructs an enumerated path. In my examples, I'll use a CTE solution, but of course you can apply the same logic to the UDF solution in SQL Server 2000.

Simply put, a cycle is detected when you follow a path leading to a given node if its parent's path already contains the child node ID. You can keep track of cycles by maintaining a *cycle* column, which will contain 0 if no cycle was detected and 1 if one was detected. In the anchor member of the solution CTE, the *cycle* column value is simply the constant 0, because obviously there's no cycle at the root level. In the recursive member's query, use a LIKE predicate to check whether the parent's path contains the child node ID. Return 1 if it does and 0 otherwise. Note the importance of the dots at both the beginning and end of both the path and the pattern—without the dots, you will get an unwanted match for employee ID *n* (for example *n* = 3) if the path contains employee ID *nm* (for example *m* = *15, nm* = *315*). Listing 9-21 shows the code that returns a subtree with an enumerated path calculation and has the addition of the *cycle* column calculation. If you run the code in Listing 9-21, it will always break after 100 levels (the default MAXRECURSION value) because cycles are detected but not avoided.

Listing 9-21   Detecting cycles, CTE solution

```
DECLARE @root AS INT;
SET @root = 1;

WITH SubsCTE
AS
(
  SELECT empid, empname, 0 AS lvl,
    CAST('.' + CAST(empid AS VARCHAR(10)) + '.'
         AS VARCHAR(MAX)) AS path,
    -- Obviously root has no cycle
    0 AS cycle
  FROM dbo.Employees
  WHERE empid = @root

  UNION ALL

  SELECT C.empid, C.empname, P.lvl + 1,
    CAST(P.path + CAST(C.empid AS VARCHAR(10)) + '.'
         AS VARCHAR(MAX)) AS path,
    -- Cycle detected if parent's path contains child's id
    CASE WHEN P.path LIKE '%.' + CAST(C.empid AS VARCHAR(10)) + '.%'
      THEN 1 ELSE 0 END
  FROM SubsCTE AS P
    JOIN dbo.Employees AS C
      ON C.mgrid = P.empid
)
SELECT empid, empname, cycle, path
FROM SubsCTE;
```

You need to avoid cycles, or in other words, not pursue paths for which cycles are detected. To achieve this, simply add a filter to the recursive member that returns a child only if its parent's *cycle* value is 0. The code in Listing 9-22 includes this cycle avoidance logic, generating the output shown in Table 9-29.

Listing 9-22   Not pursuing cycles, CTE solution

```
DECLARE @root AS INT;
SET @root = 1;

WITH SubsCTE
AS
(
  SELECT empid, empname, 0 AS lvl,
    CAST('.' + CAST(empid AS VARCHAR(10)) + '.'
         AS VARCHAR(MAX)) AS path,
    -- Obviously root has no cycle
    0 AS cycle
  FROM dbo.Employees
  WHERE empid = @root

  UNION ALL
```

```
SELECT C.empid, C.empname, P.lvl + 1,
  CAST(P.path + CAST(C.empid AS VARCHAR(10)) + '.'
    AS VARCHAR(MAX)) AS path,
  -- Cycle detected if parent's path contains child's id
  CASE WHEN P.path LIKE '%.' + CAST(C.empid AS VARCHAR(10)) + '.%'
    THEN 1 ELSE 0 END
FROM SubsCTE AS P
  JOIN dbo.Employees AS C
    ON C.mgrid = P.empid
    AND P.cycle = 0 -- do not pursue branch for parent with cycle
)
SELECT empid, empname, cycle, path
FROM SubsCTE;
```

Table 9-29 Employees with Cycles not Pursued

empid	empname	cycle	path
1	David	0	.1.
2	Eitan	0	.1.2.
3	Ina	0	.1.3.
7	Aaron	0	.1.3.7.
11	Gabriel	0	.1.3.7.11.
9	Rita	0	.1.3.7.9.
12	Emilia	0	.1.3.7.9.12.
13	Michael	0	.1.3.7.9.13.
14	Didi	0	.1.3.7.9.14.
1	David	1	.1.3.7.9.14.1.
4	Seraph	0	.1.2.4.
5	Jiru	0	.1.2.5.
6	Steve	0	.1.2.6.
10	Sean	0	.1.2.5.10.
8	Lilach	0	.1.2.5.8.

Notice in the output that the second time employee 1 was reached, a cycle was detected for it, and the path was not pursued any further. In a cyclic graph, that's all the logic you usually need to add. In our case, the cycle indicates a problem with the data that needs to be fixed. To isolate only the cyclic path (in our case, .1.3.7.9.14.1.), simply add the filter *cycle = 1* to the outer query as shown in Listing 9-23.

Listing 9-23 Isolating cyclic paths, CTE solution

```
DECLARE @root AS INT;
SET @root = 1;

WITH SubsCTE
AS
```

```
(
  SELECT empid, empname, 0 AS lvl,
    CAST('.' + CAST(empid AS VARCHAR(10)) + '.'
        AS VARCHAR(MAX)) AS path,
    -- Obviously root has no cycle
    0 AS cycle
  FROM dbo.Employees
  WHERE empid = @root

  UNION ALL

  SELECT C.empid, C.empname, P.lvl + 1,
    CAST(P.path + CAST(C.empid AS VARCHAR(10)) + '.'
        AS VARCHAR(MAX)) AS path,
    -- Cycle detected if parent's path contains child's id
    CASE WHEN P.path LIKE '%.' + CAST(C.empid AS VARCHAR(10)) + '.%'
      THEN 1 ELSE 0 END
  FROM SubsCTE AS P
    JOIN dbo.Employees AS C
      ON C.mgrid = P.empid
      AND P.cycle = 0
)
SELECT path FROM SubsCTE WHERE cycle = 1;
```

Now that the cyclic path has been identified, you can fix the data by running the following code:

```
UPDATE dbo.Employees SET mgrid = NULL WHERE empid = 1;
```

Didi will probably find herself unemployed.

Materialized Path

So far I presented solutions where paths were computed when the code was executed. In the materialized path solution, the paths will be stored so that they need not be computed repeatedly. You basically store an enumerated path and a level for each node of the tree in two additional columns. The solution applies only to trees—possibly forests.

There are two main advantages of this approach over the iterative/recursive approach. Queries are simpler and set-based (without relying on recursive CTEs). Also, queries typically perform much faster, as they can rely on indexing of the path.

However, now that you have two additional attributes in the table, you need to keep them in sync with the tree as it undergoes changes. The cost of modifications will determine whether it's reasonable to synchronize the path and level values with every change in the tree. For example, what is the effect of adding a new leaf to the tree? I like to refer to the effect of such a modification informally as the "shake effect." Fortunately, as I will elaborate shortly, the shake effect of adding new leaves is minor. Also, the effect of dropping or moving a small subtree is typically not very significant.

The enumerated path can get lengthy when the tree is deep—in other words, when there are many levels of managers. SQL Server limits the size of index keys to 900 bytes. To achieve the performance benefits of an index on the path column, you will limit it to 900 bytes. Before getting concerned by this fact, try thinking in practical terms: 900 bytes can contain trees with hundreds of levels. Will your tree ever reach more than hundreds of levels? I'll admit that I never had to model a hierarchy with hundreds of levels. In short, apply common sense and think in practical terms.

Maintaining Data

First run the code in Listing 9-24 to create the Employees table with the new *lvl* and *path* columns.

Listing 9-24 Data definition language for employees with materialized paths

```
SET NOCOUNT ON;
USE tempdb;
GO
IF OBJECT_ID('dbo.Employees') IS NOT NULL
  DROP TABLE dbo.Employees;
GO
CREATE TABLE dbo.Employees
(
  empid    INT            NOT NULL PRIMARY KEY NONCLUSTERED,
  mgrid    INT            NULL     REFERENCES dbo.Employees,
  empname  VARCHAR(25)    NOT NULL,
  salary   MONEY          NOT NULL,
  lvl      INT            NOT NULL,
  path     VARCHAR(900)   NOT NULL UNIQUE CLUSTERED
);
CREATE UNIQUE INDEX idx_unc_mgrid_empid ON dbo.Employees(mgrid, empid);
GO
```

To handle modifications in a tree, it's recommended to use stored procedures that will also take care of the *lvl* and *path* values. Alternatively, you can use triggers, and their logic will be very similar to that in the stored procedures below.

Adding Employees Who Manage No One (Leaves)

Let's start with handling inserts. The logic of the insert procedure is simple. If the new employee is a root employee (that is, the manager ID is null), its level is 0 and its path is '.' + *employee id* + '.'. Otherwise, its level is the parent's level plus 1, and its path is: *parent path* + '*employee id* + '.'. As you can figure out, the shake effect here is minor. There's no need to make any changes to other employees, and to calculate the new employee's *lvl* and *path* values, you only need to query the employee's parent.

Run the code in Listing 9-25 to create the usp_insertemp stored procedure, and run the code in Listing 9-26 to populate the Employees table with sample data.

Listing 9-25 Creation script for the usp_insertemp procedure

```
---------------------------------------------------------- ----------------
-- Stored Procedure: usp_insertemp,
--   Inserts new employee who manages no one into the table
----------------------------------------------------------------------------
USE tempdb;
GO
IF OBJECT_ID('dbo.usp_insertemp') IS NOT NULL
  DROP PROC dbo.usp_insertemp;
GO
CREATE PROC dbo.usp_insertemp
  @empid   INT,
  @mgrid   INT,
  @empname VARCHAR(25),
  @salary  MONEY
AS

SET NOCOUNT ON;

-- Handle case where the new employee has no manager (root)
IF @mgrid IS NULL
  INSERT INTO dbo.Employees(empid, mgrid, empname, salary, lvl, path)
    VALUES(@empid, @mgrid, @empname, @salary,
      0, '.' + CAST(@empid AS VARCHAR(10)) + '.');
-- Handle subordinate case (non-root)
ELSE
  INSERT INTO dbo.Employees(empid, mgrid, empname, salary, lvl, path)
    SELECT @empid, @mgrid, @empname, @salary,
      lvl + 1, path + CAST(@empid AS VARCHAR(10)) + '.'
    FROM dbo.Employees
    WHERE empid = @mgrid;
GO
```

Listing 9-26 Sample data for employees with path

```
EXEC dbo.usp_insertemp
  @empid = 1, @mgrid = NULL, @empname = 'David', @salary = $10000.00;
EXEC dbo.usp_insertemp
  @empid = 2, @mgrid = 1, @empname = 'Eitan', @salary = $7000.00;
EXEC dbo.usp_insertemp
  @empid = 3, @mgrid = 1, @empname = 'Ina', @salary = $7500.00;
EXEC dbo.usp_insertemp
  @empid = 4, @mgrid = 2, @empname = 'Seraph', @salary = $5000.00;
EXEC dbo.usp_insertemp
  @empid = 5, @mgrid = 2, @empname = 'Jiru', @salary = $5500.00;
EXEC dbo.usp_insertemp
  @empid = 6, @mgrid = 2, @empname = 'Steve', @salary = $4500.00;
EXEC dbo.usp_insertemp
  @empid = 7, @mgrid = 3, @empname = 'Aaron', @salary = $5000.00;
EXEC dbo.usp_insertemp
  @empid = 8, @mgrid = 5, @empname = 'Lilach', @salary = $3500.00;
```

```
EXEC dbo.usp_insertemp
  @empid = 9, @mgrid = 7, @empname = 'Rita', @salary = $3000.00;
EXEC dbo.usp_insertemp
  @empid = 10, @mgrid = 5, @empname = 'Sean', @salary = $3000.00;
EXEC dbo.usp_insertemp
  @empid = 11, @mgrid = 7, @empname = 'Gabriel', @salary = $3000.00;
EXEC dbo.usp_insertemp
  @empid = 12, @mgrid = 9, @empname = 'Emilia', @salary = $2000.00;
EXEC dbo.usp_insertemp
  @empid = 13, @mgrid = 9, @empname = 'Michael', @salary = $2000.00;
EXEC dbo.usp_insertemp
  @empid = 14, @mgrid = 9, @empname = 'Didi', @salary = $1500.00;
```

Run the following query to examine the resulting contents of Employees, as shown in Table 9-30:

```
SELECT empid, mgrid, empname, salary, lvl, path
FROM dbo.Employees
ORDER BY path;
```

Table 9-30   Employees with Materialized Path

empid	mgrid	empname	salary	lvl	path
1	NULL	David	10000.0000	0	.1.
2	1	Eitan	7000.0000	1	.1.2.
4	2	Seraph	5000.0000	2	.1.2.4.
5	2	Jiru	5500.0000	2	.1.2.5.
10	5	Sean	3000.0000	3	.1.2.5.10.
8	5	Lilach	3500.0000	3	.1.2.5.8.
6	2	Steve	4500.0000	2	.1.2.6.
3	1	Ina	7500.0000	1	.1.3.
7	3	Aaron	5000.0000	2	.1.3.7.
11	7	Gabriel	3000.0000	3	.1.3.7.11.
9	7	Rita	3000.0000	3	.1.3.7.9.
12	9	Emilia	2000.0000	4	.1.3.7.9.12.
13	9	Michael	2000.0000	4	.1.3.7.9.13.
14	9	Didi	1500.0000	4	.1.3.7.9.14.

Moving a Subtree

Moving a subtree is a bit tricky. A change in someone's manager affects the row for that employee and for all of his or her subordinates. The inputs are the root of the subtree and the new parent (manager) of that root. The level and path values of all employees in the subtree are going to be affected. So you need to be able to isolate that subtree and also figure out how to revise the level and path values of all the subtree's members. To isolate the affected subtree, you join the row for the root (R) with the Employees table (E) based on *E.path LIKE R.path +* '%'. To calculate the revisions in level and path, you need access to the rows of both the old manager of the root (OM) and the new one (NM). The new level value for all nodes is their current level value plus the difference in levels between the new manager's level and the old manager's level. For example, if you move a subtree to a new location so that the difference in levels between the new manager and the old one is 2, you need to add 2 to the level value of all employees in the affected subtree. Similarly, to amend the path value of all nodes in the subtree, you need to remove the prefix containing the root's old manager's path and substitute it with the new manager's path. This can be achieved simply by using the STUFF function.

Run the code in Listing 9-27 to create the usp_movesubtree stored procedure, which implements the logic I just described.

Listing 9-27   Creation script for the usp_movesubtree procedure

```
---------------------------------------------------------------
-- Stored Procedure: usp_movesubtree,
--    Moves a whole subtree of a given root to a new location
--    under a given manager
---------------------------------------------------------------
USE tempdb;
GO
IF OBJECT_ID('dbo.usp_movesubtree') IS NOT NULL
  DROP PROC dbo.usp_movesubtree;
GO
CREATE PROC dbo.usp_movesubtree
  @root  INT,
  @mgrid INT
AS

SET NOCOUNT ON;

BEGIN TRAN;
  -- Update level and path of all employees in the subtree (E)
  -- Set level =
  --    current level + new manager's level - old manager's level
  -- Set path =
  --    in current path remove old manager's path
  --    and substitute with new manager's path
  UPDATE E
    SET lvl  = E.lvl + NM.lvl - OM.lvl,
        path = STUFF(E.path, 1, LEN(OM.path), NM.path)
  FROM dbo.Employees AS E          -- E = Employees    (subtree)
    JOIN dbo.Employees AS R        -- R = Root         (one row)
      ON R.empid = @root
      AND E.path LIKE R.path + '%'
    JOIN dbo.Employees AS OM       -- OM = Old Manager (one row)
      ON OM.empid = R.mgrid
    JOIN dbo.Employees AS NM       -- NM = New Manager (one row)
      ON NM.empid = @mgrid;

  -- Update root's new manager
  UPDATE dbo.Employees SET mgrid = @mgrid WHERE empid = @root;
COMMIT TRAN;
GO
```

The implementation of this stored procedure is simplistic and is provided for demonstration purposes. Good behavior is not guaranteed for invalid parameter choices. To make this procedure more robust, you should also check the inputs to make sure that attempts to make someone his or her own manager or to generate cycles are rejected. For example, this can be achieved by using an EXISTS predicate with a SELECT statement that first generates a result set with the new paths, and checking that the employee IDs do not appear in their managers' path.

To test the procedure, first examine the tree shown in Table 9-31 before moving the subtree:

```
SELECT empid, REPLICATE(' | ', lvl) + empname AS empname, lvl, path
FROM dbo.Employees
ORDER BY path;
```

Table 9-31   Employees before Moving Subtree

empid	empname	lvl	path
1	David	0	.1.
2	| Eitan	1	.1.2.
4	| | Seraph	2	.1.2.4.
5	| | Jiru	2	.1.2.5.
10	| | | Sean	3	.1.2.5.10.
8	| | | Lilach	3	.1.2.5.8.
6	| | Steve	2	.1.2.6.
3	| Ina	1	.1.3.
7	| | Aaron	2	.1.3.7.
11	| | | Gabriel	3	.1.3.7.11.
9	| | | Rita	3	.1.3.7.9.
12	| | | | Emilia	4	.1.3.7.9.12.
13	| | | | Michael	4	.1.3.7.9.13.
14	| | | | Didi	4	.1.3.7.9.14.

Then run the following code to move Aaron's subtree under Sean, and examine the result tree shown in Table 9-32 to verify that the subtree moved correctly:

```
BEGIN TRAN;

  EXEC dbo.usp_movesubtree
  @root  = 7,
  @mgrid = 10;

  -- After moving subtree
  SELECT empid, REPLICATE(' | ', lvl) + empname AS empname, lvl, path
  FROM dbo.Employees
  ORDER BY path;

ROLLBACK TRAN; -- rollback used in order not to apply the change
```

> **Note**   The change is rolled back for demonstration only, so the data is the same at the start of each test script.

Table 9-32   Employees After Moving Subtree

empid	empname	lvl	path
1	David	0	.1.
2	| Eitan	1	.1.2.
4	| | Seraph	2	.1.2.4.
5	| | Jiru	2	.1.2.5.
10	| | | Sean	3	.1.2.5.10.
7	| | | | Aaron	4	.1.2.5.10.7.
11	| | | | | Gabriel	5	.1.2.5.10.7.11.
9	| | | | | Rita	5	.1.2.5.10.7.9.
12	| | | | | | Emilia	6	.1.2.5.10.7.9.12.
13	| | | | | | Michael	6	.1.2.5.10.7.9.13.
14	| | | | | | Didi	6	.1.2.5.10.7.9.14.
8	| | | Lilach	3	.1.2.5.8.
6	| | Steve	2	.1.2.6.
3	| Ina	1	.1.3.

Removing a Subtree

Removing a subtree is a simple task. You just delete all employees whose path value has the subtree's root path as a prefix.

To test this solution, first examine the current state of the tree shown in Table 9-33 by running the following query:

```
SELECT empid, REPLICATE(' | ', lvl) + empname AS empname, lvl, path
FROM dbo.Employees
ORDER BY path;
```

Table 9-33   Employees Before Deleting Subtree

empid	empname	lvl	path
1	David	0	.1.
2	| Eitan	1	.1.2.
4	| | Seraph	2	.1.2.4.
5	| | Jiru	2	.1.2.5.
10	| | | Sean	3	.1.2.5.10.
8	| | | Lilach	3	.1.2.5.8.

Table 9-33   **Employees Before Deleting Subtree**

empid	empname	lvl	path
6	| | Steve	2	.1.2.6.
3	| Ina	1	.1.3.
7	| | Aaron	2	.1.3.7.
11	| | | Gabriel	3	.1.3.7.11.
9	| | | Rita	3	.1.3.7.9.
12	| | | | Emilia	4	.1.3.7.9.12.
13	| | | | Michael	4	.1.3.7.9.13.
14	| | | | Didi	4	.1.3.7.9.14.

Issue the following code, which first removes Aaron and his subordinates and then displays the resulting tree shown in Table 9-34:

```
BEGIN TRAN;

  DELETE FROM dbo.Employees
  WHERE path LIKE
    (SELECT M.path + '%'
     FROM dbo.Employees as M
     WHERE M.empid = 7);

  -- After deleting subtree
  SELECT empid, REPLICATE(' | ', lvl) + empname AS empname, lvl, path
  FROM dbo.Employees
  ORDER BY path;

ROLLBACK TRAN; -- rollback used in order not to apply the change
```

Table 9-34   **Employees After Deleting a Subtree**

empid	empname	lvl	path
1	David	0	.1.
2	| Eitan	1	.1.2.
4	| | Seraph	2	.1.2.4.
5	| | Jiru	2	.1.2.5.
10	| | | Sean	3	.1.2.5.10.
8	| | | Lilach	3	.1.2.5.8.
6	| | Steve	2	.1.2.6.
3	| Ina	1	.1.3.

Querying

Querying data in the materialized path solution is simple and elegant. For subtree-related requests, the optimizer can always use a clustered or covering index that you create on the *path* column. If you create a nonclustered, noncovering index on the *path* column, the optimizer still will be able to use it if the query is selective enough.

Let's review typical requests from a tree. For each request, I'll provide a sample query followed by its output.

Return the subtree with a given root, generating the output shown in Table 9-35:

```
SELECT REPLICATE(' | ', E.lvl - M.lvl) + E.empname
FROM dbo.Employees AS E
  JOIN dbo.Employees AS M
    ON M.empid = 3 -- root
    AND E.path LIKE M.path + '%'
ORDER BY E.path;
```

Table 9-35   Subtree with a Given Root

Ina
| Aaron
| | Gabriel
| | Rita
| | | Emilia
| | | Michael
| | | Didi

The query joins two instances of Employees. One represents the managers (M) and is filtered by the given root employee. The other represents the employees in the subtree (E). The subtree is identified using the following logical expression in the join condition: *E.path LIKE M.path* + '%', which identifies a subordinate if it contains the root's path as a prefix. Indentation is achieved by replicating a string ('|') as many times as the employee's level within the subtree. The output is sorted by the path of the employee.

To exclude the subtree's root (top level manager) from the output, simply add an underscore before the percent sign in the LIKE pattern:

```
SELECT REPLICATE(' | ', E.lvl - M.lvl - 1) + E.empname
FROM dbo.Employees AS E
  JOIN dbo.Employees AS M
    ON M.empid = 3
    AND E.path LIKE M.path + '_%'
ORDER BY E.path;
```

You will get the output shown in Table 9-36.

Table 9-36   Subtree of a Given Root, Excluding Root

Aaron
| Gabriel
| Rita
| | Emilia
| | Michael
| | Didi

With the additional underscore in the LIKE condition, an employee is returned only if its path starts with the root's path and has at least one subsequent character.

To return leaf nodes under a given root (including the root itself if it is a leaf), add a NOT EXISTS predicate to identify only employees that are not managers of another employee:

```
SELECT E.empid, E.empname
FROM dbo.Employees AS E
  JOIN dbo.Employees AS M
    ON M.empid = 3
    AND E.path LIKE M.path + '%'
WHERE NOT EXISTS
  (SELECT *
   FROM dbo.Employees AS E2
   WHERE E2.mgrid = E.empid);
```

You will get the output shown in Table 9-37.

Table 9-37   Leaf Nodes Under a Given Root

empid	empname
11	Gabriel
12	Emilia
13	Michael
14	Didi

To return a subtree with a given root, limiting the number of levels under the root, add a filter in the join condition that limits the level difference between the employee and the root:

```
SELECT REPLICATE(' | ', E.lvl - M.lvl) + E.empname
FROM dbo.Employees AS E
  JOIN dbo.Employees AS M
    ON M.empid = 3
    AND E.path LIKE M.path + '%'
    AND E.lvl - M.lvl <= 2
ORDER BY E.path;
```

You will get the output shown in Table 9-38.

Table 9-38   Subtree with a Given Root, Limiting Levels

Ina
| Aaron
| | Gabriel
| | Rita

To return only the nodes exactly *n* levels under a given root, use an equal to operator (=) to identify the specific level difference instead of a less than or equal to (<=) operator:

```
SELECT E.empid, E.empname
FROM dbo.Employees AS E
```

```
JOIN dbo.Employees AS M
  ON M.empid = 3
  AND E.path LIKE M.path + '%'
  AND E.lvl - M.lvl = 2;
```

You will get the output shown in Table 9-39.

Table 9-39   Nodes that Are Exactly *n* Levels Under a Given Root

empid	empname
11	Gabriel
9	Rita

To return management chain of a given node, you use a query similar to the subtree query, with one small difference—you filter a specific employee ID, as opposed to filtering a specific manager ID:

```
SELECT REPLICATE(' | ', M.lvl) + M.empname
FROM dbo.Employees AS E
  JOIN dbo.Employees AS M
    ON E.empid = 14
    AND E.path LIKE M.path + '%'
ORDER BY E.path;
```

You will get the output shown in Table 9-40.

Table 9-40   Management Chain of Employee 14

David
| Ina
| | Aaron
| | | Rita
| | | | Didi

You get all managers whose paths are a prefix of the given employee's path.

Note that there's an important difference in performance between requesting a subtree and requesting the ancestors, even though they look very similar. For each query, either *M.path* or *E.path* is a constant. If *M.path* is constant, *E.path* LIKE *M.path* + '%' uses an index, because it asks for all paths with a given prefix. If *E.path* is constant, it does not use an index, because it asks for all prefixes of a given path. The subtree query can seek within an index to the first path that meets the filter, and it can scan to the right until it gets to the last path that meets the filter. In other words, only the relevant paths in the index are accessed. While in the ancestors query, ALL paths must be scanned to check whether they match the filter. This means performing a full table/index scan. In large tables, this translates to a slow query. To handle ancestor requests more efficiently, you can create a function that accepts an employee ID as input, splits its path, and returns a table with the path's node IDs in separate rows. You can join this table with the tree and use index seek operations for the specific employee IDs in the path. The split function uses an auxiliary table of numbers, which I covered in Chapter 4 under the section "Auxiliary Table of Numbers." If you currently don't have a Nums table in tempdb, first create it by running the code in Listing 9-28.

Listing 9-28 Creating and populating auxiliary table of numbers

```
SET NOCOUNT ON;
USE tempdb;
GO
IF OBJECT_ID('dbo.Nums') IS NOT NULL
  DROP TABLE dbo.Nums;
GO
CREATE TABLE Nums(n INT NOT NULL PRIMARY KEY);
DECLARE @max AS INT, @rc AS INT;
SET @max = 8000;
SET @rc = 1;

INSERT INTO Nums VALUES(1);
WHILE @rc * 2 <= @max
BEGIN
  INSERT INTO dbo.Nums SELECT n + @rc FROM dbo.Nums;
  SET @rc = @rc * 2;
END

INSERT INTO dbo.Nums
  SELECT n + @rc FROM dbo.Nums WHERE n + @rc <= @max;
```

Run the code in Listing 9-29 to create the *fn_splitpath* function.

Listing 9-29 Creation script for the *fn_splitpath* function

```
USE tempdb;
GO
IF OBJECT_ID('dbo.fn_splitpath') IS NOT NULL
  DROP FUNCTION dbo.fn_splitpath;
GO
CREATE FUNCTION dbo.fn_splitpath(@empid AS INT) RETURNS TABLE
AS
RETURN
  SELECT
    n - LEN(REPLACE(LEFT(path, n), '.', '')) AS pos,
    CAST(SUBSTRING(path, n + 1,
          CHARINDEX('.', path, n+1) - n - 1) AS INT) AS empid
  FROM dbo.Employees
    JOIN dbo.Nums
      ON empid = @empid
      AND n < LEN(path)
      AND SUBSTRING(path, n, 1) = '.'
GO
```

You can find details on the logic behind the split technique that the function implements in Chapter 5 under the section "Separating Elements."

To test the function, run the following code, which splits employee 14's path and generates the output shown in Table 9-41:

```
SELECT pos, empid FROM dbo.fn_splitpath(14);
```

Table 9-41   Output of the *fn_splitpath* Function

pos	empid
1	1
2	3
3	7
4	9
5	14

Now to get the management chain of a given employee, simply join the table returned by the function with the Employees table:

```
SELECT REPLICATE(' | ', lvl) + empname
FROM dbo.fn_splitpath(14) AS SP
  JOIN dbo.Employees AS E
    ON E.empid = SP.empid
ORDER BY path;
```

Nested Sets

Nested sets is one of the most beautiful and intellectually stimulating solutions I've ever seen for modeling trees.

 More Info   Joe Celko has extensive coverage of the Nested Sets model in his writings. You can find Joe Celko's coverage of nested sets in his book, *Joe Celko's Trees and Hierarchies in SQL for Smarties* (Morgan-Kaufmann, 2004).

Here I will cover T-SQL applications of the model, which for the most part work in SQL Server 2005 only because they use new features such as recursive CTEs and the ROW_NUMBER function.

The main advantages of the nested sets solution are simple and fast queries, which I'll describe later, and no level limit. However, alas, with large data sets, the solution's practicality is usually limited to static trees. For dynamic environments, the solution is limited to small trees (possibly large forests, but ones that consist of small trees).

Instead of representing a tree as an adjacency list (parent/child relationship), this solution models the tree relationships as nested sets. A parent is represented in the nested sets model as a containing set and a child as a contained set. Set containment relationships are represented with two integer values assigned to each set: left and right. For all sets: a set's left value is smaller than all contained sets' left values, and a set's right value is higher than all contained sets' right values. Naturally, this containment relationship is transitive in terms of *n*-level relationships (ancestor/descendant). The queries are based on these nested sets relationships. Logically, it's as if a set spreads two arms around all its contained sets.

Assigning Left and Right Values

Figure 9-5 provides a graphical visualization of the Employees hierarchy with the left and right values assigned to each employee.

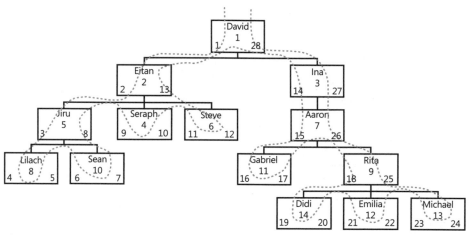

Figure 9-5 Employees hierarchy as nested sets

The curved line that walks the tree represents the order of assignment of the left and right values. Note that the model allows you to choose in which order you assign values to siblings. In this particular case, I chose to traverse siblings by employee name order.

You start with the root, traversing the tree counterclockwise. Every time you enter a node, you increment a counter and set it as the node's left value. Every time you leave a node, you increment the counter and set it as the node's right value. This algorithm can be implemented to the letter as an iterative/recursive routine that assigns each node with left and right values. However, such an implementation requires traversing the tree a node at a time, which can be very slow. I'll show an algorithm that traverses the tree a level at a time, which is faster. The core algorithm is based on logic I discussed earlier in the chapter, traversing the tree a level at a time and calculating binary sort paths. To understand this algorithm, it will help to examine Figure 9-6.

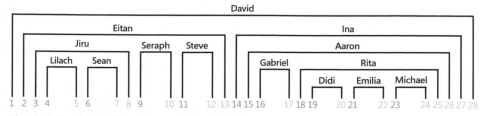

Figure 9-6 Illustration of nested sets model

The figure illustrates each employee as spreading two arms around its subordinates. Left and right values can now be assigned to the different arms by simply incrementing a counter from left to right. Keep this illustration in mind, as it's the key to understanding the solution that I will present.

Again, the baseline is the original algorithm that traverses a subtree a level at a time and constructs a binary sort path based on desired sibling sorting (for example, *empname, empid*).

> **Note**   To get good performance, you should create an index on the parent ID and sort columns—for example, (*mgrid, empname, empid*).

Instead of generating one row for each node (as was the case in the earlier solutions for generating sort values based on a binary path), you generate two rows by cross-joining each level with an auxiliary table that has two numbers: $n=1$ representing the left arm, and $n=2$ representing the right arm. Still, the binary paths are constructed from row numbers, but in this case the arm number is taken into consideration besides the other sort elements (for example, *empname, empid, n*). The query that returns the next level of subordinates returns the subordinates of the left arm only—again, cross-joined with two numbers ($n=1$, $n=2$) to generate two arms for each node.

The code in Listing 9-30 has the CTE implementation of this algorithm and generates the output shown in Table 9-42. The purpose of this code is to generate two binary sort paths for each employee, which will later be used to calculate left and right values. Before you run this code, make sure you have the original Employees table in the tempdb database. If you don't, rerun the code in Listing 9-1 first.

Listing 9-30   Producing binary sort paths representing nested sets relationships

```
USE tempdb;
GO
-- Create index to speed sorting siblings by empname, empid
CREATE UNIQUE INDEX idx_unc_mgrid_empname_empid
  ON dbo.Employees(mgrid, empname, empid);
GO

DECLARE @root AS INT;
SET @root = 1;

-- CTE with two numbers: 1 and 2
WITH TwoNumsCTE
AS
(
  SELECT 1 AS n UNION ALL SELECT 2
),
-- CTE with two binary sort paths for each node:
--   One smaller than descendants sort paths
--   One greater than descendants sort paths
SortPathCTE
```

```
AS
(
  SELECT empid, 0 AS lvl, n,
    CAST(n AS VARBINARY(MAX)) AS sortpath
  FROM dbo.Employees CROSS JOIN TwoNumsCTE
  WHERE empid = @root

  UNION ALL

  SELECT C.empid, P.lvl + 1, TN.n,
    P.sortpath + CAST(
      (-1+ROW_NUMBER() OVER(PARTITION BY C.mgrid
                        -- *** determines order of siblings ***
                        ORDER BY C.empname, C.empid))/2*2+TN.n
    AS BINARY(4))
  FROM SortPathCTE AS P
    JOIN dbo.Employees AS C
      ON P.n = 1
      AND C.mgrid = P.empid
    CROSS JOIN TwoNumsCTE AS TN
)
SELECT * FROM SortPathCTE
ORDER BY sortpath;
```

Table 9-42   Binary Sort Paths Representing Nested Sets Relationships

empid	lvl	n	sortpath
1	0	1	0x00000001
2	1	1	0x0000000100000001
5	2	1	0x000000010000000100000001
8	3	1	0x00000001000000010000000100000001
8	3	2	0x00000001000000010000000100000002
10	3	1	0x00000001000000010000000100000003
10	3	2	0x00000001000000010000000100000004
5	2	2	0x000000010000000100000002
4	2	1	0x000000010000000100000003
4	2	2	0x000000010000000100000004
6	2	1	0x000000010000000100000005
6	2	2	0x000000010000000100000006
2	1	2	0x0000000100000002
3	1	1	0x0000000100000003
7	2	1	0x000000010000000300000001
11	3	1	0x00000001000000030000000100000001
11	3	2	0x00000001000000030000000100000002
9	3	1	0x00000001000000030000000100000003
14	4	1	0x0000000100000003000000010000000300000001

Table 9-42   Binary Sort Paths Representing Nested Sets Relationships

empid	lvl	n	sortpath
14	4	2	0x0000000100000003000000010000000300000002
12	4	1	0x0000000100000003000000010000000300000003
12	4	2	0x0000000100000003000000010000000300000004
13	4	1	0x0000000100000003000000010000000300000005
13	4	2	0x0000000100000003000000010000000300000006
9	3	2	0x00000001000000030000000100000004
7	2	2	0x000000010000000300000002
3	1	2	0x0000000100000004
1	0	2	0x00000002

TwoNumsCTE is the auxiliary table with two numbers representing the two arms. Of course, you could use a real Nums table if you wanted, instead of generating a virtual one.

Two sort paths are generated for each node. The left one is represented by $n=1$, and the right one by $n=2$. Notice that for a given node, the left sort path is smaller than all left sort paths of subordinates, and the right sort path is greater than all right sort paths of subordinates. The sort paths will be used to generate the left and right values in Figure 9-6. You need to generate left and right integer values to represent the nested sets relationships between the employees. To assign the integer values to the arms (*sortval*), simply use the ROW_NUMBER function based on *sortpath* order. Finally, to return one row for each employee containing the left and right integer values, group the rows by employee and level, and return the *MIN(sortval)* as the left value and *MAX(sortval)* as the right value. The complete solution to generate left and right values is shown in Listing 9-31 and generates the output shown in Table 9-43.

Listing 9-31   CTE code that creates nested sets relationships

```
DECLARE @root AS INT;
SET @root = 1;

-- CTE with two numbers: 1 and 2
WITH TwoNumsCTE
AS
(
  SELECT 1 AS n UNION ALL SELECT 2
),
-- CTE with two binary sort paths for each node:
--   One smaller than descendants sort paths
--   One greater than descendants sort paths
SortPathCTE
AS
(
  SELECT empid, 0 AS lvl, n,
    CAST(n AS VARBINARY(MAX)) AS sortpath
  FROM dbo.Employees CROSS JOIN TwoNumsCTE
  WHERE empid = @root

  UNION ALL
```

```
    SELECT C.empid, P.lvl + 1, TN.n,
      P.sortpath + CAST(
        (-1+ROW_NUMBER() OVER(PARTITION BY C.mgrid
                            -- *** determines order of siblings ***
                            ORDER BY C.empname, C.empid))/2*2+TN.n
        AS BINARY(4))
    FROM SortPathCTE AS P
      JOIN dbo.Employees AS C
        ON P.n = 1
        AND C.mgrid = P.empid
      CROSS JOIN TwoNumsCTE AS TN
),
-- CTE with Row Numbers Representing sortpath Order
SortCTE
AS
(
  SELECT empid, lvl,
    ROW_NUMBER() OVER(ORDER BY sortpath) AS sortval
  FROM SortPathCTE
),
-- CTE with Left and Right Values Representing
-- Nested Sets Relationships
NestedSetsCTE
AS
(
  SELECT empid, lvl, MIN(sortval) AS lft, MAX(sortval) AS rgt
  FROM SortCTE
  GROUP BY empid, lvl
)
SELECT * FROM NestedSetsCTE
ORDER BY lft;
```

Table 9-43 Left and Right Values Generated with a CTE

empid	lvl	lft	rgt
1	0	1	28
2	1	2	13
5	2	3	8
8	3	4	5
10	3	6	7
4	2	9	10
6	2	11	12
3	1	14	27
7	2	15	26
11	3	16	17
9	3	18	25
14	4	19	20
12	4	21	22
13	4	23	24

The implementation of this algorithm in SQL Server 2000 is similar, but it's lengthier and slower, mainly because of the calculation of row numbers using identity values instead of the ROW_NUMBER function. You have to materialize interim results in a table to generate the identity values. For simplicity's sake, I'll show a solution with a UDF, where siblings are ordered by *empname, empid*. To create the *fn_empsnestedsets* UDF, run the code in Listing 9-32.

Listing 9-32   Creation script for the *fn_empsnestedsets* function

```
---------------------------------------------------------------
-- Function: fn_empsnestedsets, Nested Sets Relationships
--
-- Input    : @root INT: Root of subtree
--
-- Output   : @NestedSets Table: employee id, level in the subtree,
--                               left and right values representing
--                               nested sets relationships
--
-- Process : * Loads subtree into @SortPath,
--             first root, then a level at a time.
--             Note: two instances of each employee are loaded;
--                   one representing left arm (n = 1),
--                   and one representing right (n = 2).
--             For each employee and arm, a binary path is constructed,
--             representing the nested sets position.
--             The binary path has 4 bytes for each of the employee's
--             ancestors. For each ancestor, the 4 bytes represent
--             its position in the level (calculated with identity).
--             Finally @SortPath will contain a pair of rows for each
--             employee along with a sort path representing the arm's
--             nested sets position.
--           * Next, the rows from @SortPath are loaded
--             into @SortVals, sorted by sortpath. After the load,
--             an integer identity column sortval holds sort values
--             representing the nested sets position of each arm.
--           * The data from @SortVals is grouped by employee,
--             generating the left and right values for each employee
--             in one row. The result set is loaded into the
--             @NestedSets table, which is the function's output.
--
---------------------------------------------------------------
SET NOCOUNT ON;
USE tempdb;
GO
IF OBJECT_ID('dbo.fn_empsnestedsets') IS NOT NULL
  DROP FUNCTION dbo.fn_empsnestedsets;
GO
CREATE FUNCTION dbo.fn_empsnestedsets(@root AS INT)
  RETURNS @NestedSets TABLE
(
  empid INT NOT NULL PRIMARY KEY,
  lvl   INT NOT NULL,
  lft   INT NOT NULL,
  rgt   INT NOT NULL
)
```

```
AS
BEGIN
  DECLARE @lvl AS INT;
  SET @lvl = 0;

  -- @TwoNums: Table Variable with two numbers: 1 and 2
  DECLARE @TwoNums TABLE(n INT NOT NULL PRIMARY KEY);
  INSERT INTO @TwoNums(n) SELECT 1 AS n UNION ALL SELECT 2;

  -- @SortPath: Table Variable with two binary sort paths
  -- for each node:
  --   One smaller than descendants sort paths
  --   One greater than descendants sort paths
  DECLARE @SortPath TABLE
  (
    empid    INT               NOT NULL,
    lvl      INT               NOT NULL,
    n        INT               NOT NULL,
    sortpath VARBINARY(900)    NOT NULL,
    rownum   INT               NOT NULL IDENTITY,
    UNIQUE(lvl, n, empid)
  );

  -- Load root into @SortPath
  INSERT INTO @SortPath(empid, lvl, n, sortpath)
    SELECT empid, @lvl, n,
      CAST(n AS BINARY(4)) AS sortpath
    FROM dbo.Employees CROSS JOIN @TwoNums
    WHERE empid = @root

  WHILE @@rowcount > 0
  BEGIN
    SET @lvl = @lvl + 1;

    -- Load next level into @SortPath
    INSERT INTO @SortPath(empid, lvl, n, sortpath)
      SELECT C.empid, @lvl, TN.n, P.sortpath
      FROM @SortPath AS P
        JOIN dbo.Employees AS C
          ON  P.lvl = @lvl - 1
          AND P.n = 1
          AND C.mgrid = P.empid
        CROSS JOIN @TwoNums AS TN
      -- *** Determines order of siblings ***
      ORDER BY C.empname, C.empid, TN.n;

    -- Update sort path to include child's position
    UPDATE @SortPath
      SET sortpath = sortpath + CAST(rownum AS BINARY(4))
    WHERE lvl = @lvl;
  END

  -- @SortVals: Table Variable with row numbers
  -- representing sortpath order
  DECLARE @SortVals TABLE
```

```
(
  empid   INT NOT NULL,
  lvl     INT NOT NULL,
  sortval INT NOT NULL IDENTITY
)

-- Load data from @SortPath sorted by sortpath
-- to generate sort values
INSERT INTO @SortVals(empid, lvl)
  SELECT empid, lvl FROM @SortPath ORDER BY sortpath;

-- Load data into @NestedSets, generating left and right
-- values representing nested sets relationships
INSERT INTO @NestedSets(empid, lvl, lft, rgt)
  SELECT empid, lvl, MIN(sortval), MAX(sortval)
  FROM @SortVals
  GROUP BY empid, lvl

RETURN;
END
GO
```

To test the function, run the following code, which generates the output shown in Table 9-44:

```
SELECT * FROM dbo.fn_empsnestedsets(1)
ORDER BY lft;
```

Table 9-44   Left and Right Values Generated with a UDF

empid	lvl	lft	rgt
1	0	1	28
2	1	2	13
5	2	3	8
8	3	4	5
10	3	6	7
4	2	9	10
6	2	11	12
3	1	14	27
7	2	15	26
11	3	16	17
9	3	18	25
14	4	19	20
12	4	21	22
13	4	23	24

In the opening paragraph of the "Nested Sets" section, I mentioned that this solution is not adequate for large dynamic trees (trees that incur frequent changes). Suppose you stored left and right values in two additional columns in the Employees table. Note that you won't need the *mgrid* column in the table anymore, as the two additional columns with the left and right values are sufficient to answer requests for subordinates, ancestors, and so on. Consider the shake effect of adding a node to the tree. For example, take a look at Figures 9-5 and 9-6, and try to figure out the effect of adding a new subordinate to Steve. Steve has left and right values 11 and 12, respectively. The new node should get left and right values of 12 and 13, respectively. Steve's right value, and in fact all left and right values in the tree that were greater than or equal to 14, should be increased by two. On average, at least half the nodes in the tree must be updated every time a new node is inserted. As you can see here, the shake effect is very dramatic. That's why the nested sets solution is adequate for a large tree only if it's static, or if you need to run queries against a static snapshot of the tree periodically.

Nested sets can provide reasonably good performance with dynamic trees that are small (or forests with small trees)—for example, when maintaining forum discussions where each thread is a small independent tree in a forest. You can implement a solution that synchronizes the left and right values of the tree with every change. You can achieve this by using stored procedures, or even triggers, as long as the cost of modification is small enough to be bearable. I won't even get into variations of the nested sets model that maintain gaps between the values (that is, leave room to insert new leaves without as much work), as they are all ultimately limited.

To generate a table of employees (EmployeesNS) with the employee ID, employee name, salary, level, left, and right values, join the outer query of either the CTE or the UDF solution and use a SELECT INTO statement. Run the code in Listing 9-33 to create this as the EmployeesNS table with siblings ordered by *empname, empid*.

Listing 9-33   Materializing nested sets relationships in a table

```
SET NOCOUNT ON;
USE tempdb;
GO

DECLARE @root AS INT;
SET @root = 1;

WITH TwoNumsCTE
AS
(
  SELECT 1 AS n UNION ALL SELECT 2
),
SortPathCTE
AS
(
  SELECT empid, 0 AS lvl, n,
    CAST(n AS VARBINARY(MAX)) AS sortpath
  FROM dbo.Employees CROSS JOIN TwoNumsCTE
  WHERE empid = @root

  UNION ALL
```

```
SELECT C.empid, P.lvl + 1, TN.n,
  P.sortpath + CAST(
    ROW_NUMBER() OVER(PARTITION BY C.mgrid
                    -- *** determines order of siblings ***
                    ORDER BY C.empname, C.empid, TN.n)
    AS BINARY(4))
  FROM SortPathCTE AS P
    JOIN dbo.Employees AS C
      ON P.n = 1
      AND C.mgrid = P.empid
    CROSS JOIN TwoNumsCTE AS TN
),
SortCTE
AS
(
  SELECT empid, lvl,
    ROW_NUMBER() OVER(ORDER BY sortpath) AS sortval
  FROM SortPathCTE
),
NestedSetsCTE
AS
(
  SELECT empid, lvl, MIN(sortval) AS lft, MAX(sortval) AS rgt
  FROM SortCTE
  GROUP BY empid, lvl
)
SELECT E.empid, E.empname, E.salary, NS.lvl, NS.lft, NS.rgt
INTO dbo.EmployeesNS
FROM NestedSetsCTE AS NS
  JOIN dbo.Employees AS E
    ON E.empid = NS.empid;

ALTER TABLE dbo.EmployeesNS ADD PRIMARY KEY NONCLUSTERED(empid);
CREATE UNIQUE CLUSTERED INDEX idx_unc_lft_rgt ON dbo.EmployeesNS(lft, rgt);
GO
```

Querying

The EmployeesNS table models a tree of employees as nested sets. Querying is simple, elegant, and fast with the index on left and right values.

In the following section, I'll present common requests against a tree and the query solution for each, followed by the output of the query.

Return the subtree of a given root, generating the output shown in Table 9-45:

```
SELECT C.empid, REPLICATE(' | ', C.lvl - P.lvl) + C.empname AS empname
FROM dbo.EmployeesNS AS P
  JOIN dbo.EmployeesNS AS C
    ON P.empid = 3
    AND C.lft >= P.lft AND C.rgt <= P.rgt
ORDER BY C.lft;
```

Table 9-45 Subtree of a Given Root

empid	empname
3	Ina
7	| Aaron
11	| | Gabriel
9	| | Rita
14	| | | Didi
12	| | | Emilia
13	| | | Michael

The query joins two instances of EmployeesNS. One represents the parent (*P*) and is filtered by the given root. The other represents the child (*C*). The two are joined based on the child's left being greater than or equal to the parent's left, and the child's right being smaller than or equal to the parent's right. Indentation of the output is achieved by replicating a string (' | ') child level minus parent level times. The output is sorted by the child's left value, which by definition represents correct hierarchical sorting, and the desired sort of siblings. This subtree query is used as the baseline for most of the following queries.

If you want to exclude the subtree's root node from the output, simply use greater than (>) and less than (<) operators instead of greater than or equal to (>=) and less than or equal to (<=) operators. To the subtree query, add a filter in the join condition that returns only nodes where the child's level minus the parent's level is smaller than or equal to the requested number of levels under the root.

Return the subtree of a given root, limiting 2 levels of subordinates under the root, generating the output shown in Table 9-46:

```
SELECT C.empid, REPLICATE(' | ', C.lvl - P.lvl) + C.empname AS empname
FROM dbo.EmployeesNS AS P
  JOIN dbo.EmployeesNS AS C
    ON P.empid = 3
    AND C.lft >= P.lft AND C.rgt <= P.rgt
    AND C.lvl - P.lvl <= 2
ORDER BY C.lft;
```

Table 9-46 Subtree of a Given Root, with Level Limit

empid	empname
3	Ina
7	| Aaron
11	| | Gabriel
9	| | Rita

Return leaf nodes under a given root, generating the output shown in Table 9-47:

```
SELECT C.empid, C.empname
FROM dbo.EmployeesNS AS P
  JOIN dbo.EmployeesNS AS C
    ON P.empid = 3
    AND C.lft >= P.lft AND C.rgt <= P.rgt
    AND C.rgt - C.lft = 1;
```

Table 9-47   Leaf Nodes Under a Given Root

empid	empname
11	Gabriel
12	Emilia
13	Michael
14	Didi

A leaf node is a node for which the right value is greater than the left value by 1 (no subordinates). Add this filter to the join condition of the subtree query. As you can see, the nested sets solution allows for dramatically faster identification of leaf nodes than other solutions using a NOT EXISTS predicate.

Return the count of subordinates of each node, generating the output shown in Table 9-48:

```
SELECT empid, (rgt - lft - 1) / 2 AS cnt,
  REPLICATE(' | ', lvl) + empname AS empname
FROM dbo.EmployeesNS
ORDER BY lft;
```

Table 9-48   Count of Subordinates of Each Node

empid	cnt	empname
1	13	David
2	5	| Eitan
5	2	| | Jiru
8	0	| | | Lilach
10	0	| | | Sean
4	0	| | Seraph
6	0	| | Steve
3	6	| Ina
7	5	| | Aaron
11	0	| | | Gabriel
9	3	| | | Rita
14	0	| | | | Didi
12	0	| | | | Emilia
13	0	| | | | Michael

Because each node accounts for exactly two *lft* and *rgt* values, and in our implementation no gaps exist, you can calculate the count of subordinates by accessing the subtree's root alone. The count is: $(rgt - lft - 1) / 2$.

Return all ancestors of a given node, generating the output shown in Table 9-49:

```
SELECT P.empid, P.empname, P.lvl
FROM dbo.EmployeesNS AS P
  JOIN dbo.EmployeesNS AS C
    ON C.empid = 14
    AND C.lft >= P.lft AND C.rgt <= P.rgt;
```

Table 9-49 Ancestors of a Given Node

empid	empname	lvl
1	David	0
3	Ina	1
7	Aaron	2
9	Rita	3
14	Didi	4

The ancestors query is almost identical to the subtree query. The nested sets relationships remain the same. The only difference is that here you filter a specific child node ID, while in the subtree query you filtered a specific parent node ID.

When you're done querying the EmployeesNS table, don't forget to get rid of it:

```
DROP TABLE dbo.EmployeesNS;
```

Transitive Closure

The transitive closure of a directed graph G is the graph with the same vertices as G, and with an edge connecting each pair of nodes that are connected by a path (not necessarily containing just one edge) in G. The transitive closure helps answer a number of questions immediately, without the need to explore paths in the graph. For example, is David a manager of Aaron (directly or indirectly)? If the transitive closure of the Employees graph contains an edge from David to Aaron, he is. Does Double Espresso contain water? Can I drive from Los Angeles to New York? If the input graph contains the edges (a, b) and (b, c), there's a transitive relationship between a and c. The transitive closure will contain the edges (a, b), (b, c), and also (a, c). If David is the direct manager of Ina, and Ina is the direct manager of Aaron, David transitively is a manager of Aaron, or Aaron transitively is a subordinate of David.

There are problems related to transitive closure that deal with specialized cases of transitive relationships. An example is the "shortest path" problem, where you're trying to determine the shortest path between two nodes. For example, what's the shortest path between Los Angeles and New York?

In this section, I will describe iterative/recursive solutions for transitive closure and shortest path problems. In some of my examples, I will use CTEs that apply to SQL Server 2005. As with examples I presented earlier in the chapter, you can make adjustments and implement similar algorithms in SQL Server 2000 by using UDFs or stored procedures.

> **Note**   The performance of some of the solutions that I will show (specifically those that use recursive CTEs) degrades exponentially as the input graph grows. I'll present them for demonstration purposes because they are fairly simple and natural. They are adequate for fairly small graphs. There are efficient algorithms for transitive closure related problems (for example, Floyd's and Warshall's algorithms) that can be implemented as "level at a time" (breadth-first) iterations. For details on those, please refer to *http://www.nist.gov/dads/*. I'll show efficient solutions provided by Steve Kass that can be applied to larger graphs.

Directed Acyclic Graph

The first problem that I will discuss is generating a transitive closure of a directed acyclic graph (DAG). Later I'll show you how to deal with undirected and cyclic graphs as well. Whether the graph is directed or undirected doesn't really complicate the solution significantly, while dealing with cyclic graphs does. The input DAG that I will use in my example is the BOM I used earlier in the chapter, which you create by running the code in Listing 9-2.

The code that generates the transitive closure of BOM is somewhat similar to solutions for the subgraph problem (that is, the parts explosion). Specifically, you traverse the graph a level at a time (or more accurately, you are using "breadth-first" search techniques). However, instead of returning only a root node here, the anchor member returns all first-level relationships in BOM. In most graphs, this simply means all existing source/target pairs. In our case, this means all assembly/part pairs where the assembly is not NULL. The recursive member joins the CTE representing the previous level or parent (*P*) with BOM representing the next level or child (*C*). It returns the original product id (*P*) as the source, and the child product id (*C*) as the target. The outer query returns the distinct assembly/part pairs. Keep in mind that multiple paths may lead to a part in BOM, but you need to return each unique pair only once.

Run the code in Listing 9-34 to generate the transitive closure of BOM shown in Table 9-50.

Listing 9-34   Transitive closure of BOM (DAG)

```
WITH BOMTC
AS
(
  -- Return all first-level containment relationships
  SELECT assemblyid, partid
  FROM dbo.BOM
  WHERE assemblyid IS NOT NULL

  UNION ALL
```

```
    -- Return next-level containment relationships
    SELECT P.assemblyid, C.partid
    FROM BOMTC AS P
      JOIN dbo.BOM AS C
        ON C.assemblyid = P.partid
)
-- Return distinct pairs that have
-- transitive containment relationships
SELECT DISTINCT assemblyid, partid
FROM BOMTC;
```

Table 9-50 Transitive Closure of BOM (DAG)

assemblyid	partid
1	6
1	7
1	10
1	13
1	14
2	6
2	7
2	10
2	11
2	13
2	14
3	6
3	7
3	11
3	12
3	14
3	16
3	17
4	9
4	12
4	14
4	16
4	17
5	9
5	12
5	14
5	16
5	17
10	13

Table 9-50   Transitive Closure of BOM (DAG)

assemblyid	partid
10	14
12	14
12	16
12	17
16	17

This solution eliminates duplicate edges found in the BOMCTE by applying a DISTINCT clause in the outer query. A more efficient solution would be to avoid getting duplicates altogether by using a NOT EXISTS predicate in the query that runs repeatedly; such a predicate would filter newly found edges that do not appear in the set of edges that were already found. However, such an implementation will not be able to use a CTE because the recursive member in the CTE has access only to the "immediate previous level," as opposed to "all previous levels" obtained thus far. Instead, you can use a UDF that invokes the query that runs repeatedly in a loop and inserts each obtained level of nodes into a table variable. Run the code in Listing 9-35 to create the *fn_BOMTC* UDF, which implements this logic.

Listing 9-35   Creation script for the *fn_BOMTC* UDF

```
IF OBJECT_ID('dbo.fn_BOMTC') IS NOT NULL
  DROP FUNCTION dbo.fn_BOMTC;
GO

CREATE FUNCTION fn_BOMTC() RETURNS @BOMTC TABLE
(
  assemblyid INT NOT NULL,
  partid     INT NOT NULL,
  PRIMARY KEY (assemblyid, partid)
)
AS
BEGIN
  INSERT INTO @BOMTC(assemblyid, partid)
    SELECT assemblyid, partid
    FROM dbo.BOM
    WHERE assemblyid IS NOT NULL

  WHILE @@rowcount > 0
    INSERT INTO @BOMTC
    SELECT P.assemblyid, C.partid
    FROM @BOMTC AS P
      JOIN dbo.BOM AS C
        ON C.assemblyid = P.partid
    WHERE NOT EXISTS
      (SELECT * FROM @BOMTC AS P2
       WHERE P2.assemblyid = P.assemblyid
       AND P2.partid = C.partid);

  RETURN;
END
GO
```

Run the following code to query the function and you will get the output shown in Table 9-50:

```
SELECT assemblyid, partid FROM fn_BOMTC();
```

If you want to return all paths in BOM, along with the distance in levels between the parts, you use a similar algorithm with a few additions and revisions. You calculate the distance the same way you calculated the level value in the subgraph/subtree solutions. That is, the anchor assigns a constant distance of 1 for the first level, and the recursive member simply adds one in each iteration. Also, the path calculation is similar to the one used in the subgraph/subtree solutions. The anchor generates a path made of '.' + *source_id* + '.' + *target_id* + '.'. The recursive member generates it as: *parent's path* + *target_id* + '.'. Finally, the outer query simply returns all paths (without applying DISTINCT in this case).

Run the code in Listing 9-36 to generate all possible paths in BOM and their distances.

Listing 9-36   All paths in BOM

```
WITH BOMPaths
AS
(
  SELECT assemblyid, partid,
    1 AS distance, -- distance in first level is 1
    -- path in first level is .assemblyid.partid.
    '.' + CAST(assemblyid AS VARCHAR(MAX)) +
    '.' + CAST(partid     AS VARCHAR(MAX)) + '.' AS path
  FROM dbo.BOM
  WHERE assemblyid IS NOT NULL

  UNION ALL

  SELECT P.assemblyid, C.partid,
    -- distance in next level is parent's distance + 1
    P.distance + 1,
    -- path in next level is parent_path.child_partid.
    P.path + CAST(C.partid AS VARCHAR(MAX)) + '.'
  FROM BOMPaths AS P
    JOIN dbo.BOM AS C
      ON C.assemblyid = P.partid
)
-- Return all paths
SELECT * FROM BOMPaths;
```

You will get the output shown in Table 9-51.

Table 9-51   All Paths in BOM

assemblyid	partid	distance	path
1	6	1	.1.6.
2	6	1	.2.6.
3	6	1	.3.6.

Table 9-51 All Paths in BOM

assemblyid	partid	distance	path
1	7	1	.1.7.
2	7	1	.2.7.
3	7	1	.3.7.
4	9	1	.4.9.
5	9	1	.5.9.
1	10	1	.1.10.
2	10	1	.2.10.
2	11	1	.2.11.
3	11	1	.3.11.
3	12	1	.3.12.
4	12	1	.4.12.
5	12	1	.5.12.
10	13	1	.10.13.
1	14	1	.1.14.
2	14	1	.2.14.
10	14	1	.10.14.
12	14	1	.12.14.
12	16	1	.12.16.
16	17	1	.16.17.
12	17	2	.12.16.17.
5	14	2	.5.12.14.
5	16	2	.5.12.16.
5	17	3	.5.12.16.17.
4	14	2	.4.12.14.
4	16	2	.4.12.16.
4	17	3	.4.12.16.17.
3	14	2	.3.12.14.
3	16	2	.3.12.16.
3	17	3	.3.12.16.17.
2	13	2	.2.10.13.
2	14	2	.2.10.14.
1	13	2	.1.10.13.
1	14	2	.1.10.14.

To isolate only the shortest paths, add a second CTE (BOMMinDist) that groups all paths by assembly and part, returning the minimum distance for each group. And in the outer query, join the first CTE (BOMPaths) with BOMMinDist, based on *assembly*, *part*, and *distance* match to return the actual paths.

Run the code in Listing 9-37 to produce the shortest paths in BOM as shown in Table 9-52.

Listing 9-37 Shortest paths in BOM

```
WITH BOMPaths -- All paths
AS
(
  SELECT assemblyid, partid,
    1 AS distance,
    '.' + CAST(assemblyid AS VARCHAR(MAX)) +
    '.' + CAST(partid    AS VARCHAR(MAX)) + '.' AS path
  FROM dbo.BOM
  WHERE assemblyid IS NOT NULL

  UNION ALL

  SELECT P.assemblyid, C.partid,
    P.distance + 1,
    P.path + CAST(C.partid AS VARCHAR(MAX)) + '.'
  FROM BOMPaths AS P
    JOIN dbo.BOM AS C
      ON C.assemblyid = P.partid
),
BOMMinDist AS -- Minimum distance for each pair
(
  SELECT assemblyid, partid, MIN(distance) AS mindist
  FROM BOMPaths
  GROUP BY assemblyid, partid
)
-- Shortest path for each pair
SELECT BP.*
FROM BOMMinDist AS BMD
  JOIN BOMPaths AS BP
    ON BMD.assemblyid = BP.assemblyid
    AND BMD.partid = BP.partid
    AND BMD.mindist = BP.distance;
```

Table 9-52 Shortest Paths in BOM

assemblyid	partid	distance	path
1	6	1	.1.6.
2	6	1	.2.6.
3	6	1	.3.6.
1	7	1	.1.7.
2	7	1	.2.7.
3	7	1	.3.7.
4	9	1	.4.9.
5	9	1	.5.9.

Table 9-52   Shortest Paths in BOM

assemblyid	partid	distance	path
1	10	1	.1.10.
2	10	1	.2.10.
2	11	1	.2.11.
3	11	1	.3.11.
3	12	1	.3.12.
4	12	1	.4.12.
5	12	1	.5.12.
10	13	1	.10.13.
1	14	1	.1.14.
2	14	1	.2.14.
10	14	1	.10.14.
12	14	1	.12.14.
12	16	1	.12.16.
16	17	1	.16.17.
12	17	2	.12.16.17.
5	14	2	.5.12.14.
5	16	2	.5.12.16.
5	17	3	.5.12.16.17.
4	14	2	.4.12.14.
4	16	2	.4.12.16.
4	17	3	.4.12.16.17.
3	14	2	.3.12.14.
3	16	2	.3.12.16.
3	17	3	.3.12.16.17.
2	13	2	.2.10.13.
1	13	2	.1.10.13.

Undirected Cyclic Graph

Even though transitive closure is defined for a directed graph, you can also define and generate it for undirected graphs where each edge represents a two-way relationship. In my examples, I will use the Roads graph, which you create and populate by running the code in Listing 9-3. To see a visual representation of Roads, examine Figure 9-4. To apply the transitive closure and shortest path solutions to Roads, first convert it to a digraph by generating two directed edges from each existing edge:

```
SELECT city1 AS from_city, city2 AS to_city FROM dbo.Roads
UNION ALL
SELECT city2, city1 FROM dbo.Roads
```

For example, the edge (*JFK, ATL*) in the undirected graph will appear as the edges (*JFK, ATL*) and (*ATL, JFK*) in the digraph. The former represents the road from New York to Atlanta, and the latter represents the road from Atlanta to New York.

Because Roads is a cyclic graph, you also need to use the cycle-detection logic I described earlier in the chapter to avoid traversing cyclic paths. Armed with the techniques to generate a digraph out of an undirected graph and to detect cycles, you have all the tools you need to produce the transitive closure of roads.

Run the code in Listing 9-38 to generate the transitive closure of roads shown in Table 9-53.

Listing 9-38   Transitive closure of Roads (undirected cyclic graph)

```
WITH Roads2 -- Two rows for each pair (from-->to, to-->from)
AS
(
  SELECT city1 AS from_city, city2 AS to_city FROM dbo.Roads
  UNION ALL
  SELECT city2, city1 FROM dbo.Roads
),
RoadPaths AS
(
  -- Return all first-level reachability pairs
  SELECT from_city, to_city,
    -- path is needed to identify cycles
    CAST('.' + from_city + '.' + to_city + '.' AS VARCHAR(MAX)) AS path
  FROM Roads2

  UNION ALL

  -- Return next-level reachability pairs
  SELECT F.from_city, T.to_city,
    CAST(F.path + T.to_city + '.' AS VARCHAR(MAX))
  FROM RoadPaths AS F
    JOIN Roads2 AS T
      -- if to_city appears in from_city's path, cycle detected
      ON CASE WHEN F.path LIKE '%.' + T.to_city + '.%'
              THEN 1 ELSE 0 END = 0
      AND F.to_city = T.from_city
)
-- Return Transitive Closure of Roads
SELECT DISTINCT from_city, to_city
FROM RoadPaths;
```

The Roads2 CTE creates the digraph out of Roads. The RoadPaths CTE returns all possible source/target pairs (which has a big performance penalty), and it avoids returning and pursuing a path for which a cycle is detected. The outer query returns all distinct source/target pairs.

Table 9-53   **Transitive Closure of Roads**

from to	from to	from to	from to	from to
ANC FAI	IAH DEN	LAX MCI	MIA ORD	SEA ATL
ATL DEN	IAH JFK	LAX MIA	MIA SEA	SEA DEN
ATL IAH	IAH LAX	LAX MSP	MIA SFO	SEA IAH
ATL JFK	IAH MCI	LAX ORD	MSP ATL	SEA JFK
ATL LAX	IAH MIA	LAX SEA	MSP DEN	SEA LAX
ATL MCI	IAH MSP	LAX SFO	MSP IAH	SEA MCI
ATL MIA	IAH ORD	MCI ATL	MSP JFK	SEA MIA
ATL MSP	IAH SEA	MCI DEN	MSP LAX	SEA MSP
ATL ORD	IAH SFO	MCI IAH	MSP MCI	SEA ORD
ATL SEA	JFK ATL	MCI JFK	MSP MIA	SEA SFO
ATL SFO	JFK DEN	MCI LAX	MSP ORD	SFO ATL
DEN ATL	JFK IAH	MCI MIA	MSP SEA	SFO DEN
DEN IAH	JFK LAX	MCI MSP	MSP SFO	SFO IAH
DEN JFK	JFK MCI	MCI ORD	ORD ATL	SFO JFK
DEN LAX	JFK MIA	MCI SEA	ORD DEN	SFO LAX
DEN MCI	JFK MSP	MCI SFO	ORD IAH	SFO MCI
DEN MIA	JFK ORD	MIA ATL	ORD JFK	SFO MIA
DEN MSP	JFK SEA	MIA DEN	ORD LAX	SFO MSP
DEN ORD	JFK SFO	MIA IAH	ORD MCI	SFO ORD
DEN SEA	LAX ATL	MIA JFK	ORD MIA	SFO SEA
DEN SFO	LAX DEN	MIA LAX	ORD MSP	
FAI ANC	LAX IAH	MIA MCI	ORD SEA	
IAH ATL	LAX JFK	MIA MSP	ORD SFO	

Here as well you can use loops instead of a recursive CTE to optimize the solution, as demonstrated earlier with the BOM scenario in Listing 9-35. Run the code in Listing 9-39 to create the *fn_RoadsTC* UDF, which returns the transitive closure of Roads using loops.

Listing 9-39   Creation script for the *fn_RoadsTC* UDF

```
IF OBJECT_ID('dbo.fn_RoadsTC') IS NOT NULL
  DROP FUNCTION dbo.fn_RoadsTC;
GO

CREATE FUNCTION dbo.fn_RoadsTC() RETURNS @RoadsTC TABLE (
  from_city VARCHAR(3) NOT NULL,
  to_city   VARCHAR(3) NOT NULL,
  PRIMARY KEY (from_city, to_city)
)
AS
```

```
BEGIN
  DECLARE @added as INT;

  INSERT INTO @RoadsTC(from_city, to_city)
    SELECT city1, city2 FROM dbo.Roads;

  SET @added = @@rowcount;

  INSERT INTO @RoadsTC
    SELECT city2, city1 FROM dbo.Roads

  SET @added = @added + @@rowcount;

  WHILE @added > 0 BEGIN

    INSERT INTO @RoadsTC
      SELECT DISTINCT TC.from_city, R.city2
      FROM @RoadsTC AS TC
        JOIN dbo.Roads AS R
          ON R.city1 = TC.to_city
      WHERE NOT EXISTS
        (SELECT * FROM @RoadsTC AS TC2
         WHERE TC2.from_city = TC.from_city
           AND TC2.to_city = R.city2)
        AND TC.from_city <> R.city2;

    SET @added = @@rowcount;

    INSERT INTO @RoadsTC
      SELECT DISTINCT TC.from_city, R.city1
      FROM @RoadsTC AS TC
        JOIN dbo.Roads AS R
          ON R.city2 = TC.to_city
      WHERE NOT EXISTS
        (SELECT * FROM @RoadsTC AS TC2
         WHERE TC2.from_city = TC.from_city
           AND TC2.to_city = R.city1)
        AND TC.from_city <> R.city1;

    SET @added = @added + @@rowcount;
  END
  RETURN;
END
GO

-- Use the fn_RoadsTC UDF
SELECT * FROM dbo.fn_RoadsTC();
GO
```

Run the following query to get the transitive closure of Roads shown in Table 9-53:

```
SELECT * FROM dbo.fn_RoadsTC();
```

To return all paths and distances, use similar logic to the one used in the digraph solution in the previous section. The difference here is that the distance is not just a level counter; it is the sum of the distances along the route from one city to the other.

Run the code in Listing 9-40 to return all paths and distances in Roads.

Listing 9-40   All paths and distances in Roads

```
WITH Roads2
AS
(
  SELECT city1 AS from_city, city2 AS to_city, distance FROM dbo.Roads
  UNION ALL
  SELECT city2, city1, distance FROM dbo.Roads
),
RoadPaths AS
(
  SELECT from_city, to_city, distance,
    CAST('.' + from_city + '.' + to_city + '.' AS VARCHAR(MAX)) AS path
  FROM Roads2

  UNION ALL

  SELECT F.from_city, T.to_city, F.distance + T.distance,
    CAST(F.path + T.to_city + '.' AS VARCHAR(MAX))
  FROM RoadPaths AS F
    JOIN Roads2 AS T
      ON CASE WHEN F.path LIKE '%.' + T.to_city + '.%'
              THEN 1 ELSE 0 END = 0
      AND F.to_city = T.from_city
)
-- Return all paths and distances
SELECT * FROM RoadPaths;
```

Finally, to return shortest paths in Roads, use the same logic as the digraph shortest paths solution. Run the code in Listing 9-41 to return shortest paths in Roads as shown in Table 9-54.

Listing 9-41   Shortest paths in Roads

```
WITH Roads2
AS
(
  SELECT city1 AS from_city, city2 AS to_city, distance FROM dbo.Roads
  UNION ALL
  SELECT city2, city1, distance FROM dbo.Roads
),
RoadPaths AS
(
  SELECT from_city, to_city, distance,
    CAST('.' + from_city + '.' + to_city + '.' AS VARCHAR(MAX)) AS path
  FROM Roads2
```

```
    UNION ALL

    SELECT F.from_city, T.to_city, F.distance + T.distance,
      CAST(F.path + T.to_city + '.' AS VARCHAR(MAX))
    FROM RoadPaths AS F
      JOIN Roads2 AS T
        ON CASE WHEN F.path LIKE '%.' + T.to_city + '.%'
                THEN 1 ELSE 0 END = 0
        AND F.to_city = T.from_city
),
RoadsMinDist -- Min distance for each pair in TC
AS
(
  SELECT from_city, to_city, MIN(distance) AS mindist
  FROM RoadPaths
  GROUP BY from_city, to_city
)
-- Return shortest paths and distances
SELECT RP.*
FROM RoadsMinDist AS RMD
  JOIN RoadPaths AS RP
    ON RMD.from_city = RP.from_city
    AND RMD.to_city = RP.to_city
    AND RMD.mindist = RP.distance;
```

Table 9-54   Shortest Paths in Roads

from_city	to_city	distance	path
ANC	FAI	359	.ANC.FAI.
ATL	IAH	800	.ATL.IAH.
ATL	JFK	865	.ATL.JFK.
ATL	MCI	805	.ATL.MCI.
ATL	MIA	665	.ATL.MIA.
ATL	ORD	715	.ATL.ORD.
DEN	IAH	1120	.DEN.IAH.
DEN	LAX	1025	.DEN.LAX.
DEN	MCI	600	.DEN.MCI.
DEN	MSP	915	.DEN.MSP.
DEN	SEA	1335	.DEN.SEA.
DEN	SFO	1270	.DEN.SFO.
IAH	LAX	1550	.IAH.LAX.
IAH	MCI	795	.IAH.MCI.
IAH	MIA	1190	.IAH.MIA.
JFK	ORD	795	.JFK.ORD.
LAX	SFO	385	.LAX.SFO.
MCI	MSP	440	.MCI.MSP.

Table 9-54   Shortest Paths in Roads

from_city	to_city	distance	path
MCI	ORD	525	.MCI.ORD.
MSP	ORD	410	.MSP.ORD.
MSP	SEA	2015	.MSP.SEA.
SEA	SFO	815	.SEA.SFO.
FAI	ANC	359	.FAI.ANC.
IAH	ATL	800	.IAH.ATL.
JFK	ATL	865	.JFK.ATL.
MCI	ATL	805	.MCI.ATL.
MIA	ATL	665	.MIA.ATL.
ORD	ATL	715	.ORD.ATL.
IAH	DEN	1120	.IAH.DEN.
LAX	DEN	1025	.LAX.DEN.
MCI	DEN	600	.MCI.DEN.
MSP	DEN	915	.MSP.DEN.
SEA	DEN	1335	.SEA.DEN.
SFO	DEN	1270	.SFO.DEN.
LAX	IAH	1550	.LAX.IAH.
MCI	IAH	795	.MCI.IAH.
MIA	IAH	1190	.MIA.IAH.
ORD	JFK	795	.ORD.JFK.
SFO	LAX	385	.SFO.LAX.
MSP	MCI	440	.MSP.MCI.
ORD	MCI	525	.ORD.MCI.
ORD	MSP	410	.ORD.MSP.
SEA	MSP	2015	.SEA.MSP.
SFO	SEA	815	.SFO.SEA.
SEA	ORD	2425	.SEA.MSP.ORD.
SEA	JFK	3220	.SEA.MSP.ORD.JFK.
ORD	SEA	2425	.ORD.MSP.SEA.
ORD	DEN	1125	.ORD.MCI.DEN.
ORD	IAH	1320	.ORD.MCI.IAH.
ORD	LAX	2150	.ORD.MCI.DEN.LAX.
ORD	SFO	2395	.ORD.MCI.DEN.SFO.
MSP	IAH	1235	.MSP.MCI.IAH.
SFO	IAH	1935	.SFO.LAX.IAH.
SFO	MIA	3125	.SFO.LAX.IAH.MIA.
MIA	LAX	2740	.MIA.IAH.LAX.

Table 9-54   Shortest Paths in Roads

from_city	to_city	distance	path
MIA	SFO	3125	.MIA.IAH.LAX.SFO.
LAX	MIA	2740	.LAX.IAH.MIA.
LAX	ATL	2350	.LAX.IAH.ATL.
SFO	MCI	1870	.SFO.DEN.MCI.
SFO	MSP	2185	.SFO.DEN.MSP.
SFO	ORD	2395	.SFO.DEN.MCI.ORD.
SFO	ATL	2675	.SFO.DEN.MCI.ATL.
SFO	JFK	3190	.SFO.DEN.MCI.ORD.JFK.
SEA	IAH	2455	.SEA.DEN.IAH.
SEA	MCI	1935	.SEA.DEN.MCI.
SEA	ATL	2740	.SEA.DEN.MCI.ATL.
SEA	MIA	3405	.SEA.DEN.MCI.ATL.MIA.
MSP	LAX	1940	.MSP.DEN.LAX.
MSP	SFO	2185	.MSP.DEN.SFO.
MCI	LAX	1625	.MCI.DEN.LAX.
MCI	SEA	1935	.MCI.DEN.SEA.
MCI	SFO	1870	.MCI.DEN.SFO.
LAX	MCI	1625	.LAX.DEN.MCI.
LAX	MSP	1940	.LAX.DEN.MSP.
LAX	ORD	2150	.LAX.DEN.MCI.ORD.
LAX	JFK	2945	.LAX.DEN.MCI.ORD.JFK.
IAH	SEA	2455	.IAH.DEN.SEA.
ORD	MIA	1380	.ORD.ATL.MIA.
MIA	JFK	1530	.MIA.ATL.JFK.
MIA	MCI	1470	.MIA.ATL.MCI.
MIA	ORD	1380	.MIA.ATL.ORD.
MIA	MSP	1790	.MIA.ATL.ORD.MSP.
MIA	DEN	2070	.MIA.ATL.MCI.DEN.
MIA	SEA	3405	.MIA.ATL.MCI.DEN.SEA.
MCI	MIA	1470	.MCI.ATL.MIA.
JFK	IAH	1665	.JFK.ATL.IAH.
JFK	MIA	1530	.JFK.ATL.MIA.
IAH	JFK	1665	.IAH.ATL.JFK.
SEA	LAX	1200	.SEA.SFO.LAX.
MSP	ATL	1125	.MSP.ORD.ATL.
MSP	JFK	1205	.MSP.ORD.JFK.
MSP	MIA	1790	.MSP.ORD.ATL.MIA.

Table 9-54   Shortest Paths in Roads

from_city	to_city	distance	path
MCI	JFK	1320	.MCI.ORD.JFK.
LAX	SEA	1200	.LAX.SFO.SEA.
JFK	MCI	1320	JFK.ORD.MCI.
JFK	MSP	1205	JFK.ORD.MSP.
JFK	SEA	3220	JFK.ORD.MSP.SEA.
JFK	DEN	1920	JFK.ORD.MCI.DEN.
JFK	LAX	2945	JFK.ORD.MCI.DEN.LAX.
JFK	SFO	3190	JFK.ORD.MCI.DEN.SFO.
IAH	MSP	1235	.IAH.MCI.MSP.
IAH	ORD	1320	.IAH.MCI.ORD.
IAH	SFO	1935	.IAH.LAX.SFO.
DEN	ORD	1125	.DEN.MCI.ORD.
DEN	ATL	1405	.DEN.MCI.ATL.
DEN	MIA	2070	.DEN.MCI.ATL.MIA.
DEN	JFK	1920	.DEN.MCI.ORD.JFK.
ATL	MSP	1125	.ATL.ORD.MSP.
ATL	DEN	1405	.ATL.MCI.DEN.
ATL	SEA	2740	.ATL.MCI.DEN.SEA.
ATL	SFO	2675	.ATL.MCI.DEN.SFO.
ATL	LAX	2350	.ATL.IAH.LAX.

To satisfy multiple requests for the shortest paths between two cities, you might want to materialize the result set in a table and index it as shown in Listing 9-42:

Listing 9-42   Load shortest road paths into a table

```
WITH Roads2
AS
(
  SELECT city1 AS from_city, city2 AS to_city, distance FROM dbo.Roads
  UNION ALL
  SELECT city2, city1, distance FROM dbo.Roads
),
RoadPaths AS
(
  SELECT from_city, to_city, distance,
    CAST('.' + from_city + '.' + to_city + '.' AS VARCHAR(MAX)) AS path
  FROM Roads2

  UNION ALL

  SELECT F.from_city, T.to_city, F.distance + T.distance,
    CAST(F.path + T.to_city + '.' AS VARCHAR(MAX))
```

```
    FROM RoadPaths AS F
      JOIN Roads2 AS T
        ON CASE WHEN F.path LIKE '%.' + T.to_city + '.%'
                THEN 1 ELSE 0 END = 0
        AND F.to_city = T.from_city
),
RoadsMinDist
AS
(
  SELECT from_city, to_city, MIN(distance) AS mindist
  FROM RoadPaths
  GROUP BY from_city, to_city
)
SELECT RP.*
INTO dbo.RoadPaths
FROM RoadsMinDist AS RMD
  JOIN RoadPaths AS RP
    ON RMD.from_city = RP.from_city
    AND RMD.to_city = RP.to_city
    AND RMD.mindist = RP.distance;

CREATE UNIQUE CLUSTERED INDEX idx_uc_from_city_to_city
  ON dbo.RoadPaths(from_city, to_city);
```

Once the result set is materialized and indexed, a request for the shortest path between two cities can be satisfied instantly. This is practical and advisable when information changes infrequently. As is often the case, there is a tradeoff between "up to date" and "fast." The following query requests the shortest path between Los Angeles and New York, producing the output shown in Table 9-55:

```
SELECT * FROM dbo.RoadPaths
WHERE from_city = 'LAX' AND to_city = 'JFK';
```

Table 9-55   Shortest Path between LA and NY

from_city	to_city	distance	path
LAX	JFK	2945	.LAX.DEN.MCI.ORD.JFK.

A more efficient solution to the shortest paths problem uses loops instead of recursive CTEs. It is more efficient for similar reasons to the ones described earlier; that is, in each iteration of the loop you have access to all previously spooled data and not just to the immediate previous level. You create a function called *fn_RoadsTC* that returns a table variable called @RoadsTC. The table variable has the attributes *from_city*, *to_city*, *distance* and *route*, which are self-explanatory. The function's code first inserts into @RoadsTC a row for each (*city1, city2*) and (*city2, city1*) pair from the table Roads. The code then enters a loop that iterates as long as the previous iteration inserted rows to @RoadsTC. In each iteration of the loop, the code inserts new routes that extend the existing routes in @RoadsTC. New routes are added only if the source and destination do not appear already in @RoadsTC with the same or shorter distance. Run the code in Listing 9-43 to create the *fn_RoadsTC* function.

Listing 9-43   Creation script for the fn_RoadsTC UDF

```
IF OBJECT_ID('dbo.fn_RoadsTC') IS NOT NULL
  DROP FUNCTION dbo.fn_RoadsTC;
GO
CREATE FUNCTION dbo.fn_RoadsTC() RETURNS @RoadsTC TABLE
(
  uniquifier INT          NOT NULL IDENTITY,
  from_city  VARCHAR(3)   NOT NULL,
  to_city    VARCHAR(3)   NOT NULL,
  distance   INT          NOT NULL,
  route      VARCHAR(MAX) NOT NULL,
  PRIMARY KEY (from_city, to_city, uniquifier)
)
AS
BEGIN
  DECLARE @added AS INT;

  INSERT INTO @RoadsTC
    SELECT city1 AS from_city, city2 AS to_city, distance,
      '.' + city1 + '.' + city2 + '.'
    FROM dbo.Roads;

  SET @added = @@rowcount;

  INSERT INTO @RoadsTC
    SELECT city2, city1, distance, '.' + city2 + '.' + city1 + '.'
    FROM dbo.Roads;

  SET @added = @added + @@rowcount;

  WHILE @added > 0 BEGIN
    INSERT INTO @RoadsTC
      SELECT DISTINCT TC.from_city, R.city2,
        TC.distance + R.distance, TC.route + city2 + '.'
      FROM @RoadsTC AS TC
        JOIN dbo.Roads AS R
          ON R.city1 = TC.to_city
      WHERE NOT EXISTS
        (SELECT * FROM @RoadsTC AS TC2
         WHERE TC2.from_city = TC.from_city
           AND TC2.to_city = R.city2
           AND TC2.distance <= TC.distance + R.distance)
        AND TC.from_city <> R.city2;

    SET @added = @@rowcount;

    INSERT INTO @RoadsTC
      SELECT DISTINCT TC.from_city, R.city1,
        TC.distance + R.distance, TC.route + city1 + '.'
      FROM @RoadsTC AS TC
        JOIN dbo.Roads AS R
          ON R.city2 = TC.to_city
      WHERE NOT EXISTS
        (SELECT * FROM @RoadsTC AS TC2
         WHERE TC2.from_city = TC.from_city
```

```
              AND TC2.to_city = R.city1
              AND TC2.distance <= TC.distance + R.distance)
          AND TC.from_city <> R.city1;

      SET @added = @added + @@rowcount;
    END
    RETURN;
  END
  GO
```

The function might return more than one row for the same source and target cities. To return shortest paths and distances, use the following query:

```
SELECT from_city, to_city, distance, route
FROM (SELECT from_city, to_city, distance, route,
        RANK() OVER (PARTITION BY from_city, to_city
                      ORDER BY distance) AS rk
      FROM dbo.fn_RoadsTC()) AS RTC
WHERE rk = 1;
```

The derived table query assigns a rank value (*rk*) to each row, based on *from_city, to_city* partitioning, and *distance* ordering. This means that shortest paths will be assigned with the rank value 1. The outer query filters only shortest paths (*rk = 1*).

Once you're done querying the RoadPaths table, don't forget to drop it:

```
DROP TABLE dbo.RoadPaths;
```

Conclusion

This chapter covered the treatment of graphs, trees, and hierarchies. I presented iterative/recursive solutions for graphs, and also solutions where you materialize information describing a tree. The main advantage of the iterative/recursive solutions is that you don't need to materialize and maintain any additional attributes; rather, the graph manipulation is based on the stored edge attributes. The materialized path solution materializes an enumerated path, and possibly also the level for each node in the tree. The maintenance of the additional information is not very expensive, and you benefit from simple and fast set-based queries. The nested sets solution materializes left and right values representing set containment relationships, and possibly the level in the tree. This is the most elegant solution of the ones I presented, and also it allows simple and fast queries. However, maintaining the materialized information is very expensive, so typically this solution is practical for either static trees or small dynamic trees.

In the last section, I presented solutions to transitive closure and shortest path problems.

Because this chapter concludes the book, I feel I should also add some closing words.

If you ask me what's the most important thing I hope you carry from this book, I'd say giving special attention to fundamentals. Do not underestimate or take them lightly. Spend time on identifying, focusing on, and perfecting fundamental key techniques. When faced with a tough problem, solutions will flow naturally.

"Matters of great concern should be treated lightly."

"Matters of small concern should be treated seriously."

– Hagakure, *The Book of the Samurai* by Yamamoto Tsunetomo

The meaning of these sayings is not what appears on the surface. The book goes on to explain:

> *"Among one's affairs there should not be more than two or three matters of what one could call great concern. If these are deliberated upon during ordinary times, they can be understood. Thinking about things previously and then handling them lightly when the time comes is what this is all about. To face an event and solve it lightly is difficult if you are not resolved beforehand, and there will always be uncertainty in hitting your mark. However, if the foundation is laid previously, you can think of the saying, 'Matters of great concern should be treated lightly,' as your own basis for action."*

Appendix A
Logic Puzzles

Logic is at the heart of querying problems. SQL is logic, and each query problem in essence is a logic puzzle. The toughest part of solving a querying problem is usually figuring out its logical aspects. You can improve your SQL problem-solving capabilities by practicing pure logic puzzles.

A while back, I provided a couple of logic puzzles in my T-SQL column in *SQL Server Magazine* (*www.sqlmag.com*). I wanted to show the strong relationship between SQL and logic. Origi-nally, I planned on providing only those couple of puzzles. But the puzzles raised so much interest with readers—interestingly even more than the T-SQL puzzles—that I decided to con-tinue the practice and introduce a new logic puzzle every month. I'd like to thank*SQL Server Magazine*, which kindly allowed me to share the puzzles from my column with the book's readers. Most of the puzzles you will see here are a compilation from my column.

I'd also like to thank Eitan Farchi, Lubor Kollar, Gabriel Ben-Gan, Lilach Ben-Gan, Fernando G. Guerrero, Hadar Levin, Michael Rys, Steve Kass, Denis Gobo, Ken Henderson, and Erik Veerman, who originally introduced the puzzles to me.

Puzzles

The following section introduces logic puzzles. You can find the puzzle solutions in the section that follows this one.

Someone once said, "A puzzle is its own reward." Enjoy!

Puzzle 1: Medication Tablets

Imagine that you've been diagnosed with a rare disease. Your physician prescribes two medi-cations for you—call them A and B. Each bottle contains three tablets, and both medication tablets have exactly the same size, shape, color, and smell. Each bottle is marked with the medication type, one bottle with A and the other B, but the pills themselves aren't marked. You're instructed to take one A tablet and one B tablet every day for three days. Following the instructions correctly will cure you completely, but following the instructions incorrectly will result in sudden death.

The first day, you take one A tablet and one B tablet. The next day, you discover that someone has tampered with your bottles: bottle B is empty, bottle A contains one tablet, and three tablets lie on the counter. You realize that one A tablet and two B tablets are now mixed on the table, but you can't tell which is which. You call your pharmacy and learn that the tablets are out of stock until tomorrow. How can you continue following the instructions correctly and be cured?

Puzzle 2: Chocolate Bar

Imagine you have a chocolate bar made up of 40 squares arranged in 5 rows and 8 columns. Your task is to divide it into the 40 individual chocolate squares using the minimum number of cuts. You're allowed to make only one cut at a time (and you're not allowed to pile multiple layers or lay them next to each other) and only in straight lines (horizontal or vertical). How many cuts do you need at minimum? Prove your logic; don't just guess.

Puzzle 3: To a T

Copy the shapes in Figure A-1 to a piece of paper that has square gridlines, and then cut the shapes out. Use the pieces to form a T shape with the proportions that Figure A-2 shows. You might have to think outside the box for this one!

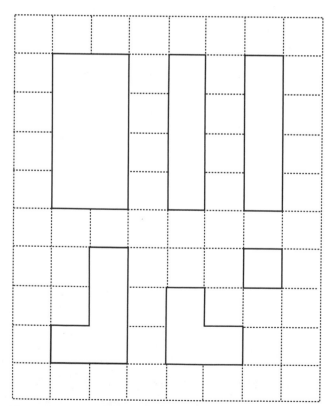

Figure A-1   T puzzle pieces

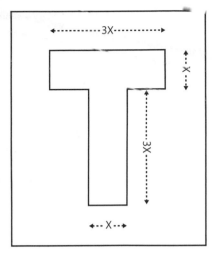

Figure A-2   T puzzle desired result

Puzzle 4: On the Dot

Two dots are marked arbitrarily on the surface of a cube. Define the shortest path along the cube's surface that connects the two dots.

Puzzle 5: Rectangles in a Square

On a piece of paper, imagine a square that has gridlines and 4 columns and 4 rows, as Figure A-3 shows.

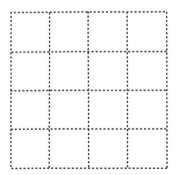

Figure A-3   The 4-by-4 square

How many different rectangles drawn on the gridlines can you identify within the square (including the outer lines forming the 4-by-4 square)?

Puzzle 6: Measuring Time by Burning Ropes

You have two ropes. Each rope takes exactly 1 hour to burn from end to end. The rope has different material densities at different points, so there's no guarantee of consistency in the time it takes different sections within the rope to burn (for example, the first half might burn in

59 minutes and the second half in 1 minute). You need to somehow measure exactly 45 minutes by using only these two ropes (and a match!). This isn't a trick question, so I'm not looking for an answer such as, "You look at your watch for 45 minutes and enjoy the light of the burning ropes." The puzzle has a logical solution that relies only on the burning of the ropes.

Puzzle 7: Arithmetic Maximum Calculation

Given the two input values m and n, calculate the maximum of the two using a single mathematical expression. Don't use conditional elements from programming, such as IF or CASE, in your solution.

Puzzle 8: Covering a Chessboard with Domino Tiles

You have a chessboard with two missing corners, as Figure A-4 shows.

Figure A-4   A chessboard with two missing corners

You have 31 domino tiles, each with a size of exactly two squares. Can you cover all the remaining 62 squares of the chessboard with domino tiles without covering the missing corners? If the answer is yes, suggest an arrangement of the domino tiles. If the answer is no, logically prove that it's impossible. Note that domino tiles cannot stick out of the chessboard, cannot be placed on top of each other, and you're not allowed to break domino tiles.

Puzzle 9: The Missing Duck

Three people arrive at a hotel and ask to share a room. The charge is $30, so each person chips in $10. Later on, the hotel receptionist finds out that he overcharged them by $5. Realizing that he can't evenly split $5 between the three guests, he pockets $2 and gives each guest $1 back. However, the receptionist finds it hard to sleep that night because the numbers don't seem to add up. Each guest eventually paid $9, and $9 × 3 + $2 = $29. Where's the missing buck?

Puzzle 10: Flipping Lamp Switches

One hundred lamps are arranged in a row (call them lamp 1, lamp 2, lamp 3, and so on). All the lamps are initially turned off, and each is equipped with an on/off switch. One hundred people—person 1, person 2, person 3, and so on—obey the following assignment: flip the switch of the nth lamp, the $2n$th lamp, the $3n$th lamp, and so on, where n is the person's number. So person 1 flips the switch of lamps 1, 2, 3, and so on; person 2 flips the switch of lamps 2, 4, 6, and so on; and similarly, persons 3 through 100 flip switches as instructed. Which lamps remain lit after all 100 people finish their assignments?

Puzzle 11: Cutting a Stick to Make a Triangle

This puzzle involves probability calculations. Suppose you cut a stick in two random places. What's the probability that you'll be able to form a triangle out of the three pieces?

Puzzle 12: Rectangle Within a Circle

This logical puzzle is a geometrical one. Examine Figure A-5. Can you calculate the length of the circle's radius?

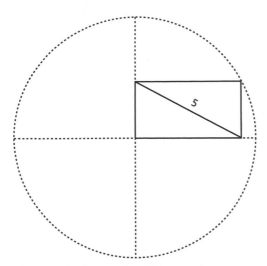

Figure A-5   Rectangle within a circle

Puzzle 13: Monty Hall Problem

You're taking part in a game show. You're standing in front of three curtains. One curtain hides a car. You don't know which is the prize curtain, but the host of the show does.

Your task is to guess which curtain hides the car. If you choose the curtain that hides the car, the car is yours. After you state your choice, the host opens one of the other two curtains, behind which he knows there is no car. The host then gives you a chance to change your mind about which curtain you think hides the car. Should you stick to your original choice, or should you choose the other closed curtain?

Puzzle 14: Piece of Cake

Suppose you have a rectangular cake with a rectangular hole cut into it in an arbitrary position, and suppose the top of the cake is frosted (but the sides are not). Figure A-6 shows a cake like this.

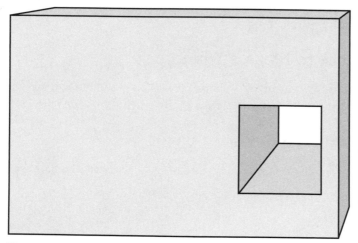

Figure A-6   Cake with a hole

You also have a knife, and you're supposed to cut the cake into two equal portions—equal in terms of the amount of cake and the amount of frosting. How can you accomplish this task with a single straight cut?

Puzzle 15: Cards Facing Up

Suppose you have a deck of 52 playing cards, and within that deck, 7 of the cards are facing up, and the rest are facing down. You don't know which of the cards are facing up and which are facing down, and you can't look at the cards to find out because you happen to be blindfolded.

Your task is to separate the cards into two piles so that each pile will contain the same number of cards facing up. Remember, you're blindfolded. How can you accomplish this task?

Here's a hint: the number of cards in each pile does not have to be the same, just the number of cards that are facing up. Also, the exact number of cards facing up in each pile is not important by itself; the important thing is having the same number of cards facing up in each pile.

Puzzle 16: Basic Arithmetic

Can you combine the integers 3, 4, 5, and 6 to yield the result 28, using only the arithmetic operators +, −, ×, and ÷ and left and right parentheses? You're allowed to use each number only once, and each of the arithmetic operators and parentheses only once as well.

Puzzle 17: Self-Replicating Code (Quine)

This puzzle was posted by Ken Henderson in his blog (*http://blogs.msdn.com/khen1234/ archive/2005/10/25/484555.aspx*), and I found it to be very interesting and challenging.

The challenge is for you to write runnable T-SQL "quine" (code that replicates itself). That is, you need to write code that generates output that is identical to the code that generated it. You're not allowed to query metadata or internal structures that give you access to the session's code buffer or stored code text. Rather, you should rely on standard SQL manipulation. For example, the following solution is not allowed, though it replicates itself:

```
DECLARE @sql AS NVARCHAR(MAX);
SET @sql = (SELECT text FROM fn_get_sql(
  (SELECT sql_handle FROM sys.sysprocesses WHERE spid = @@spid)));
PRINT @sql;
```

Coming up with any valid solution is a challenge by itself, but the shorter the code is, the more points you get.

This puzzle is not limited to T-SQL, of course. You can attempt to solve it in any programming language. You can find examples at the following URL: *http://www.madore.org/~david/ computers/quine.html*.

Puzzle 18: Hiking a Mountain

A hiker walks up a mountain, starting at the bottom exactly at sunrise and reaching the top exactly at sunset. The next day, the hiker walks down the mountain, starting at the top exactly at sunrise and reaching the bottom exactly at sunset, using the same path he used the previous day. Assume that there was no change in the sunrise and sunset times. Can you prove that there was some point along the path that the hiker visited at the same time of day in both days?

Puzzle 19: Find the Pattern in the Sequence

You're given the first few numbers in a sequence of integers: 3, 3, 5, 4, 4, 3, 5, 5, 4, 3, 6, 6, 8, 8. Can you identify the pattern in the sequence and figure out how it should continue?

Puzzle Solutions

This section contains solutions to the logic puzzles.

Puzzle 1: Medication Tablets

Cut each of the remaining four tablets in half. Consume one half of each tablet today and take the rest tomorrow.

A while back, I posted this puzzle in a SQL trainers' forum. I found one of the solutions, posted by Mary Bray from Australia, especially amusing. Mary suggested that you pour yourself a decent glass of Scotch, dissolve all the remaining tablets in it, and drink half the glass today and the other half tomorrow. Then, if you die, at least you die happy.

Puzzle 2: Chocolate Bar

Most people try to run several different scenarios—for example, first cutting on each horizontal line, and then cutting each row vertically. It's confusing to run the different scenarios in your head, so you can easily make mistakes during your calculations and obtain different results for the various scenarios. The varying results you get by mistake can create the illusion that several options exist and that one method requires fewer cuts than another. But the truth is that, whatever method you use, you'll always end up making 39 cuts.

At the start, you have one piece of chocolate. Each cut you make turns one piece (the piece you cut) into two, or in other words, each cut you make increases the number of pieces you have by exactly one. After the first cut, you have two pieces. After the second cut, you have three pieces. You will have the required 40 pieces after exactly 39 cuts.

Puzzle 3: To a T

Most people try the obvious approach—to create the T shape itself (emphasis on *itself*) by organizing the pieces in different ways. If you tried this approach, you probably couldn't come up with a solution, and for a good reason—you can't form the T shape with the desired proportions by any arrangement of the given pieces. However, if you think outside the box (literally in this case), you can form the rectangle surrounding the T shape, as Figure A-7 shows.

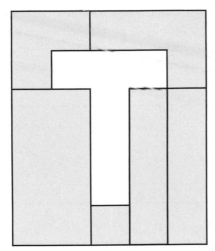

Figure A-7   T puzzle solution

Puzzle 4: On the Dot

A good way to approach this problem is to start with the simplest case—where the two dots are on the same side of the cube—and then try to generalize to more complex cases. Obviously, a straight line is the shortest path connecting two dots marked on the same side of the cube. To apply the same logic to the more complex cases in which the dots are marked on different sides, you need to visualize the cube's surface in a plane by unfolding and spreading the adjacent sides. After you have a flat surface, the shortest path between the dots is the straight line connecting them.

There are multiple ways in which you can unfold the cube's surface to generate a plane. The straight line is the shortest path in the plane of the unfolded surface between the dots, but it's not always the shortest path on the cube, nor is it always contained within the unfolded surface. (You might have "cut" the cube's surface through an edge on the actual shortest path and be forced to "jump" to the adjacent side or "go the long way around.") The goal of the puzzle was to identify the logical key, which was spreading the sides of the cube to generate a flat surface and drawing a straight line between the dots. So you don't really need to define which of the different spreads gives you the shortest straight line. It suffices to say that the shortest path on the cube's surface between the two dots is the shortest of the straight lines that connect the dots on the different unfoldings of the cube's surface.

Puzzle 5: Rectangles in a Square

To solve this puzzle, you might be tempted to simply count all the different rectangles that you can draw within the square. However, this technique is confusing and usually leads to the wrong result. I enjoy this combinatorial puzzle because the solution lies in a methodical approach.

First, determine what rectangle shapes are possible; second, determine how many rectangles there are of each shape; third, add it all up. The different types of rectangles you can draw within a 4-by-4 square are rectangles that have 1 to 4 rows and 1 to 4 columns. You can use Table A-1 as a place to write down the number of rectangles of each possible shape.

Table A-1   Number of Rectangles of Each Possible Shape

Rows/Columns	1	2	3	4
1				
2				
3				
4				

Fill each cell with the number of rectangles of the particular size (rows × columns) that you can draw within a 4-by-4 square. The number of different rectangles of a size $r \times c$ that you can draw within an $n \times n$ square can generally be expressed as $(n - r + 1) \times (n - c + 1)$. The logic behind this formula is that within n rows, there are $n - r + 1$ different vertical locations where you can position the topmost row of rectangles with r rows. Similarly, there are $n - c + 1$ possible horizontal locations where you can position the leftmost column of a rectangle with c columns. So, in total, we're talking about $(n - r + 1) \times (n - c + 1)$ different rectangles of $r \times c$ size. When you populate all cells in the matrix according to this formula, you get the matrix that Table A-2 shows.

Table A-2   Matrix Populated with Row and Column Values

Rows/Columns	1	2	3	4
1	4 4	4 3	4 2	4 1
2	3 4	3 3	3 2	3 1
3	2 4	2 3	2 2	2 1
4	1 4	1 3	1 2	1 1

Next, just add these values, and you get the answer to this puzzle:

```
4 × 4 + 4 × 3 + 4 × 2 + 4 × 1 +
3 × 4 + 3 × 3 + 3 × 2 + 3 × 1 +
2 × 4 + 2 × 3 + 2 × 2 + 2 × 1 +
1 × 4 + 1 × 3 + 1 × 2 + 1 × 1 =

4 × (4 + 3 + 2 + 1) +
3 × (4 + 3 + 2 + 1) +
2 × (4 + 3 + 2 + 1) +
1 × (4 + 3 + 2 + 1) =

(4 + 3 + 2 + 1) × (4 + 3 + 2 + 1) =

(1 + 2 + 3 + 4)² = 100
```

The solution for a more generic case with an $n \times n$ square is $(1 + 2 + 3 + ... + n)^2$.

There is another, perhaps simpler, approach, suggested by Steve Kass. In each 1-by-1 cell of the actual 4-by-4 square of the puzzle, write the number of rectangles whose "southwest" corner is at that spot. This number is easy to find—it is the number of possible "northeast" corners, or the number of cells that are neither below nor to the left of the given cell. You'll get this array of counts:

```
 4,   3,   2,   1
 8,   6,   4,   2
12,   9,   6,   3
16,  12,   8,   4
```

To get the general solution, note that the top row adds to $1 \times (1 + 2 + 3 + ... + n)$, the row below it to $2 \times (1 + 2 + 3 + ... + n)$, and so on, so the result is $(1 + 2 + 3 + ... + n) \times (1 + 2 + 3 + ... + n)$. And you get the simplified result $(1 + 2 + 3 + ... + n)^2$.

Puzzle 6: Measuring Time by Burning Ropes

Light both ends of one rope, and light one end of the other rope. As soon as the first rope is consumed (which will take exactly 30 minutes), light the unlit end of the second rope. The second rope will be consumed exactly after an additional 15 minutes, letting you measure exactly 45 minutes in total.

Puzzle 7: Arithmetic Maximum Calculation

The solution is this: $(m + n)/2 + abs(m - n)/2$. If you think about it, the greater of two values is their average plus half their absolute difference. The average of two values is equal to the smaller value plus half the difference between the two. So the average plus half the difference is equal to the smaller plus two times half the difference, which of course is the greater of the two. Said with words alone, the explanation may be hard to follow. Another way to justify the answer is to show that it is correct whether [case 1] $m >= n$ (in which case) $abs(m - n)$ is just $m - n$, and the expression simplifies to $(m + n)/2 + (m - n)/2 = 2m/2 = m$) or [case 2] $m < n$ (in which case) $abs(m - n) = n - m$, and the expression simplifies to $(m + n)/2 + (n - m)/2 = 2n/2 = n$). Because one of case 1 or case 2 is always true, the formula always works.

Puzzle 8: Covering a Chessboard with Domino Tiles

To solve this puzzle, count the black and white squares. The two missing corners are the same color—both black or both white—leaving 32 squares of one color and 30 of the other. Each domino tile covers exactly two squares—one black and one white. As a result, any arrangement of the dominoes will cover the same number of squares of each color. Therefore, it's impossible to completely cover all 62 remaining squares of the chessboard with domino tiles.

Puzzle 9: The Missing Buck

Here's where the $30 went: The hotel has $25, the receptionist has $2, and the guests have $3. What the receptionist did wrong in his calculation was that he added $27 and $2–but the reason this was wrong was that it made no sense to add these numbers because the $2 (what he pocketed) was already part of the $27 the guests paid. The original $30, if you need to account for it, is the $27 the guests paid plus the $3 change they got back.

Puzzle 10: Alternating Lamp States

All the lamps are off except for lamps number 1, 4, 9, 16, 25, 49, 64, 81, and 100, which are on. The solution to this puzzle is mathematical at its heart.

The number of times lamp n's switch was flipped equals the number of positive integer divisors of n. The final state of the lamp depends only on whether the number of integer divisors is odd or even. The only time n has an odd number of divisors is when n is a perfect square. This is because every divisor k less than the square root of n can be paired up with the divisor n / k, which is not equal to k. Thus, all lamps in positions that have an integer square root will end up in the opposite state to the one they started with, while all other lamps will stay in their original state.

Puzzle 11: Cutting a Stick to Make a Triangle

In order for the three pieces to form a triangle, all pieces must be shorter than half the length of the original stick, because in a triangle the sum of the lengths of any two sides is always longer than the length of the remaining side. If one piece is longer than half the stick's size, the sum of the other two pieces will be shorter and you will not be able to form a triangle.

Suppose the first cut is at p%. If p is between 0 and 50%, a triangle can be formed only if the other cut is above 50% (the other cut must be on the other side of the middle) and below $p + 50$% (the two cuts must be within ½ the original length of each other to avoid a too-long piece). In other words, the second cut must lie within the segment from 50% to $p + 50$%. This segment has length p, so the probability the second cut allows a triangle is p in this case.

If the first cut is between 50% and 100%, the second cut (to allow a triangle) must be at least $p - 50$% and at most 50%, or in an interval of length 50% $- (p - 50$%$) = 1 - p$. So the total probability that a triangle can be formed is:

$$\int_{0}^{0.5} p\,dp + \int_{0.5}^{1} (1-p)\,dp = \frac{1}{4}$$

You can find several formulations of the solution here: *http://www.cut-the-knot.org/Curriculum/ Probability/TriProbability.shtml#Explanation*.

Puzzle 12: Rectangle Within a Circle

We wanted to calculate the circle's radius (as shown in Figure A-5). The trick here is to recognize that the undrawn diagonal in the rectangle is a radius of the circle. Because the two diagonals in a rectangle are of equal length, the radius is 5.

When evaluating problems involving right triangles, most people assume that the solution is based on the Pythagorean Theorem, and they start calculating squares and square roots, which in this case leads to a dead end. It's easy to get confused by making quick assumptions when solving T-SQL problems, too. It's a good idea to slow down and clear your mind. In many cases, the solution you're looking for is much simpler than your first reaction leads you to believe.

Puzzle 13: Monty Hall Problem

Most people think that there's no difference in probability between sticking to your original choice and changing your choice. In other words, they think there's a 50 percent probability of winning if you stick to your choice and 50 percent if you change your choice. However, *keep in mind that your original choice was completely independent (made arbitrarily based on no prior knowledge), and that regardless of your original choice, the host will always open one of the other curtains that is empty.* So sticking to your original choice, the probability of winning remains the same regardless of the event that follows—the host opening an empty curtain. This will be the case if you chose curtain 1 twice, curtain 2 twice, or curtain 3 twice. Namely, if you stick to your original choice, you have 1/3 probability of winning. On the other hand, the host's choice of which curtain to open is dependent on your original choice, and in turn, changing your original choice is dependent on his. Thus, changing your original choice would be based on new knowledge. Having only two options left after the host opened one of the curtains, the probabilities of winning if you stick to your original choice or change your choice must add up to 1 (100 percent). Hence, the probability of winning if you change your choice is $1 - 1/3 = 2/3$. Statistically two out of three people who decide to change their choice win, while only one out of three that stick to the original choice does.

So, it's better to change your choice!

If you're not convinced yet, and I must say that with this puzzle many people don't realize the truth even after getting the explanation, I can suggest one of two things:

1. Talk with statisticians and mathematicians.

2. Write a program that simulates the game and statistically check the results. Here's an example for such a program written in T-SQL and devised by Steve Kass:

```
-- Simulating the "Monty Hall Problem" in T-SQL (2005)
--    A description of the problem can be found at
--    http://math.ucsd.edu/~crypto/Monty/montybg.html)
WITH TO AS
(
  SELECT
    -- prize_door is door 1, 2, or 3 with equal probability
    1 + ABS(BINARY_CHECKSUM(NEWID())) % 3 AS prize_door
  FROM dbo.Nums
  WHERE n <= 100000 - number of trials
```

```
    -- use any handy table that is not too small
),
T1 AS
(
  SELECT
    prize_door,
    -- your_door is door 1, 2, or 3 with equal probability
    1 + ABS(BINARY_CHECKSUM(NEWID())) % 3 AS your_door
  FROM T0
),
T2 AS
(
  SELECT
  -- The host opens a door you did not choose,
  -- and which he knows is not the prize door.
  -- If he has two choices, each is equally likely.
    prize_door,
    your_door,
    CASE
      WHEN prize_door <> your_door THEN 6 - prize_door - your_door
      ELSE SUBSTRING(
                REPLACE('123',RIGHT(your_door, 1), ''),
                1 + ABS(BINARY_CHECKSUM(NEWID())) % 2,
                1)
    END AS open_door
  FROM T1
),
T3 AS
(
  SELECT
    prize_door,
    your_door,
    open_door,
    -- The "other door" is the still-closed door
    -- you did not originally choose.
    6 - your_door - open_door AS other_door
  FROM T2
),
T4 AS
(
  SELECT
    COUNT(CASE WHEN prize_door = your_door
                THEN 'Don''t Switch' END) AS staying_wins,
    COUNT(CASE WHEN prize_door = other_door
                THEN 'Do Switch!'  END) AS switching_wins,
    COUNT(*)                             AS trials
  FROM T3
)
SELECT
  trials,
  CAST(100.0 * staying_wins / trials
      AS DECIMAL(5,2)) AS staying_winsPercent,
  CAST(100.0 * switching_wins / trials
      AS DECIMAL(5,2)) as switching_winsPercent
FROM T4;
```

The code has inline comments explaining the solution. The Nums auxiliary table was discussed in Chapter 4. But as the inline comments specify, you can query any table that has a sufficient number of rows—which are the number of trials that this solution will make.

Puzzle 14: Piece of Cake

Any straight line through the center of a rectangle splits it into two equally sized halves, regardless of the angle. First, mark the center of the cake and the center of the hole, using the fact that the center of a rectangle is the intersection of its diagonals. Then make a single straight cut through both centers—the cake's and the hole's, as shown in Figure A-8.

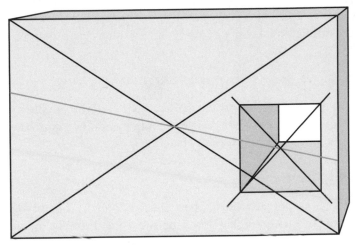

Figure A-8   Cake puzzle solution

This cut splits both the cake and the hole into equal halves. You get two pieces of the same size and the same amount of frosting.

Puzzle 15: Cards Facing Up

This puzzle is mathematical in nature. Split the deck into two piles: one pile with 7 cards, and one pile with the remaining 45 cards. At this point, the 7-card pile contains some number (possibly zero) of cards facing up. Call that number n. Since there were a total of 7 cards facing up to begin with in the whole deck, the 45-card pile must contain $7 - n$ cards facing up. Now turn over the entire 7-card pile. You're done. Before you turned over the 7-card pile, n of the 7 cards were facing up, and the rest ($7 - n$ of them) were facing down. Now that you turned it over, the numbers are reversed, and the 7-card pile contains $7 - n$ cards facing up, the same number facing up as in the 45-card pile.

Puzzle 16: Basic Arithmetic

The secret here is to generate a 7 out of 3, 5, and 6, and then multiply it by 4, because 28 (the result we need) is 7×4. This puzzle is confusing because the easy ways to generate 7 use up the number 4 ($3 + 4$, $4 + 6 - 3$, $5 + 6 - 4$, and so on). Once you realize you need to generate a 7 and multiply it by 4, you might come up with the following expression: $(6 - 2) \times (3 + 4)$. However, this solution is invalid because parentheses are used twice. A valid solution is: $4 \times (5 + 6 / 3)$.

Puzzle 17: Self-Replicating Code (Quine)

This puzzle has different solutions, all of which are quite challenging to come up with. Here's one possible solution that I came up with (note that the code wraps in text, though it should appear in a single line):

```
PRINT REPLACE(SPACE(1)+CHAR(39)+SPACE(1)+CHAR(39)+CHAR(41),SPACE(1),'PRINT REPLACE(SPACE(1)+
CHAR(39)+SPACE(1)+CHAR(39)+CHAR(41),SPACE(1),')
```

Steve Kass managed to reduce it even further by using binary values instead of the functions SPACE and CHAR:

```
PRINT REPLACE(0x2027202729,0X20,'PRINT REPLACE(0x2027202729,0x20,')
```

Another solution came to my mind—an empty batch. You might find the validity of the solution questionable, but technically it meets the puzzle's requirements: an empty batch is a runnable program in T-SQL, and it produces an empty batch.

Puzzle 18: Hiking a Mountain

I can suggest a couple of ways to approach the problem. One way is to think of two different hikers—one going up the mountain and one going down—both starting their hike the same day at sunrise and finishing at sunset. Obviously, they are bound to meet at some point. Another way is to solve the puzzle graphically. Draw a graph where the X-axis represents the time (from sunrise to sunset) and the Y-axis represents the position (from the bottom of the mountain to the top). Draw two lines representing the position and time of each hike. Obviously, the two lines must meet at some point. An example for such a graph is shown in Figure A-9.

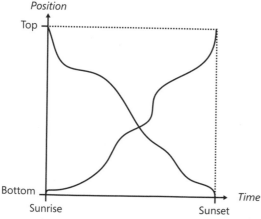

Figure A-9 Hiking a mountain

Puzzle 19: Find the Pattern in the Sequence

Each value Vn in the sequence represents the number of letters in the English name of n (without spaces and hyphens): one, two, three, four, five, six, seven, eight, nine, ten, eleven, twelve, thirteen, fourteen, and so on. Here's the first part of the sequence with a few additional numbers: 4, 3, 3, 5, 4, 4, 3, 5, 5, 4, 3, 6, 6, 8, 8, 7, 7, 9, 8, 8, 6, 9, 9, 11, 10, 10, 9, 11, 11, 10, ...

Conclusion

I hope that you find logic puzzles challenging, fun, and a great tool to improve your logic and SQL. And if you're still looking for a reason to practice them, here's one:

"Crime is common. Logic is rare. Therefore it is upon the logic rather than upon the crime that you should dwell."

–Sir Arthur Conan Doyle, 1859–1930, *The Adventures of Sherlock Holmes,* "The Adventure of the Copper Beeches"

Index

Additional SQL Server Resources for Administrators

Published and Forthcoming Titles from Microsoft Press

Microsoft® SQL Server™ 2005 Reporting Services *Step by Step*
Hitachi Consulting Services • ISBN 0-7356-2250-7

SQL Server Reporting Services (SRS) is Microsoft's customizable reporting solution for business data analysis. It is one of the key value features of SQL Server 2005: functionality more advanced and much less expensive than its competition. SRS is powerful, so an understanding of how to architect a report, as well as how to install and program SRS, is key to harnessing the full functionality of SQL Server. This procedural tutorial shows how to use the Report Project Wizard, how to think about and access data, and how to build queries. It also walks the reader through the creation of charts and visual layouts to enable maximum visual understanding of the data analysis. Interactivity (enhanced in SQL Server 2005) and security are also covered in detail.

Microsoft SQL Server 2005 Administrator's Pocket Consultant
William R. Stanek • ISBN 0-7356-2107-1

Here's the utterly practical, pocket-sized reference for IT professionals who need to administer, optimize, and maintain SQL Server 2005 in their organizations. This unique guide provides essential details for using SQL Server 2005 to help protect and manage your company's data—whether automating tasks; creating indexes and views; performing backups and recovery; replicating transactions; tuning performance; managing server activity; importing and exporting data; or performing other key tasks. Featuring quick-reference tables, lists, and step-by-step instructions, this handy, one-stop guide provides fast, accurate answers on the spot, whether you're at your desk or in the field!

Microsoft SQL Server 2005 Administrator's Companion
Marci Frohock Garcia, Edward Whalen, and Mitchell Schroeter • ISBN 0-7356-2198-5

Microsoft SQL Server 2005 Administrator's Companion is the comprehensive, in-depth guide that saves time by providing all the technical information you need to deploy, administer, optimize, and support SQL Server 2005. Using a hands-on, example-rich approach, this authoritative, one-volume reference book provides expert advice, product information, detailed solutions, procedures, and real-world troubleshooting tips from experienced SQL Server 2005 professionals. This expert guide shows you how to design high-availability database systems, prepare for installation, install and configure SQL Server 2005, administer services and features, and maintain and troubleshoot your database system. It covers how to configure your system for your I/O system and model and optimize system capacity. The expert authors provide details on how to create and use defaults, constraints, rules, indexes, views, functions, stored procedures, and triggers. This guide shows you how to administer reporting services, analysis services, notification services, and integration services. It also provides a wealth of information on replication and the specifics of snapshot, transactional, and merge replication. Finally, there is expansive coverage of how to manage and tune your SQL Server system, including automating tasks, backup and restoration of databases, and management of users and security.

Microsoft SQL Server 2005 Analysis Services *Step by Step*
Hitachi Consulting Services • ISBN 0-7356-2199-3

One of the key features of SQL Server 2005 is SQL Server Analysis Services—Microsoft's customizable analysis solution for business data modeling and interpretation. Just compare SQL Server Analysis Services to its competition to understand/grasp the great value of its enhanced features. One of the keys to harnessing the full functionality of SQL Server will be leveraging Analysis Services for the powerful tool that it is—including creating a cube, and deploying, customizing, and extending the basic calculations. This step-by-step tutorial discusses how to get started, how to build scalable analytical applications, and how to use and administer advanced features. Interactivity (which is enhanced in SQL Server 2005), data translation, and security are also covered in detail.

Microsoft SQL Server 2005 Express Edition
Step by Step
Jackie Goldstein • ISBN 0-7356-2184-5

Inside Microsoft SQL Server 2005:
The Storage Engine
Kalen Delaney • ISBN 0-7356-2105-5

Inside Microsoft SQL Server 2005:
T-SQL Programming
Itzik Ben-Gan • ISBN 0-7356-2197-7

Inside Microsoft SQL Server 2005:
Query Processing and Optimization
Kalen Delaney • ISBN 0-7356-2196-9

For more information about Microsoft Press® books and other learning products,
visit: **www.microsoft.com/mspress** *and* **www.microsoft.com/learning**

Additional Windows (R2) Resources for Administrators

Published and Forthcoming Titles from Microsoft Press

Microsoft® Windows Server™ 2003 Administrator's Pocket Consultant, Second Edition
William R. Stanek • ISBN 0-7356-2245-0

Here's the practical, pocket-sized reference for IT professionals supporting Microsoft Windows Server 2003—fully updated for Service Pack 1 and Release 2. Designed for quick referencing, this portable guide covers all the essentials for performing everyday system administration tasks. Topics include managing workstations and servers, using Active Directory® directory service, creating and administering user and group accounts, managing files and directories, performing data security and auditing tasks, handling data back-up and recovery, and administering networks using TCP/IP, WINS, and DNS, and more.

MCSE Self-Paced Training Kit (Exams 70-290, 70-291, 70-293, 70-294): Microsoft Windows Server 2003 Core Requirements, Second Edition
Holme, Thomas, Mackin, McLean, Zacker, Spealman, Hudson, and Craft • ISBN 0-7356-2290-6

The Microsoft Certified Systems Engineer (MCSE) credential is the premier certification for professionals who analyze the business requirements and design and implement the infrastructure for business solutions based on the Microsoft Windows Server 2003 platform and Microsoft Windows Server System—now updated for Windows Server 2003 Service Pack 1 and R2. This all-in one set provides in-depth preparation for the four required networking system exams. Work at your own pace through the lessons, hands-on exercises, troubleshooting labs, and review questions. You get expert exam tips plus a full review section covering all objectives and sub-objectives in each study guide. Then use the Microsoft Practice Tests on the CD to challenge yourself with more than 1500 questions for self-assessment and practice!

Microsoft Windows® Small Business Server 2003 R2 Administrator's Companion
Charlie Russel, Sharon Crawford, and Jason Gerend • ISBN 0-7356-2280-9

Get your small-business network, messaging, and collaboration systems up and running quickly with the essential guide to administering Windows Small Business Server 2003 R2. This reference details the features, capabilities, and technologies for both the standard and premium editions—including Microsoft Windows Server 2003 R2, Exchange Server 2003 with Service Pack 1, Windows SharePoint® Services, SQL Server™ 2005 Workgroup Edition, and Internet Information Services. Discover how to install, upgrade, or migrate to Windows Small Business Server 2003 R2; plan and implement your network, Internet access, and security services; customize Microsoft Exchange Server for your e-mail needs; and administer user rights, shares, permissions, and Group Policy.

Microsoft Windows Small Business Server 2003 R2 Administrator's Companion
Charlie Russel, Sharon Crawford, and Jason Gerend • ISBN 0-7356-2280-9

Here's the ideal one-volume guide for the IT professional administering Windows Server 2003. Now fully updated for Windows Server 2003 Service Pack 1 and R2, this *Administrator's Companion* offers up-to-date information on core system administration topics for Microsoft Windows, including Active Directory services, security, scripting, disaster planning and recovery, and interoperability with UNIX. It also includes all-new sections on Service Pack 1 security updates and new features for R2. Featuring easy-to-use procedures and handy work-arounds, this book provides ready answers for on-the-job results

MCSA/MCSE Self-Paced Training Kit (Exam 70-290): Managing and Maintaining a Microsoft Windows Server 2003 Environment, Second Edition
Dan Holme and Orin Thomas • ISBN 0-7356-2289-2

MCSA/MCSE Self-Paced Training Kit (Exam 70-291): Implementing, Managing, and Maintaining a Microsoft Windows Server 2003 Network Infrastructure, Second Edition
J.C. Mackin and Ian McLean • ISBN 0-7356-2288-4

MCSE Self-Paced Training Kit (Exam 70-293): Planning and Maintaining a Microsoft Windows Server 2003 Network Infrastructure, Second Edition
Craig Zacker • ISBN 0-7356-2287-6

MCSE Self-Paced Training Kit (Exam 70-294): Planning, Implementing, and Maintaining a Microsoft Windows Server 2003 Active Directory® Infrastructure, Second Ed.
Jill Spealman, Kurt Hudson, and Melissa Craft • ISBN 0-7356-2286-8

Additional SQL Server Resources for Developers

Published and Forthcoming Titles from Microsoft Press

Microsoft® SQL Server™ 2005 Express Edition
Step by Step
Jackie Goldstein ● ISBN 0-7356-2184-5

Teach yourself how to get data base projects up and running quickly with SQL Server Express Edition—a free, easy-to-use database product that is based on SQL Server 2005 technology. It's designed for building simple, dynamic applications, with all the rich functionality of the SQL Server database engine and using the same data access APIs, such as Microsoft ADO.NET, SQL Native Client, and T-SQL. Whether you're new to database programming or new to SQL Server, you'll learn how, when, and why to use specific features of this simple but powerful database development environment. Each chapter puts you to work, building your knowledge of core capabilities and guiding you as you create actual components and working applications.

Microsoft SQL Server 2005 Programming
Step by Step
Fernando Guerrero ● ISBN 0-7356-2207-8

SQL Server 2005 is Microsoft's next-generation data management and analysis solution that delivers enhanced scalability, availability, and security features to enterprise data and analytical applications while making them easier to create, deploy, and manage. Now you can teach yourself how to design, build, test, deploy, and maintain SQL Server databases—one step at a time. Instead of merely focusing on describing new features, this book shows new database programmers and administrators how to use specific features within typical business scenarios. Each chapter provides a highly practical learning experience that demonstrates how to build database solutions to solve common business problems.

Microsoft SQL Server 2005 Analysis Services
Step by Step
Hitachi Consulting Services ● ISBN 0-7356-2199-3

One of the key features of SQL Server 2005 is SQL Server Analysis Services—Microsoft's customizable analysis solution for business data modeling and interpretation. Just compare SQL Server Analysis Services to its competition to understand the great value of its enhanced features. One of the keys to harnessing the full functionality of SQL Server will be leveraging Analysis Services for the powerful tool that it is—including creating a cube, and deploying, customizing, and extending the basic calculations. This step-by-step tutorial discusses how to get started, how to build scalable analytical applications, and how to use and administer advanced features. Interactivity (enhanced in SQL Server 2005), data translation, and security are also covered in detail.

Microsoft SQL Server 2005 Reporting Services
Step by Step
Hitachi Consulting Services ● ISBN 0-7356-2250-7

SQL Server Reporting Services (SRS) is Microsoft's customizable reporting solution for business data analysis. It is one of the key value features of SQL Server 2005: functionality more advanced and much less expensive than its competition. SRS is powerful, so an understanding of how to architect a report, as well as how to install and program SRS, is key to harnessing the full functionality of SQL Server. This procedural tutorial shows how to use the Report Project Wizard, how to think about and access data, and how to build queries. It also walks through the creation of charts and visual layouts for maximum visual understanding of data analysis. Interactivity (enhanced in SQL Server 2005) and security are also covered in detail.

Programming Microsoft SQL Server 2005
Andrew J. Brust, Stephen Forte, and William H. Zack
ISBN 0-7356-1923-9

This thorough, hands-on reference for developers and database administrators teaches the basics of programming custom applications with SQL Server 2005. You will learn the fundamentals of creating database applications—including coverage of T-SQL, Microsoft .NET Framework, and Microsoft ADO.NET. In addition to practical guidance on database architecture and design, application development, and reporting and data analysis, this essential reference guide covers performance, tuning, and availability of SQL Server 2005.

Inside Microsoft SQL Server 2005:
The Storage Engine
Kalen Delaney ● ISBN 0-7356-2105-5

Inside Microsoft SQL Server 2005:
T-SQL Programming
Itzik Ben-Gan ● ISBN 0-7356-2197-7

Inside Microsoft SQL Server 2005:
Query Processing and Optimization
Kalen Delaney ● ISBN 0-7356-2196-9

Programming Microsoft ADO.NET 2.0 Core Reference
David Sceppa ● ISBN 0-7356-2206-X

For more information about Microsoft Press® books and other learning products,
visit: **www.microsoft.com/mspress** *and* **www.microsoft.com/learning**

Additional Resources for Developers: Advanced Topics and Best Practices

Published and Forthcoming Titles from Microsoft Press

Code Complete, Second Edition
Steve McConnell • ISBN 0-7356-1967-0

For more than a decade, Steve McConnell, one of the premier authors and voices in the software community, has helped change the way developers write code—and produce better software. Now his classic book, *Code Complete*, has been fully updated and revised with best practices in the art and science of constructing software. Topics include design, applying good techniques to construction, eliminating errors, planning, managing construction activities, and relating personal character to superior software. This new edition features fully updated information on programming techniques, including the emergence of Web-style programming, and integrated coverage of object-oriented design. You'll also find new code examples—both good and bad—in C++, Microsoft® Visual Basic®, C#, and Java, although the focus is squarely on techniques and practices.

More About Software Requirements: Thorny Issues and Practical Advice
Karl E. Wiegers • ISBN 0-7356-2267-1

Have you ever delivered software that satisfied all of the project specifications, but failed to meet any of the customers expectations? Without formal, verifiable requirements—and a system for managing them—the result is often a gap between what developers think they're supposed to build and what customers think they're going to get. Too often, lessons about software requirements engineering processes are formal or academic, and not of value to real-world, professional development teams. In this follow-up guide to *Software Requirements*, Second Edition, you will discover even more practical techniques for gathering and managing software requirements that help you deliver software that meets project and customer specifications. Succinct and immediately useful, this book is a must-have for developers and architects.

Software Estimation: Demystifying the Black Art
Steve McConnell • ISBN 0-7356-0535-1

Often referred to as the "black art" because of its complexity and uncertainty, software estimation is not as hard or mysterious as people think. However, the art of how to create effective cost and schedule estimates has not been very well publicized. *Software Estimation* provides a proven set of procedures and heuristics that software developers, technical leads, and project managers can apply to their projects. Instead of arcane treatises and rigid modeling techniques, award-winning author Steve McConnell gives practical guidance to help organizations achieve basic estimation proficiency and lay the groundwork to continue improving project cost estimates. This book does not avoid the more complex mathematical estimation approaches, but the non-mathematical reader will find plenty of useful guidelines without getting bogged down in complex formulas.

Debugging, Tuning, and Testing Microsoft .NET 2.0 Applications
John Robbins • ISBN 0-7356-2202-7

Making an application the best it can be has long been a time-consuming task best accomplished with specialized and costly tools. With Microsoft Visual Studio® 2005, developers have available a new range of built-in functionality that enables them to debug their code quickly and efficiently, tune it to optimum performance, and test applications to ensure compatibility and trouble-free operation. In this accessible and hands-on book, debugging expert John Robbins shows developers how to use the tools and functions in Visual Studio to their full advantage to ensure high-quality applications.

The Security Development Lifecycle
Michael Howard and Steve Lipner • ISBN 0-7356-2214-0

Adapted from Microsoft's standard development process, the Security Development Lifecycle (SDL) is a methodology that helps reduce the number of security defects in code at every stage of the development process, from design to release. This book details each stage of the SDL methodology and discusses its implementation across a range of Microsoft software, including Microsoft Windows Server™ 2003, Microsoft SQL Server™ 2000 Service Pack 3, and Microsoft Exchange Server 2003 Service Pack 1, to help measurably improve security features. You get direct access to insights from Microsoft's security team and lessons that are applicable to software development processes worldwide, whether on a small-scale or a large-scale. This book includes a CD featuring videos of developer training classes.

Software Requirements, Second Edition
Karl E. Wiegers • ISBN 0-7356-1879-8

Writing Secure Code, Second Edition
Michael Howard and David LeBlanc • ISBN 0-7356-1722-8

CLR via C#, Second Edition
Jeffrey Richter • ISBN 0-7356-2163-2

For more information about Microsoft Press® books and other learning products,
visit: **www.microsoft.com/mspress** *and* **www.microsoft.com/learning**

About the Contributors

Itzik Ben-Gan

Itzik Ben-Gan is a mentor and founder of Solid Quality Learning. A Microsoft SQL Server MVP (Most Valuable Professional) since 1999, Itzik has delivered numerous training events around the world focused on T-SQL Querying, Query Tuning, and Programming. Itzik is the author of several books on Microsoft SQL Server. He has written many articles for *SQL Server Magazine*, as well as articles and white papers for MSDN. Itzik's speaking engagements include Tech Ed, DevWeek, various SQL user groups around the world, PASS, SQL Server Magazine Connections, and Solid Quality Learning's events, to name a few.

Since 1992, Itzik has been involved in many projects covering various database and computer systems–related technologies. In addition to helping customers with their pressing needs, fixing their problems, optimizing their databases, teaching, and mentoring, Itzik has helped developers and database administrators shift to a relational/set-based mindset, improving both the performance of their code and its maintainability. Itzik's main expertise is T-SQL Querying, Query Tuning, Programming, and Internals, but he's proficient in other database areas as well. In 1999, Itzik founded the Israeli SQL Server and OLAP User Group, and he has been managing it since then.

Lubor Kollar

Lubor Kollar has been a member of the SQL Server development organization since the SQL Server 6.5 release in 1996. He was a group program manager during the SQL Server 2005 development, and his team was responsible for the "bottom" part of the Relational Engine—from query compilation and optimization to query execution, transactional consistency, backup/restore, and high availability. The major SQL Server 2005 features his team had been working on include Table and Index Partitioning, Database Mirroring, Database Snapshot, Snapshot Isolation, Recursive Query and other T-SQL query improvements, Database Tuning Advisor, and Online Index creation and maintenance. Lubor enjoys interacting with the Microsoft Research team, transforming the latest research results into product features. Before joining Microsoft, Lubor developed DB2 engines for various operating system platforms in IBM laboratories in Toronto, Canada, and Santa Teresa, California.

Among his professional achievements, Lubor especially values having solved one of the open problems in Donald E. Knuth's *The Art of Computer Programming, Volume 3* during his student years. And yes, you will find the problem and solution in the latest edition of Knuth's book.

Lubor loves the outdoors—skiing, hiking, gardening, mountain biking, fishing, and gathering mushrooms, to name his most beloved activities outside of work and home. He holds a Professional Ski Instructor license, and on winter weekends he teaches skiing at a ski resort near Redmond, Washington.

Because Lubor Kollar is not a very common name, you can use your favorite search engine to find out much more about him—his white papers, blog contributions, articles, conference papers, patents, trips, and more.

Dejan Sarka

Dejan Sarka—MCP (Microsoft Certified Professional), MCDBA (Microsoft Certified Database Administrator), MCT (Microsoft Certified Trainer), SQL Server MVP, Solid Quality Learning Mentor—is a trainer and consultant working for many Certified Partners for Learning Solutions (CPLS) centers and development companies in Slovenia and other countries. In addition to providing professional training, he continuously works on online transaction processing (OLTP), OLAP, and Data Mining projects, especially at the design stage. He is a regular speaker at some of the most important international conferences, such as TechEd, PASS, and MCT. He is also indispensable at regional Microsoft TechNet meetings, the NT Conference, which is the largest Microsoft conference in Central and Eastern Europe, and other events. He is the founder of the Slovenian SQL Server Users Group. Dejan Sarka also developed two courses for Solid Quality Learning: *Data Modeling Essentials and Data Mining with SQL Server 2005*.

Steve Kass

Steve Kass is Associate Professor of Mathematics and Computer Science at Drew University in Madison, New Jersey. Steve graduated from Pomona College and holds a Ph.D. in Mathematics from the University of Wisconsin–Madison. He is also a Microsoft SQL Server MVP.

David Campbell

David Campbell is the general manager of Strategy, Infrastructure, and Architecture for Microsoft SQL Server.

David graduated with a master's degree in Mechanical Engineering (Robotics) from Clarkson University in 1984 and began working on robotic workcells for Sanders Associates (later a division of Lockheed Corporation). In 1990, he joined Digital Equipment Corporation, where he worked on its CODASYL database product DEC DBMS and on its relational database product Rdb.

Upon joining Microsoft in 1994, David was a developer and architect on the SQL Server Storage Engine team that was principally responsible for rewriting the core engine of SQL Server for SQL Server version 7.0.

David holds several patents in the data management, schema, and software quality realms. He is a frequent speaker at industry and research conferences on a wide variety of data management and software development topics.

What do you think of this book? We want to hear from you!

Do you have a few minutes to participate in a brief online survey? Microsoft is interested in hearing your feedback about this publication so that we can continually improve our books and learning resources for you.

To participate in our survey, please visit:

www.microsoft.com/learning/booksurvey

And enter this book's ISBN, 0-7356-2313-9. As a thank-you to survey participants in the United States and Canada, each month we'll randomly select five respondents to win one of five $100 gift certificates from a leading online merchant.* At the conclusion of the survey, you can enter the drawing by providing your e-mail address, which will be used for prize notification *only*.

Thanks in advance for your input. Your opinion counts!

Sincerely,

Microsoft Learning

Learn More. Go Further.